The Development of LDS Temple Worship, 1846–2000

THE DEVELOPMENT OF LDS TEMPLE WORSHIP

1846–2000

A DOCUMENTARY HISTORY

Edited by

DEVERY S. ANDERSON

Signature Books • Salt Lake City • 2011
A Smith-Pettit Foundation Book

For Clare E. Anderson

and in memory of Cecelia Grace Anderson

Jacket design by JSK Design

The Development of LDS Temple Worship, 1846-2000: A Documentary History was printed on acid-free paper and was composed, printed, and bound in the United States of America.

www.signaturebooks.com

2020 2019 2018 2017 2016 2015 7 6 5 4 3 2

LIBRARY OF CONGRESS CATALOGING-IN-PUBLICATION DATA
The development of LDS temple worship, 1846-2000 : a documentary history / edited by Devery S. Anderson
p. cm.
"A Smith-Pettit Foundation Book."
Includes bibliographical references and index.
Summary: An edited collection of documents on the history and doctrines surrounding Mormon temples. Includes excerpts from leaders' diaries, minutes of Quorum of the Twelve meetings, pastoral letters, sermons, and official publications.
ISBN 978-1-56085-211-7 (alk. paper)
1. Mormon temples—History. 2. Church of Jesus Christ of Latter-day Saints—Doctrines—History. 3. Mormon Church—Doctrines—History. I.
Anderson, Devery S. editor.
BX8643.T4D48 2010
264'.093—dc22

2010047814

CONTENTS

A photograph section appears between chapters three and four.

ABBREVIATIONS FOR FREQUENTLY CITED SOURCES

Brigham Young Jr. diary	Brigham Young Jr. diary, typed excerpts, D. Michael Quinn Papers, Special Collections, Beinecke Library, Yale University, New Haven, Connecticut.
Buerger Papers	David John Buerger Papers, Special Collections, J. Willard Marriott Library, University of Utah, Salt Lake City.
David O. McKay diary	David O. McKay diary, photocopy, Marriott Library.
George F. Richards diary	George F. Richards diary, typed excerpts, Buerger Papers, Quinn Papers.
Heber J. Grant diary	Heber J. Grant diary, typed excerpts, Quinn Papers.
History of the Church	*History of the Church of Jesus Christ of Latter-day Saints,* 6 vols., ed. B. H. Roberts (Salt Lake City: LDS Church and Deseret News, 1902–12), plus a seventh volume added in 1932.

Journal of Discourses	*Journal of Discourses,* 26 vols. (Liverpool: Latter-day Saints Book Depot, 1854-86).
Journal History	Journal History of the Church of Jesus Christ of Latter-day Saints, a multi-volume scrapbook, original in LDS Archives, History Department, LDS Church, Salt Lake City; DVD reproduction in *Selected Collections from the Archives of the Church of Jesus Christ of Latter-day Saints* (Provo: Brigham Young University Press, 2002), vol. 2.
LDS Archives	Archives, History Department, Church of Jesus Christ of Latter-day Saints, Salt Lake City, Utah.
Marriott Library	Special Collections, J. Willard Marriott Library, University of Utah, Salt Lake City.
MFP	*Messages of the First Presidency of The Church of Jesus Christ of Latter-day Saints,* ed. James R. Clark, 6 vols. (Salt Lake City: Bookcraft, 1965-1975).
Ms. History of Brigham Young	*Manuscript History of Brigham Young, 1846-1847,* ed. Elden Jay Watson (Salt Lake City: E. J. Watson, 1971).
Perry Special Collections	L. Tom Perry Special Collections, Harold B. Lee Library, Brigham Young University, Provo, Utah.
Quinn Papers	D. Michael Quinn Papers, Special Collections, Beinecke Library, Yale University, New Haven, Connecticut.
Selected Collections	*Selected Collections from the Archives of The Church of Jesus Christ of Latter-day Saints*

	(Provo: Brigham Young University Press, 2002), 2 vols.
Thomas Bullock journal	"Journal of Thomas Bullock," ed. Gregory R. Knight, in *BYU Studies* 31 (Winter 1991), 1:15-75.
Wilford Woodruff journal	*Wilford Woodruff's Journal,* ed. Scott G. Kenney (Midvale, Ut.: Signature Books, 1983-85), 9 vols.

BIOGRAPHIES OF PRINCIPAL CHARACTERS

Anderson, Joseph. Born in Salt Lake City, Nov. 29, 1889. Graduated from Weber Stake Academy (now Weber State University), 1905. Married Norma Ettie Peterson, 1915. Secretary to First Presidency from 1922; assistant to Quorum of Twelve, 1970; member of First Quorum of Seventy, 1976; emeritus general authority, 1978. Died 1992, age 102.

Anderson, Lewis. Born in Malmö, Sweden, Oct. 24, 1850. Married Mary Ann Crowther, Nov. 18, 1870. Served as president of South Sanpete Stake for nineteen years; president of the Manti temple, 1906-33. Worked in banking as president of Manti City Savings Bank; president, Manti Livestock Company. Died 1933, age 82.

Ballard, Melvin Joseph. Born in Logan, Feb. 9, 1873. Graduated from Brigham Young College (Logan). Called as president, Northwestern States Mission, 1909. Married Martha Anable Jones, 1896. Ordained to apostleship, 1919. Opened South American mission, Buenos Aires, 1925. Died 1939, age 66.

Benson, Ezra Taft. Born in Whitney, Idaho, Aug. 4, 1899. Served LDS mission to Britain, 1921-23; graduated from BYU, 1926. Married Flora Smith Amussen, 1926. Master's degree, Iowa State University, 1927. Executive secretary, National Council of Farmers Cooperatives, 1939.

President, Washington, D.C., Stake, 1940-43. Quorum of Twelve Apostles, 1943. U.S. Secretary of Agriculture, 1953-61. President of Church, 1985. Died 1994, age 94.

Bleak, James Godson. Born in Surrey County, England, Nov. 15, 1829. Married Elizabeth Moore, Oct. 14, 1849. Baptized 1851; called as president, White Chapel Branch, 1854. Immigrated with Martin Handcart Company, 1856. Joined cotton mission in southern Utah, 1861; postmaster of St. George, 1868-72; mission to England and editor, *Millennial Star,* 1872-73; recorder, St. George temple, 1900; patriarch, St. George Stake, 1909. Married three plural wives. Died 1918, age 89.

Brown, Hugh Brown. Born in Granger, Utah, Oct. 24, 1883. Moved to Alberta, 1898; attended Brigham Young College (USU), 1901; served mission to England, 1904-06; married Zina Young Card, 1908. Became officer (major) in Canadian military, 1917; graduated from University of Alberta, passed bar exam, 1921. President, Lethbridge Stake, 1921; president, British Mission, 1937-40, 1944-46; professor, BYU, 1946-49; Quorum of Twelve Apostles, 1958; First Presidency, 1961. Died 1975, age 92.

Budge, William. Born in Lanark, Scotland, May 1, 1828. Baptized 1857; emigrated, 1860. Married Julia Stratford, 1856. Bishop, Logan, 1864-70; helped settle Bear Lake area; president, Bear Lake Stake, 1877; president, European Mission, 1878; president, Logan temple, 1906-18. Married two plural wives. Died 1919, age 90.

Burton, Theodore Moyle. Born in Salt Lake City, Mar. 27, 1907. Served in Swiss mission, 1927-30. Married Minnie Susan Preece, 1933. Earned master's degree, University of Utah, 1934; Ph.D., chemistry, Purdue University, 1951. President, West German Mission, 1957; assistant to Quorum of Twelve, 1960; First Quorum of Seventy, 1976; leader in LDS Genealogical Department, 1960s; executive director, Family History Department, 1972-78; emeritus general authority, 1989. Died 1989, age 82.

Cannon, Abraham Hoagland. Born in Salt Lake City, Mar. 12, 1859, to George Q. Cannon and Elizabeth Hoagland. Married Sarah Ann

Jenkins, 1878. Called to First Seven Presidents of Seventy, 1882; Quorum of Twelve Apostles, 1889. Married three plural wives. Died 1896, age 37.

Cannon, Angus Munn. Born in Liverpool, May 17, 1834, younger brother of George Q. Cannon. Baptized, 1840; emigrated, 1842. Missions to eastern states, 1854, 1869-70. Married Sarah Maria Mousley and Ann Amanda Harrison Mousley, 1858, then four other women, including Martha Hughes Cannon. Mayor of St. George, 1861. Helped found Call's Landing, 1864. President of Salt Lake Stake, 1876-1904; stake patriarch, 1904-15. Died 1915, age 81.

Cannon, David Henry. Born in Liverpool, Apr. 23, 1838, brother of George Q. Cannon. Emigrated 1842, baptized 1850. Worked at *Deseret News.* Served mission to California, 1856. Married Wilhelmina L. Mousley, 1859. Mission to England, 1860. Helped settle St. George (Dixie Mission), 1861. President, St. George temple, 1893-1924. Married two plural wives. Died 1924, age 86.

Cannon, George Quale. Born in Liverpool, Jan. 11, 1827. Baptized 1840, emigrated 1842. Worked at *Times and Seasons* in Nauvoo, Illinois. Missions to Sandwich Islands, 1849, eastern states, 1858-68. Married Elizabeth Hoagland, 1854. President of Oregon and California Mission, 1856-58. Published *Weekly Standard* in San Francisco, 1856. Apostle, 1860; president, European Mission, editor, *Millennial Star* and Welsh *Udgorn Seion,* 1860-64; managing editor, *Deseret News,* 1867-74; publisher, *Juvenile Instructor,* 1866-1901; superintendent of Sunday schools, 1867-1901. First Presidency, 1873. Married five plural wives. Died 1901, age 74.

Chipman, Stephen L. Born in American Fork, Mar. 18, 1864. Graduate of Brigham Young Academy, 1883. Married Sina Neilson, 1885. After her death, married Annie Maddick Jameson, 1940. Operated Chipman Mercantile Company, 34 years. BYU Board of Trustees, 1896-1939; president, Alpine Stake, 1901; president, Salt Lake temple, 1938-45. Died 1945, age 81.

Christiansen, ElRay Lavar. Born in Mayfield, July 13, 1897. Married Lewella Ann Rees, June 14, 1922. President, Texas-Louisiana Mission, 1937-41; president, Logan temple, 1943-52; assistant to Council of Twelve, 1951; president, Salt Lake temple, 1954-61; coordinator of temples, 1964. Died 1975, age 78.

Clark, Joshua Reuben, Jr. Born in Grantsville, Sept. 1, 1871. Married Luacine Annetta Savage, 1898. Bachelor's degree, University of Utah, 1898; law degree, Columbia University, 1906. Assistant Solicitor, U.S. State Department, 1906; Associate Professor, George Washington University, 1906-08; U.S. Undersecretary of State, 1928; U.S. Ambassador to Mexico, 1930-33; LDS First Presidency, 1933-61. Died 1961, age 90.

Davis, Albert Westley. Born in Columbiana, Ohio, Apr. 25, 1841. Married Melissa Jane Lambson, 1865. Served mission to Sandwich Islands. Married Annie Lois Bacon, 1884. Bishop, Salt Lake Center Ward, 1892-1906; patriarch, 1895; Salt Lake temple presidency. Died 1928, age 87.

Dyer, Alvin Rulon. Born in Salt Lake City, Jan. 1, 1903. Missionary to eastern states, 1922-24. Married May Elizabeth Jackson, 1926. Studied drafting and engineering. Founded Dyer Distributing Company, 1954. President, Central States Mission, 1954; assistant to Quorum of Twelve, 1958; president, European Mission, 1960-62; apostle (but not in quorum), 1967; First Presidency, 1968-70; First Quorum of Seventy, 1976. Died 1977, age 74.

Evans, Richard Louis. Born in Salt Lake City, Mar. 23, 1906. Married Alice Ruth Thornley, Aug. 9, 1933. First Council of Seventy, 1938; announcer for *Music and the Spoken Word* with Tabernacle Choir, 1930-71; Quorum of Twelve, 1953. Died 1871, age 65.

Gibbs, George Francis. Born in Haverfordwest, Wales, Nov. 21, 1846. Emigrated, 1866. Married Ida Snow, 1876; married Sarah Emmaline Worthen, 1884. Assistant secretary to First Presidency, 1876-1909; secretary to First Presidency, 1909-22. Died 1924, age 77.

Grant, Heber Jeddy. Born in Salt Lake City, Nov. 22, 1856. Married Lucy Stringham, 1877. President, Tooele Stake, 1880; Quorum of Twelve Apostles, 1882; president, LDS church, 1918-45. Married two plural wives, 1884. Died 1945, age 88.

Grant, Jedediah Morgan. Born in Windsor, New York, Feb. 21, 1816. Mission to southern states, 1839; presided over Church in Philadelphia from 1842. Married Carolyn Van Dyke, 1844. After her death, married Susan Fairchild Noble and Rosetta Robinson, 1849. Ordained to First Council of Seventy, 1845. Mayor, Salt Lake City, 1851 to death. Apostleship and First Presidency, 1854. Married four additional plural wives. Died 1856, age 40.

Hinckley, Gordon Bitner. Born in Salt Lake City, June 23, 1910. Graduated from the University of Utah, 1932. Mission to Britain, 1932-35. Married Marjorie Pay, 1937. Called to Deseret Sunday School Union General Board, 1937; East Mill Creek Stake presidency, 1946. Became president of stake, 1956; assistant to Quorum of Twelve Apostles, 1958; member of Quorum of Twelve, 1961; First Presidency, 1981; president of Church, 1995. Died 2008, age 97.

Hinckley, Ira Nathaniel. Born in Leeds County, Ontario, Oct. 30, 1828. Married Eliza Jane Evans, 1848. After her death, married Adelaide Cameron Noble, 1853. Emigrated, 1850. Helped build Horseshoe Fort, 1856, Cove Fort, 1867; became mayor of Fillmore; president, Millard Stake, about 1889; patriarch, 1886-1904. Married two plural wives. Died 1904, age 75.

Hunter, Howard William. Born in Boise, Nov. 14, 1907. Married Clara May Jeffs, 1931. After her death, married Inis Bernice Egan, 1990. Ordained to Quorum of Twelve, 1959; president of Church, 1994. Died 1995, age 87.

Issacson, Henry Thorpe Beal. Born in Ephraim, Utah, Sept. 6, 1898. Married Lula Maughn Jones, 1920. Member of board of regents, University of Utah; board of trustees, BYU; Presiding Bishopric, 1946-52; assistant to Quorum of Twelve, 1961-65, 1970; First Presidency, 1965-70. Died 1970, age 72.

Ivins, Anthony Woodward. Born in Toms River, New Jersey, Sept. 16, 1852. Married Elizabeth Ashby Snow, 1878. Mission to Mexico, 1875; mission to Pueblo Indians, 1877; president, Mexican Mission, 1883-84; president, Colonia Juarez Stake, from 1895; Quorum of Twelve Apostles, 1907; First Presidency, 1921. Died 1934, age 82.

Kimball, Heber Chase. Born in Sheldon, Vermont, June 14, 1801. Married Vilate Murray, 1822. Baptized in 1832. Zion's Camp militia march, 1834. Quorum of Twelve Apostles, from 1835; missionary to England, 1837-38, 1839-41; First Presidency, 1847-68. Married forty-two plural wives. Died 1868, age 67.

Kimball, Spencer Woolley. Born in Salt Lake City, Mar. 28, 1895. Mission to central states, 1914-16. Married Camilla Eyring, 1917. President of Mount Graham Stake, 1938-43; Quorum of Twelve Apostles, 1943; president, LDS Church, 1973. Announced revelation extending priesthood to blacks, 1978. Died 1985, age 90.

Lee, Harold Bingham. Born in Clifton, Idaho, Mar. 28, 1899. Married Fern Lucinda Tanner, 1923. After her death, married Freda Joan Jensen, 1963. Ordained to Quorum of Twelve, 1941; called to First Presidency, 1970; ordained president of Church, 1972. Died 1973, age 74.

Lund, Anthon Hendrick. Born in Aalborg, Denmark, May 15, 1844. Baptized, 1856; emigrated, 1862. Married Sarah Ann Preston, 1870. Served as mission president in Scandinavia, 1884-85. Called to Quorum of Twelve Apostles, 1889. Became president, European Mission, 1893; Church Historian, 1900; member of First Presidency, 1901; president, Salt Lake temple, 1911-21. Died 1921, age 76.

Lund, Christian Nielsen. Born in Kolding, Denmark, Jan. 13, 1846. Married Petra Antoine Marie Jenson, Oct. 11, 1869. After her death, married Bodil Kristiane Nielsen, 1884. President, Scandinavian Mission, 1896-98; later president, North Sanpete Stake. Died 1921, age 75.

Lyman, Francis Marion. Born in Good Hope, Illinois, Jan. 12, 1840. Married Rhoda Ann Taylor, 1857. Called as missionary to England, 1860; president, Tooele Stake, 1877; Quorum of Twelve, 1880. Married two plural wives. Died 1916, age 76.

McAllister, Duncan McNeil. Born in Glasgow, Apr. 18, 1842. Married Catherine Esther Perkes, 1866. Managed LDS business affairs in Liverpool; named to LDS Genealogical Bureau, 1888; Genealogical Society of Utah, 1894. Kept Salt Lake temple records, standardized other temple records. Died 1931, age 89.

McAllister, John D. T. Born in Sussex County, England, Feb. 19, 1827. Baptized, 1847; emigrated, 1851. Married Ellen Handley, 1847. Mission to England, 1853-56. Worked as Salt Lake City marshal, territorial marshal, Salt Lake Fire Department chief. Served as president, St. George Stake, 1877; assistant to Wilford Woodruff at St. George temple; president, Manti temple, 1893-1906. Married eight plural wives. Died 1910, age 82.

McKay, David Oman. Born in Huntsville, Utah, Sept. 8, 1873. Married Emma Ray Riggs, 1901. Ordained to apostleship, 1906; appointed to First Presidency, 1934; ordained president of Church, 1951. Died 1970, age 96.

Merrill, Marriner Wood. Born in Sackville, New Brunswick, Sept. 25, 1832. Baptized, 1852; emigrated, 1853. Married Sarah Atkinson, 1853. Helped settle Cache Valley, 1860. Director, Utah Northern Railroad; president, Logan temple, 1884-1906; board of trustees, Brigham Young College; Quorum of Twelve Apostles, 1889. Married seven plural wives. Died 1906, age 73.

Monson, Thomas Spencer. Born in Salt Lake City, Aug. 21, 1927. Graduated from University of Utah, BYU. Married Frances Beverly Johnson, 1948. President, Canadian Mission, 1959; Quorum of Twelve Apostles, 1963; First Presidency, 1985; president, LDS Church, 2008.

Moyle, Henry Dinwoodey. Born in Salt Lake City, Apr. 22, 1889. Served mission to Germany, 1909-11; attended University of Utah, University of Chicago, Harvard Law School, and mining school in Freiburg, Germany. Served in World War I. Appointed director, Petroleum Industries Council, during World War II. President, Cottonwood Stake, 1927; Quorum of Twelve Apostles, 1947; First Presidency, 1959. Died 1963, age 74.

Nibley, Charles Wilson. Born in Midlothian County, Scotland, Feb. 5, 1849. Settled in Cache Valley, 1860. Called to British Mission, 1877. Married Rebecca Neibaur, 1869. Worked in lumber business in Oregon, sugar beet industry in Utah and Idaho. Presiding Bishopric, 1907; First Presidency, 1925. Married two plural wives. Died 1931, age 82.

Nuttall, Leonard John. Born in Liverpool, July 6, 1834. Emigrated, 1852. Married Elizabeth Clarkson, 1856; married Sophia Elizabeth Taylor as plural wife, 1875. Personal secretary to Brigham Young to 1877, to John Taylor, 1879-87, and to Wilford Woodruff, 1887-92. Transcribed and helped standardize temple ceremonies, 1877. Died 1905, age 70.

Penrose, Charles William. Born in London, Feb. 4, 1832. Baptized, 1850. Served mission to England, 1852-61, 1865. Married Lucetta Stratford, 1855. Emigrated, 1861. Editor of Ogden's *Junction* newspaper; editor of *Deseret News,* 1880-85. Served in territorial legislature. Ordained to Quorum of Twelve Apostles, 1904. President, European mission, 1904. Married two plural wives. Died 1925, age 93.

Reynolds, George. Born in London, Jan. 1, 1842. Baptized, 1856; emigrated, 1865. Married Mary Ann Tuddenham, 1865. Became secretary to Brigham Young, 1865. Served in Utah's Nauvoo Legion militia. Became editor of *Deseret News, Juvenile Instructor.* Called to England to edit *Millennial Star,* 1871. Tried for polygamy, 1874, and served term in territorial penitentiary. Called to First Council of Seventy, 1890. Married two plural wives. Died 1909, age 67.

Rich, Charles Coulson. Born in Campbell County, Kentucky, Aug. 21, 1809. Baptized, 1832. Married Sarah DeArmon Pea, 1837. Served in Nauvoo Legion in Illinois, 1840s; helped settle Utah, 1847. Called to Quorum of Twelve, 1849; helped found San Bernardino, 1851; mission president, England, 1860-62; led colonization of Bear Lake Valley, Idaho, 1863. Married five plural wives. Died 1883, age 74.

Richards, George Franklin. Born in Farmington, Utah, Feb. 23, 1861. Ordained an elder at age 16, 1877. Married Alice Almira Robinson, 1882. After her death, married Betsy Hollings, 1947. Father of Apostle LeGrand Richards. Tooele Stake presidency, 1890; patriarch, 1893; Quorum of Twelve Apostles, 1906; president, European Mission, 1916-19; president, Salt Lake temple, 1921-38. Died 1950, age 89.

Richards, Stephen L. Born in Mendon, Utah, June 18, 1879. Married Irene Smith Merrill, Feb. 21, 1900. Graduated from University of Chicago law school, 1904. Called to Quorum of Twelve, 1917. Church

Radio, Publicity, and Mission Literature Committee chair, 1935-51. First Presidency, 1951-59. Died 1959, age 79.

Romney, Marion George. Born in Colonia Juarez, Mexico, Sept. 19, 1897. Served mission in Australia, 1920-23. Married Ida Olivia Jensen, 1924. Elected to state legislature, 1935. Called as assistant to Quorum of Twelve, 1941; ordained to apostleship, 1951; served in First Presidency, 1972-1985. Died 1988, age 90.

Smith, George Albert. Born in Salt Lake City, Apr. 4, 1870. Married Lucy Emily Woodruff, 1892. Ordained to Quorum of Twelve, 1903; president, LDS Church, 1945. Died 1951, age 81.

Smith, Joseph Fielding. Born in Far West, Missouri, Nov. 13, 1838. Married Levira Annette Smith, 1859, divorced in 1867. Ordained an apostle, 1866; set apart as member of Quorum of Twelve, 1867; called to First Presidency, 1866; ordained president of Church, 1901. Married five plural wives. Died 1918, age 80.

Smith, Joseph Fielding. Born in Salt Lake City, July 19, 1876. Married Louie E. Shurtliff, 1898. After her death, married Ethel G. Reynolds, 1908. After her death, married Jessie Ella Evans, 1938. Assistant Church Historian, 1906; Quorum of Twelve Apostles, 1910; Church Historian, 1921-70; First Presidency, 1965; president of Church, 1970. Died 1972, age 95.

Snow, Edward Hunter. Born in St. George, June 23, 1865. Graduated from Brigham Young Academy, 1865. Married Sarah Hannah Nelson, 1885. Served in first Utah state legislature, 1896-97. President of St. George Stake, 1901-25. Died 1932, age 67.

Snow, Erastus Fairbanks. Born in St. Johnsbury, Vermont, Nov. 9, 1818. Baptized, 1833. Mission to eastern states, 1833, 1848. Married Artemesia Beman, 1838. Entered Salt Lake Valley in advance party of explorers, July 22, 1847. Ordained to Quorum of Twelve Apostles, 1849; opened Scandinavian Mission, 1849; helped colonize southern Utah, 1861, then Arizona. Served mission to Europe, 1873. Married sixteen plural wives and went into hiding to escape arrest. Died 1888, age 69.

Snow, Lorenzo. Born in Mantua, Ohio, Apr. 3, 1814. Married four plural wives in Nauvoo, Illinois, 1845-46; later married five more. Ordained to Quorum of Twelve Apostles, 1849. Appointed to First Presidency, 1873; president of Church, 1898. Died 1901, age 87.

Stone, Oscar Leslie. Born in Teton County, Idaho, May 28, 1903. Married Dorothy Cobbley, 1924. President, Salt Lake temple, 1968-72. Assistant to Quorum of Twelve Apostles, 1972; First Quorum of Seventy, 1976; emeritus general authority, 1980. Died 1986, age 82.

Talmage, James Edward. Born in Hungerford, England, Sept. 21, 1862. Baptized, 1873; emigrated, 1876. Attended Brigham Young Academy; graduated from Lehigh University in Pennsylvania, 1883; attended Johns Hopkins University, 1883-84. Married May Booth, 1888. President, University of Utah, 1894-97. Appointed to Quorum of Twelve Apostles, 1911; president, European Mission, 1924-28. Authored *The Articles of Faith, The House of the Lord,* and *Jesus the Christ.* Died 1933, age 70.

Tanner, Nathan Eldon. Born in Salt Lake City, May 9, 1898. Settled in Alberta, 1919. Married Sara Isabelle Merrill, 1919. Worked as principal of school in Cardston, Alberta, 1929; served in Alberta legislature, 1935. Became Minister of Alberta Lands and Mines, 1936; president, Merrill Petroleum, 1952; director, Toronto Dominion Bank of Canada, 1952; and oversaw 2,000-mile pipeline to Montreal, 1954-58. President, Calgary Stake, 1953-60; assistant to Quorum of Twelve, 1960; Quorum of Twelve Apostles, 1962; First Presidency, 1963-82. Died, 1982, age 84.

Taylor, John. Born in Milnthorpe, England, Nov. 1, 1808. Married Leonora Cannon, 1833. Ordained to Quorum of Twelve Apostles, 1838; president, LDS Church, 1880. Married eight plural wives. Died 1887, age 78.

Wells, Daniel Hanmer. Born in Trenton, New Jersey, Oct. 27, 1814. Married Eliza Rebecca Robison, 1837. Sold land in Commerce, Illinois, to Mormons for city of Nauvoo. Baptized, 1846. Became mayor of Salt Lake City, 1866-76; ordained an apostle, 1857; served in First Presidency, 1857-77. President, European Mission, 1864-65; counselor to Quorum of Twelve, 1877-91; president, Manti temple, 1888-91. Married six plural wives. Died 1891, age 76.

Whitaker, Wetzel Orson. Born in Heber, Utah, Sept. 30, 1908. Married Dorothy Youkstetter, 1931. After her death, married Louise Eccles Glen, 1973. Animator with Walt Disney Studios from 1936 (*Alice in Wonderland, Cinderella,* Donald Duck films, *Peter Pan*); worked with LDS films beginning in 1946; oversaw production at BYU Department of Motion Pictures, 1953-1975 (150 films geared toward LDS youth); directed early temple endowment films. Died 1985, age 77.

Widtsoe, John Andreas. Born in Trondheim, Norway, Jan. 31, 1872. Emigrated, 1883; baptized, 1884. Studied at Brigham Young College (Logan); graduated from Harvard University, 1894. Married Leah Eudora Dunford, 1898. Earned Ph.D., University of Göttingen, Germany, 1899. Ordained to Quorum of Twelve Apostles, 1921. President of European Mission, 1926-32. Wrote books on Mormonism. Died 1952, age 80.

Winder, John Rex. Born in Biddenham, England, Dec. 11, 1821. Married Ellen Walters, 1845. Emigrated, 1853. Captain in Utah War of 1857. Called to Presiding Bishopric, 1887; First Presidency, 1901. Married three plural wives. Died 1910, age 88.

Wise, Frank Samuel. Born in Sydenham, England, Sept. 7, 1906. Emigrated in late 1930s. Served in Signal Corps Photographic Center, World War II. Worked for Deseret Film Productions; became partner in Recording Arts sound studio; hired as film editor, BYU Motion Picture studio (*Windows of Heaven, Man's Search for Happiness,* others); edited early temple films. Married Romania Meeks, 1959. Served on Sunday School General Board for 20 years. Died 1996, age 90.

Wood, Edward James. Born in Salt Lake City, Oct. 27, 1866. Missionary to Samoa, 1888-92; president, Samoan Mission, 1896. Married Mary Ann Solomon, 1892. Moved to Cardston, Alberta, 1901; called to be president of Alberta Stake, 1903-42. Married Adelaide Solomon as a plural wife, 1904, 14 years after Manifesto. Helped found Glenwood and Hillspring, 1908-1910. Called as president of Alberta temple, 1923-48; stake patriarch, 1948-56. Died 1956, age 89.

Woodruff, Wilford. Born in Avon (now Hartford), Connecticut, Apr. 3, 1807. Married Phoebe Whitmore Carter, 1837. Ordained to Quorum of Twelve Apostles, 1839; president of Church, 1889. Issued Manifesto against polygamy, 1890. Married four plural wives. Died 1898, age 91.

Young, Brigham. Born in Whitingham, Vermont, June 1, 1801. Married Miriam Angeline Works, 1924. After her death, married Mary Ann Angell, 1834. Baptized, 1832. Ordained to Quorum of Twelve, 1835; served mission to England, 1840-41; became president of Church, 1846; led Mormons to Salt Lake Valley, 1847; served as governor of territory, 1850-57. Married twenty-three plural wives. Died 1877, age 76.

Young, Brigham Jr. Born in Kirtland, Ohio, Dec. 18, 1836. Married Catherine Curtis Spencer, 1855. Ordained an apostle, 1864; served as president, European Mission, 1865, 1890-93; sustained as member of Quorum of Twelve Apostles, 1868; called to First Presidency, 1873. Married five plural wives. Died 1903, age 66.

INTRODUCTION

When Brigham Young (1801-77) helped lead the Latter-day Saints into the Great Salt Lake Valley in July 1847 to establish a home for the displaced Church, the event signaled a new beginning. Isolation meant freedom from societal expectations, and the Saints could live their controversial religion in ways not yet fully realized. This was most evident when five years later, in August 1852, Apostle Orson Pratt publicly acknowledged what most people already knew: the Latter-day Saints had long been practicing plural marriage.[1]

The freedoms envisioned in the West would also mean that they could resume their sacred temple-related ceremonies and ordinances. That the rituals were considered all-important is seen in the determination to finish the temple in Nauvoo, Illinois, at considerable cost and sacrifice, even though they knew they would have to abandon the edifice soon after its completion. It opened in December 1845 and closed two months later in February 1846. During that time, 5,583 Church members received their temple endowments.[2]

It was not the first LDS temple. In 1836, Joseph Smith (1805-44)

1. For more, see George D. Smith, *Nauvoo Polygamy: "... but we called it celestial marriage"* (Salt Lake City: Signature Books, 2008).

2. See Matthew McBride, *A House for the Most High: The Story of the Original Nauvoo Temple* (Salt Lake City: Greg Kofford Books, 2007); Lisle G. Brown, comp., *Nauvoo Sealings, Adoptions, and Anointings: A Comprehensive Register of Persons Receiving LDS Temple Ordinances, 1841-1846* (Salt Lake City: Smith-Pettit Foundation, 2006), 361.

dedicated a House of the Lord in Kirtland, Ohio, which was abandoned two years later when the Church split in two over financial and other controversies and Joseph Smith fled to Missouri. There he made plans for two more temples, one in the Mormon town of Far West where a cornerstone was symbolically laid by the Quorum of the Twelve Apostles on April 26, 1839; this was after Church members had already abandoned the town.[3] Another temple was planned for Independence (also called Zion), Missouri, but was not built because of the Mormon War of 1838 and the Church's relocation to Illinois.

Although the Saints left behind two imposing buildings they had only used briefly, what they believed they carried to their new home in the West were the necessary keys, which is to say the knowledge and authority, to resume rituals initiated by the founder. Already in Nauvoo in 1846, Young confidently promised that "this is not the last Temple that we will build—in this house we have been payed well if we were to receive no more—and I tell [you] that there will be double the anxiety manifest to build the next[,] that there was to Ericte [erect] this."[4]

When Joseph Smith first introduced temple rites, he chose not to wait for a temple's completion before performing the ordinances. For example, in Kirtland, ceremonial washings and anointings were introduced to the all-male School of the Prophets in the Newell K. Whitney general store in 1833. In early May 1842 in Nauvoo, Joseph Smith introduced the first version of what would become known as the endowment ceremony above his Red Brick Store, as well as in a few other locations in the city. He also introduced sealings (marriage for time and eternity) and the highest ordinance of the temple, the second anointing, in non-sacred settings. Proxy baptisms for the dead, introduced in 1841, were first performed in the Mississippi River long before the baptismal font in the Nauvoo temple was conceived of.[5]

The Nauvoo temple would not open for ordinance work for a year and a half after Joseph and his brother Hyrum Smith were murdered

---

3. See James B. Allen and Glen M. Leonard, *The Story of the Latter-day Saints,* 2nd ed. (Salt Lake City: Deseret Book Co., 1992), 160-61; James B. Allen, Ronald K. Esplin, and David J. Whittaker, *Men with a Mission, 1837-1841: The Quorum of the Twelve Apostles in the British Isles* (Salt Lake City: Deseret Book Co., 1992), 57.

4. Brigham Young diary, Feb. 3, 1846, Archives, History Department, Church of Jesus Christ of Latter-day Saints, Salt Lake City.

5. M. Guy Bishop, "'What Has Become of Our Fathers?' Baptism for the Dead at Nauvoo," *Dialogue: A Journal of Mormon Thought* 23 (Summer 1990): 86-88.

on June 27, 1844, and even in December 1845, the building was still under construction and the ceremonies performed in makeshift rooms separated by canvas partitions. After most of the Saints had left Nauvoo, and as workers still labored to finish the building, Apostle Orson Hyde dedicated the temple on May 1, 1846. Shortly thereafter, it was abandoned.[6]

For readers unfamiliar with LDS temple worship, the endowment, according to official public sources, includes a dramatic portrayal of the creation of the earth and its inhabitants. Using narratives adapted from the Bible and Book of Abraham (a volume of LDS scripture), the drama portrays the Fall from the Garden of Eden and the introduction of the Christian gospel, followed by what Mormons call the Apostasy and Restoration of the gospel and priesthood authority, although thematically rather than chronologically. Simultaneously, worshipers are given what Brigham Young called "the key words, the signs and tokens, pertaining to the Holy Priesthood."[7] Initiates are also charged with what Apostle James E. Talmage characterized as

> the law of strict virtue and chastity, to be charitable, benevolent, tolerant and pure; to devote both talent and material means to the spread of truth and the uplifting of the race; to maintain devotion to the cause of truth; and to seek in every way to contribute to the great preparation that the earth may be made ready to receive her King—the Lord Jesus Christ. With the taking of each covenant and the assuming of each obligation a promised blessing is pronounced, contingent upon the faithful observance of the conditions.[8]

Prior to the endowment ceremony, participants are ritually washed and anointed and given special underclothing ("garments") to wear for the rest of their lives. They are a reminder to remain pure in both thought and action. Other temple-related ordinances include proxy baptisms for the dead, marriage sealings for time and eternity, adop-

6. For the story of the Nauvoo temple in its day-to-day operations, see Devery S. Anderson and Gary James Bergera, eds., *The Nauvoo Endowment Companies, 1845-1846: A Documentary History* (Salt Lake City: Signature Books/Smith-Pettit Foundation, 2005).

7. Brigham Young, sermon, Apr. 6, 1853, in *Journal of Discourses,* 26 vols. (Liverpool: LDS Book Depot, 1854-86), 2:31-32.

8. James E. Talmage, *The House of the Lord: A Study of Holy Sanctuaries Ancient and Modern* (Salt Lake City: Deseret News, 1912), 100.

tions for eternity, and an additional anointing known variously as the second anointing, second endowment, higher blessing, or fullness of the priesthood.

Temples from Pioneer Times to the Age of Technology

For a period of time after the Nauvoo temple was abandoned, the rituals were performed in the outdoors or in temporary structures prior to completion of a proper edifice. Even though a temple site was designated on July 28, 1847, four days after the pioneer company's first arrival in the Salt Lake Valley, it would be thirty years before such a structure would be completed and it would be in southern Utah in a town named after Apostle George A. Smith, St. George, rather than in downtown Salt Lake City.

Ensign Peak

The first location in Utah where at least a portion of the endowment ceremony was performed was atop Ensign Peak, a hill named by Brigham Young on July 26 just after arriving in the valley and "consecrated for the purpose." Much of the hill's designation as a sacred site comes to us by way of legend since the only endowment documented to have been performed there was for Addison Pratt (1802-72) in 1849. Pratt was about to leave on a mission to the Society Islands (French Polynesia) and had missed an earlier opportunity to receive the ordinance in the Nauvoo temple. According to LDS historian B. H. Roberts, "this action was in harmony with the instructions of the Prophet in Nauvoo when he said that these ordinances of the temple under certain circumstances might be obtained on the mountain top, as Moses obtained them."[9] Ensign Peak is just north of the spot Brigham Young designated for a temple in downtown Salt Lake City, less than two miles away but up a steep incline that rises over 1,000 feet.[10]

---

9. B. H. Roberts, *Comprehensive History of the Church of Jesus Christ of Latter-day Saints,* 6 vols. (Salt Lake City: Deseret Book Co., 1930), 3:386-87. Roberts refers to a sermon delivered by Joseph Smith on May 1, 1842, in which the prophet, not a fan of the wealthy elite, also specified that "the rich can only get [their ordinances] in the temple, the poor may get them on the mountain top as did Moses" (Joseph Smith, et al., *History of the Church of Jesus Christ of Latter-day Saints,* 6 vols., ed. B. H. Roberts [Salt Lake City: LDS Church/Deseret News, 1902-12], 4:608).

10. Lynn M. Hilton and Hope A. Hilton, "Ensign Peak," in *Utah History Encyclopedia,* ed. Allan Kent Powell (Salt Lake City: University of Utah Press, 1994),

The Council House

With the exception of what the LDS hymn called the site of Ensign Peak "high on a mountain top," the endowment was not performed from the time of the Church's departure from Nauvoo in February 1846 until completion of one of the first buildings in the Salt Lake Valley, the Council House. As the name indicated, this stately, two-story stone building across the street to the southwest from the temple, completed in December 1850, was intended to be the site of government deliberations—specifically for the General Assembly of the State of Deseret, the legislative body of what would have been an independent country, free from the United States or Mexico. When Utah became a U.S. territory the next year, the building transitioned to become the offices and assembly room of the territorial legislature, later the territorial library and, later still, the University of Deseret.[11] But the building served a dual purpose, as a total of 2,222 Latter-day Saints received their temple endowments between February 1851 and May 1855 in the large hall on the second level.[12] The room was divided by white screens into smaller spaces, called departments, representing different stages of the endowment.[13]

The Endowment House

It soon became clear that the Council House, serving such diverse

---

170. For a fuller study of the significance of this hill to early Utah Mormons, see Ronald W. Walker, "'A Banner Is Unfurled': Mormonism's Ensign Peak," *Dialogue: A Journal of Mormon Thought* 26:4 (Winter 1993): 71-91.

11. Roberts, *Comprehensive History,* 4:13. The Council House was built by the Church's Public Works Department, an organization supervised by Superintendent Daniel H. Wells, who himself soon became Salt Lake City mayor. According to historian Eugene E. Campbell, other projects under the auspices of the Public Works Department included construction of the Old Tabernacle, a barn-shaped building with adobe walls and a broad pitched roof; Social Hall; a bath house; the General Tithing Store; and "a number of other walls, residences, schools, and church buildings." The Council House burned down on June 21, 1883 (Eugene E. Campbell, *Establishing Zion: The Mormon Church in the American West, 1847-1869* [Salt Lake City: Signature Books, 1988], 140). The Public Works Department received its financing from the Church tithing fund and employed 205 immigrants. See Allen and Leonard, *Story of the Latter-day Saints,* 283-84.

12. Gil Bradshaw, "The Council House as a House for Sacred Ordinances in the Early Church," cited in Lisle G. Brown, "'Temple Pro Tempore': The Salt Lake City Endowment House," *Journal of Mormon History* 34 (Fall 2008): 5n16.

13. Brown, "Temple Pro Tempore," 4-5.

sacred and profane purposes, could not meet the long-term needs of the Church. Therefore, LDS leaders asked architect Truman O. Angell (1810-87) to design a building that would serve as an adequate temporary sanctuary until the full temple could be built.[14] Called the Endowment House, the two-story building was constructed of adobe bricks and measured 34 feet by 44 feet.[15] The foundation was laid in September 1854. When the building was dedicated on May 5 the next year, it was exactly eight years after Joseph Smith had introduced the endowment for the first time in the room above his Red Brick Store. The next year, a twenty-foot extension was added. "Though simple," wrote historian Eugene E. Campbell, "the Endowment House contained all of the rooms modern LDS temples have and served as a structure for temple ordinances during the Saints' first three decades in the region."[16] The construction cost was $10,000.[17] At the dedication, "President [Brigham Young] Remarked the House was [ritually] clean and named it 'the House of the Lord.'"[18]

Located within the temple block in the northwest quadrant, the Endowment House functioned from May 1855 until September 1889. Each room was raised a little above the preceding one to give the sense of ascending to a higher spiritual level as one passed through the various stages of the endowment. The first floor consisted of the washing and anointing room, the Garden Room, World Room, Terrestrial Room, and two restrooms. The Celestial Room and Sealing Room were on the second floor.[19]

With the opening of the Endowment House, people from throughout the territory came to Salt Lake City to receive their personal ordinances. Writing to local leaders in Washington and Iron

---

14. James Dwight Tingen, "The Endowment House, 1855-1889," 5-6, unpublished senior paper, Brigham Young University, Provo, Utah, 1974; Campbell, *Establishing Zion,* 169; Brown, "Temple Pro Tempore," 5-6.

15. Tingen, "Endowment House," 9; Richard Neitzel Holzapfel, "Endowment House," in *Encyclopedia of Latter-day Saint History,* eds. Arnold K. Garr, Donald Q. Cannon, and Richard O. Cowan (Salt Lake City: Deseret Book, 2000), 336; Brown, "Temple Pro Tempore," 12.

16. Campbell, *Establishing Zion,* 169-70.

17. Brown, "Temple Pro Tempore," 7.

18. Minutes, May 5, 1855. For this and other sources quoted in the introduction, see fuller entries within the body of this work.

19. Tingen, "Endowment House," 9-11.

Counties in 1856, the First Presidency communicated the rules for admission:

> The persons who can get their endowments must be those who pray, who pay their tithing from year to year; who live the lives of saints from day to day; setting good examples before their neighbors. Men and women, boys and girls over 16 years of age who are living the lives of saints, believe in the plurality [of wives], do not speak evil of the authorities of the Church, and possess true integrity towards their friends, can come up after their spring crops are sown, and their case shall be attended to.[20]

In addition to "live" endowment sessions, the Endowment House also hosted proxy marriage sealings for individuals who had died or where one of a couple had died.[21] For some reason, Brigham Young waited to perform second anointings in the Endowment House until early January 1867. He may have initially assumed that the highest ordinance should only be performed in a full temple, but then decided that too much time had passed and the anointing should not be neglected.[22]

That same year, proxy baptisms for the dead were performed in the Endowment House after a pause of twenty years.[23] By the time the Endowment House closed in 1889, it had hosted 54,170 live endow-

---

20. Brigham Young, Heber C. Kimball, and Jedediah M. Grant to Stake Presidents and Bishops in Iron and Washington Counties, Mar. 2, 1856, in Parowan Historical Record, Mar. 16, 1856, 13. See also Edward L. Kimball, "The History of LDS Temple Admission Standards," *Journal of Mormon History* 24 (Spring 1998): 135-76.

21. When the Endowment House was razed in 1889, it was "a symbolic effort" to advertise the end of plural marriage (Holzapfel, "Endowment House," 337). It was also, according to David John Buerger, an effort to "refocus attention and funds upon completion of the temple" (*The Mysteries of Godliness: A History of Mormon Temple Worship* [San Francisco: Smith Research Associates, 1994], 98-99). D. Michael Quinn noted that this also made way for additional public works projects which the Church wanted to begin at the time in order to attract LDS workers to the city who would vote in a crucial election (D. Michael Quinn, "LDS Church Authority and New Plural Marriages, 1890-1904," *Dialogue: A Journal of Mormon Thought* 18 [Spring 1985]: 38). Lisle Brown thought the building was an unfortunate "casualty of the anti-Mormon polygamy crusade of the 1880s" and its destruction was not a preferable outcome (Brown, "Temple Pro Tempore," 51).

22. Buerger, *Mysteries of Godliness,* 101.

23. Campbell, *Establishing Zion,* 170.

ments, 31,052 live marriage sealings, 37,715 sealings for the dead, 694 second anointings, and 134,053 proxy baptisms for the dead.[24]

Brigham Young shuttered the revered building in 1876, telling those who wanted to be endowed that they would have to await completion of the St. George temple—even though it was 300 miles away.[25] This remained the policy until Young's death in August 1877, after which his successor, John Taylor (1808-87), reopened the Endowment House in November for young couples and older people who could not easily endure the hardship of a journey south.[26]

The first Utah temples

With the opening of the St. George temple, Latter-day Saints in that area experienced the thrill of having a permanent icon define their southern Utah community. The next temple completed was in northern Utah; the Logan temple was dedicated in 1884. It was followed in 1888 by the Manti temple in San Pete County, the area of south-central Utah that was settled by Scandinavians. These three beautiful temples were soon dwarfed in size and significance by the completion of the grand Salt Lake temple in 1893, which was four years after the second and final closure of the Endowment House.

Proxy endowments were not performed in the Endowment House. Prior to the opening of the St. George temple, one could only attend the endowment ceremony once, on behalf of oneself. The proxy ceremonies were begun by the first president of the St. George temple, Apostle Wilford Woodruff (1807-98), who also saw to the formalization of certain procedures.[27] However, as an official 1877 Church circular indicated, the protocols for attending the temple were still in flux:

> [Q] Can a brother or sister who has received Endowments in Salt Lake City or in Nauvoo, have the privilege of passing through the

24. Tingen, "Endowment House," 15.

25. Henry W. Bigler diary, Oct. 30, 1876, Utah State Historical Society, Salt Lake City.

26. Historian's Office Journal, Nov. 15, 1877, LDS Archives.

27. For Woodruff's overall influence in early Utah temple worship, see Richard E. Bennett, "Wilford Woodruff and the Rise of Temple Consciousness among the Latter-day Saints," in *Banner of the Gospel: Wilford Woodruff,* eds. Alex L. Baugh and Susan Easton Black (Provo: Religious Studies Center, 2010), 233-50.

> degrees in the St. George Temple; and if so, are they to be clothed with Temple Clothing, or in the ordinary manner?
> [A] They may have the privilege of passing through as visitors; and not wearing Temple clothing.
>
> [Q] If a person die[s] without having had endowments, is it well to bury them in garments without marks?
> [A] Such person may be buried with garments if their friends choose, but not marked, nor with robes or other Temple Clothing.[28]

In time, these issues would be smoothed out. Simultaneously, Church officials would come to see the need to standardize the endowment ceremony itself. On January 15, 1877, Wilford Woodruff, Brigham Young Jr., John D. T. McAllister, and L. John Nuttall began writing out the text of the ceremony they had previously retained by memory only. Working laboriously to avoid mistakes, it took them two months to complete the manuscript. The wisdom of committing the text to paper became evident as the Church maintained four operating temples over the next fifteen years, and the precaution guarded against careless drift in the script, as well as against unauthorized innovations.

Into the twentieth century

In 1900 the LDS membership stood at nearly 284,000. Over the next fifty years, it grew at a phenomenal rate to over 1 million. To accommodate the increase outside of Utah, Church leaders decided to dedicate temples in Laie, Hawaii, in 1919; Cardston, Alberta, in 1923; Mesa, Arizona, in 1927; and Idaho Falls, Idaho, in 1945.

Although he authorized the construction of the Hawaii temple, no new temples were dedicated during the long presidency of Joseph F. Smith (1838-1918), who presided over the Church from 1901 to 1918. However, President Smith continued to pay attention to temple-related policy. For example, he issued "Instructions Concerning Temple Ordinance Work," which stated in part:

> Those who do ordinance work have not the right to make matches [marriage sealings] between people who are deceased, except in cases of persons who were married in life. In all other instances the Presi-

28. "Questions Submitted to Pres[iden]t B[righa]m Young by the Elders Who Have Recently Been Out as Temple Missionaries," ca. 1877.

> dent of the Temple must be consulted. Persons who committed murder or suicide, or who apostatized or were excommunicated from the Church, cannot be officiated for except by special permission of the President of the Temple. He should be appealed to in all matters involving doubt or complications.[29]

In the early part of the twentieth century, the custom of abstaining from tobacco, alcohol, coffee, and tea grew in significance. As a result, it was decided in 1909 to make abstinence from such things mandatory for "all who enter the temple." Paradoxically, until July 1906, the Quorum of Twelve Apostles had spent afternoons in the temple four times a year "partaking of a sacrament" of bread and wine. The proximity to the recent change in emphasis was hinted at in the 1909 pronouncement, which recommended leniency for older people: "[When] elderly people may be found to be more or less lacking in their observance of the Word of Wisdom, and the question of their worthiness to be recommended to the temple comes before you for consideration, it will be in order for you and the Stake Presidency to consider together all such cases, deciding each on its own merits, and showing appropriate leniency to elderly people, as there can be no rigid rule for each and every case."[30] In 1917 Church leaders wrote to the board of the Idaho State Insane Asylum that, in general, Latter-day Saints committed to the asylum should not wear their temple garments. Yet again, there were exceptions: "Should any of the inmates however feel hurt in his or her feelings at being deprived of wearing the garment, we suggest that no change be made in his or her case."[31]

Perhaps nowhere was the unfinished nature of the temple ceremonies more evident than in the revisions that were made to them beginning with Brigham Young's additions to the ceremonies after Joseph Smith's death. In mid-1922, George F. Richards (1861-1950), who at the time served as the Salt Lake temple president and as a member of

29. Joseph F. Smith, *Instructions Concerning Temple Ordinance Work,* ca. 1905.

30. Joseph F. Smith, John R. Winder, and Anthon H. Lund to William H. Seegmiller and Counselors, Jan. 26, 1909; Thomas G. Alexander, *Mormonism in Transition: A History of the Latter-day Saints, 1890-1930* (Urbana and Chicago: University of Illinois Press, 1986), 261; Edward Leo Lyman, ed., *Candid Insights of a Mormon Apostle: The Diaries of Abraham H. Cannon, 1889-1895* (Salt Lake City: Signature Books/Smith Pettit Foundation, 2010), 85, 292.

31. Joseph F. Smith, Anthon H. Lund, and Charles W. Penrose to George H. Fisher, July 19, 1917.

the Quorum of Twelve Apostles, noted the changes that he was spearheading:

> Was in conference with the [First] Presidency for some time on Temple matters. Completed the rules and decisions for guidance of Temple Presidents and some changes in the ordinances. This is the fruition of a labor of months as I was able to devote myself to it. This is one of the accomplishments of my administration as Temple President of which I am greatly thankful and pleased. These rules and decisions have been gleaned from a number of books, manuscripts, and loose sheets[,] and obsolete ruling[s] have been eliminated and new rulings have been made & approved by the First Presidency. Copies of these decisions will be made and every Temple President will be supplied with a copy. The ordinances are all being rewritten and a copy will be furnished each temple. This should be the means of getting uniformity in all the temples.[32]

With approval to rewrite the ceremonies, Richards remained the most influential of anyone in advocating specific modifications. A few days later, he

> went before the [First] Presidency and presented to them an important change in the endowment ceremony by which the robes should be placed on the left shoulder first and then changed to the right shoulder once only before entering the Terrestrial room; also that Aaronic and Melchizedek be used instead of lower order of the Melchizedek and higher order of the Aaronic. I am to come back with a definite recommend of the Presidency of the Temple. This on my own suggestion.[33]

The First Presidency approved Richards's recommendations and offered rulings in areas where he posed questions and announced the changes to all temple workers on August 14, 1922. Richards's influence did not stop there. In September 1922, he noted in his diary that he "spent the day at the Temple where I read carefully all the ordinances used in the temples as changed and corrected and noted 18 times which I think need changing. It is my intention to present these to the [First] Presidency for their consideration. I also detected 7 errors in copying the ordinances." The following month, he wrote that after

---

32. George F. Richards diary, May 31, 1922.

33. Ibid., June 3, 1922.

a meeting with the First Presidency and Quorum of the Twelve, "the ceremonies, ordinances, and rules, decisions &c were approved and adopted. On these I have been working for months and for two years off and on and it is a great satisfaction to me to have them approved at this time in their present form."[34]

Record books containing corrected scripts and new instructions were delivered to all the Church's temples. "These books and their contents represent the work of months of my time and it is, I regard, a splendid accomplishment," Richards wrote. "All the temple ordinances have been considered and many changes have been made. More than 100 rules and decisions have been corr[e]lated and decided upon for the guidance of Temple presidents ... and all have been approved of the Council of the First Presidency, the Twelve and the Presiding Patriarch."[35]

Richards was not done yet. He decided to go to the temple again on September 23, 1923, to see if any other changes were needed.[36] He thought a correction was in order for the ceremony marrying couples for time but not eternity. This was approved on December 14.[37]

Although the changes were welcomed by most, some members were hesitant. David H. Cannon, president of the St. George temple since 1893, said in 1924 that Richards had "criticized [him] very severely" for not following the new guidelines regarding the unscripted portions of the rituals. Richards emphasized to him that the older precedents were obsolete.[38]

Richards then gave a nice summary, at the conclusion of his two-year task:

> I can say that since I became the President of the Salt Lake Temple we have re-written those temple ceremonies and ordinances which ha[d] been heretofore written, first at the time of the Dedication of the St. George Temple, and have put them into leatherback covers as loose leaves and provided each Temple President with a copy. Later those ceremonies known as unwritten ceremonies i.e. the covenants and the instructions given in forming the [prayer] circle and at the veil, were

34. Ibid., Oct. 5, 1922.

35. Ibid., Dec. 5, 1922

36. Ibid., Sept. 23, 1923.

37. Ibid., Dec. 14, 1923.

38. Buerger, *Mysteries of Godliness,* 141.

> written and copies furnished on loose leaf sheets for the Presidents of Temples Book. A list of 83 rules and decisions have been written[,] also for the guidance of Temple Presidents[,] supplanting all former rules not in full harmony. Each of the Temple Presidents has been supplied with copies, or rather, they were included in the Books when they [were] first sent out to the Temple Presidents.

Explaining why he, and not the First Presidency, initiated these improvements, Richards wrote that the presidency "could not be expected to be in touch with all the details of Temple work & with the needed changes only as these things are brought to their attention[,] and who should do this if not the Apostle in charge of the Salt Lake & Leading Temple of the church[?]"[39] Richards's influence over the liturgy in the twentieth century cannot be exaggerated. His actions showed the way for later leaders who would make additional modifications as well.[40]

Some new policies were quietly introduced in the pre-World War II years. The First Presidency decided in 1937 to disallow further baptisms for living people inside the temples, reserving the fonts exclusively for proxy baptisms.[41] In 1940 the ring ceremony was removed from the marriage sealing, as were rooms with altars at which individuals could pray privately.[42] By the time the Idaho Falls temple was dedicated in 1945, the ceremonies, policies, and practices seemed set in stone for the time being. However, when considering building temples in foreign countries, a new set of challenges paved the way for changes that would eventually affect domestic temples too.

World-wide expansion

Meeting the needs of Church members living abroad was the focus of temple building at mid-century under the presidency of David O. McKay (1873-1970). The first temple in Europe was in Zolikofen, a suburb of Berne, Switzerland, dedicated in 1955. In 1956 a temple was dedicated in Los Angeles, followed by two more overseas—the

39. Richards diary, July 12, 1924.

40. For more on Richards and temple work, see Dale C. Mouritsen, "A Symbol of New Directions: George Franklin Richards and the Mormon Church, 1861-1950," Ph.D. diss., Brigham Young University, 1982, 195-229.

41. Ibid., June 21, 1937.

42. Ibid., Sept. 5, 1940.

first in Hamilton, New Zealand, the second in London, England, both dedicated in 1958. There would not be another temple outside the United States for twenty years until the dedication of the São Paulo temple in 1978. Earlier, in 1964, California became the second state with more than one temple when the Church dedicated the imposing structure in the Oakland hills in 1964. This was the only temple built in the 1960s.

Taking the ceremonies overseas to meet the needs of an expanding membership was challenging and in some respects risky. New Zealand, for example, supported only 3,000 members, but President McKay believed it was the "safest" country outside of Europe where a temple could be built. McKay biographers Gregory Prince and Robert Wright show that when McKay spearheaded the overseas building, it was

> unprecedented on two levels: It was the first time temples were constructed outside North America (including Hawaii) and the first time they were constructed where stakes did not already exist. It was a calculated risk on McKay's part, but he was confident that such temples would anchor church members in their native countries, thus curtailing emigration to the United States and allowing the creation of overseas stakes.[43]

As these temples were being considered, McKay met with Gordon B. Hinckley (1910-2008), then a member of the temple department, and assigned him to devise a way to translate the ceremonies into eight languages. To accommodate this, Hinckley suggested replacing live actors with a filmed version of the endowment ceremony, which would also allow the ceremony to take place without having to move participants from room to room. Hinckley's suggestion was approved, and filming took place on the fifth floor of the Salt Lake temple. Production of later films was moved to a dedicated sound stage at Brigham Young University.[44]

With the idea of moving to film, the First Presidency wrote to the Walt Disney studios in April 1955 for permission to use three minutes of their animated movie, *Fantasia*. That portion of the Disney film portrayed the formation of the earth, which the presidency felt would

43. Gregory A. Prince and William Robert Wright, *David O. McKay and the Rise of Modern Mormonism* (Salt Lake City: University of Utah Press, 2005), 261.

44. "Swiss Temple Dedication a Bold Act of Faith," *Church News,* Sept. 17, 2005.

be appropriate to accompany the Creation narrative. Disney granted permission on May 25 for a five-year period. At the Church's pleading, Disney later granted an extension, the Church promising: "The public is never invited to these classes; no publicity is ever given, and no admission charge is ever made. This most excellent footage has become inseparably a part of the ... [temple program] in establishing a mood of reverence and awe for the Creator's work." This segment from *Fantasia* was used until the ceremony was again revised in 1989-90.[45]

One approach to making the temple accessible to members around the world was to literally take the temple to the members rather than ask the members to come to the temple. In October 1968, Mark Garff, who chaired the Church Building Committee, proposed purchasing and outfitting a ship as a sailing temple. By docking this portable temple in various countries, the costs involved in constructing temples would be avoided. It seemed like a good idea at first, but on October 11, 1968, Alvin R. Dyer, a counselor to the First Presidency, worried that "in the very early days of the Church the Prophet Joseph [Smith] had said that the waters would be cursed, that he did not know exactly what that might mean but that we should not be insensible to that." Dyer "also mentioned the fact that when the saints came to Utah they had to wait forty years before a temple was completed and he did not think it was so urgent that people who live in distant places could not wait a little for a temple."[46] On October 24, McKay responded to a question by saying that "as far as I was concerned we are not considering this proposition," advising people against planning trips around its hypothetical appearance.[47]

Temple building returned to Utah after a barren period of nearly eighty years with the completion in 1972 of structures in Ogden and Provo that were described as having a space-age look. They were dedicated by President Joseph Fielding Smith (1876-1972). Nine years later,

45. All correspondence between LDS leaders and Disney Studio are typed excerpts in the David John Buerger Papers, Special Collections, J. Willard Marriott Library, University of Utah.

46. "Minutes of President Alvin R. Dyer of a Meeting with the First Presidency held in President McKay's Apartment," in David O. McKay diary, Oct. 11, 1968. For Joseph Smith's teaching that the waters are cursed, see Doctrine and Covenants 61:14-16.

47. McKay diary, Oct. 24, 1968, qtd. in Prince and Wright, *David O. McKay and the Rise of Modern Mormonism,* 275.

the Salt Lake Valley received its second, the Jordan River temple, dedicated in 1981. This brought the number of temples in Utah to seven; by 2010, the number had risen to thirteen, with two more announced or under construction.

The first temple dedicated under President Spencer W. Kimball (1895-1985) was a towering structure near the nation's capital, called the Washington, D.C., temple. The sixteenth in operation, it ushered in an escalated era of temple building. By Kimball's death in 1985, the number of temples Churchwide had more than doubled. Of thirty-six then in operation, eighteen were located outside the United States.

In the decade after Kimball's death, his immediate successors, Ezra Taft Benson (1899-1994) and Howard W. Hunter (1907-1995), oversaw the completion of eleven more sacred buildings, and beginning under President Benson's administration Church leaders revised the endowment ceremony again, removing some of the symbolism and rewording some of the text.[48] After President Hinckley flew to Hong Kong to dedicate the forty-eighth temple in 1996, the most unprecedented building era began. Over the next three and a half years, another twenty temples would be dedicated, bringing the number to sixty-eight. Many of these were small and were located adjacent to existing Church buildings. In fact, the temple in Vernal, Utah, was fashioned out of an existing building, the Uintah Tabernacle, that was built in 1907, and refurbished in 1997.

The pace continued into the new millennium. As the Church completed construction of a new, 20,000-seat, granite-faced conference center in downtown Salt Lake City in 2000, it also raced to complete its 100th temple before October conference. In order to reach that mark, the Church had to complete thirty-two new temples that year before October; it would do so and go on to finish an additional two by year's end, bringing the count to 102. Temple building slowed somewhat thereafter, with thirty-two dedicated by August 2010. However, considering that it took the Church 154 years to dedicate its first thirty-two temples, the accomplishment in constructing as many in a ten-year period reflected positively on the Church's growth and sta-

---

48. See the articles in the *Arizona Republic,* Apr. 28, 1990; *Salt Lake Tribune,* Apr. 29, 1990; *New York Times,* May 3, 1990; and *Los Angeles Times,* May 5, June 2, 1990. For a summary, see "Comments on Temple Changes Elicit Church Discipline," *Sunstone* 14 (June 1990): 60.

bility. Of the last thirty-two temples, as of this writing, seventeen were built outside the United States.

Perhaps the symbolically most significant edifice since the 1893 completion of the monumental Salt Lake City temple was the emergence in 2002 of a temple in Nauvoo in the same design as the one the Church had abandoned there in the nineteenth century. Besides the intent to serve Midwestern (as well as vacationing) Church members, the temple serves as a reminder of the membership's pioneer heritage and as a symbol of triumph over adversity.

Modifications

Between the time when ordinances were perfected in the attic story of the unfinished Nauvoo temple and the time when that sacred edifice was rebuilt, LDS leaders saw the need to occasionally modify aspects of the temple rituals, as well as the policies surrounding performance of the ordinances. Church leaders have consistently reminded the general membership of the sacred nature of the temple and encouraged those who qualify to receive their endowments. At the same time, the Church has faced the challenge of keeping the underlying message relevant to members living in different cultural settings than existed at the time the ceremonies were conceived.

Temple garments

In the Nauvoo temple, an initiate would present himself or herself before an officiator who would proceed to cut markings into his or her underclothing. The marks were to be hemmed by the initiate at a later time, at home, to make the marks permanent. The significance of this has been explained only obliquely, giving rise to various private interpretations. Brigham Young thought the garments had magical powers, saying that Willard Richards had been protected from bodily harm when he was shot at in Carthage, Illinois, standing alongside Joseph and Hyrum Smith, who were assassinated. The Smiths had apparently removed their garments due to the heat, while Richards had not. "The balls flew around [Richards], riddled his clothes," Young said, "and shaved a passage through one of his whiskers" but did not otherwise harm him.[49]

The earliest garments were union suits that extended the length of

49. Buerger, *Mysteries of Godliness,* 148.

the arm to the wrist and the length of the leg to the ankle. They could only be made of white cotton, flax, or wool.[50] Unlike underwear today consisting of shorts and a t-shirt, or panties and a camisole, the garments were one-piece articles of clothing that had to be stepped into through the hemmed neckline. Members were warned not to let the garments be "altered or mutilated" to short-sleeved cutoffs or to give them a lower neckline. "These requirements are imperative; admission to the Temple will be refused to those who do not comply therewith," one communication read.[51] "The Saints should know that the pattern of endowment garments was revealed from heaven," President Joseph F. Smith added in 1912, "and that the blessings promised in connection with wearing them will not be realized if any unauthorized change is made in their form, or in the manner of wearing them."[52] The president could not understand why members would "mutilate them, in order that we may follow the foolish, vain and (permit me to say) indecent practices of the world."[53]

Over time, Church leaders would nevertheless accommodate long-term changes in the concept of underwear design.[54] In April 1923, they did away with the collar flap, replaced tie-strings with buttons, and allowed women to wear modified garments with sleeves as far as the elbows and legs to the knees.[55] In 1930 shorter garments were approved for men, although the First Presidency qualified this to require that when in the temple itself, men would be required to "wear the approved garment in use before the above modifications were approved."[56] The old-style, ceremonial garments remained current in the temple for another forty-five years. The idea of doing away with the traditional

50. Abraham H. Cannon diary, Dec. 7, 1893.

51. Smith, *Instructions Concerning Temple Ordinance Work.*

52. Joseph F. Smith to Bishops of Wards, ca. 1912.

53. Joseph F. Smith, "Fashion and the Violation of Covenants and Duty," *Improvement Era* 9 (Aug. 1906): 813-14.

54. According to a Church educator whose brother-in-law was in the Quorum of Twelve Apostles, the quorum once discussed doing away with garments altogether except when inside the temple. The idea originated with Apostle Melvin J. Ballard, according to the second-hand account, whose wife found the garments uncomfortable ("Conversation with George T. Boyd, July 3, 1986," Buerger Papers.)

55. George F. Richards diary, Apr. 14, 1923.

56. Heber J. Grant to Ruth May Fox, Lucy G. Cannon, and Clarissa Beesley, June 17, 1930.

style in the temple was debated for years before it was approved. For example, in 1969, President David O. McKay's office journal read:

> It seemed inconsistent to place on the individual in the temple ceremony the so-called ceremonial garment telling him that he must wear it the rest of his life and then giving permission for him to immediately replace this garment with the modified garment normally worn by members of the Church. Then too the temple ordinance workers and even the ones who place the garments on the individual are themselves wearing the modified garment. President [N. Eldon] Tanner felt that this matter should be referred to the Twelve [Apostles] before this change is made.[57]

In 1972 the First Presidency reaffirmed its commitment to "the old style garment" in the temple.[58] Then in 1975 it decided that temple patrons could wear either the old style or the new, according to their personal preference.[59] Four years later, they surprised Church members by making the bold and popular decision to allow two-piece garments consisting of a top and bottom.[60] In 1998 Church leaders discounted the idea that the garments offered a physical shield for wearers, explaining that the protection they provide is "against temptation and evil."[61]

The second anointing

Joseph Smith introduced the second anointing the same day, September 28, 1843, that women were introduced to the endowment. Prior to that time, women were not allowed into the inner sanctum of the Anointed Quorum. Even so, nineteen men and seventeen women received their second anointing in the short span of nine months before Smith's death.[62] He introduced it to trusted followers as the "fulness of

---

57. David O. McKay diary, April 8, 1969.

58. Joseph Fielding Smith, Harold B. Lee, and N. Eldon Tanner to Boyd F. Schenk, Feb. 16, 1972.

59. Spencer W. Kimball, N. Eldon Tanner, and Marion G. Romney to All Temple Presidents, Nov. 10, 1975.

60. Spencer W. Kimball, N. Eldon Tanner, and Marion G. Romney to Executive Administrators, Regional Representatives, Stake, Mission, and District Presidents, Bishops, Branch Presidents, and Temple Presidents, Dec. 15, 1979.

61. *Church Handbook of Instructions, Book 1* (Salt Lake City: Church of Jesus Christ of Latter-day Saints, 1998), 69.

62. See Devery S. Anderson and Gary James Bergera, eds., *Joseph Smith's Quo-*

the priesthood," saying it fulfilled the promise of the first anointing in confirming their appointments as kings and priests, queens and priestesses in the next life. The second anointing was said to be the "crowning ordinance" of the Restoration, a ritual that "seal[ed] their exaltation upon them while they are yet in this life."[63]

The ordinance was typically performed in two parts. The first involved an officiator, who performed the anointing in the temple. The second part was performed at home, with only the husband and wife present. According to David Buerger, "In this part of the ordinance, the wife symbolically prepared her husband for his death and resurrection, a ceremony that gave the wife a claim on her husband ... in the resurrection."[64]

After Smith's death, Brigham Young increased the number of second anointings and opened the ordinance to plural wives. Before the temple closed in February 1846, a total of 603 second anointings had been performed, nine of which were by proxy for the dead.[65] Then the ritual was curtailed for over three decades until 694 anointings were ultimately performed in the Endowment House before its closure in 1889.[66]

An interesting dilemma was the difficulty in establishing standard protocols for determining who should be invited to receive the highest temple ordinance. In 1884, President John Taylor let it be known that he alone would "designate the parties who should receive these ordinances."[67] He allowed recommendations from families for deceased ancestors but not for the living. Understandably, those who acted as proxies for the dead had to have already received the ordinance themselves.[68]

---

rum of the Anointed, 1842-1845: A Documentary History (Salt Lake City: Signature Books/Smith-Pettit Foundation, 2005), xxxvi.

63. See Glen M. Leonard, *Nauvoo: A Place of Peace, a People of Promise* (Salt Lake City: Deseret Book Co, 1992), 260-61; Bruce R. McConkie, *Mormon Doctrine,* 2d ed. (Salt Lake City: Bookcraft, 1966), 109-10; David John Buerger, "'The Fulness of the Priesthood': The Second Anointing in Latter-day Saint Theology and Practice," *Dialogue: A Journal of Mormon Thought* 16 (Spring 1983): 10-44.

64. Buerger, "Fullness of Priesthood," 26.

65. Anderson and Bergera, *Nauvoo Endowment Companies,* xxviii.

66. Tingen, "Endowment House," 15.

67. L. John Nuttall to John D. T. McAllister, Sept. 19, 1884.

68. David H. Cannon to John D. T. McAllister, Dec. 4, 1885; John Taylor to John D. T. McAllister, Dec. 9, 1885; John Taylor to Eliza Perry Benson, Mar. 4, 1886.

With a third temple in the works away from headquarters, the president decided to let local leaders submit names of candidates for the honor, although with a reminder that "unworthy persons" not be "recommended for this ordinance." Candidates would still be screened by the president himself.[69] President Taylor's successor, Wilford Woodruff, continued to discourage individuals from requesting the ordinance, for themselves or for their "faithful aged," preferring "that their names should be presented by their bishop and stake president," he wrote.[70] In 1901 bishops were told not to make recommendations, reserving the responsibility to stake presidents.[71] President Lorenzo Snow decided that only those who had gathered to Utah were worthy to receive the highest ordinance—not only among the living, but also among the dead unless they had desired to immigrate but had been prevented from doing so.[72]

In 1903 the Church presidency discovered that officiators were encouraging patrons to request a second anointing. The First Presidency instructed one temple president:

> When such persons come to their Stake Presidents and ask for this blessing, saying they were counselled to do so in the temple, it places him in the unpleasant position, perhaps, that he has to refuse their request, and he is blamed by the applicants. No person has the right to ask for this blessing. He must wait till sought out by his Stake President. If the President of a temple feels impressed with the worthiness of any person, dead or alive, he can make suggestions to the President of the Stake, but he should not mention this to the persons themselves.[73]

Because of the confidential nature of the anointing—recipients were instructed not to talk about it openly—by 1917 it was performed only on Fridays. There was also a prohibition on more than one couple per stake receiving the anointing at the same time so that acquaintances

---

69. John Taylor and George Q. Cannon to Jesse W. Crosby and Counselors, Mar. 17, 1887.

70. Wilford Woodruff to Daniel H. Wells, Sept. 28, 1888.

71. George F. Gibbs to Christian N. Lund, Feb. 25, 1901.

72. Joseph F. Smith and John R. Winder to David John and Joseph B. Keeler, Mar. 18, 1902.

73. Joseph F. Smith, John R. Winder, and Anthon H. Lund to John D. T. McAllister, Aug. 25, 1903; also George F. Gibbs to John F. Tolton, Sept. 20, 1908.

would not see each other and guess that the other couple was there for the same purpose.[74]

In 1926 stake presidents were asked to stop recommending individuals, as the Church presidency now reserved the right to do so to members of the Quorum of the Twelve. Because most members were not personally known to the apostles, recommendations were usually made when members of the hierarchy visited stakes and heard about individuals from stake presidents.[75] The change in policy, according to George F. Richards, occurred when

> about 1928 [1926] an incident occurred which so incensed the First Presidency that they had all the recommend books brought in to the President's office, and instructions were given that no recommends of that character should be given by stake presidents thereafter. …
>
> A brother who had received his Second Blessings, while speaking in a priesthood meeting in one of the Idaho stakes, told the brethren that they all should have their Second Blessings. Of course that was a serious infraction of the charge which he received when he had his Second Anointings; but I have never learned of any serious consequences to follow, except the action on the part of the Authorities, discontinuing the administration of those blessings in the Church.[76]

In time, Richards would become so distraught that the ordinance had fallen into disuse, he wrote the First Presidency and Twelve in 1949 that he could not bring himself "to feel that the Lord is pleased with us in neglecting such an important and sacred endowment." Up to that time, 32,901 second anointings had been performed throughout the Church, but during the last twelve years, Richards pointed out, there had been only eight. "It is to be hoped that this communication will not be shelved and forgotten without full consideration by this Council." He added: "For several years these matters have given me great mental anxiety and spiritual concern, and but for want of courage I would have sought an opportunity to be heard years ago."[77] The brethren listened

74. George F. Gibbs to William D. Kuhre, Mar. 17, 1917.

75. Heber J. Grant to Stephen L. Chipman, Jan. 30, 1926; Buerger, "Fulness of the Priesthood," 40.

76. George F. Richards to the First Presidency and Quorum of the Twelve, Aug. 18, 1949.

77. Richards to the First Presidency and Quorum of the Twelve, Aug. 18, 1949.

to the extent that they authorized the second anointing for general authorities who had not yet received it.[78] Richards died in August 1950.

The second anointing continues to be performed on a limited basis. In 1966, the First Presidency "went over a list of the Brethren of the General Authorities who have not had their second anointings." David O. McKay asked Joseph Fielding Smith "to officiate at these ordinances in behalf of these Brethren."[79] David Buerger interviewed three temple presidents who confirmed that the ordinance is still being performed, although it remains shrouded in secrecy.[80] And as Buerger concluded, "the current official policy initiated by Heber J. Grant suggests that Church authorities now feel that the second anointing is not required for exaltation."[81]

The status of blacks

Black members of African descent have had an unusual history in the LDS Church. Although Joseph Smith ordained at least one black man to the priesthood, Brigham Young declared in 1849, and reiterated in an address to the Utah territorial legislature in 1852, that "any man having one drop of the seed of [Cain] ... in him cannot hold the priesthood and if no other Prophet ever spake it before I will say it now in the name of Jesus Christ."[82] This priesthood restriction has been interpreted by Church leaders ever since as having come from God. Because priesthood was required of men entering the temple, blacks (men and women both) were unable to receive the endowment or temple sealing ordinances until the policy changed in June 1978. Before that date, local LDS leaders often asked for clarification regarding the extent of the priesthood ban and if it meant complete exclusion of black members from temple-related activities.

One of the earliest accommodations to a black member was that offered to Jane Manning James (1822-1908), an early convert who had lived with the Smith family in Nauvoo. In 1894, James petitioned Church leaders to be sealed to Joseph Smith, as many women had

78. Richards diary, Dec. 7, 1949; Jan. 6, Apr. 20, 1950.

79. McKay diary, Nov. 9, 1966.

80. Buerger, "Fulness of the Priesthood," 43n122.

81. Ibid., 43.

82. Qtd. in Lester E. Bush Jr., "Mormonism's Negro Doctrine: An Historical Overview," *Dialogue: A Journal of Mormon Thought* 8 (Spring 1973): 25-26.

been, but her request was denied because of the priesthood ban. As something of a compromise, she was permitted to be sealed as a servant "for eternity to the prophet Josep[h] Smith and in this capacity be connected with his family and be obedient to him in all things in the Lord as a faithful Servitor."[83] The wording suggests that little thought was given to any future changes in the status of blacks in the hereafter.

In the 1960s the First Presidency received several letters regarding black members who desired to participate in, or receive, temple ordinances. President David O. McKay denied temple admittance in 1962 to a girl whose mother was white and father black.[84] The matter of children of an interracial couple was addressed again three years later when a woman, once married to a black man and who had borne two children by him, wanted to be sealed to her current white husband and have the previous children sealed to them. McKay granted permission for the marriage sealing but withheld allowing the children to be sealed to them.[85]

The next year, President McKay addressed a similar issue regarding a woman who had been to the temple and subsequently married a black man. The woman was told by her local Church leader "that no further Temple visits would be allowed her, and that[,] because of her marriage to a Negro[,] her Temple endowments are ineffective." McKay overruled the invalidation of her endowments but did prevent her from visiting the temple again. "The [ward] Bishopric also are to be told that any children born of this marriage cannot hold the Priesthood; however, there is no reason why she cannot be active in the Ward and Stake."[86]

Eligibility for temple ordinances changed in August 1966, but the new policy did not ease the restriction against blacks. In a letter to local Church leaders throughout the world, the First Presidency stated that "after the expiration of one year from the date of death, temple ordinances may be performed for all deceased persons, except those of known Negro blood, without the consideration of worthiness or any other qualification."[87] Yet in September that year, President McKay

83. Book of Temple Ordinances, May 18, 1894, 33-34, citing Adoption Record, Book A, 26, in "Confidential Research Files," copy in Buerger Papers.

84. McKay diary, July 17, 1962.

85. Ibid., Apr. 14, 1965.

86. Ibid., Jan. 12, 1966.

87. David O. McKay, Hugh B. Brown, N. Eldon Tanner, and Joseph Fielding

"could see no objection to the sealing" of a white couple to the black children they had adopted.[88] In a mixed message seven months later, a bishop was told to discourage a couple that was considering a similar adoption.[89]

That said, in 1968, President McKay authorized the most inclusive policy yet regarding blacks:

> Attention was called to a letter from President Reuel E. Christensen of the Manti Temple reporting that a bishop and stake president in one of the BYU Stakes had inquired if they could send colored people who are members of the Church in good standing ... to do baptismal work for the dead in the temple.
>
> I ruled that worthy negro baptized members of the Church should be permitted to do baptismal work for the dead if they desire to do so.[90]

Proxy baptisms remained the only temple work that black members could perform until June 1978, when President Spencer W. Kimball extended priesthood ordination to all worthy males regardless of race. Such a change may have been anticipated as early as 1974. That year, Kimball announced that a temple would be built in Brazil, a country with a high percentage of racially mixed marriages. Many Brazilian members were descendants of interracial relationships. Had the policy not changed in 1978, very few local Saints would have been able to attend the Brazilian temple after its formal dedication the following December.[91]

The status of women

Although Joseph Smith initially introduced the endowment to men only, sixteen months later, on September 28, 1843, women were initiated into the Quorum of the Anointed, which met regularly until mid-1844.[92] Not that questions involving women were given high

---

Smith to Presidents of Stakes, Bishops of Wards, Presidents of Missions, and Presidents of Temples, Aug. 15, 1966.

88. McKay diary, Sept. 27, 1966.

89. Ibid., Apr. 26, 1967.

90. Ibid., Dec. 5, 1968.

91. For the story of the Brazilian temple, see Mark L. Grover, "The Mormon Priesthood Revelation and the São Paulo, Brazil Temple," *Dialogue: A Journal of Mormon Thought* 23 (Spring 1990): 39-53.

92. For the story of the Anointed Quorum, see Anderson and Bergera, *Joseph Smith's Quorum of the Anointed.*

priority. In 1887 the First Presidency was asked if a woman who had left her husband after receiving her second anointing could be anointed to a second man. "There is no necessity to answer this question until a case arises which may require an answer," the First Presidency responded.[93]

In 1884, President John Taylor said that a woman who married someone of another faith should not be asked to officiate at the temple, and further that "being married to a gentile, it is not proper for her to wear her garments."[94] This was reiterated by the First Presidency in 1916:

> The rule of the temple is that a woman who marries outside of the Church cannot receive a recommend to go through the temple, because her husband would be very apt to ask her to reveal the temple ordinances and if she refused to do so it would cause contention between them. If she has married a man in the Church, and she desires to receive her endowments, we do not feel that it would be wise for her to receive her endowments before her husband, and hence bishops are told not to give recommendations to wives before their husbands go with them to the temple.[95]

In 1929 the presidency held firm to this policy.[96] Yet for reasons not entirely clear, they announced four years later that a wife could receive a temple recommend if she received written consent from her non-Mormon husband. "However, women should not be urged nor requested to take advantage of this ruling," the presidency wrote. The guideline applied only to women who approached a priesthood leader with this question.[97]

Before the end of the 1930s, the First Presidency admitted that "some unfortunate and untoward incidents" had resulted from the policy. "You will not give a recommend, under any circumstances, to a wife whose husband is not a member of the Church," they emphatically told

---

93. Wilford Woodruff to Marriner Wood Merrill, Sept. 9, 1887.

94. John Taylor to Marriner Wood Merrill, Nov. 6, 1884.

95. Anthon H. Lund and Charles W. Penrose to Edward H. Snow, Mar. 11, 1916.

96. *Appointments, Instructions and Suggestions Issued by the Logan Temple, Jan. 1, 1929, for the Issue of Presidents of Stakes, Bishops of Wards and Genealogical Committees in the Logan Temple District.*

97. *Handbook of Instructions,* Number 15 (Salt Lake City: Church of Jesus Christ of Latter-day Saints, 1934), 10-11.

stake presidents. If a woman's husband was a member of the Church but had not been to the temple, he "must express his willingness and consent in writing" before the woman could attend the temple.[98] If a woman had already been to the temple before marrying outside of the Church, as the brethren explained three years later, she could continue to receive a temple recommend.[99] In 1970 the First Presidency decided that a woman married to an inactive member would henceforth be prevented from entering the temple "even though the husband is willing to give his consent in writing for his wife to receive her endowment."[100]

When Church leaders reaffirmed this policy in the 1976 *General Handbook of Instructions*, they noted that the same restriction did not apply to husbands: "A worthy man whose wife has not received her endowments may be given a recommend to receive his own endowments."[101] In such an instance, the wife's permission was not required. Over the next decade, the Church was criticized for its antifeminist positions, including for instance its public stance against the Equal Rights Amendment.[102] It is not known if sensitivity to such criticism influenced the following change, but in 1986 the First Presidency reversed itself on the policy preventing women from attending the temple if they were married to non-Mormons, and although this revision required permission of the husband, now for the first time men were similarly required to receive permission from a non-Mormon wife. In fact, the wording of the change deliberately made no mention of gender at all:

> A person who is married to an unendowed spouse may receive a recommend when he or she has provided the bishop with written consent of the spouse and both the bishop and the stake president are sat-

98. Heber J. Grant, J. Reuben Clark Jr., and David O. McKay to Presidents of Stakes and Missions, Oct. 17, 1938.

99. Heber J. Grant, J. Reuben Clark Jr., and David O. McKay to Presidents of Stakes, Bishops of Wards, and Presidents of Missions, Feb. 1, 1941.

100. *Priesthood Bulletin* 6 (Aug. 1970), 3:1, 6.

101. *General Handbook of Instructions,* Number 21 (Salt Lake City: Church of Jesus Christ of Latter-day Saints, 1976), 53-66, 98-99.

102. For more on the LDS Church's involvement in the ERA controversy, see Martha Sonntag Bradley, *Pedestals and Podiums: Utah Women, Religious Authority, and Equal Rights* (Salt Lake City: Signature Books/Smith-Pettit Foundation, 2005).

> isfied through appropriate interviews that the responsibilities assumed with the endowment will not impair marital harmony.[103]

Unlike priesthood ordination, which is restricted to males, this policy regarding temple attendance conveys the message that spiritual blessings are available to women independent of their husbands. This may well set precedent for other changes regarding women in the future.[104]

....

ABOUT THIS COMPILATION

The excerpts in the following chapters chronicle LDS temple worship from the time the Church was preparing to leave Nauvoo, Illinois, in early 1846 up to the dawn of the twenty-first century. The excerpts consist of entries from diaries and portions of minutes, letters, sermons, and official LDS publications. Every effort has been made to reproduce as faithfully as possible the text of the original documents. Where needed, I have inserted textual clarifications in enclosed brackets and provided annotations in footnotes. While I do not presume to have satisfied every reader's wishes, I hope to have struck a reasonable balance between readability and fidelity to the original texts without unnecessary intrusion.

My thanks to the early diarists who recorded their experiences in attending the temple and Endowment House and what those experiences meant to them. I am grateful to the repositories which showed foresight in preserving these documents. Thank you also to the Smith-Pettit Foundation for making available to me transcripts of and excerpts from (1) the George Q. Cannon, Spencer W. Kimball, and Joseph Fielding Smith diaries and other documents from the D. Michael Quinn Papers at Yale University; (2) the Samuel Bateman, Lorenzo Brown, Abraham H. Cannon, Esaias Edwards, Henry Eyring, Joseph

103. Ezra Taft Benson, Gordon B. Hinckley, and Thomas S. Monson to All General Authorities, Regional Representatives, Stake, Mission, and District Presidents, Bishops, and Branch Presidents, Feb. 12, 1986.

104. For more on the authority granted women by the endowment, see D. Michael Quinn, "Mormon Women Have Held the Priesthood Since 1843," in *Women and Authority: Reemerging Mormon Feminism,* ed. Maxine Hanks (Salt Lake City: Signature Books, 1992), 365-409.

Fish, Richard R. Lyman, John D. T. McAllister, and Samuel Hollister Rogers diaries, the J. Reuben Clark diary, and selected documents from the L. John Nuttall Papers, all at the Harold B. Lee Library at Brigham Young University; (3) items, including excerpts from the LDS Church Historian's Office Journal, from the 78 compact disks of *Selected Collections from the Archives of the Church of Jesus Christ of Latter-day Saints*; (4) the Book of Temple Ordinances (St. George), Temple Historical Book (Manti), Temple Historical Book (St. George), Temple Minute Book (St. George), and notes of interviews with Henry E. Christianson, T. Edgar Lyon, L. Garrett Myers, Alfonso G. Pia, George F. Richards Jr., and Frank S. Wise and other items from the David John Buerger Papers, as well as the Frederick Kesler Sr., William Henry Smart, and John M. Whitaker diaries at the J. Willard Marriott Library, University of Utah; (5) items, including transcriptions of Brigham Young's diaries and journals, in the Leonard James Arrington Papers at the Merrill-Cazier Library at Utah State University; and (6) the Henry W. Bigler diary, Thomas A. Clawson diary, and items from the Anthony W. Ivins Papers at the Utah State Historical Society. I am also indebted to the unidentified researchers who compiled "Confidential Research Files," "Research Notes on LDS Higher Ordinances," and "Research Notes on LDS Temples," which pointed me toward important concepts and documents. Unless otherwise noted, the editor has in his possession transcriptions of the letters included from the First Presidency, as well as of some of the temple presidency minutes.

The documents tell the importance of temple ordinances to LDS people. They provide context for modifications to ordinances of late, as well as to changes made in the past, and document the Church hierarchy's determination to make the ordinances understandable to a growing Church, while at the same time remaining loyal to the underlying doctrines and symbols. One may ponder the various reasons behind changes to the covenants, yet it is clear that administrative and organizational flexibility has prevented the ordinances and practices from becoming irrelevant for the majority of believing Saints.

For a documentary history of the endowment and related ceremonies during the LDS Church's Nauvoo years, readers may wish to consult my companion volumes, co-authored by Gary James Bergera, *Joseph Smith's Quorum of the Anointed, 1842-1845: A Documentary History* and *The Nauvoo Endowment Companies, 1845-1846: A Documentary*

History, both published in 2005. In all three volumes, care has been taken to limit discussion to what is appropriate, given the restrictions imposed by the LDS Church to preserve the sanctity and in some cases confidentiality of the proceedings where it is thought best to do so.

1.

"UNTIL THE COMING OF THE SON OF MAN" 1846-1880

On February 4, 1846, the first wagons were ferried across the Mississippi River from Nauvoo to Montrose, Iowa, beginning a months-long evacuation of the Mormon capital city. After the start of the exodus, the temple remained in full operation for four days, thereafter providing sacred space only for prayer circles, not for other ordinances, through September when the building was overrun by insurgents and abandoned by the Church. The following entries indicate the building's use during its decline, the continuation of prayer circles in makeshift quarters across the plains, and the renewal of temple ordinances in Utah.

President Joseph Young[1] met in the Temple with a company of saints for prayer, and organized companies[2] for prayer to meet every night. **—*History of the Church*, Feb. 11, 1846**

---

1. Joseph Young (1797-1881) was Brigham Young's brother and a convert to Mormonism in 1832. He migrated to Utah in 1850 and served a mission to England in 1870.

2. These companies of previously initiated temple worshipers were sometimes referred to as quorums. Their purpose was to dress in temple clothing, rehearse the signs and tokens of the temple endowment, and engage in ritualistic prayer, including invocations to bless the righteous and sometimes to curse the wicked.

At office until 5 [p.m.] assisting Dr. [Willard Richards][3] when I [then] went to the Temple to pray. [There were] 13 [people on hand who] met[,] and Pres. Joseph Young prayed[,] after which 15 bottles of oil were consecrated.[4] **—Thomas Bullock journal, 5 Feb. 12, 1846**

Commenced a regular meeting with the Brethren in the Temple for prayers, to continue, so long as we staid in the place, beginning near the hour of sunset. **—Samuel W. Richards,[6] Feb. 12, 1846**

Two companies met for prayer in the House of the Lord this evening, and prayed for the preservation of the Twelve [Apostles], and that they might have wisdom to guide the Saints in the paths of peace and safety; for the healing of the sick, etc.[7] **—*History of the Church*, Feb. 13, 1846**

At home until 5 [p.m.] when I went up to the Temple to pray. We assembled in the Upper Room [attic] at 6 [p.m] [There were] 29 [people] assembled for prayer and Benjamin L. Clapp[8] was leader. **—Thomas Bullock journal, Feb. 15, 1846**

Twenty-five elders met for prayer in the Temple. Elders Phineas

3. Willard Richards (1804-1854) was one of the first missionaries to England. He was called to be an apostle in 1840 and would come to serve as a counselor to Brigham Young and as Church Historian, Salt Lake City postmaster, and first editor of the *Deseret News.*

4. Consecrated oil—usually olive-based—was used in the initiatory portion of the temple ceremony, the "washing and anointing," as well as outside the temple for healing the sick.

5. The next year, Thomas Bullock (1816-1889) would keep the official pioneer camp journal for the trek west. In Utah he would also serve as clerk of the House of Representatives and work in the Church Historian's office.

6. Samuel W. Richards (1824-1909) converted to Mormonism in 1838 and moved to Nauvoo in 1842. He worked on the temple until its completion in 1846. He became a member of the first city council in Salt Lake City, a member of the Utah Territorial Legislature, and U.S. Commissioner for Davis County. He was excommunicated in 1873 and reinstated in 1878.

7. Since the death of Joseph Smith in 1844, the Quorum of the Twelve Apostles led the Church. Brigham Young would not be ordained president of the Church until late 1847.

8. Benjamin L. Clapp (1814-1860) fought at the Battle of Crooked River in Missouri in 1838; he served as one of the first Seven Presidents of Seventy from 1845 to 1859. In 1859 in Ephraim, Utah, he was excommunicated over differences with Bishop Warren S. Snow.

Richards[9] and Curtis E. Bolton[10] were mouth. —***History of the Church*, Feb. 19, 1846**

From thence to prayer meeting in the temple until 10 oclock in the evening, being one of the first quorum, numbering 15[,] which quorums regulate the order of Meeting in the Temple[,] under the direction of Orson Hyde[11] and Joseph Young, and who should there attend. **—Samuel W. Richards journal, Feb. 22, 1846**

… at sundown to the Temple, where we spent the evening in holy conversation, administering the Sacrament, and speaking in Tongues, enjoyed the fruits of the Gospel. **—Samuel W. Richards journal, Feb. 28, 1846**

At Sunset I went up to the Temple to pray. We again met in No. 1 Room of the Attic Story,[12] where the Spirit of God rested down on us. El[der] [Orson] Hyde came in to our midst … We partook of Sacrament according to the Ancient Pattern, and I thank my heavenly Father for this great privilege, and the instruction I received. **—Thomas Bullock journal, Mar. 8, 1846**

At sundown went to the Temple. [There were] 14 [in attendance, who] partook of the Sacrament[,] after which we had a most glorious time. Some of the brethren spoke in tongues. Bro. Z[ebedee]

---

9. Phineas Richards (1788-1874), a brother of Willard Richards and cousin of Brigham Young, converted to Mormonism in 1837. He came to Utah in 1848, served a Church mission to Sanpete County, and acted as a physician to the Indians. He also served in two bishoprics and a high council.

10. Curtis Edwin Bolton (1812-1890) helped build the Nauvoo temple. He later served as the French mission president and translated the Book of Mormon into French.

11. Orson Hyde (1805-1878) was a member of Zion's Camp, an LDS militia that marched from Ohio to Missouri in the 1830s. Hyde was ordained an apostle in 1835; he left the Church in 1838 but returned the following year. He was one of the first missionaries to England in 1837.

12. Room 1 served as Brigham Young's office and as the Holy of Holies where the second anointing was performed to "seal up [the individual] into eternal life and against all sin except the sin against the Holy Ghost," as Norton Jacob described it in his journal.

Coltrin[13] and [Benjamin] Brown[14] held a talk in tongues which was afterwards interpreted and confirmed. Some prophesied. Bro. [William] Anderson[15] related a vision. And all of us rejoiced with exceeding great gladness. A light was flickering over bro. Anderson's head while relating his vision, Phinehas Richards face shone with great brightness. Two men arrayed all in priestly garments were seen in the n[orth]e[ast] corner of the room. The power of the Holy Ghost rested down upon us. I arose full of the Spirit and spoke with great animation, which was very cheerfully responded to by all, and prophesied of things to come. A brother testified that our meeting was accepted of God. And we continued our meeting until after midnight, [a meeting] which was the most profitable, happy, and glorious meeting I had ever attended in my life, and may the remembrance be deeply rooted in my soul for ever and ever. **—Thomas Bullock journal, Mar. 15, 1846**

Carried a ticket to Uncle Levi [Richards][16] that he should have an admitance into the Quorum with us, and in the evening was present with us for the first time. This evening resulted in an unpleasant manner to the company, a censuring spirit arose which took several hours to quell and for a time as if to destroy the Quorum, but through faith and perseverance it was overcome, and union restored. **—Samuel W. Richards journal, Mar. 19, 1846**

Went to my Quorum meeting in the Temple. The whole Quo-[rum] being present consisting of 15 members, as follows, Zebedee Coltrain, Phineas Richards, Levi Richards, Graham Coltrain,[17] John

---

13. Zebedee Coltrin (1804-1887) was an early convert to the LDS Church. He traveled to Utah in 1847 and later resided in Spanish Fork.

14. Benjamin Brown (1794-1878) came to Utah in 1848 and served as bishop of the Salt Lake City 4th Ward. He served missions to the eastern states and to Great Britain.

15. William Anderson (1809-1846) was baptized in 1841 and soon served a mission to Chicago. He remained in Nauvoo after the majority of Saints had left and was killed defending the city during the Battle of Nauvoo.

16. Levi Richards (1799-1876) was a brother of Willard Richards and cousin of Brigham Young. He was a physician to Joseph Smith. He served a mission to Great Britain from 1840 to 1843.

17. Graham Coltrin (1796-1851) was baptized in 1831. He served a mission to Virginia.

Coltrain,[18] F[ranklin] D. Richards,[19] Abel Lamb,[20] Benj[amin] Brown, Wendell Mace,[21] Thomas B. Richards, Charles Patten,[22] Curtis E. Bolton, William Anderson, John Loveless[23] and myself. Dressing ourselves in the order of the Priesthood we called upon the Lord, his spirit attended us, and the visions of heaven were opened to our view. I was, as it were lost to my self, and [I] beheld the earth reel to and fro, and [it] was moved out of its place, men fell to the earth and their life departed from them, and at the close thereof, there appeared a great company as it were of Saints coming from the west as I stood with my back to the north and they were passing to the East, and the scripture was fulfilled which saith, "Come see the desolation which the Lord hast made in the Earth," and the company of the Saints who had been as it were from the Earth, walked in the light of the glory of the Lord [which] was around them, while darkness was on the face of the earth, and I beheld other things which were glorious while the power of God rested upon me. Others also beheld angels, and the glory of God. Having had a season of enjoyment, it was proposed by C[urtis] E. B[olton] that we pray for the Prophet Joseph [Smith] to come into our midst and converse with us, some consented to do so but the idea was first objected to as being unwise by Bro. Levi [Richards] who received a reprimand by way of [a] hint to leave the room from Bro. B[rown,] [though] not being agreed [to by the] Quorum. The matter was taken up, and after some remarks from several of the brethren, it was decided by the President, that we had no right to pray for such a thing, and all was right again. The Sacrament was administered and our great joy encreased by the gift of Tongues and Prophecy by which great bless-

18. John Coltrin (1775-1846) was baptized in 1845 and ordained a high priest by John Smith.

19. Franklin Dewey Richards (1821-1899) was ordained an apostle in 1849 and later served as president of the Quorum of Twelve Apostles and as Church Historian.

20. Abel Lamb (1801-1874) was an early convert who eventually settled in Farmington, Utah.

21. Wandle Mace (1809-1890) ran an iron foundry in Nauvoo, where he was also a member of the militia known as the Nauvoo Legion. Mace later served in the St. George temple in Utah.

22. Charles Wetherby Patten (1811-?) served as a missionary and helped aid the destitute in Nauvoo.

23. John Loveless (1807-1880) was baptized in 1831 and lived in Jackson County, Missouri, during the mob persecutions there. He traveled to Utah in 1851.

ings were spoken and made known to us. **—Samuel W. Richards journal, Mar. 22, 1846**

In the afternoon met in the attick story of the temple with the members[,] who formed a prayer circle in [Room] No. 1 and apart in [Room] No. 2[24] with our wives and had a feast of cakes, pies, wine & where we enjoyed ourselves with prayer, preaching, administration for healing, blessing children, and music and dancing untill near midnight. **—Samuel W. Richards journal, Apr. 29, 1846**

Minutes of the Dedication of the [Nauvoo] Temple April 30th, 1846. 7:45 p.m. Present at the dedication of the House of the Lord this evening[:]

Zebedee Coltrin
Graham Coltrin
John Coltrin
Thomas Bullock
Wandle Pace [Mace]
Charles W. Patten
William Anderson
Phineas Richards
Samuel W. Richards
Franklin D. Richards
Benjamin Brown
Curtis Bolton
Abel Lamb
Truman O. Angel
John S. Fullmer
Mephibosheth [S]i[rr]in[e][25] spectator through the ~~mistake~~ & invitation of Joseph Young
William W. Phelps
John Kempton
Joseph Young
Phineas [H.] Young[26]
John M. Bernhisel[27]
Jesse K. Nichols
J[acob] W Beech
John Young[28]

---

24. Room 2 was the Aaronic Priesthood room.

25. Mephibosheth Sirrine (1811-1848) was captain of the 24th Company of pioneer Saints leaving Nauvoo. He was a longtime member of the Church in good standing, so the reason for the confusion about his invitation, if that is what is implied, is unknown.

26. Phineas Howe Young (1799-1879) was a brother of Brigham Young, baptized in 1832. He served missions to Canada and Britain. He would later become bishop of the Salt Lake City 2nd Ward.

27. John M. Bernhisel (1799-1881) was baptized in 1843 and resided at Joseph Smith's Mansion House in Nauvoo. He migrated to Utah in 1847 and served as the territory's representative to the U.S. Congress from 1849 to 1863.

28. John Young (1791-1870) was a brother of Brigham Young, who served as president of the Kirtland Stake in Ohio and helped to build the Kirtland temple.

As the quorum entered the room for dedication the hymn was sung in a solemn and very impressive manner and we beheld over the stand of the Melchizedek Priesthood "The Lord has beheld our Sacrifice = Come after Us"—in beautiful gold letters—[and] after conversation on the subject of "Eternity" another hymn was sung. (Orson Hyde & Joseph L. Heywood[29] entered while [we were] singing). Elder Hyde remarked that he [was] left [feeling the] same as he did as he landed at J[erusalem] & descended the Mount of Olives.[30] He was alone. Pres[iden]t [Brigham Young] was anxious and felt glad—& feels that this Temple is built to the opposition of half headed apostates and blood thirsty opponents & laughs and feels thankful to God that he sees this hour for the world preys upon [us] "and my prediction is that the poor shall be blessed" [and] we all see for ourselves the folly of Rigdonism[31] (A[lmon] W Babbitt[32] came in) [and] Strangism[33] will be a stink in their own noses. I feel solemn and childlike, that silence is the most impressive—With regarding to Major [William B.] Warren and [Illinois] Governor [Thomas] Ford[,] I feel that they are in a course [that is] impossible. We never asked them to convey [escort Mormon emigrants] They come here against our petition. Major Warren wants us to petition for 10 men to stay here where they like, we have a deal depending upon the next court at Carthage [Illinois][.] If we retain this sway it will perhaps prevent a more swarm from coming on. (I speak confidently[.] When Porter Rockwell[34] came in with mail I met him. The last time he came[,] [he] was intoxicated.) Elder Hyde then called for the brethren to clothe themselves which they did & they called

29. Joseph Leyland Heywood (1815-1910) was baptized in 1842; he would help dispose of Church property in Nauvoo. In 1849 he became postmaster of Salt Lake City.

30. A reference to Hyde's trip to Jerusalem to dedicate the Holy Land.

31. Sidney Rigdon (1793-1876) converted to Mormonism in 1830 and was called as a counselor in the First Presidency in 1833. After Joseph Smith's murder in 1844, Rigdon presented himself as guardian of the Church but was ultimately excommunicated for rejecting the leadership of the Quorum of the Twelve.

32. Almon W. Babbitt (1813-1856) was a member of Zion's Camp in 1834. He was president of the Kirtland Stake from 1841 to 1843.

33. A reference to James J. Strang, who said Joseph Smith appointed him as Smith's successor.

34. Porter Rockwell (1813-1878) was a bodyguard to Joseph Smith and Brigham Young, a hired gun who enforced the will of the Church leadership during the period of the Church's infancy.

for a hymn when "Glorious Things of Thee Are Spoken" was sung. Elder Hyde then requested the brethren to form a circle [and] offer the signs and then dedicate the House, they moved to the front part of the Melchizedek Stand and formed a circle. Elder O[rson] Hyde President (Elder Wilford Woodruff entered). This temple has been built in 5 years and the Gov[ernmen]t has oppressed us more and more every year and now they drive us away from it and now—"I prophesy in the name of the Lord God of Hosts that this Government shall begin to be oppressed and be oppressed more and more every year and at the end of five years they shall be as badly oppressed as this people now is and they shall not know which way to look for Sunday"—"It is the general government." (Amen.) The circle again formed & offered the signs. After the signs were offered Joseph Young was appointed mouth who offered prayer to our Father in Heaven … & all responded heartily. J[oseph] Young said he felt real praise and not feather praise[.] Felt well. O[rson] Hyde [said] if we take a course to break down [the] unruly and aid the—the Lord will * *

W[ilford] Woodruff[:] I feel well and happy that I am in the house of my friends and that there has been a great victory gained over the devil and that there are many evil people and now coming into Nauvoo[.] We have gained a great victory building this Temple and as great as any in the world [have] received [persecution][,] [none] have borne as much as the Latter Day Saints. I have seen hours at midnight when I have offered up the signs in the closet alone and not a soul in all the east room. I could enter into [a] connection with [these signs] as to the blessings of God. I am thankful to be in the Council of the Honored Ones of Israel—when we can't wade[,] let no one swim. God is on our side. I have felt that the prayers of this circle have been offered up for me * * W[illiam] Anderson says as Brother Hyde has prophesied he would tell what was spoken in tongues and give the translation of it and he fully believed it. I rejoice in this thing and am willing to do all in our power to accomplish these things [and] get away [with] the brethren * *

The following are designations of where the people sat in the Stands: PH [Presiding High Priesthood] Wilford Woodruff[,] Orson Hyde[,] Joseph Young[;] PSQ [Presiding Seventies Quorum] Almon W. Babbitt[,] Joseph L Heywood[,] John S. Fullmer[;] PHQ [Presiding High Priests Quorum] John M. Bernhisel and A[bel] Lamb[,] Zebedee

Coltrin[;] PEQ [Presiding Elders Quorum] F[ranklin] D Richards[,] C[urtis] E Boltin[,] Wandle Mace[,] W[illiam] W Phelps[,] Thomas Bullock[;] PAQ [Presiding Aaronic Quorum] Phineas Young[,] Truman O Angell[,] Jesse K Nichols[;] PPQ [Presiding Priests Quorum] C[harles] W Patten[,] John Coltin[,] W[illiam] A Anderson[;] PTQ [Presiding Teachers Quorum] Phineas Richards[,] John Thompson [Kempton?][,] Samuel W. Richards[,] Benjamin Brown[;] PDQ [Presiding Deacons Quorum] M[ephiboseth] Irvine [Sirrine][,] John Young[,] Graham Coltrin[,] Jacob Beech[.]

O[rson] Hyde[:] May we rise before we close. We shall offer up our Hosannahs and where there's [time, to] shout out the ranks of the [priesthood this] evening. The order of it is Hosannah, Hosannah, Hosannah to God and the Lamb Amen Amen and Amen[,] and I don't know that there'll be any hour [available] if we should speak it out [in] the angels voices [tongues]. We belong to God. [I] feel like giving one shout in the House of God. If this is your mind signify it by rising upon your feet (all upright). The signs and shouts (thank God [for] being [here][.] You are dismissed with the blessings of thy Lord and your God Amen.) * *

The brethren adjourned to the attic story where a table was spread and loaded with "A Feast of Fat Things For the Righteous" in the shapes of wine, grapes[,] intestines [?] cakes &c &c which made a delightful banquet & was blessed by Elder Wilford Woodruff after which the feast was partaken of in great good harmony & happiness in testimony of the occasion of the dedication of the House of the Lord.

Elder Hyde gave out for the Temple hands [officiators] to enjoy themselves tomorrow at 2 p.m. F[ranklin] D. Richards received [gave] thanks to Elder Hyde in behalf of the Quorum #1 for the invitation to meet with them in the dedication of the House of the Lord. Elder Hyde met to reciprocate the kindness and desired [for it] to be continued[,] to be remembered that God may bless us & so in the day when he shall bring the righteous to himself. **—Minutes, Apr. 29, 1846**

The Temple at Nauvoo was dedicated this evening. Elders Orson Hyde, Wilford Woodruff, John [Young], Joseph [Young][,] and Phineas H. Young, J[ohn] M. Bernhisel, J[oseph] L. Heywood, and several others were present. Elder Joseph Young [Orson Hyde] offered up the dedicatory prayer, dedicating the Temple, and all that pertained thereto to the Lord, as an offering to Him, as an evidence of the willingness of His people, to fulfill His commandments, and build His holy house, even at the risk of their lives, and the sacrifice of their labor and earthly goods. He prayed for the Twelve [Apostles] and all the authorities of the Church, and for the workmen that had wrought upon the Temple in the midst of persecution, want and suffering, for the deliverance of the poor; that the Lord would direct the brethren of the camp of Israel, open the way before them and lead them to a place of His own appointment for the gathering of all the Saints, that God would avenge the blood of His servants, the prophets and of the Saints who had been slain for the testimony of the truth and mete out to our enemies the same measure which they had meted out to us. **—Manuscript History of Brigham Young, Apr. 30, 1846**

At the edge of Evening I repaired to the Temple And dressed in our Priestly robes in company with Elder Orson Hyde And about 20 others of the ^Nobility^[35] Elders of Israel. We dedicated the Temple of the Lord built by the Church of Jesus Christ of Latter Day Saints, unto His Most Holy name. We had an interesting time. Notwithstanding the many fals[e] Prophecies of Sidney Rigdon and others that the roof should not go on nor the House be finished and the threats of the mob that we should not dedicate it yet we have done both and we had an interesting time.

At the close of the dedication we raised our voices in the united Shout of Hosannah to God and the Lamb which entered the Heavens to the joy and consolation of our hearts. We prayed for the Camp of Israel, for good weather, that we might not be disturbed by any mob untill the dedication was over. I returned home thankful for the privilege of assisting in the dedication of the Temple of the Lord. **—Wilford Woodruff journal, Apr. 30, 1846**

Met at sundown in the temple for prayers as usual, after which (with our [temple] clothing) we repaired to the lower room for the purpose of dedicating the same. [A total of] 30 men selected for that purpose were present. After some conversation and singing[,] a prayer circle was formed immediately in front of the Melchizedek stand. O[rson] Hyde was President, and Joseph Young, mouth, after which

35. Carets indicate a supralinear addition.

those present were seated in the stands to represent the order of the Priesthood; myself being seated in the Teachers Stand, and a Dedicatory prayer was offered by O[rson] Hyde to which all responded "amen." After the prayer ended all shouted with a loud voice, "Hosannah, Hosannah, Hosannah to God and the Lamb, Amen, Amen, Amen!" which was repeated three times … After the services of the evening were over, by proposition of Bro. Hyde, we all went into the attick storey of the Temple and enjoyed a feast of rasins, cakes, and wine … and there decided that the temple hands should meet [the] next day at 2 oclock to enjoy themselves with cakes and wine. When about 12 we dispersed having enjoyed the blessings [and] privilege of dedicating the second Temple,[36] built upon the Land of Zion in the last days, unto the Lord, and it was accepted by him. **—Samuel W. Richards journal, Apr. 30, 1846**

The Temple at Nauvoo [Illinois] was publicly dedicated by Elder Orson Hyde; Elders W[ilford] Woodruff, A[lmon] W. Babbitt, and Joseph A. Stratton[37] were present and took part in the services. Fee for admission one dollar, to pay the hands employed on the Temple. **—Manuscript History of Brigham Young, May 1, 1846**

We met for a public dedication of the Temple this Morning. Entrance was $1 each to pay the hands that worked on the Temple. I paid $7 for 7 tickets. My company consisted of myself, wife, Father, Mother, one Cousin and Mary Jackson. At the appointed hour I opened the Meeting by prayer. Was followed in remarks by Br [Orson] Hyde who also offered up the dedicatory prayer after which Elder Almon Babbit was called upon to address the meeting which he did to the edefycation of the Saints. **—Wilford Woodruff journal, May 1, 1846.**

[Orson Hyde's dedicatory prayer:] Holy and Everlasting Father, before Thee this morning we present ourselves and acknowledge Thy mercy that has been extended to us since we have been on Thy footstool, and [give thanks] for this opportunity of dedicating this house. We thank Thee that Thou hast given us strength to accomplish the

36. The first was built in Kirtland, Ohio.

37. Joseph Albert Stratton (1821-1850) was baptized in 1840 and came to Utah in 1847. He served a mission to England from 1844 to 1846 and was later a counselor in the Salt Lake City 6th Ward.

charges delivered by Thee. Forgive us our sins and the sins of thy people. Thou hast seen our labors and exertions to accomplish this purpose. By the authority of the Holy Priesthood now we offer this building as a sanctuary to Thy Worthy Name. We ask Thee to take the guardianship into Thy hands and grant that Thy Spirit shall dwell here and may all feel a sacred influence on their hearts that His Hand has helped this work. Accept of our offering this morning, and that soul that blesses this temple[,] let blessings rest on his posterity to the latest generation, and that soul that shall practice evil against this temple and Thy House, set Thy face against him and let evil take the portion of his inheritance. Administer to Thy people and let Thy honor and glory fall on our heads, not in the eyes of men but in the day when the world shall become Thy dominion. May we have the honor to tune the lyre [in thanks] that Thou hast redeemed us from every nation and made us holy and pure and that we have washed our robes and made them white in the blood of the Lamb. [If] it must needs be that offenses come, we offer it as the fruit of our labors and may the oppression under which they [we] groaned be to our good. We ask that the angel of mercy may be round about this temple and that light may descend upon us and let us pass to the courts of the heavenly [host]. Let Thy Spirit rest upon those who have contributed to the building of this temple, the laborers on it that they may come forth to receive kingdoms and dominions and glory and immortal power. Accept of us we pray Thee, inspire every bosom to do Thy will, cause that truth may lead them[,] for [at] the glorious coming of the Son of God when you come in the name of the King, the Lord of Hosts shall be the King. Gather us in Thy Kingdom through Jesus Christ, our Lord, Amen. **—Minutes, May 1, 1846**

Went and borrowed A[aron] Farr's ornaments and robe. Then rode with Dr. Richards about 3 miles on the prairie.[38] There were 5 others and carriages[.] President Young [brought our two tents]. We fixed them up and then met and clothed. There was President B[righam] Young, H[eber] C. Kimball, P[arley] P. Pratt,[39] W[illard] Richards,

38. William Clayton and other leading men and their families had arrived at Mt. Pisgah, about 100 miles east of Council Bluffs, Iowa, which was their foreseeable destination.

39. Parley Parker Pratt (1807-1857) was called as an apostle in 1835. He was murdered in Arkansas by the husband of Eleanor McLean, whom Pratt was courting as a plural wife.

O[rson] Pratt,[40] J[ohn] Taylor, Geo[rge] A. Smith,[41] A[masa] Lyman,[42] John Smith, N[ewel] K. Whitney,[43] D[aniel] Spencer,[44] O[rson] Spencer,[45] C[harles] C. Rich,[46] E[zra] T. Benson,[47] W[illia]m Huntington and myself. Clothed and having offered up the signs [and then] offered up prayer[,] H. C. Kimball being mouth. We then conversed a while and prayed again, G. A. Smith being mouth. A[lbert] P. Rockwood[48] and W[illiam] Kimball were guarding the tent. Prayers were offered that we might be delivered from our enemies and have teams to go on our journey &c. About 2 o'clock we returned to camp. Many of the teams were coming in[,] and among the rest the teams [that were] sent back for my loading[,] which all arrived tonight. **—William Clayton diary, May 30, 1846**

Sunset I went to the Temple. J[udge] Higbee[49] [presided][,] Pres. Z[ebedee] Coltrin mouth. [blank] present. There is quite a revival in attendance. **—Thomas Bullock journal, June 8, 1846**

---

40. Orson Pratt (1811-1881) was ordained an apostle in 1835, excommunicated in 1842, and restored to the Quorum of the Twelve the following year. He served several missions and was appointed Church Historian in 1874.

41. George A. Smith (1817-1875), a cousin to Joseph Smith, was ordained an apostle in 1839. He later served as a counselor to Brigham Young.

42. Amasa Mason Lyman (1813-1877) was ordained an apostle in 1842. He later helped to colonize San Bernardino, California, where he presided from 1851 to 1857. He was excommunicated in 1870.

43. Newel K. Whitney (1795-1850) was the bishop of Kirtland from 1831 and was appointed Presiding Bishop of the Church in 1840.

44. Daniel Spencer (1794-1868) converted in 1840, served a mission to Canada, became mayor of Nauvoo, and in Utah served as president of the Salt Lake Stake.

45. Orson Spencer (1802-1855), Daniel's brother, was a Baptist minister who converted to Mormonism in 1840 and taught school in Nauvoo, served as president of the British Mission, worked as an editor at the *Deseret News,* and became chancellor of the University of Deseret (University of Utah).

46. Charles C. Rich (1809-1883) was an early convert, an apostle, co-founder of San Bernardino, president of the British Mission, and colonizer of southern Idaho.

47. Ezra T. Benson (1811-1869) was ordained an apostle in 1846 and served several missions. He was a member of the Utah Territorial Legislature. He helped settle Cache Valley, Utah.

48. Albert Perry Rockwood (1805-1879) served as one of the Seven Presidents of Seventy from 1845 and was a member of the Utah Territorial Legislature.

49. Isaac Higbee (1797-1874) was baptized in 1832. After migrating to Utah, he served as president of the Utah Stake in Provo for a short time.

After supper I, Henrietta[50] and Lucy[51] [Thomas Bullock's wives] robed ourselves, prayed, and had sacrament. I gave them much instruction in regard to their duty. **—Thomas Bullock journal, June 11, 1846**

About 6 [p.m.] went to the Temple to pray. Tarelton Lewis[52] [presided][,] Pres. Isaac Higbee mouth. **—Thomas Bullock journal, June 20, 1846**

....

About 9 [a.m.] I was washed in salaratus[53] and water from head to foot, afterward in spirits,[54] then [was] anointed in like manner by Louisa [(Free) Lee] and Rachel [Andora (Woolsey) Lee] (as I told them) preparatory to my burial. They both were very kind and attentive to me. **—John D. Lee[55] diary, Feb. 5, 1847[56]**

The morning fair and somewhat more pleasant, although there is yet appearance for more rain.[57] I felt quite unwell through the night and also this morning, having severe pain in my bowels. At 9 o'clock most of the brethren retired a little South of the camp and had a prayer meeting and as many as chose to, expressed their feelings. At a little before 12 they met again in the same spot to partake of the sacr[a]ment. Soon afterwards all the members of the council of F[ifty] or Kingdom

50. Henrietta Rushton Bullock (1817-1897) married Thomas Bullock in 1838 and was baptized in 1841. The Bullocks emigrated from England and made their way to Utah with the early pioneers.

51. Lucy Caroline Clayton Bullock (1820-1879) was one of the earliest converts in England, a midwife who was active in the Relief Society.

52. Tarleton Lewis (1805-1890) was baptized in 1836. One of the first pioneers to enter the Salt Lake Valley, he served as a bishop in Salt Lake, helped found Parowan and Minersville, and became bishop of Richfield, Utah.

53. Saleratus, baking soda, was used as a cleaning agent. Lee is describing a second anointing, the first part of which was administered to Lee on January 14 and to his plural wives on January 20 (Lisle G. Brown, comp., *Nauvoo Sealings, Adoptions, and Anointings* [Salt Lake City: Smith-Pettit Foundation, 2006]).

54. That is, distilled alcohol, used for cleaning.

55. John Doyle Lee (1812-1877) was a clerk in the Nauvoo temple. An adopted son of Brigham Young, he was executed in 1877 for his role in the 1857 Mountain Meadows Massacre.

56. This took place in Winter Quarters, Nebraska.

57. William Clayton, one of the vanguard pioneer company traveling from Winter Quarters to the Great Basin, explained that they were camped near Chimney Rock, Nebraska, and waiting for a storm to pass.

of God in the Camp except Brother Thomas Bullock, went onto the bluffs and selecting a small, circular, level spot, surrounded by bluffs, and out of sight, we clothed ourselves in the priestly garments and offered up prayer to God, for ourselves, this Camp and all pertaining to it, the brethren in the army [Mormon Battalion], our families and all the Saints, President Young being mouth. We all felt well and glad for this privilege. The names of those present, members of the above council are, Brigham Young, Heber C. Kimball, Willard Richards, Orson Pratt, George A. Smith, Wilford Woodruff, Amasa Lyman, Ezra T. Benson, Phineas H. Young, John Pack, Charles Shumway, Shadrack Roundy,[58] Albert P. Rockwood, Erastus Snow,[59] myself, Albert Carrington[60] and Porter Rockwell. The two latter having no clothing with them stood guard at a little distance from us to prevent interruption. When we started for the bluffs, there was a heavy, black thunder cloud rising from the South west, and to all appearance, it might rain any minute, but the brethren believed it would not rain till we got through and if it did we chose rather to take a wetting than to be disappointed of the privilege. It kept off remarkably till we got through, and got our cloth[e]s on, but soon after began to rain and after we got to Camp it rained considerable accompanied by strong wind. I never noticed the brethren so still and sober on a Sunday since we started as today. There is no jesting, nor laughing, nor nonsense. All appear to be sober and feel to remember their covenant, which makes things look far more pleasant than they have done heretofore. I spent most of the afternoon in Elder Kimball's wagon with Elder Kimball, President Young, Lorenzo and Phineas Young. Read the minutes of President Youngs discourse yesterday. About 5 o'clock President Young, Kimball, Benson and others walked out together to the bluffs. They invited me to go with them but

---

58. Shadrach Roundy (1789-1872) was a bishop in Winter Quarters, a member of the advance pioneer company in 1847 (at 58 years, the oldest), and a bishop in Salt Lake City.

59. Erastus Snow (1818-1888) was a member of the Quorum of Twelve Apostles and leader of the Mormon colonization of Arizona. Snow College in Utah and the Arizona town of Snowflake were both named after him. He and Orson Pratt were the first two Latter-day Saints to enter the Salt Lake Valley.

60. Albert Carrington (1813-1889) served in the Utah Territorial government and was an editor of the *Deseret News.* He was ordained an apostle in 1870 and later presided over the European Mission. In 1885 he was excommunicated, then readmitted in 1887.

I was so afflicted with Cramps I could scarcely walk, and after drinking a cup of tea prepared by Ellen Sanders[61] I went to my wagon and retired to bed early. **—William Clayton diary, May 30, 1847**

....

Sat[urday] July 21st, 1849, Ensign Hill,[62] 6 A.M.

B[righam] Y[oung][,] Isaac Morley,[63] P[arley] P. P[ratt][,] L[orenzo] Snow, E[rastus] Snow, C[harles] C. Rich, F[ranklin] D. R[ichards], Levi Hancock,[64] Henry Harriman,[65] J[edediah] M. Grant, and Addison Pratt.[66] Prayer at 6 by Isaac Morley. All but br[other] Addison clothed and Pres[iden]t B[righam] Young prayed, consecrated the spot for the present purpose of giving br[other] A[ddison] Pratt his endowment, that we might have power to erect a standard that should be glorious in the eyes of all its beholders, that no unholy thing might come here, that thy servants may come here to offer up their prayers and obtain the ministration of angels, &c., &c. Pres[iden]t B[righam] Y[oung], C[harles] C. Rich, and E[rastus] Snow undressed and proceeded to wash and anoint ^br[other]^ A[ddison] Pratt[,] (C[harles] C. R[ich] to wash, E[rastus] S[now] to anoint.) Elder [Heber C.] Kimball, [Newel K.] Whitney, and [John] Taylor came after the ordinances. C[harles] C. Rich and A[ddison] Pratt were blessed by all, H[eber] C. K[imball] being mouth. Closed at 9 a.m. **—Minutes, July 21, 1849**

---

61. Ellen Sanders (1823-1871) was born in Norway as Aagaat Ysteinsdatter Bakka and changed her name on emigration. A plural wife of Heber C. Kimball (her sister Harriet Sanders was also married to Kimball), she was one of three women who traveled with the pioneer company of 1847.

62. To the north of downtown Salt Lake City. This is the only known occurrence of the endowment ceremony being performed outdoors.

63. Isaac Morley (1786-1864) was a counselor to Edward Partridge, the first LDS bishop, and helped settle Manti, Utah. He also served in the Utah Territorial Legislature.

64. Levi Ward Hancock (1803-1882) was a member of Zion's Camp, and soon after was called as one of the Seven Presidents of the Seventy. He helped settle Manti. He was a member of the Mormon Battalion, one of about 500 soldiers recruited by the U.S. Army in Winter Quarters, Nebraska, to march to Tucson and San Diego in the 1846-1848 Mexican-American War.

65. Henry Harriman (1804-1891) was a member of Zion's Camp and in 1838 was called as one of the Seven Presidents of the Seventy.

66. Addison Pratt (1802-1872) served several missions. When he received his endowments on Ensign Peak, it was in preparation for his departure to the Society Islands. He later became disaffected, affiliated with spiritualists, and died in California.

I accompanied brother P[arley] P. Pratt[,] Erastus Snow[,] Levi Hancock & Henry Herriman on to Ensign Hill & made some preparation for the next morning at which place at 6 Oclock Pres[ident] B[righam] Young[,] the 6 members of the 12, 3 presidents of the 70s[,] with father [Isaac] Morley[,] consecrated the Hill for the erection of a standard thereon a place of prayer & the giving of Ad[d]ison Pratt his endowment which was then immediately bestowed upon him & the Co[mpany] left at 9 A.M. **—Franklin D. Richards diary, July 20-21, 1849**

Addison Pratt received his endowments on Ensign Hill on the 21st [of July 1849], the place being consecrated for the purpose. Myself and Elders Isaac Morley, P[arley] P. Pratt, L[orenzo] Snow, E[rastus] Snow, C[harles] C. Rich, F[ranklin] D. Richards, Levi W. Hancock, Henry Harriman, and J[edediah] M. Grant being present. Pres[ident] H[eber] C. Kimball, B[isho]p N[ewel] K. Whitney and Elder John Taylor came after the ordinances were attended to. Elder C[harles] C. Rich, and P[arley] Pratt were blessed by all, Pres[ident] Kimball being mouth. **—Manuscript History of Brigham Young, July 21, 1849**

....

In the Evening met several brethren in a prayer meeting at the upper room in Council House [in Salt Lake City][.] The endowment is commenced there & this was a meeting after the order of the Priesthood. **—Hosea Stout[67] diary, Feb. 26, 1851**

....

Pres[ident] Heber C. Kimball, Willard Richards, Tho[ma]s Bullock, W[illia]m C. Staines,[68] James Ure,[69] James W. Cummings,[70] Samuel L.

---

67. Hosea Stout (1810-1889) was captain of the Nauvoo police force and chief of police in Winter Quarters, Nebraska. He later served in the Utah Territorial Legislature.

68. William Carter Staines (1818-1881) joined the LDS Church in England and came to Utah in 1847, then served as an immigration agent for the Church in New York City.

69. James Ure (1817-1897) served twice as an LDS missionary to Europe (1856-1858, 1864-1867) and was a counselor in the Tooele stake presidency.

70. James Willard Cummings (1819-1883) joined the Mormons in 1841, served missions to Illinois and to the Oneida Indians, and settled in Salt Lake City.

Sprague,[71] W[illia]m W. Phelps,[72] each with a wife met in the Temple room. The brethren annointed each other. The wives were annointed by Sister [Elizabeth Ann] Whitney[73] and [Eliza R.] Snow;[74] afterwards all partook of cakes and wine.

Some spoke in tongues, etc. **—Journal History, Nov. 8, 1852**

....

Your endowment is, to receive all those ordinances in the House of the Lord, which are necessary for you, after you have departed this life, to enable you to walk back to the presence of the Father, passing the angels who stand as sentinels, being enabled to give them the key words, the signs and tokens, pertaining to the Holy Priesthood, and gain your eternal exaltation in spite of earth and hell. **—Brigham Young, Apr. 6, 1853, *Journal of Discourses,* 2:31-32**

....

Five brethren and three sisters met to receive their endowments at 8 o'clock a.m.

At 10 a.m. the First Presidency, with Orson Pratt, Orson Hyde, Wilford Woodruff, Ezra T. Benson, Daniel H. Wells, Edwin D. Wool[l]-ey,[75] William W. Phelps, James W. Cummings and Samuel L. Sprague met and clothed in upper room [of the Endowment House] for the purpose of dedicating the house.

At ¼ to 11 o'clock Pres[ident] Brigham Young called on Ezra T. Benson to open the meeting by prayer, and after other ceremonies he called upon Heber C. Kimball to dedicate the house. This was done by first naming each room separate[ly] there, [then] the material, each

---

71. Samuel Lindsey Sprague (1805-?) lived in Nauvoo and practiced medicine in Salt Lake City.

72. William Wines Phelps (1792-1872) worked for the LDS Church's printing offices in Kirtland, Ohio, and Independence, Missouri, before leaving the Church in 1838. He returned in 1840, came to Utah, and was elected to the territorial legislature where he was named Speaker of the House.

73. Elizabeth Ann Whitney (1800-1882) was a counselor to Emma Smith in the Female Relief Society in Nauvoo before emigrating west. She was the wife of Newel K. Whitney.

74. Eliza Roxcy Snow (1804-1887) was a plural wife of Joseph Smith and, after Smith's death, a wife of Brigham Young. She was the first president of the Relief Society in Utah.

75. Edwin Dilworth Woolley (1807-1881) came to Utah in 1848. He served in the Utah Territorial Legislature and as bishop of the Salt Lake City 13th Ward.

part separate[,] from stone to lumber, from adobes to sand mortar, including every kind of metal from the foundation to the chimney tops.

The president remarked the house was clean and named it "The House of the Lord." Said the spirit of the Lord would be in it, for no one would be permitted to go into it to pollute it. Also said: "When the temple is built, we will call that the Temple of our God." A quarter past 11 o'clock a.m. Commenced washing and anointing at half past 11 a.m., Heber C. Kimball presiding. Jedediah M. Grant, Orson Pratt, Ezra T. Benson, William W. Phelps, James W. Cummings, Samuel L. Sprague, William C. Staines, and James Ure, [and] Eliza R. Snow and [Elizabeth Ann] Whitney attended to the ordinances, after which Heber C. Kimball lectured to the company and about fifteen brethren who were immediately going on missions.

The spirit of the Lord was made manifest in our midst; all testified to the truth of what had been said by raising their right hands and saying "I." Jedediah M. Grant dismissed the meeting at a quarter past 5 p.m., when three couples were sealed in the sealing room.

The day was fine with a cool north west wind.

William C. Staines, clerk. **—Journal History, May 5, 1855**[76]

Then go on and build the Temples of the Lord, that you may receive the endowments in store for you, and possess the keys of the eternal Priesthood, that you may receive every word, sign, and token, and be made acquainted with the laws of angels, and of the kingdom of our Father and our God, and know how to pass from one degree to another, and enter fully into the joy of your Lord. **—Brigham Young, July 8, 1855, *Journal of Discourses,* 2:315**

....

To the presidents and the bishops in the counties of Iron and Washington. I write to inform you that the persons who can get their endowments must be those who pray, who pay their tithing from year to year; who live the lives of saints from day to day; setting good examples before their neighbors. Men and women, boys and girls over 16 years of age who are living the lives of saints, believe in the plurality [of wives], do not speak evil of the authorities of the Church, and pos-

---

76. This was thirteen years to the day since Joseph and Hyrum Smith received their endowments.

sess true integrity towards their friends, can come up after their spring crops are sown, and their case shall be attended to. …

P.S. Send us word 10 days before you send your company that we may have the rooms vacant for them. **—Brigham Young, Heber C. Kimball, and Jedediah M. Grant to Stake Presidents and Bishops in Iron and Washington Counties, Mar. 2, 1856**

I want you to forward 20 persons to receive their endowments[,] to be at the Endowment House next Friday, 23rd inst., at 7 o'clock in the morning precisely.

Also Bishop Hami[l]ton of American Fork to forward 20, to be at the Endowment House at the same time on Friday.

Bishop Henson Walker of Pleasant Grove is also requested to send 20 to be at the Endowment House Tuesday following (27) at 7 o'clock in the morning. And Bishop Blackburn of Provo to send 20 to be here at the same day and hour.

Bishop Aaron Johnson to send 40 on Friday 30th to be on hand by seven o'clock in the morning.

These men and women whom you recommend, must be individuals, who pay their tithing from year to year; who pray in their families, and do not speak against the authorities of the Church and Kingdom of God; nor steal; nor lie; nor interfere with their neighbors things; nor their neighbors wives or husbands; who attend strictly to meetings and prayer meetings, and those who pay due respect to their presiding officers, and Bishops and those who do not swear.

We shall expect you to pickup the old and infirm; the lame and blind and the righteous poor, but not the devils poor.

We would like to see many of the young and sprightly young persons who are strict to obey their parents.

We shall require the Bishops to send their names in a letter fully recommended and tell them to qualify themselves by washing their bodies in pure water and bringing Temple clothing and oil for their anointings. As they live in the country, we want them to bring their eggs, butter, meat, bread and flour, and the luxuries of [the farm] fit to grace the tables of the House of the Lord, to feed the men and women who administer unto them; and if there should be any left, that we may give it to the poor; and in so doing God will bless you and we will bless you. This by order of the First Presidency. **—Heber C. Kimball to David Evans, May 19, 1856**

....

I Attended the prayer Circle. The presidency & W[ilford] W[oodruff][,] G[eorge] A. S[mith][,] A[masa] Lyman[,] & C[harles] C Rich of the Twelve were present. There was much confersation upon various subject[s][.]

President [Brigham] Young said I shall not seal the people as I have done. Old Father Allred[77] brough[t] three young girls 12 & 13 years old. I would not seal them to him. They would not be equally yoked together. The devel can get as many recommend[ed] as He can[.] Many get their endowments who are not worthy[,] but this is the way devils are made. There will be some needed in the next world. **—Wilford Woodruff journal, June 14, 1857**

Giving endowments to a great many proves their overthrow through revealing things to them which they cannot keep. They are not worthy to receive them. Brother Heber [C. Kimball] takes the lead in giving endowments, and you may ask, "Why do you give such folks their endowments?" To qualify them to be devils, if they wish to be. The plan of salvation is calculated to make devils as well as Saints; for by and by we shall need some to serve as devils; and it takes almost as much knowledge to make a complete devil as it does to fit a man to go into the celestial kingdom of God, and become an heir to His kingdom. **—Brigham Young, June 28, 1857, *Journal of Discourses,* 4:372-73**

On the seventeenth of July 1857 we received our sealing by Brigham Young the prophet of the Lord in the house of endowments at the Alter of the Lord, Belinda [Miles] acting [as] Proxy. I first had Elizabeth Cam[p]bell sealed to me for eternity. Afterwards I had Sarah Catharine Gibbs sealed to me for eternity. Afterwards I had Belinda Miles sealed to me for time and all eternity. Brigham also blessed me and my wives with an endless Priesthood and posterity and the gift of eternal lives through faithfulness. **—Esaias Edwards[78] diary, Perry Special Collections**

---

77. Probably James Allred (1784-1876), who was a member of Zion's Camp in 1834 and was later a bodyguard to Joseph Smith. He settled in Utah in 1851, leading the settlement now called Spring City in Sanpete County.

78. Esias Edwards (1812-1897) participated in the Utah War in 1857 and later was a member of the School of the Prophets in Logan.

Some of the Brethren inquired upon Pres[ident] [Brigham] Young to make inquiries upon certain teachings of Joseph [Smith] concerning the endowments. Elder Geo[rge] A. Smith said that Joseph taught that but one king and priest could be anointed at one meeting in a private room dedicated by permission to anoint in, and but one person could be anointed in a day, but in the Temple several could be anointed in a day, but at each anointing the meeting was dismissed and then came together again.[79] Pres[ident] Young said that Joseph taught him to take the quorum and anoint them kings and priests to God, and when he got through with that begin at the beginning again to administer for the dead. When the Temple is finished and a place duly prepared we should not be confined to any particular number in sealing and anointing. The rooms next to the east pulpit, or over it[,] will be the place to attend to the second anointings. Under the pulpit in the west end will be the place to offer sacrifices; there will be an altar prepared for that purpose so that when any sacrifices are to be offered they should be offered there.[80] **—Journal History, Dec. 18, 1857**

....

[Heber C. Kimball:] We have the true Masonry. The Mason[ry] of the day is received from the apostasy which took place in the days of Solomon and David. They know[,] now and then[,] a thing that is correct[,] but we know the real thing[;] but how many comprehend it and see the propriety of being true to each other[?][81] **—Journal History, Nov. 13, 1858**

....

Those who are counted worthy to dwell with the Father and the

79. Elder Smith refers to the second anointing.

80. Although the Old Testament ordinance of animal sacrifice was contemplated as part of the "restoration of all things," it was never performed in LDS temples, as far as is known.

81. Nineteenth-century Mormons sometimes referred to the endowment ceremony as "true Masonry," a view that Joseph Smith encouraged by saying, in concert with Kimball, that Freemasonry was a corrupted form of ancient Hebrew temple ceremonies. Smith introduced the endowment right after becoming a Mason himself, and the others who first received the endowment were Masons. See Michael W. Homer, "'Similarity of Priesthood in Masonry': The Relationship between Freemasonry and Mormonism," *Dialogue: A Journal of Mormon Thought* 27 (Fall 1994): 1-113.

Son have previously received an education fitting for that society; they have been made fully acquainted with every password, token and sign which has enabled them to pass by the porters through the doors into the celestial kingdom. **—Brigham Young, May 24, 1863, *Journal of Discourses,* 10:172**

There are some of the sealing ordinances that cannot be administered in the house [Endowment House] that we are now using; we can only administer in it some of the first ordinances of the Priesthood pertaining to the endowment. There are more advanced ordinances that cannot be administered there; we would, therefore, like a Temple, but I am willing to wait a few years for it. I want to see the Temple built in a manner that it will endure through the Millennium. This is not the only Temple we shall build; There will be hundreds of them built and dedicated to the Lord. This Temple [in Salt Lake City] will be known as the first Temple built in the mountains by the Latter-day Saints. And when the Millennium is over, and all the sons and daughters of Adam and Eve, down to the last of their posterity, who come within the reach of the clemency of the Gospel, have been redeemed in hundreds of Temples through the administration of their children as proxies for them, I want that Temple still to stand as a proud monument of the faith, perseverance and industry of the Saints of God in the mountains, in the nineteenth century. **—Brigham Young, Oct. 6, 1863, Journal of Discourses, 10:251**

....

Most of you, my brethren, are Elders, Seventies, or High Priests; perhaps there is not a Priest or Teacher present. The reason of this is that when we give the brethren their endowments, we are obliged to confer upon them the Melchizedek Priesthood; but I expect to see the day, when we shall be so situated that we can say to a company of brethren, You can go and receive the ordinances pertaining to the Aaronic order of Priesthood, and then you can go into the world and preach the Gospel, or do something that will prove whether you will honor that Priesthood before you receive more. Now we pass them through the ordinances of both Priesthoods in one day, but this is not as it should be and would [be], if we had a temple wherein to administer these ordinances. But this is all right at present; we should not be satisfied in any other way, and consequently we do according to the circumstances we are placed in.[82] **—Brigham Young, June 11, 1864, Journal of Discourses, 10:309**

....

I met with The Presidency and Twelve at President [Brigham] Youngs Office at about 12 oclok. The subject of the Endowments & 2d Anointings was presented when President Young said that the order of the 2d anointing was for the persons to be anointed to be cloathed in their Priestly robes the man upon the right hand and wife or wifes upon the left hand. The Administrator may be dressed in his usual Clothing or in his Priestly Robes as he may see fit. The meeting should be opened by Prayer then the Administrator should anoint the man A King & Priest unto the Most High God. Then he should anoint his wife or wives Queens & Priestess[es] unto her husband. There should be but one man anointed at any one meeting. If more than one man is anointed in a day, they should Come together and open by Prayer as though their had not been any meeting before and thus Continue to the end.

President Young said when a woman was Anointed a Queen to a good man and he died & the woman was sealed to another man for time it was not necessary for her to be anointed a Queen again but if she was Anointed a Queen to a man who was not worthy of a wife & she is sealed to another man she should be anointed a Queen unto him. When a good man dies & his wives have not been anointed Queens unto him they may be anointed Queens to him after his death without any Proxey.

In speaking of the Endowments Preside[n]t Young said that all persons who wished strickly to observe the law of the Celestial [plural] Marriage should not get married untill they got their Endowments & are sealed at the Altar. There may be instances whare persons are Aged & infirme and not Able to get to the Endowment House [and] if they have not had their Endowments may be sealed[,] and in some instances I have given this permission[,] & others have taken the advantage of it & urged [people][,] to be sealed without Coming to the Endowment House. I gave A[masa] Lyman the privilege of sealing some in Sanber-

82. This sermon was delivered at a priesthood meeting in Logan. Young's vision of separating the Aaronic and Melchizedek priesthood elements of the endowment into two separate ceremonies was never accomplished.

nadeno [San Bernardino] by his urgent request but it will ^not^ avail anything.[83]

Some may ask the question why may we not seal & give Endowments abroad? Because it would destroy the object of the gathering. The People Should be gathered at head Quarters whare they Can be taught in the things of the kingdom of God & be under the direction of the Priesthood.

Preside[n]t Young said that when Persons Came to get their Endowments [they] Should be Clean & pure. A man should not touch a woman for 10 days before getting their Endowments. And the Twelve while travelling should hold meetings with the male members as priesthood meetings & teach these [things] but they have to [be] handled in wisdom or Evil will grow out of it. **—Wilford Woodruff journal, Dec. 26, 1866**

Presidents Brigham Young, Heber C. Kimball, Daniel H. Wells, Elders Orson Hyde, John Taylor, Wilford Woodruff, Geo[rge] A. Smith, C[harles] C. Rich, Brigham Young Jun[ior], Joseph F. Smith, Geo[rge] Q. Cannon, Lorenzo Snow & Erastus Snow met at the endowment house at 12 m. (noon)

The above named brethren clothed and prayed[,] Pres[ident] [Daniel H.] Well's four wives uniting in the circle. After prayer Pres[ident] Young proceeded to anoint Daniel Hamer Wells and his four wives (second anointing). The brethren then sang ["]Glorious things of thee are spoken.["] Elder Orson Hyde closed by prayer.

The brethren rejoiced at the commencement again of the administration of these ordinances which had not been administered since they were in the Temple at Nauvoo.

Pres[iden]t Young had procured and perfumed the oil which was consecrated at the circle on Sunday evening for the purpose. **—Historian's Office Journal, Dec. 31, 1866**

In company with Pres[iden]t [Brigham] Young went to the Endowment house; the Twelve were there. Bro[ther] D[aniel] H. Wells &

83. San Bernardino was settled by Amasa M. Lyman and Charles C. Rich in 1851 after Brigham Young called them on a mission for that purpose. Young discontinued the settlement in 1857, mostly because of dissension, and recalled the colonists back to Utah. See Edward Leo Lyman, *San Bernardino: The Rise and Fall of a California Community* (Salt Lake City: Signature Books, 1996).

four of his wives were anointed a King & Priest unto God and Queens and Priestesses unto God under the hands of Pres[iden]t B[righam] Young sen[ior][.] **—Brigham Young Jr. diary, Dec. 31, 1866**

....

Attended meeting at the Endowment House. Bro[ther] Geo[rge] Quale Cannon & three wives were anointed to the same blessings which bro[ther] [Daniel H.] Wells received under the hands of Pres[iden]t [Brigham] Young. **—Brigham Young Jr. diary, Jan. 1, 1867**

I met with the Presidency & 8 of the Twelve & Joseph F Smith[,] Joseph A. Young[,][84] & Brigham Young Jr. Dressed & Prayed. Then Presid[en]t Brigham Young gave his Son[,] Joseph A. Young[,] his second anointing.

It was decided by Preside[n]t Young that we dress & offer up the signs of the Holy Priesthood before we give the 2d Anointing & ownly Anoint one man & his wives in one day at one place. **—Wilford Woodruff journal, Jan. 2, 1867**

Jos[eph] A Young received his second anointing under the hands of his father. **—Brigham Young Jr. diary, Jan. 2, 1867**

Went to the Endowment House at 12 where I received my second anointing under the hands of my father, he ordaining me to [be] a King & Priest to the Most High God. **—Brigham Young Jr. diary, Jan. 3, 1867**

Met again with the Twelve at the endowment house. Jos[eph] F Smith and his two wives were present. He was anointed a King & Priest unto God and his two wives Queens & Priestess[es] unto their husband. **—Brigham Young Jr. diary, Jan. 4, 1867**

I met in the Prayer Circle with the Presid[en]t & Twelve. C[harles] C. Rich Prayed & E[zra] T. Benson was mouth. …

While at Presidents [Brigham] Youngs House in the Evening for Prayer He divid[ed] the Twelve in 3 companies to attend to the second Anointings. Lorenzo Snow, C[harles] C. Rich & G[eorge] Q. Cannon was to meet at Preside[n]t Youngs. H[eber] C. Kimball[,] D[aniel] H.

---

84. Joseph Angell Young (1834-1875) was a son of Brigham Young and Mary Ann Angell. He served a mission to Great Britain from 1854 to 1856 and was the first president of the Sevier Stake in Utah.

Wells[,] O[rson] Hyde[,] J[ohn] Taylor[,] E[zra] T. Benson & Erastus Snow was to meet at the Endowment House. W[ilford] Woodruff & G[eorge] A. Smith was to meet at the Historians office to attend to the Anointing in the Prayer Circle Room.[85] **—Wilford Woodruff journal, Jan. 6, 1867**

Met with Pres[iden]t [Brigham] Young and several others in a room in the Beehive house where bro[ther] [Albert] Carrington and ... his two wives[86] received their second anointing. **—Brigham Young Jr. diary, Jan. 7, 1867**

....

Record of Second Anointing
Historian's upper room
G[reat] S[alt] L[ake] city, Jan. 7th (Monday) 1867
1:00 p.m.

Present—Wilford Woodruff & Geo[rge] A. Smith, also Albert P. Rockwood, Aaron Johnson,[87] Thomas Callister,[88] W[illia]m B. Pace[89] & Robert L. Campbell[90] who with Joseph W. Young[,][91] born Jan. 12th 1829 in Mendon, Munroe County, New York[,] and Lurana Eldridge Young (his wife)[,] born Feb. 21, 1838, near Indianapolis City, Marion Co[unty] Indiana[,] and Julia Thankful Adams Young[,] born Aug. 11th, 1847 [in] Pottawatomie Co[unty] Iowa[,] clothed and prayed, W[ilford] Woodruff being mouth. After which the above persons formed a cir-

---

85. Dividing the quorum for the administration of the second anointing was apparently in keeping with Joseph Smith's counsel that only one man be anointed at a time. These separate gatherings allowed for multiple second anointing ceremonies to take place at the same time.

86. The document reads nonsensically "several of his two wives".

87. Aaron Johnson (1806-1877) was founder, postmaster, and first bishop of Springville, Utah, and a member of the territorial legislature.

88. Thomas Callister (1821-1880) was a colonel in Utah's Walker and Black Hawk Wars and president of Millard Stake.

89. William Byron Pace (1832-1907) served in the Black Hawk War, as well as being a member of the Utah territorial House of Representatives.

90. Robert Lang Campbell (1825-1874) was a prominent educator who clerked in the Church Historian's office and in the territorial legislature.

91. Joseph Watson Young (1828-1873) was a son of Lorenzo Dow Young and Persis Goodall and a nephew to Brigham Young. He served a mission to Europe and was an LDS bishop.

cle (including bro[ther] Joseph's two wives) and prayed[,] Geo[rge] A. Smith being mouth.

Wilford Woodruff then anointed Joseph Watson Young and his wives Lurana & Julia above named. Albert P. Rockwood held the horn [of oil].[92] After singing a hymn A[lbert] P. Rockwood dismissed by prayer.

Rob[er]t. L. Campbell

Recorder. **—Historian's Office Journal, Jan. 9, 1872 (entered into the historian's scrapbook retrospectively)**

Br[other] W[ilford] Woodruff notified me in person that I could receive my 2nd anointing on Saturday Feb. 9th at 2 ocl[ock] P.M. Accordingly I sent to my wives Emeline & Abigail. According[ly] they arrived on Friday afternoon at my Residency in the city.

9th Saturday all being Ready we proceeded to the Historian's Office & there Received in Regular Order My 2nd anointing & Blessings also my Wives Emeline[,] Jane Elizabeth[,] & Abigail all there in Regular Order with there Blessings. ... Br[other] George A. Smith & Woodruff officiated. Br[other] Smith being mouth. **—Frederick Kesler Sr.[93] diary, Feb. 9, 1867, Marriott Library**

Went with wife to President B[righam] Youngs Mansion to receive our blessings or second anointings which is a fullness of our endowments. President E[rastus] Snow presided[,] assisted by Robert Gar[d]ner[,][94] John M Moody[,] [and] F[ranklin] B. Wool[l]ey[,][95] J[esse] W Crosby[96] assisting. **—Lorenzo Brown[97] diary, Oct. 2, 1867, Perry Special Collections**

---

92. A ram's horn held the consecrated olive oil used in the second anointing.

93. Frederick Kesler Sr. (1816-1899) came to Utah in 1851. He served as bishop of the Salt Lake City 16th Ward for forty-three years.

94. Robert Gardner (1819-1906) operated a saw mill at Mill Creek in Salt Lake City. In 1861 he helped settle St. George, where he served two terms as mayor and helped build the temple.

95. Franklin Benjamin Woolley (1834-1869) was a son of Bishop Edwin D. Woolley, who was killed by Indians while returning to St. George from a business trip to San Bernardino.

96. Jesse Wentworth Crosby (1820-1893) served several missions for the LDS Church and was one of the first Mormon pioneers to arrive in the Salt Lake Valley in 1847.

97. Lorenzo Brown (1823-1902) helped build the Nauvoo temple, and after his arrival in Utah he was sent to Las Vegas, Nevada.

....

Pres[iden]ts [Brigham] Y[oung][,] [Heber C.] K[imball] & [Daniel H.] W[ells] Spoke on the impropriety of our youth marrying [for time], instead of getting sealed [for eternity]; also spoke of cleanliness in person before going to get their endowments; a woman should not go for a week after her menses were upon her; a man should not have intercourse with his wife for several days; but should be clean in body and exercised in spirit previous thereto. His clothing should be changed once or twice before going there. **—Historian's Office Journal, Jan. 31, 1868**

The school of the prophets met in the 14th Ward School House. Pres[idents] Brigham Young, Heber C. Kimball and Daniel H. Wells and the Twelve Apostles and others were present. Pres[ident] Brigham Young and counselors spoke; also Hiram B. Clawson,[98] B[isho]p Edwin D. Woolley, Daniel Evans and Erastus Snow. Pres[iden]ts Young, Kimball and Wells spoke on the impropriety of the youth of Zion marrying [for time] instead of getting sealed [for eternity][.] He also spoke of cleanliness of person, before going to get their endowments; a woman should not go for a week after her menses were upon her, a man should not have intercourse with his wife for several days, but should be clean in body and exercised in spirit previous thereto; his clothing should be changed once or twice before going there. **—Journal History, Jan. 31, 1868**

West room 6 p.m.
City Hall, S[alt] L[ake] City Oct. 10, [18]69.

Present—of the [First] Presidency—B[righam] Y[oung], G[eorge] A. S[mith].

[Present] of the Twelve. O[rson] H[yde], O[rson] P[ratt], W[ilford] W[oodruff], L[orenzo] Snow, F[ranklin] D. R[ichards], C[harles] C. Rich, E[rastus] Snow, Geo[rge] Q. C[annon].

B[righam] Y[oung][:] Some enquiry [was] made as to how many have their shirts marked—[A] few rose with them marked—Pres[ident Y[oung] said he took the scissors & soon made the marks. [Even] if [the] shirt [is] colored[,] mark it—[I]f [there is] flannel or buckskin between

98. Hiram Bradley Clawson (1826-1912) was the first treasurer of Salt Lake City and first superintendent of Zion's Co-operative Mercantile Institution (ZCMI).

[the] shirt & garment[,] that also should be marked. An overshirt worn as a vest should not be marked.[99]

The Twelve & first Presidency of the Seventies set the Missionaries apart.

R[obert] L. Campbell

Clerk **—Minutes of a Meeting, Oct. 10, 1869**

At 9 eve met as notified and 4 of my wives received their 2d anointing. **—Franklin D. Richards diary, Sept. 15, 1870**

....

There are many of the ordinances of the house of God that must be performed in a Temple that is erected expressly for the purpose. There are other ordinances that we can administer without a Temple. You know that there are some which you have received—baptism, the laying on of hands, the gifts of the Holy Ghost, such as the speaking in and interpretation of tongues, prophesying, healing, discerning of spirits, etc.[;] and many blessings bestowed upon the people, we have the privilege of receiving without a Temple. There are other blessings that will not be received, and ordinances that will not be performed according to the law that the Lord has revealed, without their being done in a Temple prepared for that purpose. We can, at the present time, go into the Endowment House and be baptized for the dead, receive our washings and anointing, etc., for there we have a font that has been erected [and] dedicated expressly for baptizing people for the remission of sins, for their health[100] and for their dead friends; in this the Saints have the privilege of being baptized for their friends. We also have the privilege of sealing women to men, without a Temple. This we can do

99. The markings on the underclothing, symbols intended to remind the endowed member of covenants made during the ceremony, were once cut out of the fabric during the ritual but are now pre-sewn onto white cloth with white thread as a subtle embroidery. For more on this, see the entry for Aug. 31, 1894, herein.

100. Baptism for health was one of several reasons Latter-day Saints practiced rebaptism. According to historian D. Michael Quinn, the practice "was particularly prominent during the Nauvoo years and served many functions," including a renewal of covenants, remittance of sin, and preparation to enter into plural marriage (Quinn, "The Practice of Rebaptism at Nauvoo," *BYU Studies* 18 [Winter 1978]: 226-32; also James B. Allen and Glen M. Leonard, *The Story of the Latter-day Saints* [Salt Lake City: Deseret Book Co., 1992], 430-31; Jonathan A. Stapley and Kristine Wright, "'They Shall Be Made Whole': A History of Baptism for Health," *Journal of Mormon History* 34 [Fall 2008]: 69-112).

in the Endowment House; but when we come to other sealing ordinances, ordinances pertaining to the holy Priesthood, to connect the chain of the Priesthood from father Adam until now, by sealing children to their parents, being sealed for our forefathers, etc., they cannot be done without a Temple. But we can seal women to men, but not men to men, without a Temple.

When the ordinances are carried out in the Temples that will be erected, men will be sealed to their fathers, and those who have slept [died] clear up to father Adam. This will have to be done, because of the chain of the Priesthood being broken upon the earth. The Priesthood has left the people, but in the first place the people left the Priesthood. **—Brigham Young, Sept. 4, 1873, *Journal of Discourses,* 16:186–87**

....

It is my desire to be buried in the garments and Robes of the Holy Priesthood, everything pertaining thereto properly made and put on my body. [I] do not want any extravagance, a medium coffin[,] no expense for funeral clothing such as the gentiles mourn in. [I] would like my Brethren of the Priesthood to dictate [to] my family in this matter, and see me buried as I ought to be, that my body can rest in peace. [I] do not want my coffin short or too long, deep enough to lay in without mashing my nose, and cramping my arms or crushing my stomach, a good strong one that it will hold together. I pray that I may so live that the Holy Priesthood will feel it a pleasure to put me away, and a pleasure to receive me in their society in the morning of the glorious resurrection. **—John D. T. McAllister, statement dated Nov. 10, 1873**

....

Attended meeting this morning in the Basement of St. George's Hall. Bro[ther] Geo[rge] A [Smith] said [he] wanted to finish [the] Temple for the President (B[righam] Y[oung]) to finish giving the Twelve and people what Joseph [Smith] instructed him to give them. **—Brigham Young Jr. diary, Dec. 25, 1874**

Spent the evening with Father [Brigham Young][.] Had a splendid time. He seems to feel well and talked over the plan for [the] next temple which he proposes building somewhere in Sanpete;[101] and the next one in Logan[.] He says the next plan will be more expressly

101. The reference here is to the Manti temple.

adapted to the labors of sealing men to men; men to women, baptisms, anointings, washings and other ordinances. **—Brigham Young Jr. diary, Dec. 27, 1874**

....

Endowments ceased in the Endowment House. President [Brigham] Young said, "If the people wish to receive their endowments and sealings they must go to Saint George and receive them in a Temple." **—Henry W. Bigler[102] diary, Oct. 30, 1876, Utah State Historical Society, Salt Lake City**

....

Bro[ther] Wilford Woodruff kneeled near the top of West steps [of the St. George temple], and read a lengthy prayer[;] time[:] 24 minutes. He expressed hope that it would not weaken the faith of any to hear or see him read his prayer from manuscript. All very good and satisfactory.

Adjourned to [the] main upper room which was quite full. Pres[iden]t [Brigham Young] sat directly in front of [the] lower Melchisedeck stand on which Sat bro[ther]s Woodruff[,] [Erastus] Snow and myself, and from which bro[ther] Snow read his prayer[,] 17 minutes [and] very good.

I delivered or read the dedication prayer. Returned to [the] main room—Bro[ther]s W[oodruff] & S[now] spoke a few words. Pres[iden]t B[righam] Y[oung][,] leaning on his cane and one crutch[,] came into the lower M[elchizedek] stand and addressed the saints for some 20 M[inutes][.] He said, the saints may be satisfied with this dedication—as it was good. But he would never be satisfied until he had whipped the devils and drived them off from this earth, bringing his cane down on the stand [in] front [and] making three dents which will remain as long as board remains. **—Brigham Young Jr. diary, Jan. 1, 1877**

The President, members of the Twelve and a few others including myself then repaired to the Sealing Room[,] where after Singing "Come let us anew" Elder B[righam] Young J[r] offered the dedicatory prayer for the Sealing Room & its appertenances—after which [we] returned to the lower court[,] when Bro[ther]s [Erastus] Snow &

102. Henry W. Bigler (1815-1900) was a member of the Mormon Battalion, who served as a missionary to the Sandwich Islands. He also helped colonize St. George and worked as an officiator in the temple there.

[Wilford] Woodruff spoke a short time pertaining to the workings in the Temple [and] calling on all who desired to come forth and attend to the ordinances for themselves & their dead. **—L. John Nuttall diary, Jan. 1, 1877, Perry Special Collections**

The corner stones were laid on the 10th day of March, 1873, and labor was continued thereon until Jan[.] 1st, 1877, when it was dedicated to God. (See W[ilford] Woodruff's Journal of Jan[.] 1st, 1877, which contains the dedicatory prayers of W[ilford] Woodruff, Erastus Snow, and B[righam] Young Jr., also the speech of President [Brigham] Young.) I, Wilford Woodruff, bear testimony, that Pres[iden]t B[righam] Young told me to go to work and prepare the Temple for giving Endowments, and I had made the preparations according to his acceptance; and on the 9th of Jan., 1877, we repaired to the Temple and for the first time the ordinance of baptism for the dead was performed in the Temple of St. George[.] Wilford Woodruff went into the font by the direction of Pres[iden]t Brigham Young and administered the ordinance of baptism for the first 140 persons, and confirmed the first person, Pres[iden]t Young laying on hands at the same time. John L. Smith[103] administered the ordinance of baptism for the next 83 persons, making 223 baptisms and confirmations during that day. Wilford Woodruff Confirmed one 1. J[ohn] D. T. McAllister confirmed 64, A[lonzo] H. Raleigh[104] 15, H[enry] W. Bigler 123, and Erastus Snow 20. Susie Amelia Young Dunford[105] was the first baptized and confirmed by W[ilford] Woodruff.

Pres[iden]t Brigham Young requested me to take charge of the Temple, which I did. He also requested me to write all the ordinances of the Church from the first baptism and confirmation through every ordinance of the Church. Geo[rge] Q. Cannon assisted some in this writing, and when I had finished it to the satisfaction of the

---

103. John Lyman Smith (1828-1898) came to Utah in 1847. He took part in the Indian wars, later serving two missions to Europe and becoming president of the Swiss-Italian Mission.

104. Alonzo Hazeltine Raleigh (1818-1901) was an officer in the Nauvoo Legion, served in the Utah legislative council, and helped open the St. George temple.

105. Susie Amelia Young Dunford Gates (1856-1933) was a daughter of Brigham Young and Lucy Bigelow Young. She founded the *Young Women's Journal,* the *Relief Society Magazine,* and the Utah Woman's Press Club.

President, he said to me, "Now you have before you an ensample to carry on the endowments in all the temples until the coming of the Son of Man."

On the 8th of April, 1877, W[ilford] Woodruff was appointed in the public assembly to take charge of the Temple and preside over it, and in private conversation with the President, he said he wanted me to take the whole charge of the Temple and attend to all affairs connected with the endowments, sealings &c. I told him I was not able to go to the altar and do all the sealings as I had injured myself at that labor in the Salt Lake Endowment House. Pres[iden]t Young told me to go to work and ordain some men to help me to do the sealing[s]. He told me to set apart J[ohn] D. T. McAllister and David H. Cannon for that purpose and, if I needed more, to set them apart. I set apart Br[other] McAllister to that work April 14th, 1877. I set apart David H. Cannon for the same purpose on the 27th of April. I also set apart James G. Bleak to officiate at the altar some time afterward (I do not recollect the date). (2d March 1881.)

Pres[iden]t Young gave me power and authority to give second anointings and seal women to men as I might be led by the Spirit of God. I parted with Pres[iden]t Young for the last time in the flesh at 9:30 A.M. on April 16th, 1877, when he started for Salt Lake City. Brigham Young Jr., was very sick at the time.

When I left St. George, I placed the presidency of the Temple in the hands of John David Thompson McAllister, who was to preside over it in my absence.

This is the testimony which I Wilford Woodruff bear to all whom it may concern. **—Wilford Woodruff, "History of the St. George Temple, Its Cost & Dedication and the Labor Thereon," compiled Mar. 26, 1883**

I have taken the part of Adam [in the endowment dramatization in the St. George temple]. **—Brigham Young Jr. diary, Jan. 11, 1877**

We herein embody a few instructions which we wish you to <u>strictly enjoin</u> upon the brethren and sisters who come to the [St. George] Temple to officiate for themselves or their friends:—

Those who wish to receive endowments for themselves, or friends, should be provided with oil or means to purchase it.

The sisters should be provided with two or three white skirts; and the brethren should have their garments to button from the back clear round and up the front; and shirts made to reach down to the knees, or a little below, or one may be pieced to this length for the occasion.

Before the brethren or sisters go into the Temple to receive Endowments they must wash themselves all over perfectly clean so as to enter the Temple clean.

Men and women should have no sexual connection for a week or More previous to their going into the Temple to receive Endowments. **—Brigham Young, John W. Young, Wilford Woodruff, Erastus Snow, and Brigham Young Jr. to Bishops, Jan. 13, 1877; emphasis in original**

Brigham Young jr & Myself wrote out a part of the Ceremony of the Endowment. …

I spent the Evening with President [Brigham] Young. He told me their was No Necessity of dressing in the Temple Clothing while giving the second Anointing any more than in administering the first Anointing or Ordaining. He also said that we should use the Bible in the garden & Bible & Book of Mormon in the Telestial room and add the [Doctrine and] Covenants to it in the Terrestial Room. **—Wilford Woodruff journal, Jan. 15, 1877**

Busy [in the St. George temple] writing with bro[ther]s [Wilford] W[oodruff] & J[ohn] N[uttall] on ceremonies. **—Brigham Young Jr. diary, Jan. 16, 1877**

Spent the evening reading to father [Brigham Young] what we—Bro[ther] [Wilford] Woodruff, [L. John] Nuttall & myself have written in relation to endowment. He made a number of corrections. —**Brigham Young Jr. diary, Jan. 17, 1877**

I dressed in pure white Doe skin from head to feet to officiate in the Priest Office, white pants vest & Cap[,] the first example in any Temple of the Lord in this last dispensation. Sis[ter Lucy] B. Young also dressed in white in officiating [as] Eve. President was presant and delivered a lecture at the veil some 30 att[e]nd[in]g. **—Wilford Woodruff journal, Feb. 1, 1877**

After supper went to President [Brigham] Youngs[;] present Pres[iden]t Young, W[ilford] Woodruff, E[rastus] Snow, B[righam] Young

Jr.[,] J[ames] G. Bleak[,] E[van] M Greene[106] & myself[.] Work[ing space] in the Temple being under consideration, Pres[iden]t Young was filled with the spirit of God & revelation & said when we got our washings and anointings under the hands of the Prophet Joseph [Smith] at Nauvoo we had only one room to work in with the exception of a little side room or office w[h]ere we were washed and anointed[,] had our garments placed upon us[,] and received our New Name. And after he had performed these ceremonies, he gave the Key Words[,] signs, tokens and penalties. Then after we went into the large room over the [Red Brick] store in Nauvoo, Joseph divided up the room the best that he could [and] hung up the veil. [He] marked it [and] gave us our instructions as we passed along from one department to another[,] giving us signs, tokens, [and] penalties[,] with the Key words pertaining to those signs. And after we had got through, Bro[ther] Joseph turned to me (Pres[iden]t B[righam] Young) and said Bro[ther] Brigham[,] this is not arranged right but we have done the best we could do under the circumstances in which we are placed, and I wish you to take this matter in hand and organize and systematize all these ceremonies with the signs, tokens[,] penalties[,] and Key words. I did so[,] and each time I got something more so that when we went through the Temple at Nauvoo I understood and knew how to place them there. We had our ceremonies pretty correct—

In the creation the Gods entered into an agreement about forming this earth & putting Michael or Adam upon it. These thing[s] of which I have been speaking are what are termed the mysteries of godliness but they will enable you to understand the expression of Jesus[,] made while in Jerusalem. This is life eternal that they might know thee the only true God and Jesus Christ whom thou hast Sent. We were once acquainted with the Gods & lived with them but we had the privilege of taking upon us flesh that the spirit might have a house to dwell in. We did so and forgot all and came into the world not recollecting anything of which we had previously learned.

We have heard a great deal about Adam and Eve, how they were formed &c. Some think he was made like an adobie and the Lord breathed into him the breath of life. For we read "from dust thou art and unto dust shalt thou return." Well he was made of the dust of the

---

106. Evan Melbourne Greene (1814-1882) came to Utah in 1852. He served as mayor of Provo and compiled a list of laws for Utah Territory.

earth but not of this earth. He was made just the same way you and I are made but on another earth. Adam was an immortal being when he came on this earth. He had lived on an earth similar to ours. He had received the Priesthood and the Keys thereof and had been faithful in all things and gained his resurrection and his exaltation and was crowned with glory[,] immortality[,] and eternal lives and was numbered with the Gods[,] for such he became through his faithfulness. And [he] had begotten all the spirit[s] that was to come to this earth. And Eve[,] our common Mother who is the Mother of all living[,] bore those spirits in the celestial world. And when this earth was organized by Elohim, Jehovah & Michael[,] who is Adam our common Father, Adam & Eve had the privilege to continue the work of Progression [and] consequently came to this earth and commenced the great work of forming tabernacles for those spirits to dwell in. And when Adam and those that assisted him had completed this Kingdom[,] our earth[,] he came toil and Slept and forgot all and became like an Infant child. It is said by Moses the historian that the Lord caused a deep sleep to come upon Adam and took from his side a rib and formed the woman that Adam Called Eve—this should be interpreted that the Man Adam like all other Men had the seed within him to propagate his species. But not the Woman. She conceives the seed but she does not produce it, consequently she was taken from the side or bowels of her father. This explains the mystery of Moses' dark sayings in regard to Adam and Eve. Adam and Eve when they were placed on this earth were immortal beings with flesh, bones[,] and sinues [sinews], but upon partaking of the fruits of the earth while in the garden and cultivating the ground their bodies became changed from immortal to mortal beings with the blood coursing through their veins as the action of life. Adam was not under transgression until after he partook of the forbidden fruit. This was necessary that they might be together[,] that man might be. The woman was found in transgression[,] not the Man—Now in the law of Sacrifice we have the promise of a Savior[,] and man had the privilege and showed forth his obedience by offering of the first fruits of the earth and the firstlings of the flocks—this is a showing that Jesus would come and shed his blood.

Father Adam's oldest son (Jesus the Saviour) who is the heir of the family is Father Adams first begotten in the spirit World, who according to the flesh is the only begotten[,] as it is written. (In his divinity[,] he having gone back into the spirit World and come in the spirit to Mary[,] and she conceived[,] for when Adam and Eve got through with their Work in this earth, they did not lay their bodies down in the dust, but returned to the spirit World from whence they came.[)][107]

—L. John Nuttall diary, Feb. 7, 1877, Perry Special Collections

In January 1877, shortly after the lower portion of the St. George Temple was dedicated, President Brigham Young, in following up in the Endowments, became convinced that it was necessary to have the formula of the Endowments written, and he gave directions to have the same put in writing.

Shortly afterwards he explained what the Lecture at the Veil should portray, and for this purpose appointed a day when he would personally deliver the Lecture at the Veil. Elders J[ohn] D. T. McAllister and L. John Nuttall prepared writing material, and as the President spoke they took down his words. Elder Nuttall put the same into form and the writing was submitted to President Young on the same evening at his office in residence at St. George. He there made such changes as he deemed proper, and when he finally passed upon it said: This is the Lecture at the Veil to be observed in the Temple.[108]

A copy of the Lecture is kept at the St. George Temple, in which President Young refers to Adam in his creation &c.

L. John Nuttall [signed]

For Presidents W[ilford] Woodruff[,] Geo[rge] Q. Cannon[,] Jos[eph] F. Smith

—L. John Nuttall Papers, dated June 3, 1892, Perry Special Collections

We herein embody a few instructions which we wish you to strictly enjoin upon the brethren and sisters who come to the Temple to officiate for themselves or their friends: Those who wish to receive

107. This is a portion of the "lecture at the veil" (see next entry) which is no longer part of the endowment but for half a century was delivered at the end of the ceremony. It lasted about a half hour and offered participants ideas about the meaning of what they had just experienced (David John Buerger, *The Mysteries of Godliness: A History of Mormon Temple Worship* [San Francisco: Smith Research Associates, 1994], 110-13). Brigham Young's teaching about Adam was later repudiated (Buerger, "The Adam-God Doctrine," *Dialogue: A Journal of Mormon Thought* 15 [Spring 1982]: 14-58).

108. According to Buerger, "it is uncertain whether the St. George lecture with its Adam-God teaching was included in all temples" or if officiators elsewhere were free to extemporize (*Mysteries of Godliness,* 113).

endowments for themselves or friends should be provided with oil or means to purchase it. The sisters should be provided with two or three white skirts and the brethren should have their garments to button from the back, clear round and up the front, and skirts made to reach down to the knees or a little below or one may be pieced to this length for the occasion.

Before the brethren or sisters go into the Temple to receive their endowments; they must wash themselves all over, perfectly clean, so as to enter the Temple clean.

Men and women should have no sexual intercourse for a week or more previous to their going into the Temple to receive their endowments. **—Brigham Young, John W. Young, Wilford Woodruff, Erastus Snow, and Brigham Young Jr., "Special Instructions to Bishops," January 13, 1877**

[M]yself and wives received our sec[on]d anointing under the hands of Elder Wilford Woodruff, to whom we were subsequently adopted as son and daughter[s].[109] **—Henry Eyring[110] diary, Feb. 24, 1877, Perry Special Collections**

In reply to your questions: as you and your wife received your Endowments before being sealed as husband and wife there is no need of the children being sealed to you.

As to the [issue of your wife's] New Name[,] when you and your wife get to the Temple and to the proper place[,] you can get it from your wife, but not till then. **—Brigham Young to Abraham Washburn, Mar. 9, 1877**

Went to the temple this morning and received an endowment for my [deceased, namesake] father, George Cannon. This is a blessed privilege which I desire to appreciate. It seemed that my father was near to me while going through, and I was peculiarly affected. There was a

109. The "law of adoption" was a temple-related practice begun in Nauvoo that allowed members to be sealed to prominent Church leaders instead of to their biological parents. This was reversed by Wilford Woodruff in 1894 (Gordon Irving, "The Law of Adoption: One Phase of the Development of the Mormon Concept of Salvation, 1830-1900," *BYU Studies* 14 (Spring 1974): 291-314.

110. Henry Carlos Ferdinand Eyring (1835-1902) was born in Germany, migrated to the United States with his sister, and converted to Mormonism in 1855. He later settled and died in Colonia Jaurez in the Mexican state of Chihuahua.

holy influence plainly felt. **—George Q. Cannon diary, Apr. 10, 1877,[111] typed excerpt in Quinn Papers**

Pr[e]s[ident] E[rastus] Snow said, when we can get time, we will give [the] Endowment for Each Priesthood separate[ly], and after a while when Temples [are] built we will give [the] Endowment to each according to what Priesthood they hold; then we will give men the Endowment of the Aaronic Priesthood and nothing else [at first]. **—Jens Christian Andersen Weibye[112] diary, July 9, 1877**

[Q] How shall little children be dressed in attending to the Temple Ordinance of being sealed to their parents?

[A] They should be clothed in White.

[Q] Can a brother or sister who has received Endowments in Salt Lake City or in Nauvoo, have the privilege of passing through the degrees in the St. George Temple; and if so, are they to be clothed with Temple Clothing, or in the ordinary manner?

[A] They may have the privilege of passing through as visitors; and not wearing Temple clothing.

[Q] If a person die without having had endowments, is it well to bury them in garments without marks?

[A] Such person may be buried with garments if their friends choose, but not marked, nor with robes or other Temple Clothing. **—"Questions Submitted to Pres[iden]t B[righam] Young by the Elders Who Have Recently Been Out as Temple Missionaries," ca. 1877**

I will say here, before closing, that two weeks before I left St. George, the spirits of the dead were gathered around me, wanting to know why we did not redeem them. Said they, "You have had the use of the Endowment House for a number of years, and yet nothing has ever been done for us. We laid the foundation of the government you now enjoy, and we never apostatized from it, but we remained true to it and were faithful to God."

---

111. On the next day, April 11, Cannon returned and stood as proxy for his grandfather, also named George Cannon, and wrote similarly that "there was an holy influence felt by me, as on yesterday, that the dead for whom I officiated were with me" (Quinn Papers).

112. Jens Christian Andersen Weibye (1824-1893) was born in Denmark, where he converted to Mormonism. He migrated to America in 1862, arriving in Salt Lake City that same year.

These were the signers of the Declaration of Independence, and they waited on me for two days and two nights. I thought it very singular, that notwithstanding so much work had been done, and yet nothing had been done for them. The thought never entered my heart, from the fact, I suppose, that heretofore our minds were reaching after our more immediate friends and relatives. I straightway went into the baptismal font and called upon Brother [John D. T.] MacAllister to baptize me for the signers of the Declaration of Independence, and fifty other eminent men, making one hundred in all, including John Wesley, Columbus, and others; I then baptized him for every President of the United States, except three; and when their cause is just, somebody will do the work for them.[113] **—Wilford Woodruff discourse, Sept. 16, 1877, *Journal of Discourses*, 19:229-30**

Your favor of the 22nd, inst.[,] asking the form of ceremony you ought to use in rebaptizing persons who wish the ordinance, and also the form of ceremony in confirming the same, has been received. Your letter was read to the Council, and it has been decided that the proper form to be used in rebaptizing persons who have not been cut off the Church or dealt with for their fellowship is as follows: the person who has authority from the Lord to baptize shall go down into the water with the person to be baptized, and shall say, calling him or her by name, "Having been commissioned of Jesus Christ, I baptize you for the remission of your sins, and for the renewal of your covenants, in the name of the Father and of the Son and of the Holy Ghost. Amen." In confirming[,] it is proper to reconfirm the members of the Church and to seal upon them all the former baptisms, confirmations, ordinations, patriarchal blessings, and if they have had their endowments, their washings, anointings and their sealing ordinances. **—John Taylor to Moses Thatcher, Sept. 25, 1877**

113. In fact, the founders of the United States had been baptized by proxy already by John M. Bernhisel in the Endowment House in August 1876—although proxy endowments had not been performed for the founders. The three presidents omitted by Woodruff were Martin Van Buren, who had refused to assist the Mormons in Missouri in 1838; James Buchanan, who sent 2,500 troops under the direction of Colonel Albert Sidney Johnston to Utah in 1857 to tame the secessionist spirit there; and Ulysses S. Grant, who was still alive. See Brian H. Stuy, "Wilford Woodruff's Vision of the Signers of the Declaration of Independence," *Journal of Mormon History* 26 (Spring 2000): 64-90.

A communication was read from President John Taylor to [Salt Lake Stake] Pres[ident] Angus M. Cannon, that the Twelve had decided to open the Endowment House on the last Thursday in each month for marriage sealings. President John Taylor said this was done because many young people and the aged and infirm could not arrange to go to St. George[.] The priesthood was not made for Temples, but Temples for the priesthood. **—Historian's Office Journal, Nov. 15, 1877**

[A]fter a very free expression of the members of the Quorum [of Twelve], it was obvious that it was the feeling of all present that the [means] to lawful marriage according to the sealing ordinance of the Holy Priesthood should not be diminished amongst the Latter-day Saints, but that marriage should be encouraged in our midst by every means within our power not inconsistent with the revealed will of God. It was also deemed salutory to have the Priesthood discountenance wherever practicable, the marriages of Latter-day Saints in any place not especially dedicated and set apart for the performance of the ordinances of the House of the Lord, of which the ceremony which unites the sexes in the bonds of matrimony is a very important part.

To aid in the accomplishment of this object, it was unanimously resolved by the Councils of the Apostles to re-open the Endowment House in this city for the performance of certain ordinances of the House of the Lord, namely:—

First, for the sealing of those in full fellowship in the Church of Jesus Christ of Latter-day Saints, who have been married for time by any Apostle, Bishop, Elder, Justice of the Peace, etc. since the close of the Endowment House in October, 1876.

Secondly, for the sealing of the members of the Church in good standing who have not been married but who desire to be sealed, and to whom a journey to the Temple at St. George for this purpose would not be convenient or practicable.

Thirdly, for the purpose of giving endowments to the very aged, sick, or infirm, such, and such only as their Bishop may think will probably not live until the Temple at Salt Lake City, Manti, or Logan is completed and opened.[114]

---

114. The temple in Salt Lake City was not opened until 1893. The Logan temple opened in 1884, the Manti temple in 1888.

Those desiring to receive the benefit of these ordinances must obtain a recommend from the Bishop of the Ward or settlement in which they reside, or in the absence of the Bishop, the recommend may be signed by the President of the Stake.

It will be well for persons presenting themselves at the Endowment House to receive the ordinances thereof, to be prepared to reply to the following questions:—

"When were you born?"

"Where were you born?"

"When were you first baptized?"

"What is your Father's name?"

"What was your Mother's maiden name?"

No person will be eligible to receive these blessings except they have been rebaptized.[115]

The Endowment House will be open for the performance of the ordinances mentioned on the last Thursday in November and thenceforth, until otherwise ordered, on the last Thursday of every month. All parties interested should be at the House not later than 8 o'clock a.m.

Please notify the Bishops in the Stake over which you preside of these instructions. **—John Taylor to Angus M. Cannon, Nov. 15, 1877**

....

It was a long time after the Prophet Joseph Smith had received the keys of the kingdom of God, and after Hyrum [Smith][116] and others had received many blessings, that the Lord gave Joseph a revelation, to show him and others how they could ask for and receive certain blessings. We read in the [R]evelations of St. John, that the Saints are to receive a white stone, "and in the stone a new name, which no man knoweth save him that receiveth it." Joseph tells us that this new name is a key-word, which can only be obtained through the endowments. This is one of the keys and blessings that will be bestowed upon the Saints in these last days, for which we shall be very thankful. **—Charles C. Rich discourse, Feb. 10, 1878, *Journal of Discourses,* 19:250**

115. Rebaptism as a requirement to enter the temple was discontinued in 1893. See Allen and Leonard, *Story of the Latter-day Saints,* 431.

116. Hyrum Smith (1800-1844) was a brother of founder Joseph Smith, who served as Presiding Patriarch and counselor in the First Presidency. He was murdered in the Carthage jail along with his brother.

You understood Bro[ther] Joseph F. Smith rightly with regard to those only being accepted at the Endowment House who have been re-baptized. We do not think that the blessings of the House of the Lord are for those who are either too careless or too indifferent to give heed to the servants of God, when a call is made for repentance and renewal of covenants. The only exceptions that we make to this rule are with those whose first baptism has occurred within a few (say six or eight) months. **—John Taylor to F. Spencer, Mar. 25, 1878**

Sis[ter] Caroline Carter an aged lady has my permission to receive her Second Anointings at your convenience. Her husband has received his first endowments and is dead. She was sealed to him. Bro[other] D[on] C[arlos] Thompson will act in behalf of bro[ther] Carter. **—John Taylor to Joseph F. Smith, Oct. 10, 1878**

Elder Brigham Y. Baird, of Kanab, has our permission to receive his Second Anointings, being recommended by his Bishop as worthy of receiving this blessing. **—John Taylor to Wilford Woodruff, Oct. 21, 1878**

....

[T]he evening of the fifty second Anniversary of the Angel delivering of the Plates of the Book of Mormon to Joseph Smith the Prophet of the Lord, I dedicated [my] house and room[;] also blest the Oil[,] after which my Ruth Anointed my feet and wiped them with the hair of her head, then kissed them after the pattern as written in the Testament of the Lord Jesus Christ.[117] **—Samuel Hollister Rogers[118] diary, Sept. 22, 1879, Perry Special Collections**

....

In regard to the three couples of young people, who have lately been married and desire their endowments and to be sealed, I would state that these things are not according to the order which has long been established among us. Some time ago when the Endowment House was closed, it was permitted, under the circumstances that then

117. Rogers refers here to the second part of the second anointing, which is performed at home.

118. Samuel Hollister Rogers (1819-1891) was a member of the Mormon Battalion in 1846 and later helped settle Iron County, Utah, where he served as a probate judge.

existed, for persons desirous to be married to have the ceremony performed by certain parties appointed in this City for that purpose; and, under instructions, the Bishops, in some instances, were permitted to officiate in that ordinance. This was done, however, as a matter of necessity, and is not in accordance with the order of the Holy Priesthood, and it was expected, and the parties were so informed, that as soon as the ordinances could be attended to properly, that all parties, thus married, would have to be sealed, either in the Temple or in the Endowment House. This state of things continued for a short time, when the Council [of the Twelve], on deliberation upon the subject, concluded that it was proper to re-open the Endowment House that these ordinances might be attended to properly. That House has now been opened for some two years, hence you will perceive that all ordinances performed, since that time, in the manner indicated by you, are out of place and should not be performed and cannot be tolerated, except under peculiar circumstances, and by instructions from the proper authorities; for we must maintain intact those sacred principles which God has committed to us. In the case of one young man, which you refer to, it might be excusable, but still we ought to have been consulted in the matter. However, we will let these things pass on this occasion, but hope there will not be a recurrence of this nature in the future; and if you will inform those brethren, and they come properly recommended, the matter can be attended to as per your request. **—John Taylor to Leonard E. Harrington, Feb. 13, 1880**

In regard to the second anointing of your father, we have no objections to offer in your having the privilege of officiating in that ordinance for your father and mother at the St. George Temple. **—John Taylor to Warren Cote, Feb. 13, 1880.**

These additional powers [second anointing] include all the keys that belong to the holy priesthood on the earth, or were ever revealed to man in any dispensation, and which admit men and women within the veil. They enable them to pass by the angels and the gods, until they get into the presence of the Father and the Son. They make of them kings and priests, queens and priestesses to God, to rule and reign as such over their posterity and those who may be given to them by adoption, in the great jubilee of rest which is near at hand. It gives them the right to the tree of life, and the "seal of the living God in their foreheads," spoken of by John the revelator. **—Daniel Tyler,[119] "Temples," *Juvenile Instructor,* May 15, 1880, 111.**

Pres[iden]t J[ohn] D. T. McAllister expressed his pleasure to meet with us, and to be one, with us in our desires to go forward and Minister before the Lord in Sacred things, in His Stead upon the Earth. We are called to do this work before the Lord, [to] act for him just as much as any man that was ever called. Aaron was not called any more of God, than we have been who labor in this House. I am glad of the unity, that we can live together and work together. ... We will work towards perfecting ourselves and be guarded in our acts and Sayings, that God will accept of us and our labors. Those having charge of the Rooms will please to See that there is no loud talking or laughter in their rooms, avoid making a noise and [to] Jar with the pipes in using the water &c. With regard to new Names, give easy names to be understood: Scripture names or names not in the Scripture, there are many good names of those who have lived upon the earth which are easy to understand[;] don't give any fanciful names, [and] be Sure they get the New Name and that they understand it. Avoid all you can having a noise with the Steam or Engine during prayer: Every person called to work in this house Should Notice the time and be in their Seats at prayer time. Brethren notice the prayer Roll and try and be here when your time comes for prayer, even if you have to be excused afterwards: Door Keepers See that there is no loud talking or laughter at the door. During the time of the Endowments, there Should be no knitting or Sewing in any of the rooms, no loud talking or noise. Workers who are called to take parts, commit [their parts to memory] so as not to have to read them but have your book with you So you can refer if necessary. **—Minutes, Meeting of Workers in St. George Temple, Aug. 31, 1880, typed excerpt, Buerger Papers**

119. Daniel Tyler (1816-1906) was a sergeant in the Mormon Battalion and served as president of the Swiss-Italian Mission from 1854 to 1856.

2.

DRAWING THE LINE ON POLICIES AND PROCEDURES 1881–1900

Your letter of January 20th was received this morning. And in answer to your inquiry as regards the adoption of the children of yourself and wife: Under the circumstances as you represent them, it will be proper, if the children are old enough, that they express their choice as to which parent they would rather be sealed; or, if agreeable to all parties, these children can be sealed to you as their natural father, inasmuch as they were born out of the covenant. **—John Taylor to K. M. Englestad, Jan. 26, 1881**

You say, "If parties are to be rebaptized regardless of how recent their first baptism may have been, &c. &c. we will cheerfully comply."

In the first place we think it extremely riskey to send persons to the [Endowment] House &c. who are only "recently baptized." We think people should have an opportunity to prove themselves, before coming to the House or going to the Temple, especially [in]experienced people. They should at least "summer and winter" in the Church, and then if deemed worthy to come for sacred ordinances, agreeable to [the] letter of instructions sent to the Bishops and Presidents on this subject when the House was re-opened, they should be rebaptized for the renewal of their covenants before being recommended by the bishop. **—Joseph F. Smith to William Bringhurst, Oct. 11, 1881; emphasis in original**

President Joseph F. Smith desires me to draw your attention to the rules governing the recommendations of persons desiring to receive their endowments [in the Endowment House]. Only faithful couples about to be married (or any other marriages,) or couples still bearing children, should receive recommends, with the exception of very aged persons, whose age and infirmities make desirable a departure from the strict observance of the above rule, and then, it should be stated on the recommend, that age or ill health is the reason why it is given. All others will have to wait for their blessings until one of the temples, now in the course of construction, is finished and work commenced therein, or they must go down to the temple at St. George. **—George Reynolds to Amos Maycock, Nov. 11, 1881**

Permit me to draw your attention to the fact that a few days ago you signed a recommend in favor of a young man, residing in Brigham City, who had not been re-baptized, and whose first baptism took place as long ago as 1863. The consequence was we were compelled to re-baptize him before he could receive his blessing. When such things occur it causes inconveniences and delay to the whole company passing through on that day, and is also contrary to the rules that govern in such matters. Will you please notify the Bishops in your Stake that all persons whose first baptisms have not taken place within a very recent period must be re-baptized before they receive their recommends to pass through the House of the Lord. **—Joseph F. Smith to Oliver G. Snow, Nov. 18, 1881**

Pres[ident] Erastus Snow arose and read Par[agraphs] 12, 13, 14, & 15 of Section 128 of the D[octrine] & C[ovenants]. He said the general features of the St. George Temple are in conformity to those of the Kirtland Temple which was dedicated in April 1836.

That temple may be said to have been built to show forth the order of the priesthood, Aaronic and Melchizedek—the priesthood there received the ordinance of the washing of feet and the anointing of the head with oil. This was confirmed to those holding the priesthood. There was no baptismal font in the temple at Kirtland for that ordinance had not been revealed to the people.

By the time the Nauvoo Temple was being built the doctrine of the baptism for the dead was revealed and one of the first thing[s] attended to there was the preparation of the font for the Baptism of the Dead.

It was revealed here in St. George to the prophet Brigham Young that there should be variations made in the temples to be built. This was given unto the Prophet Brigham in answer to his question, "Oh Lord show unto thy servants if we shall build all temples after the same pattern?"

The answer came. "Do you all build your houses after the same pattern? Do you[,] after increasing your families[,] build after the same pattern used when your family is small? So shall the growth of the knowledge of the principles of the Gospel among my people cause diversity in the pattern of Temples." **—St. George Stake Historical Record, Nov. 20, 1881, typed excerpt in Buerger Papers**

....

Mrs Elizabeth Gilbert,[1] (who is in her Eighty-second year) is here for the purpose of obtaining her Second Anointing, together with her husband, Algernon Sidney Gilbert,[2] who Died when Zion's Camp went up to Missouri—My Brother Henry Rollins, Stands as Proxy for her husband—his uncle.

I also wish to know if the sealing of My Mother to Mr. John M. Burk, in Nauvoo can be changed. As she did not wish to be Sealed to him—But Brother Young told her to let it be so for the present, and it could be changed afterward, (or words to that effect).

Must her sealing remain as it was in Nauvoo? Or [can] she be sealed to Joseph—For that is our Desire[.] Henry desires to be adopted into Josephs Kingdom[.][3] **—Mary Elizabeth Rollins Lightner[4] and James Rollins[5] to John Taylor, May 22, 1882**

As I understand[,] you are well acquainted with Bro[ther] James A. Rollins and his sister Mary E. who is the [plural] wife of Joseph [Smith]

---

1. Elizabeth Van Benthusen Gilbert (1800-1891) joined the LDS Church with her husband in 1830. After her husband's death, she lived with her niece, Mary Elizabeth Lightner, and family.

2. Algernon Sidney Gilbert (1789-1834) was a merchant in Kirtland, where he converted to Mormonism. Before his death during the march of the Church militia to Missouri, he was told by revelation to open a store in Missouri.

3. That is, adopted into Joseph Smith's family line for the sake of the hereafter.

4. Mary Elizabeth Rollins Lightner (1818-1913) married Adam Lightner in 1835 and became a plural wife of Joseph Smith in 1842 while still married to Adam.

5. James Henry Rollins (1816-1899) was born in Lima, New York, and raised by his aunt, Elizabeth Gilbert, after his father died. He was baptized in 1832 and came to Utah in 1849.

the Prophet. It does not require a great deal of writing from me [because] he has had his Second Anointing, and can act for his uncle if approved. They are very much exercised about their Mother. He informs me it was understood when living at President Smith's that he was to be in his family, and would like his mother sealed to him. …

N[ota] B[ene]. Please [know that I will wait for you] to answer by wire if the Mother is to be sealed to Joseph. Please [let me know whether] to say to Henry Rollins [that he should act as proxy for] Gilbert [in the] second [anointing], and all [has been] approved. If the mother remains where she is, I will understand the usual form. **—John D. T. McAllister to John Taylor, May 22, 1882**

Regarding the Lamanites [Native Americans] receiving their endowments, we should like to receive further details from you with regard to them before answering definitely. Certainly none but entirely reliable ones should have this privilege, those whom you know to be worthy according to the light they possess. **—John Taylor to Lot Smith,[6] Oct. 31, 1882**

....

By direction of Pres[iden]t John Taylor I mail to you two copies of the Revelation asked for in your letter of Feb. 4th 1883. And in reply to your 2nd question: Can you receive Second Anointings for your Brother David R. Crosley who died in the faith? Yes. Also in answer to your 3rd question, Can we receive Second Anointings for our dead fathers and mothers and others who we are proxy for? If your fathers and mothers were members of the Church in their lives and died as faithful members, Yes you can obtain Second Anointings for them, but if they and others who you are proxy for were NOT members of the Church in their lives, and for whom you have had certain ordinances performed in their behalf, it will be well to let that suffice for the present, as further opportunities may be granted hereafter. **—L. John Nuttall to J. Crosley, Feb. 6, 1883, emphasis in original**

I have read your letter and noted its contents. I am of the opinion that the parties should have ample time to prove their sincerity and

6. Lot Smith (1830-1892) was a member of the Mormon Battalion, who then served a mission to Great Britain from 1869 to 1871 and was later president of the Little Colorado Stake, named after the Little Colorado River in eastern Arizona and western New Mexico.

repentance before they are recommended to the House of the Lord. "The way of the transgress[o]r is hard," and I know of no way to make it easy. If people will transgress the laws of God they must abide the consequences. I never believed a transgressor can jump from crime to innocence in one leap. The road back from vice to virtue is a long one, lost confidence returns but slowly and very cautiously, and then only when room for doubt and distrust is fully removed by a life of unimpeachable integrity, humility, honesty & sincerity. I should want them to prove themselves worthy before giving a recommend, if I were their Bishop. **—Joseph F. Smith to Henry Tingey, Aug. 28, 1883; emphasis in original**

....

Applications are, as you are aware, being constantly made for the privilege of having women sealed to their husbands who have heretofore been sealed to other men who were not their husbands.

Similar applications are being made in the cases of sealing children to parents who have heretofore been sealed to men who were not their natural fathers.

I have been unofficially informed that when such cases are pla[i]n, and when the applications are in harmony with the teachings given at the last April Conference, the rule in the Temple should be to proceed without application to President [Wilford] Woodruff.

If this be the decision of the First Presidency, I would be obliged if I could be so informed officially by the placing of a plain "yes" or "no" upon this sheet.

[Written in pencil:] yes, W[ilford] Woodruff **—John Nicholson to Lorenzo Snow, June 18, 1884**

During my absence from the city I have authorized President Joseph F. Smith to sign all recommends for temple work with the exception of those for second anointings which I prefer to attend to myself and wish them forwarded directly to me, or have them postponed until after my return. **—John Taylor to John D. T. McAllister and Marriner Wood Merrill, Aug. 4, 1884**

Our Bishops and Presidents of Stakes cannot be too particular in giving [temple] recommends to parties, so that those who are unworthy may not have the privileges and blessings which are to be had in the house of the Lord. It is desirable that all recommends for sealings, adoptions and other anointings shall first be sent to the City for my signature as has been heretofore set forth in instructions given on those points. **—John Taylor to John D. T. McAllister and David H. Cannon, Sept. 13, 1884**

By direction of President [John] Taylor I return herewith the request of Brother David B. Ott without the signature of the president who directs me to say that in regard to the second anointings it used to be usual for others to appoint and designate who should receive them. They now seem to come wrong end first. By this I infer that the president desires to designate the parties who should receive these ordinances without the application of the parties or other persons in their behalf. There may be some instruction given upon this matter at some of our meetings during the coming conference. **—L. John Nuttall to John D. T. McAllister, Sept. 19, 1884**

I should be pleased to receive from you, for my own information, a statement of the rules you have adopted in the house of the Lord, touching the eligibility of candidates for ordinances, with such other matters relating to your administration as would enable me to correctly and [adequately] consider the numerous questions propounded by persons who are about to do work in the temple.

So you will better understand what kind of information I need, I will state a case or two. Elder William Moss of this city [Salt Lake City] was officiating in the Logan temple last September; he is now returning to do further work; he enquired of me if he would need another recommend. I told him I thought not, that the previous one would still hold good. ... Also he wants to know "how rigidly he [should draw] the line with regard to details" when performing marriages. Do you need a maiden name for the wife or can it just be "Mrs. John Morgan ... or as the case might be."

Also a man on the high council said that he had not had his endowments and went to the temple to get them and was refused entrance because he could not recollect the date of his baptism. **—John Taylor to Marriner Wood Merrill, Nov. 6, 1884**

In regard to the enquiries made by you in your letter as to the propriety of your sister officiating in the Logan temple in the ordinances for the dead, I have to say that under the circumstances stated by you it would not be proper for her to do so; and being married to a gentile, it is not proper for her to wear her garments. **—John Taylor to Joseph Hunter, Dec. 1, 1884**

In reply to your letter of Dec. 5th pertaining to telegrams and the payment thereof, I am directed by President [John] Taylor to say that in all cases such as Bishop Jones and widow Thomas, it is his understanding, and wishes you to so understand it, that no matter what may be stated in recommends as to what is desired, his initials, "J. T.," thereon is all that is meant. If he places "J. T. 2nd [anointing]" on, then he approves it in that manner. Hence the recommends of Jones and Thomas only having his "J. T."[,] that was all he intended for them. So that in future it will not be necessary for you to inquire by telegram or otherwise as to what is meant when you see his endorsement. **—L. John Nuttall to John D. T. McAllister, Dec. 10, 1884**

....

Some busybodies having made it their business to find out how long it took for a recommend left at this office to go to the president, receive his signature, and be returned, thereby calculating the whereabouts of the president,[7] he has directed me to forward all recommends left personally at this office for his signature to you at the temple after they have been signed by him, and not to return them to those in whose favor they are made out; in this way avoiding such calculations as those intimated above. **—George Reynolds to Marriner Wood Merrill, Mar. 11, 1885**

President Joseph E. Taylor[8] read a letter which he had received from Pres[ident] M[arriner] W. Merrill, who presides in the Logan Temple, naming as qualifications to be possessed by those who desire the blessings of God's House.

That they should be tithe payers, attenders of Fast meetings, and donators to temples; observers of the Sabbath day, firm believers in plural marriage, etc.

---

7. John Taylor was at the time in hiding to escape prosecution for plural marriage, which is why there was concern about anyone calculating his proximity to Church headquarters.

8. Joseph Edward Taylor (1830–1913) came to Utah in 1852. He served a mission to England and was later appointed to the Salt Lake Stake presidency and Salt Lake temple presidency beginning in 1893.

The bishops were instructed to question, very closely, all applicants who desired to go to the "House of God." The following being among the questions: Do you attend all the public meetings of the Saints: Do you observe the Word of Wisdom according to the meaning and spirit thereof; pay tithing, donate to the poor, etc.?

[The bishops were] not to recommend any young m[a]n for ordination to the Priesthood who does not observe the word of Wisdom.

Have you committed any grievous offences by breaking the laws of God? Have you lived the life of a Saint and preserved your chastity? Have you had any criminal intercourse with the opposite sex?

The Bishops were instructed not to recommend any person to any Temple unless they answered all questions in a satisfactory manner.

If applicants perjured themselves then they were amenable to God for their acts.

The subject of the celestial law of marriage was dwelt upon. It was shown that the faithful must live it, otherwise they could not attain to a fulness of glory.[9]

The Lord has said that "it is not meet that men who have not observed this law should preside over His Priesthood." **—Minutes, Special Bishops' Meeting, Nov. 6, 1885**

Since Pres[iden]t [Brigham] Young's death, while Bro[ther] D[avid] H. Cannon and myself [John McCallister] were at [the] Logan Temple (Bro[ther] [James] Bleak being in St. George) Pres[iden]t John Taylor thought those officiating in these ordinances should be set apart by the Pres[iden]t of the Church, as the authority by which they had heretofore acted was only delegated, and we were set apart by Pres[iden]t John Taylor to officiate in this Holy Calling [on] 17 June 1884. **—Temple Minute Book, St. George, Nov. 1885, typed excerpts in Buerger Papers**

To satisfy a feeling which has been on my mind for some time, I submit the following: My Son George Q. who died in this City when he was 18 years and 21 days old, was very faithful to us as a son, and also in the Holy Priesthood so far as he had opportunity[.] When a Deacon, he was 1st Councilor to the President of the Quorum, which position he filled honorably, untill ordained an Elder, previous to receiving his Endowment. He was appointed Cl[er]k of the 1st Quorum of Elders in

9. The "celestial law of marriage" refers to plural marriage.

the Stake. Being naturally of a religious turn of mind it seemed natural for him to perform his spiritual duties. He acted as a Teacher in the Ward, with entire satisfaction to the Saints up to the time of his death.

When on his death bed I asked him if there was anything that he would like me to do for him, he said "I would like you to have some wives sealed to me." According to this request I have had two girls who died in the Church sealed to him. Two others, apreciating his worth[,] have expressed a desire to have their daughters sealed to him, which will be done. These tokens of respect fills our hearts with joy feeling as we do, that our dear boy was worthy.

Now the question is, do you think he was old enough to receive his 2d Anointing?

Bro[ther] McAllister it is not my desire to seek blessings for my sons that they are not entitled to. But I had great hopes in this son, for I fully appreciated his worth, and would like to see that every blessing was put in his reach, to which his faithfulness entitled him.

You as the Pres[iden]t of the St George Stake knew him, hence I submit the question to you. **—David H. Cannon to John D. T. McAllister, Dec. 4, 1885**

I can fully endorse the words expressed by B[isho]p D[avid] H. Cannon in relation to his son George Q. He lived and died a good young man.

I think you are acquainted with him, as also his Uncle George Q.

I address this to you personally. **—John D. T. McAllister to John Taylor, Dec. 4, 1885**

Though the deceased son of Bishop David H. Cannon—George Q.—was quite young when he died, still as he is so highly recommended, you may administer to his representative and the representative of the deceased [women] who have been seal'd to him the ordinance of Second Anointing. **—John Taylor to John D. T. McAllister, Dec. 9, 1885**

....

It is not adviseable to fall into the fashion of issuing certificates of the character you describe. The parties themselves should keep a record of the transaction and the names of the witnesses, and beyond this nothing more is necessary unless it should be required to prove the marriage for the purposes of heirship to property, when it can be procured. We do not think it proper for a young man of the age you mention and an old lady, such as you describe, to marry for time and eternity, [but] there would be no objection to a union for eternity [only], even where such a disparity of ages exist[s]. **—John Taylor to Marriner Wood Merrill, Jan. 27, 1886**

Your letter asking the priviledge of 2nd anointing for your parents John Perry and Grace Williams Perry who are deceased, has been received.

You are at liberty to have them officiated for and receive their 2nd Anointings; but those who officiate for them must be those who have already had that sacred ordinance.

By presenting this to Bro[ther] M[arriner] W. Merrill[,] he will have the Ordinance attended to. **—John Taylor to Eliza Perry Benson, Mar. 4, 1886**

We are in receipt of your letters of the 5th and 6th inst. and have [perused] with interest the condition of the work on the Temple.

Respecting the painting and other ornamentations of the Temple[s] at St. George and Logan[,] my recollection is not sufficiently distinct, it having been some time since I saw them, to make any particular suggestions to you upon the subject.

However, it is important that Brother Weggeland[10] be impressed to so arrange the painting in the Garden that the Tree of Life will be convenient for the purpose for which it is used, and that the whole scenery be arranged so that the person at the Altar in giving his lecture can make convenient reference to the various objects.[11] Complaint has been made respecting these points at Logan[,] and before painting the Garden at Manti someone of experience who is familiar with the work and the giving of lectures in the Garden should be consulted as to the proper position for everything to be placed in with reference to the Altar and the Cherubim &c.

We have no objection to the employment of Bros Weggeland and

---

10. Danquart Anthon Weggeland (1827-1918) was born in Norway and converted to Mormonism in 1854. He arrived in Utah in 1862 and painted murals in the St. George, Manti, Logan, and Salt Lake temples.

11. Although painted murals depicting scenes in the Garden of Eden and other rooms of the endowment ceremony would eventually replace the use of physical scenery, the early Utah practice mirrored that of the Nauvoo temple in this regard.

Morris. Enclosed please find a permit for you to go to the Temple at Logan. **—John Taylor to William H. Folsom,[12] Apr. 18, 1886**

Advised all to get recommends from their Bishops signed by their President and by Pres[iden]t [John] Taylor and return[ed] to them before they leave home. Said those who marry outside of the church could attend to adoptions if they were recommended but should not [be] give[n] their endowments, because when they get their endowments they enter into covenants to have no sexual intercourse with the sons of Adam, except their lawful husbands, to whom they are given in the authority of the Holy Priesthood. (Pres[iden]t [John D. T.] McAllister Temple Pres[iden]t.) **—Temple Minute Book, St. George, Apr. 20, 1886**

President John Taylor may I ask a favor of You. I wish to have my father adopted to President Joseph Smith[;] it was my Fathers wish when he was alive.

I am here to do some work and would be very much pleased to have this work done.

I also wish to give my Bro[ther] Graham and his two wives their second annointing. **—Zebedee Coltrin to John Taylor, May 1, 1886**

The theme of my correspondence on the present occasion will be a subject that has engrossed my mind for many years and especially of late.

I have just returned from St George wither I had been with a portion of my family to work for my dead relatives and friends in the Temple of the Lord.

I find in looking over my record that my Father died an Elder; I rec[eive]d for him some 7 years ago his second anointings. He was a good man and was called hence without a moments warning by a St[r]oke of lightning at the age of 63. He was Killed [i]n Beaver City some 27 years ago and I am very desirous to receive for him the ordination as an High Priest that he may belong to the same quorum as my Brother Joshua and myself if it meets with your approval. Bro Erastus Snow was some little acquainted with Father and to him I refer as his advocate.

12. William Harrison Folsom (1815-1901) came to Utah in 1860. He was a carpenter and helped build the St. George temple.

My Brother Joshua had his failings, like many more, but my mind has been set at rest for many years in regard to his present condition and situation in the spirit world. He was never cut off [from] the Church altho he demeaned himself very improperly for some time before his death and no doubt brought about his early demise thro[ugh] his bad habit of drinking. Nevertheless from manifestations I have received since his death I am satisfied that he has sorrowfully repented and is now engaged in doing all the good he can on the other side. If it meets with your approval I would very much like him to receive his second anointings. I was rebaptized for him in the Temple at St George some 8 years ago[.] I take pleasure in mentioning the names of Judge Elias Smith and Pres[iden]t Daniel H. Wells as his advocates.

I have another Brother dead named Benjamin[.] He lived in Greenville Beaver Co[unty] [and] also died in the faith. I should be pleased to receive for him his second anointings and will mention the name of Pres[iden]t John R. Murdock[13] of Beaver Stake as his advocate.

I hope dear brother you will not deem me presumptous in asking for blessings for my dead relatives—they are very dear to me and I am fully satisfied that the three I have mention'd are doing all they can according to their calling and Priesthood to further on the work of the Lord where they are—I have done for them all I can—I have recd the blessings mention'd for myself and earnestly wish that these near and dear to my heart should share in the same blessings and privileges that I by the clemency of the Priesthood have been permitted to receive.

Praying the Lord to shield and protect you and the brethr[e]n with you in the future as he has in the past and with due respect I desire to subscribe myself you[r] Brother in the Gospel. **—Christopher J. Arthur[14] to John Taylor, May 11, 1886**

Three years ago I got ready by the council of Apostle George Teasdale[15] to go to St. George, to attend to Temple work also to get my sec-

13. John Riggs Murdock (1826-1913) was a member of the Mormon Battalion, later the president of Beaver Stake from 1877 to 1891.

14. Christopher Jones Arthur (1832-1918) was born in Wales. After coming to Utah, he served as a city councilman and mayor in Cedar City and was a patriarch in the Parowan Stake.

15. George Teasdale (1831-1907) was born in London; he was ordained an apostle in 1882.

ond anointings in connection with my wives. One of my wives Maria was taken sick which hindered me from going at that time, afterward my wife Eliza now seventy nine years old, became too feable to travel that distance. I have been in hiding Seventeen months past but I think I can go safely to the Logan Temple.[16] I ask if I now with my wives can have the privilege of this great blessing. I therefore think and feel as if I ought not to neglect this matter any longer if the privelege is mine[.] I would also like my first wife Ann who is dead, [who] died three years and a half ago, to recieve the blessing through one of my living wives acting for her.

Please endorse upon the recommends, if you will grant me this privilege and return [them] to me that I may know how to prepare. As I am not known by my right name here[,] please send the recommends to Brother Joseph E. Taylor with whom I am acquainted.

I will see him and ask him to recieve them for me. **—John S. Hawkins to John Taylor, June 6, 1886**

Owing to the peculiar circumstances in which we are placed, there has been some confusion and delay connected with the sending of recommends to the House of the Lord, to be endorsed by me.

To obviate this difficulty, we desire you to instruct the Saints who intend to have Temple work done, to procure their recommends sufficiently early, that they can receive them properly endorsed by me, at their own homes, before they start, instead of going to the Temple and awaiting the receipt of the recommend there by mail. If they have them in their possession before they start, they can make their arrangements for going, and for the time they will remain, and for their return, and the expense they will be at, with some degree of certainty.

We therefore urge this upon your attention, and desire that you represent the advantages of this system to all the Saints in your Stakes and Wards. **—John Taylor, circular letter, July 31, 1886**

Enclosed please find the endorsed recommends of the two widows of your father-in law for them to get their Second Anointing; and you are at liberty to act for him and receive this ordinance with them in his behalf.

---

16. Hawkins was apparently in hiding to escape prosecution for plural marriage.

Enclosed is seen a certificate for Marion Brown Arthur. As we suppose this was your wife[,] I have endorsed it for her to receive her second anointing; though you do not mention [it], or ask [for it] in the letter. If this is not your wife, she ought not to receive her second anointing on the strength of this recommend. **—John Taylor to Christopher J. Arthur, Sept. 18, 1886**

Pres[iden]t J[ohn] D. T. McAllister said, again, brethren and sisters we are permitted to meet in the House of God to labor for mankind and also for ourselves. There are but few here[,] but we can enjoy the Spirit of God. Said this is the straight and narrow path and those who are privileged to enter here are blessed above all others. Said, some time ago, on account of an expected raid by our enemies, the Temple was closed and the records taken away, and transcripts of work done could not be given. He could not lay his hands on them, but they are in a safe keeping.[17] [He] felt the time would soon arrive when we can have access to the records again and accomodate the Saints. Said the word is now given, that those who come into this Temple must keep the Word of Wisdom. Wines, liquors &c are good in sickness and should be kept in the house for medicine but not [as] beverages; they are forbidden. **—Temple Minute Book, St. George, Sept. 22, 1886**

In reply to your letter of the 12th of November, there is no objection to Brother Noah Brimhall[18] receiving his second anointing and I have endorsed his recommend accordingly. But his present wife cannot be anointed to him as she is only his wife for time, and when she receives her anointings to her deceased husband, Bailey Lake, his [Lake's] other two wives should also receive theirs.

If Brother Brimhall were to act for Bailey Lake and she were to be anointed to him as proxy, it might lead to confusion. The better way, in order that the records may be straight, is for someone to act for Brother Lake and the three wives [to] be anointed at the same time. Brother

17. The reference is to when the U.S. Army arrived in the valley in 1857 to unseat Brigham Young as governor. In response, Young declared martial law and sent guerrillas to Wyoming to attack the supply trains, forcing the army to winter in Wyoming. In the meantime, mediators from Washington, D.C., negotiated a truce, and the troops bypassed Salt Lake City, setting up Camp Floyd in Cedar Valley to the southwest, which was abandoned in 1861.

18. Noah Brimhall (1826-1918) came to Utah in 1850 and helped settle Oxford, Idaho, in 1864.

George Lake[,] having one [of] these wives and being his brothers heir[,] could do this with the greatest propriety, if he should be worthy of the ordinance.

Under the circumstances I think Brother Brimhall had better get a relative of his own, or of his deceased wifes, or in the absence of such a relative, some friend who has had her second anointing to act as proxy for his deceased wife, and let Sister Lavina Jones Lake Brimhall wait for this ordinance until arrangements can be made for the other wives of Brother Lake to join her in obtaining this ordinance[.] **—John Taylor to John D. T. McAllister, Nov. 18, 1886**

You state in your letter of the 24th that you understand from the teaching of the brethren of the apostles, that such as do not fully keep the Word of Wisdom, should not be recommended for ordinances to the temple; and you ask whether such persons shall be excluded from the House of the Lord.

The Word of Wisdom as originally given was sent not by commandment or constraint; but "by revelation on the the [sic] Word of Wisdom, for the temporal salvation of all Saints in these days," and no rule has been formulated, nor law proclaimed, nor counsel given since that time which makes its strict observance, necessary to receive ordinances of life and salvation in the temples. There are many cases where people may violate the strict letter of the Word of Wisdom, and yet be following its spirit in doing so. To say that aged people who have been accustomed to the use of tea and coffee in early life, and who feel that in their old age they need beverages of this character, shall not receive the blessings of the House of the Lord, is going beyond that which we think proper. The same may be said about other points; and yet … we are opposed to the common use of these articles by Latter-day Saints. A man or a woman who disregards the Word of Wisdom and still profess to be a Latter-day Saint ought to be ashamed of their conduct. A judicious bishop will not give a recommend to such a person without first taking up a labor with him or her against the indulgence in the habits mentioned in the Word of Wisdom. No person who flagrantly violates that word should ask for a recommend[.] **—John Taylor to John D. T. McAllister and David H. Cannon, Nov. 30, 1886**

I think President [John] Taylor will recollect a young English sister in Nauvoo by the name of Hannah Ells.[19] She was sealed to Joseph [Smith] the Prophet before his death. She died in Nauvoo in sister Sarah Kimball's[20] house. I loved her very much—was present at her death. I have had endowments for her. Sister Zina [D. H. Young][21] is in Logan and will, with your permission, have [the] second anointing for her. **—Eliza R. Snow to John Taylor, Dec. 12, 1886**

....

I again come to you for Temple Priviledges for Those I feel asured are of the <u>Worthy Dead</u>.

... May He Rec[e]ive his 2d Anointing through me as Proxy and may some of my wives rec[eive] for her?

... and as I have great Love for him as a friend I do wish to do his further work and get for him & wife his 2d anointings & if it would be right—and so wait and hope, for <u>another</u> favorable Reply. ...

PS And now it has come to me to ask the Priviledge of 2d anointing for my son James Francis, who is the Present Bishop at Tempe, and I think B[isho]ps Agent of that Stake. He is over 30 years of age and apears really one of the comeing young men of Zion. And as he expects to come for me the coming spring or early Summer, I should much like if you felt it [was] his priviledge, that he too have his 2d anointing while Here. **—Benjamin F. Johnson[22] to John Taylor, Jan. 29, 1887; emphasis in original**

Respecting second anointings, too great care cannot be observed in selecting and recommending persons for this sacred ordinance. Men and women who receive it should have proved by years of faithful service in the cause of God and unshaken loyalty to the principles of

---

19. Hannah Ells (1813-1845) was born in England and emigrated in 1841. She operated a dressmaking business in Nauvoo, where she married Joseph Smith as a plural wife in 1843.

20. Sarah Melissa Granger Kimball (1818-1898) was a member of the Nauvoo Relief Society and a counselor in the general Relief Society presidency in Utah in 1892.

21. Zina Diantha Huntington Young (1821-1901) married Joseph Smith as a plural wife in 1841, and after Smith's death she married Brigham Young in 1846. She served as the Church's third general Relief Society president.

22. Benjamin Franklin Johnson (1818-1905) was an aide to Joseph Smith, a member of the Council of Fifty, and served fourteen terms in the Utah legislature. He helped settle Santaquin, Utah, in 1851.

righteousness, that they are fit subjects to receive it. If the door were opened and the authorities were permitted to recommend freely those whom they thought suitable, we fear that many unworthy persons might be recommended for this ordinance. If you know of men in your stake whom you can thus recommend, you are at liberty to present their names for consideration. **—John Taylor and George Q. Cannon to Jesse W. Crosby[23] and Counselors, Mar. 17, 1887**

The enclosed letter from Sister [Eliza] Platt, the wife of the late Francis Platt contains a request for [a] second anointing for her husband, herself[,] and his deceased wife. What is the character of their son? It would be better to have someone else act, on account of his being young, unless he is a superior man who has proved himself to be worthy of the ordinance. **—John Taylor to Angus M. Cannon, Mar. 25, 1887**

If you will send us a recommend for yourself, properly signed, I will endorse it for your deceased husband, yourself[,] and his deceased wife to receive your second anointings. I hear that your son is a worthy young man, but he ought to have more experience and had more opportunities that age brings before receiving this important and sacred ordinance. You will, therefore, have to select some person who has already had his second anointings to act as proxy for your husband. **—John Taylor to Eliza Platt, Apr. 1, 1887**

Parties who have been married previous to going to the temple to receive their endowments and who are sealed in the temple should sign certificates[,] and the elder performing the sealing ceremony should also sign them[,] and have them properly filed in the probate court. This law is abominable in many of its features, the design of its framers was to entrap us [and] we must not let it serve this purpose. You ought not to be required to certify to sealing ordinances performed for persons who have been married previously; but if you do not, there is danger of the law being put in force against you. Therefore, to be safe it is better to make out the certificate. Sealings for the dead need not be certified to. **—John Taylor and George Q. Cannon to Marriner Wood Merrill, Apr. 7, 1887**

---

23. Jesse Wentworth Crosby (1820-1893) served several missions for the LDS Church and was one of the first pioneers into the Salt Lake Valley in 1847.

The most successful missions that have been performed in the Church, have been through the labors of elders who had not received their second anointing. Those who receive this ordinance at the present time are men well advanced in years, who have been faithful for long years in the Church and who are almost ready to pass away. **—John Taylor to Robert Henry Ford, May 9, 1887**

Your letter of the 1st [June 1887] reached me last night. I arrived here [St. George] last night to have an interview with S[amuel] Snow, as he will be here to attend Conference.

I have read your letter carefully. Now concerning endowments in all its phases: my own views are these—that we ought to follow out, as far as we can, the pattern laid down by our leaders. I consider that if there ever was any man who thoroughly understood the principle of the Endowments it was Brigham Young. He had been with Joseph Smith from the beginning of the Endowments to the end; and he understood it if any man did. And before his death he required me to write in a book every Ordinance in the Church and Kingdom of God, from the first to the last; beginning with Baptism to the last Ordinance performed through every department of the Endowments. I was several weeks doing this writing, and President Young corrected it all until he got through. Then he said to me, "Now, there you have a pattern of all the Ordinances and Endowments for every Temple we shall build, until the coming of the Son of Man." Now if I ever have anything to do, or to say, in any Temple on the earth, concerning Endowments, I would say: follow the pattern that President Young has set us; and [do] not deviate from it one iota. And if we do that, we may have a hundred Temples at work, and all the work and ceremonies will be alike in every Temple. While on the other hand, if every man who is called to preside over a Temple has his own way, and introduces his own form and ceremonies, our Temple work would be as diverse as the sectarian world and God would not appro[ve] it.

Brother Roskelley, I have given Endowments in Salt Lake City for twenty years, and I received my Endowments under the hands of the Prophet Joseph Smith. I directed the fixing up of the Temple in St. George for giving Endowments under the direction of President Young; and since the rules are written for our guidance in all future time, I feel very strenuous that in our giving Endowments we should all work alike, and not deviate from the written word.

You say, "we are told here so and so concerning sealings and adoptions." Who is it that has told you these things and given these instructions? I don't think it can be President Taylor, for neither he nor I have ever received such teachings from either Joseph Smith or Brigham Young. But I have been taught quite the reverse by President Young. He told me to have single women of my father's and mother's households sealed to me. I asked him "how many?" He said if there was not over nine hundred and ninety-nine to take them. I had some three hundred sealed to me by his instructions. I don't know whether I shall have to build them each a palace in the Celestial Kingdom of God or not. If I do, I shall have time to do it. I did as I was told. So in relation to Adoptions, most, if not all, of the Presidency and Twelve, have had men adopted to them, and all these Sealings and Adoptions are for the Salvation of the living and the dead. I have never asked any man to be adopted into my family that I can recollect of; but I have had a number of families of friends adopted into my family, as have other men, without any regard as to whether it will, in the future, cost me one dollar or a million. What we have done in this matter has been for the salvation of man. It may possibly be a correct doctrine that a man's kingdom will consist of only the fruit of his own loins. Yet J[e]sus Christ died to save the whole world, and if we, as Apostles and Elders, do nothing for the human family only for the fruit of our own loins, we shall not do much towards magnifying the Holy Priesthood God has given us for saving the souls of man—either the living or the dead.

Brother Roskelley, we must not get our minds too puckered up in these principles. We are ordained and appointed Saviors upon Mount Zion, and we must not be afraid to administer the Ordinances of Life and Salvation to our fellow man—living or dead, for fear it will cost us a dollar. I have adopted this rule in Sealings and Adoptions: to take such as the Lord has given me, and leave the result in His hands.

I think there is a Book in [the] Logan Temple containing all the Ordinances as directed by President Young. I should recommend following that strictly, that our work in both Temples may be alike.

Now concerning what Joseph Smith the Prophet said about children: In the first place he said children would rise from the grave, as they were laid down, and their parents would receive as they laid them away. This, I believe. He conveyed an idea in the first place, that they would not grow, but after more mature reflection, he conveyed the idea that they eventually would grow to the full stature of man.[24] It was a good deal upon the same principle that it was when he got the first revelation on baptism for the dead. He did not at first get the whole of it, but he went into the Mississippi River with myself and a number of others, and we baptized for the dead, without regard to males acting for males only, and females acting for females only, also without any Recorder. But the Lord revealed more to him, and gave him to understand that there should be a Recorder who should strictly record all the baptisms and Ordinances and that man should act for man, and woman for woman.[25] So with regard to his views on the Resurrection—they enlarged before he got through, and he said children would grow to full stature. That I believe.

Now anything I have said in this letter in giving my views in relation to what you have asked, need not be treated as a private matter, as you suggest. You may make whatever use of them you please.

There has got to be a welding link of some kind before we get through with this work that will adopt man to man, and weld all dispensations from Father Adam down to the last Saint. But in all this matter, I do not go around electioneering to get men adopted to me. I don't want any of this work done for me, only what the Lord wants. Paul talked a good deal about Adoptions, but we did not understand much about it, until the Lord revealed it to Joseph Smith, and we may not, perhaps, understand it now as fully as we should. Still the Sealings and Adoptions are true principles, or our Prophets have been badly deceived. **—Wilford Woodruff to Samuel Roskelley,[26] June 8, 1887**

Elder James G. Bleak speaking[:] When we receive endowments

---

24. Joseph Smith's teaching that those who die as children would be resurrected as children was first taught in the King Follett Discourse. According to one researcher, "no sources contemporary with Joseph Smith have been found which in any way contradict or modify this publicly and privately stated position" (Van Hale, "The King Follett Discourse: Textual History and Criticism," *Sunstone,* Sept.-Oct. 1983, 5-12).

25. According to historian M. Guy Bishop, "Gender distinctions [in] proxy [ordinances] were not made until after the Prophet's 1844 martyrdom, when Brigham Young assumed leadership of the majority of the saints." See Bishop, "'What Has Become of Our Fathers?': Baptism for the Dead in Nauvoo," *Dialogue: A Journal of Mormon Thought* 23 (Summer 1990) 85-97.

26. Samuel Roskelley (1837-1914) was called as bishop of Smithfield, Utah, at age twenty-four and became the Logan temple recorder in 1884.

for the dead[,] be particular to get all the signs and tokens. President [Brigham] Young told us it takes just as much to save a dead person as it does to save a living one. **—Temple Minute Book, St. George, June 15, 1887**

The Indian girl Viroqua Johnson[,] concerning whose second anointings you write to me, I think is a case that should be deferred for the present. You are at liberty to have her baptized for and have someone have Endowments for her: but at present I think it is improper for the ordinance of Second Anointing to be administered in her behalf. **—Wilford Woodruff to James H. Martineau,[27] Sept. 2, 1887**

You ask if you are right in doing temple work for some noted Indian chiefs who are deceased. I am glad that you have asked this question because in officiating for those whom you mention, you have gone too fast. A man has a right to officiate for his own dead ancestry, if he be the heir, or if it be done with a knowledge and consultation of the heir, but he has no right to go into other families and officiate for them, even though they may have no representatives in the Church[,] without in the first place consulting the presidency of the Church. **—Wilford Woodruff to James H. Martineau, Sept. 5, 1887**

We send the enclosed letter to you for Brother James H. Martineau, and send it unsealed that you may read its contents and obtain therefrom our views concerning the principle alluded to by him.

We must be more strict in enforcing the rule which is here mentioned in regard to heirship in our Temples, and people must not be permitted to follow their whims in being baptized for any and every body whom they may choose to officiate for; and persons should be questioned upon this subject of being baptized for those not of their own kin. We are satisfied that no man has a right[,] outside of his own kindred[,] to attend to ordinances for the dead without consultation and permission from the Presiding authority of the Church. But as this, perhaps, would lead to great delay and large correspondence, you as President of the Temple are authorized to exercise a wise discretion in permitting persons to be baptized for friends, when they satisfy you

27. James Henry Martineau (1828-1921) was called as a counselor in the St. Joseph Stake in Arizona in 1888. He moved to the Mormon colony of Colonia Juarez in Mexico and served as a patriarch there.

that they have no representative in the Church. **—Wilford Woodruff to Marriner Wood Merrill, Sept. 5, 1887**

Your communication of the 6th inst., asking questions respecting ordinances, has been received and considered.

You ask: Is it proper, under any circumstances, for persons to receive endowments the second time?

No, it is not proper, under any circumstances, to administer endowments twice to the same person.

You also asked: can a woman who has been anointed to her husband and afterwards leaves him to be sealed to another man, be anointed the second time—that is, to her second husband?

There is no necessity to answer this question until a case arises which may require an answer. We cannot anticipate all cases of this kind, and prefer to give no decision upon a question of this character until there is a necessity for it and all the circumstances connected with it are known. **—Wilford Woodruff to Marriner Wood Merrill, Sept. 9, 1887**

Your letter of the 14th inst., in which you suggest the propriety of Sister Adeline B. Benson,[28] wife of Brother E[zra] T. Benson, deceased, acting for the wife of Brother Joel H. Johnson, who is deceased, in receiving second anointings, has been received and considered.

I see no objection to Sister Benson acting in this capacity for Sister Johnson inasmuch as she is the latter's friend and Sister Johnson has none other kin who are in a position to receive this ordinance for her. **—Wilford Woodruff to James H. Martineau, Sept. 19, 1887**

Your letter of the 18th inst. in which you express your wishes concerning an Indian girl who has been sealed to you receiving her second anointing, and also respecting her doing work for 7 or 8 of the early martyrs, unmarried women, and having them sealed to you, has been received.

I think it is better for you to defer the ordinance of second anointing for this Indian girl who has been sealed to you since her death. It will be no los[s] to her for the present.

As to the martyrs of whom you speak, we see no impropriety in having the ordinance of baptism attended to for them, especially if you

28. Adeline Brooks Benson (1813-98) was born in Hartford, Connecticut, and married Ezra T. Benson in Nauvoo in 1844.

know who they are: but before having them sealed to you, you should certainly have some knowledge of them and of your right to have them, as others may claim that they have a better right than you hereafter. **—Wilford Woodruff to James H. Martineau, Oct. 26, 1887**

The question which you ask respecting the wearing of the veil by deceased sisters in preparing them for burial is one that was submitted by President M[arriner] W. Merrill to President [John] Taylor some time since, and his reply was, in which we fully agree, that it is proper to cover the faces of deceased sisters before burial with the veil. **—Wilford Woodruff to John R. Barns, Nov. 3, 1887**

Got up at half past 6 o'clock. After breakfast we all went to the [Logan] Temple. I was ordained an elder by Bro[ther] A. Peterson in behalf of my dead Father and got endowments for him and took my Mother through the veil and also stood proxy for my Father at the altar for my mother to be sealed to him; also took both of my wives through the veil; also my daughter, Marinda, and had our 4 oldest children sealed to us. And my wives and I received our second anointings under the hands of President [Marriner W.] Merrill and Bro[ther] Moore. **—Samuel Bateman[29] diary, Nov. 30, 1887, Perry Special Collections**

Pres[iden]t [John D. T.] McAllister speaking. Read special instructions to Bishops & others, in regard to the clothing and other matters, connected with the work here, written 13 Jan. 1877 and signed by Pres[iden]t B[righam] Young and others. **—Temple Minute Book, St. George, Dec. 1, 1887**

James Pexton died 1st May 1887, born 9th March 1831.

His wife Hannah Pexton married him in England and they were sealed in the Endowment House [in] 1855. He took another wife [and] considerably neglected his first and she obtained a divorce from him through the courts. Now comes the question of Second Anointing raised by the eldest son who [is] doing work in the Temple [and] wished his father to receive his full blessings with his mother Hannah Pexton. She reports t[hat] James Pexton came to her in a dream and asked her to forgive him. She is willing to forgive him. Wishes to know

29. Samuel Bateman (1832-1911) was a policeman and bodyguard to John Taylor.

if she should be resealed to him, and whether it would be proper for him to have his full blessings and she enjoy the same with him. The son James D. Pexton is 39 years of age [and is the] 2nd Counselor to B[isho]p Tho[ma]s H. G. Parks of the North Ward [in] Nephi. Is he old enough to receive his full blessings? and then stand for his father[?] Sister Hannah Pexton who lives in Nephi, called upon Pres[ident] [Wilford] Woodruff and asked these questions and it was taken under advisement. **—George Teasdale statement, ca. 1887**

....

Your letter in reply to mine upon the subject of second anointings for Brother George Lufkin and Brother James Townsend, has been received and considered.

Whoever attends to the ordinances for Brother Townsend should certainly take his last wife to the Temple with them, so that she might receive the blessing as well as the deceased wife. Is Brother George Lufkin the proper person [to act as proxy for Brother Townsend][?] Who is as worthy as he, who is nearer a[n] heir to the Townsend Family than he is? If he is the proper party to represent Brother Townsend, under the circumstances you are at liberty to inform him that if he will get his recommendation properly signed, I will endorse it for him to receive his second anointing and to act for Brother Townsend, on condition, also, that he takes Brother Townsend's surviving wife with him.

Now, in relation to the other subject which you mention—the cases of worthy men and women who are aged who have not had their second anointings, and who, are waiting to have this privilege accorded to them, being counseled by you not to ask for the privilege. We think such cases deserve consideration, and where you know of aged men and woman who are worthy to receive this ordinance, I would like you to forward their names to me for consideration: and these that we decide as proper persons to receive this ordinance can have their recommendations signed to that effect. **—Wilford Woodruff to Angus M. Cannon, Jan. 24, 1888**

Your letter of the 4th, describing your case in past relations and your wish concerning receiving your second anointings again, came duly to hand and has been considered. I think you should be permitted to have your second anointings with your husband, Brother Townsend, and if a recommendation be forwarded to me, properly signed by your Bishop and the president of the stake, I will have it endorsed for you to receive that ordinance with your husband. **—Wilford Woodruff to Mrs. E. J. D. Townsend, Feb. 7, 1888**

Will you please answer a few questions I wish to ask you. I am the widow of Thomas C. Jones of your Circle.[30] He died soon after we came from [the] Logan Temple working for our Dead and having our 2d [an]o[i]nting[s] where we [were] told to attend to the Washing of Feet at home. The baby was sick after we came home so I asked Bro[ther] Jones when we should attend to it and he said we had better wait till the baby is better but he was taken sick and Died before it was attended to. Can that be done by Proxy or not as I feel sorry about it for he was a good man and I gave him 2 living Wives and 3 Dead ones and worked hard to help him to keep them. **—Eliza I. Jones to Wilford Woodruff, Feb. 24, 1888**

The ordinance of which you speak, and which you say you failed to attend to before the death of your husband, is one that should not be written about, and it cannot be attended to by proxy. Your husband is dead and, so far as the ordinances is concerned, it is all right. If there are any of his children who were not born in the covenant and they are dead, a living child, or children can officiate for them in being sealed to their parents.

You ask a question whether a sister can be sealed to her first husband, who never heard the gospel, if she has embraced it and has married and [has been] sealed to another.

We do not consider it safe for a woman in the Church to be sealed to a man who died before receiving the gospel. **—Wilford Woodruff to Eliza I. Jones, Feb. 24, 1888**

Sister Zina D. H. Young has written to me concerning two of your father's deceased wives receiving their second anointings. She desires to officiate for them, to which I have consented. As you are the heir, some arrangements should be made by yourself and her for some person to act in your father's stead in this ordinance. She will probably try to see you. If you can communicate with her and let her know where you

30. This is, no doubt, a reference to a prayer circle.

can be found,[31] no doubt she will appreciate it. **—Wilford Woodruff to Brigham Young Jr., Mar. 8, 1888**

Enclosed please find a letter to Brother [Marriner Wood] Merrill, President of the Logan temple, authorizing him to administer to you the ordinance of second anointing for the deceased persons in whose behalf you wish to officiate. I have dropped a note to Brother Brigham Young [Jr.], informing him of your desire to consult with him concerning the proper person to act for his father in this ordinance. He probably will try to see you, if you can get word to him where you can be found. **—Wilford Woodruff to Zina D. H. Young, Mar. 8, 1888**

Sister Zina D. H. Young desires to officiate for Sister Sarah Mahu Young and Sister Muryett Jacobs Young (both deceased) in receiving the ordinance of second anointing, also for Sister Elizabeth Hughes Jones Smith. **—Wilford Woodruff to Marriner Wood Merrill, Mar. 8, 1888**

Brother Lyman O. Littlefield[32] has applied to me for the ordinance of second anointing for himself and his wives, whom he represents as 8 in number. Brother Littlefield is one of Zion's Camp and I think that he is entitled to this sacred ordinance. You will, therefore, please administer it to him and his living wife or wives, and to them also on behalf of his deceased wife. **—Wilford Woodruff to Marriner Wood Merrill, Mar. 29, 1888**

Brother Lyman O. Littlefield's wife was the widdow of Bro[ther] Luman Heath, a faithful elder in the Church, who died many years ago. She was sealed to her husband in the Nauvoo Temple and at that time acted as proxy for a deceased wife of Brother Heath's. Bro[ther] Littlefield has applied to me to have the privilege granted to officiate for Bro[ther] Luman Heath, that he and his deceased wife and Sister Littlefield should receive their second anointing. You are hereby authorized to administer this ordinance to Bro[ther] Littlefield for Bro[ther] Heath, and to his wife (who is Bro. Heath's wife for eternity) for the

31. Brigham Young Jr. was apparently in hiding to escape prosecution for plural marriage.

32. Lyman Omer Littlefield (1819-1890) journeyed with the Kirtland militia known as Zion's Camp when he was still a teenage boy. He later served a mission from Winter Quarters, Nebraska, to England.

sister Heath who is dead, and for herself. **—Wilford Woodruff to Marriner Wood Merrill, Apr. 23, 1888**

I have read with interest your favor of the 16th, in which you set forth the circumstances connected with the life and demise of your son Samuel Henry.

I have no doubt that he was a most excellent young man, as what you say about him is fully corroborated by Brother George Q. Cannon, who appears to have been well acquainted with him. It would give me pleasure to grant the request which you make concerning his receiving his second anointing if I did not have a feeling that there is an impropriety in administering this ordinance to young men, either living or dead, at the present time. In the days of the Prophet Joseph [Smith] and Brigham [Young] this ordinance was not sought for and would not have been administered to any who did seek for it. It was administered only to aged people, or men who were advanced in life, who had been well tried and proved. I have received since President [John] Taylor's death a number of requests from parents and others whose sons have died, asking me to grant them the privilege of officiating in this ordinance on behalf of their sons. I have invariably declined to grant these requests, because I have felt under the circumstances it would not be proper to do so. Your son will lose nothing by not having this attended to now, and you can comfort your heart with the reflection that you have done all that you can for him at the present.

You ask whether a person who has once been married in the Endowment House or Temple, and is left a widow or a widower, commit[s] adultery by marrying again when the ceremony is performed by a justice of the peace or civil officer.

There is a manifest impropriety, which every Latter-day Saint who has had his or her endowments should perceive, in such a person going to a civil officer to have a ceremony of marriage performed. The fact that such a person does so is an evidence that he or she is falling away, because if in good standing a recommendation could be obtained for the Temple, where the ceremony could be performed according to the order which God has instituted. But a person marrying under such circumstances does not commit adultery.

You ask some other questions concerning how many living wives a man must have to fulfil the law.

When a man, according to the revelation, marries a wife under the holy order which God has revealed and then marries another in the same way, he enters into the new and everlasting covenant, and so far as he has gone he has obeyed the law. I know of no requirement which makes it necessary for a man to have three living wives at a time.

I enclose herewith the answer to Sister Fail. I sent it to you that you may see its contents and then hand it to her.

The case of Henry Lovesey and Emma Townsend, which you describe, is not [a] very savory one in all its particulars, and I feel that she had better let the matter rest for the present. I do not feel clear in my mind about breaking the seal "with the old man" or consenting to the change that she seems anxious to make. **—Wilford Woodruff to Samuel A. Woolley,[33] May 22, 1888**

I take the liberty of making the following suggestions to you respecting the Temple as they now occur to us, and it is proper that they should be before you for your consideration, that you may be able as you progress to make the necessary arrangements to carry out these suggestions:

A room should be prepared, convenient to the entrance, for the President of the Temple to hold private interviews with parties who may wish his counsel.

Care should be taken to have the Recorder's Room conveniently situated for the work they have to do, be well lighted, and should have at least one vault immediately connected with it. It must not be understood from this that one vault only is needed in this Temple. The vaults which are to contain books and papers should be well ventilated, and have communication with the outside air.

In the Logan and Manti Temples the rooms designed for the ordinance of [the] second anointing are quite plain. In this Temple the rooms should be as well situated and at least as elegantly decorated as any other room in the building, so as to impress those who receive this sacred ordinance with its importance and elevated and solemn character. It would be well if two small dressing rooms could be nearby or connected with it.

A good room convenient for its purposes should be provided for

33. Samuel Amos Woolley (1825-1900) was bishop of the Salt Lake City 9th Ward.

the President of the Temple; also suitable rooms for the Presidency of the Church and the leading authorities.

We shall from time to time, probably, make further suggestions as they may occur to us in regard to the interior arrangements of the Temple. We desire that the greatest pains will be taken by yourself to have everything done in the most perfect manner, and so carefully considered beforehand that we will not be under the necessity of making changes or tearing down work that has already been done. We know that you have labored under disadvantages because of the incompleteness of the plans turned over to you, and also because of the improvements that you have felt compelled to make in those plans. We would much prefer holding the work in abeyance till you can feel sure that whatever is required to be done is done properly, than to have it pushed forward without the plan being well matured. At any time when you wish to submit any questions concerning the work we shall be glad to accord you an interview upon your notifying us to that effect.

It will be well for you to keep this letter where you can refer to it. **—Wilford Woodruff to Don Carlos Young,[34] May 24, 1888**

You mentioned the name of Brother Lewis Anderson, assistant [temple] Recorder. I infer that he is a young man: I have felt impressed not to grant permission for this ordinance (2nd Anointing) to be administered to any but aged and faithful men, and if you can get along without administering this ordinance to him, it would be better. **—Wilford Woodruff to Daniel H. Wells, June 26, 1888**

Yourself and wives are approved for Second Anointing.

The Temple will open for ordinance work on the 4th of September next. Bring Temple clothing and two towels each. **—John D. T. McAllister to Alonzo Russell, Aug. 7, 1888**

Gave instruction to give nothing but the proper wording when washing, anointing, etc. Pres[ident] [Brigham] Young once said that Free Masonary is the corruption of the keys and powers of the Holy Priesthood. So would these Endowments be changed if we were not particular about the proper wording of these ceremonies. Instructed

34. Joseph Don Carlos Young (1855-1938) was a son of Brigham Young and Emily Dow Partridge. He served as Church Architect from 1887 to 1893.

the recorders to be careful, for a great responsibility rested upon them. **—John D. T. McAllister, in Temple Minute Book, St. George, Sept. 3, 1888**

There is a tendency at the present time amongst some of the Saints to ask for the privilege of receiving their second anointings, which feeling I consider should be discouraged. I am entirely willing that the faithful aged should receive this great blessing, but I prefer that their names should be presented by their bishop and stake president, or by yourself as president of a temple, for my consideration than by themselves. It has not been customary in times past for brethren to make application in their own behalf. They were selected by reason of their known faithfulness and I think it better that this method should be continued than the opposite of men presenting their own names for consideration. **—Wilford Woodruff to Daniel H. Wells, Sept. 28, 1888**

Our young people come here to be married to be husband and wife through all eternity taking upon them covenants to observe all the laws, rites and ceremonies pertaining to the Holy order of matrimony, this is the way God has established, and the ceremony that seals one wife to a man seals other wives. And when a man takes a wife they enter this sacred order and covenant to observe all the rites in this. The man covenants to take more wives, the woman covenants to do the part of Sarah and gives her consent for him to take more wives.[35] Hoped the young people would understand these things. A covenant not kept is a covenant broken. When we enter that covenant we must continue in it. Still there is no one here who will say you shall take more wives, that is left entirely with yourselves. Said we ought to express ourselves freely upon these things here for no one dare say any thing about them on the outside of this house. You take upon yourselves covenants to not speak outside of what takes place here. It is a grand thing to have a little common sense to guide us in these things. **—James G. Bleak, in Temple Minute Book, St. George, Oct. 4, 1888**

Your pencil memoranda, dated Oct[.] 18th, showing a list of names

35. The Church (LDS D&C 132:61) taught that plural marriage could only be performed if the man's first wife gave her consent. However, this was often more theory than reality, beginning with Joseph Smith, who regularly took additional wives without Emma's consent.

of persons in Morgan Stake deemed worthy to receive their second anointings, came duly to hand.

There seems to be some misunderstanding in these matters by you in sending such a formidable list, and in such a manner as the one received. In such an important matter as second anointings it is not expected that the Stake or the Wards are to be hunted over to find names to recommend for such an ordinance. It is only contemplated that we be furnished with the names of those who are deemed worthy by the Presidency of the Stake, and who are quite aged, and whose life and labors in the Church have been such as to entitle them to this blessing. When such names are submitted[,] the ages of the parties should be noted, and you will be informed as to their acceptance before the parties receive any information or their recommends are endorsed to go to the Temple. **—Wilford Woodruff to Willard G. Smith, Oct. 22, 1888**

In such sacred matters as second anointings it must be understood that those only who are quite aged, and whose life and labors in the Church entitles them to this blessing shall be recommended by the Presidency of the Stake, and in submitting such names the ages of the parties should be noted. **—Wilford Woodruff to Charles Sperry, Oct. 24, 1888**

One of the obligations we assume here is not to repeat anything we see or hear in this House; for instance if we see a person who we think is here to take another wife, we should not talk about it for there is [a] danger of him doing so. At the time the Tucker Edmunds bill[36] became Law, President [John] McAllister sent me to Salt Lake City to see President [John] Taylor and learn what we should do as the penalties were very heavy for the person who performed an illegal Marriage and this class of cases would be illegal under this new law.

The President of the Church said, There must be no more Plural Sealings in the Temple and we will leave the responsibility upon our enemies and I can give you my word that the instructions then given ha[ve] been faithfully carried out.[37] Keep a correct Record of all the

36. The Edmunds Tucker Act of 1887, which President Grover Cleveland allowed to become law without his signature, established penalties for Mormon polygamists, repealed Utah's female suffrage, forfeited all LDS property to the federal government, and declared that children of polygamous marriages were illegitimate.

37. President John Taylor, who was in hiding at the time, sent a letter to the

work you may do here today. God bless you in the name of Jesus Christ. Amen. **—David H. Cannon, Temple Minute Book, St. George, Nov. 8, 1888**

Your letter of Nov. 9th representing the wishes of Sister Sarah Clarke who was sealed to David Wood in Salt Lake City in 1854 to have her second anointings, also to officiate for Brother Wood's First wife who is dead, has been received.

You say that Brother David Wood received his second anointing in 1867, but neither of his wives was anointed to him at that time because his first wife was not present. You are hereby authorized to administer that ordinance in behalf of Brother Wood's first wife, and afterwards Sister Smith can also be anointed to Brother Wood. It will be necessary for some persons who have received this ordinance to officiate for Brother and Sister Wood, deceased, and Sister Smith can act for herself. You can arrange about that.

In regard to establishing a rule in such cases as this one, as you intimate in your letter, I do not desire it [to] be so; but prefer that all matters pertaining to this ordinance shall first be referred to me, as also all cases where a living man has had his blessings and brings his wife or wives to receive theirs: he and they should first have permission before the ordinance is performed. **—Wilford Woodruff to Daniel H. Wells, Nov. 13, 1888**

....

[I]n these matters which are of a very sacred character [second anointings], names must be selected with great care, and extends only to those aged brethren who have proven themselves worthy through their continued faithfulness and labors in the Church[.] **—Wilford Woodruff to George C. Parkinson, Jan. 2, 1889**

This will authorize you to attend to the ordinance of second anointing for the wives of Elder David M. Stuart, of Ogden, which have not been anointed to him, and are now living; also to those of his wives who are dead that were sealed to him, and lived with him in the flesh. **—Wilford Woodruff to Marriner Wood Merrill, Jan. 23, 1889**

Church in April 1887, a month after the Edmunds Tucker Act became law, announcing that recommends for new plural marriages would be suspended. This letter was read in general conference that month (Richard S. Van Wagoner, *Mormon Polygamy: A History* [Salt Lake City: Signature Books, 1989], 130).

Remembered when the Nauvoo Temple was near completion, the saints look[ed] forward with fond anticipation to the time when they could go forth and do a work for their dead; but many were driven from Nauvoo before their anticipations could be realized and some of the last company, who did go through[,] never got further than the Terrestrial Room. Remember when men and women were baptized in the Miss[issippi] River, men for women and women for men, but they were told that this was wrong and that men should be baptized for men and women for women[,] which they did, in a Temple, in a font resting upon 12 wooden oxen, after which [it was] changed to stone oxen.[38] In those days people flocked to the House of God by thousands to do a work for their dead. **—David H. Cannon, Temple Minute Book, St. George, Feb. 21, 1889**

The enclosed recommend for Christian P. Boreguard and his wife Anna to obtain their second anointings, is returned herewith for corrections.

In regard to these matters, I will say that it is not expected that the Bishops will take these cases in hand and recommend persons for this ordinance.

The instructions which have been given on this subject are, that the <u>President of the Stake</u>, as they shall find from time to time in their Stake those br[e]thren who are <u>aged</u>, and who have been faithful in the Church during their lives, and through their untiring energies have proven themselves worthy of this blessing, will take note of such cases and, through the President, will submit to me the names of such persons and their wives, both living and dead, who have also been faithful and are worthy for consideration. In forwarding to me the names of such persons, I must have the age, in years, of each one named. It is not expected that any person will be informed of what action is being taken until after their names are approved and their recommends properly endorsed by me. Faithful and worthy aged br[e]thren who have died without this blessing, should be remembered with their wives in this connection.

After names of worthy aged persons have been submitted by the

38. It was Brigham Young who put a stop to men being baptized for women and vice versa. Joseph Smith presumably didn't have a problem with it (Bishop, "'What has Become of Our Fathers?'" 85-97).

President of the Stakes and been approved by me, the usual recommend can then be forwarded, with a slip of paper calling my attention to the fact. **—Wilford Woodruff to Ira N., Mar. 16, 1889; emphasis in original**

Your letter of Feb. 27th, asking certain questions pertaining to Temple ordinances, has been received and considered.

In regard to your last question, pertaining to a woman having been sealed and anointed [second anointing] to her husband, but subsequently divorced from him, he continuing a faithful, good man, etc, is she to be anointed to a second good man as though she never had been anointed? I answer, No. In such a case it will not be proper for the sister to be again anointed.

Your second question as to my having any word for you in relation to adoption—

I would say it will be well to leave the matter of adoption for the present as they have been, and not make any changes. This will also answer your question in regard to going back as far as records can be obtained correctly in adoptions.

In relation to children who are old enough to be baptized & who are dead, receiving their endowments. I will say that in performing ordinances for the dead it is safe to follow the rules observed in regard to the living, unless there may be special occasions which can be attended to when the circumstances require. **—Wilford Woodruff to John D. T. McAllister, Mar. 19, 1889**

Your letter of May 5th has been received, in which you set forth the expressed wishes of your sister, made before her death and after your explaining to her the true order of marriage and of adoption of her children, to be sealed to you for eternity, instead of to her husband; and if that was not admissable, that she be sealed to your son, M[ahonri] M. Steele. You also say "I told her I did not know how that would be; such things had been done, but I did not know how it would be again."

Of course, I am not conversant with what information you may have on this subject; but I am not aware of any such sealings or adoptions in this Church. I do not consider it proper for any such sealings or adoptions to be administered in the Temples of the Lord. It is not any more proper for your sister to be sealed to you as her husband, now that she is dead, than it would be if she were alive; neither should she be sealed to your son, because such a marriage is too near of kin.

If your sister, while alive, did not feel that she wished to be sealed to her living husband for eternity, and if she did not express any preference on that matter other than the ones you mention, you should then make a choice in her behalf, and have her sealed to some faithful man in the Church, either living or dead, and have her children adopted into his family. Trusting this will be satisfactory to you. **—Wilford Woodruff to John Steele, May 9, 1889**

[James G. Bleak speaking:] We should give our full attention to the rendition of the different parts and see and hear all pertaining to the ordinances. No matter how familiar we ourselves may be with them we are instructed to receive them anew, when we represent the dead, as though we had never received them before.

The person for whom we are officiating knows nothing about these ordinances except through us. As soon as we are anointed for the dead our own identity ceases, and we who are workers then leave our official calling and should not attempt to act in administering ordinances until we have finished our representation of the dead for whom we are receiving endowments. **—James G. Bleak, Temple Minute Book, St. George, May 30, 1889**

I with my youngest wife, have received our 2d anointing, but the 2 older ones have not yet been able to get to the temple, to attend to theirs but intend to as soon as circumstances will permit. I was informed there was another ordinance which might be given at some future time in an upper room. Can we not pass through them all for that is my blessing given by the Patriarch. So I feel to ask for all, ["]although the day may be breaking, I cannot let thee go, except thou bless me.["] So said our father Jacob. I have one wife who died in the faith. She was a good saint, she had her endowment in the Endowment house in Salt Lake, and was sealed to me by permission of President [John] Taylor. Can she receive the 2d anointing by Proxey[?] Should not those wives that have been sealed to me who died out of the church, be adopted to their parents who will have done the work for [her] in the temple[?] And should not those parents [be] adopted to us who have done this work for them, as we have been adopted[?] I suppose none of these receive a 2d anointing who have not received the gospel in the flesh.

Please excuse me, for so much inquisitiveness for I know not where else to apply for this information. The spirit prompts me to ask is there not another ordinance yet concerning a rod, if so can I receive it. I do not know that there is, but I feel to ask for all that is for me. Your brother

Phineas W. Cook

Jesus said seek and ye shall find, knock and it shall be opened unto you, I feel that a blessing that is not worth asking for is not worth having, and if I ask and am refused I hope it will not injure me. P. W. C.

[In pencil and different handwriting]: He has got all the ordinances he has a right to. **—Phineas W. Cook to Wilford Woodruff, June 11, 1889**

I have received your letter of the 11th inst., in which you speak of another ordinance in addition to the second anointing, which might be given at some future time in an upper room.

You have received all the ordinances which we administer. The ordinance to which you refer is one between yourself and your family, and which doubtless was explained to you when you received your second anointing.

Your wife who is dead, and who, you say, was a faithful woman, can receive her second anointing. One of your other wives can act for her. Those who died out of the Church, and who have been sealed to you since, need not at the present time receive this ordinance. We do not administer it to those who are in this condition.

As to the ordinance connected with the rod, we know nothing of that. You will have to wait for awhile or until we meet Aaron.

Of course, your present living wives, if they are worthy and can obtain recommendations from the Bishop, can receive the ordinance of second anointing, whenever it will be convenient to you and to them. **—Wilford Woodruff to Phineas W. Cook, June 18, 1889**

The questions which you ask me in your [letter] of the 20th inst. concerning the giving of endowments to persons of negro descent, have been considered. We feel that you should not administer the ordinance of endowments to any in their behalf. Their relatives can be baptized for them and also confirmed; but beyond this we think nothing more should be done.[39] **—Wilford Woodruff to David H. Cannon, June 27, 1889**

39. Beginning in 1849, five years after the death of Joseph Smith, black men of

[W]e have an objection to laying down rules which may be construed so rigidly as to do at times great injustice to worthy people, and therefore do not like to answer questions of this kind [dietary proscriptions] in a categorical manner, because cases may arise where a strict application of the rule might do injury.[40]

... as a general proposition, young men who will not refrain from the use of tobacco or liquor do not manifest such a faith as ought to be expected. ... Hot drinks are also spoken of in the Word of Wisdom and the excessive use of meat. When a rigid rule is laid down concerning this matter it cannot with propriety be confined to one article such as tobacco or liquor. Every young man in the Church should refrain from the use of hot drinks, as well as tobacco and liquor, and from the use of meat except in the way that the Lord has directed. But you can see what the result would be if we were to enforce a rigid rule of this character.

... we should be reluctant to give recommends to young men who would refuse to abstain from the use of tobacco. There might be some cases, however where to[o] strict an application of this might not be wisdom. You and all men holding authority among the people should be able to judge. ... At the same time you cannot, to use a common phrase, make fish of one and flesh of another. **—Wilford Woodruff, George Q. Cannon, and Joseph F. Smith to O. G. Larsen and counselors, Nov. 25, 1889**

I was endowed for Emma's brother, Edwin Whitham, and Emma for her stepmother, Sarah Patience Rollins Whitham, and had Sarah P. R. Whitham sealed to Emma's father George Whitham.

I had received a recommend from Stake President Ira Hatch. (Apostle F[rancis] M. Lyman having kindly helped me) to receive my second anointings. Through misunderstanding it was not signed by

---

African descent were no longer given the priesthood, and blacks of both sexes were not allowed to receive temple ordinances. See Lester E. Bush Jr., "Mormonism's Negro Doctrine: An Historical Overview," *Dialogue: A Journal of Mormon Thought* 8 (Spring 1973): 11-68.

40. Attitudes about the Word of Wisdom (LDS D&C 89) were more moderate in the nineteenth century and did not yet require total abstinence from tobacco, alcohol, coffee, and tea. Strict observance became a requirement during the administration of President Heber J. Grant (Paul H. Peterson, *A Historical Analysis of the Word of Wisdom* [Salt Lake City: Benchmark Books, 2005]).

President W[ilford] Woodruff. By Brother Daniel H. Wells' kindness I sent it from the temple to Brother Woodruff, but did not receive it back in time. So I had to come home without that great blessing. **—Thomas Memmott journal, Dec. 13, 1889**

....

Your favor of 16th inst. suggesting that Elder John Hollister and his wife Lovina, both deceased, be granted the privilege of Second Anointings is received and the request granted.

Brother [George] Reynolds says, that if he informed Sister Cox she had not received her Second Anointing[,] he was in error as according to the record Cordelia C[alista] Morley[41] born at Kirtland 28th Nov. 1823 was anointed to the Prophet Joseph Smith in the Temple at Nauvoo 27th Jan. 1846; Elder Parley P. Pratt officiating. **—Wilford Woodruff to Daniel H. Wells, Jan. 21, 1890**

At the Gardo House the question arose this morning as to whether the face of a woman who has had her endowments should be veiled or not when her coffin is closed on her dead body. Pres[ident] Woodruff did not decide in absence of any written law on the subject, but Bro[ther] Joseph F. [Smith] thought the face should be covered as this was the course pursued in the early days of the Church, and it was doubtless done in accordance with some instructions of the Prophet [Joseph Smith]. **—Abraham H. Cannon diary, Jan. 31, 1890, Perry Special Collections**

At Manti Temple. I was endowed for my Uncle Thomas Wilson, and Emma for his wife, Aunt Mary Emily Wilson, and [we] were sealed for them.

After that ordinance I and my wife Emma had the great privilege of receiving our second anointings at the hands of President Daniel H. Wells and shortly after I and my wife administered to each the ordinance of washing of feet. **—Thomas Memmott journal, Feb. 13, 1890**

We went up to the [Logan] Temple, which is a magnificent building standing on the bench above the city. We did some work in the

41. Cordelia Morley rejected Joseph Smith's marriage proposal but was sealed to him for eternity after his death, while marrying Frederick Walter Cox for mortality. She outlines this in her 16-page autobiographical sketch in BYU's Perry Special Collections (George D. Smith, *Nauvoo Polygamy* [Salt Lake City: Signature Books, 2008], 586, 642).

temple. I had my father adopted to the prophet Joseph Smith. I would have been sealed to my father, but as my sisters who were in the church were not present, it was thought best to postpone this work. I received my second anointing[,] also my wife Eliza did. She also acted for my wife Mary Campbell in having her second anointing. **—Joseph Fish diary, Apr. 8, 1890, p. 200, Perry Special Collections**

I take pleasure in sending you, herewith, a Recommend for yourself and wives to get your 2d Anointings. It will be good either at [the] Logan, Manti, or St. George [temples]. **—Joseph F. Smith letter to John Cottam, Apr. 22, 1890**

The following brethren and sisters have been recommended by President Canute Petersen,[42] and approved by me, to receive their second anointings. When they present themselves at the Temple, with their recommends[,] you are authorized to perform that ceremony in their behalf:

David Candland, Chester, age	71
Annie Candland	52
Hannah	50
Mary Ann [dead]	44
Mary Jane "	22
Carline Margaret Olsen, Mayfield, [dead] age,	66
Jonathan Midgley, Wales, age	68
Ann K.	66
Peter M. Olsen, Spring City, age	64
Karen Marie Olsen,	66
Jonas Ottenstrom, Ephraim, [dead] age	64
Marie Kaisq	65
Sildq Amela	56
Peter Nela [dead]	50
Slen Marie	67

—Wilford Woodruff to Daniel H. Wells, Apr. 23, 1890

The rule has been, for the woman to be Sealed to a man in the Priesthood, and the children Sealed to them, and the former husband

42. Canute Petersen (1824-1902) was one of the founders of Lehi and later a bishop in Ephraim. He became a member of the Council of Fifty in 1882.

be Adopted into the family. And where Such Sealings have taken place heretofore, the matters have been Submitted and [the] former Sealing Cancelled ... We do not now Seal women to men out of the Church, but some few cases were done in the Endowment House Sometime Ago. Whatever you may feel pleased to direct in these matters, we will carry out. **—Daniel H. Wells to Wilford Woodruff, May 26, 1890**

Elder H. S. Palmer of Freemont [Utah] writes to us that you have refused to give him a recommend to the House of the Lord because at his late trial he promised to obey the law.[43] If this is the only reason you have for withholding his recommend, and if he is otherwise in good standing in the Church, and were it not for this action of his you could freely recommend him, we do not think it advisable for that reason alone to withhold from him the privileges of the temple. **—Wilford Woodruff to William H. Seegmiller, Sept. 26, 1890**

I understand that Bro[ther] Solomona Piipiilani and Sister Maria Kamalo [Hawaiians] have gone to Logan to do some work for themselves and their dead.

They are THE FIRST who have been privileged to receive their 2d An[oin]t[ing]s. And this will authorize you to allow Solomona and John Kamalo (deceased husband of Maria) to be adopted or sealed to Joseph [Smith] the Prophet—if it reaches you in time, which I hope will be the case. **—Joseph F. Smith to Marriner Wood Merrill, Oct. 20, 1890; emphasis in original**

....

On the 13th of January 1877 a letter was sent to the Bishops, on preparation for Endowments, Signed by President [Brigham] Young, yourself and others. A Copy of which I enclose. To lay before you the matter pertaining to the garment, a very few have carried out these instructions, so far as the buttoning of the garment is concerned. I read now and again to the people this letter of instruction, as a great share of them from all parts come unprepared. Some wear drawers, and quite a number do not. The garment is left open only so far as the strings are used to fasten them in the front. The navel mark is opposite that

43. Apparently Seegmiller thought LDS people should stand firm in violating the law against polygamy. Notice that President Woodruff doesn't support Palmer's decision to obey the law; rather, he finds the sin of obedience in this case to be venial rather than fatal.

part of the body, but when the garment is closed[,] [f]lapped over to button, or tied, my feelings are, it should be in sight opposite that part of the body. Now our instructions are that the mark should be on one side of the opening. But we have not been instructed as to which side. Have you any word in relation to this?

I feel that we should be uniform in all these matters, and I am thus particular to lay them before you, and have the word from the head, in relation to them. **—John D. T. McAllister to Wilford Woodruff, Feb. 25, 1891**

In reply to yours of the 9th inst. I am directed to say that the late Elder Newton Daniel Hall and his two wives are approved for further blessings. This does not include his wife Sarah who married Peter Markin.

In all these cases I am requested to remind you that President Woodruff wishes to know the ages of all who are thus recommended. Upon receipt of the proper recommends for Bro[ther] Hall & wives the Pres[iden]]t will endorse it. **—L. John Nuttall to Daniel D. McArthur, Mar. 13, 1891**

The condition of many of the saints in Arizona in connection with their marriages has been brought to the attention of the First Presidency. We understand that there are many couples in that Territory who are prevented by poverty and other circumstances from going to the Temple to have their sealings, and that many of the children are being born out of the covenant because of this.

We feel to take some action upon this, as it is a great deprivation for Latter-day Saints to not have the privilege of marrying and bearing children in the covenant. In view of this, we have decided to authorize you, as one of the Apostles[,] to dedicate rooms which are now used for prayer according to the holy order,[44] and in those rooms solemnize

44. It was common for chapels and homes to have a room set aside for people to dress in robes and conduct prayer circles. For instance, see *Wilford Woodruff's Journal, 1833-1898,* ed. Scott G. Kenney (Midvale, Ut.: Signature Books, 1983), 5:73 ("I attended the prayer Circle[,] there being 24 in the Circle. We occupied Preside[n]t Young['s] new upper Room in his new House for the first time."), 6:319 ("I met at the Prayer Circle room at the Historians Office at 12 oclok. We gave [Leonard Wilford Hardy & 4 wives] their Second Anointing."), 8:138 ("I dedicated the Prayer Circle room at Kayesvill [sic] on Sunday Dec. 10"). See also "Prayer Circles Discontinued," *Sunstone,* "News" section, July 1978.

marriages such as are properly recommended, and which are of the class referred to—that is, marriages of those who are unable, through poverty or some other serious impediment, to go to the Temple of the Lord to be sealed for time and for eternity. The authority is hereby conferred upon you during this present visit to Arizona to attend to cases of this kind, and perform the sealing ordinances for time and for eternity. In doing this, we desire you to be very careful and make a proper record of all such sealings, that every case may be reported here; and in order that this may be done, we furnish you a book in which you will have entry made of all these sealings. **—Wilford Woodruff to John Henry Smith,[45] Sept. 21, 1891**

At a meeting of the First Presidency, Twelve Apostles, Presiding Bishops, First Presidents of Seventies, Presidents of Stakes and Bishops, held at the 18th Ward Chapel, Salt Lake City, October 7, 1891. President Wilford Woodruff related the following:—

["]Over fifty years ago, while in Boston, ^I^[46] dreamed that the Saints migrated to the Rocky Mountains, built a Temple and dedicated it; that at the dedicatory services Elders were set apart to go among the Gentile nations to bind the law and seal the testimony. That when after our arrival here, the question was discussed, as to what material should be used in the Temple building, some suggesting brick and others adobe, ^I^ made the remark that it never would be built of anything else than cut Granite. This, so far has come to pass as ^I^ saw it. Just before the death of Pres[iden]t [John] Taylor, too, ^I^ dreamed that the Temple was finished; and ^I^ saw the grounds around filled with the Priesthood; and while wondering why the people did not go into the Temple, Pres[iden]t [Brigham] Young came up and ^I^ asked why the brethren did not enter the building; with that Pres[iden]t Young took from his pocket the keys and handed them to ^me^ ... telling ^me^ to open the Temple and let the people in. In thinking the matter over the following morning, ^I^ wondered why it was that Pres[iden]t Young

45. John Henry Smith (1848-1911) was ordained a member of the Quorum of the Twelve Apostles in 1880 and sustained as a counselor in the First Presidency in 1910.

46. President Woodruff's remarks were written in third person and later changed to first-person extralinearly as indicated. For the sake of clarity, the superfluous third-person pronouns have been removed. Where there are now ellipses, it originally read "Pres. Woodruff" and (twice) "Pres. Woodruff said."

handed the keys to ^me^, seeing that Pres[iden]t Taylor was alive and that they were not given to him.

["]The following night, ^I^ received the same manifestation; and addressing ^myself^ to Pres[iden]t Taylor, ^I^ asked him, why he did not come in (to the Temple); he answered that he could not walk. In the morning, … ^I^ felt that Pres[iden]t Taylor would not live to see the Temple finished. A short time before Pres[iden]t Taylor's death, … ^I^ received a letter from Pres[iden]t [George Q.] Cannon informing ^me^ of the illness of Pres[iden]t Taylor; it also stated that Pres[iden]t Taylor's legs were swollen." As to this[,] Pres[iden]t Woodruff remarked, it was of little consequence whether he lived or not to witness the completion of the Temple; those were things wholly in the hands of the Lord. **—Minutes, Oct. 7, 1891, in L. John Nuttall Papers, Perry Special Collections**

It has been decided that it is no longer necessary for those going to the Temples to attend to ordinances therein to send their recommends to President Woodruff to be by him endorsed. The signatures of the Bishop and Stake President will be all that is required.

This decision applies to all ordinances attended to in the House of the Lord, except Second Anointings, which last named will still require the approval of the President of the Church before they can be administered. This being the decision, Bishops of Wards and Presidents of Stakes will see the increased necessity for care, so that no unworthy person will be recommended for ordinances in the Temples. **—Wilford Woodruff, George Q. Cannon, and Joseph F. Smith, circular letter, Nov. 6, 1891, in *MFP*, 3:228**

....

It was agreed that when the coffin is closed containing the body of a sister who has been through the temple, her veil should be placed so as to hide her face, so that when her husband meets her on the other side he may lift the same from her countenance. This is in accordance with the instructions which President [Brigham] Young gave during his life. The carelessness of the Saints in regard to their Temple clothing was talked about, and it was voted that instructions be sent to each Temple that those who receive the ordinances of the house of God be told especially to be careful not to expose their clothing to the public gaze. The clothing is as sacred as the ordinance[s] themselves. **—Abraham H. Cannon diary, Jan. 7, 1892, Perry Special Collections**

[W]e have [had] the two rooms [in the Salt Lake temple] measured which we have decided to have artistically decorated, and enclose herewith the plans of the same. They are what we call the Garden and Telestial Rooms. By sending these to you and giving you our ideas of the character of the rooms, and that which is to be represented therein, we thought you would have an excellent opportunity at Paris to get up suitable designs for them, even better, probably, than you could at home, because of the advantages which an art center like Paris furnishes in the way of suggestions, etc.

The walls of the Garden ought to represent as well as can be done, the garden of Eden in the condition in which it was when the Lord placed our first parents therein, as described in the scriptures, filled with the most beautiful vegetation, and with animals of every kind dwelling together without enmity. ... We would like the designs to be as beautiful as it is possible to obtain. The Telestial Room is the dark and dreary world into which Adam and Eve are driven out of the Garden after their transgression. It is the world under the curse. All is changed, for it is a world in which sin has made its appearance. Animals have become ravenous; they prey upon each other, and even the fowls of the air have partaken of the spirit of antagonism. The earth has become cursed for man's sake. Thorns and thistles and noxious weeds have sprung up, and the whole face of nature shows the effect of the change ... These are the scenes to be depicted upon the walls of this room. There are no human figures upon the walls of either the Garden or the Telestial world; the scenes are confined to the vegetable and animal kingdoms.

It may be practical for several of you to work in each room. ... We see no serious reason why several should not work in the same room, working of course at different details and upon different walls.

... Our experience in the Logan temple is not very encouraging for painting on the walls. The work which was first done there had all to be done over again, the paint having peeled off in consequence of the walls having become damp through defective guttering in the roof of the building. ... [You will want to] cover the wall with canvass, and paint on the canvass. Will you please examine into this question thoroughly[?] **—Wilford Woodruff, George Q. Cannon, and Joseph F. Smith to John W. Clawson, Lorus Pratt, John B. Fairbanks, Henry Evans, and Herman Haag, Jan. 26, 1892**

I went to the [Logan] Temple with the folks at 7:30 o'clock, and after the names of those who desire to work for themselves and their dead had been registered, I spoke, by request of Bro[ther] [Marriner W.] Merrill, to the Saints, and sought to impress upon them the importance of the step they are about to take. I then went to Bro[ther] Merrill's room where he gave me the marriage service to study so that I could perform the same, it being to officiate in the case of Amelia and her husband that I came to Logan. After having dinner I went to the sealing room and sealed for time and eternity fourteen couples in addition to W[illia]m H. Chamberlain, Jr.,[47] and my sister Amelia. In their case I laid my hands upon their heads, as Father [George Q. Cannon] had suggested I should do, but in the case of the others I merely repeated the ceremony. It is as follows: The hands are clasped ... while the parties are kneeling at the altar. ["]Bro[ther] W[illia]m H. Chamberlain, Jr., you take Sister Amelia Telle Cannon by the right hand and receive her unto yourself to be your lawful and wedded wife for time and for all eternity, with a covenant and promise that you will observe and keep all the laws, rites and ordinances pertaining to this Holy Order of Matrimony in the new and the everlasting Covenant, and this you do in the presence of God, angels and these witnesses of your own free will and choice?" —(Answer, "Yes") —"Sister Amelia Telle Cannon[,] you take Bro[ther] W[illia]m Henry Chamberlain, Jr., by the right hand and give yourself to him to be his lawful and wedded wife and for him to be your lawful and wedded husband, for time and for all eternity, with a covenant and promise that you will observe and keep all the laws, rites and ordinances pertaining to this holy order of Matrimony in the new and the everlasting Covenant; and this you do in the presence of God, angels and of these witnesses of your own free will and choice?" (Answer, "Yes.") —["]By virtue of the Holy Priesthood and the authority vested in me I pronounce you W[illia]m Henry Chamberlain, Jr., and Amelia Telle Cannon legally and lawfully husband and wife for time and for all eternity, and I seal upon you the blessings of

47. William H. Chamberlin Jr. (1870-1921) was president of the Church's Tahiti-Papeete Mission from 1899 to 1900. When he returned home, he studied philosophy at the University of California-Berkeley and University of Chicago, then taught at BYU, where he was reproved, beginning in 1911, for introducing students to higher criticism. When the school closed the philosophy department in 1916, Chamberlin left and thereafter taught extension courses at the University of Utah (James M. McLachlan, "W. H. Chamberlin and the Quest for a Mormon Theology," *Dialogue: A Journal of Mormon Thought* 29 [Winter 1996]: 151-67).

the holy resurrection with power to come forth in the morning of the first resurrection clothed with glory, immortality and eternal lives, and seal upon you the blessings of kingdoms, thrones, principalities, powers, dominions and exaltations, with all the blessings of Abraham, Isaac and Jacob (and say unto you, be fruitful and multiply and replenish the earth, that you may have joy and rejoicing in the day of the Lord Jesus Christ) (all these blessings) together with all the blessings appertaining unto the New and Everlasting Covenant, I seal upon you by virtue of the Holy Priesthood, through your faithfulness, in the name of the Father, and of the Son, and of the Holy Ghost, Amen." The parties then kiss each other, which ends the ceremony. —When all the sealing was done Bro[ther] Merrill said I had done the best of any person who had sealed in the Temple for the first time. —It was about 2:30 o'clock when I left the Temple. **—Abraham H. Cannon diary, Sept. 28, 1892, Perry Special Collections**

Took Breakfast at the House & drove ... through Leeds to Harrisburg to dinner then to St George before night. ... For a few days looking around town then commenced work in the Temple. Wife has found a list of names to work for & I am assisting her. I find the ceremonies the same as ever & am informed that the ceremonies as revised & corrected [and] are used in Logan & Manti have not been altered one whit but [are] word for word & [are] the same [as] will be used in the Salt Lake [temple]. **—Lorenzo Brown diary, Oct. 16, 1892**

....

At 5 o'clock I went to the [Salt Lake] Temple where I met my folks, we having received permission from Pres[ident] [Wilford] Woodruff to receive our second anointings. Father [George Q. Cannon] was there to perform the ceremony. Bro[ther] [Francis M.] Lyman was also there to be with his wife Susan D. Callister Lyman as she received this blessing. Father anointed and spoke the words, John D. T. McAllister held the horn, and Lorenzo Snow and John R. Winder were the witnesses. Sister Lyman was first anointed in the presence of us all, she thus being the first to receive this blessing in this building.[48] I then received mine, and my wives followed in the order of their marriages. I felt very much pleased to be thus favored. The ordinance of the wash-

48. The Salt Lake Temple was dedicated two months earlier in April.

ing of feet was explained by Bro[ther] McAllister, after the anointings had been given. **—Abraham H. Cannon diary, June 7, 1893, Perry Special Collections**

It is deemed necessary that the following instructions should be imparted to the brethren and sisters of the Salt Lake Temple District who intend entering the House of the Lord to attend to ordinance work for themselves or their dead.

(1) The Saints who enter the sacred building should be properly prepared. Their bodies should be scrupulously clean; and those who feel it necessary to renew their covenants before beginning their work ought to attend to this previous to entering the Temple, it being in the nature of a preparation.

(2) The Saints who come to attend to baptism for the dead should be amply dressed in white before entering the font. All participants in the ordinance of Sealing Children to Parents should also be dressed in white.

(3) Couples who come to the Temple to be married must bring Licenses from the Probate Clerk. When this is not complied with the ceremony will not be performed.

(4) In the performance of work for the dead the rights of heirship (blood relationship) should be sacredly regarded, when practicable. When an heir empowers another person to do the work in his or her stead, he or she should give the acting proxy a written authorization to that effect.

(5) Each person or family should keep an accurate individual or family record of work done; such books can be procured at the Deseret News Office.

(6) Those who do ordinance work have not the right to make matches between people who are deceased, except in cases of persons who were married in life. In all other instances the President of the Temple must be consulted. He should be appealed to in all matters involving doubt or complications.

(7) The Temple is open on all working days at 7:30 a.m. Monday is devoted to taking the record of Baptisms for the Dead, which are performed on Tuesdays. Baptismal records are not taken after twelve o'clock on Mondays. On Tuesdays all ought to be in the building by 8 a.m.

(8) The higher ordinances are attended to on Wednesdays, Thurs-

days, and Fridays. The record of this work is taken between the hours of 7:30 and 9 a.m., of the day it is performed. After the last named hour none will be admitted, as the doors will then be permanently closed for the day. The earlier the Saints come to [turn] in record[s] the better.

(9) The Saints, before coming to the Temple, should consider well the work they propose doing, and have the necessary dates, &c., in each individual case submitted to writing. The information has to be repeated, as a rule, in each case of work done for the dead. **—Lorenzo Snow, President of the Salt Lake Temple, "To Whom it may Concern," June 23, 1893, reprinted in the *Church News,* Dec. 5, 1964**

It has been the rule in [the] Logan Temple not to allow any person who had not been married under the covenant to officiate at the marriage alt[a]r in behalf of the dead. This rule, he said was wrong and must not be acted upon in the future. The reception of the endowment enabled a person to act in behalf of the dead in any of the ordinances in the house of the Lord, except the highest [second anointing]. **—Wilford Woodruff, Special Meeting of the Workers of the St. George Temple, temple annex, June 23, 1893, typed excerpt in Buerger Papers**

[I see] that your father died without having heard the gospel, and that your mother, in 1872, was sealed to him; and that in 1889, desiring the ordinance of adoption attended to, she wanted to be sealed over again, and that Pres[iden]t [Daniel H.] Wells said it could not be done, and advised that your mother be sealed to some good man, and her children adopted to him, etc. In regard to this I would say that I take it for granted that you fully appreciate the risk which a woman runs in being sealed to a man, who is dead, who had not received the gospel; and appreciating this I feel to allow your mother her own choice in the matter, but I see no reason whatever for a repetition of the sealing ordinance. In the event, however, of her allowing the sealing to remain uncancelled and you being adopted to your father I would advise that you, immediately after the adoption, have your father adopted to some good faithful man, dead or alive. **—Wilford Woodruff to William H. Evans, Aug. 11, 1893**

We have made the following ruling which is self-explanatory, and send it to you for your guidance as President of the Manti Temple.

"Persons having received their endowments, who are otherwise qualified, may act for the dead in the ordinances, of sealing and adoption, without having been Sealed or adopted themselves. But in Second Anointings, none shall be eligible to act for the dead, unless they have received this blessing themselves." **—Wilford Woodruff, George Q. Cannon, and Joseph F. Smith to John D. T. McAllister, Aug. 26, 1893**

On Wednesday Nov. 15th 1893 Presidents [Wilford] Woodruff and [George Q.] Cannon, at their office, in answer to the question put to them by Pres[iden]t Lorenzo Snow[,] made the following ruling.

"In cases where the heads of families deceased have had the necessary ordinance work done for them and they have been adopted into a family whose relationship in the covenant connects with the Prophet Joseph [Smith], the children of such parents can be sealed to the latter. This decision includes children who are in the Church and parents were not." **—Book of Temple Ordinances, Nov. 15, 1893, p. 16, copy in Buerger Papers**

It was decided [by the First Presidency and Twelve Apostles] in answer to a question that people should wear only white garments whether they be cotton, woolen, or linen. Colored garments should, however, not be used. **—Abraham H. Cannon diary, Dec. 7, 1893, Perry Special Collections**

[Six] questions submitted by the recorder through President [Lorenzo] Snow[,] answered by President Woodruff, written by his own hand.

1. When dates of death are unknown [and the] relationship absent or uncertain[,] and it is not known that the deceased reach[ed] maturity, what work, if any can be done for the dead?

Ans[wer]. It is v[e]ry [possible] that [when] a name is presented for Work for the dead[,] ... [no] evidence [exists] to show whether the person [was] a child or of mature age[.] For [the] endowment[,] wh[e]re such evidence cannot be obtained[,] do nothing. But endowments may be given w[he]re dates of birth & death cannot be found [but it is known that] they [were] of sufficient age for [the] ordinance.

2. What age must a dead female have attained before she can be endowed?

Ans[wer]. She must at least be 8 years of age before she can be baptized[,] [and] for an endow[ment][,] and [the same] if living[,] not less than 12 years [but] unless for some special reason not less than 16.

3. What age must a dead male have attained before he can be endowed?

Ans[wer]. Same as number 2.

4. What age must a dead female have attained before she can be sealed as a wife?

Ans[wer]. Not less than 12 years.

5. What age must a dead male have attained before a female can be sealed to him as a wife?

Ans[wer]. Not less than 12 years.

6. Is it proper when desired by children who are in the Church that the latter should be sealed to parents who did not hear the Gospel in life and consequently did not embrace it?

Ans[wer]. Yes—unless th[ere] is some special reason why it should not be done. (There [is] no specific date given when these questions are answered. They appear in the book for the year 1893.) **—Book of Temple Ordinances, 1893, p. 42**

....

President [Lorenzo] Snow reported that the First Presidency and Twelve [Apostles], at a meeting held in the [Salt Lake] temple, Jan. 4th, 1894, decided as follows:

"If, by mistake, a person is sealed in the temple before being endowed, it is not necessary for the sealing to be cancelled. All that is necessary is for the person to be endowed, unless the person, or the individual representing him or her, is dissatisfied." **—Book of Temple Ordinances, Jan. 4, 1894, p. 17**

[S]till-born children do not need any temple ordinances performed for them. Such was the ruling of President Brigham Young and that decision is honored in all the temples and confirmed by the instructions of the present authorities. **—George Reynolds to Jed Tomlinson, Jan. 8, 1894**

The father of W[illia]m S. Brighton was born out of wedlock and the parents were never married together. The male parent (Brother Brighton's grandfather) married, consecutively, 3 women and raised a family. His illegitimate son was reared by relatives.

The mother, when somewhat advanced in years, married a widower, who already had his family.

1st question. —To whom should the woman be sealed—the father of her child or the widower whom she married.

The decision by the council of the First Presidency and Twelve [Apostles]—She should be sealed to her husband left (the widower).

2nd question. —To whom should Brother Brighton['s] father be sealed as a child? Decision—to the mother and the man to whom she is to be sealed.

Decision rendered by the First Presidency[,] 19 April 1894. **—Book of Temple Ordinances, Apr. 19, 1894, p. 18**

Howard Egan's[49] wife committed adultery with James Monroe. Howard Egan killed Monroe on account of the crime. W[illia]m M. Egan is the issue of the adultery.

Question. —To whom does W[illia]m M. Egan go as a child—to Howard Egan or his father?

Decision of the First Presidency and 12 [Apostles][,] April 19, 1894. He belongs to Howard Egan, by virtue of the mother being Howard Egan's sealed wife, and no ordinances needed. **—Book of Temple Ordinances, Apr. 19, 1894, p. 37**

Jane Elizabeth Manning [James][50] (a Negro [woman])[:] Do you wish to be attached as a Servitor for eternity to the prophet Josep[h] Smith and in this capacity be connected with his family and be obedient to him in all things in the Lord as a faithful Servitor? (Answer[:] Yes.)[51]

Pres[iden]t Joseph F. Smith acting for and in behalf of the Prophet Joseph Smith: Do you wish to receive Jane James as a Servitor to yourself and family: (Answer[:] Yes.)

---

49. Howard Egan (1815-78) was born in Ireland and converted to Mormonism in 1842. He was arraigned in U.S. District Court in 1851 for the murder of James Monroe and found not guilty by a jury. Soon after, the Utah Territorial Legislature passed the Justifiable Homicide Act to guarantee that anyone else who killed an adulterer would be legally protected.

50. Jane Elizabeth Manning (1822-1908) lived with the Joseph Smith family in Nauvoo and was the first known black woman to enter the Salt Lake Valley. She married Isaac James, who later left her and her eight children.

51. Because blacks could not receive temple ordinances, this sealing of Manning as a servant was a compromise. Manning claimed that Emma Smith, Joseph Smith's wife, had promised her years earlier that she would be adopted and sealed to the Smith family. In 1895, Church leaders revoked Manning's sealing, but it was restored in 1902 with Bathsheba Smith acting as proxy.

By the authority given me of the Lord I pronounce you, Jane James, a Servitor to the Prophet Joseph Smith (President Joseph F. Smith acting for and an[d] in his behalf) and to his household for all eternity, through your faithfulness in the new and everlasting covenant, in the name of the Father and of the Son and of the Holy Ghost. Amen. **—Book of Temple Ordinances, May 18, 1894, pp. 33-34, citing Adoption Record A:26**

Dear Brother: applications are, as you are aware, being constantly made for the privilege of having women sealed to their husbands who have heretofore been sealed to other men who were not their husbands.

Similar applications are being made in the cases of sealing children to parents who have heretofore been sealed to men who were not their natural fathers.

I have been unofficially informed that when such cases are plain, and when the applications are at harmony with the teachings given at the last April Conference, the rule in the Temple should be to proceed without application to President [Wilford] Woodruff.

If this be the decision of the First Presidency, I would be obliged if I could be so informed officially by the placing of a plain "yes" or "no" upon this sheet. [There is a pencil-written "yes" at the bottom.] **—John Nicholson to Wilford Woodruff, June 14, 1894**

It was decided as being unnecessary to mark the shirts of those who pass through the temple and receive their endowments. The marks in their garments are sufficient.[52] … Concerning the proper position of the altar in a prayer circle—as to whether it should face the east or south—there is no rule, though the custom is to generally have them face the south. Pres[ident] [Lorenzo] Snow says he always aims to face the chief temple in offering his prayers. It was decided that the circles over which the Twelve preside be permitted to meet in the Elder's room, instead of in the basement where the ventilation is so bad, and the room so small. **—Abraham H. Cannon diary, Aug. 16, 1894, Perry Special Collections**

As a result of the conference of the brethren engaged as ordinance workers in the several Temples, held at Salt Lake Temple, some time

---

52. See the next entry for reference to marking outerwear.

ago, the following slight corrections have been adopted by us, which you will please note:

In the creation on the fifth day a grammatical error occurs. The word "their" is used instead of "its"; the word "their," therefore, is change[d] to its. In the lecture the words "next room" are used in the Terrestrial room when that same room is referred to; the words "the next" therefore have been changed to "this," as the appropriate form.

In the placing of the girdle [sash], it should be placed on the outside of the apron strings.

In the ceremonies at the veil, the practice has been to use the words, "this man Adam," while in the Logan Temple the words, "this man, representing Adam," are used. It was decided to drop the words, "this man representing," and say "Adam, &c."

The word "christian," referred to in the lecture, in connection with [a person's given] name, is dropped and the word "given" is substituted.

The words "and some have to go away on business," which occur at the end of the lecture, were expunged.

The words, "new name," were substituted for the pronoun "it," to avoid ambiguity, where it reads in the lecture, "You must remember "it," that is, your new name.

The people, when being put under covenant, should signify their assent by bowing and saying, "yes."

It was left optional with the Temple President to use persons as witnesses who were receiving endowments or to use workers as such. ...

It has been the practice to mark the shirt, but we think this unnecessary as it is not strictly a part of the Temple clothing. The marking of the garment should be done in the washing room and not at the veil; and the greatest care should be taken to see that no person is permitted to leave that room wearing an unmarked garment.[53]

In the Salt Lake Temple the practice in the Garden is for the couple at the altar to remain kneeling while the covenant relating to the ... Aaronic Priesthood is being administered, while the practice in the other Temples is for the couple to arise. The reason given by

53. At the time, the marks were still being cut into an initiate's clothing at the end of the ceremony, as opposed to the modern practice of purchasing pre-marked garments and putting them on in the initiatory ritual in the dressing room. This change in procedure made it possible to mark the underwear without affecting the outerwear. During an intermediate period beginning in about 1899, companies like Cache Knitting Works manufactured approved, but still unmarked, garments.

the Salt Lake Temple for not arising is that the couple would have to descend three steps, and as a matter of convenience they were permitted to remain on their knees. It was decided that the couples should rise. **—Wilford Woodruff, George Q. Cannon, and Joseph F. Smith to Lorenzo Snow, Aug. 31, 1894**

Pres[iden]t [Lorenzo] Snow informed me he had not been able to obtain information why women were required to vail their faces when at prayer in the Temple. **—Samuel W. Richards diary, Sept. 12, 1894**

Augusta[54] and I went to the Temple this A.M. and she had her second anointings. Pres[iden]t Lorenzo Snow officiated. He married her father and mother on the plains as they were coming to Utah and I was pleased to have him officiate in giving Gusta her anointings. Bro[ther] Jno. [John] R. Winder & John Nicholson were present. **—Heber J. Grant diary, Sept. 26, 1894**

President [Wilford] Woodruff's garments are made of cotton, he not being able to wear anything woollen next to the skin. **—George F. Gibbs to John A. Hendrickson, Dec. 5, 1894**

John Willoughby and Eliza Fox, both of them members of the Church, were married in England, and had three children, he died there, and she came to Utah with her children, where she married a member of the Church, named David Moore. She was afterwards sealed to her dead husband (Willoughby,) Moore acting as Proxey and the three children were sealed to her and Willoughby. She had five children by Moore, two of them are now living and they expressed a desire to be sealed with the three dead ones, to their father (Moore) and to their mother. What should be done about this?

This question was answered, as follows, by the First Presidency, to whom it was referred by President Lorenzo Snow: Taking the old Israelitish law as a basis, the children ought to be sealed to the first husband and the mother. Although the woman was not sealed to John Willoughby while he was in life, that was no fault of his as he was not within reach of facilities for the performance of that ceremony, and he did the best he could under the circumstances. When David Moore

54. Hulda Augusta Winters Grant (1856-1952) was born in Payson, Utah, and married Heber J. Grant in 1884 as a plural wife.

married Eliza Fox he did so with an understanding of the prior claim of the first husband, which he appears to have recognized. The sealing to the first husband was also evidently according to the desire of the woman. **—Book of Temple Ordinances, ca. 1894, p. 18**

....

Before me is your communication of Feb. 28th 1894, which has lai[n] upon my table, or in my desk, with many other letters, now for a very long time. I now recall the hasty reading of it when it came to hand, and owing to pressure of other things it was laid by for a more careful reading and proper attention at a more convenient time. And by some means the matter of the 2d Anointings, escaped my memory, while I recollected something about adoptions being referred to therein, and the decision of Pres[ident] [Wilford] Woodruff on that Subject coming soon after your letter, … settl[ing] in my mind the whole question with reference thereto. Today however on carefully reading your letter again, I saw my great mistake, And, altho[ugh] it may now be too late, I hasten to make such reparation as may lie in my power. First of all, I hope you will kindly forgive my inattention to this matter, which must as I know, be of great interest and importance to you. But if the work has not been done, I thank God it is not too late for it to be done, and I herewith Send you President Woodruffs authorization and Approval and Authorization of the Same. And if this is not Sufficient—or there is still anything lacking, if you will kindly let me know [and] you shall have my best effort to obtain it for you.

As to the matter of adoptions, you understand that children are to be sealed to their own parents so far as possible, and when not any further possible, the chain (Genealogical chain) is to be linked on to the Prophet who stands at the Head of this great dispensation. In this latter I will cheerfully help you so far as may be needed, if you will kindly let me know when my assistance may be needed. **—Joseph F. Smith to Charles F. Middleton, Sept. 18, 1895**

I am directed by the First Presidency to say in answer to your favor of [the] 10th inst., that in the cases to which you refer, the same rule holds good with regard to both living and dead. For those who have associated with any upon whom rests the curse of Cain[,][55] baptisms

55. That is, blacks of African descent.

can be performed, but endowments cannot be received. The fact of them being dead does not make any difference in regard to this law. **—George Reynolds to Levi Savage, Dec. 17, 1895**

SEALING ORDINANCE.

Brother __________ [,] you take Sister __________ by the right hand, and receive her unto yourself, to be your lawful and wedded wife, for time and ^for^ all Eternity, with a covenant and promise that you will observe and keep all of the laws, rites and ordinances, pertaining to this Holy order of Matrimony, in the New and the Everlasting Covenant, and this you do, in the presence of God, Angels and these witnesses, of your own free will and choice?

Answer[:] Yes.

Sister __________[,] you take Brother __________ by the right hand, and give yourself to him, to be his lawful and wedded wife, and for him to be your lawful and wedded husband for time and ^for^ all Eternity, with a covenant and promise that you will observe and keep all the laws, rites and ordinances pertaining to this Holy order of Matrimony, in the New and the Everlasting Covenant, and this you do in the presence of God, Angels and these witnesses of your own free will and choice?

Answer[:] Yes.

By virtue of the Holy Priesthood, and the authority vested in me, I pronounce you[,] __________ and __________ legally and lawfully, husband and wife, for time and for all Eternity, and I seal upon you the blessings of the Holy Resurrection, with ~~the~~ power to come forth in the morning of the First Resurrection, clothed with glory, immortality and eternal lives, and I seal upon you the blessings of kingdoms, thrones, principalities, powers, dominions and exaltations, with all the blessings of Abraham, Isaac and Jacob, and say unto you be fruitful and multiply and replenish the earth that you may have joy and rejoicing ^in your posterity^ in the day of the Lord Jesus Christ. All these blessings, together with all the blessings ^ap^pertaining unto the New and Everlasting Covenant, I seal upon you, by virtue of the Holy Priesthood, through your faithfulness, in the name of the Father, and of the Son, and of the Holy Ghost, amen. **—document, ca. mid-1890s, in Anthony W. Ivins Papers, Utah State Historical Society, Salt Lake City**

....

In baptizing for the dead in the Temples we understand that the form of words used is as follows:

> Having been commissioned of Jesus Christ, I baptize you[,] __________[,] for and in behalf of[,] __________, for the remission of your sins, and in the name of the Father, and of the Son, and of the Holy Ghost, Amen.

We might go into explanations as to the reasons which have caused this form of baptism to be adopted; but it is not necessary, further than to say that baptisms for health and baptisms for the renewal of covenants, etc., have led doubtless to the adoption of this form of ceremony to distinguish it from others.

We have had this matter under consideration from time to time, and supposed that our views had been made known to the Presidents of the Temples; but we understand that they have not been informed upon this point, and that the form above given is still the one used in administering baptisms for the dead.

The form we think proper, and that we desire to have used hereafter in administering the ordinance of baptism for the dead, is as follows:

> Having been commissioned of Jesus Christ, I baptize you[,] __________[,] for and in behalf of __________, in the name of the Father, and of the Son, and of the Holy Ghost, Amen.

We understand that in some instances baptisms have been administered in the Temples with something like the following ceremony:

> Having been commissioned of Jesus Christ, I baptize you for the remission of sins, for the renewal of your covenant, and for the restoration of your health, in the name of the Father, and of the Son, and of the Holy Ghost, Amen.

We do not know upon what authority this form of administering baptism has been adopted, but we think it improper. There have been times in the Church when the First Presidency have felt it necessary to call upon all the members of the Church to renew their covenants, and at such times it was suggested that the words "for the renewal of your covenant" be used in the ceremony; but it does not follow that at other times, and in individual cases, that form should be used.

We think it improper, speaking generally, for the words "for the remission of sins" or "for the renewal of your covenant" to be used in administering the ordinance of baptism.

Where it may be necessary to baptize a person who is already a member of the Church, the form of ceremony which the Lord revealed to the Nephites, and which has been revealed also to us in our day, is sufficient. It is sufficient for a sinner who joins the Church—for through that ordinance and the words of the ceremony which the Lord has given[,] his sins are remitted—and it certainly is for a man who is already a member of the Church, if it should be deemed necessary to administer the ordinance of baptism to him.

The practice which has prevailed in some instances where members of the Church are baptized, of using the words "re-baptize" and "re-confirm," we think unnecessary. When we strictly follow the form the Lord has given us we are sure to be right.

In cases where people are baptized for their health, we see no impropriety in using the words "for the restoration of your health" in the ceremony. There is a difference between baptism for such a purpose and baptism for admission into the Church. One is an ordinance of salvation—the door provided by the Lord through which His children must enter into His Church and become entitled to the blessings of the new and everlasting covenant; the other, while it may be termed in some respects an ordinance, is not imperative upon the members of the Church. If they have faith and believe, when they have an ailment, that the administration of baptism in that form will be beneficial to them, the privilege is granted to them. But there is a clear distinction between that form of baptism and the form of baptism which the Lord requires His children to obey to become members of His Church.

—Wilford Woodruff, George Q. Cannon, and Joseph F. Smith to Temple Presidents, May 20, 1896

It has been represented to me that Mary and Lucy Whitney, deceased, wives of Horace K. [Whitney][,][56] have never been annointed to their husband, who has received his [second anointing]—as I am told.

56. Horace Kimball Whitney (1823-1884) was an early Utah pioneer who worked in the LDS printing and tithing office. He was the husband of Helen Mar Kimball Whitney.

Also that Helen Mar Kimball[57]—sealed to the Prophet [Joseph Smith], has never had her 2d and she is very feeble.

Now I suggest that these are all worthy women, and if you saw proper to recommend it, I have no doubt Pres[iden]t [Wilford] Woodruff would be pleased to grant them the privilege at once. **—Joseph F. Smith to Angus M. Cannon, Oct. 31, 1896**

It is the mind of the First Presidency and Apostles expressed at one of their late regular Council Meetings, that you adopt as soon as it can be done conveniently the practice of brethren wearing white pants while doing Temple work.

This change would necessarily do away with the long white Shirt usually worn [b]y them, and admit of their wearing the regular white shirt, with collar and white tie if they choose to do so. The adviseability of this change will at once suggest itself to you. …

P.S. This change in dress need not be introduced into prayer circles. **—George F. Gibbs to John D. T. McAllister, Nov. 3, 1896**

You Ask the question, Are members of the A[ncient] O[order] [of] U[nited] W[orkmen],[58] who are members of the Church of Jesus Christ of Latter-day Saints[,] entitled to recommends to the Temples for marriages and Temple work?

In reply, we would say that we are not in favor of our Brethren joining organizations of any kind outside of our Church. But we are more especially impressed with the wrongfulness of their joining organizations which interfere with the rights of their fellow citizens in regard to labor. To illustrate: We think it is wrong, contrary to our religion, and contrary to good citizenship, for men to combine together in any organization to prevent their fellowmen from working because they do not join them or work for such an amount as they think workmen ought to have. This, we think, states our position clearly in regard to those organizations. But this A.O.U.W., as we understand, is not in

57. Helen Mar Kimball Whitney (1828-1896) was the daughter of Heber C. Kimball and Vilate Murray Kimball, and was married to Joseph Smith as a plural wife when she was fourteen years old.

58. The Ancient Order of United Workmen was founded by Freemason John Jordan Upchurch in 1868. By 1895 he had over 318,000 members in his fraternity. The organization lifted the lives of workers and provided such benefits as life insurance, while retaining overriding Masonic influences.

the strictest sense an organization of that kind. Still we think it would be better for our brethren not to join it. It would not do, however, to refuse a young man who wanted to be married in the Temple a recommend because of his being a member of that organization. We do not wish to drive our people away from the Church and from its ordinances. At the same time we would not like this to be a precedent and for others to say, "Well, the Church has no objection to our belonging to the A.O.U.W., because So and So has received a recommend and he is a member of that Order." From this we think you will understand our position. If a man desires a recommend, and this is the only objection, we think you should grant it to him, at the same time giving him these views. **—Wilford Woodruff, George Q. Cannon, and Joseph F. Smith to Abraham Hatch, 1896, in *MFP,* 3:278.**

....

Pres[ident] [Wilford] Woodruff declines to give Seconds [second anointings] to any members of the Church excepting those who have gathered to Zion; he says he must draw the line somewhere, and this is where he draws it.[59] He says too that all faithful saints who have died without having the privilege of gathering with the body of the Church will receive all the blessings they are entitled to hereafter. **—George F. Gibbs to John D. T. McAllister, Mar. 6, 1897**

It having come to the knowledge of the First Presidency that children and adults who had not received their endowments had been permitted to witness the marriage ceremony of their friends in one of the temples, the propriety of this was considered by the council of First Presidency and apostles; and I was instructed to request the president of temples to strictly forbid any person who had not received his or her endowments from witnessing the sealing ordinance. **—George F. Gibbs to Marriner Wood Merrill and David H. Cannon, Sept, 24, 1897**

The question was considered today in the council of First Presidency and apostles, whether adults who had not received their endowments should be permitted to enter the temple to be sealed to their parents. The question was decided in the negative. **—George F. Gibbs to Lorenzo Snow, Oct. 14, 1897**

---

59. The Mormon practice of "gathering" taught that converts should relocate to live with the main body of the Church.

....

At a meeting of the First Presidency and Apostles, held in the Salt Lake Temple December 16th last[,] the following question, submitted by Elder David H. Cannon, of the St. George Temple was considered:

"A couple were sealed by competent authority outside the Temple [but] one or both of them had not received endowments; are children of such unions born in the covenant, it being understood that they were born before their parents received their endowments, or should they be sealed to their parents?"

In connection with the above question Bro[ther] David H. Cannon remarked that, following instructions given by the late President Brigham Young on this point, the St. George Temple did not regard the children of such marriages as being in the covenant, and therefore required that they be sealed to their parents.

By way of explanation it may be well to state that some members of the Quorum of the Twelve Apostles had sealed couples in Arizona and Mexico by authority of President Wilford Woodruff, which had been done because of the great distance to be traveled in order to get to a temple, as well as impropriety of young people travelling [together] by wagon to a temple to be married; and some parties thus sealed had since presented themselves at the St. George temple to do temple work, hence the question.

The discussion of this subject was quite lengthy, each member present expressing his views thereon. President Woodruff decided, and the Council unanimously supported the decision, that the children of such unions were born in the covenant, and it was not necessary therefore that they should be sealed to their parents, and the records of [the] St. George Temple containing the above instructions were ordered to be made to agree with this ruling. It was the unanimous feeling of the Council that if President Brigham Young were now alive and this question were brought fully before him[,] he would modify the instructions said to have been given by him to agree with this decision. **—George F. Gibbs to Temple Presidents, Apr. 13, 1898**

At the regular meeting of the First Presidency and apostles on Thursday last, it was learned that a rule existed in the Logan temple, established by President John Taylor at the opening of that temple, permitting endowments to be given on behalf of deceased children who had attained the age of eight years before their death. At the opening of the St. George temple[,] this age was fixed by President Brigham Young at fifteen, and is still in force there, and the same rule was adopted by and is in force at the Salt Lake temple.

That uniformity may obtain in all the temples, [and] I give it as my opinion that the age fixed by President Young should be adhered to, and this became the sense of the council by formal action. **—Wilford Woodruff to Temple Presidents, June 7, 1898**

....

Some question now arose as to temple aprons, the shape and number of the leaves, and so on. Answer. Joseph [Smith] said [that] when they could be, they should be made of lambskin with three, nine, five or seven leaves on [them]—an odd number anyway. **—Minutes, Temple Sisters Meeting, Salt Lake City, June 16, 1899, typed excerpt in Buerger Papers**

Yours of the 24th enclosing a circular issued by the Cache Knitting Works, advertising their knitted garment, and informing the public that the garment had been approved by the First Presidency of the Church, is received. You now desire to know if it be true that the approval of the First Presidency has been given as stated. In answer I will say that I understand that the pattern of the garment referred to did receive the approval of the First Presidency in the lifetime of President [Wilford] Woodruff. **—Lorenzo Snow to John D. T. McAllister, June 26, 1899**

....

Elder James G. Bleak dwelt upon the opening scenes of this [St. George] Temple when our beloved President [Brigham] Young was carried by his brethren through this holy house, going from room to room speaking words of comfort and at times reproof to the people and then of the organization of this work for the dead—the Endowments which were for the first time imparted to the people in this dispensation for the dead on the 11 day of January, 1877. After speaking a short time, [Brigham Young] called for those to arise to their feet who had received their blessings in the Kirtland Temple. None arose. Now all those who had received their blessings in the Nauvoo Temple. Five males and four females arose. Then all who had received endowments in the Salt Lake Endowment House or other places where endowments were given [prior to completion of the St. George temple]. Twenty-two males and thirty-two females arose. Now all who have received their endowments in this temple. Thirteen males and eighteen females arose to their feet. **—Temple Minute Book, St. George, Jan. 11, 1900**

President [David H.] Cannon said it was gratifying to receive these kind acknowledgements. Felt glad to be here in this Temple. It is a God-blessed place to be. President Brigham Young and Geo[rge] A. Smith took the first shovelful of earth out of the foundation for this Temple to be built upon. After this Temple was completed and Pres[iden]t Young was organizing the Endowments, he could see the anxiety on the countenance of President Young that everything should be done properly. Every part of this building was set apart and made holy. **—Temple Minute Book, St. George, Jan. 25, 1900**

During the lifetime of the late President Wilford Woodruff a rule was established by him not to permit a woman to be anointed to a man unless she had lived with him as a wife. This was a restriction of the rule in such cases which obtained during the lifetime of Presidents Brigham Young and John Taylor. After considering the matter we have concluded to restore the practice as expressed in the following, and which will govern in such cases in the future:

Any woman, who has been sealed to a man in life or by proxy, whether she has lived with him or not, shall have the privilege of being anointed to him inasmuch as he shall have had his second blessings [second anointing]. **—Lorenzo Snow, George Q. Cannon, and Joseph F. Smith to David H. Cannon, Apr. 14, 1900, in *MFP*, 3:325-26**

Now with regard to your full blessings[,] you will have to see Bro. [Anthony W.] Ivins [president of the Colonia Juarez Stake] and get your recommends to the blessings of the House of the Lord for your full blessings. They will have to be endorsed by Pres[iden]t [Lorenzo] Snow, which I shall be pleased to get for you[,] and that will all be O.K. for you all to get your blessings. Anything I can do for you at any time I shall be happy to do. **—George Teasdale to Joseph C. Bentley, May 11, 1900, in Joseph T. Bentley, *Life and Letters of Joseph C. Bentley: A Biography* (Provo: By the Author, 1977), 108**

You evidently misunderstood Brother [George] Reynolds in regard

[to] recommending for the temple. What he aimed to convey to you was that it was not in order for presidents of missions to recommend for temple work; this prerogative is confined to bishops and presidents of stakes. How long this rule will obtain we do not know, but for the present it must be adhered to. **—Lorenzo Snow to Franklin S. Bramwell, June 4, 1900**

The mission presidents have nothing whatever to do with recommending their people to the temple, for the reason that it is understood that only Saints living in a gathered condition, that is, in a ward and stake organization are recommended for temple work.

... It does not necessarily follow there should not be exceptions to it. For instance, a mission president might know of Saints of long standing and experience in the Church under his jurisdiction possessing all the qualifications of worthiness for temple blessings and he might see special reasons why such parties should have the blessings of the temple; ... [he] would be at liberty to present such cases to us on their individual merits without the knowledge of the parties so recommended, and if we should see fit to make an exception ... he could then be authorized to issue recommends accordingly, to be countersigned by us. **—Lorenzo Snow to Franklin S. Bramwell, June 8, 1900**

Thursday the 19th of September 1900 was the OUTSTANDING DAY OF OUR LIFE, President Frank Y. Taylor was authorized by the First Presidency of the Church to invite Ida and I TO RECEIVE OUR SECOND ANNOINTINGS, AND IN THE TEMPLE, ON THIS MOMENTOUS DAY, President John R. Winder, President of the [Salt Lake] Temple, explained fully what the 2nd annontings were and told us of the glorious promises offered to those who keep the commandments of the Lord and live a worthy and holy life: that these were the highest of all earthly blessings and no one receives them but those selected by the President of the Church. No one else has that right. How wonderful they were, what hopes they inspire, what a strength they give, what anticipations they awaken in our hearts and how wonderful it is to feel a nearness to the Lord by righteous living. We were thrilled in expectancy and joyous in hopes of living worthy to secure all that was promised us. We have started on an everlasting journey and all depends on whether we endure until the end. **—John M. Whitaker journal, Sept. 19, 1900, Marriott Library; emphasis in original**

In harmony with the wishes of President [Lorenzo] Snow, to the effect [that] the leading brethren and sisters of the several Wards and Stakes of Zion, should be granted the privilege of receiving their second blessings [second anointings] in the House of the Lord, and in view of your continued faithfulness and untiring activity in the great cause our Father has established, for the exaltation of his children,—it affords us true pleasure to enclose you herewith your Temple recommend, duly signed, with the invitation to proceed to the Temple at your earliest convenience and receive this great blessing[,] your second annointing.

May the Lord bless and preserve you in the purity of these high covenants, we are with warmest regards. **—George C. Parkinson, Solomon H. Hales, and Joseph S. Giddes to Adelbert Henderson and wife, Sept. 25, 1900, copy in Buerger Papers**

[David H. Cannon speaking:] When a person is taking a part [in the endowment drama] it is not the province of one going through the House to correct him. **—David H. Cannon, in Temple Minute Book, St. George, Nov. 19, 1900**

With respect to Zadok K. Judd's letter (herewith enclosed) asking for second blessings [second anointings] for his father and grandfather, Pres[iden]t [Lorenzo] Snow says that many faithful people have gone into the spirit world without those blessings, and they will lose nothing by it; and all such cases he prefers to refer to the future than to undertake to endorse recommends for persons who cannot be regularly recommended. **—George F. Gibbs to David H. Cannon, Dec. 22, 1900**

3.

"INNOVATIONS MUST NOT CREEP IN" 1901–1918

President [Lorenzo] Snow has requested me to call your attention to the instructions given to Presidents of Stakes at their meeting immediately after conference in regard to recommends for second anointings. The Stake Presidents have on more than one occasion been told that for such recommends they alone are held responsible, that their bishops have nothing whatever to do with them and therefore their names should not appear on them. Instructions have been given, too, that as much as possible Presidents of Stakes should personally know the parties recommended for second anointings, but that in cases where their personal acquaintance is not sufficient to cover all cases, it would be proper for them to confer with their Bishops respecting the worthiness and fitness of any in their ward to receive these blessings with whom they may not be personally acquainted; and this is as far as Bishops should have anything at all to do in connection with such recommends. **—George F. Gibbs to Canute Peterson, Feb. 23, 1901**

[David H. Cannon] gave instructions in regard to Adam offering signs at the altar. Adam does not offer signs at the altar in the Telestial Room.

He did not want any innovations in the endowments. Spoke of

Pres[iden]t [Brigham] Young coming to him in vision and giving him important information in relation to his duty; visiting him three times in one night. **—Temple Minute Book, St. George, Mar. 5, 1901, typed excerpts in Buerger Papers**

There could be no objection to the wife revealing to her husband her new name outside of the temple, but it is at all likely that he will not need to know it outside of the temple. **—Lorenzo Snow to E. H. Rhead, Mar. 13, 1901**

After the opening exercises Pres[iden]t Lorenzo Snow spoke upon the Subject of the giving of Second Anointings. He said that this blessing brought a person to a greater knowledge of the things pertaining to God and his purposes in the earth, that the glorious things of the kingdom were made clear to the understanding of man. Therefore it would be a very serious thing for a man to apostatize after he had received this great blessing. He warned the Presidents of Stakes that they should exercise great care when giving recommends to those of his stake to receive these great blessings and should know by their work their integrity and devotion to the cause of the Gospel, for the responsibility would rest upon them if any were recommended unworthily or that apostatized. …

Pres[iden]t Jos[eph] F. Smith then made a few remarks on the Subject of the Second Anointing. He said that it was the crowning blessing of and the highest gift to be conferred by the Melchizedek Priesthood. Elders should do something to be worthy to receive this great blessing and there are many ways out of the ordinary routine duties by which a man could earn the good will of God to the obtaining of this blessing. Every man should be determined to place everything on the altar even to the laying down of life itself for the gospel sake in order to be truly worthy of this blessing. **—Thomas A. Clawson[1] journal, Apr. 8, 1901, Utah State Historical Society**

Meeting of Presidency, Apostles & Church Officers. Pres[iden]t [Lorenzo] Snow said that persons who are recommended for second anointings should be those who have made an exceptional record, that

1. Thomas Alfred Clawson (1862-1942) was bishop of the Salt Lake City 18th Ward and a dentist by profession. In 1939 he was called as patriarch of the Ensign Stake.

they are persons who will never apostatize. Pres[iden]t[s] of Stakes assume a great responsibility when they recommend persons for second anointings. …

Bro[ther] Jos[eph] F. Smith said[,] No man receives a fullness of the Melchizedek Priesthood till he has received his second anointings. Men recommended for this sacred ordinance should be men of God whose faith and integrity are unquestioned. **—Anthony W. Ivins diary, Apr. 8, 1901, Utah State Historical Society**

Pres[iden]t [Lorenzo] Snow has instructed me to say to you in answer to yours of the 3rd inst. in which you ask that the ordinance of second anointing be conferred on Brother Hjort in behalf of his deceased father, that he cannot consistently grant the request. The President says that the line must be drawn somewhere, and that he can only feel justified in approving recommends, which Stake Presidents may make, of persons known personally by them to be both suitable and worthy to receive this great blessing. **—George F. Gibbs to Christian N. Lund, Apr. 11, 1901**

In my opinion the man who pays but twenty five percent of his tithing and has been in the habit of using tobacco and getting drunk, but who is trying to quit these bad habits, and has partially succeeded, should be encouraged to continue in well doing until he is fully worthy to go to the temple before he should be recommended. **—Lorenzo Snow to William H. Smart, May 14, 1901**

President David H. Cannon said he wished to talk to us this morning. When a person is anointed, the towel should not be taken to wipe off the oil from the face or the hands or any portion of the body. Oil should not be used too profusely by the workers and should not be wiped off. There are probably some who do not understand this correctly. If they did they would not do it. It must not be done. [The] speaker wanted to say this to the people. When people come here to be baptized for their health who have not been endowed, they should be gotten out before the ceremonies commence.

No persons here should see or hear these ceremonies without they are going through, nor should they be allowed to remain in the room. **— Temple Minute Book, St. George, May 23, 1901**

Went to Temple this morning[,] presenting [the] recommend which Pres[iden]t [Lorenzo] Snow gave me about 3 months ago. We had not come [to the temple] before [to receive] our second anointing as the baby was young, and because we desired to become settled in our new home.

I was called to speak during the services of the temple. Dwelt principally upon the necessity of keeping awake during temple services and keeping awake in our duties. I consider this a very great honor to be called to speak in the House of the Lord. B[isho]p John R Winder annointed us and Elder [Adolph] Madsen[2] instructed us. These are the greatest blessings that are bestowed upon man in the flesh. We were both melted in tears and I felt the patriarchal spirit of pure affection more than I have done before. The witnesses to the annointing were John R. Winder[,] [who] annointed. Adolph Madsen assisted. John Nicholson [was the] Recorder. **—William Henry Smart diary, May 31, 1901, Marriott Library**

This evening from about 9-30 to 12 O.C[lock], my wife and I attended to the second part of the ordinance of second anointings. We besides the ordinance itself sang "We thank thee O God for a prophet," conversed concerning our duties to each other and children, read from John XII:1-8 verses, read the Rev[elation] on the Eternity of the Marriage Covenant, Section 132. We dedicated [the] room [in our house] for the purpose of this meeting [and] closed by singing: "Oh my father thou that dwellest." Anna was mouth in [the] preliminary prayer [and] I gave the dedicatory prayer and the benediction. The spirit of the Lord was with us and we felt nearer together than usual: were much encouraged in pressing onward in an endeavor to succeed in life. We fasted during the day and broke our fast together a little after 12 O.C[lock]. **—William Henry Smart diary, June 21, 1901, Marriott Library**

The following question has recently been asked us by one of our Stake Presidencies:

How strict shall we be with young men who wish to go to the temple who have united themselves with secret orders?

---

2. Adolph Madsen (1841-1924) served in the Salt Lake temple presidency under temple president Lorenzo Snow beginning in 1893.

That our views might be known and acted upon by Presidents of Stakes generally, we send you herewith a copy of the same, as follows:

"The counsel of the First Presidency in all such cases has been against our brethren joining secret organizations, and where any of them have already done so [our] counsel to them is to withdraw themselves from such organizations as soon as circumstances permit and wisdom dictate.

"It is true that many of our people have been led to join some of these societies on the ground that their aims and objects are purely charitable and social in their character, and besides, inducements are held out of procuring life insurance at greatly reduced rates. But however worthy their aims and objects may be, this fact remains: They are outside the pale of the church and kingdom of God, and brethren in allying themselves with them divide their allegiance with organizations that are manmade, and which have not been devised of the Lord for the building up of Zion; and in doing this they render themselves liable to have their feelings alienated, in whole or in part, from the church which requires their all. We may say on this point, that it is the testimony of brethren who have joined organizations of this character and severed their connections with them, that their tendency [was] to draw away from the church; and it may be said and expected, without question, if the lines were sharply drawn between Mormon and non-Mormon, that all such organizations would be found in the ranks of our enemies, on the principle set forth in the saying of our Savior, 'Those who are not for us are against us.'

["]We understand that plausible excuses are given for joining these organizations which amount to certain financial advantages which it is expected our brethren will obtain either for themselves during their lifetime or for their families, at their death. Like excuses might reasonably be given by brethren who have run after the things of the world in the hope of accumulating wealth and who, by doing so, have as a general thing made shipwreck of their faith. While we cannot consent to aught calculated to bring division and consequent weakness to the church, at the same time we have no desire whatever to deal harshly with brethren who have been led to become members of lodges or secret societies; but to all such who have faith enough to receive our advice, we would say, shape your affairs so you can withdraw from them, and never be found again associating yourselves with any organization which has not been instituted of the Lord for the building up of His Zion in the earth, and to all brethren who manifest a desire to receive this advice we would give temple recommends, also permit them to join prayer circles if found otherwise worthy.

[“]In addition to the above we feel to direct your attention to the importance of the young men under your jurisdiction receiving proper instruction on this subject before they join secret societies; and we would suggest, instead of making this a subject for public discourse, that it be talked of at priesthood and quorum meetings.[”] **—Lorenzo Snow and Joseph F. Smith to Angus M. Cannon and counselors, Aug. 29, 1901, in *MFP,* 3:340-41; emphasis in original.**

I am in receipt of a letter from sister Susie Miller, of Parawon [Utah], who is to be married in the St. George Temple the latter part of this month. Her letter sets forth in substance that she was previously married, that her husband, by whom she had children, died about 4 years ago without taking her and the children to the temple for the purpose of having the sealing ordinance performed in behalf of him and her, and having her children sealed to them, and that when reminded by her that these ordinances had not been attended to he treated the matter indifferently and died without sensing the mistake he had made. [She writes] that she now desires to be sealed to her intended husband, and have her children adopted to to [sic] him, and [to] ask my consent that this be done.

This will authorize you to seal Sister Miller to her intended husband and adopt the children by her former husband to the man she is about to marry. But in giving you this authorization I desire you to frankly state to these parties that I consent to this being done wholly on the ground that Sister Miller requested it, leaving the justness of this course (that is, adopting the children of her former husband to her intended husband) to be settled in the hereafter where everything which may be done here not strictly in harmony with justice and righteousness will be corrected. **—Lorenzo Snow to David H. Cannon, Sept. 17, 1901**

Pres[iden]t Brigham Young left St. George on 16 April 1877 for Salt Lake City and on the 17[th] [of] April Pres[iden]t Young blessed me and set me apart to do sealings—adoptions, 2nd Anointings[,] and all work in this holy Temple. This was done in Bellevieu [Bellevue,

Nebraska] at the house of Brother Jacob Gates.[3] I rejoice in this work and hope the time is not far distant when the temple will be filled with saints laboring for their dead. Be attentive and calm; see and hear what is done and said. Keep a record of what you do. **—David H. Cannon, Temple Minute Book, St. George, Sept. 18, 1901**

....

[R]ecommends for second blessings [second anointings] are not Bishop's recommends and their names therefore should not appear on them at all. The President[s] of Stakes alone are held responsible for people recommended for second annointings, and where they are not personally acquainted with the parties to be recommended, it would be in order for them of course to satisfy themselves through other reliable sources. In the next place we would say that it is not expected that people shall be found asking that this most sacred ordinance shall be administered to them, but you should take pains to seek out the worthy people under your Jurisdiction, and this by means of your counselors and Bishops. In this particular case however you will be perfectly safe in issuing the recommends sought for, as we personally know the parties to be worthy. **—Joseph F. Smith, John R. Winder, and Anthon H. Lund to Moses W. Taylor, Jan. 4, 1902**

It is not in order for people to ask for recommends for second blessings. They should be chosen through the Stake Presidency because of their faithfulness, fitness and worthiness to receive this higher ordinance of the house of the Lord. It is understood of course that you have received second anointings yourself, otherwise you had better refrain from recommending for the present. We may say however that second blessings are not administered to single individuals of either sex, but to men and their wives. **—Joseph F. Smith, John R. Winder, and Anthon H. Lund to Thomas E. Bassett,[4] Jan. 5, 1902**

Yours of the 21st inst. is received, in which you ask, in substance, the following question.

If a woman be sealed to a man who provides for her, and is kind

3. Jacob Gates (1811-1892) was one of the Seven Presidents of Seventy from 1860 to his death.

4. Thomas E. Bassett (1853-1926) was named president of the Fremont Stake in Rexburg, Idaho, in 1901.

to her, and who is a good Latter-day Saint; but she [grows] tired of him and does not love him, and obtains a legal separation from him, and [becomes] married [to] another man who is also a good Latter-day Saint, whom she loves, but her first husband still loves her and claims her for eternity, who shall she belong to in the next world?

The simple answer to this question would be thus: The husband who has the best claim on her.

But we would not have it understood that we use the word "claim" in the ordinary s[e]n[s]e, the s[e]n[s]e, for instance, in which it is used in referring to a chattel, a piece of land or an animal; for it must be borne in mind that a woman is a free agent and that she will forever enjoy the freedom of that agency, as man himself does and will. For instance, a couple who are properly married and in whom the principle of love is begotten and developed through the marital relation may claim each other in this life as husband and wife and the propriety of the use of the word claim[ed] in this instance never be questioned, for the reason that the principle of love has united them as one. But if either of them should for some reason or other, with or without justification, take it into his or her head to separate, and be fixed in that determination and remain in this state of mind, to claim each other under such conditions would amount to nothing at all. If the separation should be found to be justifiable it would be within the power of the injured party to make the state of separation perpetual or to condone the transgression and become reunited, provided of course both parties [who] desire to be reunited should be and are worthy of each other. But if the separation should be found to be unjustifiable, say, on the part of the woman, no self respecting man would want to compel her to live with him against her will, even if he had the power to do so. After reaching the perfected state of life[,] people will have no other desire than to live in harmony with the righteousness of every wrong, including that which united them as husband and wife. It is true a woman may say, I do not love my husband in this world, and I know I shall not love him in the world to come. This may or may not be true. It will depend entirely upon his worthiness. Those who attain to the first or celestial resurrection must necessarily be pure and holy, and they will be perfect in body as well. In other words every man and woman that reaches this unspeakable condition of life will be as beautiful as the angels that surround the throne of God; and therefore there will be no reason then for a woman not loving her husband; she will be able to love him in the first place because he will be a perfect being, and she would have no desire to associate in the marriage relation with anyone else, for the weakness of the flesh will then have been overcome and forgotten; and both be in harmony with the laws that united them. **—Joseph F. Smith, John R. Winder, and Anthon H. Lund to Christine Eggleston, Jan. 28, 1902**

[A]s far as possible[,] the person recommended [for the second anointing] ought to be personally known [to] you[,] and persons recommended should be instructed to regard their business to the temple as strictly private. It is taken for granted that you will confer with your counselors about such matters; also in cases where the parties are not sufficiently known to you to justify your recommending them, it is understood that you will be free to talk with their bishops or anyone else in whom he may have confidence about them for the purpose of satisfying yourself as to their worthiness to receive these higher blessings, but it should not be known why you make your inquiry about them. It was never intended that bishops should recommend for second blessings; neither that people should ask for recommends to obtain them. On the contrary, they should be sought out, and the strictest privacy should be observed in everything pertaining to this matter. **—Joseph F. Smith, John R. Winder, and Anthon H. Lund to Thomas E. Bassett, Feb. 4, 1902**

President David H. Cannon … read a letter that he wrote to the First Presidency and also one in answer to his, to the effect that persons, who have had endowments and afterwards wish to be married for time only must go to a temple to be married or they will violate the law of chastity and the children born to such parents will not be in the covenant. **—Temple Minute Book, St. George, Feb. 28, 1902**

President [David H.] Cannon said I wish to talk to you about the habit we have acquired as ordinance workers in this temple. I was coming into the house a few mornings ago at the same time a brother and his wife entered. The doorkeeper told them to take off their shoes. I felt that he should have said the same words to me. I am no better than the people who come here, neither are the rest of you brethren and sisters who labor here. We should take off our shoes before entering this house for it is a holy Place. This is the Lord's House. He said to

Moses when Moses drew near to Him on the Mount: Moses, "take off thy shoes for the ground whereon thou stand[est] is holy." I say brethren and sisters take off your shoes for this is a holy House. **—Temple Minute Book, St. George, Mar. 7, 1902**

We are often requested to grant the privilege, or rather to give recommends, to persons to get second annointings for worthy persons who are dead. Up to the month of December, 1900, there was no question, so far as we know, in our Stake about granting this privilege for the worthy dead.

On December 1, 1900, however, the Presidency of this Stake received a letter from President [Lorenzo] Snow, in which he made the following remarks:

"I would also suggest that for the present you will confine your names to men who are living, and their wives, living and dead, who are worthy,—to assist them to be more faithful and energetic in the future, and not so much for the dead. The time will come when the dead will be properly cared for."

Since the receipt of the above mentioned letter, the Presidency of this Stake have followed President Snow's instructions. But yesterday we received a very pressing request from the family of Brother Franklin Merry Whitmore, of Springville Third Ward, who died Feb. 15, 1902. He leaves one wife living; one died before him. The family has requested that he be permitted to receive his second annointings. Shall we give recommends for this purpose or not. **—David John and Joseph B. Keeler[5] to Joseph F. Smith, Mar. 15, 1902 [handwritten note: "If in their judgement he is worthy[,] it will be O.K. to do so."]**

Referring to yours of the 15th inst. we would say that President [Wilford] Woodruff's instructions to Stake Presidents on the subject of recommending for second anointing[s] limited them to persons who had gathered with the Church, whether dead or alive, and this was the policy adopted by President [Lorenzo] Snow, although he may have made exceptions to it. And it is our mind that faithful men who have gathered with the Church, who can be recommended as worthy to receive these higher blessings, but who through death were deprived of them, should receive them by proxy. It would be in order therefore to

5. Joseph Brigham Keeler (1855-1935) was president of Utah Stake and a professor at Brigham Young University.

extend your recommends to Franklin P. Whitmore, deceased, inasmuch as you knew him to be worthy. …

P.S. Names of wives of deceased persons recommended for second blessings must be given recommends. **—Joseph F. Smith and John R. Winder to David John and Joseph B. Keeler, Mar. 18, 1902**

RULES FOR THE REGULATION OF TEMPLE WORK

Adopted by the First Presidency and Quorum of the Twelve Apostles, at a meeting held in the Salt Lake Temple; April 24th, 1902.

(1) Males of 21 and females of 18 years of age can receive their endowments, provided they are properly recommended.[6]

(2) A deceased female who has attained, in life, the age of 10 or 12 years, may be sealed to a male as a wife. The same rule applies in the case of a male having a wife sealed to him.

(3) Males should possess the Melchizedek Priesthood before coming to the Temple to receive their Endowments.

(4) No male over the age of 21 years can be admitted to the Temple, to do ordinance work, except baptisms, until he has received his endowments. The same rule applies to females over the age of 18 years.

(5) Males under 21 and females under 18 can be baptized for their health. They can also be baptized for the dead, and sealed to their parents. All over 8 years old must be properly recommended by the Bishop of the Ward and the President of the Stake in which they reside.

(6) A female who has a husband or marries a man not in the Church cannot be admitted to the Temple to receive her endowments. The same rule applies to a Man who marries a wife not in the Church.

(7) Couples who come to the Temple to be married must bring licenses issued by County Clerks of the State of Utah. Those who have already been legally married do not, in order to be sealed, need licenses.

(8) If of a naturally ripe and early development, of mind and body, living children may receive endowments at the age of twelve years; but as a rule, fifteen years old is sufficiently early.

---

6. The age limits given here, 18-21 years old, conflict with rule 8 where they are said to be 12-15 years old for those "of a naturally ripe and early development." The exception, allowing twelve- to fifteen-year-olds, must have been intended to allow young women to marry early—something no doubt so obvious at the time that no further explanation was thought necessary.

(9) A dead female, in order to be baptized and endowed must have in life attained at least to the age of 8 years. The same applies to dead males.

(10) Children who die under the age of 8 years, not born in the covenant, should receive no other Temple Ordinances than to be sealed to their parents.

(11) Still born children who, their mothers state, have been quickened, are all right without having anything done for them.

(12) Children who were born out of the marriage relation, and are dead, should be sealed to the parent who has received the Gospel and lived it. In either case the parent must be sealed to a husband or wife.

(13) Children who were born to parents who had been sealed but not endowed, should be sealed to their parents, provided the opportunity should ever be given them to be sealed over an altar. Otherwise the first sealing would stand.

(14) It is necessary (when possible) that all children, married or single, born out of the covenant, should be present at the same time, to be sealed to their parents.

(15) A woman who has been born out of the Covenant, and who is married should be sealed to her parents, unless they yield up their right to her as a daughter and wish to surrender her to some other family.

(16) Where a woman has been sealed to two men and had children by both, and each of the men have a good standing in the Church[,] the children go to their respective fathers. Why? Because the children were born under the covenant to their respective fathers and bear their respective names.

(17) When desired by children who are in the Church, it is proper that they should be sealed to parents who did not hear the Gospel in life and consequently did not embrace it, unless there is some special reason why it should not be done.

(18) In cases where the heads of families (deceased) have had the necessary ordinance work done for them and they have been adopted into a family whose relationship in the covenant connects with the Prophet Joseph Smith, the children of said parents can be sealed to their own parents without annulling the ordinance first performed. This rule includes children in the Church and their parents [who] were not.

(19) Where a husband and wife are both members of the Church

and they have children, the husband dies, the wife afterwards marries another man, is sealed to her deceased husband[,] and has children by the second, all of the children should go to the first husband.

(20) No person, male or female, living or dead, can receive the highest blessings in the House of the Lord without a special recommend for this purpose, signed by the President of the Stake and endorsed by the President of the Church. The recommend, for dead as well as living, should be based on competent evidence of faithfulness, and, in cases of those who were not members of the church at their death, on evidence of their chaste and moral conduct in life. Any woman who has been sealed (in life or by proxy) to a worthy man, whether she has lived with him or not, may have the privilege of being anointed to him, provided he has had his second blessings.

MISCELLANEOUS

(21) Persons who die without having been endowed may be buried (if their friends choose) with un-marked garments, but not with robes or other Temple clothing.

(22) Unmarried people, who have been endowed, can act in sealing for the dead. Those who have been endowed may act for the dead in any of the ordinances of the House of the Lord, except Second Anointings.

(23) If, by mistake, a person is sealed in the Temple before being endowed, it is not necessary for the sealing to be cancelled. All that is necessary is for the person to be endowed, unless he or she representing him or her is dissatisfied.

(24) Words used in baptizing for the dead: "Having been commissioned of Jesus Christ, I baptize you for and in behalf of [blank space] who is dead, in the Name of the Father, and of the Son, and of the Holy Ghost. Amen."

CASES WHICH NEED NO CANCELLATION

(25) In cases where women have been sealed to other men than their husbands (the latter having died without having embraced the Gospel) and they are afterwards sealed to their husbands, it is unnecessary to cancel the first transaction. Both may stand on record. ...[7] The

7. The ellipses replace the words "(25 Concluded)".

same rule applies to cases of sealing children to parents who have heretofore been sealed to men who were not their natural fathers.

(26) All who come to the Temple to perform ordinance work are expected to make donations, according to their circumstances, to aid in meeting necessary expenses; but the poor who have nothing to give are equally welcome.

(27) No person, male or female, who has not had his or her endowments shall be permitted to witness the sealing, or any other Temple ordinance.

Adopted by the First Presidency and quorum of the Twelve Apostles, at a meeting held in the Salt Lake Temple: April 24th., 1902.
—Manti Temple Historical Record, pp. 107-10

In answer to yours of the 29th ult, we would say that under the following ruling by the Council of First Presidency and Apostles you would be authorized to administer Second Anointings in behalf of deceased women, after receiving the usual Special temple recommends in their favor signed by the Stake President and endorsed by the President of the Church.

—Ruling.—

No person, Males or female, living or dead, can receive [the] highest blessings in the House of the Lord without [a] special recommend for this purpose signed by the President of the Stake and endorsed by the President of the Church. The recommend, for dead as well as living, should be based on competent evidence of faithfulness and, in cases of those who are not members of the Church at their death, on evidence of their chaste and moral conduct in life.

Any woman who has been sealed, in life or by proxy, to a worthy man, whether she has lived with him or not, may have the privilege of being anointed to him, provided he has had his Second Anointings.
—Joseph F. Smith, John R. Winder, and Anthon H. Lund to John D. T. McAllister, June 11, 1902

We mailed you last evening a copy of certain rules applicable to Temple work, adopted by the Council of First Presidency and Apostles at their meeting in the Salt Lake Temple on the 24th of April last, which you will please receive with all others heretofore made which may be in your possession. We would like you to add to the last rule (No. 27) the following words; "excepting that of baptism. **—Joseph F. Smith, John R. Winder, and Anthon H. Lund to John D. T. McAllister, July 16, 1902**

Brethren recommended to the temple for second anointings should be men of experience whose integrity to the work of the Lord is beyond question, and who are known for their continued faithfulness, as it would be [a] very unfortunate thing indeed for a man to receive the higher blessings and afterwards apostatize. The question of age would naturally be a consideration in recommending for the higher ordinances, but it is not to be understood for a moment that you should wait until brethren become old before recommending them to receive these blessings. The chief qualifications are worthiness, fitness and unshaken integrity, and these should be combined in m[e]n thus recommended whether they occupy presiding positions or not: but as a matter of course the brethren occupying presiding positions, such as those of the stake presidency, high counsilor[,] president of the high priest's quorum, patriarch[,] and bishop are suppose[d] to be in possession of these qualifications.

The usual form of recommend should be used containing the name of the brother recommended, also the name of his wife or those of his wives, dead or alive, as the case may be, to be anointed to him, and all such recommends should be sent this office for endorsement accompanied by a letter of explanation. **—Joseph F. Smith, John R. Winder, and Anthon H. Lund to Collins R. Hakes, Aug. 1, 1902**

We take the earliest opportunity of informing you that presidents of missions are not competent to recommend to the House of the Lord; this prerogative is confined to bishops only. This is the general rule, which would convey the idea that only members of the Church living within the jurisdiction of a bishop are eligible to receive temple ordinances. But for your information we may say also that the[re] may be exceptions to this rule. For instance, you may have living under your presidency members of the Church of long standing and of good integrity, entirely worthy to receive the blessings of the House of the Lord; but it may not be wisdom for them to break up their homes and come to Zion for the purpose of making new ones, as they may be more helpful in the work of the Lord situating where they are than they would were they to gather with the saints. In all such cases it would be your privilege to correspond privately with us about them without letting the parties know of your intent and purpose; and after learning from you all about their antecedents, their worthiness, &c., if we should feel it right to permit such people to receive their endowments, a special recommend might be given to them by ourselves, w[h]ich would enable them to come to the House of the Lord to receive their blessings and return in pleasure to their homes. Such correspondence should be done by you as president of the mission. Conference presidents and branch presidents have nothing whatever to do with such matters, and the people thus recommended to us by you should be personally known to you for their worthiness to receive temple blessings. This means of course that they should be men and women of experience in the Church, strong in the faith and helpful in their way as well as tithe payers. **—Joseph F. Smith, John R. Winder, and Anthon H. Lund to Joseph E. Robinson, Aug. 9, 1902**

In the absence of [stake] President Joseph Morrell, I take the liberty of endorsing the following named Brethren and Sisters for their Second Anointing, they being recommended for that blessing by their Bishop. [Handwritten notation from President Smith: "The B[isho]p's are not expected to recommend members for their 2d blessings. This matter devolves upon the Stake Presidency."] **—Isaac Smith to Joseph F. Smith, Sept. 8, 1902**

It is for you to use your own discretion in the matter of giving recommends to the temple. You may consistently decline to give recommends to men who openly and flagrantly disregard the Word of Wisdom. ... Very old men in whom the tobacco habit may have become part of their nature, and who may regard it as a great hardship to be required to abstain from its use in order to receive your recommendation to the temple, should at least be willing to curtail themselves as much as they possibly can, and promise to cleanse themselves from the tobacco odor and not to use it at all the days they do work in the temple. As to drunkenness, we certainly think you should draw the line there. Let all such men know that they are unworthy to enter the temple and if they feel themselves too weak to overcome this sinful practice they had better acknowledge themselves failures and turn their temple work over to their children to do it for them. **—Joseph F. Smith, John R. Winder, and Anthon H. Lund to John W. Hess, Oct. 31, 1902**

Pres[iden]t [David H.] Cannon said I expect you people think I am cross: I want those who work in the wash-rooms to follow the text given you and allow no person to cloth[e] themselves. To do so is wrong and it must not be allowed.[8] If you want to make changes I must be consulted as the Presidency of the Church holds me responsible. **—Temple Minute Book, St. George, Dec. 19, 1902**

Pres[iden]t [David H.] Cannon wanted to talk to the workers: When we come to the vail, a list of names is generally prepared or one for each vail. I want Peter, James and John[9] to call up to the vail the first name of the list given to each one of them, then hand it to the sister and let her call the next; while she is going through another can be called and so on until all on the papers are through. This is the Lord's House and as such is a house of order. We are responsible for all that we do. We should be united as the heart of one. **—Temple Minute Book, St. George, Dec. 26, 1902**

HIGHER BLESSING

For females. In cases of those who are not members of the Church at their death. On evidence of their chaste and moral conduct in life any Woman who has been sealed, in life or by proxy to a worthy man, whether she has lived with him or not may have the privilege of being anointed to him, provided he has had his second blessings.

Signed by the First Presidency under date of 11 June 1902. **—John D. T. McAllister journal, Dec. 31, 1902, Perry Special Collections**

....

Mission presidents are not authorized to recommend the Saints under their presidency to the temple … [T]he portals of the temple must be safeguarded, and this can only be done by the strictest kind of watchfulness on the part of the responsible officers of the Church appointed to recommend for its ordinances, namely, the bishops of wards

---

8. This is in reference to the washing and anointing, after which the officiator slips the garment onto the initiate, a procedure that is carried out in the dressing room.

9. Brigham Young added Peter, James, and John to the endowment in Nauvoo as veil prompters, meaning that they helped initiates with memorized lines. See Devery S. Anderson and Gary James Bergera, eds., *The Nauvoo Endowment Companies, 1845-1846* (Salt Lake City: Signature Books, 2005), xxiv, 11-21.

and presidents of stakes. … [W]hile temple jurisdiction does not extend to missions, it can only be a question of time for missions contiguous to stakes to so increase in numbers as to justify us in extending to them stake organizations, and that as soon as this change shall be effected the people then will have equal privileges with those of other stakes.

In this connection we would say to you personally and privately, that where we find staunch and worthy families who are assisting in building up branches and furnishing homes for elders, and with whose integrity you are perfectly satisfied, and to whom it would be wise to extend temple privileges, you may write to us in regard to all such Saints, recommending them to the House of the Lord, and it will then be for us to endorse your recommends or otherwise as we may deem proper. In exercising this discretionary power the Saints whom you may thus favor should not know anything at all about it beforehand, and after they get their recommends through you personally they should be counseled not to talk about it. **—Joseph F. Smith, John R. Winder, and Anthon H. Lund to Nephi Pratt,[10] January 10, 1903**

This is in answer to yours of the 29th ult., asking for second blessings in behalf of your parents who died in England without hearing the gospel.

[A] second anointing is given as a reward of faithfulness to those who receive the gospel in their lifetime, and our predecessors went so far as to limit these higher blessings to those who proved themselves faithful after gathering with the body of the Church or who died faithful members of the Church on their way to Zion.

Your parents are in the hands of the Lord, and he will deal with them in the matter of second blessings as seemeth him good, after it shall be known that they have received the gospel by taking advantage of the temple work you have already done in their behalf. **—Joseph F. Smith, John R. Winder, and Anthon H. Lund to David Udall, Feb. 3, 1903**

You have our permission to do the necessary temple work in behalf of your deceased brother who died an excommunicated member of the Church after receiving his endowment and having his wife sealed to him who is also dead.

10. Nephi Pratt (1846-1910) was president of the Northwestern States Mission.

It will be an order for you, being the heir, to be baptized in behalf of your brother, to be ordained to the priesthood he formerly held, and to have his former blessings reconferred upon you in his behalf. And this will authorize the president of the temple to permit this to be done. …

P.S. If the children born to your brother before his wife was sealed to him have not been sealed to their parents, this part of his work should also be attended to.

But this matter should be laid before the High Council[,] by whom James L. Dee was excommunicated[,] for its approval; and an expression in writing in favor of this work being done in behalf of the deceased [should] be given and the same presented at the Temple, in connection with your own [temple recommend] when you go there.[11] **—Joseph F. Smith, John R. Winder, and Anthon H. Lund to Thomas D. Dee, Mar. 27, 1903**

[T]ook train at Elsinore [Utah] to attend the general Confer[e]nce of the Church of Jesus Christ of Latter Day Saints in Salt Lake City. … Some important rulings of Pres[ident] J[oseph] F. Smith[:] B[isho]ps ha[ve] nothing to do with recommending of second anointings. … [Temple] Garments made by any manufacture[r] not having an approved lab[el] upon them are not approved by the Church and no color but white is approved, and therefore will not be accepted. People going to the Temple should be scrupulously clean. Temple clothing should not be sent to a laundry. Temple apron[s] should be covered with fig leaves[,] one lap[p]ing over the other[,] to resemble a comple[te] covering of leaves. Leaves to hang downward. Question was asked if a man commits suicide, should he be buried in his Temple clothing; answer NO, unles[s] it could be proven that the person had become insane, in which event they may be buried in their Temple Clothing. …

No sister living with an outsider as her husband, can be recommended to the Temple.

All Young Men going to the Temple to do work should be ordained an Elder before going to the Temple. **—Samuel William Goold diary, Apr. 2, 1903[12]**

---

11. Apparently Dee neglected to follow through on these instructions until Oct. 17, 1906.

12. This diary is available online at "Sarah and Ida Goold," *Welsh Mormon History,* www.welshmormonhistory.org/index.php?/resources/view/1307.

I have a pair of garments here that the Presidency of the Church have had arranged for the Saints and all must conform to the same and the brethren and sisters who are engaged in the washrooms should see that the garments there are the proper ones for the Saints. **—David H. Cannon, Temple Minute Book, St. George, May 12, 1903**

[Y]ou desire to know if it would be proper to give a temple recommend to a faithful brother to receive his endowments whose wife is not a member of the Church, and who is about to make his home in Idaho. Our answer is, yes, provided he married his wife before gathering to Zion; and no, if he married her after coming to Utah. **—John R. Winder to Stephen L. Chipman, June 3, 1903**

[S]econd blessings are administered only to adults. **—Joseph F. Smith, John R. Winder, and Anthon H. Lund to Thomas E. Bassett, June 15, 1903**

From the inquiries you make in relation to recommending for [a] second anointing, we take it for granted that you yourself have not received your second blessings. If we are correct we suggest that you receive these blessings in your own behalf before recommending others to receive them, and we extend the same invitation to your counselors. Please therefore make out recommends in favor of yourself and wife or wives, and the same for your counselors and their wives, and we will take pleasure in signing them. **—Joseph F. Smith, John R. Winder, and Anthon H. Lund to Alonzo A. Hinckley,[13] June 18, 1903**

In answer to the question, if members of the Church can enter the temple who do not keep the Word of Wisdom, we would say that that is a matter to be judged of by those who issue temple recommends, namely, ward bishops and stake presidents. And while our answer to the question would, in a general way, be in the negative, it would really belong to the officers of the Church named to pass upon such a question at the time the party interested makes application to them for temple privileges. But we would suggest that it would be unprofitable in you to borrow trouble on account of supposed inability on the part of your husband to enter the temple because of pres-

13. Alonzo Azra Hinckley (1870-1936) was ordained a member of the Quorum of the Twelve Apostles in 1934.

ent failure on his part to keep the Word of Wisdom; for the reason that temple blessings are designed only for the Saints in their gathered condition; that is, for members of the Church known for their faithfulness after they have gathered to Zion. It will readily occur to you that it would be dealing unkindly with people to permit them to take upon themselves the sacred obligations of the House of the Lord without being fully prepared to do so; and it would seem that as a general thing the people must gather with the body of the Church and live among the Saints in a gathered condition before they themselves really know whether they are Saints in very deed or not. In other words, people must be rooted in the faith of the everlasting gospel before they are prepared to take upon themselves the obligations of the House of the Lord. For this, and other reasons, temple blessings are, as a rule, given only to Church members in good standing living in the regularly organized stakes and wards of Zion, and the presidents and bishops thereof are the judges as to their worthiness and fitness to receive the ordinances of the House of the Lord. **—Joseph F. Smith, John R. Winder, and Anthon H. Lund to Mrs. S. F. Zimmerman, July 18, 1903**

Complaints have reached us from Presidents of Stakes that persons doing temple work have been advised by temple workers to speak to the President of their Stake about obtaining their Second Anointing. This must not be done, or suggested by any one laboring in our temples. None but Stake Presidents have the right to suggest and recommend persons to obtain their Second Annointings. The reason is plain: those working in the temples see people in their Sunday clothing only, and are not acquainted with their everyday life. When such persons come to their Stake Presidents and ask for this blessing, saying they were counselled to do so in the temple, it places him in the unpleasant position, perhaps, that he has to refuse their request, and he is blamed by the applicants. No person has the right to ask for this blessing. He must wait till sought out by his Stake President. If the President of a temple feels impressed with the worthiness of any person, dead or alive, he can make suggestions to the President of the Stake, but he should not mention this to the persons themselves.

Please have these instructions repeated to all laboring in you[r] temple. **—Joseph F. Smith, John R. Winder, and Anthon H. Lund to John D. T. McAllister, Aug. 25, 1903**

In yours of the 21st inst. we desire to know if a regular recommend should be used for deceased people, when recommending to the temple.

Our answer is that in recommending for second blessings the same form of recommend should be used for the dead as for the living, but when people are recommended who are dead, the fact that they are dead should be so stated in the recommend. It is needless for us to say that you should recommend no deceased person to receive his second anointing without satisfying yourself of his worthiness to receive those great blessings. **—Joseph F. Smith, John R. Winder, and Anthon H. Lund to J. S. Paige Jr., Sept. 22, 1903**

Pres[iden]t [David H.] Cannon said washing and anointing the sick is not a temple ordinance.[14] **—Temple Minute Book, St. George, Oct. 26, 1903**

We return herewith [the] recommend, endorsed for second blessings, in favor of Sister Dorthy Tompsen.

We note that you say that this sister is making a desperate effort [to do] some temple work this winter. The question has arisen in our minds, whether or not she now has, or has had[,] a husband: and if a married woman, whether her husband has had his second anointing. If not, her husband, dead or alive, if worthy, should also be recommended, as she cannot have hers alone. **—Joseph F. Smith, John R. Winder, and Anthon H. Lund to Thomas E. Bassett, Nov. 16, 1903**

We have also a bulletin assigning the different parts [in the drama to] brethren and sisters who also work at the vail, excepting the preacher[15] and Lucifer. The preacher is used as a witness [at the altar]. Two witnesses are needed, we get one from the company [of initiates] going through the house. [The] speaker [David Cannon] had never thought it proper for him to take his wife through the vail when at the altar [witnessing], for there are brethren assigned to the vails and they should attend to that duty. If one of the witnesses happens to be a worker, he should not leave till we [all] get through [the veil]. **—David H. Cannon, Temple Minute Book, St. George, Dec. 30, 1903**

---

14. In other words, this ordinance was regularly performed elsewhere and was not restricted to the temple.

15. Until 1990 the endowment drama included the portrayal of a Protestant minister.

....

[T]he sister referred to in your letter may be sealed to her first husband without interfering in any way with the record of the sealing to her present husband. This is being done in other cases as well as hers, in consequence of permission not having been given to her to be sealed to her first husband at the time she married her present husband. —**John R. Winder to F. H. Wright, Feb. 1, 1904**

In regards to recommends to the Temple, the bishops should only give them to saints to receive their first endowments and they should exercise more care and caution in giving [the] same, as some unworthy persons have been admitted to the Temple and even some who were not members of the Church. **—Thomas A. Clawson diary, quoting Joseph F. Smith, Apr. 5, 1904, Utah State Historical Society**

In the first place it is your privilege to select whomsoever you choose out of your stake[,] deemed worthy by you, and recommend them for second blessings, and this may be done without the knowledge of anyone else excepting your counselors; and the parties recommended by you should be cautioned not to speak about these things to anybody outside of the temple, and not let their neighbors know their business in going to the temple.

... It is your privilege to select worthy brethren for these blessings, but it is the privilege of no one to ask you for [a] recommend to receive them, and second blessings should not be a topic of general conversation. **—George F. Gibbs to Alonzo A. Hinckley, June 8, 1904**

Pres[ident] [David H.] Cannon said that none but the proper pattern of knit garments, with the brand approved by the First Presidency, will be accepted as garments of the Holy Priesthood[,] [and] other than a white garment the President of the Church cannot be responsible for. None but the President of the church has original jurisdiction of Sealing powers. **—Temple Minute Book, St. George, Aug. 31, 1904**

As you are aware, until within a few years ago, the custom prevailed in Canada, Arizona and Mexico for our young people residing in those countries to marry for time only on account of the inconvenience and expense of attending a journey to a temple, and that in order to save this great expense, and to encourage marriages, among our young people, President Woodruff and President Snow, each in his time, authorized some of the Apostles, and perhaps others, to perform sealings for time and eternity in behalf of young couples of those places, and that this authority has been exerci[s]ed quite freely to the present time.

The council of the First Presidency and Apostles have now deemed it expedient and wise to withdraw the authority from those brethren, leaving it so[le]y in the hands of him who holds the keys thereof, and a resolution to this effect has been unanimously passed by the council.

We write you, in connection with all the other members of the Council not present when this action was taken, that you may be informed of the same, and with the request that you will, on receipt of this letter, strictly govern yourselv[es] accordingly.

We may say also in this connection that there is not [an] objection whatever to you performing the common marriage ceremony in behalf of any who may desire you to serve them in this respect; but in doing so all such couples should be given to understand that their marriage is simply a legal marriage for time only, performed under the laws of the land, and they should be urged to look forward to the time when the way shall be opened for them to come to a temple to be properly sealed and to have their children also sealed to them. **—Joseph F. Smith, John R. Winder, and Anthon H. Lund to John W. Taylor,[16] Oct. 22, 1904**

Referring to yours of the 1st inst., recommending Sister Harri[e]t B. Rowberry for [a] second anointing, we would say that a woman cannot receive those blessings except in connection with her husband: and a man so indifferent to the ordinances of the House of the Lord as to neglect doing his own temple work in his lifetime, although, as you say, he might have done so had he been so inclined, can scarcely be considered worthy of [a] second anointing and we do not see how you can consistently recommend him to receive those blessings.

For these reasons we have withheld your endorsement from the recommend sent by you in favor of Sister Rowberry. **—Joseph F. Smith, John R. Winder, and Anthon H. Lund to Thomas R. Bassett, Nov. 4, 1904**

---

16. John Whittaker Taylor (1858-1916) was ordained a member of the Quorum of the Twelve in 1884 and resigned in 1905 over his continued performance of plural marriages. He was excommunicated in 1911.

Pres[ident] Cannon: Stated, when the work here started [in 1877] there were no written parts. President [Brigham] Young asked him to take the part of preacher, and he, [the] speaker [Cannon], made a lengthy speech. Pres[ident] Young said, "You would not do for a sectarian preacher, you preach Mormonism." He told me to preach of a "Hell without a bottom[,]" "A topless throne," "A God without body, parts and passions, etc. etc.. **—David H. Cannon, Temple Minute Book, St. George, Dec. 22, 1904**

....

INSTRUCTIONS CONCERNING TEMPLE ORDINANCE WORK

At least one year should be allowed to elapse after death of individuals before Temple ordinances are performed in their behalf, unless it is known the deceased persons were faithful members of the Church, or that they were prepared to obey the Gospel before their death.

Individuals who were members of the Church, at time of death, do not need to have the ordinance of baptism performed in their behalf, unless they had become unworthy of membership. …

A living woman cannot receive endowments while her husband is alive, if the husband has not been endowed. …

Baptisms, or other ordinances, must not be performed in behalf of any individual whose death is not positively known, except one hundred years, at least, have elapsed from date of birth. When there is no evidence of the dead having attained a sufficient age in life, (fourteen years or over), ENDOWMENTS should not be performed in behalf of such persons until after the evidence is obtained.

The ordinance of endowment must not be repeated in behalf of any individual who has once been endowed, living or dead. …

The dead who have been endowed can only be represented in any vicarious work by those who have themselves been endowed. A living person cannot be represented by proxy in any Temple ordinances.

When baptisms for the dead have been attended to, the other ordinances to which the individuals are eligible should be performed without delay. Husband and wife, dead, should be sealed on same day they are endowed, if possible.

Those who do ordinance work have not the right to make matches between people who are deceased, except in cases of persons who were married in life. In all other instances the President of the Temple must be consulted. Persons who committed murder or suicide, or who apostatized or were excommunicated from the Church, cannot be officiated for except by special permission of the President of the Temple. He should be appealed to in all matters involving doubt or complications.

Before children are sealed to parents or adopted, all the other ordinances to which they are eligible should first be attended to. All the members of a family should be sealed to their parents at the same time, if possible. If the sealing is to another person than the father or mother, that fact must be stated.

Children under eight years of age do not need to have any Temple ordinances performed in their behalf, other than being sealed to parents if they were not born in the Covenant. Those eight years of age must be baptized, and dead children, who attained over fourteen years of age in life, should be endowed before being sealed to parents. No persons should have the ordinance of Sealing of Children performed for those who are not of their own lineage.

Those who do Temple work, or get it done, should be careful to designate their proper relationship to each one of the dead. A clear distinction should be made between blood kindred and those to whom they are married; the latter whom are known as relatives in law, thus a man is nephew-in-law to his uncle's wife, cousin-in-law to his cousin's wife, etc. If the dead are known to be blood relations, but the degree of relationship cannot be stated, the word RELATIVE is to be given. When there is no family connection, the word FRIEND should be used. The relatives, or friends[,] of a wife should be listed separately from those of her husband, and the work for her kindred should be at the instance of her brother, if he is a member of the Church, or of her eldest son.

In the performance of work for the dead, the right of heirship (blood relationship) should be sacredly regarded. When practicable, relatives should represent the dead. The name of the individual at whose instance (by whose authorization or permission) the work is done, and his or her relationship to each of the dead is required for [the] record, if the relationship is known. As a rule, the eldest living MALE representative of the family, who is a member of the Church, is the recognized heir. Any individuals who are eligible may act as proxies for the dead but, unless the proxy is the heir, their relationship to the dead, if any, is not to be entered.

It is advised that individuals having Temple ordinances performed should limit that work to persons bearing the SURNAMES of their parents and grandparents, and who resided in localities where those ancestors lived; that provides four family lines. To include other lines than those involves the probability of repeating Temple ordinances that individuals representing other families may have a better right to have performed. Every possible precaution should be taken to prevent such undesirable repetition. Temple work may be done for dead individuals who were married to your blood relations, but the family lines of such relatives-in-law must not be included in that work. …

The Saints who enter the sacred building should be properly prepared. Their bodies should be scrupulously clean. Those who are to be baptized, or officiate in endowments, should each bring a towel for personal use. Shoes worn out of doors should be removed from the feet, in the Temple Annex, and slippers substituted therefor. Males should be ordained Elders before they come to the Temple to receive their own endowments.

The Saints who attend to baptisms for the dead should be amply dressed in white before entering the font. All participants in the ordinance of sealing children should also be dressed in white. Males over 21 or females over 18 years of age, are not permitted to witness or take part in any Temple ordinances, except baptism for the dead, until they have received their own endowments.

Each individual should be provided with the endowment clothing they need. The garments must be white, and of the approved pattern; they must not be altered or mutilated, and are to be worn as intended, down to the wrist and ankles, and around the neck. These requirements are imperative; admission to the Temple will be refused to those who do not comply therewith.

The living who receive their own endowments are required to state their names in full, date and place of birth, date of baptism, and names of parents. Couples who come to the Temple to be married (sealed), must bring Licenses issued by County Clerks of this State; if this is not complied with the ceremony will not be performed. Those who have been legally married before do not require such licenses. Marriages of first cousins are prohibited by state law. Personal permission, or authorization by legal affidavit, of parent or guardian is required by County Clerks before issuing a license for marriage of a man under 21 or a woman under 18 years of age. Marriages can not be performed in the Temple unless the individuals are endowed. Husbands and wives must be sealed before their children can be sealed to them.

Individuals, or families, who cannot conveniently attend personally to the performance of Temple work in behalf of their dead kindred, or friends, can make arrangements to have such work done at their instance. There is no charge made by the Temple authorities for performance of the ordinances, but, when proxies have to be obtained to act in endowments for the dead, which occupies the time of an entire session in Temple work, it is customary to pay such proxies a small sum, to partly remunerate them for personal expenses; usually a man receives 75 cents, and a woman 50 cents, for such service.[17]

Persons who desire to perform Temple ordinances in behalf of the dead, but have not names of their own kindred, or friends, for that purpose, can be provided with names from lists that are on file in the Temple Recorder's office.

The Saints residing in Missions of the Church, who desire to have Temple ordinances performed in behalf of their dead kindred, can have arrangements made therefor by applying to their respective Mission Presidents. Those who reside in Stakes of Zion are advised to have their Temple work performed in the Temple that is nearest the locality where they reside. …

The Temple is open on all working days at 7:30 a.m., and all ought to be in the building not later than 8:30. Monday is devoted to taking the record[s] of Baptisms for the dead, which are performed on Tuesday. Baptismal records are not taken after eleven o'clock Mondays. The higher ordinances are attended to on Wednesdays, Thursdays, and Fridays; the record of this work is taken between the hours of 7:30 and 9:00 a.m. on the day it is performed. The earlier the Saints come to [turn] in record[s] the better. Children who are to be sealed to parents should not be brought to the Temple before 12 m. [noon]

A second company, taking endowments for the dead only, is received in the Temple at 12 m. on Wednesdays, Thursdays, and Fridays. The morning company includes all who are to receive their own endowments, or who have sealings to perform, and those who reside outside of Salt Lake City.

17. Payment for proxies was financed through donations. The intent was to help poor members spend more time in the temple, while assisting those who were too busy to attend.

All who enter the Temple must patiently observe good order and proper decorum; loud and irrelevant conversation should be avoided.

ALL WHO COME TO THE TEMPLE TO PERFORM ORDINANCE WORK ARE EXPECTED TO MAKE DONATIONS ACCORDING TO THEIR CIRCUMSTANCES, TO AID IN MEETING NECESSARY EXPENSE, BUT THE POOR WHO HAVE NOTHING TO GIVE ARE EQUALLY WELCOME.

Recommends for the privilege to work in the House of the Lord must be renewed every six months. Each individual needs a recommend, including children over eight years of age. **—Joseph F. Smith, ca. 1905; emphasis in original**[18]

It affords us much pleasure to hand you herewith a recommend for yourself and wife to the Manti Temple to receive your Second Anointing.

We feel that your devotion and service to the Church merits this special favor, and we are sure that you will appreciate it. However, should there be any reason why you cannot avail yourself of this blessing, kindly return the recommend to me.

You may visit the Temple for this purpose at any time, but it would not be well to delay it very long.

You will, of course, understand that this should not be made a matter of conversation. **—Lewis Anderson to Lars M. C. Christensen, Jan. 10, 1905, copy in Bueger Papers**

Pres[iden]t [David H.] Cannon said we should seek to do our own work for our immediate relatives when we are able so to do. If we engage proxies, let them labor for those not so closely related to us. Our relatives in the other world will ask, why <u>we</u> did not [do] the work for them; by this we shall certainly be confronted. It is a fact that

18. These instructions would be re-issued five years later under the signature of Logan temple president William H. Budge, with small changes. For instance, the words "or adoptions" would be added to "sealing of children." Some clerical requirements would be added in 1910 to assure that an individual's proxy ordinances were performed in the right order and that an heir was given first chance to perform them. Some instructions would be removed, such as the amount proxies were paid by individuals who did not have time to attend the temple, with directions to simply consult the temple recorder about making such arrangements. The hours of operation would be shortened by a half hour, the doors opening at 8:00 instead of 7:30 a.m.

while we represent the dead, they have, at times, manifested themselves[,] to his knowledge, in this temple. **—Temple Minute Book, St. George, Jan. 25, 1905**

There is a rule in the temple forbidding girls over 18 years entering that building unless they have either had their endowments or are going there for that purpose, and this rule is being strictly adhered to. But in the case of Sister Christy Ellingson, we thought, under the circumstances, we would make her an exception to the rule. You may therefore issue a recommend in her favor stating thereon the nature of the work to be done by her, namely, to be baptized for her health.[19] **—Joseph F. Smith, John R. Winder, and Anthon H. Lund to Andrew Fjeld, June 6, 1905**

Second blessings [anointings] are intended for those only who have borne the heat and burden of the day, and endured faithful to the end: and, as a general thing, they are administered only to people who have gathered with the body of the Church. And in recommending such people it is expected that their worthiness is personally known to the Stake President who recommends them. The case referred to in yours of the 12th inst. cannot for a moment be considered as eligible for these higher blessings. **—Joseph F. Smith, John R. Winder, and Anthon H. Lund to Stephen L. Chipman, June 16, 1905**

During the life of President Wilford Woodruff, Bro[ther] Isaiah Cox of St. George died, and his wives, not feeling satisfied with the course their husband had taken, represented their case to the then First Presidency, and permission was given them to be released from their husband, and acting upon this permission the sealings were cancelled.

About 2 or 3 weeks ago Sister Martha Cox called upon us in behalf of herself and the other two wives, Henryeta and Elizabeth in relation to their present condition; and after du[ly] considering the matter, and at the same time paying due respect to the personal feelings of these sisters we suggested the advisibility of their being sealed to the Prophet Joseph Smith or some other one of our leading men, deceased, with

19. This recommend was issued after health baptisms had begun to fade in importance. According to D. Michael Quinn, the majority of such baptisms, 22,403 in all, were performed in LDS temples "from 1877 through 1893" (D. Michael Quinn, *The Mormon Heirarchy: Origins of Power* [Salt Lake City: Signature Books/ Smith Research Associates, 1994], 633).

the understanding that in the hereafter a proper and righteous disposition should be made of their case. Sister Martha conveyed our mind in writing to sisters Henryetta and Elizabeth, all of whom have since elected to be sealed, with the understanding expressed, to the Prophet Joseph Smith, and you are hereby authorized therefore to perform the sealings accordingly. **—Joseph F. Smith, John R. Winder, and Anthon H. Lund to David H. Cannon, Aug. 22, 1905**

Recommends to the temple should not be given by Bishops except they and their Counselors know that he is a worthy man. Suicides or murders should not receive temple ordinances.[20] **—Anthony W. Ivins diary, quoting Joseph F. Smith, Oct. 9, 1905, Utah State Historical Society**

Pres[ident] [David H.] Cannon remarked that in the part taken by Peter, James and John[,] [temple workers] may prompt [participants at the veil] in anything [they may have] left out[,] but when they return and report their labors to Jehovah, neither Jehovah [n]or Eloheim should prompt them but, if prompting or correction is necessary anywhere at any time, the president of the temple may do so. **—Temple Minute Book, St. George, Nov. 28, 1905**

....

Your letter of the 21st of November last I suppose came duly to him [Joseph F. Smith], but was mislaid and only opened a few days ago. In it you state that a young woman of the London conference, who had returned from here on account of ill health after having received her endowments, was not likely to live long, and in the event of her death you desire to know what ought to be done about dressing her body in temple clothing, that is, whether she might order a temple suit from this city and keep it on hand to be used in case of her death, and whether or not her sister, who had not received her own endowments, might be allowed to be instructed how to cloth[e] the body.

After conferring with Presidents [Joseph F.] Smith and [Anthon H.] Lund in regard to this matter, we concluded that it would not be a wise thing for this sister to keep on hand [her] suited temple clothing as she might not pass away, and in that event the clothing might be

20. According to the document labeled "Instructions concerning Temple Ordinance Work" above, only the Church president could authorize ordinances for murderers or suicide victims.

subjected to the view of people not entitled to look upon it; and for this reason we concluded to say to you that the services of the wife of the president of the mission might be utilized in making the suit and clothing the body. **—John R. Winder to Heber J. Grant, Mar. 15, 1906**

We entered into covenants with the Lord that we will keep ourselves pure and unspotted from the world. We have agreed before God, angels and witnesses in sacred places, that we will not commit adultery, will not lie, that we will not steal or bear false witness against our neighbor, or take advantage of the weak, that we will help and sustain our fellow men in the right, and take such a course as will prove most effectual in helping the weak to overcome their weaknesses and bring themselves into subjection to the requirements of heaven. We cannot neglect, slight, or depart from the spirit, meaning, intent and purpose, of these covenants and agreements, that we have entered into with our Father in heaven, without shearing ourselves of our glory, strength, right and title to his blessings, and to the gifts and manifestations of his Spirit.

The Lord has given unto us garments of the holy priesthood, and you know what that means. And yet there are those of us who mutilate them, in order that we may follow the foolish, vain and (permit me to say) indecent practices of the world. In order that such people may imitate the fashions, they will not hesitate to mutilate that which should be held by them [to be] the most sacred of all things in the world, next to their own virtue, next to their own purity of life. They should hold these things that God has given unto them sacred, unchanged and unaltered from the very pattern in which God gave them. Let us have the moral courage to stand against the opinions of fashion, and especially where fashion compels us to break a covenant and so commit a grievous sin. **—Joseph F. Smith, "Fashion and the Violation of Covenants and Duty," *Improvement Era,* Aug. 1906, 813-14**

Pres[ident] [David H.] Cannon ... remarked, it was designed to have all [officiators] stick to the [scripted] text and all unwritten parts to be given [acted out] exactly alike in all the temples. He wished there would be no corrections made in the wording by any one, except by those accompanying them in the ceremonies as Eloheim may prompt Jehovah and vice versa, then only in very important errors and in a manner not to give offense or that exception may be taken. **—Temple Minute Book, St. George, Oct. 15, 1906**

We herewith submit answers to the questions contained in yours of the 14th inst.

Question: Where we grant a brother and sister the privilege of second blessings, and they desire the same blessings in behalf of their deceased parents who were true and faithful members of the Church while they lived, shall we grant their request?

Answer: Yes, provided they can be properly recommended.

Question: Where the husband is dead and his widow living, is it alright for her to receive these blessings and have someone who has received them to stand for him, provided of course he was a worthy man?

Answer: Yes.

Question: A brother who was recommended for this purpose a year or two ago asked permission to receive this ordinance in behalf of his son, a worthy young man who had died. Would you approve of this request being granted?

Answer: Not at present.

Question: If the good record of a man is broken by his falling into transgression, say adultery or fornication, and he repents and makes restitution as far as he can do so, and has received forgiveness, can he afterwards, by living a faithful and good life, be entitled to receive these higher ordinances?

Answer: Every such case should stand on its own merits. In some instances it may be highly proper to recommend for second anointings, in others improper. For instance, a man who commits adultery after receiving his endowments should not be recommended to receive second blessings. Let the cases of all such men be considered and determined by the authority on the other side of the veil. But where a man commits adultery before joining the Church or even after baptism but before receiving his endowments his condition is different, and yourself and counselors must be the judges as to his worthiness to receive these blessings.

Question: We have not recommended anyone, only in exceptional cases, who have not reached the age of 50. Is that age limit alright?

Answer: If a man 50 years of age has been faithful he may be recommended for higher blessings. **—Joseph F. Smith, John R. Winder, and Anthon H. Lund to Christian N. Lund and counselors, Nov. 21, 1906**

....

Please present our complements to Brother [John D. T.] McAllister and say to him that it is not customary for wom[e]n to be anointed to men, to whom they may have been sealed after death, but with whom they had not lived in their lifetime as husband and wife in the marriage relation. Both of you will at once perceive the consistency and wisdom of this when you call to mind the fact that the second anointing consists of positive blessings bestowed only upon people who are known, and who can be recommended, for their long and steadfast faithfulness in the Church. And indeed, so particular have the Presidencies been at administering second anointings, that they drew the line between faithful members of the Church who died without gathering with the Church, and faithful members who gathered with the body of the Church and remained faithful afterwards, leaving the faithful people who have died in a scattered condition to be dealt with by the authority on the other side of the veil. But the main thought intended to be conveyed by us in this particular case is that the parties receiving the blessings must not only be known for their fidelity and faithfulness, but they must be, or have been, husband and wife as well, or one flesh, to use the scriptural expression. **—Joseph F. Smith, John R. Winder, and Anthon H. Lund to Lewis Anderson, Mar. 14, 1907**

Some years ago the Presidents of the various foreign and home missions were instructed to hunt up the names of faithful saints who have died in their native lands without children or blood kin in the Church to represent them in Zion and do the temple work in their behalf, together with the genealogies of all such people as fully as they could be obtained; and to place their names and genealogies on a record specially provided for the purpose, which record should be kept for use and reference in the office of the mission. And they were also instructed to send transcripts of such records to our office from time to time so that we might refer the same to one of the temples least engaged, to perform the work, with the understanding that a report be made to the Mission President after such temple work shall have been done, so that they may make the necessary entries of explanation in the mission records going to show when and by whom the temple ordinances were performed in behalf of the deceased people acted for.

Now, dear brethren and sisters, we feel that this instruction applies to you in your far-off vast India land, as some of you may never have the privilege of gathering to Zion, and in that event we feel in our hearts that you and your dead should have the blessings of the House of the Lord conferred upon you, and in the economy of your Heavenly Father the plan prepared will provide for the worthy saints who are and may be denied the privilege of gathering with the body of the Church.

We send you herewith enclosed a blank form as a guide for the preparation and making of the record referred to, and after the record shall have been made it must be understood that it shall become the property of the Karachi Branch, or in the event of your Branch growing into a mission comprising other Branches of the Church, in that event it shall become the property of the Mission, to be carefully and sacredly kept by the President thereof as such. **—Joseph F. Smith, John R. Winder, and Anthon H. Lund to Robert Marshall,[21] president of the Karachi Branch, India,[22] Mar. 18, 1907**

You should now take pains to fix the right name firmly in your mind, and having done so the memory of it should be sacredly kept locked up in your own heart. The name under which, you say, you acted by mistake served the purpose for which it was used merely as a password and inasmuch as your intent was honest and sincere the Lord will accept of what you have done as though no mistake had been made. **—Joseph F. Smith, John R. Winder, and Anthon H. Lund to Joseph G. Allred, Mar. 29, 1907**

Inasmuch as you can recommend Bro[ther] Robert Henderson and wife, deceased, to receive their second blessings, it will be in order for you to do this. And in fact, this instruction applies to any other faithful members of the Church of your Stake whom you can recommend as worthy to receive these blessings but who passed away without them.

In the case of Bro[ther] and Sister Henderson, Sister Peters can of-

21. Robert Marshall (1827-1912) was born in Bombay and baptized in Karachi (now Pakistan) in 1903.

22. The first missionaries in Karachi, A. Milton Musser and Truman Leonard, built a chapel there in 1855. The branch vacillated in membership between a high in 1903 when John H. Cooper baptized thirteen people to 1908 when there were only four members. See R. Lanier Britsch, *From the East: The History of the Latter-day Saints in Asia, 1851-1996* (Salt Lake City: Deseret Book, 1998), 8-30; Britsch, *Nothing More Heroic: The Compelling Story of the First Latter-day Saint Missionaries in India* (Salt Lake City: Deseret Book, 1999).

ficiate for Sister Henderson (her mother), and she and the family can agree among themselves as to who shall stand proxy for Bro. Henderson. **—Joseph F. Smith, John R. Winder, and Anthon H. Lund to Oleen N. Stohl, Apr. 13, 1907**

No member of the Church, male or female, who, after leaving off his or her garments, would be justified in putting them on again without consent of the proper authority, and that authority is the First Presidency of the Church; and this consent would, as a general thing, involve the renewal of covenants by baptism. Where sisters cast off their garments, and give themselves in marriage to non-members of the Church, they must not, under any circumstances, be permitted to wear their garments again while living in such marriage relationship, and therefore all such sisters must be content to continue to live without wearing the garment of the holy priesthood during the existence of their present marital relationships. This practice obtains in the stakes of Zion and must be strictly adhered to in the missions. **—Joseph F. Smith, John R. Winder, and Anthon H. Lund to Nephi Pratt, Apr. 20, 1907**

[T]emple recommends should be issued to none excepting on the grounds of known worthiness, and it is understood generally by our bishops that new comers cannot establish a knowledge of their worthiness to the satisfaction of their bishops under an acquaintance of about two years. **—George F. Gibbs to Serge F. Ballif,[23] Oct. 31, 1907**

In view of the circumstances narrated in yours of the 2nd inst., we suggest that you issue a temple recommend in favor of sister Aaron Harrop and children who wishes to be sealed to her deceased husband and have their children sealed to them.

When Sister Harrop goes through the temple to have the necessary work done for her husband, it will be in order for her to explain that her husband had not been ordained to the Melchizedek Priesthood, and therefore he should be ordained an elder by proxy before receiving endowments in his behalf. And this letter when presented at the temple with her own recommend, will be authority for permitting this work to be done. **—Joseph F. Smith, John R. Winder, and Anthon H. Lund to George A. Browning, Dec. 12, 1907**

23. Serge Frederick Balliff (1859-1942) was president of the Cache Stake, as well as, from 1920 to 1923, president of the Swiss-German Mission.

....

INSTRUCTIONS TO THE SAINTS WHO ARE PRIVILEGED TO ENTER THE SALT LAKE TEMPLE

At least one year should be allowed to elapse after the death of individuals before Temple ordinances are performed in their behalf, unless it is known the deceased were prepared to obey the Gospel before their death. ...

Baptisms, or other ordinances, must not be performed in behalf of any individual whose death is not positively known, except one hundred years has elapsed from date of birth.

When there is no evidence of the dead having reached a sufficient age[,] endowments should not be performed in behalf of such persons. ...

The dead who have been endowed can only be represented in any vicarious work by those who have themselves been endowed. A living person cannot be represented by proxy.

Before children are sealed to parents or adopted, all the other ordinances to which they are eligible should first be attended to. All the members of a family should be sealed to their parents at the same time, if possible. If the sealing is to another person than the father or mother, that fact must be stated.

No person should have the ordinances of Sealing to Parents, or Adoptions, performed for those who are not of their own lineage.

Those who do Temple work, or get it done, should be careful to designate their proper relationship to each one of the dead. A clear distinction should be made between blood kindred and those to whom they are married; the latter are known as relatives in law, thus, a man is nephew in law to his uncle's wife, cousin in law to his cousin's wife, etc. If the dead are known to be blood relations, but the degree of relationship cannot be stated, the word *Relative* is to be given. When there is no family connection the word *Friend* should be used. The relatives, or friends, of a wife should be listed separately from those of her husband, and the work for her kindred should be at the instance of her eldest brother, if he is a member of the Church, or of her eldest son. ...

The Saints who enter the sacred building should be properly prepared. Their bodies should be scrupulously clean, and those who feel it necessary to renew their covenants before beginning their work ought to attend to this previous to entering the Temple, it being in the nature of a preparation.[24] Males should be ordained Elders before they come to the Temple to receive endowments.

The Saints who attend to baptisms for the dead, should be amply dressed in white before entering the font. All participants in the ordinance of sealing children should also be dressed in white. Males over 21 or females over 18 years of age, are not permitted to witness or take part in any Temple ordinances until they have received their own endowments. ...

Couples who come to the Temple to be married (sealed), must bring Licenses issued by County Clerks of this State. When this is not complied with the ceremony will not be performed. Those who have been legally married before do not require such licenses. Husbands and wives must be sealed before their children can be sealed to them.

In the performance of work for the dead, the right of heirship (blood relationship) should be sacredly regarded. When practicable, relatives should represent the dead. When an heir empowers another person to do the work in his or her stead, he or she should give the acting proxy a written authorization to that effect.[25] The name of the individual at whose instance the work is done, and his, or her, relationship to each of the dead is required for [the] record. As a rule, heirship is determined by the patriarchal order,[26] the eldest son.

Individuals, or families, who cannot conveniently attend personally to the performance of Temple work in behalf of their dead kindred, or friends, can make arrangements to have such work done at their instance. The necessary instructions regarding this matter will be imparted on application to the Recorder.[27]

24. This document follows, almost verbatim, the Instructions concerning Temple Ordinance Work, ca. 1905, both of which appeared under the signature of Joseph F. Smith. The text here is streamlined so that general principles are stated without all of the qualifiers that graced the original version. In some cases, a new provision has been added. Notice, for instance, that re-baptism is not now a prerequisite and seems to be discouraged, although not yet forbidden.

25. This requirement is new—or newly stated—compared to the 1905 list of guidelines.

26. The term "patriarchal order" is new to this version.

27. Notice that in the earlier version, the price for hiring someone—for those who were too busy to attend the temple—was given, whereas here the Church member is directed to make unspecified arrangements with the temple recorder.

When baptisms have been attended to, the other ordinances to which the individuals are eligible should be performed without delay. ...

Those who do ordinance work have not the right to make matches between people who are deceased, except in cases of persons who were married in life. In all other instances the President of the Temple must be consulted. Persons who committed murder or suicide, or who apostatized or were excommunicated from the Church, cannot be officiated for except by special permission of the President of the Temple. He should be appealed to in *all* matters involving doubt or complications.

The Temple is open on all working days at 7:30 a.m., and all ought to be in the building not later than 8:30. Monday is devoted to taking the record of Baptisms for the dead, which are performed on Tuesday. Baptismal records are not taken after eleven o'clock Mondays.

The higher ordinances are attended to on Wednesdays, Thursdays, and Fridays. The record of this work is taken between the hours of 7:30 and 9:00 a.m. of the day it is performed. The earlier the Saints come to give in [their] record[s] the better.

All who enter the Temple must observe good order and proper decorum; loud and irrelevant conversation should be avoided.

All who come to the Temple to perform ordinance work are expected to make donations according to their circumstances, to aid in meeting necessary expense, but the poor who have nothing to give are equally welcome.

Recommends for the privilege to work in the House of the Lord must be renewed every six months. Each individual needs a recommend, including children over eight years of age. **—Joseph F. Smith, signed statement, ca. 1908; emphasis in original**

Please find enclosed recommends for second blessings endorsed by President [Joseph F.] Smith.

The First Presidency direct me to call your attention to the printed form used by you in this instance recommending for second blessings, and would thank you to let them know if this particular form was prepared by yourself, or purchased by you of the printer already prepared? Their reason for eliciting this information is this, the form is unauthorized, and not in accordance with their mind in recommending for the second anointing. In other words the word "second" should not be in the recommend at all, and you are therefore requested to discard this particular form, and in fact to destroy it.

Instructions have been given so many times in regard to this matter, that it has been taken for granted that every Stake President is fully informed in relation to it. The way to do it is to use the common form of temple recommend, and write a letter in connection with it explaining who the people are [who are] thus recommended, and giving, as near as you can, their ages and a brief account of their lives so that the presidency may by this means gather some idea of their suitableness and worthiness to receive the endorsement of the President. And it is taken for granted that you take pains to become personally acquainted with everybody recommended by you for second blessings, and you are of course at liberty to adopt every necessary means to acquire the information; and strict privacy should be enjoined by you and all so recommended by you. **—George F. Gibbs to Alma Merrill, Jan. 14, 1908**

People who are not members of the Church during their lifetime are not eligible to receive second blessings [anointings]. They should not only have been members of the Church, but their faithfulness and worthiness to receive these blessings should be unquestioned, and besides the line has been drawn in favor of those who have either gathered with the body of the Church or died on their way to the gathering place, all others are left to be dealt with by the authority on the other side of the veil. ...

The case of the grandfather of Sister Owens of Willard City, with his wife who died before the Church was organized, comes within the rule, and it will be for you to therefore to [sic] satisfy yourself from the best evidence obtainable as to his worthiness and govern yourself accordingly. If he should be found worthy[,] his wife, in this instance, would be an exception to the rule. **—Joseph F. Smith, John R. Winder, and Anthon H. Lund to Oleen N. Stohl, May 22, 1908**

We have just returned to President [Oleen N.] Stohl two temple recommends, given by him for second blessings in behalf of two women, one of whom was not a member of the Church, the other was but she died also in a foreign land without having gathered with the body of the Church. A brother, living in Box Elder Stake, who had recently been doing work in the Logan Temple in behalf of the women referred to, was told, while there[,] that it was in order now for him to have those women anointed to him, and he therefore procured recommends from his Stake President to have this work done for them.

We have just informed President Stohl that a rule of the temple forbids deceased women who were not members of the Church prior to their demise, or who did not gather with the body of the Church, being anointed to men, therefore, we could not endorse the recommends of the sisters referred to.

We write this for your information: also to say that it is not becoming in brethren to suggest that second blessings be given to anybody, living or dead, unless they are delegated by the President of the Church to act in this capacity, and it would be well therefore for you to so inform your Temple workers. **—Joseph F. Smith, John R. Winder, and Anthon H. Lund to William H. Budge, May 22, 1908**

We note by yours of the 19th inst. that Bishop William M. Dye had requested you to sign a recommend for second blessings in favor of Sister Emma Edwards, she having asked the Bishop for such a recommend. We also note that you had signed the recommend without knowing personally as to whether or not she is a suitable woman to receive the second anointing.

Stake Presidents generally have been instructed to the effect that they alone are held responsible by us for recommends issued by them for second blessings. They have also been instructed that it is not in order for Bishops to recommend for the second anointing, neither is it in order for people to ask that they be recommended to receive those blessings; that it is for the Stake President to become personally acquainted with the members of his stake who may be recommended by him to receive the higher blessings. He may of course confer with his counselors, also with his bishops with a view to satisfying himself as to the suitableness and worthiness of people to be recommended by him, but even then he should do all he possibly can to satisfy himself personally before acting in this matter. **—Joseph F. Smith, John R. Winder, and Anthon H. Lund to James Duckworth, July 23, 1908**

You have recommended Sister Ruth Reese to receive second blessings, and the recommend is signed by her Bishop and yourself.

In the first place it is not usual to issue a recommend of this character to a woman alone, and therefore it will be proper for you to make the necessary explanations.

And in the second place it is not in order for Bishops to sign such recommends, for the reason that you alone are responsible for the worthiness of the parties recommended by you.

It is taken for granted that you yourself have had your second blessings. If not[,] you had better not sign any more such recommends until you have seen President [Joseph F.] Smith. **—George F. Gibbs to John F. Tolton, Sept. 20, 1908**

....

This is in answer to yours of the 14th inst., asking if the use of tobacco debarred a member of the Church, single or married, from the temple.

The rule of the Church on this question is that all who enter the temple should be observers of the Word of Wisdom. And the rule of the Church is also that all of its members should receive the revelation called the Word of Wisdom, and be guided by it in their lives.

But in this connection we may add by way of illustration that the fulness of the gospel has been restored to us, and it is our duty to preach it to the whole world; but because of this, it does not necessarily follow that all who receive it and yield obedience to its requirements by baptism afterwards live in strict accordance to its precepts. And so it is with reference to the Word of Wisdom among the members of the Church.

Where elderly people may be found to be more or less lacking in their observance of the Word of Wisdom, and the question of their worthiness to be recommended to the temple comes before you for consideration, it will be in order for you and the Stake Presidency to consider together all such cases, deciding each on its own merits, and showing appropriate leniency to elderly people, as there can be no rigid rule for each and every case. …

P.S. Our idea is that the cases to be referred to the Stake President for his and your consideration are those only that you yourselves cannot feel clear to act on. **—Joseph F. Smith, John R. Winder, and Anthon H. Lund to William H. Seegmiller and counselors, Jan. 26, 1909**

The general rule adopted by the First Presidency in regard to the second anointing, is in effect that those blessings should be confined to the faithful members of the Church who have gathered with the body of the Church, or who died on the way in an effort to do so. Inasmuch therefore as you shall be able to satisfy yourself through the testimony of such men as Elders E. W. and Ralph Smith that their father, who died in Australia, where he is said to have gone for the purpose of making money to immigrate himself and family to Zion, … died in a state of worthiness. You may consider yourself at liberty to recommend him and his wife for second blessings. **—Joseph F. Smith, John R. Winder, and Anthon H. Lund to Isaac Smith, Feb. 16, 1909**

Please find enclosed [the] temple recommend [in] favor of William Greenwood, which you sent President [Joseph F.] Smith to be endorsed for second blessings.

You will perceive that Brother Greenwood's wife is not recommended. If he has a worthy wife she should also be recommended; if he is not a married man, it is not in order to recommend him for second blessings. **—George F. Gibbs to Franklin S. Bramwell, Feb. 25, 1909**

We regret to say that we could not possibly find time to give second blessings to the large number of brethren and sisters mentioned in yours of the 23rd inst., during the coming conference. The Logan Temple will re-open on the 12th of April, and it may be that Pres[iden]t [William H.] Budge will be able to accomodate your people within the conference date, and we suggest that you write him on the subject. …

P.S. There were no temple recommends enclosed in your letter. Of course you understand it to be in order that temple recommends should be issued to each man and his wife or wives, and sent here for the endorsement of the President before presenting them at the temple.

If you had consulted us beforehand we should have advised not giving recommends for second blessings to so many at the same time, as privacy [in] regard to this matter is strictly required, and this you should charge them with, if they all come at one time especially. **—John R. Winder and Anthon H. Lund to Don C. Walker and counselors, Mar. 24, 1909**

All of the children who are of age have [the] right to express their own individual choice as to whom they desire to be sealed, while those who have not yet attained to their majority should wait before expressing their choice. In fact in such an important matter as this it would be well for all the younger children to wait until their judgment becomes mature before deciding to leave their father. **—Joseph F. Smith and Anthon H. Lund to Don C. Walker and counselors, Mar. 29, 1910**

President [David H.] Cannon was very pleased with the privilege of greeting the saints this morning. Wished more were here. Spoke a few words about the garment. We are told the garment is a pattern of one given to Adam and Eve in the garden. If the sleeve is cut off it will not be the proper garment. Said, President [Brigham] Young once told a young woman that they could turn in the collar and roll up the sleeves but they must not cut them off.[28] President Cannon instructed the Ordinance Workers to clothe the people with the proper garments. Spoke of the responsibility of those taking names to see that the dead are properly endowed and of those taking [dramatic] parts to render them correctly and of those engaged in any manner in this work. **—Temple Minute Book, St. George, Dec. 7, 1910**

....

President [David H.] Cannon spoke concerning the new name: Said, it is not proper to give a New Name like the name already held; however, if such thing is done, it must not be changed for that is the name by which that person will be admitted into the presence of God. If the new name given is misunderstood and another name is used [by the initiate] in the endowment—the name assumed but not given, there is provision made to correct such error. **—Temple Minute Book, St. George, Jan. 24, 1911**

President [David H.] Cannon said, A new order has been issued concerning recommends. No recommend dated earlier than Aug. 1910 will be received here, and all [who] come to this Temple after 1 Jan. 1911 must have new recommends of the new kind. The Doorkeeper here is to place his name and date of its being received upon each recommend, which is only good for 6 months.

The Doorkeeper is responsible for the carrying out of this requirement and no one should feel offended when he strives to faithfully perform his [i]ncumb[e]nt duty, but all service here should be given patiently, kindly. **—Temple Minute Book, St. George, Feb. 10, 1911**

In answer to the first question we have no hesitance in saying that every member of the Church should endeavor to observe the Word of Wisdom as near as he and she can do so consistently; and inasmuch as

28. At the time, garments ran the entire length of the arm to the wrist and down the leg to the ankle.

a member does this and is otherwise worthy he should not be denied the blessings of the house of the Lord.

Answering the second question we will say that an adult male member of the Church who does not believe in the law of tithing is unworthy to bear the holy Melchizedek priesthood, and without that priesthood he is not qualified to enter the house of the Lord. A member of the Church who is an elder and a non-tithe-payer is not worthy [of] the fellowship of the quorum to which he belongs, and the quorum might consistently withdraw their fellowship from such a member. …

In this connection we perhaps ought to say that bishops can well afford to be lenient and merciful, especially to young men who may have been neglectful in obeying the law of tithing, who give promise of doing better and of keeping the law. **—Joseph F. Smith and Anthon H. Lund to Robert D. Young, Mar. 8, 1911**

President [Joseph F.] Smith requests you to not send more than one family represented by the enclosed recommends for second blessings to the temple in one week, this as a precaution against it being known one by the other that they are recommended for the higher blessings, as strict privacy should be observed in regard to this matter. **—George F. Gibbs to Robert D. Young, Oct. 16, 1911**

The custom has developed in some of the temples of selling consecrated oil, books and records, and of renting temple clothing, the object being to accommodate persons who come to do work in the House of the Lord. Trafficking in these commodities is hardly in keeping with the sacredness of the temple, and we would, therefore, like you to discontinue this practice after December 31, 1911.

In the meantime, arrange with the Bishops to sell consecrated oil and records and to rent temple clothing, all profits (if any) over and above expenses to be turned in as temple donations once a month.

In view of the sacredness of temple work the Latter-day Saints should be encouraged to prepare temple garments, the workmanship of their own hands, and every effort should be made to discourage the practice of renting such clothing. **—Joseph F. Smith and Anthon H. Lund to Temple Presidents, Oct. 30, 1911**

In the first place you should know that the second anointing is not intended for every male member of the Church, and goodness alone is not a sufficient recommendation to receive the higher blessings.

Recommends for the second anointing should only be given to men and women who have lived together as husband and wife, and who through long years of faithfulness are still found to be worthy before the Lord and their brethren. They should be men of good report, men whose faith has never been shaken, whose integrity to the Lord and his servants has been beyond question, men who have been valiant for the truth, men who have either defended the servants of the Lord or would do so at all hazards should circumstances require it at their hands. They should be men who have done what they could whether in preaching or working or otherwise helping their file leaders in the building up of Zion, and who are ever ready and willing to labor in the interests of Zion at home or abroad. And all those thus recommended must be in harmony with the First Presidency and general authorities of the Church, also those immediately presiding over them. And this spirit also must characterize their wives in order to make them eligible to be associated with their husbands in receiving these blessings.

… [I]t is not for you to take your bishops into your confidence in having them recommend brethren to you for these blessings, because they are in no wise responsible for such recommends. It is you as stake president, and you alone, who are held responsible … [A]ll brethren recommended by you should be instructed to regard this matter in the utmost privacy. … [N]either should [bishops] take the liberty of advising any to ask you to be likewise recommended, as it is not for any man to seek for these blessings, but for those worthy of them to be sought out.

You must be exceedingly careful in recommending for the second anointing, careful as to the character of the men recommended, also careful with a view to maintaining privacy, and in order to avoid attention being drawn to recommends of this character, we suggest that you do not recommend more than one couple at a time, and that not more than one couple from your stake come to the temple during any one week.

… Deceased men or women recommended by you must of course also be likewise worthy …

P.S. We take it for granted that you and your counselors have received higher blessings. **—Joseph F. Smith and Anthon H. Lund to William C. Partridge, Oct. 23, 1911**

President [David H.] Cannon read [a] letter received 6 November 1896 from the Presidency of the Church in regard to apparel to be worn in the temple by those being endowed. This does not apply, he said, to Prayer Circles of the Brethren. There must be no innovation of these things from the instructions herein given, except it come through the proper source. He also spoke in relation to taking our shoes from our feet before entering the temple. A habit is obtaining contrary to this and it is not right. He read a letter from [the] Presidency of the Church in regard to the same and said, none but aged or sick persons are exempt from obedience to this given rule; but who will be the judge? The Doorkeeper must be the judge. Speaker did not wish to assume the r[o]le of grumbler, but let us do as we should and rejoice in the contemplation and reception of blessings that are ours united to enjoy. **—Temple Minute Book, St. George, Dec. 7, 1911**

President [David H.] Cannon said, if the sisters find it necessary to wear shoes while going through endowments, they should put moccasins on over their shoes. This is the order of this temple and we are not controlled by Salt Lake Temple. … This temple has the original of these endowments which w[ere] given by President Brigham Young and we have not nor will we change anything thereof unless dictated by the President of the Church. **—Temple Minute Book, St. George, Dec. 14, 1911**

[S]econd blessings are not given to women who do not live with their husbands. That is, a deceased woman may be sealed to a man without having lived with him as his wife, but would not be entitled to second blessings. **—George F. Gibbs to Thomas B. Evans, Dec. 20, 1911**

....

If you have not already adopted the practice of calling attention to the following regulations, when you issue recommends to individuals going to the Temple, you will please do so hereafter, in every instance.

FIRST: The garments worn by those who receive endowments must be white, and of the approved pattern: they must not be altered or mutilated, and are to be worn as intended down to the wrist and ankles, and around the neck.

Please inform all to whom you issue recommends that these requirements are imperative, and that admission to the Temple will be refused to those who do not comply therewith. The Saints should know that the pattern of endowment garments was revealed from heaven, and that the blessings promised in connection with wearing them will not be realized if any unauthorized change is made in their form, or in the manner of wearing them.

SECOND: All who come to the Temple to perform ordinance work are expected to make donations according to their circumstances, to aid in meeting necessary expenses, but the poor who have nothing to give are equally welcome.

The rule has been a part of the printed instructions, since the commencement of work in the Salt Lake Temple, but is repeated here with the request that you will mention it to all to whom you issue recommends, because the aggregate amount received is very small. It may properly be suggested to a man, who is going to the Temple to be married, that the amount of his donation should approximate or be equal to what he would be required to pay if he had the ceremony performed elsewhere, if he could afford to donate that much.

The following important items are also submitted for your careful attention: …

Recommends should be issued only to those who are worthy and faithful. A sufficient time should elapse after baptism to prove worthiness. Children under eight years of age do not need recommends, when they accompany their parents or guardians. Recommends should not be given to persons afflicted with any kind of infectious disease, or with serious or offensive skin disease.[29]

Before being recommended to receive endowments, each individual should be informed concerning the purpose, and importance, of that sacred ordinance.

Living boys and girls as young as sixteen years of age may receive endowments if, in each case, the character and condition of the individual is such that the Bishop feels justified in issuing a recommend for that purpose.

Males over twenty-one years of age, and females over eighteen, are not permitted to take part in, or witness, Temple ordinances until they receive their own endowments, except that they may be baptized for the dead, [and] in that event the recommend must show that it is is-

29. This is no doubt because of the officiator's minor contact with the initiate's skin during the ritualistic washing and anointing.

sued for Baptisms only. If they are to receive endowments at the time they are to be sealed to parents, the fact that they are authorized to be endowed then must be stated on the recommend.

A living woman cannot receive endowments while her husband is alive, if the husband has not been endowed.

Men should be ordained to the Melchizedek Priesthood before they come to the Temple to receive endowments.

Recommends for the privilege to work in the House of the Lord must be renewed every six months. Each individual needs a recommend, including children over eight years of age.

Individuals who have been endowed, and afterwards have been excommunicated, and subsequently joined the Church again, should not be recommended to the Temple until former blessings have been sealed upon them by special permission of the President of the Church.

Robes, etc., may be hired at the Temple, but all are advised to provide themselves with their own, if they can do so conveniently. The sisters should not have long "trains" on the white dresses they wear in the Temple, nor decorate with colored ribbons or gaudy ornaments.

Each person who is to receive endowments should bring a towel for their own use. All should be perfectly clean in body and clothing, not offensive to others.

Small children who are to act only in the ordinance of sealing to parents, or adoptions, need not be brought to the Temple Annex before 12 m. [noon]; all other persons should be in the building not later than 8:30 a.m., for the first company, and not later than 1 p.m., for the second company. The second company is composed of those only who are taking endowments for the dead.

It should be clearly made known[,] to those who can receive recommends to be married in the Temple, that they should not have the marriage ceremony performed before coming to the Temple, unless there is some good and justifiable reason for doing so, such as having to delay an undesirable length of time before they could come, or having to travel alone, by team, to reach the Temple.

Bishops are not to issue recommends for second anointings; that is the province of Presidents of Stakes, under approval of the President of the Church, and the individuals selected must not be informed until after the issuance of such recommend. As a general rule, such recommends are issued only in behalf of those who have had endowments in their lifetime, and have been sealed and lived together faithfully as husband and wife, and who have been valiant in the defense of truth and active in all good works. **—Joseph F. Smith to ward bishops, ca. 1912; emphasis in original**

President [David H.] Cannon spoke concerning shoes worn while receiving endowments. He said, put your moccasins on over your shoes. This is the word from the Authorities. A sample of this was given by President [Brigham] Young; he wore his moccasins over his shoes when receiving endowments for [the] deceased and we should follow his example.

Baptisms cannot be administered by persons standing out of the water. Innovations must not creep in, in any manner of thing. [The] speaker said, "It is my business to see that right is maintained here no matter what is done elsewhere. If what is done is done right, they, the dead[,] and we can pass to our exaltations, otherwise not. **—Temple Minute Book, St. George, Jan. 10, 1912**

President [David H.] Cannon remarked that yesterday in the prayer circle held by the brethren a question arose as to the requirements made by the Doctrine and Covenants of the recorder at the baptismal font. I hold the right in this temple to decide that matter and President Joseph F. Smith has the right to reverse my conclusions on this or any other point whatever.

He [Cannon] read of Doctrine and Covenants, Sec[tion] 127, sixth verse and from [the] 128th Section regarding the duties of the Recorder at the baptismal font and said, The Lord has never given a revelation to his people that the terms thereof could not be carried out in the spirit thereof. The witnesses to the baptisms in this temple faced the east end of the font. The candidate for that ordinance is brought by the baptisor with his face toward the witnesses and is placed under the water eastward—the baptisor standing between the applicant and the Recorder [and] mak[ing] it impossible for the Recorder to see that the applicant is completely immersed. The Recorder however should distinctly call [out] in the hearing of the Administrator and see the person or proxie answering thereto. [He should] see that the person baptizing repeats the name without variation. The witnesses should be satisfied that the person is totally immersed; then in confirmation the name given should be distinctly heard by the Recorder and he records the baptism and confirmation of the said person[,] [and] the name of the person administering in each ordinance[,] the names of witnesses[,] and his own name as Recorder are attached. This[,] President Cannon said[,] is the plain duty of the Recorder and constitutes the eye and ear witness [...] at the Baptismal Font. **—Temple Minute Book, St. George, Jan. 19, 1912**

At a meeting of the First Presidency and Twelve held January 25th last, it was unanimously decided to ask each of the temples to keep a card index of the names of families for whom work is being done; also that a duplicate of each card be sent to the Genealogical Society of Utah that they, as a central office, may keep on file all information of this character for the use of those interested who are constantly making inquiry, and to aid the society in their work as well.

The proposed card index will also [serve] another good purpose, that of enabling the different temples to prevent in future the duplication of temple work, as each temple, by this means, will be kept posted as to the names of the families for which work is being done in other temples. **—Joseph F. Smith, Anthon H. Lund, and Charles W. Penrose to Lewis Anderson, Feb. 16, 1912**

Members of the Church who join secret societies after having been made acquainted with the attitude of the Church with respect to secret organizations bar themselves from the temple ... [T]hey also render themselves ineligible to hold presiding positions in the priesthood, and should not be used as Teachers of the people, for the simple reason that an unwritten rule of the Church forbids its members from teaching to others that which they themselves do not practice. **—Joseph F. Smith, Anthon H. Lund, and Charles W. Penrose to Robert D. Young and counselors, Feb. 17, 1912**

He [David H. Cannon] had been asked to explain the law of retribution: The law of retribution is: To pray the Father to avenge the blood of the prophets and righteous men that has been shed, etc. In the endowment house this was given [as a personal responsibility] but as persons went there only once, it was not so strongly impressed upon their minds; but in setting in order the [script for] endowments for the dead it was given as it is written in [the] 9th Chapter of Revelations[,] and in that language we importune our Father, not that we may, but that He, our Father, will avenge the blood of martyrs shed for the testimony of Jesus.[30] **—Temple Minute Book, St. George, Feb. 22, 1912**

No sealing can be done in behalf of children born under the covenant of the Priesthood where the parents of such children separate with just cause, that is, without either the father or the mother breaking the covenant through transgression as in the case of yourself and husband, but children, after they mature through age and understanding, may choose for themselves as between their father and mother. **—Joseph F. Smith, Anthon H. Lund, and Charles W. Penrose to Sarah Whitaker, Feb. 23, 1912**

We desire to inform you that the General Board of Relief Society has been instructed by us to take charge of the business of supplying temple clothing to all members of the Church coming to the temple from time to time in need of it, also for burial purposes; and that the Society has appointed a responsible committee to attend to this business who is now prepared to furnish suits or parts of suits at its headquarters in the Bishop's Building, 49 North Main Street, this city.

The committee referred to will take this matter up with the … President of the Relief Societies of your Stake, and impart to her all the information necessary in regard to this matter.

And we would thank you also to inform your Bishops of it, and at the same time request them to instruct all those coming to the temple from their respective wards to supply themselves with temple clothing before leaving home if they can do so conveniently, otherwise to call at the office of the Relief Society in the Bishop's Building where it may be purchased or rented.

On account of the sacredness of the character of our temple cloth-

30. The "oath of vengeance" had its origin in Nauvoo when the shock of the assassinations of Joseph and Hyrum Smith were still fresh. The oath was retained in the Endowment House and in the first four temples in Utah. It received national attention in the U.S. Senate committee hearings to seat Apostle Reed Smoot. "Negative publicity from the Smoot Hearings led to a de-emphasis of this oath in the temple endowment," wrote historian David John Buerger. When Salt Lake temple president George F. Richards headed a committee in the 1920s to revise the temple ceremony, the oath of vengeance was removed. See entry for Feb. 15, 1927; Buerger, *The Mysteries of Godliness: A History of Mormon Temple Worship* (San Francisco: Smith Research Associates, 1994), 133-36; Kathleen Flake, *The Politics of American Religious Identity: The Seating of Senator Reed Smoot, Mormon Apostle* (Chapel Hill: University of North Carolina Press, 2004).

ing we have felt for some time past that a safeguard ought to be thrown around it with a view to preventing it from being loosely handled or unnecessarily exposed, and it has occurred to us that the duty of handling the clothing may very properly be imposed upon and entrusted to our Relief Society, under supervision of the proper authority. **—Joseph F. Smith, Anthon H. Lund, and Charles W. Penrose to Nephi L. Morris,[31] June 4, 1912, in *MFP*, 4:274-75**

In recommending for second blessings, the purpose of the recommend should not be written [o]n the form ... nothing in fact should be written excepting the names. A letter of explanation should always accompany such recommends, in which the recommend for higher blessings should be made. **—Joseph F. Smith, Anthon H. Lund, and Charles W. Penrose to John F. Tolton, Aug. 24, 1912**

Please perform the sealing ordinance in behalf of Elder Hyrum Richards and his wife Agnes on their presenting to you their temple recommend. This may be done without disturbing the record of the former sealing of Sister Richards to William Findley, her deceased husband, by whom she had one child born under the covenant of the holy Priesthood. Under the circumstances attending this marriage, the children born to Brother Richards by his wife Agnes may be sealed to their parents (Bro[ther] Hyrum Richards and wife Agnes), but [in the instance of] Sister Richards' first child, born to her deceased husband, Brother Findley, having been born under the covenant, nothing of course need be done in her case. **—Joseph F. Smith, Anthon H. Lund, and Charles W. Penrose to William H. Budge, Nov. 23, 1912**

The Temple Endowment, as administered in modern temples, comprises instruction relating to the significance and sequence of past dispensations, and the importance of the present as the greatest and grandest era in human history. This course of instruction includes a recital of the most prominent events of the creative period, the condition of our first parents in the Garden of Eden, their disobedience and consequent expulsion from that blissful abode, their condition in the lone and dreary world when doomed to live by labor and sweat, the plan of redemption by which the great transgression may be atoned,

31. Nephi Lowell Morris (1870-1943) attended Brigham Young Academy and the University of Utah and eventually served as president of the Salt Lake Stake.

the period of the great apostasy, the restoration of the Gospel with all its ancient powers and privileges, the absolute and indispensable condition of personal purity and devotion to the right in present life, and a strict compliance with Gospel requirements. ...

The ordinances of the endowment embody certain obligations on the part of the individual, such as [a] covenant and promise to observe the law of strict virtue and chastity, to be charitable, benevolent, tolerant and pure; to devote both talent and material means to the spread of truth and the uplifting of the race; to maintain devotion to the cause of truth; and to seek in every way to contribute to the great preparation that the earth may be made ready to receive her King,—the Lord Jesus Christ. With the taking of each covenant and the assuming of each obligation a promised blessing is pronounced, contingent upon the faithful observance of the conditions.

No jot, iota, or tittle of the temple rites is otherwise than uplifting and sanctifying. In every detail the endowment ceremony contributes to covenants of morality of life, consecration of [the] person to high ideals, devotion to truth, patriotism to nation, and allegiance to God. The blessings of the House of the Lord are restricted to no privileged class; every member of the Church may have admission to the temple with the right to participate in the ordinances thereof, if he comes duly accredited as of worthy life and conduct. ...

The Holy of Holies: The central of the three small apartments connected with the Celestial Room,—situated therefore between the Sealing Room for the Living and the Sealing Room for the Dead,—is of all the smaller apartments within the Temple walls by far the most beautiful. Yet its excellence is that of splendid simplicity rather than of sumptuous splendor. It is raised above the other two rooms and is reached by an additional flight of six steps inside the sliding doors. The short staircase is bordered by hand-carved balustrades, which terminate in a pair of newel-posts bearing bronze figures symbolical of innocent childhood; these support flower clusters, each jeweled blossom enclosing an electric bulb. On the landing at the head of the steps is another archway, beneath which are sliding doors; these doors mark the threshold of the inner room or Holy of Holies of the Temple, and correspond to the inner curtain or veil that shielded from public view the most sacred precincts of Tabernacle and Temple in the earlier dispensations.

The floor is of native hard-wood blocks, each an inch in cross-section. The room is of circular outline, eighteen feet in diameter, with paneled walls, the panels separated by carved pillars supporting arches; it is decorated in blue and gold. The entrance doorway and the panels are framed in red velvet with an outer border finished in gold. Four wall niches, bordered in crimson and gold, have a deep blue background, and within these are tall vases holding flowers. The room is practically without natural light, but it is brilliantly illumined by a large electrolier and eight side clusters of lamps. The ceiling is a dome in which are set circular and semi-circular windows of jeweled glass, and on the outer side of these, therefore above the ceiling, are electric globes whose light penetrates into the room in countless hues of subdued intensity.

On the south side of this room, opposite the entrance doorway, and corresponding in size therewith, is a window of colored glass depicting the appearance of the Eternal Father and His Son Jesus Christ to the boy Joseph Smith. The event here delineated marked the ushering-in of the dispensation of the fulness of times. The scene is laid in a grove; the celestial Personages are clothed in white, and appear in the attitude of instructing the boy prophet, who kneels with uplifted face and outstretched arms. Beneath is inscribed the scripture through which Joseph was led to seek Divine instruction: "If any of you lack wisdom, let him ask of God, that giveth to all men liberally, and upbraideth not; and it shall be given him."

And below: "This is my beloved Son, hear Him." This room is reserved for the higher ordinances [second anointings] in the Priesthood relating to the exaltation of both [the] living and dead. **—James E. Talmage, *The House of the Lord: A Study of Holy Sanctuaries Ancient and Modern* (Salt Lake City: Deseret News, 1912), 99-101, 192-94; emphasis in original**

....

Sometime in February, 1857, Sister Romania Bunnell Pratt received her second anointing with Parley P. Pratt Jr. You are hereby authorized and instructed to cancel the record of this anointing, and report to me. **—Joseph F. Smith to John D. T. McAllister, May 15, 1913**

President [Joseph F.] Smith invites you with your wife to come to the temple to receive your second blessings. If you prefer to go to Logan, please let the president know and he will send you the usual recommend. These blessings are administered on Fridays in the Salt Lake temple. **—George F. Gibbs to John W. Hart, June 14, 1913**

During the early history of the Church, as well as the early settlement of Utah, second blessings [anointings] were adminsitered only to those chosen by the president of the Church, and this continued all through the administration of President Brigham Young, but later the authority [was] vested in the stake presidents to recommend to the First Presidency such men presided over by [the stake presidents and] deemed worthy by them to receive the second anointing, this for the reason that the Church had increased in numbers so that it had become a matter of impossibility for the President of the Church to be personally acquainted with every man suitable and worthy to be thus honored.

... [It is suggested that] men [be recommended] whose faith has never been shaken, whose integrity to the Lord and his servants has been beyond question, men who have been valiant for the truth, men who have defended the servants of the Lord and never betrayed them, men who have done what they could, whether in preaching or in working to help their file leaders to build up Zion, and who are ever ready and willing to labor in the interests of Zion at home or abroad, and who are in harmony with[,] and [who] sustain by their faith and prayers and good works[,] the First Presidency and general authorities of the Church, and those immediately presiding over them, and the same with respect to the character of their wives. **—Joseph F. Smith, Anthon H. Lund, and Charles W. Penrose to David Halls, June 25, 1913**

What are known as temple ages are 18 years for girls and 21 years for boys; that is, when boys and girls have attained these years they are eligible to receive their endowments, provided of course they bring to the temple regular temple recommends. **—George F. Gibbs, Letter to Mrs. M. E. Corbet, Nov. 1, 1913**

....

Recommends should be issued only to those who are worthy. A sufficient time should elapse after baptism and after arrival in the ward to prove worthiness. Children under eight years of age do not need recommends when they accompany their parents or guardians. Recommends should not be given to persons afflicted with infectious disease, or with offensive skin diseases.

Individuals who have been endowed, and afterwards have been excommunicated, and who have subsequently entered the Church again, should not be recommended to the Temple except by special permission of the President of the Church. Women married to men who are not members of the Church should not receive endowments. Males over twenty-one years of age who have not received their endowments, and females over eighteen are not permitted to take part in, nor witness temple ordinances, except that they may be baptized for the dead. In every such case the recommend must show that it is issued for Baptisms only. If persons are to receive endowments at the time they are to be sealed to parents, the fact that they are so recommended must be stated on the recommend.

Men should be ordained to the Melchisedek Priesthood before they come to the Temple to receive endowments.

Those who go to the Temple should provide themselves with suitable clothing, as the Relief Society does not keep sufficient clothing on hand to meet the entire demand. Latter-day Saints should be encouraged to prepare and keep their own temple clothes.

Those who receive recommends to be married in the Temple should not have the marriage ceremony performed before they come to the Temple, unless there is some justifiable reason for doing so, such as having to delay an undesirable length of time before they could come, or having to travel alone, by team, to reach the Temple.

When persons go to the Temple to be married, the name of the bride must be given on the groom's recommend and the groom's name on the bride's recommend. It must also be understood that the marriage ceremony will not be performed unless the contracting parties have complied with the law in securing a proper license from the county clerk within the state where the Temple is located. …

Presidents of Missions should not issue recommends to the Temple, as a residence of at least six months in one of the wards of the Church is necessary before such recommends may be issued. Recommendations relating to temple matters in which members of missions are concerned must be sent directly to the First Presidency. ***—Circular of Instructions,* No. 12, ca. 1914**

....

Arrangements are now being made to assist the Saints residing in the various missions of the Church, and in other places remote from the Temples, who are thereby unable, personally, to perform Temple ordinances in behalf of their dead kindred, or friends[,] [or] to obtain the needed services of proxies. It is our desire that faithful members of the Church, in the condition stated, shall be helped, to the fullest possible extent, to accomplish this sacred duty that all Latter-day Saints are required, by Divine injunction, to fulfill. …

Members of the Church in missions, and localities a great distance from the Temples, who desire to comply with the gospel requirements for salvation of the dead, should confer with the President of the mission, or district, in which they reside, stating what ordinances they wish to have performed and they will then be provided with the blank [forms], and instructions needed. …

Donations are thankfully received at the Temples, to assist in meeting the heavy expense of their maintenance, but the poor, who can give nothing, are cheerfully accorded all the privileges that the most liberal donors receive.

There is no charge made by the Temple authorities for performance of the ordinances, but, when proxies have to be obtained to act in endowments for the dead, which occupies the time of an entire sess[i]on in Temple work, it is customary to pay such proxies a small sum, to partly remunerate them for personal expenses; usually a man receives 75 cents, and a woman 50 cents, for such services.

Arrangements are already made whereby faithful members of the Church who have died in various missions or who may die therein thereafter, without having received Temple ordinances in life, will have those ordinances attended to in their behalf. The names and genealogies of all such worthy individuals are now being sent to the St. George Temple, by the mission Presidents. **—Joseph F. Smith, Anthon H. Lund, and Charles W. Penrose, "Temple Work for Church Members Abroad," 1915, in *MFP*, 4:335-37**

No member of the Church beyond temple age (18 years for females and 21 years for males) are permitted to be sealed to their parents without first receiving their own endowments. **—Joseph F. Smith, Anthon H. Lund, and Charles W. Penrose to Stephen L. Chipman and counselors, Feb. 6, 1915**

(1) The pattern of the temple garment was given by revelation to the Prophet Joseph Smith[,] exact date as to month or year unknown.

(2) The garment with buttons instead of strings, referred to by you, is not the temple garment, and should not be worn as such.

(3) It is not right to leave off wearing the temple garment during the day because of hot weather; it should not be taken off at all excepting to be renewed by another, or for the purpose of bathing, or for work or other purposes requiring the baring of the body. **—Joseph F. Smith, Anthon H. Lund, and Charles W. Penrose to Arthur C. Smith, Mar. 10, 1915**

I read with interest what you write concerning your mother's having been sealed to your father and then, after his death, married another man and had seven children with him, and that she now desires to be sealed to her living husband. [Regarding] the question you ask, whether the children she had with your father, who were born under the covenant, should be sealed to the man she now desires to be sealed to for eternity, I will say in answer that children born under the covenant cannot be sealed to any other man so long as the father has been faithful in the Church, and has not been excommunicated.

In regard to your mother's being sealed to her present husband, permission must be given by President [Joseph F.] Smith, who is the only one who holds the keys to that ordinance, and he will want to know some reason why this should be done. In regard to the children born under the covenant however there is no sealing ordinance necessary for them. **—Anthon H. Lund to Hyrum Johnson, June 8, 1915**

In recommending brethren and sisters under your jurisdiction to receive temple ordinances, it is suggested that instead of mailing the letter of recommendation direct to President [Joseph F.] Smith that you hand it to the person recommended, with instructions to present it at the president's office as soon as convenient after his or her arrival in this city. This suggestion is made at the instance of the First Presidency. **—George F. Gibbs to All United States Mission Presidents, Dec. 23, 1915**

Young men or middle aged men who have had experience in the Church should not be ordained to the Priesthood nor recommended to the privileges of the House of the Lord unless they will abstain from the use of tobacco and intoxicating drinks. This is the rule of the

Church and should be observed by all its members. **—Joseph F. Smith to C. Elmo Cluff, Dec. 28, 1915**

....

Church members who knowingly ally themselves with secret organizations against the advice and counsel of the Church should not be recommended to the temple, and we may add that such brethren also render themselves ineligible to hold presiding offices in the priesthood, and cannot consistently be recognized as teachers among the people. But brethren who join secret societies without knowing the attitude of the Church in regard to such organizations, may be recommended, if otherwise worthy, on a promise to withdraw therefrom as soon as they can do so consistently. **—Joseph F. Smith, Anthon H. Lund, and Charles W. Penrose to Peter C. Larsen, Feb. 3, 1916**[32]

The rule of the temple is that a woman who marries outside of the Church cannot receive a recommend to go through the temple, because her husband would be very apt to ask her to reveal the temple ordinances and if she refused to do so it would cause contention between them. If she has married a man in the Church, and she desires to receive her endowments, we do not feel that it would be wise for her to receive her endowments before her husband, and hence bishops are told not to give recommendations to wives before their husbands go with them to the temple. If a wife received her endowments before she married[,] she showed her weakness in not keeping her covenants, but still if she afterwards proves herself a staunch Latter-day Saint and tries to live as such and has not cast off her garments, we think the bishop may give her a recommend to do work in the temple. However, if she cast off her garments when she married, we do not feel that she should be entitled to receive a recommend to the House of the Lord. **—Anthon H. Lund and Charles W. Penrose to Edward H. Snow, Mar. 11, 1916**

The rumor referred to in yours of the 3rd inst., that the Church sanctions the taking off of the sleeves and collar of the temple garment and replacing them with thin, gauzy material, in order to meet the re-

32. A note accompanying the letter expressed concern by President Penrose that an individual who had a fraternity-sponsored insurance policy might lose his investment by resigning his fraternity membership.

cent style of dress worn by ladies, is not true, and anyone resorting to such proceeding mutilates the garment, and is guilty of wrongdoing. **—Joseph F. Smith, Anthon H. Lund, and Charles W. Penrose to Stephen L. Chipman, May 6, 1916**

The garments worn by those who receive endowments must be white and of the approved pattern. They must not be altered and mutilated and are to be worn as intended, down to the wrist and ankle, and around the neck. Admission to the temple will be refused those who do not comply with these requirements. The Saints should know that the pattern of endowment garments was revealed from heaven, and the blessings promised in connection with wearing them will not be realized if any unauthorized change is made in their form or in the manner of wearing them. **—Joseph F. Smith, statement issued June 28, 1916, published in the *Improvement Era,* Aug. 1916, p. 812**

"The Lecture," which is given in the Temple from time to time, as circumstances require, was first delivered by President [Brigham] Young in this [St. George] Temple. It was written down as he spoke it, and was subsequently revised by him. The ordinances were written [down] by Presidents Wilford Woodruff and George Q. Cannon, under the direction of President Young[,] and, when completed, he said "Now you have before you an ensample to carry on the endowments in all the Temples, until the coming of the Son of Man. **—David H. Cannon to Joseph F. Smith, Anthon H. Lund, and Charles W. Penrose, Oct. 21, 1916**

....

In presenting the enclosed recommendations for second blessings to the brethren interested, the First Presidency would thank you to instruct each of them separately in regard to the sacredness of the ordinance to be administered to them, and that they must regard themselves under obligation not to speak about it to anybody outside the temple. Second blessings are administered on Fridays, and not more than one family from your stake should come to the temple on any one day to receive [the] second anointing, this in the interest of privacy, so that no one family of your stake may know that the other or others have received or are about to receive second blessings. **—George F. Gibbs to William D. Kuhre, Mar. 17, 1917**

We are informed that the rules of the [United States] Navy do not permit its men to wear any other clothing than that provided by the Navy, and it is quite possible, therefore, that our brethren who have received their endowments who join the Navy may not be permitted to wear the temple garment. In that event there would be no wrongdoing on their part in ceasing to wear the garment while serving in the Navy, as it is ceasing to wear the garment from choice that constitutes the wrong. But of course it will be their duty to wear the garment whenever free to do so. **—Joseph F. Smith, Anthon H. Lund, and Charles W. Penrose to Hans P. Ipson, June 12, 1917**

[I]n regard to the inmates of the Idaho insane asylum, members of the Church [there] wearing the temple garment, ... we will express ourselves on this subject at the next general priesthood meeting, and in the meantime would thank you as chairman of the board of directors of the Idaho insane asylum to do what you can consistently by way of correcting this practice. Should any of the inmates however feel hurt in his or her feelings at being deprived of wearing the garment, we suggest that no change be made in his or her case, and that this be an exception. **—Joseph F. Smith, Anthon H. Lund, and Charles W. Penrose to George H. Fisher, July 19, 1917**

The rule is that all sealings such as yours, performed under the stress of circumstances outside the temple,[33] be solemnized again over the altar whenever the parties so married are able to come to the temple, and that the children of such unions be also sealed to their parents over the altar, and it will therefore be in order for your wife to meet you at the temple (as suggested in your letter) to be sealed to you over again, also that your children with her [come] to be sealed to their parents, if your circumstances admit of this being done. **—Joseph F. Smith to Cyrus Robinson, Aug. 21, 1917**

[S]hould circumstances arise in your army experience to justify

33. Cyrus Robinson had written to President Smith that he was married in Thatcher, Arizona, in June 1904 in the house of stake president Andrew Kimball. The ceremony was performed by Apostle Matthias Cowley. Robinson had previously received his endowments, but his wife had not. Now returning from a mission to England, Robinson wanted to know "if this our marriage is legal or not? as we supposed we were being sealed for eternity," also whether their five children needed to be sealed to them (Cyrus Robinson to Joseph F. Smith, July 30, 1917).

you in ceasing to wear the garment, such deprivation will in no way affect your religious status, living or dead, taking it for granted of course that your worthiness to wear the garment remains unchanged, as it is ceasing to wear it of one's own free will and choice that constitutes the wrong-doing, not from doing it in obedience to legitimate authority or from justifiable circumstances . **—George F. Gibbs to J. Garfield Bastow, Dec. 17, 1917**

....

TEMPLE INSTRUCTIONS TO THE BISHOPS

If you have not already adopted the practice of calling attention to the following regulations, when you issue recommends to individuals going to the Temple, you will please do so hereafter, in every instance.

FIRST: The garments worn by those who receive endowments must be white, and of the approved pattern; they must not be altered or mutilated, and are to be worn as intended, down to the wrist and ankles, and around the neck.

Please inform all to whom you issue recommends that these requirements are imperative, and that admission to the Temple will be refused to those who do not comply therewith. The Saints should know that the pattern of endowment garments was revealed from heaven, and that the blessings promised in connection with wearing them will not be realized if any unauthorized change is made in their form, or in the manner of wearing them.

SECOND: All who come to the Temple to perform ordinance work are expected to make donations according to their circumstances, to aid in meeting necessary expenses, but the poor who have nothing to give are equally welcome.

This rule has been a part of the printed instructions, since the commencement of work in the Salt Lake Temple, but is repeated here with the request that you will mention it to all to whom you issue recommends, because the aggregate amount received is very small. It may properly be suggested to a man, who is going to the Temple to be married, that the amount of his donation should approximate or be equal to what he would be required to pay if he had the ceremony performed elsewhere, if he could afford to donate that much. ...

Recommends should be issued only to those who are worthy and faithful. A sufficient time should elapse after baptism to prove worthiness. Children under eight years of age do not need recommends, when they accompany their parents or guardians. Recommends should not be given to persons afflicted with any kind of infectious disease, or with serious or offensive skin disease.

Before being recommended to receive endowments, each individual should be informed concerning the purpose, and importance, of that sacred ordinance.

Living boys and girls as young as sixteen years of age may receive endowments if, in each case, the character and condition of the individual is such that the Bishop feels justified in issuing a recommend for that purpose.

Males over twenty-one years of age, and females over eighteen, are not permitted to take part in, or witness, Temple ordinances until they receive their own endowments, except that they may be baptized for the dead; in that event the recommend must show FOR BAPTISMS ONLY. If they are to receive endowments at the time they are to be sealed to parents[,] the fact that they are authorized to be endowed then must be stated on the recommend.

A living woman cannot receive endowments while her husband is alive, if the husband has not been endowed.

Men should be ordained to the Melchizedek Priesthood before they come to the Temple to receive endowments.

Recommends for the privilege to work in the House of the Lord must be renewed every six months. Each individual needs a recommend, including children over eight years of age.

Individuals who have been endowed, and afterwards have been excommunicated, and subsequently joined the Church again, should not be recommended to the Temple until former blessings have been sealed upon them by special permission of the President of the Church.

Robes, etc., may be hired at the Temple, but all are advised to provide themselves with their own, if they can do so conveniently. The sisters should not have long "trains" on the white dresses they wear in the Temple, nor decorate with colored ribbons or gaudy ornaments.

Each person who is to receive endowments should bring a towel for their own use. All should be perfectly clean in body and clothing, not offensive to others.

Small children who are to act only in the ordinance of sealing to parents, or adoptions, need not be brought to the Temple Annex before 12 m. [noon]; all other persons should be in the building not later than 8:30 a.m., for the first company, and not later than 1 p.m., for the second company. The second company is composed of those only who are taking endowments for the dead.

It should be clearly made known to those who can receive recommends to be married in the Temple, that they should not have the marriage ceremony performed before coming to the Temple, unless there is some good and justifiable reason for doing so, such as having to delay an undesirable length of time before they could come, or having to travel alone, by team, to reach the Temple.

Bishops are not to issue recommends for second anointings: that is the province of Presidents of Stakes, under approval of the President of the Church, and the individuals selected must not be informed until after the issuance of such recommend. As a general rule, such recommends are issued only in behalf of those who have had endowments in lifetime, and have been sealed and lived together faithfully as husband and wife, and who have been valiant in the defense of truth and active in all good works. **—Joseph F. Smith, 1918, in *MFP,* 5:110–13; emphasis in original**

Presidents of Missions are not authorized to give temple recommends; these are issued by the President of the Church for mission members upon obtaining suitable letters of recommendation from Mission Presidents for such members. Letters of recommendation should be given only to those who have been members of the Church at least a year, and in good standing for one year prior to giving the recommend. It must be known that they keep the Word of Wisdom, pay their tithing and otherwise are good members. Each letter of recommendation should specify what particular blessing the person is recommended to receive. **—Statement, ca. 1918, in *MFP,* 5:163**

President [Joseph F.] Smith directs me to say: Many of our soldier boys wearing the temple garment took it off soon after entering the service, thinking it better to do that than to have it ridiculed through exposure. Others have continued to wear it, some of whom have taken it off while drilling, and wearing it again afterwards, also on Sundays and holidays. Some have continued to wear it until after their arrival in France, and have written back to their families to send them new garments, thus showing that it is possible to wear the garment in the

Army. A rule in the Navy however forbids the wearing of the garment, but we know of no such rule in the Army. Should you be deprived of wearing the garment during your army experience through circumstances over which you have no control … the Lord will accept the [desire of your heart] . **—George F. Gibbs to Walter Welti, July 1, 1918**

… It is thought wise by the committee that the garments should be marked before they are put on the body [in the temple], as in some instances, the marks have been forgotten. You, of course, understand that the important thing is to have them marked.

In answer to the questions if it is proper for anybody who has not been through the Temple, to work on Temple clothing, I am authorized by the Chairman of the Committee to state that this depends entirely on whether such person is worthy or not. In far away places where women are faithful and good, and are unable to go to the Temple, it is permissible for them to work on the clothing. This is especially permissable where these sisters are good needle wom[e]n. As a general rule, the Authorities of the Church prefer that this work be done by those who have been through the Temple, but they are willing, under the above circumstances, to make an exception to this rule.

SPECIAL INSTRUCTIONS BY 1st PRESIDENCY

The following questions have been asked pertaining to the clothing of the dead:

[Q:] Should the veil cover the face, or should it be left up?

Ans[wer]: It should cover the face always, before burial.

[Q:] Is it right to slant the robe on the shoulder?

Ans[wer]: Yes.

[Q:] Should the robe be ironed in pleats?

Ans[wer]: Not necessarily, but it is better that way. …

[Q:] Which shoulder should the robe cover?

Answer: The right shoulder.

[Q:] How many leaves should be on an apron?

Answer: as many as desired.

[Q:] Should the stems of the leaves point up or down?

Answer: alway[s] up, the natural way.

[Q:] Would it be wrong to put garments that are unmarked on persons who have not received their endowments?

Answer: There is nothing especially wrong about it, but we advise that it be not done.

[Q:] Should the girdle be tied on the right side or on the left?

Answer: Always on the left side.

—Joseph F. Smith

In the Council House, built in 1850 on the southwest corner of Main and South Temple Streets in Salt Lake City, territorial business was conducted on the main floor and temple rites were performed upstairs for four years. The building was destroyed by fire in 1883. The bottom level was constructed of sandstone and the upper level was adobe. Photo 1869. *Courtesy Utah State Historical Society.*

The Endowment House served as a temporary temple from 1855 to 1889 except for a year of inactivity in 1876-1877. It was located on the northwest corner of the temple block in downtown Salt Lake City. *Photo by Charles R. Savage. Courtesy Utah State Historical Society.*

Jane Manning James was a servant in the Joseph Smith home in Nauvoo in the 1840s, where she was affectionately known as "Aunt Jane." In Utah she asked to be sealed to Joseph Smith. Eventually she was sealed to him but as a servant rather than a wife.

The St. George temple was completed in April 1877. The cupola, shown here, was soon damaged by lightning and replaced by the tower it is now known for. The roofline battlements included chimneys for top-floor apartments where visitors could spend the night. In the foreground one can see the water tower from which the baptismal font was filled. Photo 1877. *Susa Young Gates Collection, Utah State Historical Society.*

John D. T. McAllister helped Wilford Woodruff, George Q. Cannon, Brigham Young Jr., and L. John Nuttall write out and refine the temple ceremonies. McAllister was president of the St. George Stake, assistant St. George temple president, and later president of the Manti temple.

Brigham Young died in August 1877, four months after the St. George temple was dedicated—however, not before assigning a committee to write out and standardize the ceremonies or before contributing his own "lecture at the veil." *Photo courtesy Utah State Historical Society.*

As president of the St. George temple, Wilford Woodruff introduced vicarious endowments and shifted the focus of temples to families, encouraging members to be sealed to their ancestors instead of to friends and Church leaders as had been the custom.

The Manti temple was built in the castellated gothic-revival style of the other nineteenth-century Utah temples. It was completed in 1888. In this image one can still see the construction supervisor's home and workshop in the foreground. The Manti temple is one of only two that today continue to use live actors. *Photo courtesy Utah State Historical Society. All rights reserved.*

This sealing room of the Manti temple is designed to look like the apse of a cathedral. In more modern temples, the sealing rooms are less ornate and less spacious. *Photo courtesy Utah State Historical Society. *

The Logan temple was dedicated in 1884. As beautiful as the historic exterior is, the interior remodeling of the 1970s removed the decorative details for which the temple was known. The renovation was undertaken to facilitate the filmed portions of the endowment. *Photo courtesy Utah State Historical Society. *

As a secretary to the First Presidency for over thirty years, George F. Gibbs (back row, left) handled much of the Church correspondence with temple presidents. He is joined in the back row (l-r) by another Church secretary, L. John Nuttall, and future apostle Charles W. Penrose. In the front row are Church lobbyist John T. Caine and wife Margaret, Church President Joseph F. Smith, Emily Tanner Richards, and Emily's apostle-husband, Franklin S. Richards. The photo was taken in Washington, D. C., on May 29, 1888, at the Charles Parker Gallery. *Photo courtesy Utah State Historical Society. *

In this view of the Celestial Room in the Salt Lake temple, one can see the curtain that covered the veil when not in use. The veil represents the transition from mortal life to heaven and is only visible during an endowment session. *Photo courtesy Utah State Historical Society.*

On November 8, 1852, Elizabeth Ann Whitney (l) and Eliza R. Snow (r) anointed the wives of eight prominent LDS men in the Council House, after which they and their husbands "all partook of cakes and wine. Some spoke in tongues." Emmeline B. Wells (center), wife of First Presidency counselor Daniel H. Wells, referred to her work in the temple as "officiating in the character of a priestess." *Photo by Charles C. Savage, ca. 1876.*

Apostle George F. Richards was tasked with rewriting large portions of the temple rituals that had been identified as problematic. He spent two years thoroughly studying and revising the scripts. *Photo from the Widtsoe Family Collection, Utah State Historical Society.*

Church President Heber J. Grant introduced changes to the temple in an indirect way. Unaware of practices his predecessors had considered essential but which had become less prominent, he viewed these "innovations" as the work of revisionists and prevented their continuance as unnecessary or heretical. The emphasis of his administration was on practical matters unrelated to the temple.

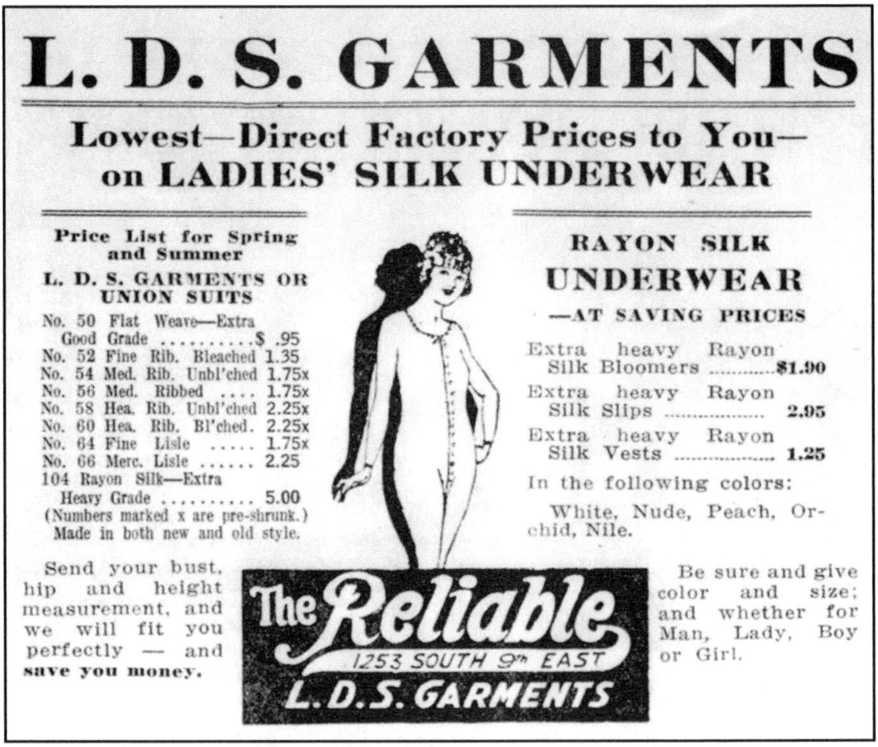

In the late 1920s, advertisements for temple garments appeared in the *Relief Society Magazine* and elsewhere. Notice that in this ad garments are available in French cotton (lisle) or imitation silk (rayon). *Courtesy Ardis E. Parshall, Keepapitchinin.org*

NEW GARMENTS

The "Temple Brand" Garments are handled only by your leading merchants. We make a Variety of Grades and Weights to meet every requirement, with strings and buttons, long or short sleeves and legs as you want them according to seasonable desires. Samples submitted on request.

For Ladies

No. 1—Flat Weave Light	.95
No. 2—Ribbed Weave Light	1.25
No. 15—Extra Quality Flat	1.45
No. 803—Extra Quality Ribb	1.50
No. 825—Med. Weight Cotton	1.85
No. 800—Silk Stripe Med	2.00
No. 850—Imp. Lisle	2.50

For Men

No. 902—Ribbed Light Weight	1.25
No. 903—Ribbed Extra Quality	1.75
No. 925—Med. Light Weight	1.85
No. 975—Med. Heavy Weight	2.25
No. 990—Heavy Ecrn. Cotton	2.50
No. 9107—Wool & Cotton	4.00
No. 970—Silk & Wool & Cotton	4.50

To insure a good fit give bust measure, height, and weight, specify whether garments are for men or women, and state whether long sleeves ankle length or short sleeves three quarter legs are desired. Double Backs 25c extra. Garments marked 15c pair extra. We prepay postage to all parts of United States.

Oldest Knitting Company in Utah

SALT LAKE KNITTING STORE, 70 Main St., Salt Lake City

The Salt Lake Knitting Store filled demand for old and new styles of garments with ankle-length legs and wrist-length arms or slightly shorter varieties in cotton, silk, or wool, flat or knitted. A stretch-panel back cost an extra quarter. *Relief Society Magazine, 1927; courtesy Ardis E. Parshall, Keepapitchinin.org*

Before becoming Church president, David O. McKay served on the committee to revise the endowment ceremony. One concern he expressed was that the committee "consider the effect upon many young people" in the endowment drama of God's "use of elevators," whereby deity descended into the Garden Room on wings of steel, resulting in repressed giggles. *Photo by George Bettridge, Saans Photography, October 1959. Courtesy Utah State Historical Society.*

The temple the Church built in a suburb of Bern, Switzerland, has lines similar to domestic temples but a simplified modern style. The first foreign temple, it led to the production of a movie with soundtracks in several languages, and the audio portion available on headphones. The temple was dedicated by David O. McKay in 1955. *Photo courtesy Utah State Historical Society.*

The man behind the camera in filming the endowment ceremony at Brigham Young University was Wetzel O. Whitaker, who had previously worked at Walt Disney Studios in the 1930s–40s. The first film of this type was directed by Harold I. Hansen and was shot inside the Salt Lake temple. Thereafter, the films were produced at a special sound stage at BYU. *Photo courtesy Perry Special Collections, Lee Library, Brigham Young University*

The look of the Oakland temple in California brings to mind a Central American pyramid, on which a large bas-relief panel depicts Jesus visiting the Americas. The Oakland temple was the first to offer a wide-screen presentation of the endowment ceremony. *Photo courtesy Utah State Historical Society. All rights reserved.*

LDS President Spencer W. Kimball, flanked here by secretary Arthur Haycock, was concerned about not diluting the moral standards required of those who attend the temple. He is nevertheless most notably remembered for removing the prohibition against blacks entering the temple. *Photo courtesy Utah State Historical Society. All rights reserved.*

4.

"A SPLENDID ACCOMPLISHMENT" 1921-1940

At our council meeting [Quorum of the Twelve] it was decided that the old form of ordaining be used in the Temple and elsewhere. It was also decided that we disorganize the temple choir at once.[1]
—George F. Richards diary, Apr. 7, 1921[2]

Attended the temple meeting as usual and after the meeting Elder Jos[eph] F[ielding] Smith[3] and I met with the temple choir members, thanked them for their faithful services of the past and released them

1. Sometimes temple choirs performed before endowment sessions.

2. For more on Richards's involvement with the temple liturgy, see Dale C. Mouritsen, "A Symbol of New Directions: George Franklin Richards and the Mormon Church, 1861-1950," Ph.D. diss., BYU, Dec. 1982, pp. 195-229; also Thomas G. Alexander, *Mormonism in Transition: A History of the Latter-day Saints, 1890-1930* (Urbana: University of Illinois Press, 1986), 298-302, for historical context.

3. Joseph F. Smith died in 1918, and his son of the same name, whose middle initial is usually spelled out as Joseph Fielding Smith to avoid confusion (he is also called Joseph F. Smith Jr.), was by now forty-four years old and a member of the Quorum of the Twelve, as well as a counselor in the Salt Lake temple presidency. Elder Richards was similarly both an apostle and a member of the temple presidency.

with our blessing. Congregational singing will be engaged in exclusively. ...[4] **—George F. Richards diary, Apr. 8, 1921**

We led our first temple [session] without a choir this morning. Am working with Bro[ther] D[uncan] M McAllister on records trying to get uniformity of ordinances, decisions & with a view to having the [First] Presidency pass on our suggestions and have them go out to all the temples. **—George F. Richards diary, Apr. 12, 1921**

One of the practices in the temple when I first went to the temple was that you were expected to make a donation as you went in the door to help temple work. That was eliminated later. I don't remember a time when to my knowledge it wasn't customary to allow a certain amount of money for the indigent people who would spend their time in the temple, going through for the dead for endowment work. It used to be fifty cents for a man or fifty cents for a woman, I think.[5] Then people like my father who didn't often have the privilege of going through the temple paid a lot of folks for doing that kind of service for them. It helped some of the elderly people to live, to have groceries to eat and places to rent. **—George F. Richards Jr.[6] oral history, Jan. 16, 18, 23, 25, 1973, p. 58, excerpt in Buerger Papers**

I obtained the ear of Presidents Heber J. Grant and Anthony W. Ivins and presented the following matters to them which they approved:

First, the changing of the place for administering to the sick from the garden room of the temple to the assembly room of the temple annex.

Second, in listing names of children for sealing to parents whether they be living or dead, they are to be listed in the order of their birth and sealed in that order and that in the sealing ceremony after the

---

4. Eventually all music would be eliminated from the temple. Meanwhile, Elder Richards would go on to note that the First Presidency had eliminated the words, "we confer upon you the holy Melchesidek Priesthood" from the temple ceremony, no doubt because of its redundancy with the requirement for attendance for men.

5. Men were paid seventy-five cents, women fifty cents.

6. Elder Richards's son, George F. Richards Jr. (1883-1974), served as a counselor in the Salt Lake temple presidency. On October 1, 1924, he received his second anointing from his father and Joseph Fielding Smith.

prox[ies] have been arranged, it is not necessary to make a distinction between the living and dead children by saying who are dead &c.

Third, that young people going through for their endowments with the intention of marrying in the temple some future day, the young man is not entitled to bring the young lady through the veil and receive her new name until they come to the temple to be married.

Fourth, that in the ceremony of the Second Endowments [anointing] the name of the husband should be given after the words, your husband[,] in the anointing and again in the sealing of the ~~wife~~ anointing. **—George F. Richards diary, June 22, 1921, emphasis in original**

I have signed the seven recommends for second blessings contained in yours of the 22nd inst., and have forwarded the same to President Shepard[7] of the Logan Temple, as requested by you.

The following is one of the instructions given to Stake Presidents in connection with their issuing temple recommends for second blessings:

"Send each and every recommend direct to the President, not by the hand of anybody, the person recommended included.[8] After the President returns the recommend to you bearing his signature of approval, it will then be in order for you to deliver it in person to the head of the family thus recommended, explaining to him in a private confidential way the sacredness of the ordinance, cautioning him at the same time not to speak of it to anybody outside the temple: and in the interest of privacy you are requested not to send more than one family to the temple the same week bearing a recommend of this character."

If you and Pres[iden]t Sheperd of the Logan temple can agree between yourselves that these blessings can be administered to each family recommended by you[,] without other families so recommended knowing anything at all about it, you have my consent that the recommends be acted on during the week of the visitation of yourself and [others] at the temple, otherwise the instruction in regard to this matter

---

7. Joseph Russell Shepherd (1865-1935) was president of the Logan temple from 1918 to 1935.

8. Notice the difference between this and the procedure for people living outside of the Wasatch front. The latter were told to bring a recommend with them and present it directly, in person, "at the [Church] president's office as soon as convenient after [your] arrival in this city" (entry for Dec. 23, 1915, herein).

should be strictly adhered to. **—Heber J. Grant to William L. Rich, June 23, 1921; emphasis in original**

We, the Presidency of the Salt Lake Temple, respectfully recommend the following for your approval:

First: that people coming to the temple to be administered to for their health are to receive that ordinance in the assembly room of the annex, rather than in the Garden Room of the temple, where such ordinances have heretofore been administered regularly on Tuesday of each week.

Second: That a man should not be permitted to take his intended bride through the veil and receive her new name except on the day they are to be married in the temple.

Third: In sealing of children to parents it is not necessary to use the word "Heiress." The word "Heir" applies alike to both male and female.

Fourth: In sealing children to parents, whether the children be living or dead, they should be listed and sealed in order of their birth, where possible.

Fifth: In sealing children to parents, where there are both living and dead children to be sealed by the same ceremony, use only the words of the ceremony heretofore used for living children. It is not necessary in the ceremony to otherwise designate those who are dead. Neither is it necessary in cases where one of the parents is dead to add the words "who is dead" after that name in the ceremony.

Sixth: In the ceremony of the second anointing, both in the anointing and the sealing of the anointing, add the name of the husband after the words, "to your husband."

Seventh: The president of the temple may decide questions of restoration of blessings for the dead; the question of restoration of blessings to the living to be decided by the President of the Church.

Eighth: That in the ceremony of sealing a woman to a man, or children to parents, it is not necessary to repeat the word "you" before each name. **—George F. Richards, Joseph Fielding Smith, and Albert W. Davis of the Salt Lake Temple Presidency to Heber J. Grant, Charles W. Penrose, and Anthony W. Ivins, Oct. 11, 1921, copy in Buerger Papers**

I went to the temple and worked at my desk until about 4 P.M. I have been for some time correlating rules and decisions by appointment of the First Presidency to be considered and approved for guidelines of all temple presidents. **—George F. Richards diary, Dec. 10, 1921**

I went to my office and to the temple and did some work on compilations of decisions & rulings and [now] have them ready to submit to Bro[ther] [Duncan M.] McAllister[9] for inspection before presenting [them] to the [temple] Committee & then to the Presidency. They comprise 25 pages[,] foolscap size pages.[10] **—George F. Richards diary, Dec. 27, 1921**

....

Met with Pres[iden]t George F. Richards of the Salt Lake Temple, Elders Joseph Fielding Smith and Duncan M. McAllister. The Presidency went over a lot of suggestions with these brethren regarding temple ceremonies, etc., and some slight changes were suggested. Our meeting lasted from 10:30 [a.m.] until 2:30 [p.m]. **—Heber J. Grant diary, Jan. 27, 1922**

Was in conference with the [First] Presidency for some time on Temple matters. Completed the rules and decisions for guidance of Temple Presidents and some changes in the ordinances. This is the fruition of a labor of months as I was able to devote myself to it. This is one of the accomplishments of my administration as Temple President of which I am greatly thankful and pleased. These rules and decisions have been gleaned from a number of books, manuscripts, and loose sheets[,] and obsolete rulings have been eliminated and new rulings have been made & approved by the First Presidency. Copies of these decisions will be made and every Temple President will be supplied with a copy. The ordinances are all being rewritten and a copy will be furnished each temple. This should be the means of getting uniformity in all the temples. **—George F. Richards diary, May 31, 1922**

This day I went before the [First] Presidency and presented to them an important change in the endowment ceremony by which the robes should be placed on the left shoulder first and then changed

9. As temple recorder, McAllister would work closely with Richards and the temple committee to revise and standardize the ceremonies. The committee consisted of Apostles David O. McKay, George F. Richards, Stephen L. Richards, Joseph Fielding Smith, John A. Widtsoe, and from mid-1924 James E. Talmage.

10. Foolscap sheets of paper measured approximately thirteen by sixteen inches.

to the right shoulder once only before entering the Terrestrial room; also that Aaronic and Melchizedek be used instead of lower order of the Melchizedek and higher order of the Aaronic. I am to come back with a definite recommend of the Presidency of the Temple. This on my own suggestion. Other members not accessible today. **—George F. Richards diary, June 3, 1922**

I attended to my duties as usual at the Temple. I had 33 marriages solemnized. I filled an appointment made with the [First] Presidency other brethren being present as follows: Jos[eph] Fielding Smith, Albert W. Davis, Duncan M. McAllister, Willard Young,[11] Israel Call[12] & Patriarch Hyrum G. Smith.[13]

I presented the suggestions of a change in the order of robing and in the wording of the ordinances and lecture which were by vote approved. This order is to place the robe on the left shoulder at that point in the Telestial room when formerly it was placed on the right shoulder, and change [it] onto the right shoulder at that point in the ceremony in the Telestial room where at present it is changed onto the left shoulder—there will be no other changing of the robes. The ceremonies and Lecture will be changed to conform [to this convention]. Full explanation will be given in [the] Temple Historical Record. This will clarify some matters which at present are obscure and will shorten the services. **—George F. Richards diary, June 7, 1922**

A MEMORANDUM OF SOME OF THE EVENTS AND OF SOME OF THE THINGS ACCOMPLISHED IN AND ABOUT THE SALT LAKE TEMPLE DURING THE PERIOD OF MY ADMINISTRATION AS PRESIDENT ... FROM MARCH 14, 1921 to APRIL 30, 1937. ... June 7, 1922—REGARDING THE ROBES OF THE HOLY PRIESTHOOD IN THE ENDOWMENTS CEREMONY: Taken from the minutes of a meeting at the office of the First Presidency. Presidents [Heber J.] Grant,

---

11. Willard Young (1852-1939) was a son of Brigham Young and Clarissa Ross. He served as an assistant to the president of the Logan temple from 1916 to 1917. In 1919 he was made superintendent of Church building construction.

12. Israel Call (1854-1938) was an ordinance worker in the Salt Lake temple for thirty years until his death and a patriarch in the South Davis Stake for ten years.

13. Hyrum Gibbs Smith (1879-1932) was Presiding Patriarch of the LDS Church from 1912 to 1932.

[Charles W.] Penrose and [Anthony W.] Ivins being present. I represented[,] having discussed with associates in the temple[,] the advisability of instituting a change in the procedure of placing the Endowment Robes on the individuals receiving endowments[,] the present method being to first place the robe on the right shoulder, [and] subsequently change it to the left shoulder, and later again back to the right shoulder. The proposed change would be to place the robe first on the Left shoulder, … then to change it to the Right shoulder, … thus obviating one of the changes heretofore made, and more effectively indicating transition from the lower to the higher orders of the Priesthood.

After considering carefully the proposed change, the Presidency decided unanimously that from that time on the Robe should first be placed on the Left shoulder, and be changed to the Right shoulder at the time the Endowment candidates are going to enter the Terrestrial World room. The necessary changes in the text, to conform with this decision, are to be made in the new books of rules, etc. that are to be issued to the Temple Presidents. (Announced to Temple workers in [a] meeting held 14 Aug. 1922). **—George F. Richards memorandum, June 7, 1922, copy in Buerger Papers; emphasis in original**

Soon after the dedication of the St. George Temple[,] Pres[iden]t Brigham Young and Apostles Wilford Woodruff and Erastus Snow called some of the leading brethren of this part of the country and administered to us what was said to be the endowment as administered in the Kirtland Temple. At the same time Pres[iden]t Young explained to us that after their arrival in Nauvoo the Lord revealed to the Prophet Joseph Smith in a meeting held in the Prophet's brick store, the present endowment as subsequently administered in the Nauvoo Temple and other places where endowments were given until the completion of the St. George Temple.

That at that time it was tho[ugh]t that the endowment was to be administered in two degrees, the first degree to include the Aaronic Priesthood only and that … the robe would be on the right shoulder and that when the applicant had received the higher or Melkesedic Priesthood the robe would be on the left shoulder.

Sometime after this meeting and during the month of March Elders Wilford Woodruff and ~~Geo[rge] Q. Cannon~~ ^Brigham Young Jr.^ were appointed by Pres[iden]t Brigham Young to write the ceremonies of the endowment in their entirety.

On the 11th of January 1877, Pres[iden]t Young announced in the Temple in the presence of the company who was receiving endowments that this was the first time that the endowments had been administered for the dead (of which there was any record) in this dispensation. Later at a council meeting held in the Temple when Pres[iden]t Young was present Apostle Erastus Snow asked the question how it was that the endowment was not administered by degrees as contemplated and Pres[iden]t Young answered that it might be at some time in the future.

Since we were together in the St. George Temple on July 4th, 1922 I have spent considerable time in trying to find minutes of the two meetings to which I made reference but without success. I can't call to mind at the present time any person living who was present at either of these meetings so that I am giving you what was said according to my recollections[,] and while I may not use the exact phrasiology I give it to you as my mind serves me[,] and with this in view I can see how it is possible that the robe was placed on the right shoulder before ascending to the Terrestrial room to commence service under the Melkesedic Priesthood.

I have tho[ugh]t much upon this subject since we were together and I thot [it] better that I submit them to you[,] as I believe that I am the only man living today who was present during the winter of '[18]77 until the 16th of April where Pres[iden]t Young spent most of his time giving instructions to the elders on this important subject.

I don't know if I related to you a circumstance that occurred in the Logan Temple in June 1884 when [there were] parties who came from Bear Lake to do work in the Temple, [but] a woman among these people had been married previous to leaving Salt Lake City for Carson Valley in the spring of 1856, [and] her husband subsequently went over the mountains into California where his remains were found a few days after just above Plaserville badly mutilated by the hogs who were very numerous around the mining camps at that time. She had 4 children to this man, [and] she subsequently married again and had 4 children by the second marriage. She came to the Temple for the purpose of being sealed to the second husband for time and eternity and having the 8 children sealed to the second husband for time and eternity and having the 8 children adopted to them[.] The relatives of the first husband were opposed to this and came to the temple in force to see that justice was done their kinsman. Pres[iden]t John Taylor called a High Council to try the case. It was shown by the evidence that the first husband's death had occurred through foul play, that the coroners jury had found that a bullet had penetrated one of the ribs, [and] further evidence established the fact that the young man had been an exampilary Latter-Day Saint and that the children could not be taken out of their l[i]n[e]age except for cause, that the 4 children born before[,] <u>as the second man[,] knew he was marrying into another man's wife</u>. The 8 children were to go to the first husband and that if she wanted to be sealed to the second husband for eternity she could do so and any children that comes to them after this such sealing[,] they could belong to her and her second husband. As I remember the pill was too large for her to swallow and she was not sealed to her second husband.

From that time until the present children are not taken out of their l[i]n[e]age of their progenitors, in the St. George Temple, without just cause.

I felt impressed to write you as above indicated as a friendly communication and not an attempt to direct anything that the leaders of this Church have in view. With kind personal regards, your brother in the gospel. **—David H. Cannon to George F. Richards, July 18, 1922, copy in Buerger Papers; emphasis in original**

Attended the regular weekly Council of the Twelve and [First] Presidency [meeting] where the Temple ordinances and rulings were considered as a final consideration and the books were put into the hands of Bro[ther] D[uncan] M. McAllister to be written up for all the temples. This is a great relief to me. I have been engaged on this work for months. **—George F. Richards diary, Aug. 31, 1922**

I spent the day at the Temple where I read carefully all the ordinances used in the temples as changed and corrected and noted 18 times [where there are issues] which I think need changing. It is my intention to present these to the [First] Presidency for their consideration. I also detected 7 errors in copying the ordinances. **—George F. Richards diary, Sept. 16, 1922**

Attended 8:30 temple meeting and my weekly council meeting in the temple which began at 1 P.M. and closed at 3:30 P.M. At this meeting the ceremonies, ordinances, and rules, decisions &c were approved and adopted. On these I have been working for months and for two years off and on and it is a great satisfaction to me to have them approved at this time in their present form. **—George F. Richards diary, Oct. 5, 1922**

INSTRUCTIONS TO TEMPLE WORKERS

Temple workers should be recommended the same as other people, and their recommends should be renewed every six months.

Temple workers should, in all things, be worthy examples to others who come to the temple to do work. Every regulation of the temple should be carefully observed by them.

Cleanliness is next to Godliness and in the House of the Lord that principle must be strictly observed. This applies alike to both person and apparel.

Workers may wear their shoes into the Temple but they should be kept polished and clean from dust and mud. In the ante-room to the Annex will be found materials which may be used for this purpose when necessary.

Those who come to the Temple for ordinance work should remove their shoes from their feet before entering the Temple. A checking room has been provided where, without charge, shoes, wraps, and valuables should be checked to avoid losses through mistake or otherwise.

People coming to the Temple to witness sealings should be ushered into the reception room next to the sealing room where they may be comfortable while waiting. They should not enter the celestial room, except where it becomes necessary in order to sign their names as witnesses.

Persons going through for Endowments may wear white house-slippers instead of moccasins when desired, but where this is done, the slippers should be kept clean the same as the other parts of the Temple clothing. Where moccasins are used, white house-slippers may be used over the moccasins if desired.

Temple workers taking character parts should wear white clothing and white shoes.

Persons coming to the Temple should have their minds upon the work they have come to do, and the workers should neither say nor do anything to detract their attention therefrom.

All unnecessary conversation should be dispensed with, and all necessary conversation should be in an undertone.

There should be no unnecessary standing around or wandering about the halls or rooms of the Temple. Each person should do his or her part in carrying forward the work as expeditiously as possible.

Those who wait upon others should be careful to keep their breath sweet and their fingernails clean. Foul breath may be caused through neglect of the teeth, or over eating; through lack of exercise or of pure air or by neglecting to drink plenty of water.

Those in the wash rooms should not invite those who come to the Temple for Endowments to come to their room. There should be no discriminating for or against any person or class of persons. Those who are most in need of aid should be the first to receive assistance.

Modesty should characterize the actions both of workers and of those who come to the Temple to do their own work.

At the Veil, special care should be taken to adhere strictly to the instructions and the spirit of that part of the Endowments. Pure thoughts and circumspect behavior is imperative.

Be to those who come to the Temple a servant, and serve such as if he or she were your dearest friend.

Avoid everything that savors of selfishness. The work we are called to is one of unselfish, generous service to others, and we should be looking for the opportunity to thus serve.

The affairs of the Temple should not be talked abroad.

In ordinance work, speak to be heard by those who are concerned, but avoid speaking unnecessarily loud.

Gum chewing should not be indulged in within the Temple or its approaches.

Hats must not be worn in the Temple. Men should remove their hats before entering the Annex. We would be pleased if the sisters would observe the same rule.

Punctuality is a virtue which every Temple worker should possess and practice.

Brethren and sisters who have been set apart as regular temple workers may have access, while in the temple, to the books containing the ceremonies, but neither the books nor a transcript therefrom should be taken away from the Temple.

We are sure the Lord is pleased with those who so willingly serve him by serving their fellowmen, whether living or dead, and we are just as sure he will abundantly reward them for their services. **—George F. Richards, Oct. 26, 1922**

INSTRUCTIONS CONCERNING TEMPLE ORDINANCE WORK

At least one year should be allowed to elapse after death of individuals before Temple ordinances are performed on their behalf, unl[e]ss it is known the deceased were faithful members of the Church or that they were prepared to obey the Gospel before their death.

Individuals who were members of the Church, at time of death, do not need to have the ordinances of baptism performed in their behalf, unless they had become unworthy of membership. …

A living woman cannot receive endowments while her husband is alive, if the husband has not been endowed. …

Baptisms, or other ordinances, must not be performed in behalf of any individual whose death is not positively known, except one hundred years, at least, have elapsed from date of birth.

The ordinance of endowment must not be repeated in behalf of any individual who has once been endowed, living or dead. …

The dead who have been endowed can only be represented in any vicarious work by those who have themselves been endowed. A living person cannot be represented by proxy in any Temple ordinances.

When baptisms for the dead have been attended to, the other ordinances to which the individuals are eligible should be performed without delay. Husband and wife, dead, should be sealed on [the] same day they are endowed, if possible.

Those who do ordinance work have not the right to make matches between people who are deceased, except in cases of persons who were married in life. In all other instances the President of the Temple must be consulted. Persons who committed murder or suicide, or who apostatized or were excommunicated from the Church, cannot be be [sic] officiated for except by special permission of the President of the Temple. He should be appealed to in all matters involving doubt or complications.

Before children are sealed to parents or adopted, all the other ordinances to which they are eligible as children should frist [sic] be attended to. All the members of a family should be sealed to their parents at the same time, if possible. If the sealing is to another person than the father or mother, that fact must be stated, and approved by the President of the Temple.

Children under eight years of age do not need to have any Temple ordinances performed in their behalf, other than being sealed to parents if they were not born in the Covenant. Those eight years of age must be baptized, and dead children, who attained over fourteen years of age in life should be endowed, before being sealed to parents. Those between the age of 8 and 14 may be endowed at the discretion of the parents, or those concerned. No person should have the ordinance of Sealing of Children performed for those who are not of their own lineage. ...

In the performance of work for the dead, the right of heirship (blood relationship) should be sacredly regarded. When practicable relatives should represent the dead. The name of the individual at whose instance (by whose authorization or permission) the work is done, and his or her relationship to each of the dead is required for [the] record if the relationship is known. As a rule the eldest living MALE representative of the family, who is a member of the Church, is the recognized heir. Any individuals who are eligible may act as proxies for the dead but, unless the proxy is the heir, their relationship to the dead, if any[,] is not to be entered. ...

The Saints who enter the sacred building should be properly prepared. Their bodies should be scrupulously clean. Shoes worn out of doors should be removed from the feet in the Temple Annex, [and] slippers may be substituted therefore. Males should be ordained Elders before they come to the Temple to receive their own endowments.

The Saints who attend to baptisms for the dead should be amply dressed in white before entering the font. All participants in the ordinance of sealing children should also be dressed in clean, white clothing. Males over 21 or females over 18 years of age, are not permitted to witness or take part in any Temple ordinances, except baptism for the dead, until they have received their own endowments. Children under the ages specified, may be sealed to their parents before having their endowments, but they are not permitted to witness any other ceremonies except baptism for the dead.

Each individual should be provided with the endowment clothing they need. The garments must be clean and white, and of the approved pattern; they must not be altered or mutilated, and are to be worn as intended, down to the wrists and ankles, and around the neck. These requirements are imperative; admission to the Temple will be refused to those who do not comply therewith.

The living who receive their own endowments are required to state their names in full, date and place of birth, date of baptism, and names of parents. Couples who come to the Temple to be married (sealed), must bring Licenses issued by County Clerks of this State; if this is not complied with, the ceremony will not be performed. Those who have been legally married before do not require such licenses. Marriages of first cousins are prohibited by state law. Personal permission, or authorization by legal affidavit, of [a] parent or guardian is required by County Clerks before issuing a license for marriage of a man under 21 or a woman under 18 years of age. Marriages can not be performed in the Temple unless the individuals are endowed. Husbands and wives must be sealed before their children can be sealed to them.

Individuals, or families, who cannot conveniently attend personally to the performance of Temple work in behalf of their dead kindred, or friends, can make arrangements to have such work done at their instance. There is not [a] charge made by the Temple authorities for performances of the ordinance, but, when proxies have to be obtained to act in endowments for the dead, which occupies the time of an entire session in Temple work, it is customary to pay such proxies a small sum, to partly remunerate them for personal expenses; usually a man receives 75 cents, and a woman 50 cents for such service.

Persons who desire to perform Temple ordinances in behalf of the dead, but have not names of their own kindred, or friends, for that purpose, can be provided with names from lists that are on file in the Temple Recorder's office.

The Saints residing in Missions of the Church, who desire to have Temple ordinances performed in behalf of their dead kindred, can have arrangements made therefor by applying to their respective Mission Presidents. Those who reside in Stakes of Zion are advised to have their Temple work performed in the Temple that is nearest the locality where they reside. …

The Temple is open on Monday and Tuesday at 8:30 a.m., on Wednesday, Thursday and Friday at 6:30 a.m. Record taking commencing at 7 a.m. Monday is devoted to taking the record of Baptisms for the dead which are performed on Monday and Tuesday. Baptismal records are not taken after eleven o'clock Mondays. The higher ordinances are attended to on Wednesdays, Thursdays and Fridays. The earlier the Saints come to give in [their] record[s] the better. Children who are to be sealed to parents should not be brought to the Temple before 12 m. [noon]

Four sessions are held each endowment day. [The] first session record [is] taken [at] 7 a.m.; [the] second session record [is] taken [at] 8 a.m.; [the] third session record [is] taken [at] 11 a.m., and [the] fourth session record [is] taken [at] 1 p.m. Sealings can be attended to in all but the last session. As far as possible, those who go through for [their] own endowments and marriage, should attend the second session.

All who enter the Temple must patiently observe good order and proper decorum; loud and irrelevant conversation should be avoided.

ALL WHO COME TO THE TEMPLE TO PERFORM ORDINANCE WORK ARE EXPECTED TO MAKE DONATIONS ACCORDING TO THEIR CIRCUMSTANCES, TO AID IN MEETING NECESSARY EXPENSE, BUT THE POOR WHO HAVE NOTHING TO GIVE ARE EQUALLY WELCOME.

Recommends for the privilege to work in the House of the Lord must be renewed every six months. Each individual needs a recommend, including children over eight years of age. …

The foregoing instructions are issued by the authority of the First Presidency. **—George F. Richards, ca. 1920s; emphasis in original**

Spent a busy day there [Salt Lake temple] considering the ordinances and suggested changes for harmony's sake and for clarification. **—George F. Richards diary, Nov. 20, 1922**

Spent an hour or more with the First Presidency considering the ordinances & ceremonies of the Temple. Some changes made. **—George F. Richards diary, Nov. 24, 1922**

I took [the] 8:00 A.M. train for Logan and arrived there at noon. I took with me 12 books of temple ordinances, rules &c for the use of the Logan temple. The Temple Presidents' Book containing all the Temple ordinances and eleven books of parts written from the Presidents' books. We have eight such sets of books, one for each of the temples. I brought the old books back with me. Going to Logan I read all the ordinances, ceremonies and rules and while there I read them all to the workers in the temple. These books and their contents represent the work of months of my time and it is, I regard, a splendid accomplishment. All the temple ordinances have been considered and many changes have been made. More than 100 rules and decisions have been corr[e]lated and decided upon for the guidance of Temple presidents and these, some o[ld] & many new ones are written in the Presidents Book, and all have been approved of the Council of the First Presidency, the Twelve and the Presiding Patriarch. **—George F. Richards diary, Dec. 5, 1922**

We feel constrained to call your attention to the custom prevailing to some extent in our temples of baptism for health, and to remind you that baptism for health is not part of our temple work, and therefore to permit it to become a practice would be an innovation detrimental to temple work, and a departure as well from the provision instituted of the Lord for the care and healing of the sick of His Church.[14] And in this connection we desire to say that the practice of Church members going to Temples to be administered to is a departure from the way instituted of the Lord, and we are desirous that these things should be corrected and receive attention of the proper authorities in the branches, Wards, and Stakes of the Church where they belong, and it will be for you to so inform your temple workers and those who may come to you from time to time for baptisms for health and to be administered to. **—Heber J. Grant, Charles W. Penrose, and Anthony W. Ivins to Temple Presidents, Dec. 15, 1922, cited in Anthony W. Ivins to Frank Y. Taylor and counselors, Jan. 18, 1923**

....

14. From entries in the current collection, readers may recall that Brigham Young spoke about temple ordinances in September 1873 and said: "We can, at the present time, go into the Endowment House and be baptized for the dead, receive our washings and anointings, etc., for there we have a font that has been erected [and] dedicated expressly for baptizing people for the remission of sins, for their health and for their dead friends." In a letter to temple presidents on May 20, 1896, the First Presidency set the wording for health baptisms. In the "Rules for the Regulation of Temple Work" issued in April 1902, the First Presidency allowed "males under 21 and females under 18" to enter the temple to be "baptized for their health," adding that they could "also be baptized for the dead [and] sealed to their parents."

After meeting I remained with members of the Twelve and later[,] with Pres[ident] [Rudger] Clawson[,][15] visited absentees Jos[eph] F[ielding] Smith & O[rson] F. Whitney[16] and discussed proposed changes in the garment which had been considered before the Council of the Presidency, the Twelve & Patriarch, the matter having been referred to the Twelve for recommendation. **—George F. Richards diary, Apr. 5, 1923**

At the regular weekly meeting of the Council of the twelve the matter of changing or permitting some changes to be made in our temple garments.—Four changes are proposed & nearly all the brethren seem to favor them.—1. closing the crotch & using a button and a flap. 2. Eliminating the loose collar. 3. Using buttons instead of strings. 4. Shorter sleeves for women. **—Richard R. Lyman diary, Apr. 5, 1923, Perry Special Collections**

President George F. Richards of the Salt Lake Temple called on the [First] Presidency this morning and we discussed the unwritten ceremonies of the temple and also the question of allowing some changes in the style of the garments that the people who have been through the temple should wear. There was no decision made. **—Heber J. Grant diary, Apr. 14, 1923**

I spent 1½ hours with the [First] Presidency where I read to them the ceremonies connected with the giving of the 1st and 2nd lectures of the Aaronic Priesthood as I had written them after hearing them repeated and after I had revised them. I asked if all the ceremonies could not be written, revised and approved and go into the Presidents' Book held only by the Temple Presidents. The Presidency were all present and thought favorably of these. The matter is to be submitted to the Council of the First Presidency, the Twelve & Patriarch. This would give us a standard to go by that these ceremonies might be kept uniform.

The subject of the garment was again brought up and considered and certain changes thought favorably of[:] the permis[s]ibility of dispensing with the collar, using buttons instead of strings, using the closed

15. Rudger Clawson (1857-1943) was ordained to the Quorum of the Twelve in 1898 and became its president in 1921.

16. Orson Ferguson Whitney (1855-1931) was ordained to the Quorum of the Twelve in 1906.

crotch and fl[a]p, and for the women wearing elbow sleaves and leg length legs just below the knee.

I spent about seven hours at the temple—President E[dward] J. Wood[17] was given a full set of Temple books to take home with him to Cardston for the Temple. **—George F. Richards diary, Apr. 14, 1923**

I spent [the day] at the temple writing what ha[ve] heretofore been [the] unwritten ceremonies of the temple. My son George assisted me all the afternoon. **—George F. Richards diary, Apr. 16, 1923**

I spent at the Temple [a] busy [day] at my desk and meeting callers, answering questions. Pres[ident] Jos[eph] F[ielding] Smith & Albert M. Davis, my assistants[,] read and approved the form of ceremonies which I have been preparing. **—George F. Richards diary, Apr. 17, 1923**

I was the speaker at the temple this morning, prayed at the altar in Council—Our Council [of the Twelve Apostles] meeting lasted from 10 a.m. to about 4 p.m. I read in the council meeting [the parts] which [are] known as the unwritten ordinances of the temple[,] prepared by me[,] and it was decided to have copies made and one each entered inside the Presidents' Book of each Temple. **—George F. Richards diary, Apr. 19, 1923**

I spent some time with the [First] Presidency and [Presiding] Bishopric considering improvements to be made at the temple. It was left in the hands of the Bishopric & Presidency of the Temple.

I had the unwritten ordinances of the Endowments typed today by Bro[ther] Jos[eph] Anderson under the direction of Duncan M. McAllister. This is done by the authority of the First Presidency. A copy is to be kept in the Presidents' Book at each temple. **—George F. Richards diary, Apr. 20, 1923**

Coming not as an order, nor as a rule to be rigidly enforced, but rather permissive in character, is a recent outgiving of the First Presidency of the Church of Jesus Christ of Latter-day Saints. It concerns the garments worn by members of the church who have been married in the temple, or who have participated in other ceremonies performed or rites observed therein.

---

17. Edward James Wood (1866-1956) was the first president of the Cardston, Alberta, temple, serving from 1923 to 1948.

While minor modifications of the temple garment, it is said, have been made at various times during past years, the latest order in permission is regarded by younger members of the church as most liberal and acceptable. Among the older membership the optional change is variously received. Some of the pioneer stock look upon any deviation from the old order as a departure from what they had always regarded as an inviolable rule. Others of long standing in the church accept the change as a progressive move intended to add to personal comfort.

OLD STYLE UNCOMFORTABLE

In the old days the temple garment was made of plain, unbleached cotton cloth. Unbleached linen was as far afield in "finery" as the devotee was permitted to go. No buttons were used on the garment. Tape tie-strings took their place.[18] The garment itself was uncomfortably large and baggy. But despite these imperfections, the old-style garment is faithfully adhered to by many of the older and sincerely devout members of the church. These regard the garment as a safeguard against disease and bodily harm, and they believe that to alter either the texture of cloth or style, or to abandon the garment altogether would bring evil upon them.[19]

One good woman of long membership in the church, hearing of the change that has recently come about, went to the church offices and uttered fervid objection. "I shall not alter my garments, even if President Grant has ordered me to do so. My garments now are made as they were when I was married in the endowment house long before the temple was built. The pattern was revealed to the Prophet Joseph and Brother Grant has no right to change it," she said.

Explanation was made that the first presidency had merely issued permission to those who so desired to make the modifying change;

---

18. In the nineteenth century, "tape" referred to a narrow band of fabric, sometimes woven, for curtain ties and string (Noah Webster, *An American Dictionary of the English Language,* 1828).

19. The idea of the garment as a shield against physical harm goes back to Nauvoo where the story was told of Willard Richards escaping gunfire unharmed when wearing his garments in the Carthage Jail, while Joseph Smith and his brother Hyrum were killed and John Taylor injured while not wearing theirs. In 1996 J. W. "Bill" Marriott, CEO of the Marriott Hotel chain, told Mike Wallace on CBS's *60 Minutes* news program that he was spared physical harm when wearing his garments during a boat fire.

that any member of the church who preferred to adhere to the original style was at perfect liberty to do so.

President Charles W. Penrose says that modification of the garment is elective with each individual member of the church who has gone through the temple. The change in style is permitted for various good reasons, chief among which are promotion of freedom of movement in the body and cleanliness. Formerly the sleeves were long, reaching to the wrists. While doing housework the women would roll up the sleeves. If sleeves were to be rolled up they might as well be made short in the first place for convenience, it was argued. Permission to abbreviate is now given, but it is not an order and is not compulsory, it is explained.

IS GENERALLY WELCOMED

Encasing the lower limbs the old-style garment reaches to the ankles and is looked upon by young members as baggy, uncomfortable and ungainly. The young of the gentler sex complained that to wear the old style with the new and finer hosiery gave the limbs a knotty appearance. It was embarrassing in view of the generally accepted sanitary shorter skirt. Permission is therefore granted by the first presidency to shorten the lower garment. Also buttons are permitted to take the place of the tie-strings.

Young men of the church, especially those who take exercise or play games at gymnasiums, favor the shorter garment. The permission granted is hailed by them as a most acceptable and progressive one. Altogether, and except in few instances, the permissive modification is welcomed as a sanitary move and a change looking to the comfort and health of those who wear temple garments.

Instead of the old-style coarse, unbleached, irritating material of which temple garments were once made, the finer knitted goods, and even silks, are now used. These materials and modified styles are officially approved, but such alterations are optional with each individual, and by no means compulsory, church officials desire it understood. **—"Temple Garments Greatly Modified, Church Presidency Gives Permission, Style Change Optional with Wearer,"** ***Salt Lake Tribune,*** **June 4, 1923**

For some time past the First Presidency and Council of Twelve have had under consideration the propriety of permitting certain modification in the temple garment, with the following result:

After careful and prayerful consideration it was unanimously decided that the following modifications may be permitted, and a garment of the following style be worn by those Church members who wish to adopt it, namely:

(1) Sleeve to elbow.
(2) Leg just below knee.
(3) Buttons instead of strings.
(4) Collar eliminated.
(5) Crotch closed.

It may be observed that no fixed pattern of Temple garment has ever been given, and that the present style of garment differs very materially from that in use in the early history of the Church, at which time a garment without collar and with buttons was frequently used.

It is the mind of the First Presidency and the Council of Twelve that this modified garment may be used by those who desire to adopt it, without violating any covenant they make in the House of the Lord, and with a clear conscience, so long as they keep the covenants which they have made and remember that the garment is the emblem of the Holy Priesthood designed by the Lord as a covering for the body, and that it should be carefully preserved from mutilation and unnecessary exposure, and be properly marked.

It should be clearly understood that this modified garment does not supersede the approved garment now in use, that either of these patterns may be worn, as Church members prefer, without being considered unorthodox, and those using either will not be out of harmony with the order of the Church.

In order that there may be uniformity in temple work, and that the expedition in the administration of the ordinances of the House of the Lord may not be impeded, we recommend that people doing temple work, whether it be ordinance work for the dead or first endowments for the living, wear the approved garment now in use. If persons appear at the temple with the modified style, however, they should not be refused admittance, provided they come properly recommended. Bishops, in giving recommends to the temple should call attention to this recommendation.

Will you advise the Bishops of your Stake of these changes, being careful to give the matter no unnecessary publicity.

This letter is not to pass from your hands, nor are copies to be furnished to any other person. …

NOTE: We send you this copy of a letter addressed to Stake Presidents for your personal information, and to be used by you in connection with the instructions contained in it. **—Heber J. Grant, Charles W. Penrose, and Anthony W. Ivins to Stake and Temple Presidents, June 14, 1923**

Now in one of these meetings [a prayer circle presided over by George F. Richards] before I went on my mission, President Richards had announced to the brethren that at the meeting that day they had come to the final conclusion that a modified garment was to be allowed.

Now I was to go to the temple the next day to get my endowments. This would have been sometime in May or June [July 13] of 1923 because I was getting ready to go on my mission. Father was going to go with me the next day and Mother had purchased the old fashioned garments for me. He came home and said [he had just learned] that they could wear a new garment and ZCMI had them in stock. They had ordered them in and they were available. It would now be announced [through priesthood channels] as the brethren announced it [to stake leaders] at stake conferences; there was never a public announcement made of it but they would simply notify the stake presidencies and the bishops in the stake.

Well, Mother said, "I think it is a lot better for you to take the new garments in the mission field than these old ones with the strings which will cause comments everywhere you go." ZCMI opened at eight o'clock in those days; we were going to the nine o'clock session. She came down with us and went to ZCMI and got two pairs of these garments. Father and I went to the temple and met Mother.

We had quite a scene in the temple because I was the first one that had ever appeared in the temple with these new garments. When I went into the washing and anointing rooms, Brother Snow, who lived up here on Canyon Road and who was one of the Church attorneys, I think, that used to officiate in a session there in the washing and anointing room, would not let me put them on. He said, "That isn't a temple garment. You can't wear them."

There I was stuck and I said, "Well, my father got the word that this was to be allowed. Here I am. What can I do?" Father had finished and was outside waiting for me to come. So Brother Snow put his head outside of the room and said, "Bishop Lyon," and he came over. Brother Snow said, "This young man doesn't have a temple garment." My father said, "Well, last night at the meeting President Richards said that the new garment, the modified garment, should be allowed and this is it." Brother Snow said he had not been authorized to do this. "He cannot go through." They didn't have a clothing rental service then as far as I know. It was "bring your own" pretty well in those days.

Father said, "Well, is President Richards in the building?" He said, "Yes." So I just stayed there and Father went out and put his clothes on and went up and called for President Richards. President Richards came down and I can remember President Richards came down in the washing room and called the men out of the washing and anointing rooms and he said, "Now brethren, you know this morning when we met in meeting, I told you that there had been a change made yesterday in the meeting. It's not right for you to make the decision. The decision has been made and it's all right. This is the decision that has been made and this is going to be it."

So we went back in and put the garments on. In those days they marked them right on you the first time. You couldn't buy them marked at that time. At any rate, so far as I know[,] I am the first person at least in the Salt Lake Temple that ever wore the modified garment. It came down to the ankle and down below the elbow.

[Question]: But it did not have the strings?

L: It had not strings. It had buttons. It was just basically a one-piece union suit made by one of the knitting mills here. That's what I took on my mission. I know I was the first one with them going over. All the other missionaries had the old fashioned garments; I was the first over there with them. They quizzed my going over on the boat. They thought I was a renegade or something. **—T. Edgar Lyon[20] oral history, Jan. 20, 1975, pp. 249-50, excerpt in Buerger Papers[21]**

BLESSING UPON THE HEAD OF SISTER ARMENIA WILLEY LEE,[22] PRESIDENT ANTHONY W. IVINS BEING VOICE, SETTING HER APART TO BE THE PRESIDING WOMAN IN THE ALBERTA TEMPLE.

---

20. Thomas Edgar Lyon (1903-1978) taught at the LDS Institute at the University of Utah and was a research historian at Nauvoo Restoration, Inc.

21. See also T. Edgar Lyon Jr., *T. Edgar Lyon: A Teacher in Zion* (Provo: Brigham Young University Press, 2002), 39-41.

22. Armenia Willey Lee (1881-1965) was a widow at the time of her calling to the Alberta temple. She later married Mark Anthony Coombs in 1936.

Sister Lee, we lay our hands upon your head in the name of the Lord, and inasmuch as you have been chosen to act as the presiding woman in the temple, working in harmony with and under the direction of President [Edward J.] Wood, we bless you with the spirit of this calling, that the Lord may give you an understanding heart, that you may know, as you come in contact with women, both old and young, their necessities and their requirements, to answer the questions which they may ask, under the inspiration of the Spirit of the Lord, and to give them the necessary instructions for their guidance, and to direct the labors of other women, each in their proper place and in their proper sphere.

We pray our Father in Heaven that He will qualify you for this work, that you may come to understand thoroughly the plan of human redemption, which is typified in the ordinances that are administered here, that He will give you bodily strength and mental understanding, so that this mission which we now place upon you may be properly discharged.

We bless you, Sister Lee, with the spirit of this calling, and promise you that if you shall go to the Lord, He will hear and answer your prayers and will qualify you and you shall have great joy in the performance of this duty, all of which we seal upon you, and set you apart to this work in the name of Jesus Christ, our Redeemer. Amen. **—Typescript dated Aug. 29, 1923, in the Anthony W. Ivins Papers, Utah State Historical Society**

I went to the Temple soon after 10 A.M. and considered the temple ordinances with a view to recommending to the Presidency a number of changes. **—George F. Richards diary, Sept. 23, 1923**

I spent the day at the Temple. Jos[eph] F. Smith Jr. & Stephen L. Richards spent two hrs. with me in the Temple going over the Temple ordinances, considering proposed changes. Adjourned until 2 P.M. tomorrow. **—George F. Richards diary, Oct. 29, 1923**

Elders Jos[eph] F. Smith Jr & Stephen L. Richards spent an hour with me in going over some suggestions I have to offer of change[s] in the ordinances[,] including a rewriting of them. **—George F. Richards diary, Oct. 30, 1923**

Elders Jos[eph] F[ielding] Smith & Stephen L. Richards sat with me as a committee in examining the ceremonies and ordinances [and] suggested changes. In the evening Bro[ther] Israel Call assisted me in indicating more fully the actions as they are practiced. I now am prepared to present to the [First] Presidency & Twelve my recommendations. **—George F. Richards diary, Nov. 2, 1923**

Worked on Temple ordinances to get them in shape to present suggestions of changes for the consideration of the Council. **—George F. Richards diary, Nov. 15, 1923**

Called on the First Presidency and attended to some business with them. I presented to them the corrected form of [the] Ceremony for time marriage [sealings][23] … which received their approval. **—George F. Richards diary, Dec. 14, 1923**

Now, my dear sisters, in receiving your blessings you will go into a room, having removed your clothing and having placed a shield around you to protect your body, and there you will receive the greatest blessings that any woman on this earth ever had that we have any account of. Then you will be clothed in a garment by the sister who has authority. This garment that you receive is given symbolically as was the garment given to Adam & Eve in the Garden of Eden. On it will be placed sacred marks. These are the marks of the Holy Priesthood. Some look upon it as a very trifling thing and say "What difference does it make [to] just to cut a hole in a piece of cloth?" Girls, you might say the same thing when you go to meeting and take the sacrament. There is this difference, we are carrying out the commands of God through our symbols of the things our Father in Heaven bestowed on his children that entitles them to the blessings they could not have if it were not for that garment on the body and the marks placed upon it.

When Joseph Smith received the endowments and revelation from the Lord to be given to his people by authority, he also received instructions as to how to make this garment. None had ever seen anything like it and the sisters who made it were under his direction and when it was submitted to him, he said that it was right and the way it had looked to him [in his mind] and he accepted it. This garment had a collar and it had strings to tie it and sleeves that came to the wrist,

23. Some sealings are performed for the duration of the couple's earth life and not for eternity.

not to the hand, but about an inch above, and the leg came down to the ankle joint. This was the pattern given and it is right[,] for Aunt Eliza Snow was the governess and seamstrees in his house at the time the first garments were made and heard the instructions to the sisters. Thus the Kingdom of God rolls on and the living authorit[ies] are the ones who can make changes in the revealed work of the Lord to answer the purposes of the day in which they live. Today there is a change in the garments that can be made outside of this Holy House in the garments we wear on our bodies. This garment is called the modified or permitted garment and the pattern of this garment I will point out to you, but first I want to explain to you about the little mark we have in the back of our garment, the little woven design which we have looked upon as desig[n]ating the things we buy as being the right kind of a garment. Now, sisters, I want to tell you the way we came by this mark of approval. In days past there was a great variety in the way they made the garments as then they were always made from cloth. President [John] Taylor prayed to the Lord that they might be permitted to use the knitted garment and they could all be of the same pattern. They might vary a little, but the garments were all similar and when they made these garments, many people questioned the change from the cloth garment to the knitted garment. It was because the living authority said we might and it was this mark that was used to tell us that the garment was approved. Today, these marks of approval can be purchased by the thousands and are placed upon anything their customers will buy and for that reason, today this mark means nothing to us.

You know what is the right kind of a garment. The garment to be worn outside of the House of the Lord has been approved by authority and I have a written statement signed by President [Heber J.] Grant to this effect. The garment is not too low in the neck, just a nice, modest neck, but with [the] collar omitted. Instead of being to the wrist, they come to the elbow, and the leg instead of coming to the ankle, comes below the knee, always covering the knee so that the mark placed by the holy Priesthood can come over the knee, for that is where i[t] should be worn. This pattern can be worn and you are not doing anything contrary to the Priesthood, but it must be worn only outside this house and cannot be worn in the House of the Lord.

Some people who do not understand this very well will tell you that anything that has the marks placed upon it is a garment of the

Holy Priesthood. (And some make these marks about like a button hole, but they should be about one inch each way.) But this is false, for you are desecrating our covenants and deceiving yourself by putting on anything of this kind. There are two kinds of garments and two only; the one given by the Prophet Joseph Smith to be worn in the Temple and the one given by President Grant to be worn outside the House of the Lord. Wear this modified garment and be happy if it adds to your happiness to wear it this way. When you wear anything besides these two approved patterns you are wearing only a piece of underwear which is not a garment and you are placing upon your body something with the marks of the Holy Priesthood where these marks should not be placed for it is not approved of nor accepted by the authority of God. These are vital questions and thousands of people are being deceived and are wearing something that exposes their bodies and des[e]crates the marks of the Holy Priesthood.

Now, Dear Sisters, are there any questions[?]

Garments should be worn all the time. When you understand the covenants, you will understand that you cannot take them off at night. **—Zina Y. Card, "Garments," *Temple Instructions,* ca. 1923**

....

I went to the Temple as usual and after disposing of the mail & other necessary desk work I called upon the [First] Presidency and arranged that President [Anthony W.] Ivins should go over the Temple ordinances with me and Jos[eph] F[ielding] Smith and give consideration to changes I have proposed, before the Presidency take them up. **—George F. Richards diary, Mar. 10, 1924**

President David H. Cannon presiding. Stake President Edward H. Snow and Counselor George F. Whitehead[24] of the St George Stake were present by invitation of President Cannon.

After Roll Call, President [David] Cannon stated [the] object of meeting.

After making some explanations, he referred to the Presidents Book which he said contained all the ceremonies of the various ordinances except the unwritten parts[,] which he explained.

24. George Frank Whitehead (1863-1961) was president of the St. George temple from 1932 to 1937.

Pres[iden]t Cottam then read the ^what was called^ unwritten parts, [temple] pres[iden]t Cannon making comments as they were read.

Pres[iden]t Cannon stated that President George F. Richards was appointed to see that there was a uniformity of method and system in all the temples. Said when Pres[iden]t Richards came and talked to him, he ^Pres[iden]t Richards^ criti[ci]zed him very severely for not adhering to the unwritten part of the ceremonies as he had been instructed to do. Said he told Pres[iden]t Richards that President [Brigham] Young had 20 men revise the ceremonies of the ordinances. Pres[iden]t Young said "we are going to give endowments for ^the dead^ the first time and we want to give you the ceremonies as they were given by the Prophet Joseph Smith in the Nauvoo Temple."

These endowments were received ^from the Lord^ by the Prophet Jos[eph] Smith in the Nauvoo Temple and the key word of the endowment was revealed to him (here he gave the key word).

Pres[iden]t Cannon referred to the President's book which contained all the ceremonies of the Temple ordinances, except the unwritten part, which we have been using since this Temple opened 47 years ago, and when we came to talk to President Richards, he said that was wrong, that the unwritten part should be written and rendered the same as the other parts.

President Cannon stated that President Richards [confronted him] at Hurrican[e][,] when they [were at] the St George June quarterly conference[.] [Elder Richards] criti[ci]zed him again[,] and said "you must either conform to our method or we to yours." Said Pres[iden]t Richards told him that the [First] Presidency of the Church and the twelve Apostles were the presiding authorities of in [sic] the Church at present, and they must stand at the head and be responsible for the direction of the affairs of the Church, and the [dramatic] parts in the ordinances of the Temples must be rendered as they have directed.

Said Pres[iden]t Richards instructed him to gather up all the old rulings and instructions and burn them up, and if he did not want to do this, to bundle them up and send them to him.

Said Pres[ident] Richards suggested that a good capable man be selected to render a [dramatic] part and keep him on this particular part continuously and not change the parts every two weeks, as had been the practice. In devotional don[']t ask men to speak in turns, but invite in other men, the president of the Stake and other men, bishops of wards etc to speak. … In the creation room, where Eve makes covenant with Adam[,] they clasp hands and remain so till Eloheim instructs them what to do.

[President Cannon] gave as a reason [for] having this meeting, the precarious state of his health. Said Pres[iden]t Richards told him that he should be in harmony with the President of the Stake (here Pres[iden]t Cannon asked Pres[iden]t [Edward H.] Snow if he had not been in harmony with the President of the Stake and Pres[iden]t Snow answered "Yes".)

Mentioned the fact of having given instructions from time to time in regard to the ordinance workers having no authority to do any thing [outside of the temple] in the different wards and stakes on the strength of them being ordinance workers in the Temple. If a man comes recommended from the wards and stakes, the president of the Temple had no authority to debar him [from entrance to the temple], for any d[e]rel[i]ction of duty. The [temple] president's authority was only ministerial.

There is to be a custodian for these books, containing the parts including the unwritten part. We are to appoint a man to take charge of these books, and every book is to be put into the hands of this man and they will be locked up after being used.

If we want any information, not contained in the "Presidents Book" we will refer to the authorities of the Church for that information, but not refer to any of the old rulings.

President Edward H. Snow of the St George Stake presidency was invited to speak. Said he was not familiar enough with all the ordinances to say much about them, but thought the changes have been made from the experience they have had. One change he mentioned is in no longer praying that the blood of the prophets and righteous men, might be atoned for, because this prayer has been answered and is no longer necessary. Mentioned a book exposing Mormonism that he took out of our library to read. This book was ful[l] of falsehoods, and exag[ge]ration and not fit for our people to read and he had the book taken out of the library entirely.

Thought the changes made in the temple ordinances have all the essentials necessary and are made in order to have a uniformity in all the temples. Said the grammar is poor and the construction bad in some of the ceremonies. Spoke of the bad language in the parts as first written; as now written, the same ideas are preserved as formerly expressed.

Approved the idea of one man for one part permanently. Said the men working at the vail should be neat and shaven[,] with sweet breath etc etc.

Pres[iden]t Cannon stated that President Anthony W. Ivins at a conference in Enterprise took exception to the wa[y] the Law of Retribution was worded, and said he thought the language was harsh and that the authorities thought of changing that. If there is anything we wished to be noted for, it was for our uprightness and obedience to authority.

Made further remarks in regard to his dealings with those who are employed in this Temple. Said he has never had any trouble with any one. Spoke of his handling the funds of the Temple in an economical manner. "All we do here is done open and above board, there is nothing hidden." Considered the changes made in the ordinances are an improvement and we are going to conform to them to the very best of our ability.

Benediction. Pres[iden]t George P. Whitehead 2nd counselor in the St George Stake Presidency. **—Minutes of a Meeting Held in the St. George Temple, June 19, 1924, copy in Buerger Papers**

Obtained an interview with Pres[iden]ts [Heber J.] Grant & [Charles W.] Penrose, Elder M[elvin] J. Ballard present. They consented to Bro[ther] [James E.] Talmadge [sic] being on the Committee for Temple Ordinances. I advised Bro[ther] Talmage accordingly. **—George F. Richards diary, July 10, 1924**

Thoughts about my journal. When I think that someone may undertake to look through my journals after I shall have gone hence with a view to accumulating information for a book on my Biography, I feel ashamed that I have written so much into my journal that is of so little worth and so lacking of interest. I have thought that notwithstanding I have been closely associated with others in the making of Church history[,] I would leave the making or writing of such history to the Church, its Stakes, & wards, & missions and that leaves me but little to say about such matters. When pouring over the Temple Ceremonies alone and with a committee appointed to consider them with me I usually mention that I have been working at my desk or in the

Temple, yet in time great changes have evolved which as a whole may not be mentioned by me in my journal. Of that character of work I can say that since I became the President of the Salt Lake Temple we have re-written those temple ceremonies and ordinances which have been heretofore written, first at the time of the Dedication of the St. George Temple, and have put them into leather back covers as loose leaves and provided each Temple President with a copy. Later those ceremonies known as unwritten ceremonies i.e. the covenants and the instructions given in forming the circle and at the veil, were written and copies furnished on loose leaf sheets for the Presidents of Temples Book. A list of 83 rules and decisions have been written also for the guidance of Temple Presidents supplanting all former rules not in full harmony. Each of the Temple Presidents has been supplied with copies, or rather, they were included in the Books when they [were] first sent out to the Temple Presidents.

The Temple Committee have gone over the ceremonies of the Endowments with a view to more perfectly put them in proper form and we are still working on them and I am in hope that in due time these will be considered by the Presidency and as far as is right the suggestions will be approved and the ceremonies be re-written[,] having all the written ceremonies appear in their most perfected form and regular order in the Presidents' Books and in the past books. I am delighted with what has been done thus far and am hopeful that the future will see the other changes made which are very much needed. As these things originated on my recommendations and I have had more to do with them than anybody else[,] I feel that I have had [an] important part in the splendid accomplishment which the saints generally know not of. I have felt that since I have been called to preside here in the Temple that if I should live and labor here acceptably to the Lord, He would use me as an instrument in advancing the work in these lives and I believe he has thus blessed me, and used me. The First Presidency could not be expected to be in touch with all the details of Temple work & with the needed changes only as these things are brought to their attention[,] and who should do this if not the Apostle in charge of the Salt Lake & Leading Temple of the church. The first committee appointed on this work consisted of in order of seniority, Geo[rge] F. Richards, David O. McKay, Jos[eph] Fielding Smith, Stephen L. Richards and John A. Widtsoe. Since David O. McKay is away, in Europe, Bro[ther] James E. Talmage has been appointed a member of that committee.

Pres[ident] A[nthony] W. Ivins has been appointed to go over the work with the Committee before it is presented to the [full Church] Presidency. To date we have had two sittings with Pres[ident] Ivins.

A small sheepskin binding book is kept in my desk which shows progress of the work at the Salt Lake Temple since I became President. This book gives valuable information but is not as complete as I could wish. **—George F. Richards diary, July 12, 1924**

I [sat] with the Temple ordinance Committee for several hours in my office room in the Temple considering the ordinances with a view to suggesting changes to be made in the reading of the ordinances of the Temple. **—George F. Richards diary, Sept. 2, 1924**

....

If you have not already adopted the practice of calling attention to the following regulations, when you issue recommends to individuals going to the Temple, you will please do so hereafter, in every instance.

The garments to be worn in the Temple by those who are receiving endowments for themselves or for the dead must be white, and should be of the unaltered pattern.

All who come to the Temple to perform ordinance work are expected to make donations according to their circumstances, to aid in meeting necessary expenses, but the poor who have nothing to give are equally welcome. This rule has been a part of the printed instructions, since the commencement of work in the Salt Lake Temple, but is repeated here with the request that you will mention it to all whom you issue recommends, because the aggregate amount received is very small. It may properly be suggested to a man, who is going to the Temple to be married[,] that the amount of his donation should approximate or be equal to what he would be required to pay if he had the ceremony performed elsewhere, if he could afford to donate that much.

The following important items are also submitted for your careful attention: ...

Recommends should be issued only to those who are worthy and faithful. A sufficient time should elapse after baptism to prove worthiness. Children under eight years of age do not need recommends when they accompany their parents or guardians. Recommends should not be given to persons afflicted with any kind of infectious disease, or with serious or offensive skin disease.

Before being recommended to receive endowments, each individual should be informed concerning the purpose, and importance, of that sacred ordinance.

Living boys and girls as young as sixteen years of age may receive endowments if, in each case, the character and condition of the individual is such that the Bishop feels justified in issuing a recommend for that purpose.

Males over twenty-one years of age, and females over eighteen, are not permitted to take part in, or witness, Temple ordinances until they receive their own endowments, except that they may be baptized for the dead, [and] in that event the recommend must show that it is issued <u>for baptisms only</u>. If they are to receive endowments at the time they are to be sealed to parents, the fact that they are authorized to be endowed then must be stated on the recommend.

A living woman cannot receive endowments while her husband is alive, if the husband has not been endowed, without special permission of the President of the Church. The same rule applies to men as to women.

Men should be ordained to the Melchizedek Priesthood before they come to the Temple to receive endowments.

Recommends of the privilege to work in the House of the Lord must be renewed every six months. Each individual needs a recommend, including children over eight years of age.

Individuals who have been endowed, and afterwards have been excommunicated and subsequently joined the Church again, should not be recommended to the Temple until former blessings have been sealed upon them by special permission of the President of the Church.

Robes, etc. may be hired at the Temple, but all are advised to provide themselves with their own, if they can do so conveniently. The sisters should not have long "trains" on the white dresses they wear in the Temple, nor decorate with colored ribbons or gaudy ornaments.

All should be perfectly clean in body and clothing, so as not to be offensive to others.

Small children who are to act only in the ordinances of sealing to parents, [or] adoptions, need not be brought to the Temple Annex before 12 m [noon]. Record[-]taking for the first company, on endowment days, begins at 6:30 a.m. All persons intending to go through the Temple with the first company should be in the building not later than 7:00 a.m. To go through with the second company they should be in not later than 8:00 a.m.; with the third company at 11:00 a.m.; the fourth at 1:00 p.m.; and the fifth at 5:30 p.m.

It should be clearly made known to those who can receive recommends to be married in the Temple, that they should not have the marriage ceremony performed before coming to the Temple, unless there is some good and justifiable reason for doing so, such as having to delay an undesirable length of time before they could come, or having to travel alone long distances to reach the Temple.

Persons going to the temple to be married should be instructed that the placing of a ring on the lady's finger is no part of the wedding ceremony and must not be done while at the altar in the sealing room of the temple.

Bishops are not to issue recommends for second anointings; that is the province of the President of the Church. As a general rule, such recommends are issued only in behalf of those who have had endowments in their lifetime, and have been sealed and lived together faithfully as husband and wife, and who have been valiant in the defense of truth and active in all good works. ...

The foregoing instructions are issued by the authority of the First Presidency. **—George F. Richards to bishops, ca. 1925, copy in Buerger Papers; emphasis in original**

REPORT OF TEMPLES FOR THE SIX
MONTHS ENDING JUNE 30, 1925 COMPARISONS

		1925	1924	Increase	Decrease
Special Ordinances[25]		26	52		26
Nature of Work		Logan	Manti	Salt Lake	Total
SPECIAL ENDOWMENTS:[26]					
Living	Male	1	1	9	11
	Female		1	11	12

25. The reference here is to second anointings.

26. This section gives more detail for the "special ordinances" line preceding it.

Dead	Male				
	Female	1		2	3
Total number of Special Ords.		2	2	22	26

—Anthony W. Ivins Papers, Utah State Historical Society

There exists at present a lack of uniformity in recommending Saints from the Missions to do work in the temples.

Following are some of the points we should like you to note when issuing recommends:

(1) Whenever possible brethren should be ordained Elders before coming to the temple for endowments.

(2) Sisters married to non-members should not be recommended to the temple to receive endowments.

(3) Bearers of temple recommends should be instructed that such must be endorsed by the President of the Church before being presented at the temple. As it now is[,] brethren and sisters often go direct to the temples with their recommends and there find they must be endorsed, and thus confusion and delay result.

(4) Brethren and sisters coming to the temples should bring their recommends with them. Sometimes people come from a distance to this city expecting to enter the temple immediately upon their arrival, and then have to wait on expense until their recommends are received. It would be far better for them to wait at their homes until they receive their recommends than to be delayed here.

(5) As far as possible Presidents of Missions should be personally acquainted with each person recommended, or at any rate be fully assured of the entire worthiness of the brother or sister recommended to enter the House of the Lord.

(6) The Deseret News publishes the dates of the closing of the temples during the summer, and it would be well to keep informed as to those dates and thus avoid having saints come long distances to do their temple work only to find the temple closed.

(7) The following form is suggested as sufficient for the purpose of recommending to the temple:

> Elder (or Sister) __________ is recommended as worthy to enter the temple for (endowments) (sealing) (work for the dead). He (or she) is a member of the __________ Branch, __________ Mission.

It will then be proper to add any necessary explanation or instructions as to where the recommend is to be sent, etc. The names of a family may all be inserted on one recommend.

We feel sure that adherence to these rules will be the means of saving our time, also that of the Saints coming to the temples, and those officiating therein. **—Heber J. Grant, Anthony W. Ivins, and Charles W. Nibley to B. H. Roberts,[27] July 25, 1925**

....

Had an appointment with Temple ordinance Committee at 8:00 A.M. and made good progress. **—George F. Richards diary, Jan. 18, 1926**

Second Blessings are only given by the President of the Church upon recommendation of a member of the Council of the Twelve.[28] **—Heber J. Grant to Stephen L. Chipman, Jan. 30, 1926**

I met D[avid] O. McKay, Jos[eph] F[ielding] Smith, S[tephen] L. Richards and J[ohn] A. Widtsoe of the Twelve at the Temple as a committee at 8:00 A.M. where we spent about 1½ hours in consideration of the Temple ordinances with the purpose of suggesting certain changes in the reading of the Ritual of End[owment] & the ceremonies of the Temple. **—George F. Richards diary, Apr. 20, 1926**

At five o'clock went to the temple with my wife and did endowment work for and on behalf of Warren Gamaliel Harding[29] and Sister Grant went through for his wife, after which we stood in behalf of President Theodore Roosevelt's father and mother[30] and also stood for President Harding and wife and were sealed for eternity for these

---

27. Brigham Henry Roberts (1857-1933) was one of the Seven Presidents of Seventy from 1888 to 1933.

28. This change in policy, where previously stake presidents had suggested candidates for the second anointing, resulted in a dramatic decrease in the number of such ordinances. David John Buerger found that Heber J. Grant, whose administration spanned the years 1918-45, "apparently authorized only a few hundred for an annual average of one-tenth that of his predecessor" (Buerger, *The Mysteries of Godliness: A History of Mormon Temple Worship* [San Francisco: Smith Research Associates, 1994], 160).

29. Warren G. Harding (1865-1923) was twenty-ninth president of the United States. He was inaugurated in 1921 and died in office two years later. His wife, Florence King Harding, died in 1924.

30. Theodore Roosevelt (1858-1919) was twenty-sixth president of the United

two couples, George F. Richards performing the ceremonies. **—Heber J. Grant diary, Sept. 10, 1926**

We find upon inquiry that it has been some years since ordinances bestowing second blessings have been performed in cases where both parties are dead.

Where people are sealed in the temple for and on behalf of the dead, or in cases where people who are dead were themselves sealed while living, the feeling has always been that every privilege, power and blessing of every description will be given to them, if they have lived worthy of same, and that they could not have more even if they had additional blessings sealed upon them. We, therefore, feel that there is no necessity of performing the ordinances that Sister Smith requests. **—Heber J. Grant, Anthony W. Ivins, and Charles W. Nibley to Joseph W. McMurrin,[31] Oct. 19, 1926**

[We] reached the temple at ten A.M. and were there until five P.M. The regular endowment ceremonies were read over and discussed. **—Heber J. Grant diary, Dec. 9, 1926.**

Attended temple meeting at 8:15 a.m. and the Weekly Council meeting at 10:00 a.m. The latter continued until about 5 P.M. We had under consideration a revision of the Temple ordinances.

The question of [the oath of] Retribution took considerable time. **—George F. Richards diary, Dec. 9, 1926**

Attended to my regular duties at the Temple as usual—

Attended a meeting of the Twelve [Apostles] from 9 to 10 o'clock and a meeting of the [First] Presidency and Twelve from 10:— a.m. to about 3:— P.M.

This was a very important meeting. At this meeting the Report of the Committee of Apostles on Temple Ordinances was accepted with a few minor changes. This necessitates the printing[32] of the Ceremonies

---

States. His father, Theodore Roosevelt Sr., died in 1879, and his mother, Martha Bulloch, died in 1884.

31. Joseph William McMurrin (1858-1932) was sustained as one of the Seven Presidents of Seventy in 1897.

32. Although he says "printing," the documents will be hand-written, not printed, for distribution to the temples.

for all the Temples. It is helpful to have these ready for the beginning of the New Year. **—George F. Richards diary, Dec. 16, 1926**

....

I went to the Temple as usual. Pres[ident] [Heber J.] Grant called me over to his office[,] and the First Presidency then decided several important points pertaining to the Temple ordinances[,] making a finish of the work which has been under consideration of a committee of five of the Twelve for several years. These points today decided will be reported to the Council for their approval next Thursday. **—George F. Richards diary, Jan. 25, 1927**

At the Council meeting the last of the committee's recommendations concerning the endowment ceremonies was approved. There remains to have them written for all the temples. **—George F. Richards diary, Jan. 27, 1927**

We have the Temple ordinances written into the books for the Presidents of Temples and are preparing the [actors'] Part books and will get them to you in the near future, or at conference time.

At request of President [Heber J.] Grant[,] we have already adopted some of the changes decided upon, and it will be in order for you to do the same.

In sealing for the dead, whether one or both be dead, omit the kissing. Omit from the prayer in the circle all references to avenging the blood of the Prophets.

Omit from the ordinance and lecture all reference to retribution. This last change can be made with a day's notice to those taking parts that contain such reference.

This letter is written with the approval of the [First] Presidency. **—George F. Richards to the President of the St. George Temple,[33] Feb. 15, 1927, copy in Buerger Papers**

It is not customary now for presidents of Stakes, as you know, to recommend people for higher blessings. That matter should be taken up by the visiting apostle at your quarterly conference, and all recommendations of this kind should come direct from the apostles. **—Heber J. Grant to Levi S. Udall, Apr. 6, 1927**

33. This would have been Edward H. Snow (1865-1932), who served as president of the St. George temple from 1926 to 1932.

The only proper place for [a film] presentation [on the life of Jesus Christ] would be a holy temple, if the time could ever come when it might be deemed wise and proper to use the motion picture in these sacred places. We have no such intention at the present time. **—Heber J. Grant, Anthony W. Ivins, and Charles W. Nibley to Pearl W. Peterson, Aug. 27, 1927**

....

[Relief Society] president [Clarissa S.] Williams[34] reported that a second [inquiry] had been received regarding the wearing of L.D.S. garments in hospitals during confinement and other illnesses. She stated that this second letter had come from Arizona. Upon receiving the letter she asked the [First Presidency's] secretary to confer with President [Anthony W.] Iv[i]ns in the matter, and President Iv[i]ns stated that it is perfectly alright and proper for women to remove their garments during lying-in at hospital or during other hospital illnesses. President Williams stated further that in the conference with the Presiding Bishopric this morning the matter was reported to the Presiding Bishop and the Relief Society executive committee were informed by the Bishopric that they have understood for some time that it was allowable for women to remove their garments during the time they are confined in the hospital, if they so desire. They quoted the following ruling, which was made by the First Presidency of the Church: "On March 16, 1925, the Presidency ruled that, in response to an inquiry asking if it was proper to remove garments from patien[ts] during operations, that the wishes of the patients should be considered, but that there had been a ruling of the Presidency some time ago that because of sanitary reasons it might be wise to remove the garments from the patient, and where it is thought best to do so, this may be done." **—Minutes of a Meeting of the General Board of the Relief Society, May 23, 1928, typed excerpt in the Buerger Papers**

According to a recent ruling of the First Presidency and the Council of the Twelve, it will [not] be necessary in the future for temple recommends issued to saints of record in the missions of the United States, Canada and Mexico, to bear the endorsement of the President of the Church or one of his counselors.

---

34. Clarissa Smith Williams (1860-1930) was the daughter of Apostle George Albert Smith and Susan West and was general president of the Relief Society, 1921-1928.

You are therefore hereby authorized to honor such recommends when properly signed by the Branch President and the Mission President.

Temple recommend forms similar to those in use in the wards and stakes of the Church are being printed, and the various missions will be provided with them at an early date. **—Heber J. Grant, Anthony W. Ivins, and Charles W. Nibley to George F. Whitehead, June 28, 1928**

....

APPOINTMENTS, INSTRUCTIONS AND SUGGESTIONS ISSUED BY THE LOGAN TEMPLE

RECOMMENDS

All persons over eight years of age must present recommends signed by the Bishop of the Ward and President of the Stake before being admitted to the Temple, no matter for what purpose they come.

Recommends must be renewed on the 1st day of January or the 1st day of July in each year, as all recommends expire on the 30th day of June and the 31st day of December following the date of their issue. …

Recommends must state the specific work to be performed. Such general terms as "Temple Work," "Work for the dead," "Vicarious work," etc. cannot be accepted. …

Persons coming to the Temple from Missions must bring recommends signed by the Branch President and the President of the Mission.

Recommends should not be given to persons to do Temple work, who after having received their endowments have been excommunicated from the Church, even though they subsequently join the Church, until their former blessings have been conferred upon them by special permission of the President of the Church.

Males over 21, and females over 18 years of age should not be recommended to the Temple to take part in, or witness any of the Temple ordinances, except baptisms, until they have had their own endowments.

BAPTISMS

Although it is preferable that baptisms for the living be not performed in the Temples, yet because of local conditions, permission has been given the Logan Temple to do so. These baptisms are performed on Tuesdays only, and it is necessary that all who come for this purpose, as also the parent or guardian who may accompany the child, to bring recommends. A certificate of baptism is always given the child, and also a copy sent to the Bishop of the Ward who issues the recommend.

Baptisms for health are not performed in the Temple.

The Saints who attend to do baptisms, whether for themselves or for the dead, should be amply dressed in white before entering the font.

Baptisms or other ordinances must not be performed in behalf of any individual whose death is not positively known, except one hundred years at least have elapsed from date of birth.

ENDOWMENTS

A living woman cannot receive endowments while her husband is alive, if the husband has not been endowed.

The ordinances of endowment must not be repeated in behalf of any individual who has once been endowed, living or dead. ...

The dead who have been endowed can only be represented in any vicarious work by those who have themselves been endowed. ...

MARRIAGES

Couples who come to the Temple to be married (sealed), must bring Licenses issued by County Clerks of this State; if this is not complied with, the ceremony will not be performed. Those who have been legally married before do not require such licenses. Marriages of first cousins are prohibited by state law. Personal permission, or authorization by legal affidavit, of parent or guardian is required by County Clerks before issuing a license for marriage of a man under 21 or a woman under 18 years of age. Marriages cannot be performed in the Temple unless the individuals are endowed.

Those who are worthy of receiving recommends to be married in the Temple should not have the marriage ceremony performed before coming to the Temple, unless there is some good and justifiable reason for doing so, such as having to delay an undesirable length of time before they could come, or having to travel alone a long distance to reach the Temple.

SEALINGS

Husband and wife, dead, should be sealed on the same day they are endowed if possible, and their children, if any, sealed to them as soon thereafter as possible.

Before children are sealed to parents or adopted, all the other ordinances to which they are eligible as children should first be attended to. All the members of a family should be sealed to their parents at the same time, if possible. If the sealing is to another person than the father or mother, that fact must be stated, and approved by the President of the Temple.

Children under eight years of age do not need to have any Temple ordinances performed in their behalf, other than being sealed to parents, if they were not born in the Covenant. Those eight years of age must be baptized, and dead children, who attained over fourteen years of age in life[,] should be endowed, before being sealed to parents. Those between the age of 8 and 14 may be endowed at the discretion of the parents, or those concerned. No person should have the ordinance of Sealing of Children performed for those who are not of their own lineage.

Those who do ordinance work have not the right to make matches between people who are deceased, except in cases of persons who were married in life. In all other instances the President of the Temple must be consulted.

Living husbands and wives must be sealed before their children can be sealed to them.

It is not necessary for small children, who are to be sealed to their parents, or to be adopted, to be at the Temple before 12 o'clock (noon).

GENERAL INSTRUCTIONS

... In the performance of work for the dead, the right of heirship (blood relationship) should be sacredly regarded. When practicable[,] relatives should represent the dead.

The name of the individual at whose instance (by whose authorization or permission) the work is done, and his or her relationship to each of the dead is required for [the] record if the relationship is known. As a rule the eldest living MALE representative of the family, who is a member of the Church, is the recognized heir. Any individuals who are eligible may act as proxies for the dead but, unless the proxy is the heir, their relationship to the dead, if any[,] is not to be entered.

It is advised that individuals having Temple ordinances performed should limit that work to persons bearing the SURNAMES of their parents and grandparents, and who resided in localities where those ancestors lived; that provides four family lines. To include other lines than those involves the probability of repeating Temple ordinances that individuals representing other families may have a better right to have performed. Every possible precaution should be taken to prevent such undesirable repetition. Temple work may be done for dead individuals who were married to your blood relations, but the family lines of such relatives-in-law must not be included in that work.

Each individual should be provided with the endowment clothing they need. The garments to be used in the Temple must be of what is known as the old style, clean and of white material.

At least one year should be allowed to elapse after [the] death of individuals before Temple ordinances are performed in their behalf, unless it is known the deceased were faithful members of the Church or that they were prepared to obey the Gospel before their death.

A living woman cannot receive endowments while her husband is alive, if the husband has not been endowed.

Persons who committed murder or suicide, or who apostatized or were excommunicated from the Church, cannot be officiated for except by special permission of the President of the Temple. He should be appealed to in all matters involving doubt or complications.

When baptisms for the dead have been attended to, the other ordinances to which the individuals are eligible should be performed without delay. Husband and wife, dead, should be sealed on [the] same day they were endowed, if possible.

The Saints who enter the sacred building should be properly prepared. Their bodies should be scrupulously clean. Shoes worn out of doors should be removed from the feet in the Temple Annex[;] slippers may be substituted therefor. Males should be ordained Elders before they come to the Temple to receive their own endowments.

The Saints who attend to baptisms for the dead should be amply dressed in white before entering the font. All participants in the ordinance of sealing children should also be dressed in clean, white clothing. Males over 21 or females over 18 years of age, are not permitted to witness or take part in any Temple ordinances, except baptism for the dead, until they have received their own endowments. Children under the ages specified, may be sealed to their parents before having their endowments, but they are not permitted to witness any other ceremonies except baptism for the dead. …

Individuals, or families, who cannot conveniently attend personally to the performances of Temple work in behalf of their dead kindred, or friends, can make arrangements to have such work done at their instance. There is no charge made by the Temple authorities for performance of the ordinances, but, when proxies have to be obtained to act in endowments for the dead, which occupies the time of an entire session in Temple work, it is customary to pay such proxies a small sum, to partly remunerate them for personal expenses; usually a man receives 75 cents, and a woman 50 cents for such service.

Children who are to be sealed to parents need not be brought to the Temple before 12 m [noon]. **—For stake presidents, bishops, and genealogical committees in the Logan Temple District, Jan. 1, 1929; emphasis in original**

Two weeks ago tonight[,] Th[ursday][,] M[ar]ch 28, 1929[,] I met with my prayer circle for the last time—and disbanded it. The [first] presidency & the Council of the Twelve decided March 28th that only official prayer circles be continued—that is[,] circles which have other business to do as for example [the] high council—& our weekly councils meeting. It is nearly 33 y[ea]rs since Francis M. Lyman invited me into the circle. President [Heber J.] Grant presided over it after the death of F[rancis] M. L[yman] until he became president of the church—since then I have been its president. While I feel relieved[,] I hated to say good bye to those fine brethren. I have been associated with them so long. We all said good bye & God bless you—but not without shedding some tears. **—Richard R. Lyman diary, Apr. 11, 1929, Perry Special Collections; emphasis in original**

Dr. Fred Clawson called and asked permission to give a recommend to J--- A. G-------- and his wife to witness the marriage of their daughter. I told him I would give him an answer later in the day. J--- is a full tithe-payer and has been for years, but on account of the use of tobacco has never had a recommend to the temple. I think he is a man of absolute honesty and integrity, and personally I have no objection to his witnessing the marriage of his daughter in the temple. **—Heber J. Grant diary, Oct. 31, 1929; hyphens added to conceal identity**

In the year 1899, Feb[.] 20 at Thatcher, Grahym [sic] Co[unty] Ariz[ona], my Parents were Sealed for time & all eternity at the Sealing house. Being such a long way from the Temple the Church had this sealing done for the convenience of the People. Later the Sealing house & Records were burned. Does this Sealing still hold? Or will it have to be done over? **—Maud Y. White to Heber J. Grant, Dec. 13, 1929**

Any sealings for eternity that I may have performed in Arizona or elsewhere—unless they have been cancelled by the proper authority—are in full force and effect. I have been a uthorized by the President of the Church to solemnize such sealings. The fact that the records may have been lost or destroyed does not affect the validity or efficacy of those ordinances. **—Heber J. Grant to Maud Y. White, Dec. 16, 1929**

The Salt Lake Temple was dedicated April 6, 1893. Ordinance work commenced May 23, 1893. At that time the Salt Lake Stake, presided over by President Angus M. Cannon[,] with Joseph E. Taylor and Charles W. Penrose, included all of Salt Lake County.

In September, 1898, an invitation was issued to the presidents of the twen[t]y-two Elders Quorums in the stake to attend a meeting to arrange to hold a Prayer Circle of the presidencies of the Elders Quorums of the stake.

The first Prayer Circle meeting was held September 23, 1893 in the Elders' room in the Temple. Elder Edward W. Davis, President of the First Quorum of Elders, and his counselors George M. Cannon and John N. Matheson, was appointed to preside at the meetings. Levi W. Richards was appointed secretary. This organization continued until the death of Edward W. Davis, September 10, 1896. Elder George M. Cannon was sustained president of the Circle January 9, 1897.

Funds for the furnishing of the room—the altar, table, chairs, desk, wardrobes, carpets, curtains, etc., were furnished at a cost of about $300.00 by the early members of the Circle.

Up to this time the meetings had been held on Saturdays, but a Sunday Circle was started August 15, 1897, to meet at 4:15 p.m. President George M. Cannon having been ordained a High Priest, was released February 17, 1900, and James W. Ure was appointed to succeed him, and Elder Levi W. Richards was to preside in the absence of Elder Ure.

Elder David A. Smith was appointed secretary September 16, 1900.

July 1, 1900, it was agreed to meet hereafter on Sundays at 8 a.m.

March 6, 1904, Herbert J. Shimming was appointed secretary. March 17, 1907, Samuel Holmes was appointed to act as counselor to the President of the Circle and to succeed Herbert J. Shimming who had been released to join another circle, as secretary. Albert J. Ellgren was appointed assistant secretary on the same date, and on July 4, 1909, Elder Anthony W. Ivins of the Council of the Twelve was appointed by the First Presidency to preside over the Circle.

James W. Ure died December 10, 1912. Levi W. Richards died March 30, 1914. Elder Melvin J. Ballard of the Quorum of the Twelve was appointed president of the Circle March 27, 1921, to succeed President Anthony W. Ivins who had been appointed Counselor in the First Presidency.

August 24, 1924, Samuel Holmes was released as secretary and Theodore A. Shoenfeld was appointed to succeed him. March 27, 1927, Jesse M. Drury was appointed secretary to succeed Brother Schoenfeld who had withdrawn.

March 31, 1929, President Melvin J. Ballard met with the members of the Circle and stated that at a meeting of the First Presidency and the Quorum of the Twelve it had been decided to discontinue all prayer circles presided over by a member of the Quorum of the Twelve Apostles. This action was taken after careful investigation and discussion. He expressed his appreciation of the faithfulness and the good attendance of the members of the Circle and told of his desire that we should devote ourselves to Temple work for the dead and continue to receive the spirit of Temple work.

The final meeting was held Sunday, April 14, 1929 where it was announced that it had been arranged for the members of the Circle to meet Sunday, April 21, at 9 A.M., to be shown through the Temple by a Temple worker, Brother William Howells. Ninety-two members of the Circle and their friends participated in this most enjoyable and memorable occasion.

During the 35 years of the existence of this Circle, some 286 men bearing the High Priesthood, have partaken of its influence and have been benefit[t]ed by the splendid spirit of Brotherhood that has been manifest. We have enjoyed the Spirit of the Lord in our meetings together. We have received wise counsel and good instructions for our duties as presiding officers in the Priesthood Quorums. We have received instructions in the doctrines of the Gospel of Christ. Our Faith has been increased and we have imbibed the Spirit of Temple Work.

We especially appreciated and enjoyed the associations of President Anthony W. Ivins and Melvin J. Ballard who have always been willing to help us with our problems and teach us the things pertaining to the restored Gospel.

We regret the discontinuance of the Circle, but we shall always hold dear our associations together and remember our wonderful experiences. **—*History of the Elder's Quorum Prayer Circle, Salt Lake City, 1893-1929* (Salt Lake City, 1929)**

REQUIREMENTS AND INSTRUCTIONS FOR SETTING UP PRAYER CIRCLES IN STAKES

1. Approval from First Presidency and Twelve first secured.
2. One or more of the Twelve will be appointed to organize and instruct.
3. An elevated room used only by Stake Presidency and High Council of sufficient size to accommodate lockers for storage of Temple clothing is required.
4. The Prayer Circle is normally confined to the Stake Presidency and High Council, which includes Stake Clerks.
   (a) Presidency to nominate others (Patriarchs, Bishops, Pres. of High Priests Quorum) and invite those approved for the Prayer Circle.
      1. They should be men who are true, tried, active, devoted, strong in testimony, integrity, faithful, honest, obedient, submissive, prayerful, loyal, sustain authority without hard feelings and without guile, whose houses are in order. No contention in the home, but love and affection; also no envy, harshness or backbiting but a full love of the people. No hatred or strife, willing to reconcile differences, appealing to proper Church tribunal where necessary.
   (b) Uniform seating arrangement according to seniority.
      1. Excuse those released from positions that formerly entitled them to membership in the Prayer Circle.
      2. Even and odd in the circle.
5. All participating are to be robed in Temple clothing. Two prayers are

to be given, first kneeling and the second standing about the altar. An altar is required.

(a) Provide roll [of][:]

1. Those who dress.

2. Those who do not dress.

3. Recommend all should dress and participate.

4. Those in circle must be clothed.

a. Wear approved garments only and Temple clothing with white tie and white socks—not over colored [clothing].

b. Body clean coming before the Lord.

(b) Roll also is to assure rotation in offering prayers.

1. Person leading in prayer while kneeling prays for the one who will be voice in the circle.

2. The person who is voice in the circle will incorporate the first prayer in the prayer at the altar.

3. Avoid duplication in prayer substance and those who are voice are to be led by the Spirit.

6. All signs are given … to precede the prayer at the altar.

(a) President or Bishop leads in signs.

7. The purpose of the prayer circle:

(a) The true order of prayer.

(b) Get close to the Lord.

(c) [One's] spirit is drawn out to God and His Son.

(d) Hearts humble, contrite and at peace.

(e) Softens hearts of participants and draws them near to God.

(f) Perfect love and harmony.

(g) Pray for the sick.

(h) Pray for the advancement of the Lord's work with His blessings upon the people and His leaders.

(i) Pray reverently.

8. Members of the circle may nominate people who are sick or otherwise afflicted for the prayer list, which list should be revised quarterly.

(a) President or Bishop to read list, which list of persons is to be remembered in the prayer at the altar. List to be placed on the altar.

9. Four great covenants.

(a) Sacrifice and obedience

(b) Gospel

1. Four standard works.
2. Refrain from lightmindedness.

(c) Chastity
(d) Consecration

10. Prayer Circles should teach us to be better husbands, fathers, devoted Church members, etc.
11. Change back to street clothing for such business as needs to be transacted. **—ca. 1920s**

....

Brother Charles H. Hyde, former president of the Netherlands Mission, called, in regard to a woman who is visiting Utah. She is from Australia and her husband does not belong to the Church. We agreed to let her have the privilege of viewing the interior of the temple without going through for her endowments. **—Heber J. Grant diary, May 10, 1930**

During the summer of 1927 R--- S---- applied for a church divorce from R--- S---- accusing her of self afflicted abortion.[35] You referred them to us and after our investigation we reported by letter to you.

Both of these parties applied for divorce at a later date, and on March 28th, 1928 you cancelled their marriage.

Both of these people have left our ward, but because of our knowledge of the case they do return for information. At this time R--- S---- has come, stating that she desires to be married again and wants to know if she can be married in the temple.

Not being sure whether the abortion would hinder her from further temple work, if her life since has been right, I refrained from committing myself but advised her I would let her know later.

Can you kindly advise what should be done in her case. **—Arias G. Belnap to Heber J. Grant, June 17, 1930; hyphens added**

If the Bishop of the Ward where Sister R--- S---- resides and the President of her stake see fit to give her a recommend to the temple, from their knowledge of her life since her separation from her former

35. In the 1930s abortion was illegal in the United States.

husband, I would raise no objection to their doing so. **—Heber J. Grant to Arias G. Belnap, June 18, 1930; hyphens added.**

In the evening I performed the ordinance of sealing Maud May Babcock to President Brigham Young, Willard Young acting for his father. I also administered Seconds [second anointing] to her. **—George F. Richards diary, Sept. 3, 1931**

[Question]: Did people at one time pay a small remuneration for doing endowments?

[L. Garrett] M[yers]:[36] Yes.

[Question]: What was that program?

M[yers]: Well, for instance, they did during the early stages of the Depression. President [Heber J.] Grant deputized, I think, seven women, widows, busy going through the temple ordinances in behalf of his deceased ancestry. He paid them maybe fifty cents a name. Many people who couldn't get to the temple—you see we didn't have them scattered as widely then as they a[re] now—would want to hire someone to go through the temple in behalf of the ancestors of these individuals who were out of state. They'd pay them the standard which I think was fifty cents a name to take them through the temple for endowments. That way it didn't cost anything for baptisms or sealings. President Grant had 100,000 names gathered on his lines. I think I wouldn't be far wrong when I say that he acquired the biggest collection of anyone else in the Church in names of the progenitors and relatives that died when he was alive. He had a special researcher that spent her full time doing work in his behalf.

Brother [Sterling W.] Sill[37] said, "If President Grant can do 100,000 I can do 40,000." So he set his goal for 40,000. He would pay them to do the endowments because he didn't have the opportunity or time to cover those. That kept them busy full time working on his.

[Question]: Was this true of all temples in existence at that time?

M[yers]: Yes.

[Question]: The people could be paid.

---

36. Myers was superintendent of the Genealogical Society during the 1950s.

37. Sterling Welling Sill (1903-94) was called as an Assistant to the Quorum of the Twelve in 1954 and later made a member of the First Quorum of Seventy in 1976. He was given emeritus status in 1978.

M[yers]: They could earn a dollar a day going through twice. Maybe sometimes they would go three times but not very often.

[Question]: When people submitted names did they give money at the same time they submitted the names?

M[yers]: Yes. As a general rule they left the money with the clerks at the desk where they received the names. They would bring their slip back showing they'd performed an endowment, and they'd receive their money.

[Question]: Now if someone sent in names would they just send in the money with the names to pay for this?

M[yers]: Yes. Or many of them would give donations to the temple. And they'd say, "I've done all I can on my lines. I'm working on research now. I don't have any names. But there may be some in the same fix who have time and I'll just give $100 to the temple. You can pass it out as you see it's needed." There was nothing harmful in that because many people lived very cheaply in the Depression years, and they enjoyed going to the temple. They would, as a general rule, only do that when they had no names of their own. When for instance they'd worked constantly on their own genealogy, maybe they would go through once or twice and would give the carfare at least [for someone] to come in to the genealogical research department or library or to the temple.

[Question]: Do you remember when that policy was brought to an end?

M[yers]: Oh, that was carried up to comparatively recent times I imagine because it entailed perhaps changes in temple procedures which made it difficult to handle the cash that was received and distributed. But the way they used to pay them I know was just by a person bringing up his slip showing he's gone through the temple on that session, and they would just turn it over and give them money. There was a great spirit of cooperation during the Depression years particularly. And they lasted for ten years. And they didn't get better until the war came on and they started to prepare for World War II. I don't know when they stopped that in the temples. It would be a temple problem. **—L. Garrett Myers oral history, 1976, p. 21, excerpt in Buerger Papers**

....

At a recent meeting of the First Presidency and the Council of the Twelve it was decided that women who are in good standing in the Church and have been faithful and devoted members, but whose husbands are not members of the Church or are not worthy of a temple recommend, may, with the written consent of their husbands, be granted the privilege of receiving their endowments and doing temple work for the dead.

The written statement of the husband should be presented at the temple together with the usual temple recommend from the Bishop of the Ward and the President of the Stake, and filed with the recommend.

We neither urge nor request women to take advantage of this ruling, and it is a privilege that should be given to those only who have proven themselves worthy and are desirous of receiving these blessings. **—Heber J. Grant, Anthony W. Ivins, and J. Reuben Clark Jr. to Stake Presidents, Apr. 17, 1933**

We refer to the letter of the First Presidency of June 14, 1923, regarding the pattern and wearing of garments. We wish to reaffirm here the directions, principles, counsel and admonitions contained in that letter.

The question has arisen regarding the labels appearing upon garments sold as Temple garments by various mercantile establishments in this region. The Church discontinued the use of all Temple garment labels several years ago. Notwithstanding this fact garments are still sold to the public bearing labels reading in some such form as the following:

"This Garment Approved 1st Presidency. No knitted garment approved which does not bear this label;" or "This garment approved by the Presidency: Always look for this label on an approved garment;" and similar formulae.

You will direct all Bishops in your Stakes to advise every person who applies for a recommend to enter the Temple, that the Church has no label of any sort for Temple garments; that it has not authorized, nor does it sanction, the placing of any label of any sort on Temple garments; and that the use of all such labels by any and all mercantile establishments is a misrepresentation of fact. The Church has not approved any particular design or pattern of garment otherwise than as set out in the letter of June 14, 1923, and in this letter.

You will direct all Bishops also to instruct every applicant for a Temple recommend, that Temple garments with shoulder straps instead of sleeves do not meet the requirements of a proper garment, nor do they meet the obligations assumed in the endowment ceremony by those endowed. Temple garments with straps are disapproved. In order to conform to the requirements already given in the letter mentioned above and to the obligations assumed in the endowment ceremonies, Temple garments must have a sleeve at the shoulder.

You will instruct Bishops also carefully to explain to all persons recommended to the Temple, that anyone wearing Temple garments which do not conform to the required standards does so upon his own responsibility. **—Heber J. Grant, Anthony W. Ivins, and J. Reuben Clark Jr. to Stake Presidents, Aug. 23, 1933**

Answering your questions[,] [I] will say that the Church has no objection at all to a woman remarrying. In fact if she is a young woman we have rather urged her, if she has a good opportunity to do so, to remarry. If she does marry we advise[,] that if she has been sealed to her husband or her first marriage [was] performed in the Temple[,] that it would be a nice thing for her to marry in the Temple again but that [this second] marriage would only be for time. If she cannot go to the Temple for her second marriage there is no objection nor does she violate her covenants under the new ruling if she marries one not of the Church providing she is married by a Bishop or President of a Stake. If she has children by a second marriage[,] certainly it is with the understanding that the children and the wife belong to the man to whom she is sealed. A girl who has already received her endowments and marries outside of the Church naturally cannot have her children sealed to her until such time that she has secured either here or hereafter a worthy husband to whom she and the children may be sealed. The same thing is true with a man who has not married for time and eternity.

The modification of the garments was approved by the [First] Presidency and it is as equally acceptable to wear them as the old garments. There is no line drawn between the two except for uniformity sake and for that reason the old style is still used in the Temple. **—Melvin J. Ballard to Lloyd J. Ririe, Dec. 1, 1933, copy in Buerger Papers**

The Salt Lake Temple receives forty thousand or more recommends annually. Since most of these are received during January, and thousands of members require the redating of their admission cards, it is no small task to maintain the readily accessible file required. Since the full cooperation of all bishops is necessary to properly operate this department[,] the following suggestions are offered on the issuing of recommends. ...

Where individual recommends are issued members should be instructed to obtain the signature of the stake president without fail. Members receiving their own endowments require an individual recommend and must provide the information required, including their complete and accurate baptism date. In no case should individuals who are to receive their own endowments be included on a group recommend list.

Special recommends are required for marriage, but this may be included with a living endowment recommend or one issued for regular ordinance work. Where members who are being married have received their endowments previously, this endowment date is required and should be obtained before coming to the Temple.

Recommends are in force for the entire year of issue: expiring Dec. 31. Care should be taken to avoid duplication, since this renders the report of the bishop as well as that of the Temple inaccurate. **—*Deseret News,* Dec. 30, 1933**

....

Bishops are authorized to issue temple recommends to all faithful members of the Melchizedek Priesthood and adult women members of their wards. Recommends for the performance of the ordinance of baptism for the dead may also be issued to exemplary young people. Recommends must be countersigned by the president of the stake. It is important that all those who may desire to enter the temple for endowments or other ordinances, should observe the law of tithing. The applicant should also observe all other principles of the Gospel, should keep the Word of Wisdom, not use profanity, should not join nor be a member of any secret oath-bound organization and should sustain without reservation the general and local authorities of the church. The privileges of the temple should come as a reward for faithful and diligent service.

In addition to the foregoing, women who are in good standing in the church and have been faithful and devoted members, but whose husbands are not members of the Church or are not worthy of a temple recommend, may, with the written consent of their husbands be granted the privilege of receiving their endowments and doing temple work for the dead. The written statement of the husband should be presented at the temple, together with the usual temple recommend from the bishop of the ward endorsed by the president of the stake, to be filed with the recommend. However, women should not be urged nor requested to take advantage of this ruling. It is a privilege to be granted those who have proved themselves worthy and who are desirous of receiving these blessings. **—*Handbook of Instructions,* Number 15 (Salt Lake City: Church of Jesus Christ of Latter-day Saints, 1934), pp. 10-11**

OFFICIAL INSTRUCTIONS ON THE PREPARATION OF TEMPLE SHEETS

1. Recommends. (a) All persons eight years of age and over are required to present a Temple recommend (or, for adults, a properly dated admission card) to the door-keeper before entering the Temple.

(b) When a recommend has been secured from the Bishop, or Branch or District President, the **holder must get it signed** by the Stake President or Mission President before it will be accepted at the Temple. In wards using group recommends, members are required to make application to the Bishop each year to have their names included on the list. Recommends are now issued annually and are in force during year of issue only, expiring December 31st. …

2. Donations. Donations are accepted at the door of the Temple. A consistent donation by couples being married, who can afford it, would be the amount of the fee required for a civil ceremony.

3. Living Endowments and Sealings. Members going to the Temple for their own endowments should obtain, if possible, **before leaving home,** all of the data called for on the reverse side of their recommends. The Bishop or Ward Clerk can often times assist the individual members by supplying the needed information from the Ward records. Baptism dates (day, month and year) must be obtained without fail. Members who are already endowed and who are going to the Temple for marriage or sealing must have their own endowment date (day, month and year). …

9. Paid Work. When proxies have to be obtained to act in endowments for the dead, it is customary to pay 50 cents for a male name and 40 cents for a female name. …

12. Heir. The full name of the proper heir is required on every sheet. The name should be written the same each time. Initials only are not sufficient. If the heir is dead indicate it thus[:] (d). The heir should be determined according to the following rule: "The oldest male in that direct (blood) line to have joined the Church in life." If there is no male in the line, who was baptized in life, then the oldest female to have joined the Church in life in that direct (blood) line may be designated as heir, using her full maiden name. If she has been sealed to her husband, then (and then only), add her married name to her full maiden name. Be careful to keep different lines under their proper heirship. Any question on establishing an heir may be submitted to the Temple Recorder. If it becomes necessary to change the heir on your line or lines, notify the Recorder of the Temple at once. Special signed permission from the Temple Presidency is required to make a non-member the heir.

13. Relationship. The relationship of the heir to each individual must be stated, using [the] exact relationship, if possible; for example, if the heir is John Henry Jones and you are giving the names of his grandparents and aunts and uncles, the relationship would be given respectively as grandson, nephew, etc., in the right hand column. Always state what relation the heir is to the dead and not the relationship of the dead to the heir. If [the] exact relationship is not known then use relative or relative-in-law[,] but care should be taken to keep within the rule covering the use of such names. Relationship[s] may be dittoed.

14. Work for Friends. Ordinance work for "friends" cannot be performed without permission from the Presidency of the Temple. Such permission and the written approval on the sheet should be obtained before presenting such sheet to the Temple Index Bureau for checking.

15. Infants Exempt. Children under eight years of age are not eligible for baptism and endowments[,] and their names should not be entered on these sheets. …

43. Year must elapse. One year should elapse from date of death before Temple ordinances are given if the individual heard the Gospel and did not accept it, or if a member of the Church and did not take advantage of the privilege to have his own endowments. Exceptions to this rule must be approved by the Presidency of the Temple. …

58. Rule of Sealing. In sealing the dead, a **woman is to be sealed**

to her first husband; any exceptions to this rule must be by permission of the Temple Presidency.

59. Must have been married in life. Only those who were married in life should be sealed. Sealings of persons who were not married in life cannot be performed, except by the permission of the Temple Presidency. …

68. Data for children. The names of all the children who are to be sealed at the same time must be placed in the order of their birth (oldest first), whether they are living or dead. If they are eligible for baptism and endowment those ordinances should be attended to first with the complete endowment date given as required. State sex of each child as indicated in the column following the name.

69. Complete family. All members of one family should be sealed to their parents at the same time, if possible. …

71. Ordinances required. The dead who lived to the age of eight years or over are eligible for baptism and also endowments. Living males 21 years and over, or living females 18 years and over are to receive their own endowments before being sealed to their parents.

72. Adoptions. If the intended sealing of a child is to a person other than the natural father or mother, this fact must be explained to the Temple Presidency and answered by them. …

74. Respect rights of others. Sealings should not be performed for [anyone] other than relatives. (See paragraph 14.)

75. Bring nurse. When children are brought to the Temple for sealing, the parents should provide a nurse, if possible, who is properly recommended to the Temple, to care for the small children. In no case are children to be brought to the Temple except when required for their own sealings to parents. (This does not include children eight years of age and over who are brought in as proxies for baptisms for the dead on baptismal days.) **—Salt Lake temple presidency, Jan. 1, 1934; published in the *Deseret News,* Jan. 5, 13, 20, 1934, emphasis in original**

I wrote Pres[iden]t Heber J. Grant as fol[lows]:

Dear Pres[ident] Grant:

If the following named brethren, General Authorities of the Church, and their wives have received their Second blessings, the Salt Lake Temple Records do not disclose that fact. I therefore conclude that they have not except possibly Pres[ident] Hart who may have received his blessings in the Logan Temple: J. Reuben Clark Jr., Charles H. Hart,[38] Antoine R. Ivins,[39] Samuel O. Bennion,[40] John H. Taylor[.][41]

I understand that it is in order for a member of the Council of Twelve to recommend worthy members to the President of the Church to receive their Second blessings. Accordingly, I recommend that these brethren and their wives be invited to receive their blessings. **—George F. Richards diary, Apr. 19, 1934**

The garment is like the ordinary union suit in most cases. I do not hear anyone howl throughout the length and breadth of the land about union suits. They are so much better than the two-piece suits our grandfathers and grandmothers grew up with. As for Masonry, we have taken nothing from the Masons any more than we took baptism by immersion from the Baptists. Corrupted truth is found everywhere. The temple ordinances were revealed as many other things have been revealed to the Prophet [Joseph Smith]. …

There have been no changes in the garment. Fundamentally it is like it was in the beginning. Lengthening or shortening of the sleeve is not a change really. It is just a minor thing, in line with our needs, especially in the summer time; but that does not make any difference to the garment itself. It is a covering for my body, representing covenants I have made. We make entirely too much of the so-called changes. There have been no changes in the ideas. **—John A. Widtsoe, "Answers to Seminary Teachers' Questions, Summer School, 1934," pp. 32, 33**

....

The rites and ceremonies performed in the temples are sacred, not secret, and are not open to the public[,] no more than are those which are performed in the Masonic temples. There is no place in the temple that a faithful, worthy Latter-day Saint cannot go, nor is any ordinance administered therein that a worthy Latter-day Saint cannot receive. **—Heber J. Grant to Dorothy C. Alexander, Jan. 18, 1935**

---

38. Charles Henry Hart (1866-1934) was called as one of the First Seven Presidents of Seventy in 1906.

39. Antoine Ridgeway Ivins (1881-1967) became one of the First Seven Presidents of Seventy in 1931.

40. Samuel Otis Bennion (1874-1945) became one of the First Seven Presidents of the Seventy in 1933.

41. John Harris Taylor (1875-1946) was one of the First Seven Presidents of Seventy from 1933.

I recall that when you were in my office some days ago you inquired if it were necessary for brethren who officiate as temple workers to be ordained to the office of high priest, and I promised to give you a definite answer to your question at a later date.

The brethren of the Twelve, with whom I have discussed this matter, agree with me that this is NOT necessary, except when they are called to do sealing work, and then they should be ordained high priests and specially set apart for that work. **—Heber J. Grant to Lewis R. Anderson, Mar. 5, 1935; emphasis in original**

During the last year particularly we have been more deeply impressed than ever with the need of Stake and Ward officers exercising more care and of giving deeper personal inquiry into the lives of those who are promoted in the Priesthood and to those who are recommended to go through the temple. That there is too much moral laxity in the Church today, as in the world generally, is apparent to anyone who will give the least thought to the matter. Unfortunately we have some psychologists in our leading institutions of learning and some teachers in our high schools who by their unwise instructions and sometimes by in[n]uendos and sneers lend encouragement to wilful youth to disregard the tried and proved laws of chastity and virtue.

There are three things which we can do—(1) raise the standard of parental instruction, and try to improve home conditions; (2) encourage more chaperonage of youth; (3) choose more competent Ward Teachers whose duty it is to "watch over the Church always and to see that no iniquity exists," &c. **—David O. McKay to Joseph F. Merrill,[42] June 15, 1935**

In reply to your request that the scope of your duties be at least briefly outlined, we take pleasure in offering the following suggestions:

(1) Please consider the possibility of preventing, or at least of reducing to a minimum the parading before the public and the blatant advertising of the "L.D.S. Garment."

Note: The garment is associated with some of the most sacred covenants which members of the Church make. Neither the covenants nor the garment should be known by anyone who does not understand to a degree at least their true significance.

42. Joseph Francis Merrill (1868-1952) was ordained a member of the Quorum of the Twelve in 1931.

May we not be held accountable if through our negligence, things which should be held in reverence are subjected to sneers and ridicule?

(2) Another matter that deserves most careful thought is having men represent in person Divine Beings.[43] Is it promotive of faith and reverence for imperfect mortals to attempt to personify perfection?

a. With this phase of the ceremony, please consider the effect upon many young people of the use of elevators in this ceremony.[44] **—David O. McKay to George F. Richards, Joseph Fielding Smith, Stephen L. Richards, and Melvin J. Ballard (Members of the Committee on Temple Ceremonies), June 29, 1935, copy in Buerger Papers**

....

At 8:15 a.m. held a brief consultation with Joseph Fielding Smith regarding our imperative duty to attach more reverence for Temple apparel by withdrawing the garment from commercial institutions. Gave him my views and suggestions in writing on reverence for the Garment. **—David O. McKay diary, March 23, 1936**

[A]t ten o'clock attended the regular weekly meeting of the [First] Presidency and [Twelve] Apostles at the temple. A long report was read at the meeting submitted by a committee of the Twelve, regarding temple ordinances. Some discussion followed the reading of this report. **—Heber J. Grant diary, Apr. 2, 1936**

Supplementing our report under date of March 31, 1936, which was in the nature of a r[é]sum[é] of our deliberations up to that time, we, your committee appointed to give consideration to matters relating to temple work and ordinances, we [sic] beg leave to submit the following recommendations with reference to Temple garments:

1. That the present requirement for the use of the old form of garment exclusively in doing temple work be modified so as to permit the wearing of all approved patterns of the garment within the temple for endowment work. This recommendation is made in the belief that

43. The issue here seems to be whether individuals portraying deities in the dramatic portion of the ceremony should remain off-stage and speak their lines without being seen.

44. In the Salt Lake temple, the actors representing the godhead began using the elevator to descend into the Garden Room, representing the Garden of Eden, while Peter, James, and John, by contrast, descended by means of a staircase.

the present practice tends to build up in the minds of the people an unwarranted distinction between the old form of the garment, now used exclusively for temple work, and the modified form which has now been authorized for a number of years. It is thought that this distinction may serve in the minds of many people to invest the old form with far more of sanctity than the modified or new form of the garment, and that in consequence many may be induced to take liberties in unwarranted modifications of the new form of the garment which they might not otherwise take were the new or modified form of the garment permitted in the temple for endowment service. It is pointed out that in the beginning of the use of the new or modified form of the garment no such restriction against its use in the temple was contemplated, and that, although modified somewhat from the old garment, it is still the garment of the holy priesthood just as much as the old form of garment is, and should therefore be accepted for any use which may be made of the old form. The matter of uniformity [in the temple] is perhaps one of convenience but we may be sacrificing much in the way of reverence and respect for the garment which is worn outside of the temple to obtain this uniformity.

Three members of the committee favor this recommendation, one is opposed to it.

2. We recommend that we authorize the wearing of garments without sleeves which conform in all other respects to the pattern at present agreed upon, provided, however, that this modification, if adopted, shall not be construed to permit the wearing of mere shoulder straps. It is our thought that that portion of the garment covering the shoulders should be of the same material as the body of the garment, as illustrated by the sample herewith submitted. We make this recommendation somewhat reluctantly and with deference only because we have convinced ourselves that it will tend to bring about more respect for instructions given for the wearing of the garment on the part of many members of the Church, and in the second place because we are sure that it will obviate undesirable exposure of the garment which now so frequently occurs through the wearing of present-day patterns of clothing. We feel sure that such a modification will greatly please many good women throughout the Church, and we have not been able to see that we are yielding any vital thing in this slight change. Very short sleeves are now permitted, but such short sleeves are just

enough to carry an undesirable display of the garment with modern styles of clothing.

Three members of the committee concur in this recommendation, one does not assent to it.

3. We recommend that a definition be given in the temple of the symbolism and significance of the various marks in the garment. We believe that an understanding on the part of those entitled to wear the garment of these sacred makings will tend greatly to bring about more reverence for the garment itself. The best interpretation which has come to us up to this time has been supplied by President [David O.] McKay. It is as follows:

A. The square: Honor, integrity, loyalty, trustworthiness.

B. The compass: An undeviating course in relation to truth. Desires should be kept within proper bounds.

C. The navel: That the spiritual life needs constant sustenance.

D. The knee: Rever[e]nce for God, the source of divine guidance and inspiration.

To this last one might be added that which is now in use: That every knee shall bow and every tongue confess that Jesus is the Christ.

All concur in this recommendation.

4. We recommend that there be an understanding that when occasions arise that necessitate the exposing of the garment to the gaze of the curious, the unbeliever or the scoffer, the wearer is justified in laying it aside temporarily and that the wearer must be the judge as to what circumstances warrant this action.

5. We recommend that an effort be made to collect immediately all trademark labels signifying official approval of garments manufactured, and that hereafter we endeavor to prohibit their use entirely. We recommend also that an attempt be made to dissuade merchants and manufacturers from advertising L.D.S. garments.

6. We recommend that an effort be made, through selected agencies of the Church, to dissuade all members of the Church from asking for L.D.S. garments when purchasing from mercantile institutions, and that the people be instructed never to have the markings placed on the garments at such places; that all markings be placed on garments either by those entitled to wear them, the Relief Society, or other persons specially authorized to do this work, and then an understanding be had that no underwear becomes a temple garment

until after it has been properly marked by those having authority to do the marking.

One member of the committee does not favor the restriction against mercantile institutions marking garments. **—George F. Richards, Joseph Fielding Smith, Stephen L. Richards, and Melvin J. Ballard, Committee Report to the First Presidency and Council of the Twelve Apostles, Apr. 22, 1936, copy in Buerger Papers**

There are nine temples in the Church ... You will be interested to know what has been done in these temples covering the period from Nauvoo days until the present time, or until the end of 1935. The statement follows:

	Living	Dead
... Special ordinances [second anointings]	14,777	6,208

—Rudger Clawson, general conference sermon, in *Conference Report of the Church of Jesus Christ of Latter-day Saints,* Oct. 1936, p. 118

....

During March 1937 Elder George F. Richards and wife, Supervisors of Temples, visited officially at the [Manti] Temple. His suggestions and instructions consisted of the following: ... When marking the garments place the garment on the person unmarked, place pins in the marked space, take the garments off and proceed to cut the marks. **—Manti Temple Historical Record, Mar. 1937, typed excerpt in Buerger Papers**

The rule of the Church with respect to marriages outside of the Temple is that the ceremony shall be performed either by a Bishop or a Stake President, or, in the absence or disability of one of these, by his counselor, who, under such circumstances, is the acting presiding authority. In special cases Stake and Ward officials have heretofore been authorized to grant permission to other Elders to perform marriage ceremonies.

Experience has demonstrated the inadvisability of making these exceptions. We recommend, therefore, that marriage ceremonies outside of the Temple be performed only by the authorities named above. Presidents of Stakes and Bishops of Wards are now advised not to transfer this authority to any other Elders in the Church.

When circumstances seem to justify that a marriage ceremony be performed by an Elder other than the President of the Stake or the Bishop of the Ward, permission to perform such should be obtained from the First Presidency of the Church. **—Heber J. Grant, J. Reuben Clark Jr., and David O. McKay to "Dear Brethren," Mar. 11, 1937**

For several years I have been trying to get before the [First] Presidency for their consideration, about 80 proposed decisions & Rules for the Temples in addition to what they already have. The President assured me he would try and get the time before I have to go to Hawaii. **—George F. Richards diary, Apr. 20, 1937**

Pres[ident] [David O.] McKay also said that he would formulate a letter to all Stake Presidents informing them that living baptisms in the Temples should be discontinued. I suggested that Temple Presidents be also notified. **—George F. Richards diary, June 21, 1937**

Reports received at this office indicate that there is an increasing practice in some districts of baptizing and confirming children and adults in temples even where baptismal fonts are conveniently accessible.

This matter was recently considered by members of the First Presidency and Council of the Twelve, and after due deliberation it was unanimously decided to confirm a former ruling that baptisms for the living should not be performed in any temples where there is a convenient place for baptisms outside of the temple, and that temple fonts, excepting in case of real necessity, be used only for the purpose of baptizing for the dead.

Will you please give this information to the Bishoprics in your Stake so that they may govern themselves accordingly.

It is understood of course that there may be exceptions to this rule, for example, where there [is] no baptismal font within a convenient distance, or when extreme cold weather might justify a modification of this recommendation.

In general, however, the instructions given above should be carefully followed. **—David O. McKay to "Dear Brethren," June 25, 1937**

This [temple] endowment comprises a course of instruction relating to the journey of man from the creation, through the Garden of Eden, his struggle when driven out into the world, and the exaltation to which he may attain. ...

The ordinances of the endowment embody certain obligations of chastity, charity, consecration and service. Blessings are pronounced conditioned upon faithful observance of these obligations.

In every detail the endowment is uplifting and sanctifying, obligating him who receives it to moral, religious and patriotic endeavor.[45] **—*Latter-day Saint Temples* (Salt Lake City: Church of Jesus Christ of Latter-day Saints, 1937), no pagination**

....

At ten o'clock I attended the meeting of the [First] Presidency and [Twelve] Apostles. Brother [David O.] McKay was absent on account of lumbago.[46] We had quite a discussion about the temple ceremonies. **—Heber J. Grant diary, Feb. 17, 1938**

The increased use by some Church members, young and old, of garments that do not conform to the standard prescribed, and the actual disuse of any garment at all by a few, are cause for deep concern and call for definite instructions and guidance regarding this matter. ...

For the guidance and protections of these and of members of the Church generally, it has been deemed advisable to copyright a different label which will be placed only upon those garments which conform to approved regulations. ...

The marks should never be placed on garments except by one who is entitled to wear them. [W]hen garments are marked before being sold, the marking must have been done by one officially authorized. ...

So far as the Lord has revealed His will on this matter, it is far better not to receive the endowment than to receive it and then to violate the undertakings and obligations and covenants that pertain thereto.

Young people who declare that they will not wear the garment after they shall have received their endowment should not be given

45. Notice the close paraphrase of James E. Talmage's 1912 *The House of the Lord* asserting that the ceremony "comprises instruction relating to ... the creative period, the condition of our first parents in the Garden of Eden, ... their condition in the lone and dreary world ... [and] the plan of redemption ... The ordinances of the endowment embody certain obligations on the part of the individual, such as [a] covenant and promise to observe the law of strict virtue and chastity [and] to be charitable ... In every detail the endowment ceremony contributes to covenants of morality of life, consecration of [the] person to high ideals, devotion to truth, patriotism to nation, and allegiance to God" (see chapter 3 herein).

46. Lumbago is a term for lower back pain.

recommends. **—Heber J. Grant, J. Reuben Clark Jr., and David O. McKay to Hyrum B. Calder and counselors, Mar. 25, 1938**

Letter from First Presidency pertaining to the garment was read by Brother Poulson. "Authorized pattern" is the new copy-right pattern which was exhibited to those present.

Sister Young told of a meeting held in the Logan Temple where the late Pres[ident] [Anthony W.] Ivins stated that the full meaning of the marks of the garment has not been revealed. All garments worn must have the approved mark.

When receiving your endowments the garment should not be placed on the individual until after it is marked. All ordinances should be given with closed eyes. **—Manti Temple Historical Record, May 1, 1938**

IN RE[GARD] [TO THE] GARMENT LABEL

Under date of March 25, 1938 we sent to all Stake Presidents a letter announcing the adoption of a new registered label called the label of "authorized pattern," which is designed for the aid and protection of our people in the purchase of garments. So many questions have been brought to our attention by Presidents of Stakes and others with reference to this subject that we deem it advisable to again write all Stake Presidents, Bishops, and Mission Presidents in relation thereto. We trust that this letter will serve to answer the inquiries which have reached us without the necessity of corresponding individually with those who have written us about the subject.

STAKE PRESIDENTS, BISHOPS, AND MISSION PRESIDENTS TO GIVE INFORMATION TO THE PEOPLE.

When the Presidents of Stakes, Bishops of Wards, and Mission Presidents are fully advised as to the policy and procedure of the Church in relation to this subject, it is hoped that they will then give to the members of the Church who have received their endowments in the Temple and who are entitled to wear the garment such information as these members of the Church may require to guide them in their purchase and use of the garment. This information should be disseminated among the members of the Church who are entitled to it in a proper way. The High Council, Presidencies of Quorums, Relief Society Stake and Ward Officers, and perhaps some other trusted members of the Church may be called into private session and there receive the instructions, with counsel to treat the matters [under] consider[ation] confidentially. It is deemed inadvisable to present such items in the Sacrament Meetings or in any other meetings to which the public generally and those who have not received their endowments may be in attendance.

MATTERS TO BE EXPLAINED

1. The New Label

Ten copies of the new label are attached to this letter. These copies may be passed around among persons mentioned hereinbefore in order that they may become acquainted with the label and be able to distinguish it from any other label which may be attached to garments. After the labels have been shown, they should all be collected and retained with this letter in the official files of the Stake, Ward, or Mission. Under no circumstances must these labels be permitted to go beyond the custody of the Presidents of Stakes, Bishops of Wards, and Mission Presidents.

It will be observed that no mention is made on the label of the word "garments" and that the sole words of designation are "authorized pattern." These words should be so emphasized that the people will become fully familiar with them.

2. Objects in Securing and Using New Label

The purpose of the Church in registering and distributing the new label is two-fold:

a. To aid and protect the people of the Church in securing garments of authorized patterns and materials as distinguished from patterns and materials which are not approved but which are frequently offered for sale by merchandising establishments; and

b. To promote merchandising practices in the sale and distribution of garments which shall tend to conserve sanctity and reverence for them and which it is hoped, will bring about a discontinuance and suppression of certain advertising display and sales practices which have been highly repugnant to the faithful members of the Church.

3. How These Objects Are to be Accomplished

a. By License of Manufacturers to Use Label. Certain manufacturing establishments, chiefly those controlled and operated by members of the Church, will be granted the privilege to attach the label of "authorized pattern" to types of underwear manufactured by them after the several patterns shall have first been submitted to and approved by the First Presidency. In such manner a large proportion of all knit garments which are made by western manufacturers will be distributed with the registered label attached. The manufacturers of these goods will be required to exact an agreement from all the retail establishments and sales people who distribute garments made by them to the effect that the garment shall not be advertised through any advertising medium whatsoever and that they shall not be displayed on counters or elsewhere within stores but that they shall be kept for sale within containers which shall obscure them from public gaze and scrutiny, to be designated only by prescribed words and figures which the manufacturers may place on the containers for shipment. The manufacturers themselves also agree that they will not advertise garments.

b. Education of Church Members in Purchasing. If the members of the Church are educated when purchasing garments to ask for garments of "authorized pattern," the foregoing method of handling them will be greatly facilitated. To this end, instruction as hereinbefore mentioned should be discreetly given to all of those who are interested in the purchase of garments.

4. Underwear Not Manufactured by Manufacturers Licensed to Use the Label

As heretofore explained, it is not the purpose of the Church to grant licenses to use the new label to others than local manufacturers, but that does not mean that types of underwear which conform in all respects to approved patterns may not be legitimately used for garments. Any member of the Church who is entitled to wear the garment is also entitled either to make his own garments or procure them wheresoever he pleases. If he secures underwear to be made into and used as garments from sources other than from the manufacturers who are licensed to use the new label, it is his personal responsibility to see that such underwear conforms to patterns approved by the Church. Any member of the Church can learn of the approved patterns from his Stake President, Bishop, or Mission President, or by comparison with patterns bearing the label of "authorized pattern."

5. The Label is Not Indispensable to the Garment

Its purpose has been hereinbefore stated. If desired, a member of the Church may cut the label from the garment to which it is attached. The label is not a part of the garment. It is merely designed for aid and protection to the purchaser. Under no circumstances should labels which are taken from the garments be distributed to others. They should be destroyed.

6. Marking Garments

The marks on the garments are perhaps their most sacred feature. It is highly desirable that the placing of these marks be kept out of the commercial field as much as practicable. Where the members of the Church are prepared to mark their own garments in their own homes it is well that they do so. In the event they are not so prepared, they may call upon the Relief Societies for this service. In the larger cities where garments are sold in great quantities[,] arrangements will be made by the First Presidency for the appointment of certain members of the Church in some of the major establishments dispensing garments to do marking. In these centers, the purchasers may arrange with such establishments where persons are duly appointed for the service, to have garments marked. In all cases the manufacturers and merchandisers of garments under license from the Church to use the label of "authorized pattern" will be required not to hold marked garments in stock.

After the garment has been properly marked it is permissible to stitch the marks in order to keep them neat and less conspicuous.

It is in reality the sacred markings and the intention of the wearer that convert underwear into garments. It is therefore of the utmost importance that the marks be understood and sacredly regarded.

7. Garments for Use in the Temples

In order to establish and preserve a uniformity of practice in the Temples it has been deemed advisable to ask members of the Church doing Temple work to wear in the Temple only the so-called old style garments including long sleeves and legs, collars, and strings. A pair of such garments may always be kept with a person's Temple ceremonial clothes. Such garments may be either of the knit type or made of white cloth. This request is made not because the modified patterns of garments which have been authorized are not deemed adequate for Temple use but because it is felt that a uniformity of pattern would simplify and be more desirable for Temple use. The Temples themselves supply many garments for ceremonial purposes and these garments conform to the old type and style. Young people coming to the Temples for their first endowments should be carefully instructed in this particular. They should be advised either to provide themselves with the old style garments or that they may procure the same in the Temple but they must be also instructed that they must have with them garments of "authorized pattern" to wear after they have received their endowments.

8. Disposition of Worn-out Garments

That worn-out and discarded garments may never come to the notice of those who would scoff and ridicule, it is suggested that the marks may be cut from them and that thereafter they may be put to such uses as may be made of cloth. They cease to be garments, and it is not necessary that they be burned or otherwise completely destroyed as some have supposed.

9. Obtaining Garments in Mission[s] and Remote Places—Mail Orders—and Canvassers

Mission Presidents should be prepared to supply all information concerning garments required by members of the Church in the Mission fields. They whose fields of labor are in the United States, Canada or Hawaii should supply themselves with lists of manufacturers and merchants from whom garments of "Authorized pattern" may be obtained. Such manufacturers will undoubtedly be pleased to keep on file with the Mission Presidents price lists of various patterns and quantities which can be made available to Church members desiring to order from such establishments. Mission Presidents will also be prepared to advise members where their garments may be marked if purchasers are not prepared to mark them in their homes.

Members of the Church are cautioned in purchasing garments from mail order houses or canvassers to be careful to secure for their protection goods bearing the registered label of "authorized pattern." They may well beware of all advertisements which may be sent to them by letter or otherwise with solicitation that they make purchases, for it is against the policy of the Church to permit such advertisements.

10. Education of Young People

One of the most important obligations of the Church is to prepare its youth to receive their endowments. Boys and girls should be taught to look forward to going to the Temple as one of the richest opportunities of their lives. They should understand that here are given the highest blessings which men obtain in this world. They should be early impressed with the sanctity of the marriage covenant and with its fundamental place in our concept of eternal welfare and happiness.

They should also be made to know that the garment of the holy priesthood will be given to them in the Temple ceremony, and that it represents something very sacred which is not to be looked upon lightly nor sacrificed to the dictates of fashion and worldly opinion. It must be made clear to them that it is such an indispensable part of the Temple ceremony that if they do not make up their minds to always wear it, and respect it, they are not entitled to the endowments of the Temple.

Such education can be properly given to the young without disclosing the Temple ceremonies. It should be made the subject of constant teaching not only by the officers and organizations of the Church but by the homes of the Latter-day Saints.

11. General Specifications for Garment Patterns

a. The material used shall be of such texture as to constitute a "covering" of the body. (Transparent nets and similar materials not permitted.)

b. The pattern shall in general conform to that of the ceremonial garment used in the Temple with the following express modifications thereof permitted:

The legs of the garment may be shortened from ankle length to a length extending merely below the knee. The sleeves may be shortened from wrist length to a length extending on a garment of size 36, 8 inches from the neck band to the end of the sleeve, with appropriate and corresponding lengths for different sizes of garment. Collars, as provided for the ceremonial garment, may be eliminated. Buttons may be substituted for strings. The crotch may be closed. Side-leg or shoulder openings may be provided instead of front and back openings[,] or any combination of these openings is permissible.

c. The so-called shoulder strap is not allowable.

12. What to Do with this Letter

a. It should first be carefully studied by each Stake Presidency, each Bishopric, and each Mission President.

b. It may be then read to select groups at private meetings as hereinbefore set out.

c. It should be preserved in the official files of Stakes, Wards, and Missions for future reference.

d. Whenever questions arise with reference to the garment, the letter should be carefully perused before answer is given and before the inquirer is referred to any source of information other than the letter.

e. If any inquiries reach the First Presidency or other General Authorities of the Church from members of the Church, these questions, if they may be answered by referring to the letter, and those submitting them, will be referred to Stake Presidents, Bishops, and Mission Presidents for answer. If items arise not covered in the letter, Stake Presidents, Bishops, and Mission Presidents will be informed in due course.

Now, brethren, we have written you at length in this matter not only with the intent to supply information which will enable you to answer questions about the garment, but also with the purpose of soliciting your fullest cooperation in a determined effort to educate our people to a sacred regard for the garment of the holy priesthood and the ceremonies in the House of the Lord. More than anything else, we want the members of the Church to keep their covenants. The steps we have taken are designed to help them so to do, but they can become effective only as the people maintain faith sufficient to follow counsel and cleave unto the Lord. We wish you, in presiding over the people, to be kind and sympathetic and charitable in enforcing the regulations of the Church, and we wish you also to uphold without compromise those standards and truths which we know to be indispensable for eternal welfare and exaltation. **—Heber J. Grant, J. Reuben Clark Jr., and David O. McKay, Circular letter, July 20, 1938**

Some unfortunate and untoward incidents following the giving of endowments to wives of Church members who have not been through the temple, and to the wives of non-members, have brought this matter again in review by the Council of the First Presidency and the Twelve. After fully considering the whole matter the following decision has been reached:

Hereafter you will not give a recommend, under any circumstances, to a wife whose husband is not a member of the Church. You may use your own good judgment and wisdom in explaining to those who apply that our experience has shown that the results of giving endowments to women whose husbands are not members of the Church have led to regrettable and unfortunate conditions, which frequently have made most difficult the lives of the women receiving their endowments.

You will give recommends to wives of members of the Church who have not had their endowments only if the husband is absolutely willing that the endowment should be given to his wife. You will therefore be expected personally to interview the husband in order to assure yourself that he has no objection whatever, and, in addition, he must express his willingness and consent in writing. This written consent must be attached to the recommend itself, which must be signed by the Bishop of the Ward and the President of the Stake, or, in the case of people living in the missions, by the President of the Branch and the President of the Mission. Unless these requirements are fully complied with, it will not be possible for the woman so recommended to go into the Temple.

In order to avoid all embarrassment, we must ask you to carry out these instructions explicitly.

P.S. Please convey this message immediately to your Bishops and Branch Presidents. **—Heber J. Grant, J. Reuben Clark Jr., and David O. McKay to Stake and Mission Presidents, Oct. 17, 1938, in *MFP,* 6:60-61; emphasis in original**

Brother George F. Richards called at the office and showed us a sample of a temple apron, which President [David O.] McKay and I approved. I very much like the appearance of it. It looks more expensive than the others and yet it is cheaper. It is worked on a [sewing] machine instead of by hand. **—Heber J. Grant diary, Dec. 17, 1938**

....

As you are aware, a few years ago the Temple Covenant of chastity was modified so as to permit faithful, worthy women of the Church whose husbands have not received the Endowment to go to the Temple for their own endowments and not be violating their covenant by living with their husbands thereafter, to whom they have not been given of the Lord in the authority of the Holy Priesthood.

Young unmarried women are also affected by the foregoing named action, so, if they marry outside the Temple after receiving their endowment they will not be violating their covenants. **—George F. Richards to Heber J. Grant, Mar. 13, 1939, copy in Buerger Papers**

A case had been referred to us in which a woman whose father and mother had been through the Temple was applying to go through the Temple herself. She was from the Southern States Mission, and the Church records showed that opposite her name someone had placed the endorsement, "negro blood." Brother [David O.] McKay talked with me yesterday or the day before about it, and I suggested that he get her patriarchal blessing and see what the patriarch said her lineage was. Brother McKay did that, and found the blessing had been given by Elder George F. Richards, that he had told her she was of the lineage of Israel through Joseph and Ephraim. We decided that under those circumstances she could not be denied admission to the Temple. **—J. Reuben Clark office diary, Aug. 18, 1939, Perry Special Collections**

....

Sealings After Civil Marriages—Permission may be granted to couples who have been married by civil law to have their marriages solemnized in the Temple, at such time as local authorities feel assured of their personal purity and worthiness and of the genuineness of their desire for the blessings of the House of the Lord.

Couples who have associated together illicitly should not be recommended to the Temple until they have satisfied their bishops that they have thoroughly repented, and have shown their repentance by living righteously for a prolonged period of time. Mere sorrow is not repentance. It is urged that the desirability of Temple marriages be continually emphasized.

Marriages in the Temple following civil ceremonies are sealings only, and should not be reported as Temple marriages. A Temple marriage is one in which the parties enter into the marriage relationship for the first time.

Dissolution of Temple Marriages—The Church has no authority to grant civil divorces. That is a concern of the State. The Church, however, may dissolve that part of a marriage for time and eternity which pertains to the life after this. The power to "bind on earth and in heaven" is power also to "loose on earth and in heaven." Each request to have an eternal marriage annulled, must come before the president of the Church for action.

Undue Publicity of Garment Should be Avoided—It is the duty of all persons who have been through the Temple to see that the garment is not subjected to undue publicity, and to unite in an earnest effort to re-establish and to maintain the reverence it merits.

To this end it is recommended that leading stake and ward officers discretely dissuade all members of the Church from even asking for "L.D.S. garments" when purchasing from mercantile institutions, and from buying garments that have been un-authoritatively marked. Authorized manufacturers and distributors of the garment will be requested not to advertise or openly to display the garments, but to keep them in boxes or other closed retainers. A request by the purchaser for "garments of the authorized pattern" is all the designation necessary.

The marks should never be placed on garments except by one who is entitled to wear them. Where garments are marked before being sold, the marking must have been done by one officially authorized.

TEMPLE RECOMMENDS

How and to Whom Recommends Are to Be Issued—Every Church member eight years of age and over requires a recommend to enter the Temple.

Temple recommends are to be issued in triplicate—the originals to be sent to the Temple, the duplicates given to the applicants, and the triplicates to remain in the recommend books for the bishops' records. The original copies of the recommends should either be mailed or be delivered personally to the Temple by the bishops and are not to be given to the persons in whose favor they are issued. The duplicate copies will identify members when they arrive at the Temple.

A bishop should not issue a recommend to any person who has not been a member of record of his ward for at least one year, except upon receipt of a letter written by the bishop of the ward, president of the branch, or president of the mission of which the applicant was a member during the year immediately preceding the date of application for a recommend, stating that the person requesting a recommend is worthy to enjoy the privileges of the Temple. But a bishop, branch or mission president will not certify to another bishop, branch or mission president as to the worthiness of any person to receive a Temple recommend, unless the person has been a member of record of his ward, branch, or mission for at least one year, and is otherwise considered worthy.

No person should be given a recommend to the Temple who does not uphold the General Authorities of the Church; who is not an honest tithepayer or who does not undertake to become an honest tithe payer, as distinguished from a part tithepayer or a token payer; who does not either observe the Word of Wisdom or express a willingness to undertake to observe the Word of Wisdom; and who is not otherwise fully worthy by believing in and living the Gospel. Young people going to the Temple to receive their own endowments should agree to wear the garment properly before receiving a recommend.

Temple recommends, properly signed, may be issued by bishops and presidents of independent branches to members of record who meet the foregoing requirements, to receive ordinances for themselves or for the dead. When a member wishes to visit several Temples during the year, a recommend to each Temple will be required.

Applicant's Statement—Space is provided on the back of the Temple recommend for the applicant to state his qualifications and Church standing. The statement is to be filled in and signed personally by the applicant. Recommends will not be accepted at the Temple if the Statements are not filled in and signed when presented. The applicant must sign all three copies of the recommend.

When recommends are issued to persons who have not paid tithing or who have not kept the Word of Wisdom, or who have not observed any of the other requirements listed in the various items of the Statement, the bishop should carefully point out that the promise contained in item VI of the Statement will require that they amend their lives in the ways in which they fall short, and he will render such aid as may be possible to help such persons in their efforts to live righteously; **provided, however, no one who cannot honestly make the affirmations contained in items numbered I and II on the Statement shall receive a recommend to the Temple**. In no case will a recommend be given to an applicant merely because he has had a recommend before; each applicant must show his worthiness for a recommend each time he applies therefor.

To safeguard bishops and presidents of Temples, and to provide shorter periods when those who enjoy the privileges of the Temple may be interviewed by their bishops, recommends will expire June

30 and December 31 of each year. Church members will therefore be required to make application each six months for recommends. Any person becoming unworthy during the period shall have his recommend immediately revoked. …

Special Cases—Recommends may be given to wives of [men who are] members of the Church [but] who have not had their own endowments only if [their] husbands are absolutely willing that the endowments should be given to their wives. Before such recommends are issued presidents of stakes will be expected to personally interview [the] husbands in order to assure themselves that the husbands have no objection to the endowments being given to their wives. Husbands must express their willingness and consent in writing, and this written consent is to be attached to the Temple recommend, which must be signed by the bishop of the ward and the president of the stake, or, in the case of people living in the missions, by the president of the branch and the president of the mission. Recommends will not be accepted at the Temple for these special cases unless the letters of consent accompany them. Women should not be urged nor requested to take advantage of this rule. It is a privilege to be granted those who have proved themselves worthy and are desirous of receiving these blessings.

Under no circumstances is a recommend to the Temple to be issued to a wife whose husband is not a member of the Church. Experience has shown that the results of giving endowments to women whose husbands are not members of the Church have led to regrettable and unfortunate conditions.

Witnessing Marriages or Viewing Interior of Temples—Do not issue recommends for witnessing Temple marriages, or for the purpose of being shown through a Temple, to children or adults who have not received their own endowments.

Adoptions—Living children should be adopted through legal proceedings of an established court before being sealed to adopted parents by Temple ceremony. This rule applies irrespective of age. Parents who desire to adopt children should indicate a willingness to make the adopted children legal heirs to property on a par with their natural children. Legal adoption papers should be shown to the Temple presidency at the time the request for adoption of children is made. **—Handbook of Instructions, Number 16 (Salt Lake City: Church of Jesus Christ of Latter-day Saints, 1940), 123-25, 129-33; emphasis in original**

[Rudger Clawson] asked my opinion as to whether a man was violating his covenants who having once married a wife in the temple, wife being now dead, he married a second wife civilly. I asked what he thought. He said he thought he was not violating his covenants but was weak in the faith. I agreed. **—J. Reuben Clark office diary, June 10, 1940, Perry Special Collections**

I had a meeting with the Temple Presidency of [the] Salt Lake Temple instructing them as counseled by the [First] Presidency & the Twelve this day to discontinue [the] ring service in sealing, i.e., marrying couples where such ring service, or ceremony is used; also to discontinue prayer rooms provided with altar &c for individual use. — **George F. Richards diary, Sept. 5, 1940**

President [J. Reuben] Clark reported in brief to President [David O.] McKay the report which was made by Brother George F. Richards a few weeks ago regarding information which had come to him of misconduct of temple workers, involving apparently illicit sexual relations, and also the intimation that Brother George F. Richards made that possibly the "new polygamists" were trying to operate there by performing marriages in the temple. President Clark suggested that it seemed to him the only way to meet this situation was for the [First] Presidency to appoint two people—one brother and one sister—who were thoroughly reliable, alert and not gullible, as workers here in the temple, and to watch and report to the First Presidency what they found to be going on in such matters. **—J. Reuben Clark office diary, Dec. 30, 1940, Perry Special Collections**

5.

"A PERSONAL RESPONSIBILITY" 1941–1960

There appears to be some confusion as to the course which Presidents of Stakes, Bishops, Presidents of Branches and Presidents of Missions should follow with reference to making out, signing, and delivering the new temple recommends. In the following instructions—

Presidents of Independent Branches will follow the procedure laid down for Bishops.

Presidents of Dependent Branches will work through their respective Bishops.

No recommends should be granted to anyone in the Mission except he has been first interviewed by the President of the Mission, who must fully satisfy himself as to the worthiness of the person applying for the recommend. The Mission President should have the Branch President sign the recommend with him.

That this whole matter be handled in an orderly way we call your attention to the following matters:

The giving of a recommend to enter into the House of the Lord and to participate in the ordinances therein performed, is a most serious matter, not a mere formality to get the member past the entrance to the temple. Bishops should, of course, urge all members of their wards to fit themselves by right thinking and living, to enter the temple to do temple work, and should urge the worthy members to get recommends; nevertheless, Bishops should not indiscriminately urge all members of their wards to come and get recommends for that purpose. Bishops should always remember that only those who are really worthy members of the Church should be given recommends.

The rather loose supervision which it appears has in some cases been exercised in these matters by Bishops has resulted in some persons going into the temple who are not worthy.

The Bishop should interview every applicant who applies for a temple recommend. He should see that the statement on the back of the recommend is signed by the applicant in triplicate. That is, the statement on the original recommend should be signed, the statement on the duplicate which is given to the applicant should be signed, and the statement on the copy retained in the office of the Bishop should be signed, so that there shall be no mistake as to the actual signature by the applicant.

If the Bishop feels that the statement has not been honestly made and signed, or if he feels for any other reason that the applicant is not worthy to go to the temple, he will, of course, not sign and issue the recommend.

After the Bishop has so examined the applicant and, being satisfied of his worthiness, has had him sign the statement, and has himself signed the recommend in triplicate, he will forward to the President of the Stake the original recommend, and the duplicate which is to be delivered to the applicant after its countersignature by the President of the Stake. Upon receiving them, the President of the Stake will examine them and determine whether or not he believes the applicant is worthy of a recommend. In case he has any doubt about the matter, either because he is not acquainted with the applicant or because the statements as signed by the applicant are not satisfactory to him, the President of the Stake will call in the applicant, interview him, and make his own determination as to whether or not the applicant should be given a recommend.

If the President of the Stake decides that the applicant should not be given a recommend he will return to the Bishop the original and the duplicate, without his signature and with a statement that he does not approve of the issuing of the recommend, and the recommend will in such a case not be issued by the Bishop.

If the President of the Stake decides, after such investigation and interview, that the recommend should be issued, then he will sign both the original and duplicate and return them to the Bishop; or, if contributive to the applicant's convenience, the Stake President may give the applicant the signed duplicate and return the original to the Bishop. The Bishop will thereupon forward the original recommend to the temple and, if it has not already been given, will hand the duplicate to the applicant.

Neither the President of the Stake nor the Bishop will sign the recommend unless and until the applicant has fully made out the statement and signed it.

Furthermore, it is not intended that these recommends should cover more than one applicant. Bishops should not issue these recommends, for example, to a man and his wife, but each person going to the temple should have a recommend by himself.

The only exception to individual recommends is where groups of children are sent to the temples to do baptismal work for the dead. There the regular group form of recommend may still be used. However, in this case the Bishop should satisfy himself that each child recommended is a good child who is exemplary in his life and is attending to such Church duties as are incident to his age. Great care should be taken to see that the children of apostates, as also children of parents belonging to or affiliating with apostate groups, are not included in such groups nor given individual recommends. The President of the Stake will also sign this recommend. But, as stated above, in all other cases, except only where such groups of children are involved, there must be an individual recommend given to each person who is to go to the temple. **—Heber J. Grant, J. Reuben Clark Jr., and David O. McKay, circular letter, Jan. 6, 1941, in *Progress of the Church,* Jan. 1941, 47**

DIRECTIONS FOR CLOTHING THE DEAD WHO HAVE RECEIVED THEIR ENDOWMENTS

The Body should be thoroughly washed, and, if a man, the face shaved, or the beard trimmed, according to the practice of the person while living.

The clothing should be white throughout, and scrupulously clean. The garments should be of the old style approved pattern, properly marked. White hose should be used, and should be placed outside the garment leg.

For a man, a white shirt, collar, and tie should be used, also white trousers. A coat is not a part of the temple-burial clothing.

The robe should be placed on the right shoulder, and tied with a draw-string, with the bow of the girdle on the left side. The length of the robe should be to, or near, the ankles.

The cap should be placed on the head with the bow over the left ear, and tape [fabric] string attached to the opposite side of the cap, the other end of the string being attached to the robe at the shoulder. If desired the cap may be left off until time to close the casket.

The apron should be tied about the waist in a bow.

The girdle [sash] should be placed around the waist and tied in a bow over the left hip. It should be so placed as to cover the top of the apron, the ribbon strings of the apron, and draw-string of the robe.

White moccasins, with a cuff, should be used over the hose.

A white or pale ivory dress, and white under-clothing and hose, should be used for a woman.

The woman's veil should be placed with the short ruffled part in the back of the neck, and the veil drawn over the face when the casket is about to be closed. When the woman's veil is properly adjusted on the head, a part of the hair should show below the veil over the forehead. The veil may be softly draped on the pillow back of the head until time to close the casket, at which time it is drawn over the face.

The apron should be covered with a piece of white linen.

Please preserve these instructions and transmit them to your successor. **—General Board of the Relief Society, Feb. 1941**

There seems to be some misunderstanding of the instructions given concerning the issuance of temple recommends to wives of nonmembers of the Church.

In the latest handbook, page 132, is found the following paragraph pertaining to this subject:

Under no circumstances is a recommend to the temple to be issued to a wife whose husband is not a member of the Church. Experience has shown that the results of giving endowments to women whose husbands are not members of the Church have led to regrettable and unfortunate conditions.

The question has arisen as to whether this restriction applies to women who are married to non-members but who have taken out their endowments before this rule was given. It should be understood that the rule applies specifically to those who are seeking their own endowments. Women who have previously been in the temple and who are worthy, though their husbands may be non-members, may still be granted the privilege to go through the temple. **—Heber J. Grant, J. Reuben Clark Jr., and David O. McKay, circular letter, Feb. 1, 1941**

Your attention is called to our letter under date of July 20, 1938, in which matters pertaining to the garment and "Authorized Pattern" labels are set out in considerable detail. It is felt that this letter should be reviewed by you to the end that you may again direct the attention of members of the Church to the instructions given therein. In case some letters may have been mislaid or otherwise lost, we are enclosing herewith another copy of the letter for your files.

There are two additional items containing slight modifications of which we wish to advise you:

1. It has been decided to permit regularly licensed manufacturers to supply licensed merchants and distributors with a small sign, 4½ by 8½ inches, on which will appear a replica of the "Authorized Pattern" label. These signs may be placed by such licensed merchants and distributors in front store windows and/or in the store department where garments bearing the "Authorized Pattern" label are sold. It is felt that this sign will aid members of the Church in finding authorized distributors.

We are forwarding to each Stake President and Mission President a sample of the signs that will be found in the stores of licensed distributors. This sample should be obtained by the Bishops from the Stake Presidents and displayed to those hereinafter designated so that the Church membership generally may be informed as to the appearance of this sign designating licensed distributors. Any distributor displaying any other sign or advertising display of L.D.S. Garments will be understood to be violating his Merchant's Agreement.

All members of the Church who see in any store or distributing agency whatsoever any sign or insignia other than the insignia of "Authorized Pattern" may know that such signs or insignia are in violation of the policy of the Church, and such members are invited to inform the Advisory Committee, addressing their communications to Joseph Anderson, Church Office Building, Salt Lake City, Utah.

2. It has been further decided to restrict the use of the label to garments which are manufactured by licensed manufacturers for sale to the trade through regularly licensed distributors only, deliveries to be made to such distributors in containers as provided for in their Agreements. Garments bearing the label of "Authorized Pattern" are not to be sold by agents or distributors in a house-to-house or personal canvass. It is permissible, however, for garments bearing the "Authorized Pattern" label to be ordered from and delivered by licensed manufacturers or distributors to mail order or special order customers, so that members of the Church residing in missions and distant stakes and branches may be supplied with their requirements out of regularly manufactured stocks of licensed manufacturers. If you discover that the needs of your people are not adequately supplied by the licensed distributors, you are requested so to advise us and to make suggestions as to the setting up of an agency or agencies which will be adequate for the purpose.

3. We are pleased to announce the appointment of an Advisory Committee, to whom problems relating to the manufacture and sale of garments bearing the "Authorized Pattern" label will be referred. Communications on these matters should be addressed to Joseph Anderson, Church Office Building, Salt Lake City, Utah, in order that these problems may receive prompt attention by this Special Committee. **—Heber J. Grant, J. Reuben Clark Jr., and David O. McKay, circular letter, Mar. 3, 1941**

… I have come over here this morning particularly because I have met so many young people who have been disappointed after they have gone through the House of the Lord. They have been honest in that disappointment. Some of them have shed tears as they have opened their hearts and expressed heart-felt sorrow that they did not see and hear and feel what they had hoped to see and hear and feel.

I have analyzed those confessions as I have listened to them, and I have come to the conclusions that in nearly every case it was the person's fault. He or she has failed to comprehend the significance of the message that is given in the Temple. And so this preliminary meeting is held that we might, in a way, preview the ceremony and present, in a way, the significance of the ordinances given this day.

Now the only purpose, as I say, is that we might see more clearly, understand more thoroughly, the message of the Temple ceremony. If we can do that, then our time here this morning will not have been spent in vain.

These young people to whom I refer have become absorbed in what I am going to call the "mechanics" of the Temple, and while criticizing these they have failed to get the spiritual significance. …

After the preliminaries, you will be asked to go into a room where you will be washed. Now that act of washing in itself will be insignificant. There may be some things associated with it which you might criticize, and in your heart there will be a tendency to criticize. But what is the significance of it? Cleanliness. And the message of this: "Cleanliness is next to Godliness"; not just cleanliness of body alone, but cleanliness of mind, and that cleanliness of mind should have preceded your entrance into this Temple by the eradication of every ill feeling, by the elimination of every vulgar thought.

That is what it means to be clean to enter the House of God. And even as cleanliness of body, clean linen gives to man a sense of dignity, of purity, all through life. Men who will not keep the Sabbath Day, who let their boys put on their old work clothes on Sunday and go out and work, have not a sense of the value of cleanliness upon the character of their boys. The consciousness of clean linen is, in and of itself, a source of moral strength, second only to that of a clean conscience. Some of our young people fail to see the significance of that little simple ceremony.

And then you listen to why you are washed. The blessing that will come to your eyesight, to your mind, to our hearing: all based upon the cleanliness of the thought and the cleanliness of your acts and your deeds.

The next little simple ceremony, I will call it little and simple because you might in your heart so consider it, is the Annointing. That, too, is performed with acts which may be done in a way that will merit criticism. I am not saying that they do not merit it if you have criticism in your heart. But let your spiritual eyes see the significance of that annointing, and then you will realize what it means to be initiated into the House of God and all its mysteries, to have in your heart as young people the spirit of emulation, the realization that anything which any other man or any other woman has accomplished, you may, through the help of God, also accomplish. You know what that means to the human soul! If you do not, then listen to what a young girl said down here in one of our institutions recently. Discouraged, down-hearted, and despondent, she said to her attendant: ["]Leave me alone. Nobody cares for me."

Emulation dead. No place in the world for her, so she thought. That is the depth to which a person through discouragement may fall, and many have so fallen.

Not so with one who is annointed to become a king and priest of the Most High; a queen and priestess in the realms of God. Now that is what it means. I do not know how long it will take you or me to achieve that, but we are annointed that we may become such. Do not shut your eyes to the glories and open them to the mechanics that seem so simple and are performed so awkwardly sometimes.

The prophet said: "What is man that thou art mindful of him? and the Son of man that thou visited him? For thou hast made him a little lower than the angels, and hast crowned him with glory and honor."

With these preparations we then enter upon a [dramatic] presentation of the truest philosophy of life ever given to man. What did the Savior say to His Apostles? "Teach them all things whatsoever I have commanded you."

You are going out to teach people the true philosophy of life, the restored Gospel of Jesus Christ, which is the power of God unto salvation. The world is longing for it.

Now in a few short hours, here, today, will be presented to you in symbolic form that philosophy, that upward climb into the presence of God. I have used the word "mechanics," now I am going to use the word "symbolism." These ordinances will be presented in an outward way. Men with ordinary expressions, with ordinary features, in simple dramatic form, will present this philosophy. You may sit in your seat and criticize the man or the woman, if you wish; you may look at his dress and count the buttons; you may look at her dress and criticize. If you do, I am sorry for you. Or you may sit there and see through the symbolism the glory which God has given you.

For example: You will first be asked if you are willing to obey the law of Eloheim; are you willing to take upon yourself the responsibility of making God the center of your lives? That is what it means. Then you will be asked if you will obey the law of sacrifice, and you will covenant to do it. Well, now, those are just simple words, aren't they? But what does it mean to obey the law of sacrifice? Nature's law demands us to do everything with self in view. The first law of mortal life—self-preservation, selfishness—would claim the most lu[s]cious fruit, the most tender meat, the softest down on which to lie.

I am taking you back to the Garden of Eden, when man entered into mortality; the Tree of Life, and the Tree of Good and Evil, and everything which man desired was placed before him. And selfishness, the law of nature, would say, "I want the best; that is mine." But God said: "Take the firstlings of the flock and offer a sacrifice unto me."

That is the story. The best shall be given to God; the next you may have. God is the Center. …

You can go through the movements of that law of sacrifice and see nothing but mechanics if you will, but if you do you will be disappointed. But you can sit there and commune with the Spirit and receive a message that there is a law that will help me to see spiritually through my entire life.

In the presentation of the Law of the Gospel, "the power of God unto salvation," you will be told where to find these laws specifically, which you are expected to obey—in the Bible, the Book of Mormon, the Doctrine and Covenants, and the Pearl of Great Price; the Bible and the Book of Mormon particularly, and these others are equally important. God does not leave you without a guide. Too many of our young people throw them aside. If you are to teach, you are to study also, and today you covenant that that is what you are going to do. You cannot waste your time in the field looking after pleasure and the sights, or lounging around headquarters. You are studying to teach men the Gospel of Jesus Christ.

With these steps we rise to one of the most significant [covenants] in all the world. There will be presented to you the law of chastity, and you are going to hold up your right hand that you will obey it. What is that law of chastity which will be given to you?

I am going to tell you young people now, particularly you who have heard professors say something else, that obedience to that law of chastity in this world is the source of virile manhood, and you keep it with your life, young man! It is the crown of beautiful womanhood, and you should treasure it as you treasure your life, young woman. It is the foundation of the happy, contented home. Divorce proceedings bear witness to the fatal result of the violation of that law. It is the chief contributing factor to the strength and perpetuity of the race. That is part of the philosophy of life to be presented in the House of God this day. And if you violate it, then you will bring sorrow upon your heads. Poignantly a young man knows that fact today, who sat in this building four years ago and listened to some such admonition as I am giving you this morning.

If in our souls we can accept these laws, we are then ready, spiritually prepared, to enter the presence of God, provided we can obey the law of consecration, the next step.

The law of consecration—"my time, my talents, all that I possess, are placed upon the altar for the advancement of the kingdom of God," and when men can attain to that spiritual achievement, they can merit what Christ said to Zacchaeus, a money-maker, a man who I think sometimes had dealt dishonestly with his fellowmen. He was a publican, a tax-collector. One day the Lord said unto him: "Zacchaeus, make haste, and come down; for today I must abide at thy house [Luke 19:5]."

I do not know what happened at that dinner table. Nobody knows, except by inference, but we do know that Zacchaeus' heart was touched, and he recognized Jesus as a man of God, and when that testimony, even that glimmer of a testimony entered his heart, he said:

"Behold, Lord, the half of my goods" (I wish he had said "all," but he did not) "I give to the poor [Luke 19:8]."

That was a wonderful thing for a rich man to say—"take half of what I have." "And if I have taken anything from any man by false accusation, I restore him fourfold." And Jesus said unto him: "This day is salvation come to this house."

And when you and I can stand at a certain place in the House of God and say conscientiously and truly, "I will consecrate my life, my time, my talents to the advancement of the Kingdom of God," we are prepared through inspiration to enter into His presence.

And that is what you do at the veil, symbolically, when the veil is drawn asunder and you enter into the Celestial Room.

There, brethren and sisters, I have just briefly previewed the ordinances in the Temple of God. You will make covenants. There are certain things which belong to the priesthood, signs and tokens that belong to the priesthood, which will emphasize the importance of the covenants you make. …

Today you make promises with uplifted hand, and I pray God that you will have power to keep them. Go through the House of God today seeing the spiritual significance of the ordinances, that you may not come out disappointed, but filled with a desire and determination to walk uprightly before God, and thus merit His divine inspiration, not only while you are on your mission where you will need it—oh, how you will need it—but all through life when you come back to make a success of your vocation in your own life—that you may "Seek first the kingdom of God and his righteousness, that all these things may be added unto you." **—David O. McKay, a speech ("The Temple Ceremony") to departing missionaries, Sept. 25, 1941**

Administration of Second Anointings to December 31, 1941

Temple	Living	Dead	Total
Nauvoo and other sites (1843-46)	591	0	591[1]
Endowment House (ded. 1866)	694	0	694
St. George (ded. 1877)	1,814	1,615	3,429
Logan (ded. 1884)	3,040	1,243	4,283
Manti (ded. 1888)	2,412	1,134	3,546
Salt Lake City (ded. 1893)	6,368	2,211	8,579
Laie (ded. 1920)	0	0	0
Alberta (ded. 1923)	13	1	14
Mesa (ded. 1927)	0	0	0
TOTAL	14,932	6,204	21,126[2]

—from "Temple Ordinance Statistics," Books A, B, C

1. According to Lisle G. Brown, second anointings were performed for 603 individuals in Nauvoo, 594 living and 9 dead (Brown, comp., *Nauvoo Sealings, Adoptions, and Anointings: A Comprehensive Register of Persons Receiving LDS Temple Ordinances, 1841-1846* (Salt Lake City: Smith-Pettit Foundation, 2006), 361.

2. Different numbers appear in "Temple Ordinance Statistics," Book C, which has a total of 20, 990 ordinances, with 14,781 for the living and 6,209 for the dead. See also Salt Lake temple recorder Joseph Christensen's "Report of Ordinances

....

Primarily the wearing of the garment is an individual responsibility. It is associated with sacred obligations entered into by the wearer with the Lord in the temple; consequently, the conscience of the wearer must guide when circumstances seem to justify a modification of these obligations. The sacredness of the garment should ever be present and uppermost in the wearer's mind.

One way to protect this sacredness is not to expose it to the view of scoffers, and where conditions arise making such exposure unavoidable, it would seem best reverently to lay aside the garment and then put it on again when such conditions pass. The First Presidency has felt that this policy might be followed by soldiers during their enlistment. **—Heber J. Grant, J. Reuben Clark Jr., and David O. McKay, circular letter, Oct. 30, 1942**

....

I attended regular Thu[rsday] meetings. At the 10:00 A.M. meeting of the [First] Presidency, the Twelve and the Patriarch held in the Temple, the matter of allowing the administration of second blessings was considered. I brought up the subject at our last Quarterly meeting of the Twelve held in the Temple Sept. 29th last. I made quite an extended talk on the subject at that time at the conclusion of which it was decided by vote to present the question to the Council of the First Presidency, the Twelve and the Patriarch. To-day all were present except Geo[rge] Albert Smith, Richard R. Lyman and Sylvester Q. Cannon and I suggested to Pres. [Rudger] Clawson that he bring the question forward, which he did. I had a chance to explain, and it was decided that the four members of the Council, viz. J. Reuben Clark Jr., Albert E. Bowen, Harold B. Lee and the Patriarch Jos[eph] F. Smith should be privileged to receive theirs and others whom the members of this council may recommend and the Council sustain. Pres. [Heber J.] Grant appointed me to administer these blessings. I suggested that Jos[eph] Fielding Smith be appointed to assist me in this work. We are to make the appointment, i.e. Jos[eph] Fielding & I, for the brethren.

I have anxiously looked forward to this action.

The records show that there have been 32,495[3] such blessings ad-

Performed," *Genealogical and Historical Magazine*, 1939, 10-11, which has a total of 20,998 second anointings, with 14,779 for the living and 6,209 for the dead.

3. This total differs from that given in a previous entry.

ministered in the Church and that during the last 12 years there have been but 8 administrations.[4] Thirteen of the 32 General Authorities had not had theirs and at least two others who have had them with their first wives have later wives not yet anointed to their husbands. **—George F. Richards diary, Dec. 10, 1942**

I obtained permission of Pres[ident] [Heber J.] Grant to see him at his home. I found him in bed and his condition seemed worse than I had expected to find. I gave him a blessing, and recommended that he issue recommends to all the General Authorities and their wives who have not received their second blessings and give it [to] them for Christmas which he approved and authorized[,] also approved Stephen L. Chipman & Wife whom I recommended. I reported to Joseph Anderson, who had recommends made. These I took to the President and he signed them. I returned the signed recommends to Joseph Anderson, the President's Secretary, for distribution. I feel that this day's accomplishment has been inspired and is a wonderful accomplishment. May the Lord be praised for ever.

This is one of the most happy days of my life. I am sure it will endure over Christmas. **—George F. Richards diary, Dec. 24, 1942**

This has been a wonderful year for me and my family. ... I have also been instrumental in renewing the former practice in the Church of administering Second Anointings to faithful members, the practice having gone practically into disuse, only eight such blessings having been administered in the past twelve years. Up to twelve years ago there had been administered in the Church thirty-two thousand plus of such blessings. The day before Christmas I was instrumental in getting Pres[ident] [Heber J.] Grant to sign recommends for thirteen of the general authorities and their wives and the wives of two others of the Council to [be anointed with] their husbands; also a recommend for Stephen L. Chipman and wife, he having had his previously. I am sure that the Lord has inspired what I have been able to do along these lines. Pres[ident] Grant, in our council meeting of a few weeks ago appointed me to administer these blessings and at my request appointed

4. These twelve second anointings were all performed in the Salt Lake temple. The decline was the result of the 1926-1927 change in policy that required apostles, rather than stake presidents, to recommend people for the ordinance. See Buerger, *Mysteries of Godliness*, 164.

Elder Jos[eph] Fielding Smith to assist me. We are the only ones in the Church having this authority by appointment. **—George F. Richards diary, Dec. 31, 1942**

....

I was in the regular council meeting of the [Twelve] Apostles in the Salt Lake Temple a good part of the day. Some matters of importance were considered regarding Temple ordinances. The matter to be submitted to the First Presidency. **—Joseph Fielding Smith diary, Jan. 5, 1943, typed excerpt in Quinn Papers**

At 10:00 A.M. the Twelve met the [First] Presidency in their office in the Church offices building and Pres[ident] [Heber J.] Grant ordained Spencer Kimball and Ezra T. Benson apostles and set them apart members of the quorum of the Twelve. We then repaired to the Temple excepting Pres[ident] Grant & Pres[ident] [J. Reuben] Clark, the latter being out of the State. By request of Pres[ident] [David O.] McKay, I instructed the brethren on the tokens &c. **—George F. Richards diary, Oct. 7, 1943**

Attended 10:00 A.M. meeting of the First Presidency, the Twelve & the Patriarch. The council approved my recommendation that 2nds [second anointings] be offered the following: Harold S. Snow of St. George Temple, El Ray Christiansen Pres[ident] of [the] Logan Temple and David Smith, Pres[ident] of [the] Idaho Falls Temple. **—George F. Richards diary, Oct. 14, 1943**

....

Who May Issue and Receive Recommends: Bishops of wards and presidents of independent branches are authorized to issue temple recommends. Members of dependent branches will obtain them from the bishops of the wards to which the branches are attached.

Every Church member eight years of age or over must have a recommend to enter the temple. Each person must have his own recommend. It is not proper, nor acceptable, to issue a joint recommend to a man and his wife. When a member wishes to visit several temples during the year, a recommend to each temple is required.[5]

---

5. This is the first time temple tourism was raised. Notice that the policies and procedures in the 1944 *Handbook of Instructions* parallel the guidelines offered in the First Presidency's circular letter of January 1941 with some additions and clarifications.

The giving of recommends to enter the House of the Lord and participate in the ordinances therein performed is a most serious matter, not a mere formality to get members past the temple entrance. Bishops should, of course, urge members of their wards to fit themselves by right thinking and living to enter the temple and do temple work, and encourage worthy members to obtain recommends. Bishops should not, however, persuade all members of their wards to get recommends. Bishops should always remember that only those who are really worthy members of the Church should be given recommends. They are not to be issued to persons who do not sustain the General Authorities of the Church; who are not honest tithepayers or who do not undertake to become honest tithepayers, as distinguished from part tithepayers or token payers; who do not observe the Word of Wisdom or express a willingness to undertake to observe the Word of Wisdom; and who are not otherwise fully worthy by believing in and living the gospel. …

Candidates to be Interviewed: Bishops should interview every applicant for a temple recommend and see that the statement on the back of the recommend form is signed by the applicant in triplicate, that is: the statement on the original copy should be signed; the statement on the duplicate copy which is given to the applicant should be signed; and the statement on the copy retained by the bishops should be signed, so that there will be no mistake as to the actual signature by the applicant.

If a bishop feels that the statement has not been honestly made and signed, or if, in his opinion, the applicant, for other reasons, is not considered worthy to go to the temple he will, of course, not issue and sign the recommend. But if, after the applicant has been examined, the bishop is satisfied of his worthiness and the statements have been properly signed, he will sign the three copies of the recommend and send the original and duplicate copies to the stake president.

Stake President's Responsibility: Upon receiving the original and duplicate copies of the recommends, the stake president will examine them and determine whether or not he believes the applicant is worthy of the recommend. In case he has any doubt about the matter, either because he is not acquainted with the applicant or because the statements as signed by the applicant are not satisfactory to him, the stake president will call in the applicant, interview him, and make his own decision as to whether or not the applicant should be given a recommend.[6] If the stake president decides that the applicant should not be given a recommend, he will return without his signature the original and duplicate copies to the bishop of the ward who issued them, with a statement that he does not approve of the issuing of the recommend. The three copies of the recommend will then be cancelled.

If the president of the stake decides, after investigation and interview, that the recommend should be issued, he will sign both the original and duplicate copies and return them to the bishop who issued them; or, if convenient to the applicant, he may give him the signed duplicate and return the original to the bishop. The bishop will thereupon forward the original copy to the temple upon which it is issued and give the duplicate to the applicant, unless he has already received it from the stake president. It is recommended that the stake president interview each applicant going to the temple for his own endowments.

Record Membership of One Year Required: A bishop should not issue a recommend to a person who has not been a member of record of his ward for at least one year, except upon receipt of a letter written by the bishop of the ward, president of the branch, or president of the mission, of which the applicant was a member during the year immediately preceding the date of application for a recommend, stating that the person requesting a recommend is worthy to enjoy the privileges of the temple. But a bishop, branch or mission president, will not certify to another bishop, branch or mission president as to the worthiness of a person to receive a temple recommend, unless the person has been a member of record of his ward, branch, or mission for at least one year, and is otherwise considered worthy.

Exception to Individual Recommend: The only exception to individual recommends is where groups of children are sent to temples to do baptismal work for the dead. In these instances, the group form of recommend may be used, but bishops should satisfy themselves that each child recommended is a good child, exemplary in his life, and attending to such Church duties as are required of his age. Exceptional

6. Notice that the stake president was expected to interview a candidate only if he doubted the bishop's judgment, that the primary responsibility for determining an individual's worthiness fell to the bishop. However, in the next paragraph we read that the stake president was to "interview each applicant" going to the temple for the first time.

care should be taken to see that the children of apostates, and the children of parents belonging or affiliating with apostate groups, are not recommended to the temple, either with groups or individually. Group recommends require the endorsement of the stake president.

Applicant's Statement: Space is provided on the back of the temple recommend for the applicant to state his qualifications and Church standing. The statement is to be filled in and signed personally by the applicant. Questions are to be answered by "yes" or "no" and not by a check mark. Recommends will not be accepted at the temple if the statements are not filled in and signed when presented.

When recommends are issued to persons who have not paid tithing or who have not kept the Word of Wisdom, or who have not observed other requirements listed in the various items of the statement, the bishop should carefully point out that the promise contained in item VI will require that they amend their lives in the ways in which they fall short, and he will render such aid as may be possible to help such persons in their efforts to live righteously. **Members who cannot honestly make the affirmations contained in items I and II on the statement shall not receive recommends to the temple.** In no case should a recommend be given to an applicant merely because he has had one before. Each applicant must show his worthiness for a recommend each time he applies.

Expiration Dates for Recommends: To safeguard bishops and presidents of temples and to provide shorter periods when those who enjoy the privileges of the temple may be interviewed by their bishops, recommends will expire March 31 and September 30 of each year. Church members will, therefore, be required to make application each six months for recommends. Any person becoming unworthy during the period shall have his recommend immediately revoked.

Special Cases: Recommends may be given to wives of members of the Church who have not had their own endowments only if the husbands are absolutely willing that the endowments should be given to their wives. Before recommends are issued for this purpose, presidents of stakes will be expected to personally interview husbands in order to assure themselves that the husbands have no objections to the endowments being given to their wives. Husbands must express their willingness and consent in writing, and this written consent is to be attached to the temple recommend.

Recommends will not be accepted at the temple for these special cases unless the letters of consent accompany them. Women should not be urged nor requested to take advantage of this rule. It is a privilege to be granted to those who have proved themselves worthy and are desirous of receiving these blessings.

Under no circumstances is a recommend to the temple to be issued for endowments to a wife whose husband is not a member of the Church. Experience has shown that the results of giving endowments to women whose husbands are not members of the Church have led to regrettable and unfortunate conditions. This rule applies specifically to those who are seeking their own endowments. Women, married to non-members, who had received their own endowments before this rule was given, may still be granted the privilege of going through the temple, if they are worthy, notwithstanding their husbands are non-members.

Witnessing Marriages or Viewing Interior of Temples: Do not issue recommends for witnessing temple marriage, or for the purpose of being shown through a temple, to children or adults who have not received their own endowments.

Adoptions: Living children should be adopted through legal proceedings of an established court before being sealed to adopted parents by temple ceremony. This rule applies irrespective of age. Parents who desire to adopt children should indicate a willingness to make the adopted children legal heirs to property on a par with their natural children. Legal adoption papers should be shown to the temple presidency at the time the request for adoption of children is made. …

Temple Recommends to Divorced Persons: Bishops should make sure that in the case of a divorced person being recommended for temple marriage, a final divorce decree has been secured; and if the individual was married in the temple previously that a temple divorce has been granted in the case of a woman. However, a man married in the temple who has had a civil but not a temple divorce may be recommended for temple marriage without first having the previous sealing annulled. …

An unmarried man or woman having previously received his or her endowments, and being recommended for "All Ordinances for the Dead," may serve as a proxy in the sealing of dead couples.

It is a legal requirement that a couple obtain a marriage license within the state where the temple to which they are recommended is located. . . .

Sealings After Civil Marriages: Permission may be granted to couples who have been married by civil law to have their marriages solemnized in the temple, at such time as local authorities feel assured of their personal purity and worthiness and of the genuineness of their desire for the blessings of the House of the Lord.

Couples who have associated together illicitly should not be recommended to the temple until they have satisfied their bishops that they have thoroughly repented, and have shown their repentance by living righteously for a prolonged period of time. Mere sorrow is not repentance. It is urged that the desirability of temple marriages be continually emphasized.

Marriages in the temple following civil ceremonies are sealings only, and should not be reported as temple marriages. A temple marriage is one in which the parties enter into the marriage relationship for the first time.

Dissolution of Temple Marriages: The Church has no authority to grant civil divorces. That is a concern of the State. The Church, however, may dissolve that part of a marriage for time and eternity which pertains to the life after this. The power to "bind on earth and in heaven" is power also to "loose on earth and in heaven." Each request to have an eternal marriage annulled, must come before the president of the Church for action.

Undue Publicity of Garment Should be Avoided: It is the duty of those who have been through the temple to see that the garment in not subjected to undue publicity and to accord it the reverence it merits.

To this end it is recommended that presiding stake and ward officers discreetly dissuade members of the Church from asking for "L.D.S. garments" when purchasing from mercantile institutions, and from buying garments that have been unauthoritatively marked. Authorized manufacturers and distributors of the garment will be requested not to advertize or openly display the garments, but to keep them in boxes or other closed retainers. A request by the purchaser for "garments of the authorized pattern" is all the designation necessary.

The marks should never be placed on garments except by one who is entitled to wear them. Where garments are marked before being sold, the marking must have been done by one officially authorized. **—*Handbook of Instructions,* No. 17 (Salt Lake City: Church of Jesus Christ of Latter-day Saints, 1944), 76-83, 89-90; emphasis in original**

Later, I went over to the Temple and instructed the [First] Presidency to take steps to have more reverence in the Temple. To that end suggested: first, the removal of the desk in the Celestial Room; second, not to have witnesses to marriages enter Celestial Room in street clothing; third, it will be well to consider the advisability of the General Authorities who perform marriages to be dressed in white. **—David O. McKay diary, Feb. 28, 1944**

This is a day I shall never forget. Flora [Amussen Benson][7] and I met in the Celestial Room of the [Salt Lake] temple at 12:30 [p.m.] and in line with the recommendation of Pres[ident] [Heber J.] Grant received our second blessings under the hands of Elders Geo[rge] F. Richards and Jos[eph] Fielding Smith of the Council of Twelve. Our hearts swelled to overflowing with gratitude for the Lord's rich blessings. **—Ezra Taft Benson diary, Aug. 30, 1944**

Had long conference with Bro. Geo[rge] F. Richards re. temple work, temple rulings and the importance of the second or higher blessings. I am very grateful that my faithful and devoted wife and I have recently received these rich blessings. I wish more of the Latter-day Saints could receive these blessings. I feel sure there are hundreds who are worthy. **—Ezra Taft Benson diary, Dec. 22, 1944**

....

Where men lose their lives while engaged in military service, either by accident or in combat, their parents or other relatives desiring to have temple work done for them may do so as soon as it is definitely known that they are dead. **—Heber J. Grant, J. Reuben Clark Jr., and David O. McKay, circular letter, Mar. 9, 1945**

....

I attended a committee meeting, with Pres't David O. McKay, President George F. Richards, Stephen L. Richards, John A. Widtsoe and myself, to consider some matters pertaining to the temple ordi-

---

7. Flora Smith Amussen Benson (1901-1992) was born in Logan and married Ezra Taft Benson in the Salt Lake temple in 1926.

nances. We were in session for some time. **—Joseph Fielding Smith diary, Jan. 23, 1946, typed excerpt in Quinn Papers**

I was instructed by the First Presidency to write to Pres[ident] Edward J. Wood for the Alberta Temple at Cardston,[8] calling his attention to reported irregularities, and innovations, seances[9] &c introduced into the temple and temple ordinances with a request that such deviations must stop. **—George F. Richards diary, Aug. 29, 1946**

....

First Presidency, Harold B. Lee, Stephen L. Richards met to discuss matters pertaining to the garment. **—David O. McKay diary, Jan. 7, 1947**

[T]here is a custom in some areas and among some organizations of having group prayers in which those participating, sometimes kneeling and sometimes standing, arrange themselves in a circle and then hold each other's hands while the prayer is being offered. From these reports that come to us it would seem obvious that the effort is to duplicate as nearly as possible the procedure of the sacred prayer circle.

This innovation is not in accordance with the due order of the Church and should be discontinued at once. Where groups are assembled together, the prayers should be offered in the ordinary way we offer prayer as in our public services as at Sacrament meetings, priesthood meetings, and other like gatherings. This rule does not exclude groups from kneeling in prayer on proper occasions, but it is intended to exclude all simulations of the regular prayer circle. **—George Albert Smith, J. Reuben Clark Jr., and David O. McLay, circular letter, Jan. 30, 1947**

Following is a transcript for the minutes of the meeting [Feb. 20, 1947] of the First Presidency and the Council of The Twelve, which is self-explanatory:

Elder Joseph Fielding Smith called attention to an inquiry from President ElRay Christiansen of the Logan Temple on the following matter: A couple have adopted legally an infant child, born illegitimately, and are desirous that the names of the natural parents be not placed upon the records.

---

8. The Cardston, Alberta, temple opened in 1923. Edward J. Wood, still serving in 1946, was its first president.

9. That is, attempts to communicate directly with the dead.

"In discussing this matter the Brethren were agreed that in cases of this kind the names of the natural parents should not appear on the record, and that the names of the couple who are adopting the child should appear as parents. On motion this became the sense of the Council. President George F. Richards was requested to convey this same information to all the temples." **—George F. Richards to Edward J. Wood, Feb. 28, 1947, copy in Buerger Papers**

....

Heretofore, to wit on June 30, 1941, June 27, 1941, August 17, 1942, and January 31, 1949, we have communicated with you and issued instructions concerning the granting of temple recommends for couples to be married in our temples for time, or for time and eternity, or for eternity only, with reference to the necessity or non-necessity of securing certificates of serological tests[10] by the persons to whom the recommends are to be issued.

As we still have questions arising with reference to these matters, we have deemed it wise to summarize the various instructions heretofore given for your information and convenient use:

1. All couples marrying merely for time or for time and eternity in Utah temples, no matter where they live, must present serological certificates before the ceremony can be performed.

2. All couples applying only for sealings in the temples in Utah must if either or both of them resided in Utah at the time of the civil marriage, present serological certificates before the sealing is performed, *provided* the civil marriage was performed subsequent to February 28, 1941; if civilly married before that date, the certificate is not required for sealings.

3. Couples domiciled in States not requiring serological tests and civilly married in such a State, may be sealed in any temple without producing a serological certificate.

4. Couples domiciled in States not requiring serological tests may be married for time and eternity in any temple located in a State that does not require such tests.

Will you be good enough to be guided by the foregoing rules in the granting of all recommends and the marrying of all couples in our

10. This blood-serum examination checks for venereal disease.

temples. **—George Albert Smith, J. Reuben Clark Jr., and David O. McKay, circular letter, Feb. 28, 1949, in *MFP,* 6:281-82; emphasis in original**

I attended [the] quarterly meeting of the Twelve where I presided and presented my views respecting the non administration of seconds [second anointings], … with the request by motion made by Stephen L. Richards that I present the matter to the [First] Presidency if I could get a hearing, either to them alone or in the Council of the First Presidency & the Twelve. **—George F. Richards diary, Aug. 12, 1949**

Attended quarterly meeting of the Twelve from 9 a.m. to 2 p.m. Consideration was given to the sacred matter of second blessings. Discussion followed the reading of an important statement prepared and read by Pres. Geo[rge] F. Richards which I responded to wholeheartedly. I was happy when all of the eleven members present (Bro. [Matthew] Cowley was absent) approved of the matter for recommendation to the Twelve. **—Ezra Taft Benson diary, Aug. 12, 1949**

At the 10:00 A.M. Council meeting of the [First] Presidency and Twelve I read a paper of 5 or 6 pages deploring the neglect on our part in not administering Second blessings as formerly. The paper and other statements made by me in connection therewith were accepted 100%. **—George F. Richards diary, Aug. 18, 1949**

Dear Brethren:

For a long time I have felt that I would like to express to you the disappointment I feel[,] that we have practically discontinued the administration of Second Anointings in the Church, and to give to you some of the reasons why I feel as I do.

I have not been able to bring myself to feel that the Lord is pleased with us in neglecting such an important and sacred endowment, which He has given us to be administered in His holy temples to worthy members of His Church.

The Second Anointings were given by revelation to the Prophet Joseph Smith to be administered to worthy members of the Church, both the living and the dead; and from the days of the Prophet Joseph [Smith] to the days of President Heber J. Grant that practice continued.

… I understand [D&C 124:40-41] to mean and include the Second Anointings, a neglect to administer which[,] in the temples reared for that purpose[,] will be attended by the Lord's displeasure, and bring upon us cursings instead of blessings, wrath, indignation and judgments.

["]We [quoting Joseph Smith] calculate to give the Elders of Israel their washings, and anointings, to attend to those last and more impressive ordinances without which we cannot obtain Celestial thrones.["] …

This refers directly to the Second Anointings. Nowhere else in Church ordinances are men made kings and priests unto the Most High God.

In olden times, kings in Israel were anointed such by the Prophets of God. Should not those who are to become kings and priests and attain to Godhood be anointed thereto while here on earth? That is the nature of the work of Second Anointings.

Every man and woman who has received his or her first endowments has received a PROMISE that through faithfulness they would be privileged to receive the Second Anointings.

"Brethren and Sisters [quoting the temple liturgy], if you are true and faithful, the day will come when you will be chosen, called up and anointed kings and queens, priests and priestesses, whereas you are now anointed only to become such. The realization of these blessings depends upon your faithfulness." …

Thousands of good and faithful men and women are dying without receiving a fulfillment of the promise made them in connection with the temple ceremonies.

When living members receive their Second blessings, or anointings, they are given a charge that they must not speak of those things to anybody; that only those who are invited by the President of the Church are to receive them; and that none others are supposed to know anything about them.

Formerly, the Stake Presidents made their recommendations for Second Anointings to the President of the Church, and when approved by him the individuals so approved received their invitation from the President of the Church, and on presentation of that recommend to the Temple President of the temple district where the individuals resided, the temple president officiated for them. The Stake Presidents had SPECIAL recommend books for that purpose.

About 1928 an incident occurred which so incensed the First

Presidency that they had all the recommend books brought in to the President's office, and instructions were given that no recommends of that character should be given by stake presidents thereafter.

The Twelve were authorized to make recommendations; but their recommendations were rarely ever acted upon favorably, so that the administering [of] Seconds almost entirely ceased. In twelve years, from 1930 to 1942, when these facts were tabulated, but eight such blessings were administered in the Church. Only EIGHT blessings in twelve years!

The following tabulation of Second Blessings administered in the temples where such blessings were administered will no doubt be of interest to you:

Temple	Period	Living	Dead	Total
Salt Lake	To Dec. 10, 1942	14,847	6,226	21,073
Logan	To Oct. 13, 1931	3,139	1,229	4,368
St. George	To Jan. 13, 1938	1,885	1,619	3,504
Manti	To Dec. 12, 1929	2,407	1,143	3,550
Nauvoo	In Jan. & Feb. 1846			406
	Totals	22,278	10,217	32,901[11]

The incident above mentioned which so exasperated the First Presidency was as follows: A brother who had received his Second Blessings, while speaking in a priesthood meeting in one of the Idaho stakes, told the brethren that they all should have their Second Blessings. Of course that was a serious infraction of the charge which he received when he had his Second Anointings; but I have never learned of any serious consequences to follow, except the action on the part of the Authorities, discontinuing the administration of those blessings in the Church.

It appears to me that the mistake made by the good brother in Idaho was not so serious as to justify letting those sacred ordinances come into disuse in the Church. I think now is the time to act; with such modifications as to details as the brethren might feel to make, insuring that these blessings be administered only to those who are worthy to receive them. ...

11. See previous entries for different totals.

If there is condemnation resting upon us for our neglect, the longer we delay action the greater will be our condemnation. …

Temples under construction now and in the future should be provided with a room for the administration of these blessings alone, to be known as the Holy of Holies, for if we do not move in the matter before us, some others coming after us will do so <u>for it must be done,</u> and temples should be designed and constructed with that thought in mind.

It is to be hoped that this communication will not be shelved and forgotten without full consideration by this Council. For several years these matters have given me great mental anxiety and spiritual concern, and but for want of courage I would have sought an opportunity to be heard years ago. I do not want to leave this sphere of action without VIGOROUSLY protesting our indifference and neglect. **—George F. Richards to the First Presidency and Quorum of the Twelve, Aug. 18, 1949, typed copy in Buerger Papers; emphasis in original**

I went to the temple at 11:00 a.m. and assisted Elder Jos[eph] Fielding Smith, administered Seconds [second anointings] to Preston D. Richards and wife Barbara, and the members of [the] Emigration Stake Presidency and their wives. **—George F. Richards diary, Dec. 7, 1949**

....

I went to the Temple by appointment, and administered Second blessings to three of the general authorities and their wives, Elders Eldred G. Smith,[12] Milton R. Hunter[13] and B[isho]p Thorp[e] B. Isaacson. Bro[ther] T[horpe] B. Isaacson stood as proxy for Samuel F. Ball who is dead & Betsy Hollings Richards for Adena Christena Anderson Ball. **—George F. Richards diary, Jan. 6, 1950**

… finally, it may be said that the temple endowment is not secret. All who meet the requirements for entrance to the temple may enjoy it. Since it is sacred, it is not bandied about the streets or in gossiping parlors. It is, in the outline: the story of man's eternal journey; instructions to make the endless journey increasing and progressive; covenants

12. Eldred Gee Smith (1907-) was called as Presiding Patriarch in 1947 and given emeritus status in 1979.

13. Milton Reed Hunter (1902-1975) served in the First Council of Seventy from 1945 to 1975.

that we will so live as to make the journey an upward one; a warning that sometime we shall be called upon to show whether we have kept our covenants; and the great reward that comes to the faithful and the righteous. **—John A. Widtsoe, "Whence Came the Temple Endowment?" *Improvement Era,* Feb. 1950, 95**

I obtained permission from President Geo[rge] Albert Smith for my Sons Oliver and Ray and their wives to receive their Second Anointings. **—George F. Richards diary, Apr. 20, 1950**

It is being observed that some Latter-day Saint men and women, some of whom are presiding officers and teachers in both stake and ward positions, are removing their temple garments to wear abbreviated clothing in varying degrees when working around their homes, when traveling by auto, or camping out-of-doors. In some instances, brethren who have been through the temple are removing their shirts while mowing the lawns or performing other out-door responsibilities, thus exposing the upper garment to full view.

Such removal of the temple garment, or exposure to more or less public view, is not in keeping with its significance or sacred purpose.

It is suggested you use your influence in encouraging Latter-day Saints to avoid these practices. **—Presiding Bishopric (LeGrand Richards, Joseph L. Wirthlin,[14] and Thorpe B. Isaacson) to bishops, Aug. 23, 1950**

The renewed calling of men into military training[15] renders it desirable to reaffirm certain observations heretofore made during the last World War in the matter of *wearing the temple garment.*

1. The covenants taken in the temple incident and attached to the wearing of garments contemplate that they will be worn at all times. No exception to these covenants is found anywhere in the ceremonies. These covenants run between the one making them and the Lord. These covenants so made take on the nature of commandments of the Lord.

2. In the early days of the Church the Lord announced that where men prevented his Saints from carrying out the commandments he had given them, the Lord would relieve the Saints from rendering

14. Joseph Leopold Wirthlin (1893-1963) served in the Presiding Bishopric from 1938 to 1961.

15. The Korean War began in June 1950.

obedience to the command, and would visit the iniquity and transgression involved in such disobedience upon the heads of those who "hindered" his work. The Lord said this rule was given for the consolation of the Saints "who have been commanded to do a work and have been hindered by the hands of their enemies, and by oppression." (D&C 124:49 ff.)

3. Where the military regulations are of a character that "hinders," that is, makes impossible the wearing of the regulation garments, either in training on the drill grounds or in combat zones, [an] effort should be made to wear underclothing that will approach as near as may be the normal garment.

Where military regulations require the wearing of two-piece underwear, such underwear should be properly marked, as if the articles were of the normal pattern. If circumstances are such that different underwear may be turned back to the wearer from that which he sends to the laundry, then the marks should be placed on small pieces of cloth and sewed upon the underwear while being worn, then removed when the underwear is sent to the laundry, and resewed upon the underwear returned.

The wearing of the normal garment should be resumed at the earliest possible moment.

4. Every effort should be made to protect the garments from the gaze and raillery of scoffers. This may cause considerable inconvenience at times, but tact, discretion, and wisdom can do much to alleviate this inconvenience. If the scoffing became unbearable and the wearer should decide that the Lord would consider he was really "hindered" by the scoffers from wearing the garments, and if he should therefore lay them aside, then the wearer should resume the wearing of the normal garment at the earliest possible moment.

A certain amount of curiosity and light comment may be frequently expected, wherever, for one cause or another, the garments are brought into view, but this is not the "hindering" of which the Lord spoke as excusing obedience.

The blessings flowing from the observance of covenants are sufficiently great to recompense for all mere inconveniences.

The wearing of the garment is the subject of direct covenant between the Lord and the covenant maker, who must determine to what extent he will keep his covenants. To break our covenants is to lose the protection and blessings promised from obedience thereto. **—George Albert Smith, J. Reuben Clark Jr., and David O. McKay, circular letter, Oct. 2, 1950, in *MFP,* 6:287-88; emphasis in original**[16]

....

I HAD A VERY GREAT HONOR BESTOWED UPON ME TODAY. THE BRETHREN HAD APPOINTED ME TO SERVE WITH ELDER JOSEPH FIELDING SMITH AND ELDER JOHN A. WIDTSOE in giving SECOND BLESSINGS IN THE TEMPLE. I WAS MUCH HONORED. **—Spencer W. Kimball diary, June 7, 1951, typed excerpt in Quinn Papers; emphasis in original**

....

From 9 to 9:50 a.m.—Attended the regular First Presidency's meeting. We considered a letter from Elder John A. Widtsoe regarding the work of translating the temple ceremonies into foreign languages.[17] The Brethren felt that the Translating Committee, together with the Temple Committee, should meet with the First Presidency when consideration might be given to all questions where there is any doubt as to the adequacy of the translation. The Committee will meet with the Presidency on Monday, March 10, at 10:30 a.m. **—David O. McKay diary, Mar. 6, 1952**

This morning I assisted Pres. Joseph Fielding Smith in giving Second Blessings to Delbert Stapley[18] and John Longden[19] and wives. This was my first experience. I have been appointed by the First Presidency some months ago to assist in this great program. **—Spencer W. Kimball diary, June 30, 1952, typed excerpt in Quinn Papers**

....

Reports reaching us indicate that not infrequently divorced per-

16. This letter was reissued on Aug. 31, 1964, and Mar. 17, 1969.

17. The Swiss temple was announced in 1951 (dedicated in September 1955) as the first in a non-English-speaking country. Switzerland has 19 German-speaking cantons, 6 French-speaking, and 1 Italian-speaking—also a sizeable minority that speaks Romansh, an ancient Latin dialect. The country is centrally located, and the temple was intended to serve a large portion of western Europe.

18. Delbert Leon Stapley (1896-1978) was ordained a member of the Quorum of Twelve Apostles in 1950.

19. John Longden (1898-1969) was an Assistant to the Quorum of the Twelve from 1951 to 1969.

sons secure recommends to go to the temple who, the records of the divorce proceedings show, were guilty of conduct or practices which completely destroy their worthiness to enter the temple again for any purpose, and lastly of all to enter the temple—this applies usually only to the men—to be sealed to another person.

It is true they may affirm and feel they have repented but in some cases the misconduct involved criminal acts or perverted practices that would require a long period to show they had met the elements of repentance which the Lord has laid down,—"By this ye may know if a man repenteth of his sins—behold, he will confess them and forsake them" (D&C 58:43).

We feel we should take such steps as may be wise to forestall the possibility (so far as we can) of such unfit persons entering the temple, which is desecrated by their very presence. To accomplish this, we have decided upon two measures:

First. Whenever a divorced person applies for a recommend to the temple, the bishop shall make careful, but discreet and courteous inquiry into the causes that led to the divorce proceedings and the grounds on which the divorce was granted, and report these to the president of the stake who shall supplement the bishop's investigation if he feels such a course wise. Particular care should be exercised when the applicant for the recommend is the party whose conduct is the basis for the divorce.

Second. Before the recommend is issued[,] the case, with an accompanying statement of the facts elicited by the bishop or president of the stake, should be referred to the First Presidency for their consideration and action, either of approval or disapproval of the issuing of the temple recommend. In cases where a temple divorce has been granted or applied for, the First Presidency may have facts which the party applying for the recommend may not have disclosed. We ask bishops of wards and presidents of stakes to be most careful to observe this procedure from now on. **—David O. McKay, Stephen L. Richards, and J. Reuben Clark Jr., circular letter, Mar. 2, 1953**

We refer to our letter of March 2, 1953, regarding the matter of granting temple recommends to people who have been divorced.

The returns thus far received indicate that there are some misapprehensions and misunderstandings as to certain matters which the instructions are designed to cover. We therefore call attention to the following matters in order that the requests hereafter made of us may contain the material which we desire.

1. The instruction relates to all persons who have had divorces, no matter when the divorce occurred, and no matter whether or not they have since received recommends to go into the temple.

2. The bishop of the ward should make his investigation and write a letter giving the results thereof to the president of the stake. The bishop's letter to the president of the stake should, whenever possible, contain a short statement signed by the person making the application, covering specifically the matters mentioned in the first paragraph under item 3 below.

The president of the stake should likewise make an investigation, personally whenever possible, and either approve or disapprove the recommendation of the bishop of the ward. Both bishops and presidents of stakes should do more than merely endorse a letter of the applicant.

The president of the stake should forward the completed file to us. A separate letter should be written concerning each applicant.

3. The essential information that should be sent to us from the bishop and the president of the stake should relate to the divorce and the circumstances attending it. In the matter of the divorce the essential thing we wish to know is whether or not there was on the part of the one seeking the recommend any infidelity or other serious transgression.

We wish both the bishop and the president of the stake to make definite statements of their own feelings and impressions on these matters after their interviews with the applicants. This information should be sent to us irrespective of the fact that we may have a record here having to do with a sealing cancellation.

We are sure you understand that the Church has always looked with disfavor upon divorce, and has discouraged it wherever possible.

A statement of the present worthiness is a matter for the determination of the bishop and president of stake, acting in their sound discretion.

4. We will ask bishops of wards and presidents of stakes to understand that the work in the First Presidency's office is of such a character and quantity that it will take time to process these various applications that are made, and the applications should be made with this fact in mind.

Applications should be in the hands of the First Presidency at least three weeks before it is planned to use the recommend.

5. In the matter of keeping records of these divorce dates, each bishop should endorse in a clear hand on the first page of the membership card of the applicant and above the words "Husband and Wife (full name)," the word "divorcee." Following this word one of the three following endorsements should be made:

"First Presidency granted clearance _______ (date)," if the First Presidency did clear the applicant; or "First Presidency denied clearance _______ (date)," if the First Presidency so ruled; or "First Presidency postponed clearance _______ (date)," if that was the action taken. **—David O. McKay, Stephen L. Richards, and J. Reuben Clark Jr., circular letter, July 10, 1953**

President McKay mentioned another matter which he said is one of great importance, and that is the new method of presenting the Endowment in our Temple that will be constructed in Europe. There will be no change in the endowment ceremonies but instead of having the members move from one room to another, we will bring the rooms to the people.[20] He explained that that involves a great deal of study and preparation, and it will all have to be done here, undoubtedly in this [Salt Lake] temple before we introduce it there. The First Presidency feel that a committee should be appointed, who will be recommended by the Temple Committee, and will meet later, and probably Brother [Richard L.] Evans, assisted by Brother Gordon B. Hinckley, and some other specialists could be studying the modern use of the radio and television, and Brother Evans could render excellent service in that connection, and it would perhaps be well to have him here to partake of the spirit of this Council. **—Minutes, meeting of the First Presidency and Quorum of Twelve, Oct. 1, 1953, included in David O. McKay diary, Oct. 29, 1953; emphasis in original**

20. The problem in Switzerland was allowing people who spoke different languages to attend a common session. It was not a new dilemma for the Swiss. The solution drew on the example of the United Nations, and previously the League of Nations, in allowing people their choice of language through headphones. Introducing technology into the temple radically changed the interior design. Now, instead of a Garden Room and World Room, there was an auditorium with a movie screen. It was then decided to add a second theater to allow for staggered starting times.

Elder [Bruce C.] Hafen[21] recounted how, in 1953, a young staff member in the Missionary Department named Gordon B. Hinckley was called into the office of President [David O.] McKay and given the difficult assignment of devising a way to present the temple ordinances in eight languages.

After weeks of studying the temple ordinances, pleading with the Lord and counseling with President McKay in the Salt Lake Temple, Brother Hinckley proposed presenting the endowment ordinances in movie form. When the First Presidency and Quorum of the Twelve approved the idea, the fifth floor of the Salt Lake Temple was organized into a sacred movie set where filming took place.[22]

... In one year they finished the English-language film, then made films for each of the seven other European languages.

Moving the film of the sacred ordinances through Swiss customs without receiving the typical scrutiny and review by custom agents required faith and prayer.[23] **—"Swiss Temple Dedication a Bold Act of Faith,"** ***Church News,*** **Sept. 17, 2005**

....

At the regular meeting of the Council of the First Presidency and Quorum of the Twelve held on May 20, 1954, the following decision was reached:

That hereafter recommends may be issued to worthy young people, both young men and young women, who have not had their endowments to go to the temple to be sealed to parents at any time prior to their reaching the age of 21. This supersedes the earlier rulings on the question which made a difference between the young men and the young women in respect to the age limits governing them in this matter. **—David O. McKay, Stephen L. Richards, and J. Reuben Clark Jr. to temple presidents, June 7, 1954, copy in Buerger Papers**

---

21. Bruce Clark Hafen (1940-) was president of Ricks College, 1978-1985; dean, J. Reuben Clark Law School, 1985-1989; and provost, Brigham Young University, 1989-1996, when he was then called to the First Quorum of Seventy.

22. Elder Hinckley consulted with Elder Richard L. Evans, Paul Evans, and Joseph Shaw of KSL TV and Frank Wise of the BYU Motion Picture Department. The committee decided to hire Harold I. Hansen as the film's director, Frank Wise as editor, and Winifred Bowers as costume designer.

23. Elder Hinckley said they paid a $27 customs duty in Switzerland and "nobody ever saw a frame" of the film (Sheri L. Dew, *Go Forward with Faith: The Biography of Gordon B. Hinckley* [Salt Lake City: Deseret Book Co., 1996], 179-80).

At a meeting of the Salt Lake Temple Presidency with President [David O.] McKay[,] the following matters were discussed:

Adoptions: Seal children of divorced couple (children not born under covenant) to the parent having legal custody & to companion of that parent without formality of legal adoption to the parent's companion.

It was suggested by President [El Ray] Christiansen that [the] adoption ceremony seems incomplete and unsatisfactory. Matter taken under advisement by President McKay.

Marriage: If marriage is to be deferred more than a week after couple goes to temple, the groom should not take the bride through the veil until they come for marriage.

Going from Room to Room: Approval given by President McKay for men and women in passing from room to room to go together in double file. **—David O. McKay diary, May 21, 1954**

This morning at 8 o'clock, met with the Temple Committee, consisting of the Presidency, President Joseph Fielding Smith, Elders Harold B. Lee, and Spencer W. Kimball. I asked Howard McKean[24] to present the proposed plan of preparing the present Temple rooms in the Salt Lake Temple to experiment upon the new plan of presenting the ordinances by use of screen and visual aids. It was decided that we can use the Assembly Room in the Temple to set up a stage to make the experiment without making important changes in the present rooms. **—David O. McKay diary, June 14, 1954**

Considered a letter … about issuing temple recommends to nontithe payers. I explained that people who go to the temple should be full tithe payers and should observe the Word of Wisdom; that as a matter of fact, it is a question of their faith. Men who have a testimony of the Gospel and believe it should contribute to it and if they fail to keep their promise to observe these commandments the Bishop has a right to withhold the recommend, not wholly on the failure to pay tithing but because of their lack of faith in the Gospel. Their failure to pay tithing would indicate their lack of faith in the Gospel. **—David O. McKay diary, July 9, 1954**

24. Howard McKean (1886-1955) chaired the Church Building Committee from 1946 to 1955.

Mrs. R--- B----- S----- … called stating that she desires to go to the temple tomorrow morning to witness the marriage ceremony of her nephew, P[ri]v[a]t[e] J----- W. B-----, Jr. Sister S----- desires to take her mother, Mrs. A. L. B-----, with her to the temple to witness this marriage. If Sister S----- is not able to go to the temple, her mother would be unable to go because of her extreme old age.

Inasmuch as Sister S----- was divorced from her former husband, it is necessary for her to obtain special permission to go to the Temple to witness this marriage as there is not time for her papers to be processed normally for the regular temple recommend.

President McKay talked to [the stake president, who] … was instructed to mark on Sister S-----'s recommend that it is to witness a marriage only. **—David O. McKay diary, Sept. 14, 1954; hyphens added to obscure individuals' names**

Held a consultation with Elder Richard L. Evans of the Council of the Twelve. We considered the method of presenting the Temple ceremony, having in mind the audience sitting in the same room instead of going to three different rooms. **—David O. McKay diary, Dec. 31, 1954**

....

The announcement by President David O. McKay in the early 1950's that temples would be built in London, England; Zollikofen, Switzerland; and Hamilton, New Zealand created the need for additional translations of the temple ceremony. … [and] to accommodate the requirements of lip synchronization. In addition, experience was proving the need for certain corrections of the existing translations.

By 1969 … requests had come for consideration of Portuguese and Italian. A request had been made for the correcting of the German translation. There was dissatisfaction expressed in other languages, and it was becoming apparent that a great work lay ahead to equip each temple with translations of all the approved languages of the Church.

This was a new challenge for [the] Translation [Department]. A particular requirement existed not evident in other translation work. This work must be performed in a temple and could not be done in translation offices. The logistical challenge demanded the best thinking and planning to meet the pressing demand … to properly equip selected temples (Switzerland, London, New Zealand, Hawaii, Tokyo, Provo, Los Angeles, Washington) with appropriate translations in recorded form. All other temples were to have language cards which would allow proper administration of the ordinances in the respective languages.

It was becoming commonplace for peoples of many languages to appear at many temples where it might not have been anticipated ... This was truly an evidence of the emerging universal nature of the Church. **—John E. Carr, *"For in that Day ...": A History of Translation and Distribution, 1965-1980* (Salt Lake City: By the author, 1985), 296-97**

Dear Mr. __________:

With some awareness of what we are asking, we are, nevertheless, persuaded to write to you as pertaining to the possibility of your permitting us to purchase some three minutes of footage from Fantasia:[25] specifically that part from the third reel which ~~has to do with~~ ^portrays^ the emergence of a nebula out of the darkness of unorganized matter to the appearance of the round earth in the firmament. This footage, if the favor were granted, would be reduced to 16 millimeter film and would be accompanied by a brief citation of some scripture and other spoken lines descriptive of how the Lord God brought the earth into being.

We have been in touch with "Judge" [Wetzel O.] Whitaker, ~~recently,~~ and also by telephone within the last two or three days with Eric C. Larson,[26] and we feel that we could satisfy you as to the problems that might ordinarily suggest themselves. To begin with, our contemplated use would be without music, and would therefore~~, without any of~~ ^avoid^ the "Ascap" or ~~Tetrille~~ ^A[merican] F[ederation] of L[abor],^ complications. Our use would further be for a strictly limited group of our own Church members only, for instructional purposes, and the footage would never be shown publicly. All copyright and other protective assurances that we could give you as concerning our respect for your granting this permission would be observed.

Again we say, we think we know something of the magnitude of

25. *Fantasia* is an animated movie from 1940 that gave cartoon interpretations to eight pieces of classical music. The footage the Church sought ran three minutes and illustrated Igor Stravinsky's *The Rites of Spring* by showing the creation of the world.

26. Eric Cleone Larson (1905-1988) was an animator with Walt Disney Studios from 1933 to 1986. He worked on *Bambi*, *Cinderella, Fantasia, The Jungle Book, Sleeping Beauty*, *Snow White*, and other films.

the favor we are asking, but were much impressed by this sequence, ~~and have never seen anything of the kind done so well~~, and we know of no ~~possible~~ ^feasible^ way of duplicating it or approaching it ourselves.

Time is a pressing element with us in this hoped for use, and if you look upon this request with favor, we should be most pleased to send you one of our appointed representatives to meet with you at your convenience to arrange such documentary assurances and considerations as the circumstances suggest.

Thank you for your consideration of this request. …

P.S. Some years ago you graciously accommodated us with permission to use a minute or two of footage from ["]the Grasshop[p]er and the Ant["] for a Church Welfare film, which we were making at the time. We have not forgotten the magnitude of that favor and are grateful for it.[27] **—LDS First Presidency to Disney Studios, undated draft, ca. Apr. 15, 1955, typed excerpt in Buerger Papers**

… We have been most earnestly grateful for the use of this footage, and our need for it is urgent and will continue to be so into the future as far as we can foresee.[28]

For your information, this brief excerpt is used without identification in small restricted instruction classes, in which it introduces a discussion on the creation of the earth. The public is never invited to these classes; no publicity is ever given, and no admission charge is ever made. This most excellent footage has become inseparably a part of the brief introduction to this instruction in establishing a mood of reverence and awe for the Creator's work.[29] **—LDS First Presidency to Roy Disney, Oct. 14, 1960, typed excerpt in Buerger Papers**

---

27. Disney Studios CEO Roy Disney (Walt Disney's brother) responded on April 20 that he would "consider" the request. One month later on May 25, permission was granted for a five-year term.

28. When the Church failed to apply for an extension to its use permit, Eric Larson of Disney Studios reminded Elder Richard L. Evans on August 9, 1960, that permission had expired. Evans forwarded Larson's letter to Elder Gordon B. Hinckley, who responded to Evans that "if we were denied this[,] I don't know what we would do. Needless to say[,] we would be put in a very embarrassing situation."

29. The First Presidency requested permission "on a permanent basis if that is possible within your policies, or under any conditions which would seem to you to be fair and acceptable under the aforestated circumstances." Two weeks later, permission was granted without a time restriction.

... Our grateful appreciation to you and Mr. Disney and your associates for your most gracious consent for us to continue to use the 350 feet of film footage from "The Rites of Spring" for the purpose which we have previously defined, and for the continued full term period of copyright.

This is a most generous accommodation, and we assure you that it will be used respectfully and constructively, and that the privilege will not be abused or exceeded. **—LDS First Presidency to Gunther R. Lessing, Disney Productions Legal Department, Nov. 9, 1960, typed excerpt in Buerger Papers**

Since strict instructions had always been in existence limiting the speaking and performing of the personalities connected with the Endowment only within the sound stage [in the temple's assembly room], lighting gantries and other structures, extending out from the balcony, were fashioned to support the backdrop and necessary light fixtures. A "set" depicting the World room was then constructed lengthwise between the two rostrums.[30] **—Frank S. Wise, "A New Concept in Temple Building and Operation," 1983, p. 3**

[Q]: I noticed in the first [film] that Eve had blonde hair and Adam looked like a football player and had longish hair.

W: That was the second one that was made.[31] That was [project] 134, with the thick-necked Adam and the blonde. Then there were

30. Filming began in the winter, so while the dramatic portion was filmed inside the Salt Lake temple, the director, Harold Hansen, had nature footage shot in the more weather-cooperative southern states. For the audio portion, people were hired to read translations in Danish, Dutch, Finnish, French, German, Norwegian, and Swedish. The film was then prepared for duplication in California, although the film and the audio recordings were kept separate to guarantee against theft, also to allow for the easy addition of more language tracks. In fact, it was decided to always play the movie and sound recordings separately in the temple for the same reasons—synchronized but not joined together. The film became known for its long pauses in English, allowing for the parts to be read in languages that took longer to convey the same message.

31. Harold Burton, designer of the Oakland Temple, liked the new wide-screen concept in American movies, so he designed the endowment rooms with wide screens. This made it necessary to produce a new 35mm film. For the first few months of operation, slide projectors were used to produce murals on the screens to suggest room changes. The new movie was filmed at the BYU Motion Pictures Studio. According to Frank Wise's oral history, "one of the reasons why the second one was made was because the first one was too long. ... Then the third one was

some objections to the blonde, because they said that down in South America blondes are freaks because everybody is black haired and dark. So they said, "Make one with a dark Eve." So we didn't pick a black-haired Eve, but a dark-haired Eve.

[Q]: And that's the third one?

W: That would be [project] 198. That's the one that was made in the last five years. **—Frank S. Wise oral history, 1980-1981, p. 58**

When completed, project #100 remained in use for a number of years at Oakland and 16mm reduction prints were prepared for English-speaking patrons in foreign Temples. One attempt was made to match a German dialog track to the 16mm version of #100, and this was used with some success in Switzerland. However, the old original first versions made in the Salt Lake Temple continued to be used for other languages. …

[For the third film, the crew] journeyed up and down the west coast photographing numerous scenes for inclusion in the Creation sequence. …

[T]he fourth version of the Temple Endowment film was initiated at the Brigham Young University motion picture department and given the project #198. Much of the detail of this new production paralleled that of #134, but new sets were constructed in an attempt to give as much variation as possible.[32] A new cast was assembled for the live-action sequences but much of the Creation footage was repeated from #134. …

Early in 1976 the Temple Committee decided to transfer all film and sound operations from the Brigham Young University motion picture department to their own facilities which had been set up in the basement of the Salt Lake Temple. **—Frank S. Wise, "A New Concept in Temple Building and Operation," 1983, pp. 12, 14, 16, 26**

---

made because President [Harold B.] Lee didn't like the beards and long hair. So he wanted … Peter, James and John to be clean shaven and have short-cropped hair."

32. They had already constructed new sets for project #134 because the wooden trusses supporting stage 2's roof had collapsed, destroying the sets for project #100. The third film was completed by November 1971 in time for the dedication of the Ogden and Provo temples. For the fourth film, a greater attempt was made to accommodate foreign languages. For the Japanese version, for instance, every third frame was printed twice to allow more time for audio synchronization. New audio tapes were recorded in June 1972 in London and in early 1973 in Laie. The dubbing was done in June 1973 in a sound room at the BYU Hawaii campus.

[Q]: With all this fancy stuff, with eight tracks with the languages, and with control tracks and so on, is it difficult to make copies? Do we make them, or does some commercial lab do it for us?

W: All of the soundtracks are made right here in the [Salt Lake] temple, in the room down below the temple. They can also be duplicated in some of the temples.

[Q]: They have their own electronics staff?

W: They have all the staff and electronics that are necessary to make all the tracks that they need.

[Q]: And then the visual part can be done anywhere?

W: That is done at a lab in California. We send a man down with it and he watches it all the way through. They babysit it through, as they call it. **—Frank S. Wise oral history, 1980-1981, p. 65**

For your guidance in extending invitations to members of your missions to attend the Swiss Temple dedicatory services, and in issuing recommends for endowments and other ordinance work in the temple, we are pleased to give you the following information: …

It should be understood that wives of non-member husbands should not be recommended to the temple to receive their endowments. If they have previously had their endowments, then temple recommends might be issued to them provided they are in every way worthy, but even in such an event it is recommended that the wife receive the written consent of the husband before the recommend is issued.

Worthy female members of the Church who are married to husbands who are not worthy to go to the temple must secure the written consent of their husbands, and in addition, the branch president or mission president should interview the husband to satisfy himself that there is no objection on his part to his wife's receiving her endowments in the temple.

It is not necessary that worthy brethren receive the consent of their wives, whether the wives be non-members or unworthy of temple recommends, in order that they may be recommended to the temple for their own endowments or to do other ordinance work. **—David O. McKay, Stephen L. Richards, and J. Reuben Clark Jr. to Presidents of Missions in Europe, June 20, 1955**

....

Since the dedication of the Swiss Temple we have been giving consideration to the needs of our European Saints for temple garments and temple clothing. We are aware of the difficulties attendant on the importation of these items into the several European countries. Not only are the duties imposed very high, but the articles may be subjected to inspection.

In the hope that we may avoid, in large measure at least, such costs and hazards we are now suggesting to you and all other mission presidents in the European area that when requests come to the branch presidents and to the mission presidents for temple garments by those who have had their endowments or expect to receive them and who are accounted worthy, that the Saints making such requests be counseled to obtain through commercial channels one-piece underwear which conforms to the approved pattern of the temple garment, and that when such articles of underwear have been so secured that the Saints be authorized to place the proper markings on such underwear, and that they be given the assurance that this underwear so marked fully satisfies the requirements of an approved garment.

The mission president should in all cases be prepared to inform the branch presidents, and they in turn the Saints making the application for garments, as to what constitutes the approved pattern of garment, and the materials of which the garments may be made. In order that this information may be available to the mission presidents and the branch presidents[,] some brief specifications as to patterns and materials[,] and also as to markings, are included with this letter. These specifications should be treated confidentially and should not go beyond the branch presidents who may be safely entrusted therewith.

In case [a] question arises as to the necessity for the approved labels to be attached to the garment, it may be explained to the Saints that this label is no essential part of the garment itself, but that it has been supplied by the Church to manufacturers of garments for the sole purpose of giving assurance to our brethren and sisters that the manufactured articles to which they are attached conform to approved patterns. It may be considered desirable for mission and branch presidents to make some little investigation in mercantile houses as to types of underwear which are available to meet the requirements of the garment as to pattern and material so that they may be thereby enabled to better counsel the Saints.

As to the marking of the underwear which is purchased, the mission and branch presidents should make provision, preferably through trusted Relief Society workers, who have had their endowments, for instruction as to the proper marking of the garments, and where necessary the Relief Society may perform this service for the Saints.

This provision for a procurement of underwear to serve as garments will make it possible for the Saints in the colder countries to secure garments made of warm materials which are usually not available except on special order from our garment manufacturing institutions.

There will be maintained in the Swiss Temple a stock of the garments which are sometimes designated as ceremonial garments, which, largely for the sake of uniformity, are used in the temple ceremonies. These may be procured by the Saints and kept by them for temple ceremonial work only.

Each of the missions, we understand, is supplied with a limited number of temple clothing for burial purposes. Many of the Saints will wish to acquire their own temple clothing for endowment work. We think it will be feasible for one or more of the Relief Societies in each mission to provide the temple robes and other articles to the Saints, or to instruct them how they can make these in their homes for themselves.

If the demand for such temple clothing should be sufficiently large in any of the missions as to require the purchase of cloth and materials in larger amounts than a given Relief Society could well afford, the mission president may, if necessary, supply on a loan basis small sums for this working capital. There would be no objection to the Relief Society furnishing such temple clothing, receiving from the sales made to the Saints a price sufficient to cover the cost of materials and a reasonable cost of the labor. …

SPECIFICATIONS OF APPROVED L.D.S. GARMENTS

1. The material used shall be white and of such texture as to constitute a "covering" of the body. (Transparent nets and similar materials not permitted.)

2. The pattern shall in general conform to that of the ceremonial garment used in the temple with the following express modifications thereof permitted; but none others:

The legs of the garment may be shortened from ankle length to a length extending merely below the knee. The sleeves may be shortened from wrist length to a length extending on a garment of size 36, 8 inches from the neckband to the end of the sleeve, with appropriate and corresponding lengths for different sizes of garment. Collars, as provided for the ceremonial garment, may be eliminated. Buttons and other acceptable fasteners may be substituted for strings. The crotch may be closed. Side-leg or shoulder openings may be provided instead of front and back openings or any combination of these openings is permissible.

3. The so-called sleeveless and shoulder strap patterns are now allowable.

4. It is permissible to use a garment with a wide leg, provided it conforms in all other particulars to specifications, and provided it is not designated as a sleeping garment. **—David O. McKay, Stephen L. Richards, J. Reuben Clark Jr. to European mission presidents, Nov. 4, 1955, copy in Buerger Papers**

It has been called to our attention that there has accumulated in the various temples of the Church a large number of male names for which endowment work has not been done.

Ordinances have been performed for the corresponding female names in the families thus represented, but as you realize, families cannot be sealed until all members are endowed.

To equalize the situation and make it possible to complete this work we desire to call upon worthy holders of the Melchizedek Priesthood to assist.

With this in mind, we propose the following:

1. That two endowment sessions for brethren only be held in each temple every Saturday at hours to be announced to you by your temple president.

2. That the Melchizedek Priesthood of the Church cooperate in this temple work as a quorum project.

3. That the president of your temple district shall indicate to you as the stake president the number of men desired from your stake for particular sessions on given dates during the year.

4. That you in turn, through your stake Melchizedek Priesthood Committee and quorum presidencies, arrange for quorum members to fill these assignments.

5. That the first of these special sessions for men only be held on Saturday, January 14, 1956, with others to follow weekly until the necessary work is accomplished.

We request that the brethren plan to fill these assignments as made, going to the temple in the district in which they live, rather than to plan excursions to temples in other districts.

In addition to the above, it occurs to us that you may have in your stake many brethren who can attend the regular temple sessions on days other than Saturday, and we shall be grateful if you will give them encouragement to do so.

You may, also, have some worthy unemployed or retired brethren who could attend regular sessions if some small amount were made available to them to pay for bus fare or lunches. Temple presidents have a fund from which they are authorized to contribute such aid to brethren in this category on a basis of 90¢ for each endowment session attended. We shall appreciate your encouraging such needy brethren to participate in this phase of the program.

It goes without saying, of course, that all attending the temple must be worthy to obtain their recommends in the usual way. **—David O. McKay, Stephen L. Richards, and J. Reuben Clark Jr. to stake presidents, Dec. 15, 1955**

Based on individual worthiness and other specified qualifications as set forth herein under the general heading "Temple Recommends," the following members of the Church may be given recommends to enter the temple:

1. Converts to the Church who have demonstrated their obedience to the gospel plan for at least one full year from the date of baptism. …

2. Persons receiving their own endowments, or receiving endowments on behalf of the dead: Male members must bear the Melchizedek Priesthood.

3. Persons participating in sealing ordinances who have received their own endowments, including unmarried men or women, who have been recommended for "all ordinances for the dead."

4. Baptized children under 21 years of age who are to be sealed to their parents (1) whether or not they have received their own endowments, (2) whether or not, if male members, they have been ordained to the Priesthood. **Note:** Men and women 21 years of age, or over, must receive their own endowments before they can be sealed to their parents.

5. Unbaptized children under eight years of age to be sealed to their parents. No recommend required. …

6. Persons to be married in the temple. Male members must bear

the Melchizedek Priesthood. ... **Note:** A couple must obtain a marriage license in the state where the temple to which they are recommended is located whether they are being married for time, or for time and eternity. A marriage license is not required for sealing following a civil marriage.

7. A wife who has previously received her own endowments.

8. The wife of a Church-member husband who has not received his own endowments, *provided the husband gives his consent in writing*, which written statement must be attached to his wife's recommend.

9. Persons desiring to witness temple marriages or to view the interiors of dedicated temples. (Must have received their own endowments.)

10. Baptized members desiring to be baptized for the dead. ...

Temple Recommends will not be granted to the following persons:

1. Members of the Church judged to be unworthy to receive temple ordinances.

2. Couples desiring to be sealed in the temple, (following a civil marriage) if either of them cannot, when applying for a Temple Recommend, be legally married in his, or her, state of residence.

3. Divorced persons, who have not been given clearance by the First Presidency. ...

4. Wives who have not yet received their own endowments whose husbands are not members of the Church.

5. Children eight years of age or over who have not been baptized.

6. Children of apostates or of parents belonging to, or affiliating with, apostate groups. ...

The bishop or independent branch president is under obligation to conduct a tactful but thorough interview, *each time a recommend is applied for*, to determine the applicant's worthiness to enter the temple.

Assuming that procedures and suggestions, as outlined herein, have been followed in cases requiring special attention, worthiness to enter the temple will be determined on the premise that the applicant is morally clean; has no affiliation in sympathy or otherwise, with apostate groups running counter to the Church in any way; that he sustains local and General Authorities of the Church; is a full tithe-payer, or promises to become such; abstains from the use of tea, coffee, tobacco, and alcoholic drinks, and that he obeys the whole gospel law to the best of his ability.

Where applicants are not thus keeping the commandments of the Lord, they should repent and prove themselves worthy through a probationary period before being given a recommend.

Couples who have associated together illicitly should not be recommended to the temple until they have satisfied their bishops that they have thoroughly repented, and have shown their repentance by living righteously for a prolonged period of time. Mere sorrow is not repentance. …

Divorced persons are not to be given recommends to enter the temple for any purpose until their applications for Temple Recommends have been approved by the First Presidency.

When the approval of the First Presidency is received, such persons may thereafter be given Temple Recommends on the same premise and in the same manner as prescribed for worthy members of the Church.

If, after receiving the approval of the First Presidency, persons again become involved in divorce proce[e]dings, they are not to be given Temple Recommends until again cleared by the First Presidency. …

A recommend should not be issued to any person until he has been a member of record in the ward or branch for at least one year, except upon receipt of a letter from the bishop of the ward, president of the branch, or president of the mission, of which the applicant was a member during the preceding year, and then only when the letter affirms the person's worthiness to enter the temple. …

Living children must be adopted legally before they can be sealed to their adopted parents in the temple regardless of age. Adoption papers should be shown to the temple presidency at the time the request for sealing is made. …

Worthy Church members should be encouraged to get recommends and do temple work, but they should not be called on "missions" to the temples to perform ordinances by proxy for the dead. …

Where couples have been married by civil law, permission to have their marriages solemnized in the temple may be granted one year or more after the civil ceremony, provided that local authorities feel assured of their personal purity and worthiness and of the genuineness of their desire for the blessings of the house of the Lord. No exceptions to this one-year rule waiting period are to be made except by permission of the First Presidency. …

Any request to have a temple marriage annulled must come before the President of the Church for action. **—*Helps and Suggestions for Ward Bishoprics* (Salt Lake City: Church of Jesus Christ of Latter-day Saints, 1956), 17-23; emphasis in original**

At 4 p.m. went to the Salt Lake Temple where I went over the temple ceremony in the master book and also the various parts used by those taking part. Gord[o]n Hinckley who is getting a book ready for the Los Angeles Temple[33] called my attention to minor discrepancies between the master book and the parts used by the various participants. Found that a few errors have been made in re-typing the parts. **—David O. McKay diary, Jan. 14, 1956**

It has come to our attention that some bishops issue temple recommends to applicants not really qualified to go to the temple. In such instances they either fail to hold interviews that reveal the facts or they pass on to the stake president the distasteful responsibility of declining to sign the recommend.

The bishop's signature on a temple recommend should indicate that he has personally interviewed the applicant, has asked the necessary questions to determine the individual's qualifications, and that he believes the person is worthy to go to the temple.

A bishop should never, knowingly, issue a temple recommend which he has any reason to believe will not be cleared and approved by the stake president. **—"More Care Urged in Temple Recommends," *Messenger,*[34] Apr. 1956**

Pres[ident] Joseph Fielding Smith telephoned about second anointings for some of the brethren. I told him to send the forms and we would take care of this at the next meeting of the Council. **—David O. McKay diary, June 12, 1956**

President [David O.] McKay explained that in Switzerland the law requires that, if a person dies before noon, the body must be delivered to the appropriate officers of the government for burial before night; that all burials are under the auspices of the government of the

33. The Los Angeles temple was dedicated on March 11, 1956, by President David O. McKay.

34. *The Messenger* was published and distributed monthly by the Presiding Bishopric from January 1956 through December 1964.

canton, and that others are not permitted to handle the body. Under these circumstances, it is difficult to arrange for burial in their temple clothes of members who have had their endowments. It was agreed that burial clothes be made available in each branch where members live who have had their endowments, and that someone be assigned at once to dress the deceased person in the burial clothes before the body is delivered to the government. It was suggested that, since the presence of the apron might be misunderstood, it be placed with the body and covered from view with a shield over the clothing. **—David O. McKay diary, Dec. 11, 1956**

I do not care what office you hold in this Church—you may be an apostle, you may be a patriarch, a high priest, or anything else—you cannot receive the fulness of the priesthood [second anointing] unless you go into the temple of the Lord and receive these ordinances of which the Prophet [Joseph Smith] speaks. No man can get the fulness of the priesthood outside of the temple of the Lord. There was a time when that could be done, for the Lord could give these things on the mountain tops—no doubt that is where Moses got it, that is no doubt where Elijah got it—and the Lord said that in the days of poverty, when there was no house prepared in which to receive these things, that they can be received on the mountain tops. **—Joseph Fielding Smith, *Doctrines of Salvation: Sermons and Writings of Joseph Fielding Smith*, comp. Bruce R. McConkie (Salt Lake City: Bookcraft, 1956), 3:131-32, 178**

....

Letter read from Sister Y----- M-------- ... stating that she and her husband had adopted a baby through the Relief Society Social Service Agency; that the child was sealed to her and her husband in the temple in November, 1956; that they have had the impression that the child is theirs as though it had been born to them; that it was adopted into their family line and had all the privileges of a natural child; that they have now been told by people engaged in genealogical work who have quoted various general Authorities to substantiate their statements that the blood line has jurisdiction over the sealing, and no sealing ceremony could change the fact that she had not given birth to the child, and that he would never belong to their family line; that therefore it was his duty to do the genealogical work for his natural parents; and that in the hereafter he would have a choice as to which family he wished to belong—that of his natural parents, or that of his adopted parents.

President [David O.] McKay announced for the information of the Brethren that the First Presidency has ruled that the child belongs to its adopted parents, having been sealed to them, and that the blood line has no jurisdiction over the sealing. **—Minutes, Quorum of the Twelve Apostles meeting, Jan. 10, 1957, included in David O. McKay diary, Apr. 7, 1957; hyphens added to obscure individual's name**

Elder Richard L. Evans came in and reported that he is very much in favor of putting in all the Temples the new presentation of the endowment ceremony as now given in the Swiss Temple, and as will be given in the New Zealand Temple and the London Temple.[35] **—David O. McKay diary, Feb. 21, 1957; emphasis in original**

Your letter of July 23, 1957, addressed to President [David O.] McKay, I am asked to acknowledge for him.

I am instructed to say that people who have a right to wear the garments are at complete liberty to wear the old style garment all the time both in and out of the temple.

Care should be taken not to expose the garment to the ridicule of unbelievers. **—A. Hamer Reiser,[36] letter dated Aug. 2, 1957, copy in Buerger Papers**

This morning at 10 o'clock, I met with Elder Richard L. Evans and Brother Gordon B. Hinckley in the Salt Lake Temple where we spent two and a half hours studying the presentation of the temple ceremonies as now given in the temple at Switzerland, and as it will be given in New Zealand and in London. I feel that it was a two-hour period very well spent, and that such development in connec-

35. A close reading of this diary entry, and of the subsequent entry for Oct. 6, 1957, indicates that the decision to equip the temples in New Zealand and England with movie auditoriums had already been made and the question under consideration was whether all future temples should be similarly designed. The Hamilton and London temples were nearly complete and would be dedicated in April and September 1958 respectively.

36. Albert Hamer Reiser (1897-1981) was Assistant Secretary to the First Presidency beginning in 1955.

tion therewith will be presented to the Temple Committee before it is installed.

I have spent several Sunday mornings in the Temple studying the ceremonies, the magnificence and the significance of which (referring to the endowment) are seldom, if ever, really comprehended by our young folks when they first go through the Temple. I think the ceremony can be presented more effectively, but before any changes are made they will be presented to the members of the Temple Committee. **—David O. McKay diary, Oct. 6, 1957; emphasis in original**

....

I told Brother [Wendell B.] Mendenhall that the First Presidency had approved of his suggestion that a white cloth moccasin for use as footwear in the New Zealand [temple] be made. This will overcome the problem of fitting the feet of the native people. The Temple Committee is to be authorized to go ahead with the project.

Although Brother Mendenhall had advised that we have a stretch-type moccasin, the Brethren of the First Presidency chose a terry cloth moccasin. **—David O. McKay diary, Jan. 17, 1958; emphasis in original**

Spent many hours going through forty-five petitions for cancellation of Temple Sealings. Granted cancellations for all but two or three cases. Since April, 1954, have cancelled 620 sealings.

Number of petitions for cancellations of temple sealings considered by President [David O.] McKay since April 1954:

Dates	Cases referred to Pres. McKay	Cases denied	Cases cancelled	Cases Not Acted on or Held in Abeyance	Cases Given Permission to Be Sealed
April 1954 to May 1955	244	35	205	3	1
Aug. 1955 to Oct. 1956	175	2	172	1	
Oct. 1956 to Dec. 1957	190	4	185	1	
Feb. 1958 to June 7, 1958	59		58	1	
Totals	668	41	620	6	1

—David O. McKay diary, June 8, 1958; emphasis in original

It has come to our attention from a number of sources that the following seems to be a somewhat growing procedure in the matter of admission of people to our temples either for their own endowments or to do work for the dead, namely, people are occasionally admitted to do such work in our temples who do not have temple recommends. These people are said to offer various reasons as to why they do not have recommends. They are understood usually to assure the temple authorities that they are worthy of recommends and they add the further assurance that if they are admitted without a recommend they will secure a recommend upon their return home and forward it to the authorities of the temple to which they thus seek irregular admission without recommends. Our information is that not infrequently people are actually admitted into our temples upon such representation.

Occasionally, but apparently not always, the temple president will undertake on his own responsibility to get in touch with the president of the stake from which the individual so seeking such admission comes, and receive from him word by telephone as to whether or not the stake president regards this person so seeking irregular admission as worthy to be admitted to the temple.

It probably not infrequently happens that there is no identification of the individual by the president of the stake except perhaps such as could be by conversation over the telephone, a procedure which could be very uncertain.

It is not necessary to do more than to call the attention of our brethren, presidents and other presiding authorities in the temples—that this admission for temple work of persons without the regular and duly signed temple recommends, is a wholly irregular and unauthorized procedure and should not be followed.

Temple presidents and other temple authorities involved, will find their work most easily performed if they will confine entrance to temples for work therein to those who have with them their recommends properly signed and witnessed, and for the work authorized by the recommend. This is the rule which governs admission to temples for all ordinance work and should not be varied except upon authorization by the First Presidency.

The presidents of the temples should not undertake to exercise any discretion in the matter of admission to the temple without recommends. These cases must be referred to the First Presidency.

Furthermore, unless a temple president should know of his own knowledge that the one carrying a recommend is not worthy, all persons carrying recommends to the temple, properly authenticated, should be admitted for the purposes specified on the recommend. In the rare case where a temple president or a responsible temple official has personal knowledge of the unworthiness of an individual carrying the temple recommend, the matter should be reported to the First Presidency for their action.

All solicited exceptions to the operation of this rule that no person should be admitted by the president or temple authorities to the temple for ordinance work without a due and proper recommend, entitling on its face the individual to go into the temple and perform the work proposed, should be reported to the First Presidency for their reconsideration and determination. **—David O. McKay, Stephen L. Richards, and J. Reuben Clark Jr. to temple presidents, Aug. 15, 1958**

The matter of university stakes and wards giving recommends to students of the university for entry into the temple and doing endowment work therein was considered at a recent meeting of the Council of the First Presidency and Quorum of the Twelve and the following was the decision reached:

That where these young people have had their endowments and wish to go to the temple to do ordinance work for the dead, the bishops of student wards and presidents of university stakes may issue recommends to such young people provided they are satisfied as to their worthiness. That, however, members of their wards who wish to go to the temple to receive their own endowments should receive temple recommends from the bishops of their home wards signed also by the presidents of the stakes in which the home wards are located.

You will be good enough to be governed by this conclusion in the issuance of temple recommends in the future. **—David O. McKay, Stephen L. Richards, and J. Reuben Clark Jr. to Presidents of Stakes and Bishops of Wards Whose Membership Consist of University and College Students, Dec. 30, 1958**

....

Realizing the burden that is placed upon the stake president in the matter of signing recommends to the temple for worthy members of the Church residing in his stake, the First Presidency and Quorum of the Twelve, in recently considering the matter, decided to authorize counselors in stake presidencies to share this responsibility with the stake president, with the understanding that the brethren of the stake presidency shall make careful interrogation of and investigation regarding each one who seeks a recommend to the temple, in an effort to avoid permitting unworthy people to enter the House of the Lord.

It should be understood that this permission does not extend to bishops' counselors, except in cases where the bishop is away from the ward or otherwise unavailable. **—David O. McKay, Stephen L. Richards, and J. Reuben Clark Jr. to stake presidents, Mar. 16, 1959**

At our First Presidency's meeting this morning President Stephen L. Richards stated that Margaret Cornwall Richards, widow of Robert Richards,[37] [daughter-in-law] of Stayner Richards, was a widow when she married Robert Richards. Her first husband was killed in the war. There were no children. The first marriage was a temple marriage. She is the mother of two children by Robert Richards, who died of polio while Stayner Richards was president of the British Mission. She asks whether or not she may be sealed to Robert Richards and have the children sealed to them. President [J. Reuben] Clark stated that a nephew of his is in the same situation, having married a woman who had been sealed to her first husband, the husband having passed away.

I reviewed the case of Axel Olson, who married a young girl, 16 years of age. He was killed in Ogden Canyon shortly thereafter. She was a mother and a widow by the time she was seventeen years old. Later a man married her. He was not a member of the Church at the time. They had 12 or 13 children, all of whom were baptized in the Church and finally he, the husband, was baptized. The case was presented to President Joseph F. Smith when the mother desired to be sealed to her husband who was the father of the 12 or 13 children. I said that President Smith informed me that in this Church a woman has her choice; if she wants him (the father of the 12 or 13 children) she may have him, but she cannot take Axel's child from him, but she may be sealed to the second husband, and may have the children of the

37. Robert Stayner Richards died in 1951 after marrying Margaret Cornwall five years earlier. He was Stephen L. Richards's nephew and a son of Stayner Richards; nothing more is known about his wife's first marriage.

second husband sealed to them. They went to the Temple and had the 12 or 13 children sealed to them. **—David O. McKay diary, May 8, 1959**

We enclose herewith a copy of the adoption ceremony which has been prepared for use in the various temples in lieu of the form you have heretofore used for this ordinance. You will note that there are some changes in the copy of the ceremony as herewith enclosed, which changes we feel are vital and of such a nature as to make the form more comprehensive and to give greater significance to the ordinance.

We shall be pleased to have you replace the form that you now have in your books with this copy we are sending herewith. **—David O. McKay, Stephen L. Richards, and J. Reuben Clark Jr. to temple presidents, July 15, 1959**

[Gary] C[arlson]:[38] What happened in these early days [late 1950s], really when we started working with Brother [Hugh B.] Brown, is that they asked us to look at some basic concepts. We worked with the people in the Genealogical Society and did what [we] thought were some very simple calculations such as estimating how many people have been born on the earth. Some estimates were around seventy billion. At the time we were doing about one million endowments per year in the temples. One million goes into seventy billion an awful lot of times. We made some charts and some fancy overheads and so on to try to explain to the Brethren and help them understand that the numbers get very large, if you assume we need to do the genealogical work for everybody, not knowing who is going to accept and who isn't. I still have some of those charts and they may be in some of those papers that I've passed on to you.

The figures showed that if the Church kept on growing the way it was, then every adult member of the Church could spend eight hours a day in the temple seven days a week all of his life and we would never come up to the rate of new births in the world. Even if we were all in the temple all day, we'd still be falling behind.

We must have made a half a dozen presentations to various groups trying to just get that idea across, that the numbers were big and we needed computers to process the data and get the job done. Some of

38. Gary Carlson served on a Church data processing committee and as a director of Management Systems Corporation.

the Brethren thought we were tampering with doctrine. They were very nervous about our interferences.

[Q]: You mean doctrine in the sense of who is responsible for genealogy research, or other doctrine?

C: The family responsibility was the initial one that came up; I remember one time we made a presentation to the Quorum of the Twelve and I don't remember who it was, but one of the Brethren said, "Now Brother Carlson, you mean to tell me that you think that I am not responsible for my direct ancestors?" I said, "Now, brother, I'm not saying that at all. I'm just saying that there are seventy billion names to be done, and if you have to do them all, we're not going to make it. Something has to change."

We tried to sort of skirt the issue and point out that change was what was needed. And as brash young foolish people we had some suggestions as far as changes that could be made. One of the earlier questions, that Jack Pettit came up with really, was whether we could separate the physical processing in the temples as we could separate it in the computer. That is, could you do initiatory work separate from endowments and separate from sealings, etc.? When we suggested that idea in Salt Lake, I wasn't sure if we were going to get a paid ticket home or not. [laughter] There was a lot of discussion and I know that some of the Brethren thought we were a bunch of heretics.

Again we kept saying, "We don't want to impinge on doctrine. We just want to help you understand the problems, from a data processing standpoint, and the implications for physical processes that have to be faced sooner or later."

One other thing on that—I remember one meeting with the Quorum of the Twelve in the auditorium in the old Church Office Building. Joseph Fielding Smith was there, and as I recall he was president of the quorum at the time. Joseph Fielding Smith was pretty old at the time and very tired and rested his eyes often. We all had an interest in helping him understand. There was a little stage in the front of the room and we had a flipchart up there with some of our charts and our drawings on.

I remember I got up to give my presentation and I looked right at President Smith and I tried to talk very slow and distinct right to him. He sat in his chair with his head bowed and eyes closed as though totally sound asleep. So I changed the inflection of my voice and I'd pause and I'd almost yell and I would do everything that I could to try to wake him up, because I so wanted him to understand the concept that we were talking about. Once in a while he'd raise his head just a little bit, open his eyes a little bit, and then zonk, down he'd go. I was almost beside myself. I looked over to Jack and to Kendall sort of saying, "Hey, do I quit and wait until he wakes up or keep going? What do I do?' They didn't give me any encouragement. They just sort of hid their heads and I went on.

My part of the presentation was trying to get across the magnitude of the problem as far as the work to be done and how little we were doing in terms of the total problem.

We finished up and several of the Brethren came up and said that was fine and they appreciated the information. I got to President Smith and I said, "I hope you understand what we were trying to say. Is there anything I can answer or any questions I can help you with?" He looked me straight in the eye and he said, "Now, Brother Carlson, you may think I was asleep. I'm an old man and my eyes are tired and my body is tired and I have to rest whenever I can." I felt smaller and smaller. He said, "But I heard what you said. I don't understand it, but I have a feeling that you young men know what you are talking about and I have confidence in you."

[Q]: That was all you needed, wasn't it?

C: That was all I needed. I practically flew home without the airplane. I still remember that so vividly. He didn't understand it, he knew he wasn't going to, but he could feel that we understood the technology that [we] were talking about, and he had confidence in us. That was a humbling experience. That was one of the more striking experiences I've had in the whole thing. I thought he'd been asleep and just not heard a thing. He had heard, but not understood, but he understood that he did not understand.

… Let me mention a few recent developments … where we do the washing and anointing separately from the endowment and so on. I think that, to some extent, is a result of the computer thrust that, "We can process the records any way you want and put them back together." You do not have to take one name through baptism, washing, and anointing, endowment, and then sealing.

[Q]: Were you involved in that decision-making process?

C: Only indirectly. I've always tried to be very careful to not suggest doctrinal change. But in our committee we did try to demonstrate that the temple processing could be done in pieces and that processing could put the information back together.

[Q]: Who was the key man among the General Authorities in catching that vision and finally implementing it?

C: I'm not sure, in retrospect. I know that Brother [Harold B.] Lee was very disturbed by the idea. At a meeting when he first clearly understood what we were suggesting, I remember him saying, "Now you mean to tell me, brethren, that you can give someone his endowments before he's had the washing and anointing?" And we meekly nodded yes. And he was very unhappy with that.

[Q]: In effect that's what happens now, isn't it?

C: That's correct. In the temple now we don't care if you seal them first and baptize them next, endow them next, and wash and anoint them next. The sequence doesn't matter. But that was a conceptually very difficult task. All we said was that technically it could be done, and then it was up to them to decide what to do about the idea.

If ever a mantle of authority fell upon a man, it was on President Lee. Before he was the prophet[,] in some of our meetings he was cantankerous—I guess that's the right word. In fact, I remember one meeting with President Lee. We told him about a computer system and that it could save the Church money. I remember him looking at me and waving his finger in my face and saying, "Now Brother Carlson, don't you tell me a computer ever saves anybody any money. Do you want to tell me why [we need it]?" And so on. And I said, "Yes sir, yes sir. It can provide better service." But he was quite adamant about that and upset, and I was sorry to see him upset. You don't like to see people like that. After he was the prophet I never once saw him angry. I never once saw him shake his finger in anybody's face. The first time I met with him after he had become President, I couldn't believe he was the same man.

[Q]: Well, he probably wasn't.

C: He wasn't. There's no question of it. He was a prophet then. And the lapse of time between the finger-wagging meeting and when he was President was only about four or five months. That's why the change was so striking to me. I remember I went in with Jerry Davey, and when we came out I said, "Jerry, that is a different man." We both knew it. He was now a prophet.

Getting back to what we were talking about, … we made a number of other suggestions which we have been told are none of our business, and I accept that totally [laughing]. We felt it was our task to help the Brethren understand, data processing-wise and physical process-wise, what options they had. This change of sequence in the temple I think is the result, to some extent, of this trust. **—Gary Carlson oral history, Jan. 15, 1980, pp. 8, 10, 20, 25, excerpt in Buerger Papers**

....

Every Church member eight years of age or over must have a recommend to enter the temple.

A group recommend may be issued only to holders of the Priesthood and girls of comparable age who desire to go to the temple as a group to do baptismal work for the dead. In all other cases an individual recommend is required for each person. Separate recommends must be given for each temple. …

Worthiness a Prerequisite: No person should receive a recommend for any purpose unless he is believed to be worthy in every respect. Unworthiness disqualifies him.

Before issuing recommends bishops will assure themselves by searching inquiry that the recipients are free from all kinds of immoral practices; that they have no affiliation, in sympathy or otherwise, with any of the apostate groups that are running counter to the established order of the Church; that they sustain the local and General Authorities of the Church; are full tithepayers, or will covenant to become such; that they observe the Word of Wisdom, abstaining from tea, coffee, tobacco, and liquor; and that they are fully worthy as evidenced by their observance of the whole gospel law including abiding by all conditions of their temple obligations.

Where applicants are not keeping the commandments, they should prove themselves through a probationary period before the recommend is issued. Every person must be adjudged worthy for a recommend each time he applies for one. …

In the case of group recommends for children, bishops will assure themselves that each child recommended is a good child, exemplary in his life, and attending to such Church duties as are required of his age.

Exceptional care will be taken to see that the children of parents belonging to or affiliating with apostate groups, are not recommended to the temple, either with groups or as individuals.

Record Membership of One Year Required: Bishops and branch presidents should not issue a recommend to a person until he has been a member of record of their ward or branch for at least one year, except upon receipt of a letter from the bishop of the ward, president of the branch, or president of the mission, of which the applica[nt] was a member during the preceding year, stating that such person is worthy to enjoy the privileges of the temple. …

Recommends for Wife Only: A wife whose Church-member husband has not received his endowments will not be given a recommend to receive her endowments unless the husband expresses his consent in writing. This certification must be attached to the recommend.

Stake presidents will interview such husbands to assure themselves that the husband has no objection to the endowments being given to his wife.

Under no circumstances will a recommend be issued for endowments to a wife whose husband is not a member of the Church. This rule does not prevent such a worthy wife, whose husband is willing, from participating in baptisms for the dead in the temples.

Women who received their own endowments before this rule was given, or who were endowed before being married even though married to non-members, may still be granted the privileges of going through the temple if they are worthy.

Witnessing Marriages or Viewing Interior of Temple: Persons witnessing marriages or viewing the interiors of dedicated temples must have recommends. Recommends are to be granted only to those who have received their own endowments, and all of the requirements of personal worthiness must be met.

Adoption: Living children must be adopted legally before they can be sealed to their foster parents in the temple. Adoption papers should be shown to the temple presidency at the time the request for sealing is made. …

Recommends for Divorced Persons: No divorced person, man or woman, is to receive a temple recommend until and unless the facts of the divorce have been submitted by the bishop to the First Presidency, and the bishop receives back from the First Presidency, a letter authorizing the issuance of such a recommend and on condition of worthiness as developed in a careful interview by the bishop and stake presidency. Bishops should make sure that in the case of a divorced person being recommended for temple marriage, a final divorce decree has been secured; and if the individual was married in the temple previously[,] that a cancellation of sealing has been granted in the case of a woman. However, a man married in the temple who has had a civil divorce but not a cancellation of sealing may be recommended for temple marriage without first having the previous sealing annulled if he is fully worthy and if his divorce has been cleared by the First Presidency.

Bishops should conduct a thorough, searching interview of men and women seeking recommends to marry a second time in the temple. They should inquire into the basis of the divorce, know whether there have been more divorces than one, seek to learn where the fault lay, and issue the recommend only if they are convinced that the applicant is wholly worthy.

Whenever a divorced person applies for a recommend to the temple, the bishop shall make careful, but discreet and courteous inquiry into the causes that led to the divorce proceedings, and the grounds on which the divorce was granted, and report these in writing to the president of the stake who shall supplement the bishop's investigation if he feels such a course wise. Particular care should be exercised when the applicant for the recommend is the party whose conduct is the basis for the divorce.

Before the recommend is issued[,] the case, with an accompanying statement of the facts elicited by the bishop or president of stake, should be referred to the First Presidency for their consideration and action, either of approval or disapproval of the issuing of the temple recommend. In cases where a temple divorce has been granted or applied for, the First Presidency may have facts which the party applying for the recommend may not have disclosed.

The instruction relates to all persons who have had divorces, no matter when the divorce occurred, even prior to joining the Church, and no matter whether or not they have since received recommends to go into the temple.

The bishop of the ward should make his investigation and write a letter giving the results thereof to the president of the stake. The bishop's letter to the president of the stake should, whenever possible, contain a short statement signed by the person making the application, covering specifically the matters mentioned in the paragraphs below.

The president of the stake should likewise make an investigation, personally whenever possible, and either approve or disapprove the recommendation of the bishop of the ward. Both bishops and presidents of stakes should do more than merely endorse a letter of the applicant.

The president of the stake should forward the completed file to the First Presidency. A separate letter should be written concerning each applicant. …

The present worthiness is a matter for the determination of the bishop and president of [the] stake, acting in their sound discretion.

The work in the First Presidency's office is of such a character and quantity that it will take time to process these various applications that are made, and the applications should be made with this fact in mind. …

Temple Sealings: Sons and daughters over 21 years of age must receive their own endowments before being sealed to parents. Children under 8 require no recommend for sealing to parents, but date and place of birth are required for the temple record.

Temple Marriages Must Follow Law: A couple must obtain a license in the state where the temple to which they are recommended is located. No recommend will be given to any couple to be sealed in any temple (following a previous civil marriage) until and unless they may be legally married in the state in which they live. For instance, the performance of a sealing ceremony under the following circumstances would be WRONG:

A couple residing in State A went to State B and were civilly married. They could not at the time be legally married in State A where they lived because one of them was a divorced person and the time that must elapse between the granting of the divorce and the legal ability to marry had not expired. Having been married in State B they then obtained a temple recommend and went to another state, other than State A, to be sealed in the temple, still before the time when they could legally marry in State A. …

Calls to Do Temple Work Not Approved: Worthy Church members should be encouraged to get recommends and do temple work, but they should not be called on "missions" to the temples to perform ordinances by proxy for the dead.

Sealings after Civil Marriages: Permission may be granted to couples who have been married by civil law to have their marriages solemnized in the temple at such time as the stake president and bishop feel assured of their personal purity and worthiness and of their genuine desire for the blessings of the House of the Lord.

Where parents are not eligible to enter the temple, and yet insist on witnessing the wedding ceremony of their son or daughter, bishops must apply to the First Presidency for permission if it is desired to hold a civil ceremony first, to be followed shortly afterward by the sealing in the temple. Special permission of the First Presidency in each instance of this kind is required.

Where couples deliberately refuse temple marriages for reasons of their own, and afterward desire a sealing, they should be asked to wait for at least a year in which to demonstrate their sincerity and worthiness to receive this blessing.

If an unmarried couple, worthy of temple marriage, yet living at a considerable distance from a temple, desires to travel unaccompanied from their homes to the temple, it may be thought advisable that they have a civil marriage before leaving home, though only a few days may intervene between the civil ceremony and the sealing in the temple.

Couples who have associated together illicitly should not be recommended to the temple until they have satisfied their bishops that they have thoroughly repented, and have shown their repentance by living righteously for a prolonged period of time. Mere sorrow is not repentance. It is urged that the desirability of temple marriages be emphasized continually.

Dissolution of Temple Marriages: Any request to have a temple marriage annulled must come before the President of the Church for action. **—*General Handbook of Instructions,* Number 18 (Salt Lake City: Church of Jesus Christ of Latter-day Saints, 1960), 65-70, 74-75; emphasis in original**

One letter I dictated was to a woman in answer to her question about the wearing of the garments while sun bathing. I said to her: "The wearing of the garment is a personal responsibility, and conditions that justify temporary removal should be determined by each person." **—David O. McKay diary, Feb. 1, 1960**

The First Presidency have directed the Presiding Bishopric to instruct bishops that worthy members of the Church, desiring to be baptized for the dead, are to be twelve years of age or older. Worthy bearers of the Aaronic Priesthood 12 to 21 and young women of corresponding ages should especially be encouraged and invited to participate in this vicarious work. **—Joseph L. Wirthlin, Thorpe B. Isaacson, and Carl W. Buehner[39] to bishops, July 11, 1960**

In increasing numbers people come to the Church offices with temple recommends signed by the branch president but unsigned by the mission president. The normal course is that both signatures should be on every temple recommend.

Not infrequently mission presidents write in and ask that their people be interviewed here at Church headquarters. Obviously the only thing that the interviewer here has is whatever information the individual wishes to give. We know nothing about the past of the individuals save what is told to the interviewer here. As a matter of fact, we have only the word of the one desiring the temple recommend. In other words, we are completely ignorant about the situation.

It is unnecessary to remind you brethren that the receipt by any person of the temple endowment is a most serious matter,—the blessings promised and the covenants made relating to the living of their lives, indeed, the whole ceremony is of the very last importance. We feel that for an unworthy person to go through the temple and receive his endowments merely adds to his culpability and consequent loss of the blessings promised in the temple, and also increases the responsibility before the Lord for past misdeeds which may or may not be thoroughly repented of, and in addition to his responsibility for his conduct with reference to further transgression. In this connection you will have in mind the provisions of [Doctrine and Covenants] Section 82, verse 7: "And now, verily I say unto you, I, the Lord, will not lay any sin to your charge; go your ways and sin no more; but into that soul who sinneth shall the former sins return, said the Lord your God."

Furthermore, it is of the very last importance that any divorce situation involving the one seeking the recommend, should be cleared here, and that any sexual irregularity should be thoroughly repented of. On this point the Lord has said: "By this ye may know if a man repenteth of his sins—behold, he will confess them and forsake them." (D&C 58:43)

---

39. Carl William Buehner (1898-1974) was second counselor in the Presiding Bishopric from 1952 to 1961.

We urge you brethren, each of you, to bring these general matters to the attention of the members of your mission, and in this presentation you might consider the wisdom of adding that surely the blessings bestowed, the promises given, and the covenants[,] taken as an incident of the endowment ceremony, are of a character that justify any inconvenience that might be incident to an interview with the mission president and the securing of his signature to the recommend. **—David O. McKay, J. Reuben Clark Jr., and Henry D. Moyle to mission presidents, Aug. 25, 1960**

I reviewed a case in which restoration of blessings is requested, and in which there is a temple record of endowment, but no record of excommunication. I directed that arrangements be made at once for the Temple records of endowments to be made complete by the addition of the record of excommunication of persons endowed, and that the restoration of blessings when this action is taken be also entered upon the record of the endowments. **—David O. McKay diary, Nov. 9, 1960**

Inasmuch as our old supply of temple recommends is exhausted, we are now printing and will soon have ready for distribution, a new stock. This has afforded us the opportunity of making some changes in the form which we deem will be helpful and beneficial to the work.

Hereafter there will be two forms. It will be necessary for you to have two books, one form for recommending admission to the temple for vicarious baptism for the dead, to be issued only to children between 12 and 21 years of age; the other form to be used by those who are going to the temple for their own endowments or to do work vicariously for the dead.

In preparing these forms we have had in mind the desirability of using every precaution possible to avoid forgery by those who might seek to enter the temple unworthily, and also to provide forms that would be most convenient for the bishop and the stake president, as well as the workers in the temple. To provide a safeguard against forgery you will note we are suggesting that the one who signs the recommend, which means the bishop or the branch president or the counselors, as the case may be, will initial each ordinance for which the applicant is being recommended. The temple workers are reminded by a note at the heading of the recommend to check each recommend to make sure that the initials opposite each ordinance are in the same handwriting as the signer of the recommend. This will do away with the check mark previously used.

You will note that we have eliminated from section two of the old recommend the space provided "for those previously endowed to be present at marriages of children or kinfolk." Upon inquiry we learned that there have been frequent instances where individuals who have not been endowed, and in some cases not presently worthy of a regular temple recommend for ordinances, have been given a recommend to witness a marriage. In place of this practice, which is contrary to the rule of the temple, you will find in these forms the statement "any applicant who has been personally endowed and who is presently worthy to do all ordinances for the dead may witness a temple marriage or sealing." It is necessary for us all to comply with this rule and to issue no recommends under any other circumstances for persons to witness temple marriages.

We have changed the expiration date from September 30th, which appears on some of the older forms, to July 31st, which is the current expiration date.

On the form for recommending children only[,] we have made an insert to conform to the present ruling of the First Presidency as to the ages of those who are to be baptized for the dead. We are suggesting that this form be used for all members between the ages of 12 and 21 years, and that the regular temple recommend be used for recommending members for baptism for the dead only in cases where the individuals are 21 years of age or older. We think that the comparatively small number of those over 21 doing baptisms for the dead should not necessitate a separate form.

We hope that you will find that these new forms and the initialing rather than checking of the specific ordinances to be performed will not only be helpful and protective to you but to the temple workers also.

It is our desire that no temple recommend should be issued to persons touring the country to enter the temple merely to view the interior. It is not conducive to temple work to have visitors going through as tourists. **—David O. McKay, J. Reuben Clark Jr., and Henry D. Moyle, circular letter, Nov. 28, 1960**

6.

"STANDARDS AND PRINCIPLES" 1961–1970

There has been some uncertainty in the past arise in cases where a couple have been civilly married in a State which does not require a serological [blood] test. In all cases where a couple has been legally married in any State or Country of the world, they are entitled to go to any temple of the Church if properly recommended by their bishops and stake presidents, or branch and mission presidents, and are otherwise worthy to be sealed for time and eternity, without complying with the laws of the State or Country in which the temple is located. We give full recognition to the married status of such couples created under the laws of the land in which they were civilly married. It is this legal marital status which gives us the right to perform our temple sealings without compliance with the provisions of the laws which apply to the creation of the marital status by the civil law. Therefore, if a couple are legally married in a State or Country in which no serological test is required, they are not obligated to undergo such a test in the State or County in which the temple is located as a condition precedent to their participating in the sealing ordinances of the temple. **—David O. McKay, J. Reuben Clark Jr., and Henry D. Moyle, circular letter, May 31, 1961**

Mission, stake, and ward officers should not decide for endowed persons in the armed services what they should do relative to wearing of proper clothing, rather such endowed persons, having read or had read to them the First Presidency's letter,[1] should then determine for themselves under the circumstances facing them, what course to pursue. Servicemen who have questions relative to problems in this field should consult with their bishops or branch presidents. **—*Handbook of the L.D.S. Servicemen's Program* (Salt Lake City: General LDS Servicemen's Committee, June 1961), 6**

Temple personnel have the unpleasant duty to decline admittance to the temple to members whose recommends are not properly filled out. Bishops should avoid such unnecessary embarrassment and disappointment to their members by rechecking every recommend for accuracy and completeness before it is given to the worthy member. Typewritten recommends are not acceptable. Each recommend must be filled out by hand in ink in the same writing as the one authorized to prepare and sign it. **—"Temple Recommends Must Be Carefully Prepared," *Messenger,* Dec. 1961; emphasis in original**

It has been the policy in the past to require all divorced persons to be cleared by the First Presidency before they could be issued a recommend to the temple. Hereafter it will not be necessary to submit such cases to the First Presidency for clearance except in those instances where the person seeking a temple recommend has had more than one divorce since baptism or has been divorced from a husband or wife to whom he or she has been sealed in the temple even though the sealing has been cancelled.

Applications for divorce clearance of those persons who have had more than one divorce since baptism[,] or who are divorced from [the] one to whom they have been sealed in the temple, should be made [by filling out] the forms provided for this purpose. A supply is being sent herewith to stake and mission presidents. We call your attention to the instructions printed on each form and request that you follow these instructions specifically.

In all cases where there has been a divorce in the life of the person seeking a recommend to the temple, and clearance by the First Presidency is no longer required, the stake president, bishop, or mission president should conduct a thorough, searching interview to determine

1. See George Albert Smith, J. Reuben Clark Jr., and David O. McKay, circular letter, Oct. 2, 1950.

not only the applicant's present worthiness, but also whether or not there was any infidelity or serious transgression in connection with the divorce. **—David O. McKay, Henry D. Moyle, and Hugh B. Brown, circular letter, Dec. 18, 1961**

[George H.] F[udge]:[2] About this same time, in 1961, we were down to a point where we were so short of names [of the dead for proxy ordinances] that literally we were running backwards and forwards to the Salt Lake Temple almost on a daily basis taking the names for the next day. The alternatives were that we would have to do something drastic in providing names or we would have to close the temples or decrease the number of sessions they had. When that was placed before the Brethren, President [David O.] McKay said that the temples must not close. Therefore the Genealogical Society would be responsible for keeping those temples open and supplying names. We could not go out then with the whip and tell the Saints, "Do more and more research." The alternative was that we would begin with an extraction program ourselves. …

So then really what we were doing is performing ordinances and these were being held [in abeyance in the spirit world] until a person proved himself worthy to accept them. Now if that was a true concept, then why couldn't we go ahead and perform ordinances not necessarily in the same sequence as we had been doing for the living? This concept would enable us to take a christening record and not only perform the baptism and endowment, but also seal the child to his parents from that one record. In doing that[,] we would be sure that the child was sealed to his correct parents. We wouldn't have to worry about grouping them. In other words, if we sealed every child to his parents and assumed we had all the records of the whole world, in the end we would have sealed everyone in the world.

Well, I took that concept to the Brethren. Elder [Theodore M.] Burton was then the managing director [of the Genealogical Department]. President [N. Eldon] Tanner had been made an apostle and was not a member of the First Presidency. In turn we went to Elder [How-

2. George Henry Fudge (1919-86) was general manager of the Genealogical Society (an LDS Church department) from 1961 to 1963 and later director of the Advanced Planning department, which supervised the introduction of computer technology into genealogical and temple work. In late 1975 he was appointed director of the renamed Genealogical Department.

ard W.] Hunter, who was the president of the [Genealogical] Society.[3] Brother Burton was the managing director, or the general manager at that time. Brother Hunter felt it was a good concept, so he went to the First Presidency with it. After some deliberation by the Brethren they decided that it was a correct concept and that we should pursue it. They sent us a written statement accordingly to approve us going ahead. …

[Q]: What percentage of the names for the ordinances in the temples does the Genealogical Department now prepare?

F: Seventy-six.

[Q]: Has the percentage been about like that since you started this program?

F: Yes. It's been around seventy-five percent. …

[Q]: You mentioned that in May of 1972 a committee had been appointed to investigate endowment procedures in the temple. I was wondering what this committee did.

F: Well, I think that this was a committee probably headed by Brother Howard W. Hunter to look at some of the procedures which were being followed in the temple with some recommendations to be made to the First Presidency as to how maybe those procedures could be streamlined. That kind of a report would have gone directly to the First Presidency and I wouldn't really know what was proposed.
—George H. Fudge oral history, Jan. 29-30, 1976, pp. 15, 17, 19; excerpt in Buerger Papers

....

President [Henry D.] Moyle presented to me for my approval a letter that he had prepared in answer to a question from a stake president pertaining to the adoption by the grandparents of a child born to their daughter illegitimately, the grandparents desiring to have this child who is now six years of age sealed to them. The mother is married now but does not wish to have the child sealed to her and her present husband. The information given indicates that the grandparents took custody of the child when he was five days old, that the names of the grandparents were placed on the birth certificate as the parents of the baby, that the boy has been raised as their son, and they do not wish to take any action that would reveal to the boy now or later that these

3. The Genealogical Society became the Genealogical Department in 1975 and would later be restructured as the Family History Department.

people are not his natural parents. The grandparents wish to have the boy sealed to them as child to parents without a legal adoption. President Moyle raised the question as to whether it would be advisable for the Church to be a party to recognizing a falsified document and basing the sealing on that document, the document referred to being the birth certificate on which the names of the grandparents appear as the parents of the child.

I said that I feel the request of the grandparents should be granted, namely, that permission be given for them to have the child sealed to them as [a] child to parents without a legal adoption, that I favor the proposition that the child look upon these people who have reared him from early infancy and supported him, as his father and mother. **—David O. McKay diary, Feb. 1, 1962; emphasis in original**

Effective since March 7, 1962, the daily schedule of endowment sessions in the Salt Lake Temple has been reduced to five each day Monday through Friday by discontinuing the "D" and "E" sessions, which are recorded at 12:45 p.m. and 2:45 p.m., respectively. Furthermore, sisters will be permitted to perform not more than one endowment each day. **—"Special Salt Lake Temple Notice,"** ***Messenger,*** **Apr. 1962**

We read a letter … reciting conditions with which Brother D---- J----- is obliged to cope since he received his endowments in the Salt Lake Temple because of the amputation of his right leg above the knee and his wearing an artificial limb attached above the knee. He explained that he cannot cope with the leg of the garment over the artificial limb. His wife proposes that the knee mark be placed in the left leg of the garment and that the right leg be modified to overcome the present difficulty which Brother J----- experiences.

I said, "Since that right leg is gone, I think he meets the requirement of 'every knee shall bow and every tongue confess that Jesus is the Christ.'—the purpose of the mark, by the suggestion. I think in this case—and this is the only time we could permit a change of the garment—this fulfills the purpose of the garment. I think we should make no publicity whatever. We give special permission to place the mark in the left leg." **—David O. McKay diary, Apr. 4, 1962; hyphens added to conceal identities**

The question of whether or not a daughter whose mother is white and father negro may go to the temple was raised. I answered the question in the negative. **—David O. McKay diary, July 17, 1962**

The failure of some bishops to properly and adequately complete temple recommends creates many undesirable situations. It is imperative that every bishop be alert to eliminate faulty recommends that result in a member being delayed, disappointed, and embarrassed when attempting to enter the temple. The First Presidency's instructions are to the effect that no change, correction, addition, or deletion is to be made or repaired in a temple recommend without the authorization of the bishop or stake president who has signed the document. This requirement necessitates a contact with local recommending authorities to receive their authorization. Hence, a considerable amount of time and expense can be attached to each necessary correction. This we must avoid.

Since the defect in the recommend is usually not discovered until the member has presented it all to the admittance desk in the temple, you can imagine the anxiety and disappointment experienced when the temple officials must turn them away. A thoughtful, thorough bishop CAN save the members of his ward from experiencing this frustration. …

Occasionally, people come to the Office of the First Presidency for recommends without having gone at all to the bishop. In such cases, the people say someone has told them they can get a recommend from the Office of the First Presidency. It must, of necessity, be explained to these people that bishops and stake presidents are the local certifying and recommending officers upon whom everyone else must rely and that nothing can be done without their instructions and authorization. These cases become extremely involved and burdensome.

All bishops are requested to be sure each recommend is adequately and carefully prepared. Stake presidents are responsible and expected to determine the correctness of each recommend before signing. **—"Properly Completed Temple Recommends Required,"** ***Messenger,*** **Aug. 1962; emphasis in original**

President [Hugh B.] Brown asked if members of the General Authorities, exclusive of the First Presidency, are to be admitted to the temples to perform marriage ceremonies without a recommend. I said General Authorities have never had recommends to go to the temple for this purpose or for other temple work. Their wives should have recommends when they are not accompanied by their husbands. (This as a means of identifying them when they may go to a temple where they may not be known to be the wives of General Authorities of the Church.)

... President Brown asked if the initialing of recommends to correct them when they are incomplete or must be altered should be done only by the General Authorities of the Church. Presidents of the temples want to know whether or not they should accept recommends initialed by anyone but the First Presidency. I said that only the First Presidency and the General Authorities may initial the recommends. **—David O. McKay diary, Aug. 16, 1962**

....

With the thought in mind of reducing the time spent by bishops, branch presidents and mission presidents in preparing recommends for members of the Church who desire to go to one or more temples, a recommend form has been prepared which may be used for any and all temples.

Hereafter, one recommend acceptable in any temple will be issued to each patron rather than issuing a separate recommend for each temple. The new form will be used by those who go to the temple for their own endowments, sealings or marriages or who receive these ordinances in behalf of the dead.

You will continue to use the forms you now use for children between 12 and 21 years of age who go to the temple to act as proxies in doing baptisms for the dead.

The new forms are being printed and will be sent by July 1. You will kindly use the new form for those members who apply for recommends to be used after August 1, 1963.

You will notice that the new form is arranged in two sections. When issuing a recommend for all ordinances for the dead, use only the left hand portion. However, when the applicant is recommended for [their] own Endowment, Marriage, Sealing after Civil Marriage, or Sealing to Parents, both portions of the recommend are to be filled out.

The bishop will prepare the original, the buff and pink copies. He will retain the pink copy. The patron will present the white and buff copies to the first temple he goes to, where they will be stamped and dated. He will retain the buff copy, leaving the original (white) with the recommend clerk. If the first temple the patron attends is not in the temple district in which he resides, the temple will make a photo copy of the white (original) recommend for its own files. The temple making the photo copy will send the white (original) to the temple in the district where the patron lives for filing and for future reference.

We stress again the importance of bishops' filling out the recommends completely and accurately, giving all dates and other information called for. This should be done in ink in the bishop's own handwriting, including his initials, indicating the ordinances to be received.

To avoid disappointments and difficulties at the temple, make sure that the applicant takes the recommend to the stake president for [an] interview and for his signature.

We urge that each applicant is carefully interviewed to ascertain if he or she is worthy and prepared to enter the temple.

Please inform the applicant that he may be asked to also sign the recommend at the temple on the place provided for in the temple recommend. **—David O. McKay, Henry D. Moyle, and Hugh B. Brown, circular letter, May 29, 1963**

Every Church member eight years of age or over must have a recommend to enter the temple. A group recommend may be issued for those eight to eleven years of age, to holders of the Aaronic Priesthood, and girls of corresponding ages who desire to go to the temple as a group to do baptismal work for the dead. In all other cases an individual recommend is required for each person. ...

By Whom Issued: All recommends are issued by the bishop or branch president and endorsed by a member of the stake presidency or, if in a mission, endorsed by the mission president or a counselor to the mission president if so authorized. During their absence from the ward or branch, the bishop or branch president may assign the responsibility to his first counselor. In the event the first counselor is also absent, the second counselor may be authorized to interview and issue the recommend.

The bishop or branch president will conduct a thorough, searching interview of each applicant for a recommend every time application is made, irrespective of how well the person is known to the interviewer. Each applicant going to the temple should also be interviewed by the endorsing member of the stake presidency or mission presidency.

Worthiness a Prerequisite: No person should receive a recommend for any purpose unless he is found to be worthy in every respect. Unworthiness disqualifies him.

Before issuing recommends bishops will assure themselves by searching inquiry that the recipients are free from all kinds of immoral or unchristianlike practices; that they have no affiliation, in sympathy or otherwise, with any of the apostate groups that are running counter to the established order of the Church; that they sustain the local and General Authorities of the Church; are full tithepayers, or will covenant to become such; that they observe the Word of Wisdom, abstaining from tea, coffee, tobacco, and liquor; and that they earnestly strive to do their duty in the Church, to attend their sacrament, Priesthood, and other meetings, and to obey the rules, laws and commandments of the Gospel, including abiding by all conditions of their temple obligations.

Where applicants are not keeping the commandments, they should prove themselves through a probationary period before the recommend is issued. Every person must be adjudged worthy for a recommend each time he applies for one.

In the case of group recommends for children, bishops will assure themselves that each child recommended is at least 12 years of age, a good child, exemplary in his life, and attending to such Church duties as are required of his age.

Exceptional care will be taken to see that the children of parents belonging to or affiliating with apostate groups are not recommended to the temple, either with groups or as individuals.[4]

Record Membership of One Year Required: Bishops and branch presidents should not issue a recommend to a person until he has been a member of record of their ward or branch for at least one year, except upon receipt of a letter or letters from the bishop of the ward, president of the branch, or stake or mission president, of which the applicant was a member during the preceding year, stating that such person is worthy to enjoy the privileges of the temple. …

How to Fill Out the Temple Recommend: Typewritten recommends are not acceptable. Each recommend must be filled out by hand in

4. The subsequent edition of the *General Handbook of Instructions* (number 20, 1968) qualified this as follows: "unless it is clearly established that they are completely free from parental domination in any apostate religious matters."

ink in the same writing as the one authorized to prepare and sign it. ...

Revocation of Recommends: If at any time during the year a person is adjudged unworthy his recommend will be recalled or revoked immediately by a letter from the bishop to the temple president.

Recommends for Wife Only: A wife whose Church-member husband has not received his endowments will not be given a recommend to receive her endowments unless the husband expresses his consent in writing. This consent must be attached to the ward copy[5] of the recommend.

Stake presidents will interview such husbands to assure themselves that the husband has no objection to the endowments being given to his wife.

A recommend will not be issued for a wife to receive her endowments if her husband is not a member of the Church.[6] This rule does not prevent such a worthy wife, whose husband is willing, from participating in baptisms for the dead in the temples.

Women who received their own endowments before this rule was given, or who were endowed before being married even though married to non-members, may still be issued recommends to do work for the dead if worthy.

Witnessing Marriages or Viewing Interior of Temple: Persons witnessing marriages or viewing the interiors of dedicated temples must have recommends. Recommends are to be granted only to those who have received their own endowments, and all of the requirements of personal worthiness must be met.

Recommends for Divorced Persons: Divorces or annulments of marriage in which the applicant has been a party need not be cleared by the First Presidency unless the persons were sealed to each other in the temple, or unless the applicant has had more than one divorce or annulment since baptism. Nevertheless, bishops and stake presidents should conduct a thorough, searching interview to determine the applicant's present worthiness to go to the temple and to ascertain

---

5. In the November 1963 *Messenger,* a correction notice changed the words "ward copy" to "white (original) copy."

6. The 1968 handbook noted two exceptions: "This rule does not apply to a woman legally divorced from a nonmember husband, nor in such an unusual situation as where the husband has been missing for many years."

whether or not there was any marital infidelity or serious transgression on the part of the applicant in connection with the divorce or annulment.

Divorce Clearances: If there has been a divorce or an annulment of the marriage of persons sealed to each other in the temple, or if a person has had more than one divorce or annulment since baptism, clearance by the First Presidency must first be obtained before temple recommends can be issued to such persons.[7] …

Temple Marriage Must Comply with the Law: In order for a couple to be married in the temple they must obtain a marriage license valid in the county where the temple is located to which they have been recommended.

Before couples can be married in Utah temples, regardless of where they reside, they must present serological certificates before the ceremony can be performed. This requirement does not apply to couples who have been married civilly outside of the state of Utah and come to a Utah temple to be sealed.

Sealing after Civil Marriage: No recommend will be given to couples to be sealed in the temple after a civil marriage unless it can be determined that such civil marriage is valid.[8] If either of the parties have been previously married and divorced, the decree of divorce must have been final before the date of remarriage in order for the second marriage to be valid.

Recommends for Sealing of Children: Children under the age of 8 years are not required to have recommends to be sealed to parents. Children 8 years of age and over are required to have recommends and must have been baptized to be sealed to parents. If children are 21 years

---

7. In the 1968 handbook, the "brethren [who are] authorized to issue temple recommends" were further told that they "should carefully and searchingly interview the applicant, and if it is found that he or she is innocent of any serious wrongdoing in connection with the divorce or annulment and is otherwise worthy, a temple recommend may be issued." They were to "make sure that … a final divorce decree has been secured; and, if the individual was married in the temple previously, that a cancellation of sealing has been granted in the case of the woman."

8. However, the 1968 handbook went on to explain that "where a couple has been legally married in any state or country of the world, they are entitled, if worthy, to be sealed without complying with the marriage laws of the state or country in which the temple is located. Full recognition is given to the marriage laws of the land in which couples were legally married."

of age or over they must have received their own endowments before they can be sealed to parents.[9]

Calls to Do Temple Work Not Approved: Worthy members of the Church should be encouraged to get recommends and do temple work, but they should not be called on "missions" to the temples to perform ordinances by proxy for the dead. …

Sealings after Civil Marriages: Permission may be granted to couples who have been married by civil law to have their marriages solemnized in the temple at such time as the stake president and bishop feel assured of their personal purity and worthiness and of their genuine desire for the blessings of the House of the Lord.[10]

Where parents are not eligible to enter the temple, and yet insist on witnessing the wedding ceremony of their son or daughter, bishops must apply to the First Presidency for permission if it is desired to hold a civil ceremony first, to be followed shortly afterward by the sealing in the temple. Special permission of the First Presidency in each instance of this kind is required.

Where couples deliberately refuse temple marriage for reasons of their own, and afterward desire a sealing, they should be asked to wait for at least a year in which to demonstrate their sincerity and worthiness to receive this blessing.

If an unmarried couple, worthy of temple marriage, yet living at a considerable distance from a temple, desires to travel unaccompanied from their homes to the temple, it may be thought advisable that they have a civil marriage before leaving home, though only a few days may intervene between the civil ceremony and the sealing in the temple.

Couples who have associated together illicitly should not be rec-

---

9. The 1968 handbook stipulated that "if a daughter under the age of 21 years is married, she must receive her own endowments before she can be sealed to her parents." It also laid out conditions under which a child can be sealed to a step-parent or foster parent, stating further that "children born in the covenant cannot be sealed to anyone[,] but belong to their natural parents. This rule is not altered by adoption, consent of the natural parents, request of the child after becoming of age, or death of the natural parents."

10. In the 1968 handbook this discretion was replaced with the requirement that "where a couple are married by civil ceremony, they should not be recommended to the temple until after a year has elapsed since the civil ceremony was solemnized. Exceptions to this requirement may be granted only by the First Presidency."

ommended to the temple until they have satisfied their bishops that they have thoroughly repented, and have shown their repentance by living righteously for a prolonged period of time. Mere sorrow is not repentance. It is urged that the desirability of temple marriages be emphasized continually.

Dissolution of Temple Sealings: Any request to have a temple sealing cancelled must come before the President of the Church for action. **—*General Handbook of Instructions*, Number 19 (Salt Lake City: Church of Jesus Christ of Latter-day Saints, 1963), 73-81, 85**

Recent experiences emphasize the need of greater care and attention being exercised in the issuing of recommends to the Temple. Applicants in too many cases seem to be more appreciative of going through the House of the Lord than deeply conscious of the obligations they take upon themselves by so doing. ...

Therefore, in your careful interrogation of the applicant, you will please keep in mind the following standards and principles of the Church, and others which are equally essential to worthiness to go through the Temple of the Most High.

1. Are you morally clean and worthy to enter the temple?

2. Will you[,] and do you[,] sustain the General Authorities of the Church and will you live in accordance with the accepted rules and doctrines of the Church?

2a. Do you have any connection, in sympathy or otherwise, with any of the apostate groups or individuals who are running counter to the accepted rules and doctrines of the Church?

3. Are you a full tithe payer?

3a. Are you exempt from paying tithes?

4. Do you keep the Word of Wisdom?

5. Do you always wear the regulation garments?

6. Will you earnestly strive to do your duty in the Church, to attend your sacrament, priesthood, and other meetings, and to obey the rules, laws, and commandments of the Gospel?

7. Have you ever been denied a recommend to any Temple? If so, ascertain date of refusal, name of Bishop, Stake and obtain clearance from previous Bishop before issuing recommend.

8. Have you ever been divorced?

The Bishop is the "common judge in Israel" and upon him and his counselors rests the great responsibility of encouraging the membership of the Ward so to live as to be worthy of the blessings of the Temple. **—David O. McKay, Henry D. Moyle, and Hugh B. Brown, circular letter, ca. June 1963**

We read a letter from President Philip S. Low of the Indianapolis Stake in which he presented the case of a man who had asked for a Temple recommend, but that he is not wearing his garments where he is employed because he is engaged in pouring molten metal, and when fragments scatter and fall to his shirt and his undershirt, he can easily throw them out by raising his one-piece undershirt. If he wears garments, he cannot expel the hot pellets.

I directed that President Low be informed that the man may reverently remove his garments under these circumstances, but should replace them as soon as convenient when he leaves his employment where he is engaged as he explains. **—David O. McKay diary, July 19, 1963**

... (1) You have given us an assignment to improve the temple ceremony as it is presented in the one-room temples, and in Los Angeles, on film and sound track for the various language groups.[11]

(2) You have given us permission to do this at Brigham Young University at a time when we could dedicate the studio and set it apart for this purpose.

(3) Doing this in the Salt Lake Temple or other temple would [again] require virtually making a motion picture studio of some part of the temple, including special lighting, cameras, stage facilities, etc.

(4) Brigham Young University's motion picture facilities are crowded so they [BYU President Ernest L. Wilkinson and Wetzel O. Whitaker of the BYU Motion Picture Studio] propose to add a new sound stage at a cost of $91,000 which could be dedicated, locked up, and set apart for this purpose during the periods when these films are not being made. They have made approximately 50 Church films, and are in the process of making more, and need the additional sound stage anyway.[12] **—Richard L. Evans to the First Presidency, Sept. 13, 1963; typed excerpt in Buerger Papers**

---

11. Elder Evans was writing on behalf of the committee that had been assigned to oversee production of the endowment films.

12. The First Presidency responded on October 22 to commend the "fine work of Brother Whitaker and his staff" and give "consent to a special appropriation in the amount of $91,000 for the purpose indicated."

[Alfonso G.] P[ia]:[13] It was during the same period too, in the early '60s—'62, '63, right in there—that the question of dividing the initiatory ordinances from the endowment took place, which was very controversial. It came about as a result of recommendations made that tied into computerization. … It was done in Salt Lake and it was done in Los Angeles initially. … I'm inclined to believe that the first separation of the initiatory work was done in the Los Angeles Temple.

Well, to my knowledge, in the early stages as the Church commenced doing records tabulation work, it was played down and wasn't made public. As it became broader and broader, I think in the late '60s in reports you would start to see so many endowments performed, so many names submitted by [the] membership, and so many others, but undefined. I believe the reports came out with an "others" category. I'm not sure what the ratio is now, but I understand that well over half the work comes in through records tabulation. **—Alfonso G. Pia oral history, Aug. 2, 7, 1979, pp. 13-14, excerpt in Buerger Papers**

....

President [N. Eldon] Tanner referred to a ruling by President [David O.] McKay in 1961 to the effect that where children have been adopted by men other than their own fathers, their responsibility for sealings and research should be on their adopted father's line and not on their own blood lines.[14] The question had been raised as to whether this ruling pertained only to illegitimate children rather than the entire field of special sealings of wives to husbands. President Tanner mentioned in this connection the ruling contained in the manual to the effect that if a child is legally adopted, that adoption transfers him to the family of his adopted parents and he is considered henceforth to all intents and purposes their child, and that he should trace the lines of his adopted legal parents. Also that in a ruling dated March 17, I had indicated that in genealogical research, legally adopted children had no responsibility to the natural blood lines although there may be

13. Alfonso Gerrit Pia (1916-1994) directed the Mechanized Data Processing area of the Church's Financial Planning Department.

14. This is consistent with previous rulings by the First Presidency that in the next life, families will be organized according to their temple sealings, sometimes involving adoptive parents, and not automatically as natural family groupings. President Woodruff advised men to be sealed to their natural parents rather than to Church leaders, which was a new emphasis, but the underlying concept remained the same: in the next life, it is the sealing that counts, not the DNA.

occasions when conditions would suggest special consideration. In this connection, President [Hugh B.] Brown raised the question as an illustration as to what the situation would be where a woman was married to three husbands and there were three children each having different fathers. If they were all sealed to one man would the responsibility for research be through the blood line or through the sealing line. I said that if they are sealed for time and eternity, they will follow the sealing. I said that the same ruling should apply in all cases, legitimate or otherwise, that the person in question should act as though the adopted father was his real father. **—David O. McKay diary, Jan. 14, 1964**

As a matter of routine procedure, the bishop when issuing a recommend should instruct the applicant to deliver the necessary copies of the recommend to the stake or mission president for the required personal interview and signature.

When the signature of the stake or mission authority has been omitted, the applicant usually indicates that he did not know that this was necessary. To avoid such situations we suggest that bishops give complete instructions to each applicant. **—"Temple Recommends Require Signature of Stake or Mission President,"** ***Messenger,*** **Feb. 1964**

President [N. Eldon] Tanner presented a case that had come to him from H------ L. C----- regarding his son, W----- L--- C-----, who died in February 1953, leaving two children who were born in the covenant to him and his wife, W-----. His wife subsequently received a cancellation of the Temple sealing and has married two other men since that time. She was married to her present husband in April, 1962, by civil ceremony[,] and she and he later went to the Temple and were sealed for time and eternity and had the two children, born in the covenant to her first husband, W----- L--- C-----, sealed to her and her present husband. I said that the sealing was not valid, and I asked President Tanner to notify these people to that effect, and to write to the Temple where this sealing was performed, asking that it be cancelled, a copy of the letter to the Temple President to be sent to Brother C-----. **—David O. McKay diary, Feb. 5, 1964; hyphens added to conceal names; emphasis in original**

President [N. Eldon] Tanner brought to my attention a question that had been raised regarding temple work for [United States] Presidents Martin Van Buren, James Buchanan and Ulysses S. Grant. In this connection reference was made to President Wilford Woodruff's statement that he had done the work for all the presidents of the United States excepting these three. President Tanner referred to information that had been given to him by Henry Christiansen of the Genealogical Society to the effect that in the case of James Buchanan the records indicate that baptism was performed for him and he has been sealed to his parents, this work having been done by relatives. In the case of Martin Van Buren, baptismal work was done for him August 9, 1876 in the Endowment House, which apparently was not known to President Wilford Woodruff at the time he had the work done for the other presidents. Subsequently, the baptism was done again for Martin Van Buren in 1948 and was followed by endowments, but he is not sealed to his parents, nor has there been a sealing between him and his wife. In the case of Ulysses S. Grant, his baptism and endowment work were done in 1926 at the instance of President Heber J. Grant. President Tanner raised the question as to whether, in view of President Woodruff's attitude, these ordinances should be cancelled or if the necessary additional work should be done in each case. <u>I ruled that we should leave these cases as they are until the Lord gives us further direction in the matter</u>. **—David O. McKay diary, Feb. 7, 1964; emphasis in original**

<u>Temples—Book of Decisions for [Temple] Presidents</u>[15] ...

Presidents [Hugh B.] Brown and [N. Eldon] Tanner reported to me that they had gone through the manuscript of the proposed book of decisions as prepared by Elders Howard W. Hunter, ElRay L. Christiansen and Alvin R. Dyer, and had marked those items which they felt needed [a] decision by me. The matters were presented and I approved as follows:

(1) Endowment work need not be done for deceased children under eight years of age.

(2) Ordinances need not be performed for children under eight years of age born in the covenant.[16]

---

15. The full line reads like an entry in an index: "Temples—Book of Decisions for Presidents of."

16. Children were "born in the covenant" if their parents were married in the temple before the children were born. The wording and concept came from the Puritan "halfway covenant," by which children who were baptized as infants were considered half-members of the congregation awaiting full membership as

(3) Children born in the covenant remained sealed to their father and mother even though the sealing between their parents may be cancelled. They cannot be sealed to any other parent.

(4) All persons going through the Temple for themselves or the dead should wear the ceremonial garment. The modified approved style may be worn at any other time.

(5) In the washing and anointing and sealing rooms the full name of the individual for whom the ordinance is performed should be used when initially given in the ordinance, but the proxy's full name need not be used when otherwise mentioned in the ordinance.

(6) It was suggested that the ordinance of baptism for members of the negro race be performed by others than negroes if this can be accomplished without offense.[17]

Temple Recommend Cards for General Authorities

Consideration was given to the suggestion that a Temple card be prepared for the General Authorities and their wives to be signed by the First Presidency, indicating that they are entitled to the privileges of all Temples. This card could be presented at the Temple gate indicating that the General Authorities and their wives have an authoritative Temple card of admittance, thus eliminating the necessity of presenting a Temple Recommend. It was suggested that provision be made for the signature of the holder to appear on the back of the card for identification, and the card would not need to be renewed. I indicated my approval of this proposition.

Temple Sealings Involving Polygamous Marriages

President Tanner presented to me for my clarification the case of Ammon Meshach Tenney. Prior to the marriage in question, this man had been married twice and both of his wives were living and married

adults when they were confirmed. Their baptism "sealed" their parents' covenant (Dan Vogel, *Religious Seekers and the Advent of Mormonism* [Salt Lake City: Signature Books, 1988], 163). The way Joseph Fielding Smith articulated the Mormon idea of covenant in 1951, children of parents who had been sealed could expect "eternal lives" with their parents: "after the resurrection, [the parents] … will have a continuation of the[ir] seeds forever, and the family organization [will] not come to an end" (*Conference Report,* Oct. 1951, pp. 120-21).

17. Notice that the concern, beyond whether black children would be allowed in the temple to do baptisms for the dead, was that a white proxy might take offense at being baptized for someone whose name was recognizably ethnic.

to him when he married the third wife in Mexico. This [third] sealing was supposed to have been performed by A[lexander] F. McDonald[18] and cannot be confirmed by official records. In such cases the usual procedure is to encourage the family to have the sealing done again, wives to husbands and children to parents, with the notation on the bottom of the sheet that the family has record of the sealing, but it cannot be verified from official records. It was explained that in this case the family is willing and ready to perform the requested sealings for the purpose of having an official record. The question is raised: Should this be done because it is a polygamous marriage. Brother Christiansen of the Genealogical Society indicates that it is his interpretation of my ruling heretofore made that when no official record exists of a polygamous marriage in the Church no action is to be taken to perform sealings even if the sealings were performed before the Manifesto. President Tanner said that this ruling, as he understands it, pertains to the United States, but that so far as Mexico is concerned, it was his understanding of my ruling that if it was a polygamous marriage before the Manifesto and there was no official record the work should be done again. He asked if his understanding was correct. I said I think that is the safest thing to do, so that there would be a proper record of the sealings. **—David O. McKay diary, Feb. 14, 1964**

I, W. Cleon Anderson, do hereby certify and declare that on the 21st day of February, 1964, at nine-thirty A.M. I met for about thirty minutes with President Joseph Fielding Smith [and] he gave me some instruction in answer to a letter written February 14, 1964. I requested that he put these instructions on paper, initialing and signing those items in my presence, which he did. After President Smith finished going over the above subject with me, the following conversation ensued:

I asked President Smith, "Is it wrong to wear the string tie garments outside the temple?"

President Smith looked at me for several moments and then unbuttoning the third button in his shirt, brought out one of the ties on a pair of old style temple garments and said, "This is what we should be wearing—the Lord gave them to us, and so this is what I wear."

18. Alexander Findlay McDonald (1825-1903) was born in Scotland and migrated to Utah in 1854. He helped settle Mesa, Arizona, and in 1885 helped establish LDS colonies in Mexico.

I said, "I have worn the old style garments for two years now and some of the ignorant brethren have accused me, so now I wear a tee shirt over them."

President Smith then said, "When the Lord gave the garments to us they had strings. I have never worn a button pair; however, I don't say those with buttons are not garments." **—W. Cleon Anderson, notarized statement, Feb. 24, 1964, copy in Buerger Papers**

Brother Howard S. McDonald:[19] Esteemed friend and fellow laborer in the Church of Christ, in accordance with the inspiration of the Lord through his servants we lay our hands upon your head and bestow upon you the sealing powers given direct from our Savior to his servants now on earth, for those who have passed beyond. And we say receive this power and blessing, and may it fill your soul with thanksgiving and rejoicing and inspire you to continue your life in purity, earnestness, and devotion to the cause of eternal life as exercised in the House of the Lord, the Temple of the Most High. May the spirit of this calling rest upon you from this moment on and may it give you insight into the blessings the Lord has in store for you and your sweet wife and others [to] whom you administer, and in response to the calling which you now receive and accept as coming from on high.

Our Father in heaven, we pray thee to bless this thy servant and continue to fill his soul with rejoicing and satisfaction in accepting this special call to be exercised in the Salt Lake Temple of the Lord. May his soul be filled with thanksgiving and be filled with the revelations that come from thee to him as he discharges his duties incumbent upon him in accepting this additional blessing, crowning blessing, to be exercised as president of the Salt Lake Temple.

Brother McDonald, we say unto you, receive this power and magnify it as the Lord inspires you and associates in the temple to carry this spirit of sealing to those who will come under your jurisdiction.

We bless you with health and bless you with response to the inspiration of the Lord that will come to you through the blessings that will befall you in the discharge of your duties.

We bless you with the spirit of discernment, that you may discern the difference between those who seek personal advancement and

19. Edward Howard Stevenson McDonald (1894-1986) was president of BYU from 1945 to 1949 and president the Salt Lake temple from 1964 to 1968.

those who express a willingness to lose themselves for the good of the cause of Christ. May you have this spirit of discernment and exercise it in accordance with the inspiration that comes to you.

We bless you with a spirit of compassion, that your soul may be filled with sympathy for those who have struggled to make themselves worthy to participate in the temple and participate in the dissemination of the principles of eternal salvation. The things which come to you in this position [are] not to the physical convenience, not to personal aggrandizement, but are things pertaining to the Spirit of the Most High. You are dealing with things of the spirit that lead to life eternal.

Treasure them and realize that your service now pertains to life eternal, here and throughout the eternities. [There is] nothing [but] pertains to the things of the soul that will become comprehended in our administration of the sealing power which is now given to you to be exercised here and hereafter.

Our father in Heaven, we pray that thou wilt continue to be with thy servant, give to him thy mind and will concerning thy wishes as associated with the sealing power for the living and the dead.

All these blessings and the blessings of peace and happiness we seal upon you and your associates in the name of the Lord Jesus, our Redeemer, and by the virtue of the Holy Melchizedek Priesthood, in the name of Jesus Christ, Amen. **—blessing by President David O. McKay, setting apart Howard S. McDonald as president of the Salt Lake temple, Apr. 3, 1964, recorded in McDonald's self-published *Brief Autobiography,* 82-84**

Sister Ella Gibbs McDonald:[20] By virtue of the Holy Priesthood vested in us, we your brethren, members of the First Presidency of the Church, together with your husband who has been set apart to preside over the Salt Lake Temple and given the sealing power, lay our hands upon your head and set you apart as the Matron of the Salt Lake Temple, to labor with your husband and the other workers there for the welfare and the benefit of the living and the dead.

We seal upon you every right and privilege appertaining to this calling and pray that God will bless and magnify you in this calling,

20. Ella Gibbs McDonald (1894-1966) was born in Brigham City and married Howard S. McDonald in 1917. She served as Salt Lake temple matron from 1964 to 1966.

that they who work in the temple may see in you one of His choice servants, that He may give you the wisdom and the ability to live the Gospel so completely before these with whom you labor that they can with safety follow your example and be inspired thereby.

It will be your privilege, Sister McDonald, to work with the young women who come to the temple to be married, to advise and counsel them, to instruct them, and we pray that god will magnify you in this calling, for it is important that you impress upon them the need for virtue and chastity, the need for love and understanding, the need to carry into their homes and their regular lives the spirit of the Gospel which they will feel while they are in the temple. This is a high privilege which comes to you and we pray that you may be made equal to every emergency.

It will be part of your duty and calling to labor with the sisters in the temple. The regular temple workers, to preside over them under your husband, to advise and counsel with them and to set things in order, and do everything in your power to advance the work of our Heavenly Father in this most important calling.

We bless you that you may have health and strength to enable you to carry on, and that your family may be blessed; and we pray that God will help you and your husband to work together as one, to be united as the President has advised, so that there may be harmony and love and peace, not only while you are in the temple but in your home.

To this end we set you apart now and commit you to this work, and seal upon you every blessing which your heart can desire in righteousness, dependent upon your faith and faithfulness. This we do by virtue of the Holy Priesthood and in the name of Jesus Christ, Amen. **—blessing given by President David O. McKay to Ella Gibbs McDonald, setting her apart as temple matron, Apr. 4, 1964, recorded in Howard S. McDonald, *Brief Autobiography,* 84-85**

It was mentioned that some question has been raised in regard to the sealing of children to their mother and foster father in cases where the natural parents have been separated by divorce and the mother marries a second man. <u>I reiterated former instructions that in all such cases the children should be legally adopted before they are sealed to their mother and the foster father; that no action should be taken regarding children born in the covenant.</u> …

It was mentioned that the question has been raised as to whether brethren who have in the past received the sealing power and officiated in the Temple are now authorized to perform sealing ordinances for their friends in the Temple without special permission.

I ruled that in cases of this kind these brethren should receive special permission in each instance before performing sealings in the Temple. **—David O. McKay diary, May 13, 1964; emphasis in original**

President [N. Eldon] Tanner presented the request of Elder Theodore M. Burton [of] the Genealogical Department for instructions in the matter of sealing living persons by proxy as in cases where the living person is mentally or physically so incapacitated that he cannot come to the Temple for the ordinances, and also in cases where the mental age is not determined. He reviewed the ruling that when a person is not physically or mentally able to go to the Temple the work may be done by proxy. Problems included are: Who decides whether the mental age is eight years or over? The Genealogical Department has been informed that a competent physician may determine the mental age and if it is not eight years of age the child is not baptized, but that such a child may be sealed to parents.

I directed that each case be considered on its special circumstances. **—David O. McKay diary, June 16, 1964; emphasis in original**

A new form of temple recommend has been printed for use after August 1. This will be prepared in duplicate instead of triplicate. The original copy (white) will be given to the applicant and the duplicate copy (pink) will be retained in the book.

The recommend will be valid for admission to all temples in the Church and will expire on April 30 following the date of issuance instead of July 31 as in the past.

At the time you affix your signature[,] inform each applicant that no person will be admitted to the temple without the recommend in his possession. **—David O. McKay, Hugh B. Brown, and N. Eldon Tanner, circular letter, July 15, 1964**

A letter from President Mark E. Petersen[21] was read in which he reports comments coming from the London Temple about modifications of the sequences of Temple services when one group of partici-

21. Mark Edward Petersen (1900–84) served in the Quorum of Twelve Apostles from 1944 to 1984.

pants in the service continues session after session, in which case at first the entire procedure is given, with film, prayer circle, and the lecture; but for the sessions immediately subsequent, in which this same group and no others participate, the tape is used but the film and the lecture may not be; and if the same group wishes to continue for another session, the prayer circle is occasionally omitted. I said and advised, "I would not omit anything. The people who go through are proxies for some man or woman who should participate in the entire session without omissions." **—David O. McKay diary, Dec. 1, 1964; emphasis in original**

....

President [Hugh B.] Brown called attention to a request that had been received from a woman formerly married to a Negro, by whom she had two children. She later divorced the Negro and married a white man and wants to go to the Temple and have her children sealed to her and her present husband. We agreed that if otherwise worthy, the woman and her white husband could go to the Temple for their endowments and be sealed, but the children by the former marriage could not be sealed to them. **—David O. McKay diary, Apr. 14, 1965**

President [N. Eldon] Tanner raised a question as to what the attitude of the Church should be regarding permitting a seven-year-old boy to witness the sealing of his adopted sister to his parents. The Temple authorities had told the mother that this could not be done without the approval of the First Presidency. I said that consent might be given in this case.

In answer to the question as to whether this should be accepted as a Church policy that children under eight years of age might witness sealings, I said that each individual case should be judged upon its merits. **—David O. McKay diary, Apr. 20, 1965**

President [N. Eldon] Tanner reported that a number of Japanese Saints are coming to Hawaii in June on a Temple excursion. There are among them four members who wish to do the endowment work for[,] and have sealed to them[,] persons who have recently passed away; that is, they have been dead less than one year—four months to nearly a year. The question is raised as to whether an exception might be made granting this permission inasmuch as they may never have another opportunity to come to the Temple.

I ruled that permission could be given for this work to be done in the cases mentioned. In this connection, it was mentioned that Elder Gordon Hinckley will be in close touch with these people. ...

President Tanner mentioned the case of a sister who lives in Massachusetts who desires to be sealed to her father who is deceased. This sister can come to the Temple at this time with a family who are coming from that area, and it would seem that this may be her only opportunity. Her father, who is not a member of the Church, died December 29, 1964, and she wishes to do his endowment work and to be sealed to him as child to parents. I gave consent for the exception in this case. **—David O. McKay diary, Apr. 27, 1965**

Complaints have reached us from several sources that in many cases the men working in the temple and going through for their own endowments and working for the deceased are not careful about their appearance.

In some cases it is reported that the men's clothing and persons are not clean, that there is not proper uniformity among the men in the matter of dress, especially as it refers to the caps that they wear, and that in general they detract from the orderly and desirable atmosphere of temples and temple work.

We shall appreciate your bringing this matter to the attention of the brethren and ask that their clothing be well pressed and clean and that they take care in dressing to make sure their appearance is desirable. **—David O. McKay, Hugh B. Brown, and N. Eldon Tanner to temple presidents, Apr. 29, 1965**

According to your wishes, I am reviewing for you herein the matters that were discussed and the decisions that you made in regard to each of them. ...

I referred to another letter from President [Octave] Ursenbach[22] in which he stated that ... some[one] had reported that there was some irregularity [in the Cardston temple with] regard [to the embrace at the veil]. While the letter did not state what the irregularity is, I took the liberty of saying to you, President McKay, that I had known of cases in the past where these contacts at the veil have been made so

22. Octave Willis Ursenbach (1893-1981) was president of the Cardston temple from 1956 to 1968.

literally [as an embrace] and with such insistence by some brethren that it had become offensive and humiliating to some of the sister patrons being introduced.

I stated that I had been instructed by President George F. Richards, when he was supervising the temples, to make sure that the brethren who assist at the veil do not offend the sisters in this way and that rather than do so they should not insist on making contact with them except perhaps with the … hand on the back for fear that it would be embarrassing to them. I read briefly from minutes of meetings held with workers covering similar instructions to them.

RESPONSE: President McKay stated that the highest degree of decorum and respect should be exercised by the brethren working at the veil, particularly in relation to the sisters who are being introduced and that any person who, even in his mind, fails to have pure thoughts and who is not circumspect and wholesome in every way should not be invited to assist at the veil. President McKay felt that the brethren who receive the sisters at this point should be carefully selected for their wholesomeness and unquestioned character. It is the responsibility of the temple presidency to see that the highest type of men are selected for this service. The substance of it all is that no person should be embarrassed or humiliated through the insistence of some to make certain of these [being] literal and actual [contacts].

I agreed to give direction, as necessary, by letter to President Ursenbach. …

Some times women come into the washing and anointing rooms wearing wigs which are often unnoticed or are not easily detected. I reported that some had asked about anointing the heads of such women where the ceremony says "I pour this … oil upon your head."

SOLUTION: President McKay felt that we should not anoint a wig, but where they are being worn, the sister[']s head should be anointed as near the hairline as possible—perhaps near the temple. **—ElRay L. Christiansen to David O. McKay, May 4, 1965, in David O. McKay diary, May 4, 1965; emphasis in original**

President [N. Eldon] Tanner presented the case of a couple who were married in 1938 and divorced civilly in 1954 but had not had their temple sealing cancelled. Following the civil divorce the woman in the case gave birth to an illegitimate child by another man to whom she was not married. He reported that the child's half sister is legally adopting the illegitimate child as her child and wants to have it sealed to her and her husband. The question has been raised as to whether this illegitimate child was born in the covenant.

I ruled that inasmuch as the sealing between this sister and her first husband was not cancelled, the child born illegitimately to her following the legal divorce was born in the covenant.

Sealing of Child Born While Father Was Excommunicated—President Tanner mentioned to me the case of a man who, after having been sealed to his wife in the Temple, was excommunicated, subsequently rebaptized and his Priesthood only restored. Children were born to this couple during the time that the father was out of the Church. The parents would now like to have these children sealed to them. The question raised is whether or not the man's blessings should be restored before the sealing is performed.

I stated that it would be necessary that the endowments and sealings of the man involved be restored before these children could be sealed to their parents. Elder John Longden had officiated in restoring the Priesthood.

Sealing of Children Born Out of Wedlock—Attention was called to a question ... pertaining to a sister who before she joined the Church lived out of wedlock with a man by whom she had six children, that she joined the Church two years ago, has married a good Latter-day Saint, and they wish to go to the Temple to be sealed and to have these six children born by this previous relationship sealed to them. The father of the children refuses his permission for the children to be sealed to her and her husband. The question has been raised as to what action could be taken to have these children sealed to their mother and their stepfather.

I decided that the husband would have to legally adopt the children before they could be sealed to him and the mother. **—David O. McKay diary, May 6, 1965**

Upon request of the First Presidency Elder [Delbert L.] Stapley called and presented samples of the new ceremonial garment which is to take the place of the string garment now being used in the Temples. This new garment will have buttons instead of strings, and [a] closed crotch. It will also have a collar on it. Elder Stapley showed samples of the new ceremonial garments for men and women, and they were approved by me. Letters will be sent to the Presidents of Temples notifying them of this change. This new garment pattern had been presented to the Brethren in the meeting of the council of the First Presidency and the Twelve on January 21, 1965, at which time it was unanimously approved by the Council. **—David O. McKay diary, May 14, 1965**

President [Hugh B.] Brown reported that at the Council Meeting in the Temple yesterday, Brother [Harold B.] Lee, who is head of the Garment Committee, had raised a question about authorizing ZCMI to mark Munsingwear and other union suits as Temple Garments, which practice they have been following for some time. It was the sentiment of the Garment Committee that inasmuch as the distribution of Temple Garments has been turned over to the Relief Society[,] anyone desiring to use union suits or underwear other than the authorized pattern garment should take this underwear to the Relief Society for marking, or should mark it themselves.

I agreed with this sentiment. **—David O. McKay diary, June 4, 1965**

This will advise you that approval has been granted for limited modification in the design of the garment used in the temple to allow for better fit and greater wearing comfort.

The approved modified design for *women* has a button front rather than string ties, a brassiere top patterned after the brassiere top of garments used for day-time wear, a helanca[23] stretch insert in the back at the waist, and widened overlapping back panels with a helanca stretch piece at the top of each panel and a button to assure [the] panels remaining closed. All other features of the garment, including the collar, long legs, and long sleeves, remain the same as heretofore.

The approved modified design of the garment for *men* has a button front, closed crotch, helanca stretch insert piece in the back at the waist, widened overlapping back panels with a helanca stretch piece at the top of each panel and a button to assure [the] panels remaining closed. All other features of the men's garment also, including the collar, long legs and long sleeves, remain the same as heretofore.

Both the button-front and the string-tie-front designs for men and women

---

23. Helanca was the first synthetic stretch fabric, developed in Switzerland in 1931 and improved on in the 1950s in France. It was mostly used for socks and tights.

are approved for temple wear; either design may be used. You will note that the basic specifications for the garment remain unaltered. **—David O. McKay, Hugh B. Brown, and N. Eldon Tanner to temple presidents, June 10, 1965; emphasis in original**

It has come to our attention that in some wards marriage ceremonies have been performed for couples following their marriage in the temple, in order that non-member relatives and friends might be privileged to witness such a pretended marriage. We are also informed that in other instances relatives and friends of the newly married couple have gathered in the ward house or elsewhere following the temple marriage in a service somewhat similar to a wedding, where prayer has been offered, remarks made by the bishop or others, and at times pomp and ceremony introduced somewhat aping sectarian weddings.

These practices make a mockery of the temple marriage; they are unauthorized and contrary to Church procedures and must not be encouraged or permitted. This does not have reference to the wedding reception which customarily follows civil and temple marriages.

We shall appreciate your accepting this letter as a directive for your guidance in matters of this kind. **—David O. McKay, Hugh B. Brown, N. Eldon Tanner, Joseph Fielding Smith, and Thorpe B. Isaacson, circular letter, Dec. 20, 1965**

....

[This is to remind you that] the authority to cancel temple sealings is vested in the President of the Church, and in him only, and that no sealing of the living or the dead can be authoritatively cancelled except upon his personal authorization. Should there be on file in any of the temples information or advice that could be otherwise understood[,] we kindly ask that the instruction given in this letter be accepted as a substitution therefor. **—David O. McKay, Hugh B. Brown, N. Eldon Tanner, Joseph Fielding Smith, and Thorpe B. Isaacson to temple presidents, Jan. 4, 1966**

In order that there may be no misunderstanding in regard to the matter of the sealing in the temple of children to persons other than natural parents, we are pleased to give you the following information for your guidance.

Children who have not been born in the covenant or sealed to their natural parents may be sealed to a natural parent and stepparent, or may be sealed to foster parents, under any one of the following circumstances:

1. If the stepparent or foster parents have legally adopted minor children ... and a copy of the final decree of adoption, or Certificate of Live Birth issued in states using this form of evidence, is presented to the temple president, or

2. If the stepparent or foster parents to whom minor children are to be sealed have secured and presented to the temple president a written statement from the natural parent or parents consenting for such sealing, or

3. If the children to be sealed are of legal age [and] in the place of their residence and request the temple president for such sealing, or

4. Minor children may be sealed to a natural parent and a stepparent without the requirement of adoption in cases where the other natural parent is deceased.

Children born in the covenant cannot be sealed to persons other than their natural parents. This rule is not altered by adoption, consent of the natural parents, or request of the child after becoming of age.

Illegitimate children may be sealed to their natural mother and the husband to whom she is sealed without the consent of the natural father, and only the natural mother's consent is necessary for illegitimate children to be sealed to foster parents.

No sealing of children to persons other than natural parents will be permitted except as set forth above without written authorization of the First Presidency. **—David O. McKay, Hugh B. Brown, N. Eldon Tanner, and Joseph Fielding Smith, circular letter, Jan. 8, 1966**

Consideration was given to a letter from H---- B---- de E----, also a letter from Bishop K----F-------- S----- and Counselors ..., these letters having reference to the problems involved in this sister's marriage to a Negro. She became a member in 1961, received her endowments in 1963, and was divorced from her former husband in 1965. She has subsequently married a Negro non-member, and has been told by the Bishopric that no further Temple visits would be allowed her, and that because of her marriage to a Negro her Temple endowments are ineffective.

It was decided to write the bishopric asking that they inform this sister that the fact of her marriage to a Negro does not cancel her endowments; that, however, under the circumstances she should not be recommended to the Temple for further ordinance work. The Bishopric also are to be told that any children born of this marriage cannot hold the Priesthood; however, there is no reason why she cannot be active in the Ward and Stake. **—David O. McKay diary, Jan. 12, 1966; hyphens added to conceal names**

Mention was made of contrary rules made in the J--- W. A-------- case. On September 26, 1946, it became the action of the Council of the First Presidency and Quorum of the Twelve that Brother A--------'s children born to him and his wife following his excommunication and before the restoration of his Priesthood and blessings, were not born in the covenant and should be sealed to him and his wife. On May 19, 1960, in regard to this same matter, the First Presidency ruled that under the circumstances in the J--- W. A-------- case, the children were born in the covenant and that no further sealing was necessary.

Referring to these actions, I said the first action was correct; namely, that they were not born in the covenant and should be sealed to their parents after their father's restoration. **—David O. McKay diary, Feb. 10, 1966; emphasis in original; hyphens added to conceal identities**

In response to an inquiry from a brother as to whether his 34 year old son, who is suffering from cerebral palsy, might be permitted to refrain from wearing his garments after receiving his endowments in the Temple, it was decided to tell this brother that we think it inadvisable for his son to receive his endowments at this time under the circumstances. **—David O. McKay diary, Mar. 1, 1966**

A question having been raised by a sister in the Rodeo Ward, Walnut Creek stake, as to the attitude of the Church regarding "willing" parts of the body for medical research, it was decided to make reply to the Bishop who submitted the question that this is a matter that the individual must decide for himself; that, however, in the case of those who have been through the Temple and received their endowments, we advise against their doing this. **—David O. McKay diary, Mar. 2, 1966**

Attention was called to the application of Sister I--- R------- P----- for permission to do the sealing work in the Temple for her father, Joseph E. Robinson, and his three wives. Their names and dates of marriage are as follows: Minnie Ann Knell, December 21, 1891; Willmia Brown, April 7, 1901; and Harriet Spencer, October 3, 1901. Attention was also called to a ruling made by me on March 3, 1964, [that] … "in the case of polygamous marriages performed in Mexico before the Manifesto, and there [is] no official record, the work should be done again."

President [N. Eldon] Tanner said that … Sister P----- had spoken to various of the Brethren in regard to this matter, appealing for the work to be done for her father and his wives, and that a letter from Sister P----- addressed to me had been handed to him by Brother Hunter indicating that she had seen me and that I had told her that I would sign the papers authorizing the work to be done if she would send in the sheets which she has now submitted. (These papers were submitted by Sister P----- to President McKay's secretary, who turned them over to Paul Royal of the Genealogical Society for further checking.)

I stated that if the polygamous marriage took place prior to the statement by President Joseph F. Smith in 1904 to the effect that polygamous marriages could not be solemnized anywhere in the world, … the work could be performed for the parties concerned or the President of the Church could ratify the marriages that had been performed. It was agreed that the simpler way would be to ratify the marriages …

We reversed the decision made in our meeting of March 23, 1966, and ruled that it would be inadvisable to ratify purported sealings performed for Joseph E. Robinson and three women. In giving this matter further consideration, we had in mind that were the Church to adopt the policy of ratifying polygamous marriages that took place prior to the announcement by President Joseph F. Smith in 1904 … it would let down the flood gates and descendants of many polygamous marriages performed after the Manifesto would make application for permission to have the purported sealings of their parents or grandparents ratified, and perhaps in some cases where the individuals entering into these relationships have been excommunicated from the Church, there would be individuals such as cultists and others. The former action was therefore rescinded and it was decided to notify Sister I--- R------- P----- that the case of Joseph E. Robinson and the three women referred to would have to be left in the hands of the Lord for decision by Him in the Hereafter. **—David O. McKay diary, Mar. 23, Apr. 12, 1966; hyphens added to conceal the individual's identity**

In order that there may be no misunderstanding in regard to the matter of the sealing in the temple of children to persons other than natural parents, we are pleased to give you the following information for your guidance.

Children who have not been born in the covenant or sealed to their natural parents may be sealed to a natural parent and stepparent, or may be sealed to foster parents, under any one of the following circumstances:

1. If the stepparent or foster parents have legally adopted minor children to be sealed and a copy of the final decree of adoption, or Certificate of Live Birth issued in states using this form of evidence, is presented to the temple president, or

2. If the stepparent or foster parents to whom minor children are to be sealed have secured and presented to the temple president a written statement from the natural parent or parents consenting to the proposed sealing, or

3. If the children to be sealed are of legal age[,] in the place of their residence[,] and request the temple president for such sealing, or

4. Minor children may be sealed to a natural parent and a stepparent without the requirement of adoption in cases where the other natural parent is deceased.

Children born in the covenant cannot be sealed to persons other than their natural parents. This rule is not altered by adoption, consent of the natural parents, or request of the child after becoming of age.

Illegitimate children may be sealed to their natural mother and the husband to whom she is sealed without the consent of the natural father, and only the natural mother's consent is necessary for illegitimate children to be sealed to foster parents.

No sealing of children to persons other than natural parents will be permitted except as set forth above without written authorization of the First Presidency. **—David O. McKay, Hugh B. Brown, N. Eldon Tanner, and Joseph Fielding Smith, circular letter, June 8, 1966**

In a letter from Elder ElRay L. Christiansen, the question was raised as to whether or not men or women who have commenced divorce proceedings should be recommended to the Temple either for their own endowments or to do work for the dead while the divorce is being sought.

We understood the present policy to be, which understanding was confirmed, that where a divorce is in process, the Bishop should not issue Temple Recommends to the parties involved until after the divorce situation has been settled.[24] …

In his letter, Elder Christiansen also states that two Temple Presidents have recently inquired regarding permitting couples to be married civilly before traveling from their home to the Temple within a few days to have the sealing solemnized in the Temple.

We decided to send a letter to Presidents of Temples informing them that the First Presidency must be consulted in regard to any proposed civil marriage of couples desiring to go to the Temple to be sealed. **—David O. McKay diary, June 14, 1966**

President [N. Eldon] Tanner mentioned that at the June 9th meeting of the First Presidency and the Twelve, two questions had been considered regarding the issuing of Temple recommends—one of which pertained to granting authorization for the issuance of Temple Recommends to converts who have been members of the Church less than a year, and the other the issuing of Temple Recommends to couples who have been married by civil ceremony for less than a year. It was the sentiment of the Council that any such exception should be granted only upon the approval of the First Presidency and that when exceptions are granted a copy of the First Presidency's letter of permission should accompany the recommend to the Temple. …

Referring to the issuing of Temple Recommends to new converts and others, President Tanner mentioned that at the meeting of the Council referred to on June 9, the Brethren had mentioned that many of our young people who go through the Temples gain a wrong impression, that they do not obtain a proper understanding of the Temple

24. Accordingly, the First Presidency explained this in a circular letter dated July 5, 1966. But the next month, they remembered overlooking their "former instruction" that clearance was necessary only if the couple had been previously sealed in the temple. They were reminded by Elder Howard W. Hunter that "it sometimes happens that divorces are not fully determined for a rather lengthy period of time, and in some cases the innocent party involved would, under the instruction heretofore given, be prohibited from receiving recommends to do work in the Temple." The First Presidency therefore decided to give bishops and stake presidents discretion in determining the worthiness of an individual going through a divorce (David O. McKay diary, Aug. 23, 1966) and prepared a correction, which was sent on August 30 (see below).

work and sometimes lose their faith by reason of the Temple ceremonies. He explained that when companies of young men and young women going on missions have been through the Temple for the first time and received their endowments, it is customary to hold a meeting with these young people after the Temple session and explain to them the meaning of the Temple ceremonies and give them opportunity to ask questions. It was thought that it would be helpful if a meeting of this kind might be held with new converts, young couples and others who go through the Temples to receive their endowments so that they could ask questions and get enlightenment regarding the Temple ceremonies. I commented upon this matter at the Council meeting referred to and said I was impressed with the necessity of having missionaries and young couples meet together after the Temple ceremonies where they might ask any questions they wished, and said that there are hundreds of our boys and girls who, after going through the Temple, would like to ask questions. I feel we should make it obligatory. I said also that what we do here in the Salt Lake Temple we must do in the other Temples as well. I also stated that the First Presidency would take the matter under consideration and appoint a committee of three to make a study of this problem. **—David O. McKay diary, June 21, 1966; emphasis in original**

[Y]ou indicate that the president of the Church is the only one who administers in the holy of holies. While the president holds the keys of this sacred work, he can also delegate this authority to others, and this has been done to members of the Quorum of the Twelve, but only to such members as the president authorizes and delegates. I don't know of any presidents of temples who have this authority. **—LeGrand Richards,[25] letter dated July 5, 1966, copy in Buerger Papers**

Consideration was given to a letter from L--- B. W---- ... in which she asks three questions regarding sealings:

(1) "Does the Church permit the sealing for eternity of a single living woman to a decease[d] man, a friend but not a husband, in life?"

(2) "Does the Church permit the sealing[,] for eternity only[,] of a single living woman to a married living man?"

25. LeGrand Richards (1886-1983) was called as Presiding Bishop in 1938 and ordained to the Quorum of Twelve in 1952. He was the son of George F. Richards.

(3) "If the answer is yes to either or both of [these] questions, would you advise me to have the sealing performed?"

The proposition submitted by this sister is to the following effect: This sister, who is 82 years of age, has never been married. A few weeks ago a friend said to her in the presence of his wife, who is also a friend, that if she wanted a husband she could be sealed to him. This suggestion was reiterated on a second occasion by the man in the presence of his wife.

We decided to answer the questions submitted as follows: That the answer to the first question is yes, that a single living woman may be sealed while living to a deceased man, a friend but not a husband; that, however, each such case should be submitted to the First Presidency with the facts for their approval.

To the second question, we agreed that the Church does not permit the sealing for eternity only of a single living woman and a married living man.

In other words, in the case submitted[,] ... if Sister W---- wishes to be sealed to the man she mentions after he passes away, or if he wishes to have her sealed to him after she passes away, this may be done inasmuch as both parties have expressed their desire in life to be so sealed, this expression having been made in the presence and with the approval of the man's living wife. **—David O. McKay diary, July 6, 1966; hyphens added to obscure the woman's identity**

From time to time we receive requests from couples who desire to be married by civil ceremony before traveling from their home to the temple to have the sealing solemnized. For your guidance we are pleased to tell you that the ruling is that where couples are married by civil ceremony they should normally not be recommended to the temple until after a year or very near that period of time has elapsed since the civil ceremony was solemnized. Occasionally we receive requests for exceptions to this ruling, the reason given being that the parents of one or both of the contracting parties are non-members and are desirous of witnessing the civil ceremony. In such cases we have, as a general rule, granted permission. It should be understood, however, that this permission must be obtained in each instance from the First Presidency before authorization may be given.

Where parents of the couple to be married are members of the Church but not active or qualified to receive temple recommends, we have not felt to grant exceptions to the general rule that the marriage should be performed in the temple in the first instance. **—David O. McKay, Hugh B. Brown, N. Eldon Tanner, and Joseph Fielding Smith, circular letter, July 6, 1966**

In authorizing temple ordinances to be performed for the dead, it has been the policy to ignore the matter of worthiness of such persons during their lifetime except in cases of murder, suicide, excommunication, mental retardation, or other conditions which have been defined as restricting ordinance work. In these latter cases the work is not done and the matter is left in the hands of the Lord. These latter cases are very few and cause the laborious work of checking and investigating. Usually the only evidence available is hearsay, and decisions made are often arbitrary because of the absence of facts.

Ordinance work has been done and is being done for many deceased persons who would not qualify under the present rules for the reason that vital statistics and other records do not reveal such disqualifying matters. In these cases the work is done but the matter rests in the hands of the Lord, being little different from the cases where the work is not done and left to the Lord.

The Genealogical Society has recommended that in all cases where persons are deceased, and one year has elapsed from the date of death, temple ordinances may be performed for them without consideration of worthiness or qualification.

After careful consideration of this recommendation, the First Presidency and Council of the Twelve have decided that after the expiration of one year from the date of death, temple ordinances may be performed for all deceased persons, except those of known Negro blood, without the consideration of worthiness or any other qualification. These ordinances shall consist of those not received by such persons during their lifetime or which were taken away by excommunication. This rule will eliminate investigations and decision[s] as to worthiness and qualification[s] of deceased persons whose names are submitted for temple work, and also the necessity of restoration of blessings to those who were excommunicated in life. Therefore in the future it will not be necessary to submit to the First Presidency applications for restoration of former priesthood and blessings to those who were excommunicated before they passed away. **—David O. McKay, Hugh B. Brown, N. Eldon Tanner, and Joseph Fielding Smith, circular letter, Aug. 15, 1966**

The instructions given in this letter supercede those set forth in ours of July 5th addressed to presidents of stakes and bishops of wards on the subjects thereto treated.

Where persons who are involved in pending divorce or annulment proceedings make application for permission to go to the temple, brethren authorized to issue temple recommends should carefully and searchingly interview the applicant, and if it is found that he or she is innocent of any serious wrongdoing in connection with the divorce or annulment and is otherwise worthy, a temple recommend may be issued.

When the final decree of divorce or annulment has been entered, a divorce clearance must be obtained from the First Presidency by the parties involved, if they were previously sealed to each other in the temple, before they may be permitted to continue temple attendance or receive a temple recommend. Divorce clearances are secured by making application on forms previously furnished to stake and mission presidents. The forms contain the specific instructions.

Divorces or annulments of marriage need not be cleared by the First Presidency for persons who were not sealed to each other in the temple. Nevertheless, brethren authorized to issue temple recommends should conduct a thorough searching interview to determine the applicant's worthiness to go to the temple. **—David O. McKay, Hugh B. Brown, N. Eldon Tanner, and Joseph Fielding Smith, circular letter, Aug. 30, 1966**

Inquiry has been received from the presidency of one of the stakes in Las Vegas regarding the attitude that the Church should assume in the matter of appointing to administrative positions or issuing temple recommends to employees [of] gambling casinos, more specifically employees who are dealers, pit bosses, cashiers in tellers windows, change girls, bartenders, cocktail waitresses and cigar and cigarette girls.

This question came before the Council of the First Presidency and Quorum of the Twelve for consideration some months ago, and it was the sentiment of the Council at that time that we do not want any of our members participating in these gambling dens. President [David O.] McKay indicated that while he did not want to rule arbitrarily on this matter that we cannot handle whiskey and gambling without being scarred by it, and that our people should stay away from such places. The President further said that we had better not temporize with these things.

In a subsequent consideration of the matter it was decided to convey this information to stake presidents who are concerned with this problem and advise that we should not appoint to administrative positions nor issue temple recommends to people in these gambling places whose employment requires them to meet the public and participate in the manner indicated. We hope that our brethren and sisters can find employment in a more desirable environment.[26] **—David O. McKay, Hugh B. Brown, N. Eldon Tanner, and Joseph Fielding Smith to Stake Presidents in Las Vegas and Reno, Nevada, [and] Presidents of California Missions, Aug. 30, 1966**

President [N. Eldon] Tanner referred to a question that had arisen as to the possibility of children who have themselves been sealed to their parents or who were born in the covenant attending a sealing where other children are being sealed to their parents. As an illustration he mentioned cases where parents who have children born in the covenant go to the Temple to have sealed to them children whom they have adopted. Under these conditions the parents would like to take their family with them to witness the sealing of other children. He stated that in two or three cases we have authorized this procedure, but that the Temple rule is that children under 21 years of age and only those over 21 who have had their endowments should be permitted to witness these sealings. President Tanner said that he and President [Hugh B.] Brown had discussed this with Elder Howard W. Hunter and it was their feeling that it should be a general rule that children under 21 may, where they desire to do so, and obtain the necessary recommends, attend and witness the sealing [of] adopted brothers and sisters.[27] **—David O. McKay diary, Aug. 31, 1966**

The First Presidency urge that bishops instruct members discarding worn temple garments that any identifying symbols which might be related to the temple should be removed. The material may then be destroyed or used in the home. Garments should not be discarded

26. Three years earlier, the Church had dedicated its first stake center in Las Vegas to serve two stakes. The LDS population today is about 12 percent of the city's total, or over 100,000 members in more than twenty stakes. The Las Vegas temple was dedicated in 1989.

27. A circular letter to this effect was sent on Sept. 8.

where they will be picked up or used by others. ***—Priesthood Bulletin,* Sept.-Oct. 1966**

President [N. Eldon] Tanner called attention to some variance in decisions heretofore made regarding children born to parents while they were out of the Church who had been sealed in the Temple and subsequently excommunicated. He referred to an action taken by the Council in the days of President [Lorenzo] Snow, January 13, 1898, at which time President Snow gave it as his opinion that under these circumstances children born while their parents who had been sealed in the Temple were out of the Church because of excommunication should be sealed to their parents. He also mentioned rulings made by me to the same effect on September 26, 1946, and February 3, 1966, at which time I said these children were born out of the covenant and would have to be sealed; that, however, on May 19, 1960, in the case of J--- W. A-------- who was excommunicated from the Church and whose wife was not excommunicated, I had ruled that the children born to this couple while Brother A-------- was under excommunication were born in the covenant and remain sealed to the mother and that since the father's blessings had been restored, nothing more need be done.

I said that it was evident that in cases of this kind children born while one parent or both parents were out of the Church should be sealed to the parents after the parents have had their former blessings restored. This became the unanimous sentiment of the First Presidency. **—David O. McKay diary, Sept. 20, 1966; hyphens added to obscure the individual's identity**

After considering all the facts presented regarding the desire of a couple who have been sealed in the Temple to have sealed to them two children with Negroid blood, I indicated that I could see no objection to the sealing being done. **—David O. McKay diary, Sept. 27, 1966**

Reference was made by President [N. Eldon] Tanner to a question raised at the lunch table last Thursday following the Council meeting to the effect that someone had said that he had seen on the desk of the president of the Manti Temple a book regarding second anointings. President [Hugh B.] Brown had conferred with President Petersen of the Manti Temple who said that he has such a book, that he has always kept it in the vault in the Temple and that no one has access to it. The Brethren had not understood that there were copies of this book in the Temples other than one in the Salt Lake Temple. I asked President Joseph Fielding Smith to look into this situation and if there is such a book, it should be brought here.

President Tanner mentioned that following this discussion the question was raised about individuals in the Quorum of the Twelve who haven't received their second endowments. I asked that I be given a list of the names of the Brethren of the Twelve who have not received these blessings. **—David O. McKay diary, Oct. 25, 1966**

We went over a list of the Brethren of the General Authorities who have not had their second anointings. I asked President Joseph Fielding Smith to officiate at these ordinances in behalf of these Brethren, to be assisted by Elder Spencer W. Kimball when Elder Kimball returns from South America. **—David O. McKay diary, Nov. 9, 1966**

Clare [Middlemiss][28] came up to Huntsville with a folder full of correspondence which had accumulated for sometime now, and also with some forty cases of petitions for cancellation of Temple sealings. We went over these without any disturbance in two hours, and I was very happy that this work had been cleared away. There were one or two cases on the cancellations which were doubtful, so I allowed a second sealing for the woman, leaving to the next life and the Lord's decision which man the woman would have. **—David O. McKay diary, Nov. 23, 1966**

In counseling, the bishop is reminded that it is permissible to talk about the temple, its structure, the rooms, the ordinances, and all that the Church has *officially published* about the temple.

Do not assume that worthiness to enter the temple at one time is an excuse for a casual interview subsequently. In determining worthiness to go through the temple, make sure that careful interrogation has been made into all areas listed on the inside cover of the temple recommend book. ***—Counseling and Interviewing Guide for Bishops*** **(Salt Lake City: Church of Jesus Christ of Latter-day Saints, 1966), 10-11; emphasis in original**

....

28. Clare Middlemiss (1901-1983) was a personal secretary to David O. McKay from 1935 until his death in 1970.

Attention was called to a letter … written in behalf of a family in the branch who operate a service station, and in connection therewith a café, in which café beer is served. … [T]his family are a very active and fine family, that they pay their tithing and serve as far as possible, although during the summer months they cannot attend their meetings as frequently as they should because of their activities at the service station and café, that one of the sons of the family is attending the Brigham Young University and is expecting to go on a mission this summer. The Branch President raises the question as to whether, under the circumstances, his parents may be permitted to have recommends to go to the Temple when the son goes to the Temple after he receives his mission call.

In discussing this matter, I ruled that if the parents are otherwise worthy, as indicated by the Branch President, except for their involvement in this café operation, they may be given Temple Recommends. **—David O. McKay diary, Feb. 15, 1967**

Consideration was given to a letter from Sister V----- G----- … asking the following question: In a case where a child is being legally adopted by a couple and the child passes away before the adoption proceedings are completed, may the child be sealed to the adopting parents. It was our sentiment that under these circumstances the child could be sealed. **—David O. McKay diary, Mar. 8, 1967; hyphens added to conceal the name**

Consideration was given to the matter of the sealing to his parents of P----- R------, 15 years of age, who is retarded, the mother having inquired if this could be done by proxy. In answer to a letter from the First Presidency, [the stake president] … reports that the boy is hyperactive, his attention span is very short, he cries readily and becomes violent at times, and doesn't understand normal conversation. According to [the stake president], the American Fork Training School Chaplain suggests that the boy could possibly be brought to the Temple if accompanied by a matron to take care of him, and that they do have matrons who hold Temple Recommends.

It was our sentiment that the boy might be taken to the Temple and sealed to his parents under the conditions mentioned. …

Attention was given to a letter from [a ward bishop] … written in behalf of a sister residing in his Ward, who has been guilty of moral transgression resulting in pregnancies and abortions. She and her husband now have three children. She is repentant and attends Church regularly and wants to serve in the Church, and the children are being raised in the Church. The Bishop says she has no hope of ever going to the Temple because of the things she has done. It was decided to answer the Bishop that this sister should be encouraged to continue to repent and live a proper life in the future and leave her situation to the Lord, [but] that she should not be given a Temple Recommend. …

Attention was given to a letter from Elder Mark E. Petersen reporting that a group of people associated with the deaf organization in Southern California and Salt lake City had conferred with him relative to the possible arrangement of Temple sessions for the deaf. He stated that there are 200 faithful Latter-day Saints who are deaf in Southern California in the San Diego-Los Angeles area, 255 in Salt Lake City, and 120 in Ogden.

We were unanimous in our feelings that sessions for these deaf people should be provided in the Salt Lake and Los Angeles Temples. …

Attention was called to a letter from [a ward bishop] … stating that an Elder and his wife are considering legally adopting two Negro children. They have two children of their own. The Bishop asks for counsel on the matter. He inquires if the couple will be able to have these children sealed to them in the Temple.

We decided to answer the Bishop stating that they should discourage such an adoption. **—David O. McKay diary, Apr. 26, 1967; one name obscured (cf. Jan. 12, 1968)**

President [N. Eldon] Tanner mentioned that some of the Temple Presidents have served nine or ten years and others a briefer period of time. He was wondering if it would be well to have a policy indicating a specified period of time that a Temple President should serve. He thought that if this were done it would be easier to release them than otherwise.

I said that I do not feel there should be any limitation set on a Temple President's term of service. President Tanner inquired if I would agree with him that it might be a good thing to review the list of Temple Presidents from time to time to ascertain just how long they have served. I said that this is a good idea, and Brother [Joseph]

Anderson was asked to prepare a list for our consideration. **—David O. McKay diary, May 23, 1967; emphasis in original**

It has been called to our attention that occasionally young women come to the temple to receive their endowments or to do ordinance work for the dead wearing slacks or mini-skirts. We suggest that when interviewing sisters applying for temple recommends you kindly remind them of the sanctity of the temple and the propriety of being modestly dressed when they enter the House of the Lord. **—David O. McKay, Hugh B. Brown, and N. Eldon Tanner, circular letter, Aug. 30, 1967**

President [Hugh B.] Brown reported that in the Council meeting Thursday some complaint was made about giving temple recommends to converts of less than a year. The brethren were agreed that conditions altered cases, that sometimes exceptions may be made where people have been in the Church only seven or eight months under certain conditions.

President [N. Eldon] Tanner mentioned that a case that had given the brethren concern was an announcement that appeared in the press regarding a civil marriage by an elder of the Church in the Skaggs Baptist chapel, followed very shortly thereafter by a sealing in the temple. This was a case where the mother of the bride was not a member of the Church. The brethren felt that care should be exercised in these cases. **—David O. McKay diary, Sept. 1, 1967**

The following brethren met with President [David O.] McKay in his apartment for the purpose of presenting to the President the new temple ordinance film and tapes: Presidents Hugh B. Brown, N. Eldon Tanner and Joseph Fielding Smith; Elders Richard L. Evans, Gordon B. Hinckley, Alvin R. Dyer, Frank Wise, Judge Whittaker and Joseph Anderson. Sister [Emma Ray] McKay[29] was also present.

Following the presentation of the picture[,] Elder Evans stated that this is the first improvement that the committee had attempted to make since the President instructed them 12 years ago to prepare a film for the Swiss Temple, which film is now in use in several of the temples. He said that the nature of the construction of the Oakland Temple

29. Emma Ray Riggs McKay (1877-1970), President McKay's wife since 1901, was born in Salt Lake City and graduated in music from the University of Utah in 1898.

room prompted this improvement and that the film is a result of the further assignment given the committee to move forward and upgrade the film that is being used in New Zealand, Great Britain, Switzerland and Los Angeles. He said the committee would hope to continue its attempt to improve the film but it is proposed that this film which they had witnessed today be used until they are able to improve it further, replacing the one that was produced 12 years ago.

President Brown commented that there is very little change, that the words are the same [and] there are a few modifications and refinements [but] nothing that changes the meaning, the wording[,] or the significance of the film [presentation]. President Brown and President Tanner had reviewed it yesterday and were greatly impressed by it and thought it should be presented to the President for his consideration.

President McKay said that he approved it just as it is, and authorization was therefore given for the committee to go forward with the project. In answer to Elder Evans' inquiry as to whether they might continue to improve it, not holding up its use but [nevertheless] making improvements wherever it was thought advisable, this was authorized. Elder Hinckley commented that in the temple it would be shown to greater advantage because it would be presented on a large screen and the light and sound will be better than was the case today. President McKay commented that this is the best we have had. President Smith also said it was very well done. **—Minutes of a meeting, Nov. 16, 1967, included in the David O. McKay diary, Nov. 16, 1967**

... I [Mark Garff][30] asked the President to listen me out and see if I was foolish in what I was suggesting. He said he would be glad to listen and I told him I had just returned from the Far East; this is about the only time I have left my desk for the two and [a] half years I have been working for President [David O.] McKay and in my mind I tried to conceive a plan whereby we could bring Temple work to our people. I said cautiously to President McKay: "If you think I am out of bounds I want you to tell me, but I am proposing to you now, that The Church obtain or build a ship sufficient in size to run the oceans and we equip

30. Mark Brimhall Garff (1907-1995) began chairing the Church Building Committee in 1965. He had been president of the Danish Mission from 1937 to 1939. See also Gregory A. Prince and William Robert Wright, *David O. McKay and the Rise of Modern Mormonism* (Salt Lake City: University of Utah Press, 2005), 273-75.

this ship as a temple ship; that we take the ship and outfit it as a temple, then take the ship into the ports and harbors where our people live. We could do this around the entire continent of South America, Europe, along the coast of China, Japan, Australia and even Africa if we wanted to.["] I was sure the cost would not amount to any more than what the cost of some of our temples has been. I suggested to the President that we do not have the money to build temples all over the world and it would be an impossibility because our funds are limited and if we followed this procedure we could get at least those who want their endowments done while they are still alive, we could move [people] to the ports where we would dock this ship; otherwise it would be impossible for them to have their own endowments and we might carry it even further than their own endowments and move on to doing work for the dead, making this a continuous tour of where there are people needing the blessing of the temple and the holy endowment.

After I explained to the President my thinking he said to me: "That is not foolish thinking and I want you to pursue this thought and pursue the feasibility of it and make a report to me." He seemed to be greatly intrigued with the idea, he seemed to grasp it very quickly and thought it would be a good idea, so I am going to pursue it a little further as fast as my time will allow. **—Minutes of a Meeting, Nov. 30, 1967, included in the David O. McKay diary on the same date**

....

President [N. Eldon] Tanner mentioned that in the Temple book of instructions in London at least, and perhaps in the other Temples, the statement is made that women may be used as witnesses for Temple marriages. President Buckmiller[31] of the London Temple is asking if women can be used as witnesses for sealings for the dead in the Temple, sealing of children to parents, etc. He said that Elder [Howard W.] Hunter says that it is permitted for the living and the question is raised as to whether the same service may be performed by women for the dead.

I said that I could see no reason why the women could not so serve. President Tanner explained that in England it is very difficult to get enough men to the Temple to take care of this work for the deceased. …

31. Leroy John Buckmiller (1901-2000) was president of the London temple from 1966 to 1968.

President Tanner mentioned that sometime ago a ruling was made that where a couple had adopted Negro children, those children could be sealed to the adopting couple; that now a question comes to the following effect: A man married a Negro woman by whom he had a child. This woman died, and he married a white woman. He is now asking if his child or children by the former marriage with the colored woman may be sealed to him and his present wife, who is a white woman, after they have been properly adopted. President Tanner asked if the former ruling regarding sealing adopted children to white parents would include this situation. I said there was no reason why it shouldn't. **—David O. McKay diary, Jan. 12, 1968 (cf. Apr. 26, 1967)**

Consideration was given to a letter … regarding a question raised by R----- W---- M-E------ and his wife, E-------- M-E------. This couple wish to have their family sealed to them in the Temple. The eldest daughter, K-------, who is eighteen years of age, suffered a severe illness when she was two and one-half years of age, as a result of which her mental development was stopped at that point. She is in the hospital and her parents say that it would be practically impossible to move her any distance.

The question raised is whether or not this girl may be sealed to her parents by proxy. It was decided to answer … that under the circumstances this sealing may be done vicariously. **—David O. McKay diary, Jan. 16, 1968; hyphens added to obscure the names**

It has come to our attention that in some of the temples[,] instruction has been given to those going through to receive their endowments prior to entering into the marriage covenant that they must not remove the temple garment during the time of sexual relations.

We have authorized no such instruction or advice. We feel that this is a matter of such intimate nature that it must be left with the persons concerned. We therefore ask that you govern yourselves accordingly. **—David O. McKay, Hugh B. Brown, and N. Eldon Tanner to temple presidents, May 22, 1968**

Brother [Alvin R.] Dyer … took up the case of Brother and Sister G---- which involves the sealing of this couple and the two sons of Sister G---- by a former marriage.

I gave President Dyer permission to tell the couple they may be

sealed, but the sealing of the two boys, who have not been legally adopted by Brother G----, and who are unable to find their own father, a retired Army captain, should be held in abeyance until either the father has been declared officially dead, or they should be legally adopted, or if the father is found the father would give his consent to such action.
—David O. McKay diary, July 9, 1968; hyphens added to conceal identities

Mark B. Garff, Emil Fetzer and Fred Baker of the Building Committee met with the First Presidency ... Brother Garff mentioned that ... in the Church 52.7% of the members in the United States are within a reasonable distance from the temple, that 1,370,000 can go to the temples; that there are other members within reasonable distances outside of the United States but that is only 7.2%. There are 30%, or 785,000 people who do not have access to a temple. These people are scattered anywhere from Alaska, on the east coast, in the islands of the sea, Australia, Korea, and areas where the people haven't the money to go to the temple because they are so far away.

Elder Garff said that he felt that what we should do is bring the temple to the additional membership of the Church. He said it was the committee's proposal that we buy a ship and outfit the ship and make it a temple ship and that we take this ship to the ports of the earth where our people are. He said that with a ship we could outfit a temple and take that temple to 30%. Included in the 30% would be people in the United States who are not accessible to the temple and those throughout the world. He said that this could be done for between a million and a half and two million dollars, that a ship could be purchased and remodeled and that we could get the crew and could sail the seas at about a half a million dollars a year. This would mean that there are 50,000 Melchizedek Priesthood members in the Church that we would reach by bringing the ship to them in these ports, and in addition, their wives and children. He said there are plenty of people in the Church who would be willing and who are able to serve as captain and crew members. In this manner he said that we could take a ship to the people of the earth for less money than it costs us to build a temple anywhere in the United States or elsewhere. He thought that they could get this thing underway within a year and could buy the ship and rig it up for our purposes.

Brother Baker said that the thing that had led them to consider such a proposal was that as they looked activity-wise at our existing temples today they found that the temples outside of the United States are being utilized mostly for living endowments rather than vicarious work for the dead. He said he did not think that they had ever been in a country considering building matters that a mission president, stake president or someone else hadn't said that they had picked out a beautiful site which they thought would be wonderful for a temple.

Referring to the United States he said our temples are located in the western area which takes care of the bulk of our people, but in visualizing what a ship might do[,] it is startling to realize that in a short time making a very small circuit a ship could cover all the areas of the United States stopping at vital points along the seaboard. He said the idea would be that the ship would be scheduled in these ports for a certain length of time and that the stakes and missions would be scheduled for certain sessions so that provision could be made for living endowments to be given to worthy members in these accessible areas as well as work for the dead. He said that such a ship could travel up the Mississippi and the Missouri rivers and that the entire inland part of the United States could be covered. In this way he said that it would be possible to do away with the pressure that is being brought in the various areas away from the Church until such areas had sufficient membership to sustain a temple of their own. He said that in areas where there was unrest we could stay away from such places until the unrest subsided. He expressed the view that once every year or every eighteen or nineteen months we could touch all of these particular areas with the vessel.

In answer to a question as to whether the ship would fly the American flag it was stated that it would not be the intention to do this, that if it were to sail under an American flag it would cost three to four times the amount involved than if it flew under a foreign flag. They thought there would be no problem at all in getting temple workers who would take care of the ordinance and temple ceremonies on board ship, nor in getting members for the crew. He mentioned that we have many seamen and navy men who like the sea and would be delighted to serve on a ship of this kind. [They] stated that they had … in mind … a thousand-ton ship and that they had made investigation to see if it was possible to put a temple facility in this particular vessel, that it has four decks[.] Brother Fetzer explained to the brethren how the ship could be remodeled in such a way as to provide the necessary rooms and facilities for temple work, which would be separate and apart from the space that would be occupied by the crew and would provide necessary staterooms for passengers, waiting rooms, initiatory ordinance rooms, etc. It was stated that the complete ordinance could be presented on either tape or film, and this would be like our ordinance rooms in our new temples. In addition there would be sealing rooms provided and it was thought that it would be possible to accommodate three companies a day on the ship.

Elder [Alvin R.] Dyer mentioned a matter that he said bothered him somewhat[,] and that was [that] in the very early days of the Church the Prophet Joseph had said that the waters would be cursed, that he did not know exactly what that might mean but that we should not be insensible to that.[32] He also mentioned the fact that when the saints came to Utah they had to wait forty years before a temple was completed and he did not think it was so urgent that people who live in distant places could not wait a little for a temple.[33] Elder Dyer said he thought this was a wonderful study that had been made and he realized that it might present an answer to an existing problem.

President [N. Eldon] Tanner said it was his understanding that the brethren of the Building Committee had merely presented a program for the consideration of the First Presidency, that they were not saying this should be built or any other temple should be built, that they had made a careful survey in accordance with the President's request and are merely reporting the results of their survey and study.

Elder Garff said that if the brethren would like them to do so[,] they could pursue this matter further and bring actual costs and look for a desirable ship. The brethren said that they should not do this at the present time. The brethren were agreed that the matter was deserving of careful consideration. **—Alvin R. Dyer, minutes of a meeting with the First Presidency, President McKay's apartment, recorded in Elder Dyer's diary, Oct. 11, 1968**

---

32. See D&C 61:14-16.

33. Perhaps Elder Dyer should have emphasized that a ship would serve the Saints temporarily the way the Council House and Endowment House had while Salt Lake Valley settlers waited for the temple to be dedicated. Instead, according to a comment recorded in President McKay's diary (below), Dyer turned the argument on its head and said his parents had waited twenty-five years for the Logan temple to be completed, so if people elsewhere had to wait, so be it—it wasn't anything more than those who had come before them had done.

At 9:30 a.m. a meeting was held with President [David O.] McKay in his apartment which was attended by President [N. Eldon] Tanner, President [Joseph Fielding] Smith, myself [Alvin R. Dyer], Brother Joseph Anderson, and the three members of the Church Building Committee.

Temple on an Ocean-going Vessel

For nearly one hour the brethren from the Building Committee made a presentation suggesting the purchase of an ocean-going vessel, which vessel was to be equipped for Temple Ordinance work and then sail to the various points strategically located throughout the earth where Latter-day Saints, principally in remote places, would have access to the Temple Endowment. It was reported that this project would cost approximately two million dollars and could be maintained throughout the year at a cost of about $500,000 per year[,] that crews could be recruited by simply calling various members of the Church to a 12 or 18-month mission, and that the members of the crew on the boat would not be the same as those that would be called to officiate in the Temple Ordinances for people throughout the earth.

Comment

It is obvious that this would satisfy a need for the far away, remote places where members of the Church would not have access to the Temple Endowment, but in order for it to be successful it would have to also touch the heavier populated areas in America as well as in South America. Otherwise it would be unfeasible as to cost. The proposition thus submitted is without question worthy of consideration and this is precisely the status that it was left in. There were no decisions made. However, a great many comments were made which consisted of the following:

1. President Smith raised the question that Temples were to be constructed according to revelation in Stakes of Zion.

2. I raised the question as to the cursing that has been placed upon the waters in the last days, as to whether it would be proper in the light of that statement by the Prophet to construct a Temple to sail on the waters.

3. I also raised the question as to the worthiness of the members in far away places or as to whether their association in the Church was sufficiently experienced to have the Temple work performed for them at this time. The Building Committee stated that there were 50,000

men who held the Melchizedek Priesthood in these far away places who would have access to the Temple. I pointed out that even here in Zion only 40% of them were worthy of going to the Temple and it would be probably much less in these far away places. Then if they were not permitted to go[,] with the ship being anchored in a nearby harbor, that it would offend them.

4. The question also arose as to why we should be so pressing and introducing such urgency [in] methods to get the Temple work done for people in remote places since most of the Temple work will be accomplished in the Millennium and no one will suffer who is worthy to receive the endowment and that we sometimes were pressing these matters. I pointed out the fact that my own parents waited 25 years before they could go to the Logan Temple and even though they had the Endowment House before they constructed the Salt Lake Temple, there was no vicarious work done for many, many years after the Saints arrived here.

5. I also pointed out the fact that there were areas in the United States and in South America where Temples should be erected on a permanent basis since they would remain during the Millennium as temples are to be constructed in North and South America which the Lord has designated as Zion, for the work to be accomplished, not only prior to, but during the Millennium.

6. Finally, while this project appears to have great merit on first thought, the more it is thought about the more problems would seem to arise. However, the matter was left for further consideration by President McKay and the First Presidency.[34] **—Minutes of a meeting of the First Presidency, recorded in the David O. McKay diary, Oct. 11, 1968**

It was reported that requests have been received for permission to issue temple recommends to women to go to the temple to receive their endowments who are not divorced but have been separated from their husbands for some years and have not heard from them during that period of separation, nor do they know where they are. President [N. Eldon] Tanner said it was his feeling that where the law of the state where the parties reside says that a man who has deserted his wife and

---

34. Two weeks later, McKay wrote to an inquiring individual that "as far as I am concerned[,] we are not considering this proposition," and further discussion of the matter apparently ceased. See Prince and Wright, *David O. McKay,* 275.

has not been heard of for a designated number of years is considered dead, that the woman in such a case should be given a recommend to the temple to receive her endowments.

I concurred that under conditions of this kind the woman should be granted permission to go to the Temple to receive her endowments if she is otherwise worthy. **—David O. McKay diary, Oct. 15, 1968**

Attention was called to a letter from President Reuel E. Christensen[35] of the Manti Temple reporting that a bishop and stake president in one of the BYU Stakes had inquired if they could send colored people who are members of the Church in good standing residing in their wards to do baptismal work for the dead in the temple.

I ruled that worthy negro baptized members of the Church should be permitted to do baptismal work for the dead if they desire to do so. **—David O. McKay diary, Dec. 5, 1968; emphasis in original**

....

Elder Howard W. Hunter met with the First Presidency this morning and presented to them a problem pertaining to genealogical work which he said the committee had been discussing for several months. He explained that over the years the rule has been that if a woman has had more than one marriage in her lifetime we would seal her to her first husband, everything else being equal. This would pertain only to people who are dead. [Even] if a woman had been married two or more times and had children by each marriage, heretofore she has been sealed to the first husband. If she had no children by her first husband but had children by her second marriage, many times she was sealed to the second husband so that the children could be sealed to their own father. He said there have been cases where the family has said that the mother or grandmother, whoever it might be, did not want to be sealed to her first husband, that she did not respect him and had more affection for her second or third husband, as the case might be, and sometimes under such circumstances she was sealed to the second or third husband. He said that where we have trouble is in cases that go beyond the point of memory, that, for instance, when we go to the parish records in England, and the other registries, and we find the woman

35. Reuel E. Christensen (1904–1983) was president of the Manti temple from 1968 to 1974.

has been married to several men, we do not know what her wishes or desires were and so ordinarily she would be sealed to her first husband, except in cases when we had enough information to indicate that the second or third one would be the appropriate husband to seal her to. He said all of this is a little arbitrary and is based upon lack of facts.

He mentioned the recent decision of the First Presidency[,] going into the computer program[,] to the effect that we would go through the parish register of marriages and seal all women to their husbands wherever we found their record of marriage in the parish records. He said this results sometimes in a woman being sealed to more than one husband, that sometimes where a woman has been married more than once she is sealed to two persons. This was approved by the First Presidency. In these cases the woman would have the right of choice in the hereafter. Elder Hunter said that our brethren in the Genealogical Society who have been serving for many years have suggested the desirability of sealing women to more than one man where they have been married several times. This pertains to people who are dead. He explained that when a woman is sealed to her first husband and there have been several marriages, the matter is left in the hands of the Lord and her choice in the hereafter, but this does not give the posterity a positive line to follow. He said the brethren of the Genealogical Society have had the feeling that it would be better to seal such a woman who has had more than one husband to each of her husbands and let the children of each marriage be sealed to their parents. This would still give the woman the right to make her selection in the hereafter. He said that frequently they have people come into the Genealogical Society office and say that their great grandmother, for instance, said before she died that she loved her second husband more than the first and that they would like to have her sealing to the first man broken so that she could be sealed to the second. Elder Hunter said that they were commencing to wonder if they followed the right course through all these years. He thought it was perfectly proper that in life a woman be sealed to only one husband, but after death and many years have passed and there are posterity from the lines of several husbands, it becomes a difficult situation.

There was some discussion and explanation made regarding this proposed change. In this connection mention was made of the fact that in cases where a sealing was cancelled between a couple who have children born in the covenant that these children are not permitted to be sealed to anyone else than their natural parents and that the matter is left to the hereafter for decision as to whether they should go with the mother or the father. The brethren emphasized in the discussion that the fact that the work is done for these people does not necessarily mean that it will be accepted, that, however, the work must be done for everyone and it is like putting it in a bank as it were to be held subject to the worthiness and acceptance of the individual.

After a rather lengthy discussion of the matter President [David O.] McKay indicated his approval. **—Minutes of a First Presidency meeting, Jan. 14, 1969, included in the David O. McKay diary on the same date**

President [Hugh B.] Brown called attention to a letter that had been prepared for the First Presidency's signature ... on the action taken by the First Presidency in a recent meeting ... [when] President Brown was away, in which it was decided pertaining to work for the dead that it would be permissible to seal a woman to more than one husband in cases where there had been children by more than one husband and it was not known which husband she preferred. The decision was that the woman could be sealed to her various husbands by whom she had children and thus the way would be provided so that the children born to these marriages could be sealed to their natural parents and do the temple work for their parents. The woman would have the right to make her own choice in the hereafter as to which of the husbands she would wish to be sealed to. President Brown said he did not feel to favor this decision. He mentioned that some years ago when he was taking charge of these matters for me it was thought that the matter of the relationship of these people who were dead and concerning whom we had not knowledge should be left for solution in the next world, and not clutter our records with a lot of sealings of one woman to several husbands. He wondered if this had been given careful consideration.

President [N. Eldon] Tanner reported that this entire question had been discussed by the First Presidency a short time ago ... [and] that Brother [Howard W.] Hunter's argument, with which he agreed, was that when we seal a woman to any man in cases of those who have passed away[,] it is arbitrarily done and we do not know whether this man was the woman's choice or not, that where a woman had been married to two or three husbands the children were sometimes at a loss to know what to do about their genealogy, sealings, etc., that Brother

Hunter argued that if she were sealed to all of the husbands, no matter what her choice should ultimately be the work would be done for all of the families. He stated that it was an arbitrary action no matter what we did. He mentioned that our former practice was to seal this woman to her first husband unless it was known that she wanted to be sealed to one of her subsequent husbands, and all of this was arbitrary, that, for instance, one family wanted her sealed to their father and another family wanted her sealed to their father, and they wouldn't have any direct line to follow unless this was done; that if she was sealed to all of the husbands the work could be carried on by the different families and it was no more of a problem to let her and the Lord decide later than if we were to make an arbitrary decision now. President Tanner mentioned that President [Joseph Fielding] Smith at the time said he could see no greater problem in that event. President [Alvin R.] Dyer had at first questioned it and then thought it was the right thing to do. President Dyer commented that at first he did not think it was the right thing to do but the more he thought about it the more he realized that whenever you do any work vicariously for the dead it depends upon their acceptance on the other side and the conglomeration of marriages will have to be straightened out, that in the meantime the descendants of each of the husbands could go ahead with the temple work and the children could have the sealing blessing and know that they could be sealed to their mother and one of the husbands. President Tanner further mentioned that President Smith had made the statement in writing that there will be a transference of sealings[,] and if that is true it would be simple to make the transfer according to the woman's choice.

President Tanner asked me if I wanted to hold the matter up for the present and I said absolutely. **—David O. McKay diary, Feb. 3, 1969**

President [N. Eldon] Tanner said the suggestion has been made that the temple ceremonies for the dead be shortened to do away with repetition. This would not pertain to the living but only the dead. The brethren who have considered the matter say that it would not in any way detract from the importance of the covenants, promises and ceremonies. President Tanner said that if I felt that the suggestion is worthy of consideration there could be arranged a condensed version of these ceremonies for presentation to me for my approval. President Tanner said that Elders Howard W. Hunter, Gordon B. Hinckley and

Theodore M. Burton think it could be done very well and he believed that Brother Richard L. Evans felt the same way. President [Hugh B.] Brown suggested that these brethren be asked to bring in a copy of the present ceremony and also a copy of the proposed ceremony so that comparisons could be made.

I said this might be done. **—David O. McKay diary, Feb. 19, 1969**

Brethren who have taken upon themselves the covenants of the temple and who are asked to perform baptisms for the living should not assume, because their clothes will get wet or for any other reason, that they should not wear garments under their white baptismal clothing. Regular garments are to be worn by everyone who has received his temple endowments, while performing baptisms. ...

The continuous calling of men into military service makes it desirable to reaffirm certain observations previously made by the First Presidency in the matter of wearing temple underclothing.

Such apparel should be worn at all times unless very unusual circumstances prevent it. Under present-day conditions there are very few such occasions.

When military underclothing is required, it should be worn with the understanding that the wearing of the temple underclothing shall be resumed at the earliest possible moment.

Under these exceptional circumstances the identifying features should be placed on small pieces of cloth and attached to the military underclothing while it is being worn, and then removed when the military apparel is sent to the laundry.

Every effort should be made to keep the approved pattern from attracting the attention of those who would misunderstand. **—*Priesthood Bulletin,* Mar. 1969, 6-7**

Attention was called to a letter from Sister Belle S. Spafford,[36] General President of the Relief Society, relative to temple clothing.

The brethren agreed that temple aprons must be made under the direction of the Relief Society and only individuals who have had their own endowments and who hold current temple recommends should make the temple aprons.

36. Marion Isabelle Sims Smith Spafford (1895-1982) was president of the General Relief Society from 1945 to 1974.

I gave direction to the matter that it is not necessary to bless Temple clothing.

I also gave direction that it is permissible for individuals to be buried in laundered and clean temple clothing rather than to go to the expense of the purchase of entirely new clothing. **—David O. McKay diary, Mar. 5, 1969**

President [N. Eldon] Tanner called attention to a letter handed to him by Elder Howard W. Hunter to be handed to the First Presidency referring to a custom in the early days of the Church for a woman to be sealed to a good man in the Church, a General Authority or someone else who was still living, other than her deceased husband who died without accepting the gospel. The sealing was performed as an assurance for an eternal union in the hereafter. It is now recommended that inasmuch as President Wilford Woodruff received a revelation which altered this practice, that in such cases prior to 1890 when this ruling was made, if the woman was sealed to a deceased member of the Church or to a living member of the church but did not live with him as a wife, permission be granted for her to be sealed also to her non-member deceased husband to whom she had been married in life. The original sealing will not, however, be cancelled. President Tanner said that it would seem that this would be particularly desirable when the woman had children by the non-member husband, that under this ruling the children could be sealed to their parents. President Tanner asked me if I could see anything wrong about such a ruling, and I said no. …

Attention was given to a letter by the presidency of the Salt Lake Temple asking that consideration be given to a proposed change in the style of the ceremonial garment that is worn in the temple. The letter explains that there would be many advantages to wearing the regular garment in the temple instead of the so-called ceremonial garment, that when one goes through the temple he or she would be clothed in the garment of the Holy Priesthood by wearing the same style of garment worn when they leave the temple. Under the present arrangement the so-called ceremonial garment is placed on the individual and he or she is told to wear it throughout his or her life, and then when they leave the temple they wear the regular style garment. Then, too, considerable time would be saved because one would not need to change from the regular style into the so-called ceremonial style before going into the ordinance room. Another consideration mentioned is that when the sisters wear the ceremonial garment the bottom part of the legs of the garment shows below the dresses.

Another argument is that the garment approved for initiatory work could be the regular approved style garment with the zipper at the top, which some of the approved garments now have. This would be much more modest than the present garment with the strings and would also save time. An additional reason is that there would be a considerable saving to both the temple and the patrons; the temple would save the cost of the garments and the patrons would save the amount they pay for rental.

Again, those who officiate in the temple wear the regular approved style garment and it seems logical that the patrons should be permitted to wear the same style as those who officiate.

I gave my approval. **—David O. McKay diary, Mar. 6, 1969**

Attention was called to a letter from President [O. Leslie] Stone of the Salt Lake Temple mentioning that occasionally members come to the temple who are not properly dressed, sisters wearing slacks and mini-skirts, and brethren without ties or jackets, etc. President Stone suggests the need of correcting this. It was mentioned that a letter was sent to presidents of stakes and bishops of wards, copies of which were sent to the temples August 30, 1967, regarding the wearing of slacks and mini-skirts by women who go to the temple. The brethren agreed that a letter should be sent to stake presidents, bishops and mission presidents. It was decided to look up our former letter on the subject. **—David O. McKay diary, Mar. 10, 1969**

We reiterate the instruction given in our letter of August 10 [sic, August 30], 1967 that sisters should be advised against wearing slacks or mini-skirts when going to the temple to receive their endowments or to do ordinance work for the dead.

There are also those of our brethren who sometimes go to the temple without a necktie or jacket and who otherwise are not properly groomed.

Temple patrons should bear in mind that they are visiting the house of the Lord and that they should wear clothing suitable for the occasion, such as they would wear when attending a sacrament meeting on Sunday.

We suggest that when interviewing brethren and sisters for recommends you kindly remind them of the sanctity of the temple and the propriety of being modestly dressed and properly groomed when they prepare to enter the temples of the Lord. **—David O. McKay, Hugh B. Brown, and N. Eldon Tanner, circular letter, Mar. 17, 1969**

President [N. Eldon] Tanner referred to approval given by the First Presidency for the wearing of the new style garment in the temple. He mentioned that the question had been raised in connection therewith as to the use of the new style garment in place of the so-called ceremonial garment in the washing and anointing rooms. The question was raised as to whether the procedure which has been followed over the years as to the manner in which the garment should be placed on the individual, one leg at a time, etc., is a part of the ceremony. The brethren did not feel that this is a part of the ritual. It was agreed to announce this new policy regarding the garments to the General Authorities in their meeting on Thursday, March 27th. **—David O. McKay diary, Mar. 18, 1969**

We are very concerned that our people going to the temple for the first time have a better introduction to the temple. There are too many people who are given temple recommends with no explanation whatever. They come to the temple not knowing what to expect. Some are disappointed, many are thrilled, but we feel that people ought to have some kind of an introduction to the temple before they go to the temple and they are more likely to understand what they receive and with better understanding they are more likely to be loyal to the covenants that they make. **—Mark E. Petersen, address to the Regional Representatives Seminar, Apr. 2, 1969**

President [N. Eldon] Tanner mentioned the approval given at a recent meeting of the First Presidency for using in the temple ceremonies the new style garment in place of the so-called ceremonial garment. He said this matter had been presented by President [O. Leslie] Stone of the Salt Lake Temple and two other temple presidents, also Howard [W.] Hunter and his committee. They felt, and President Tanner agreed, that it seemed inconsistent to place on the individual in the temple ceremony the so-called ceremonial garment telling him that he must wear it the rest of his life and then giving permission for him to immediately replace this garment with the modified garment normally worn by members of the Church. Then too the temple ordinance workers and even the ones who place the garments on the individual are themselves wearing the modified garment. President Tanner felt that this matter should be referred to the Twelve before this change is made. …

President [Alvin R.] Dyer said that he would personally see no inconsistency in placing upon the person in the temple a garment that covers the knee so that the wearer will be impressed with the idea that this is the way it should be. President Tanner thought we should advise all the stake presidencies and bishops to instruct their people when recommended to the temple to be sure their garments come below the knees. **—David O. McKay diary, Apr. 8, 1969**

President [N. Eldon] Tanner referred to initiatory ordinances in the temple for the dead and proposed the adoption of the following procedure:

Perform the ordinations to the Melchizedek Priesthood in advance with the other initiatory work to follow by other proxies. Under this plan one proxy would be ordained for each individual name as at present, but at one sitting he would act as proxy for several individual names. This proposed procedure would eliminate the proxy walking back to the ordaining area after completing each initiatory ordinance. Instead, the proxy would remain in an assigned ordinance booth to complete all the names on his list. This would give three proxies for the same person instead of two.[37]

This was approved. **—David O. McKay diary, Apr. 17, 1969**

President [N. Eldon] Tanner said that President [O. Leslie] Stone of the Salt Lake Temple had called to his attention the large number of marriages in the Temple and the problems involved in requiring members of families who wish to witness the marriages to remove their street shoes and wear white shoes. President Stone mentions the

37. In other words, according to the original procedure, a proxy was washed, anointed, and ordained, and another proxy was endowed. As proposed here, the ordination would be performed in three steps, requiring as many proxies. The officiators would henceforth put their hands on the proxy's head and recite the ordination in the name of the deceased, quickly remove their hands and replace them on the proxy's head to recite the ordination for the next deceased person, and so on.

confusion that often develops, that shoes become misplaced and in some cases people take shoes that are not their own, etc. He wonders if this custom could not be changed and permit those who come to witness the ceremony to wear their street shoes. The brethren felt that we should continue the present rule that street shoes should not be worn. **—David O. McKay diary, Sept. 12, 1969**

The First Presidency has assigned to the Relief Society the exclusive distribution of authorized pattern garments. This assignment, however, does not include responsibility for directing the purchaser with regard to the proper wearing of the garment. Such instruction should be given at the time of interviews for temple recommends by the bishops and stake presidents.

In assigning garment distribution to the Relief Society, the First Presidency specifically stated: "... remember always, sisters, that your responsibility is not to regulate the wearing of the garment, but to see that it is distributed according to directives which are given by the presiding authorities of the Church."

Instructions for the proper wearing of the garment are also given in the temple at the time the endowment is received. Questions which may arise following this should be referred to the local Priesthood authorities issuing the recommend. They, in turn, may refer questions to the presiding authorities of the Church.

Any deviation from instructions issued by Priesthood authority with regard to wearing the garment bearing the authorized pattern label, or any modifications made by a person in regard to the design of the garment become the responsibility of the individual. Latter-day Saints privileged to wear this sacred clothing know the blessings attendant upon its proper wearing and care. **—David O. McKay, Hugh B. Brown, and N. Eldon Tanner to General Authorities and Regional Representatives of the Twelve, Oct. 22, 1969**

President [N. Eldon] Tanner mentioned proposed changes in the dialogue in the temple rituals, some of which he said had been implemented and some will be implemented on the tape and film that are being prepared. He said that some of these are intended to save repetition and others to clarify the statements made. He said the changes proposed were minor, and mentioned one or two changes as an illustration of what it is proposed to do. President Tanner said that a few of these suggested changes had been presented to President McKay some time ago by Elder ElRay L. Christiansen and had received his approval.

Elder [Harold B.] Lee said that we must assume that all that has been done is under the inspiration of the Almighty to the Presidency and the Twelve, which is the legislative body of the Church. He said, "If you will tell us that you have that inspiration and you now bring that for our approval, I will have no question, but when you sit down to make changes in some things that we have had for a whole century, I have some reservations."

The brethren discussed at some length the various parts of the ceremony and proposed changes, but there was some opposition expressed to the proposal to make changes at this time, especially without reading carefully and discussing the proposed changes. Elder [Marion G.] Romney said he had confidence in the President, and that everything he says he would sustain. He also had great confidence in President Tanner and the other brethren, and was willing to rest on their judgment, but he did not want to pass on anything without knowing what it is. He said he was willing to leave it to the committee if it is thought that is what should be done, but if they wanted his opinion on it he had to know what it is, and wouldn't want to vote to pass this as long as there was one person in the Council who questioned it. **—David O. McKay diary, Oct. 23, 1969**

....

Bishops and stake presidents are reminded that when they are interviewing young people for temple recommends for marriage, the young people and their families should be told there must be no rice thrown around the temple grounds. Furthermore, it should be made clear that it is improper to deface or decorate automobiles that are to be parked near the temple. Honking horns and dragging objects behind automobiles are also violations of good taste in the proximity of the temple. Such customs are not in keeping with the sacredness of the temple marriage ordinance. **—*Priesthood Bulletin*, July 1970, 3-4**

A female Church member married to a nonmember is not permitted to receive a temple recommend for her endowment blessing. The same applies to a female member married to a Church member who has not received his endowment, even though the husband is willing to give his consent in writing for his wife to receive her endowment.

Furthermore, Church leaders should not urge young unmarried female members to obtain their endowments unless they are to be married in the temple or are preparing to go on missions. An unmarried female member should be authorized to obtain her endowment only when her age and maturity justify it. … **—*Priesthood Bulletin*, Aug. 1970, 1, 6**

Frequently couples whose parents, one or more, are not members of the Church desire to be married by civil ceremony before going to the temple so that the nonmember parent may witness the marriage. It is contrary to policy to grant such requests.

In lieu thereof, if the parties concerned desire to do so, they may arrange through the bishop of the bride or groom for the holding of a meeting in a cultural hall or some room other than the chapel subsequent or prior to the temple marriage which the nonmember parents and other friends may be invited to attend. This meeting might include a musical number, such as a vocal selection, and prayer; and the bishop of the ward or some other qualified person might explain to those present the principle of eternal marriage. There would, however, be no exchanging of vows nor marriage ceremony of any kind as a part of this arrangement. Under no circumstance may a civil marriage ceremony follow a temple marriage. This would be mockery and something that cannot be condoned. **—*Priesthood Bulletin,* Sept. 1970, 3-4**

Consideration has been given to the various methods of presenting the endowment ceremonies in the temples. We have learned that in some temples the endowment ceremony has been given by voice on tapes alone, where no picture is shown by film or slide nor by live dramatization.

After giving careful consideration to this matter, we now request that hereafter the endowment not be presented merely by tape recordings. We are certain that some reflection on this matter will convince you that this is the least effective method of teaching and that other methods are much more satisfactory both for those going through for their own endowments or as proxies for those deceased. **—Joseph Fielding Smith, Harold B. Lee, and N. Eldon Tanner to temple presidents, Dec. 9, 1970, copy in Buerger Papers**

Ofttimes female members of the Church receive their endowments in a certain temple and then for varying reasons enter a different temple later on with their intended husband to whom they expect to be sealed for time and eternity.

As you know, on such occasions the sister is to convey to her intended husband in the "short veil ceremony" her new name which she received in the temple at the time she was endowed. Quite often they have forgotten what this new name is and thus she cannot give it to him and disappointment follows.

Because of its sacred and confidential nature, this information should not be transmitted by mail or by telephone; therefore, the First Presidency recommends that you use a simple code system which will be made known to each temple president who will keep it in a special file. The information requested may then be transmitted by letter or if necessary by telephone using combinations of numbers. The information will be given only by a temple president to another temple president—never to the patron directly.

Of course, the need for this applies only to those sisters who were endowed prior to January 1, 1965, when the present new name system was adopted.[38]

The method is this: Instead of spelling out the new name, the numbers corresponding to the letters in the name should be transmitted along with a person's name and date of the endowment.

example:

A	B	C	D	E	F	G	H	I	J	K	L	M	N	O	P	Q	R	S	T	U	V	W	X	Y	Z
1	2	3	4	5	6	7	8	9	10	11	12	13	14	15	16	17	18	19	20	21	22	23	24	25	26

If the name given were Martha, the numbers transmitted would be: "The information you seek on behalf of __________ is 13-1-18-20-8-1."

We ask that after January 1, 1971, all temple presidents use the simple code system herein outlined when transmitting the new name on behalf of patrons who need such information. **—Joseph Fielding Smith, Harold B. Lee, and N. Eldon Tanner to temple presidents, Dec. 21, 1970, copy in Buerger Papers**

38. On the date mentioned, names were standardized Church-wide so that those being endowed on a specific day received the same new name for women or the same new name for men.

7.

"GREAT CARE AND ATTENTION" 1971–1980

Any temples now manufacturing ceremonial clothing or other items of clothing for temple wear are requested to discontinue doing so. Sewing rooms in temples should be maintained only for the repair or reconditioning of clothing. **—Joseph Fielding Smith, Harold B. Lee, and N. Eldon Tanner to temple presidents, Jan. 6, 1971, copy in Buerger Papers**

Occasionally a serviceman desiring a temple recommend cannot be interviewed conveniently by the mission president or the stake president who presides over the area in which he serves. For this reason, we now extend to all mission presidents and stake presidents (not their counselors) who preside over areas which include or which are near operating temples, authority to interview servicemen and, if they find them worthy, to countersign their temple recommends. This authorization is expressly conditioned upon the requirement that any serviceman coming for such interview must present either a temple recommend or a letter of recommendation signed by the leader of the Church military group to which he belongs. In each instance the stake or mission president who countersigns the temple recommend should conduct a careful, searching interview to make certain that the applicant is in every respect qualified to enter the temple. …

When garments are too worn for use, the marks of the priesthood should be removed from them and burned or otherwise obliterated. Worn-out temple clothes should have the significant identifying features rendered unrecognizable. The fabrics of which garments and temple clothing were made then have no further significance as sacred clothing of the Church.

Garments and temple clothing that are freshly laundered and in good condition for wear, but for which an individual no longer has use, may be given to a worthy Church member or sent to a bishop's storehouse for distribution. Under no circumstances should this clothing be sent to the Deseret Industries for resale. …

The *General Handbook of Instructions,* No. 20, 1968, page 102, item FF, is amended to read as follows: … Temple ordinances for a deceased person, whether a member or nonmember, will not be performed until the expiration of one year from the date of death. This waiting period may be waived upon application to the First Presidency if a deceased person was a member of the Church and worthy to go to the temple but was unable to do so while alive due to circumstances beyond his control, as for example, a confining illness or an age limitation. **—*Priesthood Bulletin,* Feb. 1971, 3-5**

Enclosed are copies of the following memoranda:

"So You Are Going to the Temple"

"Important Information for the Brides and Grooms"

"Concerning Sealings for the Living"

This material is to be used in connection with your interviews with those who are preparing to go to the temple for their own blessings.

The information will, we believe, help you to help them to understand in a general way the nature and meaning of the blessings promised them through the temple ordinances. It will help them also to know what they need to do in preparing for that significant event. **—Joseph Fielding Smith, Harold B. Lee, and N. Eldon Tanner, circular letter, Feb. 12, 1971, copy in Buerger Papers**

SO YOU ARE GOING TO THE TEMPLE

It has come to our attention that many of those planning to go to the temple for the first time are not properly oriented as to what to expect there. Under such circumstances they may fail to receive adequate understanding from their experiences in the temple. Conversely, we have been made aware of the fact that a number of people have been told more than is necessary about the temple ordinances before they go there.

It is most important for bishops and stake presidents to conduct helpful and instructive personal interviews with their members who are preparing to go to the temple for their own endowments, as well as for certain other purposes.

A good number of bishops and stake presidents have asked for suggestions and some guidelines as to what should be covered in such interviews.

A searching interview should be conducted by the bishop and also by the stake president to determine whether or not—

1. The applicant has a testimony of the Gospel.
2. He supports local and General Authorities.
3. Accepts and follows the teachings and programs of the Church.
4. Keep[s] the Word of Wisdom, uses drugs.
5. He is morally clean—free from adultery, fornication, homosexuality.
6. He is in good standing in the Church.
7. He is free from legal entanglements.

Without discussing the intimate ordinances and other sacred matters which should not be spoken of outside the temple, a general explanation of the origin, purpose, and blessings of the endowment should be given. This explanation should be given after it has been determined that the applicant has met the requirements necessary to enter the temple worthily.

Guidelines for Explaining the Purpose and Blessings of Temple Ordinances:

1. Personal Commendation—The person should first of all be commended for being worthy and desirous of entering the temple and participating in the sacred ordinances. This might be done in a manner such as follows: You are to be commended and congratulated for your desire to enter the holy temple. It will be one of the most important and significant days of your life on earth, if you keep the covenants you make with the Lord. Not only are you to be commended for your desire to go to the temple, but for having lived so that you may be considered worthy to go. It is important that you continue to be worthy

because the marvelous blessings promised through the ordinances received can be realized only upon your faithfulness in keeping the commandments of the Lord. "... when we obtain any blessing from God, it is by obedience to the law upon which it is predicated" (D&C 130:20).

While most of what you will learn in the temple should be learned in the temple itself, there are some things that I, as your bishop, can tell you which should make your first visit there more enjoyable and edifying.

2. Purpose of the Temple—Most people who go to the temple the first time do so to receive their own endowments and to be sealed for time and eternity. Many members go to the temple to be baptized for the dead, or to be sealed to their parents who initially were not married in the temple. The majority of the people you will see in the temple, however, will have been there many times before. They will be doing vicarious work for the dead.

All this ceremonial work, which takes place in the temple (baptisms, ordinations, endowments, marriages, and other sealing ordinances) is necessary for the exaltation of the living and of the dead.[1] ...

3. The "Endowment"—Before a person can be married (or sealed as husband and wife) in the temple, he (or she) [must have] received the ordinances of the "endowment."

What comprises the temple endowment? The Prophet Brigham Young gave this excellent definition of the endowment:

"Let me give you a definition in brief. Your endowment is to receive all those ordinances in the House of the Lord, which are necessary for you, after you have departed this life, to enable you to walk back to the presence of the Father, passing the angels who stand as sentinels, being enabled to give them the key words, the signs and tokens pertaining to the Holy Priesthood, and gain your eternal exaltation in spite of earth and hell" (Discourses of Brigham Young, p. 637).

As you receive your endowment, you will be given instruction relative to the purposes and plans of the Lord in creating and peopling the earth. You will be taught that which must be done in order to gain exaltation. These matters are so sacred the Lord has withheld

1. This passage is credited to Elder John A. Widtsoe's lecture, "Temple Worship Is an Avenue to Exaltation in God's Kingdom," delivered to the Genealogical Society of Utah, Oct. 12, 1920, excerpted in *Temple Worship*, a pamphlet published by the BYU stake presidencies, 1964.

them from the knowledge of the world and disclosed them only to the faithful in certain places dedicated for this purpose. (D&C 95:8-9; 124:25-41; Luke 24:49.)

Elder James E. Talmage has given us a clear description of the endowment:[2] …

To endow is to enrich, to give something long-lasting and of much worth to another. The endowment ordinances enrich in three ways:

(a) The one receiving the ordinance is given power from God. "Recipients are endowed with power from on High" (Bruce R. McConkie, Mormon Doctrine [2d ed., 1966], p. 227).

(b) A recipient is also endowed with information and knowledge. "They receive an education relative to the Lord's purposes and plans …" (ibid.).

(c) When sealed at the altar a person is the recipient of glorious blessings, powers, and honors, as part of his endowment.

4. Initiatory Ordinances—Washings, Anointings, and Receiving the Sacred Garment—Associated with the endowment are washings and anointings—mostly symbolic in nature, but with definite, immediate blessings as well as future blessings promised.[3] …

Also, you will be officially clothed in the garment of the Holy Priesthood and promised marvelous blessings in connection with it.

As these ordinances are administered it is important that you listen carefully and try to remember the blessings promised and the conditions upon which they will be realized.

5. Temple Clothing—People who enter the temple to be married or to participate in other sacred ordinances change from their everyday clothes to plain, clean white clothing. President Hugh B. Brown has suggested the reason for this:[4] …

All clothing necessary for participating in the temple ordinances is available at the temple and may be rented for a nominal price. This clothing may also be purchased, if one so wishes, from Relief Society Distribution Centers where clothing for temple use may be available.

---

2. See James E. Talmage, *The House of the Lord* (Salt Lake City: Bookcraft, 1962), 99-101.

3. See D&C 124:37, 39.

4. See Hugh B. Brown, *Continuing the Quest* (Salt Lake City: Deseret Book, 1961), 3, also cited in Wilson K. Anderson, *An Endowment for the Faithful* (Provo: Privately printed, 1962), 24.

Wedding dresses for use in the temple may be rented at the temple in addition to the other clothing. If a bride wishes to bring her own wedding dress to the temple, she may do so, provided it meets the standards prescribed. The dress should be white or "off white," and should be reasonable and acceptable in length, and should cover the arms, and have a high neck. Dickeys are available at the temple to cover the arms and neck, if this coverage is not provided otherwise.

People who go to the temple for the first time should purchase beforehand part of the temple clothing referred to as the "Temple Garment," of a non-ceremonial pattern, so that he or she may have it to wear upon leaving the temple. These "garments" should be worn whenever normal clothing is worn, and will require that sisters, particularly, will select clothing that will be modest and becoming to a Latter-day Saint. Various approved styles with proper measurements may be discussed at Relief Society Distribution Centers where they are available. …

6. Sacred Nature of Temple Ordinances—The ordinances of the temple are so sacred that they are not open to the view of the public, but only to those who qualify through righteous living to participate in them. Likewise, their sacred nature is such that discussion of them outside the temple is [i]nappropriate.

7. Temple Ordinance Workers—Throughout the temple there are people who are assigned to assist you at all times. When going to the temple for the first time you may be assured that you will not be left unattended. If any of the instructions given you throughout the endowment session are forgotten, please do not hesitate to take advantage of the many opportunities given you to seek help from temple officiators while in the temple.

8. Recommends—After a thorough personal interview[,] a temple recommend is issued to the person by his bishop. The recommend is for his personal use only. Never should it be "loaned" to another. This recommend provides for admittance to all temples of the Church and authorizes participation in the ordinances specified by the bishop on the recommend. After obtaining the recommend from the bishop, the recipient should make an appointment with the stake president for approval and signature. The member of the stake presidency will interview the person in turn, and if the candidate successfully completes the interview, will sign the recommend. After signing the recommend himself, the person should take it to the temple where it will be examined

and stamped by a temple worker inside the temple. The recommend should be kept on the person while in the temple, and taken to the temple each time he or she wishes to be admitted. Make certain that each one understands that he will not be admitted to a temple without a proper recommend which has been signed by both the bishop and the stake president. …

9. Blessings of Temple Activity—Apart from the blessings coming to participants from receiving sacred ordinances necessary for exaltation of the living and the dead, are other blessings. Participation in temple ordinances, among other things, provides dynamic, vivid, useful instruction in gospel principles. It provides a place for meditation and worship—a place for contemplation and prayer. The temple is a sanctuary from the world, and is a bit of heaven on earth.

As a result of continued temple activity[,] a person is more aware of the world in which he lives, more dedicated to the purposes of God, and better equipped to deal with and overcome the trials and temptations of life. It is for this reason, that you are to be congratulated for choosing to accept the blessings of the temple, and are encouraged to return to the temple frequently and regularly. **—Attached to Joseph Fielding Smith, Harold B. Lee, and N. Eldon Tanner, circular letter, Feb. 12, 1971; emphasis in original**

IMPORTANT INFORMATION FOR THE BRIDES AND GROOMS

As you make preparations to go to the temple to be married, it is important that you heed the following information:

1. RECOMMENDS: Procure your temple recommend for marriage(s) from your bishop(s), and before leaving the bishop, be sure he has initialed[,] in the spaces provided for this purpose[,] all ordinances you desire to receive. …

If you have been civilly married for less than one year, or if your baptismal date is less than one year from your anticipated first visit to the temple, you must bring a letter of permission from the First Presidency granting permission for your sealing and/or your early endowment.

2. LICENSE: If you are to be married, you should obtain a marriage license valid in the county or other civil jurisdiction where the temple is located. For example, out-of-state licenses are not legal in

Utah. You should check on the legal requirements for marriage in the state or country in which your marriage is to be solemnized. It will be necessary to bring your marriage license with you to the temple.

3. BLOOD TESTS: In Utah and in most other states and in some countries in order to procure a marriage license, you must present an official certificate showing the results of serological (blood) tests. (Out-of-state blood tests are acceptable in Utah if they are dated within 30 days of the date you obtain the license.) There is no required waiting period in Utah for the issuance of the license or for the performance of the marriage ceremony. However, you should determine if, in other states or countries, there are such requirements for obtaining a marriage license.

4. AGE: If the groom is under 21 and the bride is under 18, a license may be obtained in Utah, provided the applicant presents a notarized statement giving the consent of his or her father, mother, or legal guardian when and if one of these cannot be present. These requirements may be different elsewhere.

5. TIME: If you plan to go on an endowment session and to be married immediately thereafter, you should be at the temple 45 minutes to one hour before the session is scheduled to begin. This will give opportunity to be made ready. No appointment is necessary for marriages performed under these conditions.

6. SCHEDULED MARRIAGES: If you plan to be married at a special time, you should make an appointment with the person at the "Marriage Desk" well in advance for the day and the hour you wish to be married. In order to be ready on time, you should be at the temple well in advance of the hour set for the marriage.

7. INVITED GUESTS: If you expect to have relatives or friends attend the marriage, please inform the "Marriage Desk" [of] the appropriate number. Bear in mind that only those who have received their own endowments and who present valid temple recommends are permitted to attend.

Will you please remind all guests to come properly dressed. Also urge them to be on time. Guests who arrive late cannot be admitted to the sealing room after the ceremony has commenced.

8. WITNESSES: If convenient, please arrange for your two male witnesses to accompany you to the temple the day of your wedding so that all papers can be signed upon your arrival at the temple. If you are coming alone and do not have witnesses, the temple will provide them.

9. APPROPRIATE CLOTHING: Your bishop can furnish you with information as to the purchase or rental of appropriate clothing while you are in the temple. Be sure to bring approved-style garments to wear when you leave the temple. These can be purchased at the Garment Distribution Center, 107 East South Temple, or the Relief Society Building, 76 North Main, or from your stake Relief Society Distribution Centers where clothing for temple use may be available.

NOTE: If you do not have sufficient funds to purchase garments to wear upon leaving the temple, inform your bishop and he, no doubt, will find ways and means to assist you.

Street clothing worn to the temple should be modest and clean. Church standards should be observed. Sisters should not come to the temple dressed in mini-skirts or slacks. Brethren coming to witness the marriage should wear a long-sleeved white, or a light-colored shirt, with a tie and jacket.

10. WEDDING GOWNS: If you have a wedding gown delivered to the temple or if you bring it yourself, it will be taken by an attendant to the Brides' Dressing Room and held for you. You are responsible for all other personal items, which can be placed in private lockers available to you. If you intend to use your own gown, it is suggested that the sleeves be wrist length. Shoes should be white or nearly so with low or medium heels. There are many shades of white, so do not be too concerned about the shade, as long as it falls in the white category.

11. After your marriage if you desire to take pictures on the temple grounds, you are welcome to do so. If desired, the bride may wear her wedding gown. When you arrive at the temple, all cameras must be checked at the recommend desk. Photographers, and anyone without recommendations, including non-members, will be welcome to wait in the outer foyer until you are ready to take pictures. They can then join the wedding party on the temple grounds. No pictures may be taken inside the annex or in the temple proper.

12. Many have found it desirable to go to the temple for their own endowments and perhaps more than once before their marriage ceremony so that they might understand more clearly the purpose of the temple ordinances and their significances with reference to the temple marriage ceremony.

13. It is urged that young married couples return often to the tem-

ple to renew their covenants and to be reminded frequently of their obligations and responsibilities.

14. Couples planning to be married in the temple should be encouraged to use the regular temple officiators who have been given the sealing power and are on duty for this very purpose. They should be discouraged from asking General Authorities to perform such marriages. **—Attached to Joseph Fielding Smith, Harold B. Lee, and N. Eldon Tanner, circular letter, February 12, 1971; emphasis in original**

CONCERNING SEALINGS FOR THE LIVING

The purpose of this memorandum is to set forth information that will be helpful to you who are coming to the temple for sealings, subsequent to your civil marriage and for those parents whose children are to be sealed t[o] them.

1. If you are coming to the temple for the first time and plan to receive your own endowments before the sealing, our receptionists will direct you to the interviewing department where all necessary arrangements can be made. In this event, you should come to the temple no later than one hour before the session on which you plan to go begins.

2. If you are coming to be sealed after a civil marriage, be sure to bring complete current temple recommends (including the right-hand side) signed by both your bishop and stake president.

3. Unless otherwise authorized, there is a one-year waiting period after baptisms and civil marriages before sealings can take place. However, if the reason for not being married in the temple was that one of the parties had not been a member for a year then, with the approval of the First Presidency, the sealing can take place any time after the year expires from the date of baptism. Any exceptions must be approved by the First Presidency. Please bring the letter of approval with you where exceptions are involved.

4. If a couple are to be sealed and one spouse is deceased, or if deceased children are to be sealed to parents, there is a one-year waiting period from the date of death before the sealings can take place. …

6. If adopted children are involved, then you must bring a final Decree of Adoption OR a Birth Certificate showing the adopting parents as the mother and father. If there are some other children in the family, please put their names on the same family group sheet with the adopted children.

7. If children of a previous marriage (living and under age 21, or deceased, who have not been legally adopted) are to be sealed, a letter of consent from the other spouse, if living, must be brought to the temple. Such names must be on a separate family group sheet showing their blood parents.

8. The only children permitted to witness the sealing of children to parents are the brother(s) and sister(s) (including adoptions) of those to be sealed.

9. Those over twenty-one (and married daughters under twenty-one) must have received their own endowments in order to be sealed or to witness sealings.

All children eight years of age and over must have been baptized and MUST have a temple recommend. (Exceptions may exist for some mentally retarded children.)

10. The temple nursery will care for the children to be sealed and the children who are permitted to witness the sealing. Necessary clothing may be obtained at a nominal rental fee; however, if desired, items of white clothing may be brought with the children: e.g. underwear, white socks, white shirts, white blouses, skirts, or dresses, etc. No shoes are required for children. The nursery attendants will see that all of the children are dressed in white before they are taken to the sealing room.

11. If a mature person comes to the temple whose name is on the family group sheet as a parent or child and who, through his or her own knowledge, can vouch for the accuracy of the information shown on the sheet, then the sheet need not be submitted to the Genealogical Society before coming to the temple to accomplish the work, even though one or more deceased persons' names are included on the sheet. All other records of deceased persons must be submitted to the Genealogical Society for processing.

12. If there are adult guests (who have received their endowments and who hold current temple recommends) coming to witness the sealing only, they should go directly to the "Marriage Waiting Room" or the linen room, where they can obtain white slippers before being directed to the sealing room.

Guests should be advised to come to the temple in clean, modest clothing in keeping with the Church standards. Brethren should wear a clean, long-sleeved white shirt, or a light colored shirt, a tie, and a suitcoat or jacket.

13. Your bishop can furnish you with information as to the purchase or rental of appropriate clothing while you are in the temple. Be sure to bring one pair of the approved-style garments to wear when you leave the temple.[5]

14. Cafeteria facilities are available in some temples for the use of temple patrons, or desired food or drink may be brought for the very young.

Volunteer workers will assist you in every possible way while you are in the temple. They are most anxious to bring joy and happiness into your lives. We are sure the Lord is pleased when we take hold of our blessings as you are doing by going to the temple. Please return often. **—Attached to Joseph Fielding Smith, Harold B. Lee, and N. Eldon Tanner, circular letter, Feb. 12, 1971; emphasis in original**

We call to your attention the following regulations as applied to [temple] garments:

1. Individuals who have received their endowments who desire to make garments for themselves or a family member may do so.
2. Individuals, as such, are not authorized to make garments for sale.
3. The practice of a group of sisters meeting together to make garments is not approved. Should a sister need help in making garments, it would be given through the stake Relief Society president in the privacy of a home.
4. Because of the sacred character of garments, Relief Society Presidents should not permit Relief Society members to sew garments during a Relief Society meeting or a Relief Society gathering; nor should they sponsor or in any way participate in organizing sewing classes for making garments.
5. The Church does not issue patterns for garments, nor does it issue instructions for making them; neither does it issue to individuals the Approved Pattern label.

Any sister choosing to make garments for herself or family, using as a pattern a pair of garments bearing the Authorized Pattern label which she may have on hand, is reminded that the garment bearing the Authorized Pattern label is made according to specifications set by

5. At this point, the "old style" ceremonial garment was still required to be worn while participating in temple ordinances. "Approved style" referred to the new design (see entry dated Feb. 11, 1972).

The First Presidency. There should be no modification in the design of a garment as approved by The First Presidency. **—Joseph Fielding Smith, Harold B. Lee, and N. Eldon Tanner to All Stake and Mission Presidents, Mar. 9, 1971, copy in Buerger Papers**

In issuing these directives [letters dated Jan. 6, Mar. 9, 1971], we had not fully contemplated the extent of the sewing being done in some of the temples, nor of the quantity of fabrics on hand or the wide variety and differing costs of fabrics being used by the various temples. These matters posed an almost insurmountable problem for the (Beehive) Mills in immediately taking over stocks on hand and in standardizing and properly pricing clothing made from these fabrics.

In light of these problems, we herewith authorize temples [to continue making garments for now and] to phase out their manufacturing on or before July 1, 1971. **—Joseph Fielding Smith, Harold B. Lee, and N. Eldon Tanner to temple presidents, Mar. 11, 1971, copy in Buerger Papers**

It came to my attention yesterday of a lovely woman who was married to a new convert to the Church. Her husband of many years had finally become a member and when she wanted to receive a temple recommendation that she might see their son married, she had not been endowed so her bishop and stake president interviewed her for endowment only and issued the recommendation that she might go to the temple and be endowed and then witness the marriage of her son.

When she arrived at the temple, of course, she was not permitted entrance inasmuch as the new ruling[6] had now been placed into effect that a woman who had not been endowed who was married to a man who has not been endowed may not be endowed until he too receives that blessing. Can you imagine the heartache of that woman as she took her temple clothing which had been purchased in the little suitcase which she had with her and returned to her home? She explained to her newly baptized husband that she was refused entrance into the temple of the Lord. This could all have been avoided if the bishop had read the letter from the First Presidency, if the stake president had read the same letter and if perhaps the Regional Representative had reviewed the contents of that letter with his stake president. **—Thomas S. Monson, address to the Regional Representatives Seminar, Apr. 2, 1971**

6. See *Priesthood Bulletin*, Aug. 1970, pp. 1, 6.

We have felt some concern over the repeated requests by temple presidents for couples from the U.S.A. to be called and assigned to serve as aid[e]s, as set-apart ordinance workers, and in some cases as sealers in the temples in England, Switzerland and New Zealand.

While we realize the necessity of having an adequate number of qualified persons, both male and female, to supervise the work and assist in various ways, it is our feeling that this privilege and obligation rightfully belongs to members living within the area designated for each temple. This was naturally taken for granted when the temples were erected. Even though [foreign volunteers] have borne it willingly, and at considerable sacrifice to themselves, the cost to these "imported" temple missionaries and to the Church is considerable and in some cases rather excessive in amount.

While a few such persons from America will be provided where conditions justify, we now ask you to look over your membership and without conferring with them, send us a list of names of worthy and otherwise qualified men and women, whom you can recommend and who, you believe, can accept such a call for up to eighteen months. If they cannot meet all of the expenses personally, you should then devise ways and means whereby some financial assistance by others will be provided.

Because of the great spread and growth of the Church, the time is here when leaders of each institution and each established unit in the Church must assume their full share of the responsibilities for that unit or institution and become self-sustaining by providing not only the leadership, but also the "man-power" and the means for most of the cost of operations. **—Joseph Fielding Smith and Harold B. Lee to stake and mission presidents in England, Switzerland, and New Zealand, July 7, 1971, copy in Buerger Papers**

....

A deceased person who is to be dressed in temple-burial clothing may be dressed by a family member who has received his or her own endowment. If a family requests dressing service from the Church, a man who has received his endowment would be assigned by the bishop to dress a man; a woman would be assigned by the Relief Society president to dress a woman.

In some areas only a licensed mortician, or his employee, is allowed to handle a deceased body. Where such a regulation exists, a member of the family or an appropriate person assigned by the bishop or Relief Society president may carefully look over the clothing after the body is dressed to make sure that it has been properly placed on the body. Morticians have always been willing to cooperate in this matter. Some morticians permit a family member or an assigned person to be present at the time the temple clothing is placed on the body of the deceased person. …

The body should be thoroughly washed, and if a man, the face shaved, or the beard trimmed, according to the practice of the person while living. A woman's hair should be dressed according to the style usually worn by her while living.

The clothing should be white throughout, except the apron, and should be scrupulously clean.

The garments should be placed on the body first.

The hose should be drawn up over the garment leg.

The other articles of clothing should then be placed on the body—white shirt and trousers or one-piece approved suit and tie for men, white slip and dress for women.

The robe should be placed on the right shoulder and tied with the drawstring at the waistline at the left.

The apron should be tied about the waist in a bow.

The girdle [sash] should be placed around the waist and tied in a bow over the left hip. It should be so placed as to cover the top of the apron, the ribbon strings of the apron, and the drawstring of the robe.

The moccasins, with a cuff, should be placed on the feet over the hose.

The man's cap is usually placed at the side of the body until time to close the casket, at which time it should be placed on the head with the bow over the left ear, and the tape tie (at the opposite side of the cap) attached to the robe at the right shoulder.

The woman's veil should be placed on the head with the short ruffled part at the back of the neck. A part of the hair should show below the veil over the forehead. The body of the veil may be softly draped on the pillow at the back of the head until time to close the casket, at which time it is drawn over the face.

In no instance should a flower or branch be placed on the temple clothing worn by a woman. If desired, a handkerchief may be placed in her hand. …

When a viewing takes place under circumstances where a number of persons attending the viewing do not understand the sacred meaning of the clothing and thus might be led to question, authorization is granted to provide a plain white coverlet to be used only insofar as necessary to cover the apron itself. Decision as to the use of such a coverlet would rest with the local priesthood authority, and an explanation regarding the decision would be made to the family. (The coverlet is to be removed at the time the casket is closed.) **—*Instructions for Making Temple Clothing and Clothing the Dead* (Salt Lake City: Church of Jesus Christ of Latter-day Saints, 1972), 13-14**

For your information we may say that some years ago the First Presidency and the brethren of the Twelve authorized certain modifications in the style of the temple garment. These modifications consisted of the following changes: (1) collar eliminated, (2) closed crotch, (3) buttons instead of strings, (4) legs to knee, and (5) short sleeves.

It is the mind of the First Presidency and the Council of the Twelve that this modified garment may be used by those who desire to adopt it without violating any covenant they make in the House of the Lord and with a clear conscience, so long as they keep the covenants which they have made. This modified garment does not supersede the old style garment. Either of these patterns may be worn, as Church members prefer, and those using either will not be out of harmony with the order of the Church.

However, in order that there may be uniformity in temple work and that expedition in the administration of the ordinances of the House of the Lord may not be impeded, the brethren have recommended that people doing temple work wear the old style garment. **—Joseph Fielding Smith, Harold B. Lee, and N. Eldon Tanner, letter dated Feb. 16, 1972, copy in Buerger Papers**

Enclosed is a copy of the letter dated February 10, 1972 to us from President Harold Glen Clark[7] of the Provo Temple. As you will see, President Clark inquires whether it is permissible for a Negro and his wife to join a group from the Brigham Young University 6th Stake to serve as proxies in the Temple Baptistry.

Provided that this couple can meet every requirement for admis-

7. Harold Glen Clark (1902-1984) was the first president of the Provo temple, serving from 1972 to 1976.

sion to the temple, there would be no reason why they should not be given temple recommends for the limited purpose of serving as proxies in temple baptisms. **—Joseph Fielding Smith, Harold B. Lee, and N. Eldon Tanner, letter dated Feb. 29, 1972, copy in Buerger Papers**

The Temple Endowment Fund enables individuals who live a long distance from the temple, or who are otherwise unable to attend, to make contributions to assist others to perform temple work. This fund is used to aid patrons who have time and are physically able to perform temple work but who need financial assistance for lunch money or transportation. This fund is important and we encourage contributions to it.

However, some have thought that by making a contribution to the Endowment Fund their temple responsibility has been fulfilled. It was never intended that the payment of money into the Endowment Fund would satisfy the obligation Church members have to do temple work. We cannot buy exaltation. It is obtained only by compliance with all of the commandments, one of the most important of which is seeking out our kindred dead and performing their work in the temple. **—*Priesthood Bulletin*, Apr. 1972, 4**

[In] the *General Handbook of Instructions,* [the section titled] "Sealings after Civil Marriages," says in part that "where a couple are married by a civil ceremony, they should not be recommended to the temple until after a year has elapsed since the civil ceremony was solemnized." This statement has raised the question whether it is in order to recommend worthy couples to attend the temple even though they have to wait for their sealing.

1) If a person has been endowed before a civil marriage and is in every respect worthily qualified to go to the temple, it is proper to issue a temple recommend within the year following the civil marriage, but not a recommend for his own sealing to a spouse until a year has elapsed from the time of his civil marriage.

2) If a person has not been endowed prior to his civil marriage, then no temple recommend may be issued until a year has expired after the civil marriage.

This instruction does not apply at those temples where the civil law requires that marriages be performed outside the temple, provided that the couple go to the temple for their sealing immediately following their civil marriage. Other exceptions may be granted only by the First Presidency ... **—*Priesthood Bulletin,* June 1972, 2**

In late July, 1972, President Harold Glen Cark of the Provo Temple called me into his office and invited me to become a sealer in the Provo Temple. This complimented me very much to be called into such an important ecclesiastical position. I gave him an affirmative answer and he proceeded to give me a very thorough examination regarding my spiritual worthiness. President Clark was pleased with the interview and immediately made an appointment for me to be in President Harold B. Lee's office at 2:00 P.M., August 14, 1972. I quote here from my Journal of the experiences in President Lee's office and subsequent events preparatory to becoming a sealer in the Provo Temple:

August 14, 1972. I had never dreamed or hoped that one day a Prophet of the Lord would lay his hands upon my head and give me a blessing. But this day at 3:00 P.M. President Harold B. Lee set me apart as a sealer in the Provo Temple for both the living and the dead. The note below over the signature of President Lee is a copy of the official record:

["]Salt Lake City, Utah, August 14, 1972. I have this date conferred the sealing power upon Wayne Brockbank Hales to be exercised in the Provo Temple in behalf of both the Living and the Dead. —Harold B. Lee["]

Brother William F. Edwards, an old B.Y.U. friend of mine, was set apart as a sealer in the Provo Temple at the same time. President Lee's prayer in my behalf was in part as follows:

"My Dear Friend and Brother, Wayne Brockbank Hales, by the power of the Holy Melchizedek Priesthood which I hold and as President of the Church of Jesus Christ of Latter Day Saints, I confer upon you the sealing power to be exercised in the Provo Temple for both the Living and the Dead." He then continued to bless me for my faithfulness for keeping God's commandments[,] my services as Bishop and Stake President[,] my help and inspiration to hundreds of young men and women over the years[,] [and] my willingness now to function as a sealer in the Provo Temple." He promised me many fine experiences: That my health would be good and life will be sustained for this service. That I would have added conviction to the efficacy of the ordinances and that my testimony would be magnified. That I would have spiritual experiences and that I would feel close to departed loved ones. That my home would be one of peace and love and that I would have the complete support of my wife and family. That I would give counsel, faith and conviction to many saints who come to the Temple to do ordinance work both for the living and the dead. That great joy would be in the heart because of the services I perform for those who come to the temple.

I do not know [if] I [ever] felt hands weigh heavier upon my head than those of President Lee as he set me apart for this service. It seemed to me he wanted to impress me with the weighty responsibilities being placed upon me by the calling. It is a great privilege and a great honor to become a sealer in one of the temples in the Church. There are twenty-four who are honored with this calling in the Provo Temple. I approach this service very humbly and pray that I can be worthy of the trust and serve both the living and the dead in the true spirit of Elijah. **—Wayne B. Hales, *My Life Story,* 1976, pp. 320–21**

One of the big problems we ran into when I was head of the records processing division was the fact that more and more[,] some of the membership of the Church were in actual fact playing one temple president against another. Under President [N. Eldon] Tanner's leadership we felt there was a need for unity on special decisions. So we gradually developed what we called a confidential section which dealt with a maze of problems in special sealings, problems with excommunications, and what to do in the cases of murder and suicides, sealing cancellations and every thing of this nature that was miscellaneous but nevertheless extremely important. It required a high degree of unity between the various temples on actions to be taken and so on. …

Presently the Temple Committee consists of several of the General Authorities appointed by the First Presidency to see that there is proper coordination between the temples and that there is unity of action. They are predominantly concerned about the performance of ordinances and the ceremonies themselves being constant and the physical structure being handled properly. In general it is concerned that everything is properly handled concerning the management of the temple. …

There were many problems which came up [with the audio recordings], and I am sure that this committee was involved with that ... [and] the problem arose whether we could seal children to parents from a birth record. We would never know for sure whether the parents had their work done and had been sealed. ... [I]n 1972, we made some shift[s] in the sealing procedures, and then still later on under President Lee it was still felt that we should not perform any sealing until we were sure that the endowments had been performed. ... Finally the First Presidency felt, after giving it full consideration, that we could still follow a non-sequential order in certain instances. But this was not finalized in its entirety until just recently. Certain bits of it were, but the entire policy was not [settled until] ... September 1975 [when] the latest decision that affected [the] sequence of ordinances [was made]. **—Henry E. Christianson oral history, Dec. 9, 1975, Jan. 27, 1976, excerpts in Buerger Papers**

We have appointed a Temple Committee to supervise and direct all matters pertaining to the operation of temples. Elder Gordon B. Hinckley of the Council of Twelve has been named Chairman of this Committee, with ElRay L. Christiansen and O. Leslie Stone, Assistants to the Twelve, and Armis Ashby as members.

We have asked that this committee assume the responsibility for the coordination of work in the temples, presentation of the temple ceremony and other matters relating to the operation of the temples, the development and installation of equipment, the supplying of films and the production of films and sound tracks, the making of translations, the preparation of master books and part books, the recruitment and interviewing of temple missionaries, and all other matters incident to the operation of our temples.

We shall ask that before proceeding with any projects related to temple operations you refer them to this committee for consideration and authorization. The committee will also schedule visits by its members to the various temples and will advise temple presidents of the same. All orders for films or other material should be sent to the committee and questions concerning temple operations referred to it. We hope that with the appointment of this committee there may come about a closer coordination of the work.

Elder Hinckley will work closely with President [Harold B.] Lee on all of these matters, so that you may be assured of our personal attention where needed. **—Harold B. Lee, N. Eldon Tanner, and Marion G. Romney to temple presidents, Wetzel O. Whitaker, and J. Thomas Fyans,[8] Nov. 6, 1972, copy in Buerger Papers**

....

As you know, all temple recommends now expire on April 30th each year. This causes members to seek renewals at or near the same time, which results in heavy loads for the bishops and others involved in issuing and approving recommends, even to the extent of not providing enough time for thorough interviews. In order to correct this condition, it is felt advisable to adopt a new plan under which recommends may be issued all during the year.

Worthy members may secure a temple recommend at any time; however, effective immediately, those previously endowed should be encouraged to apply for renewal recommends during the quarter in which their birthday occurs. If desired, husbands and wives could apply at the same time during the quarter in which either one of them has a birthday. ...

With these changes it is our hope that bishops and others who issue or countersign recommends will interview every applicant in depth so as to make sure that only those who are worthy are recommended to enter the temples.[9] **—Harold B. Lee, N. Eldon Tanner, and Marion G. Romney, circular letter, Jan. 26, 1973, copy in Buerger Papers**

The following policy supercedes the instruction included as item 10 of the October 1972 *Priesthood Bulletin.*

1) A recommend issued to a married woman who is going through the temple for her own endowments should be issued in her complete maiden name, followed by her current married name in parentheses: Louise Emma Jones (Archer), for example.

2) A recommend issued to a woman who previously has been endowed should be issued in her given name, initial, and current married name: Louise J. Archer, for example. The sealed name of a married

8. John Thomas Fyans (1918-) was called as an Assistant to the Quorum of the Twelve in 1974 and sustained as a member of the First Quorum of Seventy in 1976.

9. Beginning on November 1, 2002, temple recommends remained valid for two years rather than one year. See "Temple Recommends Change from Yearly to Biennial," *Church News*, Oct. 26, 2002.

woman will be used on a recommend only when the sealed name is the current married name. …

Church leaders should not urge young, unmarried members to obtain their endowments unless they are to be married in the temple or are called to serve as missionaries. Members should be authorized to obtain their endowments only when worthiness, age, and maturity justify it. ***—Priesthood Bulletin,* Feb. 1973, 6-7**

President Dallin H. Oaks[10] has informed me that advice relative to counseling young men and women about temple endowments is being given by either faculty and/or Church administrators which is not in agreement with Church policies.

It seems that some BYU young women are being encouraged to receive their temple endowment any time after age 19. This counsel is opposed to the Church policy which is to encourage young women to wait until the time near their marriage or prior to receiving mission calls.

I have been informed by the Council of the Twelve office that young men, many of whom are ordained elders at the age of 18, should not be encouraged nor allowed to go to the temple for their endowments. **—Roy W. Doxey[11] to All Full-time BYU Faculty Members, Mar. 9, 1973, Perry Special Collections**

Elder [James A.] Cullimore[12] has discussed with me the matter of your sealing[.] … The problem as I understand it is that you have been told in the past that after your sealing was cancelled and you were sealed to each other that the children born to you could then be sealed to you. It is unfortunate that this has not been understood properly and that there are some disappointed children now as well as disappointment in your own behalf.

10. Dallin H. Oaks (1932-) served as president of Brigham Young University from 1971 to 1980 and was called to the Quorum of Twelve Apostles in 1984.

11. Roy Watkins Doxey (1908-1992) authored several books on LDS scripture and served as BYU Dean of Religious Instruction, director of the Church Correlation Department, and president of the Eastern States mission. He also served as a regional representative of the Church.

12. James Alfred Cullimore (1906-1986) was called as an Assistant to the Quorum of the Twelve in 1966 and later served in the First Quorum of Seventy from 1976 to 1978.

But let me hasten to assure you that you need not have concern about this matter. If your lives and the lives of the children are in order and you are worthy of the blessings of eternity, these blessings will be granted to you and in the justice of the Lord, you will not be disappointed in the sealing of your children.

I can promise you that there is agency in the hereafter as there is in this life and that you will have opportunity of choice and will never need to be sealed to anyone you do not want to be sealed to and that if you are worthy you will have the blessings of your family in being together in the hereafter.

I recall President [David O.] McKay giving an account of just such a circumstance as yours to which he recounted hearing President Joseph F. Smith state to the parents, "Take no concern about the matter. Live the gospel, keep the commandments and the Lord will see to it that proper assignment of our posterity will be made and you will be very happy about it."

I can also promise you that if you accept this and live the gospel and be[come] worthy of the blessings of eternity[,] they will be yours[,] which means that you will have the blessings of posterity as well, knowing that there is a just God and that he will not deprive us of a single blessing we have earned [and] can give us great security. **—Harold B. Lee, letter dated July 18, 1973**

In several instances reported recently, members have commenced to wear temple garments before being endowed. To help prevent this unauthorized practice, the First Presidency has issued the following instructions: Those who go to the temple for the first time should purchase beforehand part of the temple clothing referred to as the temple garment, of a nonceremonial pattern, bearing the "approved pattern" label so that it can be worn upon leaving the temple. This garment should not be worn until after a member has completed the endowment in the temple. …

Next to the temple, the home is the most sacred place to hold [a marriage] ceremony. Requests to have marriage ceremonies performed in the chapel should be discouraged. Receptions following a temple or civil marriage may be held in ward cultural halls. ***—Priesthood Bulletin,*** **Dec. 1973, 1, 4**

....

This is a reply to your letter of May 2, 1974, concerning the problem which Sister H---- T------- has in wearing the temple garment due to her physical disability.

For your information we may say that individual Saints are free to make such alterations in the garment as may be dictated by unusual physical handicaps or disabilities. Where there is a problem such as the one being experienced by Sister T-------, we have taken the position that such modification as may be necessary to accommodate the wearing of the garment to the special physical disability or handicap is permissible. **—Spencer W. Kimball, N. Eldon Tanner, and Marion G. Romney, letter dated May 7, 1974, copy in Buerger Papers; hyphens added to conceal the individual's identity**

President Spencer W. Kimball called me in to notify me that Dantzel[13] and I were to report to the [Salt Lake] temple on June 9[,] [1974]. ...

Dantzel and I were privileged to enter the temple on this Sabbath day to attend a special meeting at the invitation of President Spencer W. Kimball. The sacred nature of this event precludes our mentioning more about it here other than to say that it did take place, but this experience is of the greatest importance to us and to our family.[14] **—Russell M. Nelson,[15] *From Heart to Heart: An Autobiography* (Salt Lake City: Quality Press, 1979), 360**

....

Temple recommends should not be issued to a young man being considered for a call as a missionary until he has received his mission call in a letter from the First Presidency. **—*Priesthood Bulletin*, June 13, 1975**

Those couples planning to be married in the temples should be counseled that space in the sealing rooms is limited and that they should limit the number of guests invited to witness the ceremony. They should contact the temple in advance to determine the number that can be comfortably accommodated and then *limit their invitations accordingly. Only family members and close personal friends who have temple recommends should be invited.*

13. Dantzel White Nelson (1926-2005) married Russell M. Nelson in 1945.

14. The reference here is presumably to the second anointing.

15. Russell Marion Nelson (1924-) was called to the Quorum of the Twelve Apostles in 1984.

Temple marriages are sacred occasions and should not be planned as wedding receptions. Where large groups attend, it is difficult to maintain the order and reverence that should exist in the House of the Lord. ***—Priesthood Bulletin,* Sept. 19, 1975; emphasis in original**

Garment and Temple Clothing Program
[Questions from Relief Society Representatives]

1. Question: Is it permissible to make copies of the instructions for making the men's one-piece [temple garment] suit and give them to each Ward Relief Society President?

Answer: No. The supervision of making the one-piece temple suit is under the direction of the Stake Relief Society President, who has the instructions. …

3. Question: Is there a booklet available to instruct endowed members concerning the wearing of the sacred garments? If not, who is responsible for answering questions about how the sacred garments should be worn?

Answer: No. The regulations for the wearing of authorized pattern garments are set by the First Presidency of the Church. Full instructions with regard to this are given in the temple at the time one receives his or her endowments. Individual questions should be referred to his/her priesthood authority.

It is not within the jurisdiction of [the] Relief Society to give instructions relative to the wearing of the garments or to authorize any modification of the instructions given by the First Presidency.

4. Question: When a garment representative fits the individual for garments before his/her endowments have been received, is it proper for the garment representative to tell him/her that the garment should fall to the knee?

Answer: Yes. It is permissible to inform patrons that the authorized-pattern garment should fall to the knee. …

7. Question: May Ward Relief Society presidents obtain one men's and one women's burial set and store in a locked closet at the Church for emergencies?

Answer: It is preferred that burial sets be handled on a stake basis in order to rotate the burial clothing more frequently. A stake should keep on hand at least one man's and one woman's medium size burial set. In most instances two each of men's and women's burial sets should be kept on hand for emergencies, and reordered immediately upon their use in the stake.

Multiple centers should carry at least three medium and one large burial set for men and three medium sets for women. The medium size fits most individuals.

8. Question: May individuals be buried in their regular temple clothing that has been worn to the temple?

Answer: Yes, with the exception of the shoes. A special moccasin is used in place of the regular temple-wear shoe.

9. Question: May instructions for dressing the dead in the sacred clothing be mailed, and may they be included with the clothing that endowed members request before death in order to be sure they have it when needed?

Answer: Stake/mission/district Relief Society Presidents may request copies of "Directions for Clothing the Dead Who Have Received Their Endowments" to be mailed to them from the Relief Society General Board. These copies, however, are for distribution to ward and branch Relief Society presidents only, and are not to be included with burial clothing purchased by individuals.

10. Question: Whose responsibility is it to oversee the dressing of the endowed members for burial?

Answer: A deceased person who is to be dressed in temple-burial clothing may be dressed by a family member who has received his or her endowment. If a family requests dressing service from the Church, a man who has received his endowment would be assigned by the bishop to dress a man; a woman would be assigned by the Relief Society president to dress a woman.

In some areas only a licensed mortician, or his employee, is allowed to handle a deceased body. Where such a regulation exists, a member of the family or an appropriate person assigned by the Bishop or Relief Society president may carefully look over the clothing after the body is dressed to make sure that it has been properly placed on the body. Morticians have always been willing to cooperate in this matter. Some morticians permit a family member or an assigned person to be present at the time the temple clothing is placed on the body of the deceased person. …

14. Question: How do you dispose of worn or discarded garments and temple clothing?

Answer: Under no circumstances is the sacred clothing to be given to any organization, including the Deseret Industries. Garments and temple clothing that are freshly laundered and in good condition for wear, but for which an individual no longer has use, may be given to an endowed relative or to a bishop for welfare purposes.

When garments are too worn for use, the marks of the priesthood should be cut from the garment and either shredded with the scissors or burned. The fabric of which the garments were made then have no further significance as sacred clothing of the Church, and may be used for other purposes if desired, after rendering it unrecognizable as an article of clothing. The authorized-pattern label in the garment should also be cut off and destroyed, or kept for future reference concerning size and style.

When discarding temple clothing, the significant identifying features of the robe, cap and veil are to be removed and destroyed. The fabric could then be cut so as not to be recognized as the sacred clothing and used for other purposes if desired.

When discarding the apron, the entire apron should be destroyed.

15. Question: What is the ruling on sisters making their own or their husband's temple garments?

Answer: Worthy individuals who have received their own endowments may make garments for themselves or a family member upon authorization of the stake or mission president.

The Church does not issue patterns for garments, nor does it issue instructions for making them. The individual would use a pair of garments bearing the Authorized Pattern label for a pattern. There should be no modification in the design or length of the sacred garment as specified by The First Presidency. Any violation of this regulation is an individual responsibility. ...

16. Question: Is it permissible for sisters to put zippers in garments, either for nursing purposes, or in the ceremonial garments to be worn to the temple?

Answer: Any modification of the authorized pattern garment is to be handled on an individual basis. Requests for modification of the sacred garment are to be submitted to the office of The First Presidency. ...
—Temple Clothing Program, minutes, Oct. 3, 1975, excerpt in Buerger Papers

In the future, while involved in temple ordinances, patrons will have the option of wearing either the "approved style" garment (short sleeve and knee length) or the garment with the long sleeve and long leg.[16]

Patrons receiving their initiatory ordinances may be clothed in their own "approved style" garment.

It is suggested that temple presidents not purchase any more of the long-sleeve, long-leg garments for rental purposes. **—Spencer W. Kimball, N. Eldon Tanner, and Marion G. Romney to temple presidents, Nov. 10, 1975, copy in Buerger Papers; emphasis in original**

This is an official invitation to you to present yourself and your wife to receive your Second Anointings.

This is the last and greatest of the ordinances of this life. No mention should be made to anyone. It is most sacred.

This will be given Monday, January 12, 1976, at 3:00 p.m. The place will be the St. George Temple. Please advise me by return mail or telephone if you desire this blessing and can arrange to be present.

You should be prepared with your regular temple clothing.

—Spencer W. Kimball, letter dated Dec. 12, 1975

....

No person should receive a [temple] recommend for any purpose unless found to be worthy in every respect. Interviewers should not assume that worthiness to enter the temple at one time allows for a subsequent casual interview.

Before issuing a recommend the bishop will assure himself by searching inquiry of the worthiness of the applicant in relation to the standards and principles of the Church. These may include the following questions:

1. Are you morally clean[17] and worthy to enter the temple?

---

16. Notifying temple workers of the First Presidency's letter, the Provo temple presidency drew a line in the sand and announced that it would continue to require the old-style garment in some instances. "In the case of regular proxies doing initiatory work, we will use the convenient long legged ceremonial garment," the temple presidency wrote, indicating how entrenched the tradition was and their intent to follow only the letter and not the spirit of the First Presidency's recent advice (*Provo Temple Bulletin*, Nov. 12, 1975).

17. In a supplement to the handbook issued in July 1976, this question was made more explicit to determine whether the individual had "ever been involved in a transgression relating to the law of chastity that has not been resolved with

2. Will you and do you sustain the local and General Authorities of the Church, and will you live in accordance with the accepted rules and doctrines of the Church?[18]

3. Do you have any connection, in sympathy or otherwise, with any of the apostate groups or individuals who are running counter to the accepted rules and doctrines of the Church?

4. Are you a full tithe payer?

5. Are you honest in your dealings with your fellowmen?

6. Do you keep the Word of Wisdom?

7. Do you wear the regulation garments?[19]

8. Will you earnestly strive to do your duty in the Church; to attend your sacrament, priesthood, and other meetings; and to obey the rules, laws, and commandments of the gospel?

9. Have you ever been denied a recommend to any temple? (If so, ascertain date of refusal and name of bishop, ward, and stake.)

10. Have you ever been divorced? If so what was the real reason for the divorce? If the marriage was in the temple, has the divorce clearance been obtained from the First Presidency?

11. Has there ever been a major transgression in your life that has not been confessed and adjusted?[20]

Where an applicant is not keeping the commandments, he should be required to demonstrate his true repentance before a temple recommend is issued. …

---

the appropriate priesthood authorities." By "chastity" was meant abstinence from extramarital sex, not celibacy, as the more common understanding of the word would imply.

18. In the July 1976 supplement, bishops were asked to further request a statement from the candidate proclaiming loyalty to the LDS president as "a Prophet, Seer, Revelator, recognizing no other person on the earth as authorized to exercise priesthood keys."

19. This question was expanded in the July 1976 supplement to inquire whether the candidate wore the "regularly approved garments both night and day."

20. The July 1976 supplement suggested one last question: "Do you consider yourself worthy in every way to go to the temple?" This was intended to cover such issues as "physical or emotional abuse" of one's family. The question was broadened in 1985 to determine whether a man was meeting his financial obligations to an ex-wife and children (Edward L. Kimball, *Lengthen Your Stride: The Presidency of Spencer W. Kimball* [Salt Lake City: Deseret Book Co., 2005], 169). Candidates were later also asked if they believed in "God, the Eternal Father, in his Son, Jesus Christ, and in the Holy Ghost," as well as in the atonement of Christ.

With the following exceptions, everyone who is given a temple recommend, for ordinances other than baptisms for the dead, must have been previously endowed or be presently recommended for his own endowment.

1. Properly recommended, worthy, unendowed, single children (including divorced persons, widows, or widowers with single status) regardless of their age may attend the temple to be sealed to their parents, whether the parents are living or dead. They are not to be permitted to witness the sealing of parents or participate in any other ordinance except where they are qualified to serve as proxies in performing baptisms and confirmations for the dead. *Married, unendowed children regardless of age are not permitted to enter the temple to witness or participate in such sealings.*

2. Worthy, unendowed, single children under age twenty-one [who were] born in the covenant or [were] previously sealed to their parents are permitted to witness the sealing of brothers and sisters, including those adopted, to the parents. Worthy, endowed children may attend such sealings regardless of age. ...

A man should not be recommended to receive his own endowment unless he holds the Melchizedek Priesthood. ...

Young unmarried male or female members should not be recommended by Church leaders to obtain their endowments unless they are to be married in the temple or until they have received their mission call in a letter from the First Presidency. Other young persons should be recommended to receive their endowments only when their age and maturity justify it. ...

A wife whose husband is not endowed *should not be given a recommend to receive her endowment.*[21] (A man who has received his endowment and subsequently is excommunicated from the Church is considered to be unendowed until his blessings are restored.)

Such restriction as in the above paragraph does not apply to a woman legally divorced, or legally separated, nor in such an unusual situation as where the husband has been missing and his whereabouts have been unknown for ten years or more.

Women who received their own endowment before this rule was given or who were endowed before being married, even though mar-

21. Notice that there is no longer any differentiation between husbands who are church members and husbands who are not members.

ried to non-members, may still be issued recommends to do work for the dead if worthy and living in conformity with covenants previously received.

An unendowed, worthy wife whose husband is willing may participate in baptisms and confirmations for the dead. ...

A worthy man whose wife has not received her endowments may be given a recommend to receive his own endowments. ...

A couple married by civil ceremony outside the temple are not to be issued recommends for the performance of ordinances other than baptisms and confirmations for the dead in the temple until after a year has elapsed since the civil ceremony was performed. *This rule does not apply in the following situations*:

1. A person endowed before being married in a civil ceremony, who is worthy to go to the temple, may receive a temple recommend within the year following the civil marriage to do *ordinance work for the dead*. Also a worthy person holding a current recommend may continue to perform the ordinance work for which it was issued.

2. Where civil law requires that marriages be performed outside the temple, provided the couple goes to the temple for their sealing within such reasonable time after their civil marriage as travel permits. This includes civil marriages in Japan and the temple districts of [the] London, Switzerland, and New Zealand temples.

3. Due to the complicated procedure for validating marriages of Mexican citizens that are performed outside of Mexico, it is recommended that civil marriages take place in Mexico prior to sealings in the temple in those instances where the couple plans to reside in Mexico. ... In such cases, worthy couples may come to the temple for their endowments and sealings without the usual one-year waiting period provided they do so within a reasonable time as set forth in 2 above.

4. A couple married by civil ceremony, who were worthy but could not have a temple marriage because either or both had not been members of the Church for one year, may be issued recommends for their endowments and sealing as soon as they have been members for one year. They are not required to wait one year from their marriage date.

5. Still another exception would be where couples are civilly married and travel long distances from other countries with an organized Church group to do temple work. Such situations generally result in substantial savings for the couple to come to the temple.

6. Other exceptions may be granted only by the First Presidency. …

A marriage for time only may be performed in the temple only when the woman has been previously sealed to another man and such sealing has not been cancelled. Both the man and the woman must previously have been endowed and they must present a marriage license valid in the jurisdiction of the particular temple. …

Any person married in the temple, whose spouse has died, and who subsequently marries a divorced person, or an unendowed person, does not thereby violate the temple covenants. …

Exceptional care is to be taken to see that the children of parents belonging to or affiliating with apostate groups are not recommended to the temple, unless it is clearly established that they are completely free from parental domination in any apostate religious matters.[22] …

Where a previously endowed person who is involved in pending divorce, legal separation, or annulment proceedings makes application for permission to go to the temple, brethren authorized to issue temple recommends should carefully and searchingly interview the applicant; if it is found that he or she is innocent of any serious wrongdoing in connection with the pending divorce, legal separation, or annulment and is otherwise worthy, a temple recommend may be issued. However, such recommend should be surrendered to the bishop on the date the divorce becomes final. …

If a worthy man remarries after the death or divorce of his wife, the new wife may be sealed to him. It is not necessary to cancel the sealing or receive permission of the former wife, if living, to permit the sealing of the subsequent wife provided the divorce is final and a divorce clearance has been obtained from the First Presidency. …

In cases where a couple married in the temple obtain a sealing cancellation and during mortality take no further action to restore such sealing, no subsequent request by their descendants or relatives will be approved for the restoration of the former sealing of that couple. The matter in these cases will be left in the hands of the Lord. The only exception to this rule would be where some conclusive evidence can be established by witnesses that both partners had desired to be reunited. …

---

22. The previous policy was more strict in prohibiting children of apostates from entering the temple, without exceptions.

Children may not have the sealing of a parent or parents altered at will. Any alteration of sealing of deceased couples must be … approved by the First Presidency. …

Frequently couples whose parents, one or more, are not members of the Church desire to be married by civil ceremony before going to the temple so that the nonmember parents may witness the marriage. It is contrary to Church policy to grant such requests. In lieu thereof, if the parties concerned desire to do so, they may arrange through the bishop of the bride or groom to hold a meeting in the meetinghouse subsequent or prior to the temple marriage to which the nonmember parents and other friends may be invited; this meeting may be held in the cultural hall or some room other than the chapel. This meeting might include a musical number, such as a vocal selection, and prayer; and the bishop of the ward or some other qualified person might explain to those present the principle of eternal marriage. (A temple sealer should not be asked to give these instructions.) There would, however, be no exchanging of vows nor marriage ceremony of any kind as a part of this arrangement. The above does not apply in areas where the law requires the civil marriage to be performed in a public place. …

Under no circumstance may a civil marriage ceremony follow a temple marriage. This would be mockery and cannot be condoned. …

A living, endowed, married woman, who is not sealed to anyone, can be sealed to a deceased husband only when written consent is given by her living husband. This consent must be presented to and retained by the temple. …

1. A living woman can be sealed only to one husband.

2. A living woman having had more than one civil marriage, but sealed to one of her husbands, has thereby exercised her right of choice and cannot be sealed to any other husband unless the first sealing is cancelled.

3. A deceased woman having had more than one civil marriage, but having been sealed to one of her husbands during life, cannot be sealed to any other husband by proxy because she exercised her election to be so sealed during lifetime.

4. A deceased woman having had more than one civil marriage, but not having been sealed to any of her husbands during her lifetime, may, after the death of all husbands and any of their subsequent spouses, be sealed to any one or to all of her husbands, leaving to the woman and

to the Lord the decision as to which one, if any, of the sealings will become effective.[23] Under this provision, children can be sealed to their own parents unless already sealed to others. …

Children eight years of age and over must have recommends and must have been baptized in order to be sealed to their parents. (Some mentally retarded persons are exceptions. …) Recommends are not needed for children under age eight.

A married child must receive the endowment before being sealed to parents. …

If parents have been sealed in the temple and one or both of them are subsequently excommunicated, any children born to them between the time of their excommunication and restoration of blessings are not born in the covenant and therefore would have to be sealed to their parents after the blessings are restored, providing the parents, if they are both still alive, are living together and are not divorced. …

Children born in the covenant cannot be sealed to anyone else. If children are sealed in life to parents, they are not to be sealed again to anyone else, even though the parents to whom they were sealed later received a cancellation of their sealing. This policy is not altered by adoption consent of the natural parents, request of the child after becoming of age, or death of the natural parents.

A child born to a woman who is already sealed to a husband is born in the covenant of the mother's sealing, whether or not the father of the child is the man to whom she is sealed, and provided neither the mother nor her legal husband are excommunicated at the time of the birth of the child. Birth in the covenant is a birthright blessing which guarantees eternal parentage to the child regardless of what happens to the parents, so long as the child remains worthy of that blessing. No sealing to parents is necessary for a child born in the covenant even if there is a subsequent change in the sealing status of the parents. …

---

23. This resolves the controversy discussed in the previous chapter about whether a deceased woman could only be sealed to her first husband only, or the husband with whom she had the most children, or if she could be sealed to all of her husbands and let the matter be sorted out in the next life. Here a distinction is being made between a deceased woman and one who is still living, for whom the prohibition against being sealed to more than one husband remained even if her previous husband or husbands had died. Notice also how the prerogative of being sealed to more than one individual is explicitly granted to men.

Living, single, unendowed and married, [or] endowed children who are not born in the covenant or who have not been sealed to their natural parents may be sealed to a natural parent and stepparent, or they may be sealed to adoptive parents, under any one of the following circumstances:

1. If the stepparent or adoptive parents have legally adopted the minor children to be sealed and a copy of the final decree of adoption (or certificate of live birth issued in those states using this form of evidence) is presented to the temple president.

2. If the stepparent or adoptive parents to whom the minor children are to be sealed have secured and presented to the temple president a written statement from the natural parent or parents consenting to the proposed sealing.

3. If the children to be sealed are of legal age in the place of their residence and request the temple president for such sealing.

4. Minor children may be sealed to a natural parent and a stepparent without the requirements of adoption in cases where the other natural parent is deceased, except in those instances where the natural parents either have been sealed or are to be sealed. …

Children born out of wedlock may be sealed to their natural mother and the husband to whom she is sealed without the consent of the natural father. Only the natural mother's consent is necessary for children born out of wedlock to be sealed to adoptive parents.

If a child born out of wedlock is abandoned by its mother and is totally supported and cared for by its father, the child may be sealed to the father and the wife who is sealed to him, provided that the evidence of abandonment is conclusive. …

If children are placed in the custody of their father after an action for divorce and he cares for them, these children may be sealed to him and the wife who is sealed to him provided the mother is deceased. If the mother is living, her written consent must be secured before minor children can be sealed to a stepparent. …

No other sealing of children to persons other than natural parents will be permitted except upon written authorization of the First Presidency. …

A person who has been excommunicated after being endowed is not endowed again. Such person becomes a member of the Church by baptism and confirmation, and then only after authorization of the

First Presidency may the endowment be restored to that person by a restoration of blessings to be performed by a member of the First Presidency or the Council of the Twelve. …

In the case of endowed, deceased persons who were excommunicated in life, baptism by proxy must be performed first and then be followed by restoration of former blessings.

However, where deceased persons were known to have been excommunicated for polygamist teachings and activities, vicarious work in their behalf is to be performed only upon obtaining the express permission of the First Presidency.

All restoration of blessings of deceased persons are handled or directed by the president of the Salt Lake Temple after receiving information from the Genealogical Society which processes such names under the direction of the First Presidency. …

Situations arise where an endowment may be performed either in life or by proxy, but where no valid record or proof can be found of baptism preceding the date of the endowment, in all such situations it is necessary to perform a valid baptism by proxy if the person concerned is deceased. If the person is living, he or she should be baptized so that an official record may be made of that ordinance.

Following such baptism the endowment and sealings previously performed must be reconfirmed and ratified by proper authority. …

In the case of a living person, it will be necessary for that person to go to the temple, show a written authorization from the First Presidency and receive the reconfirmation of the endowment and ratification of sealings, if any. A member of the temple presidency or a sealer designated by them will officiate. …

Individuals who cannot come to the temple due to reasons of health or distance of travel should present the letter of authorization from the First Presidency to one of the General Authorities visiting the area. Most General Authorities hold the sealing power and have authority to perform such ordinances. …

It is here emphasized that this procedure does not pertain to excommunicated persons, whether or not they have been reinstated by baptism and had former blessings restored. Actions in such cases come under special procedures …

A living mentally retarded person is judged for temple work on his own behalf on the basis of his established mental age, based on the pattern prescribed for chronological age. A person with a mental age of less than eight years would not require baptism before sealing to parents. A person with a mental age of eight years or above would require baptism before being sealed to parents.

The extent of mental retardation must be determined by special testing administered by a physician, psychiatrist, or other professionally qualified person. A current certificate from such professional person designating the mental age must be presented to the temple president when a request is made for a temple ordinance for such a living mentally retarded person. If a child is under eight years of age, or if already baptized, no certificate is required for sealing to parents.

Temple ordinances by proxy for *living* mentally retarded persons will be performed only in cases of extreme hardship where presence in the temple would be detrimental to the physical or emotional welfare of the person or members of the family, or to the atmosphere of the temple. Permission for such action may be granted only by the First Presidency. …

Temple ordinances for *deceased* mentally retarded persons will be performed in accordance with rules for all deceased persons without consideration of mental retardation. …

No temple ordinances are necessary for stillborn children, and ordinances in their behalf are not performed. …

No endowment is required or will be performed for children who die under the age of eight years. No temple ordinances other than sealing to parents will be performed for such children, provided they were not sealed to parents during their lifetime or were not born in the covenant. …

Blind persons, wherever possible, should have an escort of the same sex who can accompany them through the temple. Where this is not possible, arrangements should be worked out with the temple president to have a temple worker assigned to render such assistance as may be required for the welfare and safety of such patrons.

Seeing eye dogs are not permitted in the temple. …

The Church does not look with favor upon the tattooing of the body, but this does not restrict a person from receiving a temple recommend, unless such tattooing is obscene and unbecoming in the house of the Lord. …

Worthy young men should not be denied a temple recommend

because their hair is too long. Good grooming should be encouraged through love, kindness, persuasion, and understanding. Rigid rules must not be established that would prohibit those in this category from participation in sacred priesthood ordinances including ordinances of the temple. However, they should be counseled to keep their hair clean and presentable. **—*General Handbook of Instructions,* Number 21 (Salt Lake City: Church of Jesus Christ of Latter-day Saints, 1976), 53-66, 98-99; emphasis in original**

When a person who has been sealed previously is involved in divorce, legal separation, or annulment and is guilty of a moral transgression, clearance must be obtained from the First Presidency before that person may obtain a temple recommend. This policy includes an individual who has been divorced after a civil marriage if he (she) has been sealed in a prior marriage. To obtain such clearance, the applicant should complete in detail an Application to the First Presidency for Divorce Clearance. The bishop can obtain this form from the Office of the First Presidency. However, if a person who has been sealed to a spouse commits adultery which is the cause of a divorce or which results in the breaking up of a home or homes, such person cannot be sealed to the one with whom the adultery occurred. If any exceptions are made to this rule, they must be authorized by the First Presidency.

In all other cases involving divorce, legal separation, or annulment, permission to go to the temple may be granted by the bishop and stake president. Such persons desiring to obtain a temple recommend should go through the regular procedure of interviews regarding worthiness. These cases would include persons never sealed in the temple and persons previously sealed in the temple but not involved in moral transgression.[24] **—*General Handbook Supplement,* July 1976, p. 3**

The prime responsibility of temple presidents is to operate the temples in the best possible manner so as to properly serve the patrons. In so doing it is necessary to work closely with stake and mission presidents in the temple district. Communications with them from time to time will be both necessary and desirable, and this is in order. However,

24. In the *General Handbook Supplement* of April 1977, the First Presidency amended the July 1976 supplement to specify that "divorce clearances as set forth above (whether obtained from the First Presidency or from the bishop and stake president) are required only for the first recommend issued after the divorce."

written communications must be carefully controlled in the interest of economy of materials and postage and the time of stake and mission presidents in reading and acting upon such communications.

In suggesting schedules to stake and missions covering special temple days, baptisms, initiatory ordinances, sealings, priesthood days, etc., the term "invite" should be used rather than "assign." It should always be remembered that stake and mission presidents are not responsible to temple presidents.

Temple attendance is the responsibility of local priesthood leaders. Such motivations as may be necessary to get them to function properly is the responsibility of the Temple and Genealogy Executive Committee. Once each quarter the Genealogical Department will send a report to stakes and missions showing temple attendance for each month, and it is not desirable for temple presidents to duplicate this effort. Reports from temples on special priesthood days are permissible.

Members of the temple presidency may accept invitations to speak in regional, stake, district, ward, or branch meetings. These contacts will provide opportunities to discuss temple matters and assist local priesthood leaders in promoting temple attendance and genealogical research for the benefit of all concerned. This will also help to inform Regional Representatives of the Twelve about temple matters and influence their support. **—Spencer W. Kimball, N. Eldon Tanner, and Marion G. Romney to temple presidents, July 26, 1976, copy in Buerger Papers**

....

The temples are reserved for sacred ordinances pertaining to the living and the dead. Worthy members of the Church should go to the temples as often as possible to participate in this important work. One of the ordinances performed in the temple is that of the endowment, which comprises a course of instruction relating to the eternal journey of man and woman from the preearthly existence through the earthly experience and on to the exaltation each may attain. **—Spencer W. Kimball, "The Things of Eternity—Stand We in Jeopardy?"** ***Ensign*****, Jan. 1977, 6**

Although the Church discourages artificial insemination with other than the semen of the husband, it recognizes this is a personal matter which must ultimately be left to the determination of the husband and wife with the responsibility for the decision resting solely upon them.[25]

25. A circular letter from the First Presidency dated April 19, 1977, added a

However, a child born by means of artificial insemination after parents are sealed in the temple is born in the covenant. A child born by artificial insemination before parents are sealed may be sealed subsequent to the sealing of parents.[26] **—*General Handbook Supplement,* Apr. 1977, pp. 4, 6**

About a year before we received our [mission] call to go to Hungary [in 1978], President Spencer W. Kimball wrote us a personal and sacred letter inviting us to come to Salt Lake and receive a special blessing. So on the date specified we went to Salt Lake and[,] along with ten or twelve others[,] went to the temple and[,] in the Holy of Holies in the Salt Lake Temple[,] were given the Second Endowment. It was very sacred and very impressive and a great comfort to us. We feel so grateful for this special blessing and ... feel that if we remain true and faithful to the Church and to the Lord, our calling and election are sure. **—Joseph T. Bentley,[27] *Life and Family of Joseph T. Bentley: An Autobiography,* privately published, 1981, p. 142**

When an interview reveals a transgression not previously resolved with the appropriate priesthood leader, the length of elapsed time, the present worthiness of the individual, the extent to which the transgression is widely known, and the quality of repentance must all be carefully considered in deciding (a) whether formal disciplinary action is to be taken; and (b) the nature of any discipline to be imposed. Where circumstances warrant, including evidence of sincere repentance, a common judge [bishop] has the right to waive court action.

Confidentiality in handling all such matters is of utmost importance. **—Spencer W. Kimball, N. Eldon Tanner, and Marion G. Romney, circular letter, Aug. 29, 1977, copy in Buerger Papers**

This is an official invitation from the President of the Church for

---

caveat that "artificial insemination with semen other than from the husband may produce problems related to family harmony."

26. Couples began turning to artificial insemination in the 1940s, and by 1955 over 50,000 women had become pregnant through this method. By the 1970s the methods had become refined enough that the practice was more or less uncontroversial, prompting the First Presidency to address the issue.

27. Joseph Taylor Bentley (1906-1993) was general superintendent of the Young Men's Mutual Improvement Association, serving from 1958 to 1962, as well as an assistant to BYU President Ernest L. Wilkinson during the 1960s.

you and your wife to receive the most holy second anointings which it is planned will be given to you in the Salt Lake Temple on Sunday, October 23, 1977, at 3:00 p.m.

For this you should arrange to bring your temple clothing and come also with a temple recommend. Other instructions will be given to you at that time.

If you wish to receive these blessings, please advise me immediately by letter. These blessings are to be given only upon your total worthiness. We would like you to indicate in your reply regarding this matter.

This whole program should be totally confidential; and as a reply to family members as a reason for your leaving home that day, you may say you are going to a special meeting at the temple. …

P.S. If you do accept, please complete and return the enclosed form. **—Spencer W. Kimball, letter dated Oct. 12, 1977**

....

On Thursday mornings at 10 a.m. they [the First Presidency] join with the Council of the Twelve in the upper room of the [Salt Lake] temple, where [generally] the Twelve have been convened since 8 a.m. It is in this room that the leadership of the Church has been directed by the Lord since the temple was completed [in 1893]. …

As the First Presidency enters this room at ten o'clock on Thursday mornings, we shake hands with all members of the Twelve, then change to our temple robes. We sing, kneel in prayer, and then join in a prayer circle at the altar, after which we change to our street clothes. **—N. Eldon Tanner, "Administration of the Restored Church," an address delivered at BYU, Jan. 8, 1978, published in the *Ensign,* Apr. 1978, p. 76**[28]

Before issuing a recommend, the interviewing authorities should assure themselves by searching inquiry of the worthiness of the applicant in relation to the standards and principles of the Church. They should discuss the following with each person: …

11. In speaking of the temple, the Lord made it clear that no unclean thing should enter therein. He also said, "But if there shall come into it any unclean thing, my glory shall not be there; and my presence shall not come into it." (See D&C 94:8–9.) Our Heavenly Father is

---

28. See also N. Eldon Tanner, "The Administration of the Church," *Ensign*, Nov. 1979, p. 47, for similar comments.

very displeased when any of his children engage in impure, unholy, or unnatural sex acts. When a person has been involved in any of these situations, complete repentance is required before a temple recommend is issued. ...

When a woman is properly sealed to a husband in the temple, all children born to her while that sealing remains in effect are born in the covenant. Her sealing is no longer in effect when any of the following occurs:

1. She is excommunicated.
2. The husband to whom she is sealed is excommunicated.
3. Her sealing to her husband is cancelled.

If a woman is sealed to a husband and he is later excommunicated, that sealing (though no longer in effect by virtue of the act of excommunication) must still be formally cancelled before she can be sealed to another husband.

All children born to her while the sealing is not in effect are not born in the covenant and would need to be sealed to parents even if the sealing of the parents is restored after the birth of these children. ...

Without approval from the First Presidency, a living child may not be sealed to a natural parent and a stepparent or to foster parents if any of the following six conditions is known to exist:

1. The child is married and not endowed.
2. The child is born in the covenant while sealed to parents.
3. The child was adopted because both parents died.
4. The child's mother did not give up the child voluntarily for adoption under conditions not involving neglect.
5. The adopting parent is the stepmother, and the natural mother is sealed, or it is planned to have her sealed, to the natural father. (The natural mother can be sealed to the natural father unless she is sealed to another husband before her death.)
6. When the traditional practice (as in Asia or the Pacific) violates the laws of the country in which the child resides.

A person who is twenty-one or older at the time of a sealing request and to whom none of the preceding conditions applies—

1. May be sealed to a natural parent and a stepparent or to foster parents by making a request to a temple president for this sealing. If the person has been adopted, he should present to the temple president documentary proof of the adoption.

2. Must submit a special request to the Genealogical Department and receive clearance to be sealed to a natural parent and a stepparent or to foster parents *if the person was adopted after reaching legal age.*

3. May be sealed to a living mother and a stepfather to whom the mother has been sealed. A person has this right of election because he cannot be sealed to both natural parents in this circumstance.

A person who is under twenty-one at the time of a sealing request *and to whom none of the preceding conditions applies* may be sealed to a natural parent and a stepparent or to foster parents if the parents requesting the sealing present any one of the following documents to the temple president:

1. Copy of the final decree of adoption, or
2. Copy of the revised legal birth certificate, or
3. Written consent to the proposed sealing signed by the other natural parent. If the other natural parent is deceased or missing (as defined in the following paragraph), the consent of the remaining parent will suffice. If a court has withdrawn parental rights permanently from a natural parent because of neglect, the agency or person to whom parental rights were awarded must give written consent to the proposed sealing.

If a natural parent has been missing for more than ten years and is therefore not available to give written consent, a person under twenty-one may be sealed to the other natural parent and a stepparent, subject to future review. However, such a sealing should not be performed if the natural parents are sealed. In this context, the word *missing* means that reasonable efforts have failed to locate the parent. "Reasonable efforts" include contacting relatives and friends and checking records that might reveal the parent's location. The temple president should be satisfied that reasonable efforts have been made to locate the missing parent. …

If the natural parents of a child who has not been adopted legally are not known and cannot be determined by reasonable efforts, the foster parents of the child should request permission from the Genealogical Department to have the child sealed to the foster parents …
—*General Handbook Supplement,* Mar. 1978, pp. 4-11; emphasis in original

Over the years special permission has been given from time to time for special prayer circles to be held either in the temples of the

Church or in special rooms designated for that purpose in stake, ward, or other buildings.

Because of the increasing number of requests for such prayer circles, viewed in light of the rapid growth of the Church, and because of the complications that holding prayer circles in temples on Sunday have created and their tendency to take the participants away from their families and their other Church responsibilities, the Council of the First Presidency and the Quorum of the Twelve has decided that all such prayer circles, whether held in the temples or outside the temples, be discontinued immediately.

However, recognizing the value of these prayer circles in developing spirituality, commitment, and unity among those participating in them, we suggest that in lieu of such prayer circles, stake leaders may wish to consider the following: (1) that periodically stake leaders and their wives attend a temple session together in connection with which arrangements be made with the temple presidency for the prayer circle held during the endowment session to be composed of several stake leaders and their wives; and (2) that periodically stake leaders and their companions be called together in a special meeting where opportunity [can] be given to those present to express themselves by way of testimony or exhortation. **—Spencer W. Kimball, N. Eldon Tanner, and Marion G. Romney, circular letter, May 3, 1978, copy in Buerger Papers**

In interviewing one for a temple recommend, the individual being interviewed should be reminded that the Lord has said no unclean thing should enter His house. The procedure should be the same as for the other interviews.

When interviewing married persons, the one doing the interviewing should scrupulously avoid indelicate inquiries which may be offensive to the sensibilities of those being interviewed.

Married persons should understand that if[,] in their marital relations[,] they are guilty of unnatural, impure, or unholy practices, they should not enter the temple unless and until they repent and discontinue any such practices.[29] Husbands and wives who are aware of these requirements can determine by themselves their standing before the Lord. All of this should be conveyed without having priesthood lead-

29. This is addressed in more detail in Spencer W. Kimball, N. Eldon Tanner, Marion G. Romney, and Gordon B. Hinckley, circular letter, Jan. 5, 1982.

ers focus upon intimate matters which are a part of husband and wife relationships. Skillful interviewing and counseling can occur without discussion of clinical details by placing firm responsibility on individual members of the Church to put their lives in order before exercising the privilege of entering a house of the Lord.

Anyone guilty of verbal or physical child abuse or spouse abuse should not enter the temple.

All should be reminded that the Lord is the judge, and he knows what they are doing. They should be asked if they are worthy and qualified for a temple recommend. If not, advise them to repent and bring their lives in harmony with the teachings of the gospel. **—Spencer W. Kimball, N. Eldon Tanner, and Marion G. Romney, circular letter, June 9, 1978, copy in Buerger Papers**

With the forthcoming dedication of the Sao Paulo [Brazil] Temple[30] it is especially important that ecclesiastical leaders in the surrounding areas who are responsible for issuing temple recommends review the policies set forth [below] …

Where couples live in a foreign land and lack of the necessary funds at the time of their marriage to cover travel costs to the temple, or where a temple was not available on their continent at the time of their marriage[,] and at that time both parties were worthy to enter the temple[,] … [they] may come to the temple for their endowments and sealings without the usual one-year waiting period. While no minimum or maximum time is set between the civil ceremony and the temple sealing, it is recommended that such sealing be accomplished within such reasonable time after the civil marriage as the mode of travel permits. After a couple is legally married there is no requirement that they abstain from marital relations pending their sealing in the temple. **—Spencer W. Kimball, N. Eldon Tanner, and Marion G. Romney, circular letter, July 31, 1978, copy in Buerger Papers**

We are pleased with the increase in the amount of work being

30. The São Paulo temple was dedicated on October 30, 1978, a few months after the June 8, 1978, announcement that blacks would henceforth be given the LDS priesthood. In Brazil, it was difficult to know who had African blood and who did not, and the prohibition against black Africans was difficult to uphold. For more on this, see Mark L. Grover, "The Mormon Priesthood Revelation and the São Paulo Brazil Temple," *Dialogue: A Journal of Mormon Thought* 23 (Spring 1990): 39-53.

accomplished in the temples and hope and expect this trend to continue. However, we want to stress that while members should be encouraged to go to the temple, quotas should never be used. Quotas sometimes cause people to go grudgingly and sometimes lose the spirit of the work. The decision as to when to attend the temple must be left up to every person based on his own circumstances and desires. A visit to the temple to do work for the dead should result in a happy spiritual experience. This is possible only when patrons visit voluntarily without pressure from any source. **—Spencer W. Kimball, N. Eldon Tanner, and Marion G. Romney, circular letter, Mar. 28, 1979, copy in Buerger Papers**

Beginning the 4th of June, 1979, the first phase of a new microcomputer system for recording temple ordinances will begin in the Salt Lake Temple. The foundation of this new system will be a new (smaller size) temple recommend.

In preparation for this system, all bishops in the Wasatch Front area are being issued new recommend books late this month, or early in March 1979. On receipt of the new Recommend Books, please start using them and destroy any other recommend books on hand. …

Please advise each person receiving a recommend that when going through the Salt Lake Temple during the installation period, to allow approximately 15 minutes extra time for the processing of their new recommend. The temple staff will laminate their individual recommend, encoding special information on it which will be used in the automated system.

This recommend will, of course, be honored at <u>all temples</u>.

—Spencer W. Kimball, N. Eldon Tanner, and Marion G. Romney, circular letter, Apr. 2, 1979, copy in Buerger Papers; emphasis in original

Many of the garments (with the exception of cotton garments) are being marked electronically. As a result, the material is not cut, nor is there a need for backing.

This procedure has been approved by the First Presidency, and members, when inquiring, should be assured that the marking is proper and that they have no need to communicate with the Relief Society Distribution Center. **—Washington, D.C., Temple Presidency to All Stake and District Presidents in the Washington Temple District, June 1, 1979, copy in Buerger Papers**

After due consideration the First Presidency and Council of the Twelve have approved and authorized the Beehive Clothing Mills to manufacture two-piece garments for both men and women. These garments will be in addition to the one-piece garments. Distribution will be handled by the Relief Society through normal channels ...

As is now the case, each person who wears the garment is answering to the Lord for properly wearing and caring for it. **—Spencer W. Kimball, N. Eldon Tanner, and Marion G. Romney, circular letter, Dec. 15, 1979, copy in Buerger Papers**

Worthy individuals who have received their endowments and who desire to make temple clothing for themselves or a family member may do so upon authorization of the stake or district Relief Society president.

Individuals who have not received their own endowments, but have received recommends to go to the temple and desire to make their own temple clothing, may do so under the direction of the stake or district Relief Society president. ...

The Church has not authorized any individuals to make temple clothing for sale. This service is confined to the jurisdiction of the Beehive Clothing Mills.

Where violations of this regulation are found, neither the Relief Society nor the Beehive Clothing Mills is authorized to regulate the matter. Regulation is a priesthood responsibility exercised in harmony with counsel from the presiding priesthood of the Church. ...

Because of the sacred character of temple clothing, Relief Society presidents should not permit Relief Society members to sew on temple clothing, including the embroidering of aprons, during any Relief Society meeting or gathering. The practice of a group of sisters meeting together at other times to make temple clothing for their own use is not approved. Should a sister need help in making temple clothing, it is given through the stake or district Relief Society president in privacy. ...

All temple clothing is to be white, other than the apron, which is green as explained in the section on making aprons. Since the suggested fabrics for the robe, woman's veil, and man's cap may not be available everywhere, other white fabrics of similar weight and texture may be used. **—*Instructions for Making Temple Clothing* (Salt Lake City: Church of Jesus Christ of Latter-day Saints, 1979), 1-2**

....

This is an official invitation from the President of the Church for both of you to receive the most holy second anointings which it is planned will be given to you in the Ogden Temple on Sunday, August 24, 1980, at 3:00 p.m.

For this you should arrange to bring your temple clothing and come also with a temple recommend. Other instructions will be given to you when we meet at the temple.

If you wish to receive these blessings, please advise me immediately by letter. These blessings are to be given only upon your total worthiness. We would like you to indicate in your reply regarding this matter.

This whole program should be totally confidential; and as a reply to family members as a reason for your being away from home that day, you may say you are going to a special meeting at the temple. …

P.S. If you do accept, please complete the enclosed form and return it with your letter of reply. **—Spencer W. Kimball, Letter dated July 18, 1980**

The [temple] garment, covering the body, is a visual and tactile reminder of our covenants. For many Church members the garment has formed a barrier of protection when the wearer has been faced with temptation. Among other things it symbolizes our deep respect for the laws of God—among them the moral standard. **—Boyd K. Packer,[31] *The Holy Temple* (Salt Lake City: Bookcraft, 1980), 79**

31. Boyd Kenneth Packer (1924-) was sustained as an Assistant to the Twelve Apostles on September 30, 1961, and subsequently ordained an apostle on April 9, 1970, at age forty-five.

8.

"AN ESSENTIAL STEP" 1981–2000

The First Presidency has approved a crew-neck top for the two piece temple garment for men serving in the military forces. This top meets military requirements to wear crew-neck T-shirts. … At present, these tops will be sold only to members serving in the military forces, including active duty, reserve, and National Guard components, due to limited quantities available. Proof of military status will be required at the time of purchase. **—*Bulletin,*[1] Dec. 1981, p. 2**

The Council of the First Presidency and the Quorum of the Twelve recently approved the following changes in the procedure governing the issuance of temple recommends, where divorce, separation or annulment are involved, which supersede the procedure set forth in Supplement #3 to the *General Handbook of Instructions,* page 7:

An individual who has been a party to a divorce, legal separation, or an annulment may be granted permission to go to the temple by the stake president without clearance by the First Presidency. Such persons desiring to obtain temple recommends should be carefully interviewed by both the bishop or branch president and stake president

1. The *Bulletin,* previously the *Priesthood Bulletin,* was a monthly publication for bishops, stake presidents, and mission presidents.

to determine their worthiness. The events leading to the breakdown of the marriage should be carefully reviewed in connection with the issuing of the first recommend after the divorce, legal separation or annulment. Thereafter, temple recommends may be issued according to the usual procedure. Where serious transgressions were committed, appropriate disciplinary action should have been taken. Temple recommends issued after serious transgressions must not be granted routinely. Divorce clearances for members living in missions may be granted by mission presidents according to the same procedures.

If a worthy man who has had a wife sealed to him remarries after the wife's death or final decree of divorce, his new wife may be sealed to him, provided she is not already sealed to another man. It is not necessary to cancel the sealing of the former wife to him or to receive her permission if she is living.

If a person sealed to a spouse commits adultery that causes a divorce or contributes to the breakup of a home, that person cannot be sealed to the one with whom the adultery was committed. The First Presidency must authorize any exceptions. **—Spencer W. Kimball, N. Eldon Tanner, Marion G. Romney, and Gordon B. Hinckley, circular letter, Dec. 2, 1981, copy in Buerger Papers**

....

In interviewing one for a temple recommend, the individual being interviewed should be reminded that the Lord has said that no unclean thing should enter His house. The procedure should be the same as for the other interviews.

When interviewing married persons, the one doing the interviewing should scrupulously avoid indelicate inquiries which may be offensive to the sensibilities of those being interviewed.

Married persons should understand that if in their marital relations they are guilty of unnatural, impure, or unholy practices, they should not enter the temple unless and until they repent and discontinue any such practices. Husbands and wives who are aware of these requirements can determine by themselves their standing before the Lord. All of this should be conveyed without having priesthood leaders focus upon intimate matters which are a part of husband and wife relationships. Skillful interviewing and counseling can occur without discussion of clinical details by placing firm responsibility on individual members of the Church to put their lives in order before exercising the privilege of entering a house of the Lord. The First Presidency has interpreted oral sex as constituting an unnatural, impure, or unholy practice.[2] If a person is engaged in a practice which troubles him enough to ask about it, he should discontinue it.

Anyone guilty of verbal or physical child or spouse abuse should not enter the temple.

All should be reminded that the Lord is the judge, and He knows what they are doing. They should be asked if they are worthy and qualified for a temple recommend. If not, advise them to repent and bring their lives in harmony with the teachings of the gospel. **—Spencer W. Kimball, N. Eldon Tanner, Marion G. Romney, and Gordon B. Hinckley, circular letter, Jan. 5, 1982, copy in Buerger Papers**

The temple endowment includes certain sacred covenants which place the individual under obligation to observe these throughout life. Those who go to the temple for the first time should be both worthy and sufficiently mature to assess their capacity to keep these covenants thereafter, whether by marrying an active Church member, or by righteous living, though unmarried.

Single members who so qualify may be permitted to receive their temple blessings. Generally such unmarried individuals could be recommended as they become established in their vocations and professions and desire to be further strengthened in righteous living. **—Spencer W. Kimball, N. Eldon Tanner, and Marion G. Romney, circular letter, July 1, 1982, copy in Buerger Papers**

In the course of our visits to the temple, we are given insights into the meaning of the eternal journey of man. We see beautiful and impressive symbolisms of the most important events—past, present, and future—symbolizing man's mission in relationship to God. We are reminded of our obligations as we make solemn covenants pertaining to obedience, consecration, sacrifice, and dedicated service to our Heavenly Father. **—Ezra Taft Benson, "Temple Blessings and Covenants," Temple Presidents Seminar, Sept. 28, 1982**

---

2. Contrary to the overall caution not to probe topics of intimacy with married couples, bishops apparently began inquiring about oral sex, offending some members enough to prompt them to protest this intrusion into their private lives. See Spencer W. Kimball, N. Eldon Tanner, Marion G. Romney, and Gordon B. Hinckley, circular letter, Oct. 15, 1982, below.

Under date of January 5, 1982, we addressed a letter to you which outlined procedures to be followed in conducting worthiness interviews. Since then, we have received a number of letters from members of the Church which indicate clearly that some local leaders have been delving into private, sensitive matters beyond the scope of what is appropriate.

In conducting worthiness interviews, you should follow carefully the instructions contained in our letter of January 5, 1982. Also, you should never inquire into personal, intimate matters involving marital relations between a man and his wife. You should never deviate from or go beyond the specific questions contained in the temple recommend book. If in the course of such interviews a member asks questions about the propriety of specific conduct, you should not pursue the matter but should merely suggest that if the member has enough anxiety about the propriety of the conduct to ask about it, the best course would be to discontinue it. We feel, brethren, that if those who conduct these interviews are sensitive and wise, they can avoid such explicit questions being asked by those being interviewed. **—Spencer W. Kimball, N. Eldon Tanner, Marion G. Romney, and Gordon B. Hinckley, circular letter, Oct. 15, 1982, copy in Buerger Papers**

....

No unworthy person should receive a [temple] recommend. Interviewing officers cannot assume that a member is worthy at the present time because he has been worthy in the past. If a person is not keeping the commandments, he must demonstrate genuine repentance before he can receive a temple recommend.

During an interview, a person may confess a transgression that he has not resolved with a priesthood leader. The interviewing officer should seek divine guidance and should consider—

1. How long since the transgression occurred.
2. Whether the member is worthy now.
3. How many people know about the transgression.
4. Whether the member has repented completely.

The one conducting the interview then must decide whether to take Church court action ... All information divulged in such cases must be kept in absolute confidence.

Bishops must take exceptional care in issuing recommends to members whose parents belong to or sympathize with apostate groups.

Such members must demonstrate clearly that they are free of any influence from their parents' religious ideas. They must accept the teachings and doctrines of the Church and repudiate the doctrinal teachings of their parents that caused their parents' excommunication. …

Only the bishop may issue temple recommends in a ward unless he is absent. If he is absent, he may assign his first counselor to issue recommends. If the bishop and his first counselor both are absent, the bishop may assign his second counselor to issue recommends. …

After the bishop's interview, a member of the stake presidency interviews each applicant and signs the recommend if the applicant is worthy. The stake president should interview those seeking a temple recommend for the first time and those being married in the temple. …

A man must hold the Melchizedek Priesthood to receive a temple recommend for his own endowment.

A worthy man whose wife is not endowed may receive a temple recommend for his own endowment.

A wife whose husband is not endowed may not receive a recommend for her own endowment. (A man who has been endowed and later excommunicated from the Church is considered not endowed until his blessings are restored.) This restriction does not apply to a woman who is legally divorced, legally separated, or whose husband has been missing for ten or more years. …

Young, single adults normally receive their temple endowments when they are called to serve full-time missions or when they are to be married in the temple. The temple endowment includes sacred covenants that the member is obligated to observe throughout life. Those who go to the temple should be both worthy and mature enough to keep these covenants by righteous living, though unmarried. Single members who are qualified by worthiness and maturity may receive a temple recommend for their own endowments. Generally, such unmarried members could be recommended when they become established in their vocations and professions, and want to be strengthened further in righteous living. …

The requirements for a recommend to receive the temple endowment apply also to recommends for marriages and sealings. Even a member who is endowed and holds a valid recommend must obtain a new recommend to be married or sealed. …

A child over twenty-one who is worthy to enter the temple may receive a recommend to be sealed to his parents only if the child has received his temple endowment. …

A worthy endowed wife of an unendowed man may receive a recommend to do work for the dead. A worthy unendowed wife may receive a recommend to perform baptisms and confirmations for the dead if her husband does not object. …

When a member who has been sealed to a spouse is divorced, legally separated, or had the marriage annulled, and is guilty of sexual transgression, and when the requirements of any necessary discipline have been satisfied, then the stake president may grant a "divorce clearance" (clearance to receive a temple recommend) and give permission to go to the temple without clearance from the First Presidency. This instruction applies to those divorced after a civil marriage if they were sealed in a prior marriage. Both the bishop and stake president are to interview the member carefully to determine worthiness and must not issue a temple recommend routinely to a member who has committed a serious transgression. … The stake president's "divorce clearance" is required only for the first recommend after a divorce. A "divorce clearance" does not cancel the sealing. Only under authorization of the President of the Church can a sealing be canceled. …

When a member is divorced, legally separated, or has had the marriage annulled *and has not* committed a sexual transgression, the bishop and stake president may issue a temple recommend after a regular worthiness interview. This instruction applies both to members who have been sealed and those who have not been sealed. …

A member may receive a recommend to perform ordinances for the dead, other than baptisms and confirmations, only after being endowed or being recommended for his own endowment. Unendowed members may receive recommends to perform baptisms and confirmations for the dead.

An unmarried unendowed member over twenty-one (including a divorced member, widow, or widower) may not receive a recommend to be sealed to his parents, either living or dead, without first being endowed. An unmarried unendowed child who is eight or older may receive a recommend to witness the sealing to parents of his living brothers and sisters, including those adopted, if he was born in the covenant or has been sealed to his parents. A child under eight needs no recommend.

A married unendowed member may not receive a recommend to attend sealings, including the sealing of his parents, or to perform other ordinances except baptisms and confirmations for the dead. …

An endowed member who stops wearing garments, but who has not been excommunicated, may begin wearing them again without permission. A person who has been excommunicated is authorized to wear garments again only after a General Authority has restored his blessings. He should begin wearing them immediately, without waiting to go to the temple. …

Worthy members who have received their endowment or have temple recommends to receive their own endowment may make their own temple clothing, including the one-piece white suits for men. They should make them as instructed in *Instructions for Making Temple Clothing*, which is available from the Relief Society general office.

Neither individual members nor commercial firms may make and sell temple clothing. The First Presidency must approve any exceptions. …

Members should remove the marks from worn-out garments and burn the marks or cut them into small pieces. They then should cut up the garment so the location of the marks cannot be identified. The remaining fabric of the garments then is no longer considered sacred.

Members should burn worn-out temple clothing or alter it so the original use cannot be recognized.

Members may give garments and temple clothing that are in good condition to a worthy endowed member or to a bishop's storehouse. Under no circumstances should members send garments or temple clothing to Deseret Industries or charities for resale. …

A couple married outside the temple may not receive a recommend to be sealed until at least one year after the civil marriage.

The one-year waiting period does not apply in the following circumstances:

1. The couple lives in a country in which the laws do not readily recognize a marriage performed out of the country.

2. The couple travels with a Church-sponsored excursion to a temple in a different country than where they live.

3. The temple in which a couple will be married is located in a

country where the law requires that marriages be performed in a public place.[3]

4. An unchaperoned couple's travel to a temple would require one or more overnight stops on the way.

In the preceding circumstances, worthy couples should receive their temple endowments and be sealed as soon as the mode of travel permits, without the one-year waiting period. After a civil marriage, a man and woman need not abstain from marital relations before being sealed. ...

A living woman can be sealed to only one husband. A living woman who has been married more than once in civil ceremonies, but is sealed to one of her husbands, has made her choice. She cannot be sealed to any other husband unless the first sealing is canceled.

A living, endowed, married woman who has not been sealed to a husband may be sealed to a deceased husband with the signed consent of her living husband. ...

A deceased woman who has been married more than once in civil ceremonies, but who was sealed to one of her husbands during her life, cannot be sealed to any other husband by proxy. ...

To apply for cancellation of a temple sealing, a member must write to the President of the Church and request an Application for Cancellation of Temple Sealing form. The form contains instructions on how to proceed.

A worthy husband and wife who are waiting to have a former sealing canceled and who were married civilly in a temple may be sealed as soon as they receive a letter from the President of the Church notifying them that the former sealing has been canceled. They must present the letter at the temple where they will be sealed.

If a woman is sealed to a husband, and he is excommunicated later, their sealing, though suspended and not in effect, must be canceled before she can be sealed to another husband ...

Children have no right to change the sealing status of their deceased parents to suit themselves. Only the First Presidency can ap-

3. In 1989 the handbook added that if a country did not recognize temple marriage as legal, a couple could be sealed at any time following their civil marriage. This was confirmed in 2008 when the handbook added that the timing should be "convenient to their circumstances" ("Revisions to Policies in the Church Handbook of Instructions," attached to Thomas S. Monson, Henry B. Eyring, and Dieter F. Uchtdorf, circular letter, Apr. 22, 2008).

prove a change in sealing status, including cancellations of living sealings and reinstatement or resealing of canceled sealings.

If a husband and wife had their sealing canceled and did not attempt to have it reinstated during their lives, their descendants or relatives may not have it reinstated after their deaths. The matter will be left in the hands of the Lord. The only exception is when conclusive evidence shows that both partners wanted to be reunited. Only the President of the Church can authorize the reinstatement of the canceled sealing. ...

When a wife is sealed to a husband, all children born to her while that sealing is in effect are born in the covenant. Even if the wife remarries later and bears children whose father is not the husband to whom she is sealed, the children are born in the covenant.

A woman's sealing is suspended and not in effect if she is excommunicated or if the husband to whom she is sealed is excommunicated. Children born to her while her sealing is not in effect because of an excommunication or after the sealing has been canceled are not born in the covenant. Such children eventually must be sealed to parents.

A child born after the excommunication of either parent and before that parent's blessings are restored ... is not born in the covenant and must be sealed to parents. Neither the excommunication of either covenant parent nor the cancellation of the parent's sealing affects the status of children born in the covenant.

If a child is born in the covenant and remains worthy, his birthright guarantees that he will have parents eternally no matter what happens to the covenant parents. Such a child is never to be sealed to parents. ...

A living child who is sealed to parents receives the right to the same blessings as if he were born in the covenant and he cannot be sealed later to any other parents, even if (1) the sealing of his parents is canceled after his birth, (2) he is adopted later, (3) his natural parents give their consent, (4) he gives his consent, or (5) his natural parents die.

These instructions apply also to a deceased child who was sealed by proxy to parents when one or both of the parents were living. The only exception would be if the sealing of a child to parents were canceled by the President of the Church. ...

Members who want to be sealed to parents other than both natural parents, and parents who wish to have children sealed to them who are not the natural children of both parents, must submit their requests to the Temple Department for review by the First Presidency. This instruction also applies both to a member who was not legally adopted by the parents to whom he wants to be sealed and to a member who was legally adopted after reaching legal age. …

The First Presidency approval is not required in the following cases:

1. When a person cannot be sealed as a child to both natural parents because—

a. The child is adopted and neither he nor his parents have knowledge of the identity of his natural parents.

b. The child was born out of wedlock and the natural father is not identified.

c. The child's mother was sealed during her life to a husband other than the natural father.

In the preceding cases, the child may be sealed to the adopting parents (in case a) or to a natural parent and a stepparent (in cases b and c).

2. A living person may choose to be sealed to his natural father and stepmother. This choice is possible if his natural mother is not sealed to his natural father. The natural mother can be sealed to the natural father unless she is sealed to another husband during her life. If, after the bishop or stake president has explained the possibility of a sealing to natural parents, the natural father does not intend to have the natural mother sealed to him, the child may be sealed to the natural father and the stepmother.

If both natural parents are deceased and the mother was not sealed during her life, the natural parents should be sealed to each other and the child sealed to his natural parents.

3. A child may be sealed to foster parents if the child was legally adopted because of parental neglect, but not if the adoption was because of the deaths of the natural parents or for other reasons beyond their control.

Bishops and stake presidents should counsel families to consider the possibility of having children sealed eventually to the two natural parents even though they may have been divorced or are not worthy at the present time to receive temple blessings. Families should understand that sealing to natural parents usually is preferable when it is possible.

A child adopted by grandparents normally should not be sealed to the grandparents if an eventual sealing to at least one of the natural parents appears to be possible. Such sealing decisions are not urgent; waiting usually is in the best interest of all concerned.

If a living child under twenty-one or any deceased person born in the last 95 years is to be sealed to foster parents or to a natural parent and a stepparent, the legal parental rights of living parents not involved in the sealing must be cleared. The parents requesting the sealing must submit to the Temple Department one of the following documents with their request. If the request does not require approval of the First Presidency, the required documents must be submitted to the temple president prior to the sealing.

1. Copy of the final adoption decree or copy of the revised birth certificate (as proof of adoption) if the child is to be sealed to adopting parents.

2. Signed consent by the other natural parent, whether member or nonmember, if the child is to be sealed to one natural parent and one stepparent. The consent statement must name the child and the parents involved in the sealing and must state that the action consented to is a sealing to the one natural parent and one stepparent. If one natural parent is deceased or is missing, the consent of the remaining natural parent suffices. If a court has permanently withdrawn parental rights from a natural parent, the agency or person who has parental rights must give the consent.

The living child must be in the custody of the living parents to whom he is to be sealed. However, a court decree granting legal custody may not be used in place of the documents listed in the preceding paragraph to permit a sealing. A parent still has parental rights even though he may not have met all of his legal obligations and even though his child is in the legal custody of someone else. Also, the court may change legal custody.

If a natural parent has been missing for more than ten years, a living person under twenty-one or a deceased person may be sealed, with the temple president's approval, to his other natural parent and a stepparent. Such a sealing is subject to future review.

A parent is considered missing if reasonable efforts have failed to locate him. Reasonable efforts include contacting relatives and friends, and checking records that might reveal his location. Before the sealing can be performed, the temple president must be satisfied that the parent is missing. If families have any question about whether the requirements for a sealing subject to future review have been satisfied, they should contact the temple president or recorder for clarification well in advance of the planned trip to the temple. …

If the natural parents of a child who has not been legally adopted are not known and cannot be identified by reasonable efforts, the foster parents of the child may seek permission through the Temple Department to have the child sealed to the foster parents. …

Only members who have received their endowments may be buried in temple clothing. An endowed person who stopped wearing garments before his death may be clothed in temple clothing for burial if the family so requests, unless he was excommunicated. An endowed person who has committed suicide may be buried in temple clothing, unless he was excommunicated. Excommunicated persons whose blessings have not been restored may not be buried in temple clothing. **—*General Handbook of Instructions* (Salt Lake City: Church of Jesus Christ of Latter-day Saints, 1983), 34-44, 12; emphasis in original**

Two copies of *Instructions for Clothing the Dead* are distributed to stake Relief Society presidents and to stake and mission presidents. Ward or stake Relief Society presidents, stake presidents, or bishops may request additional copies of this information from the Relief Society General Office.

Church distribution centers do not carry burial clothing for infants or children. If the need should arise, the local Relief Society could help the family obtain appropriate clothing. The Church has not given regulations for dressing infants, children, or unendowed members for burial. **—*Relief Society Handbook* (Salt Lake City: Church of Jesus Christ of Latter-day Saints, 1983), 28**

....

Bishops are to consider the mental age instead of the chronological age of a living mentally handicapped member when deciding whether he can do his own temple work. Mental age may be established by tests given by professionally qualified persons.

A mentally handicapped member whose chronological and mental ages are eight or older must be baptized before being sealed to parents. A member whose mental age is less than eight does not need to be baptized before being sealed to parents. However, if his chronological age is eight or older, a current certification that the mental age is younger than eight must be presented to the temple president before the member can be sealed to parents.

Proxy temple ordinances may be performed for a living mentally handicapped member in extreme cases; for example, when the member's presence in the temple would be detrimental to his own or his family's physical or emotional welfare or would detract from the spiritual atmosphere of the temple. Only the First Presidency may grant permission for such ordinance work. Then written permission must be presented at the temple. …

A physically handicapped member who has sufficient mental capacity may receive his own endowment. He may do temple work for the dead if he can care for himself without help or is accompanied by a relative or friend who can provide the help he needs.

Whenever possible, a blind member should have an escort of the same sex accompany him through the temple; otherwise, he should arrange with the temple presidency to have a temple worker assist him. Guide dogs are not permitted in temples.

A member who is subject to uncontrollable seizures should not receive ordinances while he is living. Such members are not accountable to have received these ordinances. Their temple work may be completed by proxy after death. Members who have been endowed but now are subject to uncontrollable seizures should not do temple work. …

When a member who has been sealed to a spouse is divorced, legally separated, or had the marriage annulled, and is guilty of sexual transgression, and when the requirements of any necessary discipline have been satisfied, then the stake president may grant a "divorce clearance" (clearance to receive a temple recommend) and give permission to go to the temple without clearance from the First Presidency. This instruction applies to those divorced after a civil marriage if they were sealed in a prior marriage. Both the bishop and stake president are to interview the member carefully to determine worthiness and must not issue a temple recommend routinely to a member who has committed a serious transgression. The interviewer should review carefully the events that led to the breakdown of the marriage and must feel certain that the transgression will not happen again. … The stake president's "divorce clearance" is required only for the first recommend after a divorce. A "divorce clearance" does not cancel the sealing. Only under authorization of the President of the Church can a sealing be canceled …

When a member is divorced, legally separated, or has had the marriage annulled *and has not* committed a sexual transgression, the bishop and stake president may issue a temple recommend after a regular worthiness interview. This instruction applies both to members who have been sealed and those who have not been sealed. …

A child born to sealed parents who was conceived by artificial insemination is born in the covenant. Such a child who is born before his parents are sealed may be sealed to his parents after they are sealed …

No temple ordinances are performed for stillborn children. However, the family may record the birth of a stillborn child on the family group record. …

No temple endowment is performed for a child who dies before age eight. Only sealings to parents are performed for such children. If the child was sealed to parents while he was living or was born in the covenant, no ordinances are performed. …

Temple ordinances for deceased mentally handicapped persons are performed the same as for other deceased persons. Mental age is not considered. …

Temple prayer rolls provide a way to remember those who are sick, otherwise afflicted, or who need the faith and prayers of temple patrons for other reasons. Members should not submit long lists of names.[4]

No special arrangements are made for members to pray privately in the temples. However, members may remain briefly in the celestial room and meditate in silent prayer.

The sick are administered to in the temples only in emergencies. **—*General Handbook of Instructions* (Salt Lake City: Church of Jesus Christ of Latter-day Saints, 1985), 6-2 to 6-11; emphasis in original**

A deceased person who is to be buried in temple clothing may be dressed by a family member who has been endowed. If a family requests this service from the Church, a man who has been endowed is assigned by the bishop or branch president to dress a man; a woman

4. Church members are invited to call the temple to submit names for prayer circles or to add a name to the prayer roll while attending the temple. The names are prayed for by those who make up a prayer circle during an endowment session.

who has been endowed may be assigned by the Relief Society president to dress a woman.

In some areas only a licensed mortician or his employee is allowed to handle a deceased body. Where such a regulation exists, a member of the family who has been endowed or another endowed person assigned by the bishop, branch president, or Relief Society president should carefully check the clothing to make sure that it has been properly placed on the body.

Morticians are usually willing to cooperate in this matter; some permit a family member or an assigned person to be present at the time the temple clothing is placed on the body.[5] …

If a viewing takes place under circumstances where a majority of the persons attending the viewing will not understand the sacred meaning of the clothing and thus might be led to question, authorization should be given by the local priesthood authority, after consultation with the family, to use a plain white covering over the apron. The covering should be removed at the time the casket is closed. …

In no instance should a flower or jewelry be placed on the temple clothing. If desired, a white handkerchief may be placed in a woman's hand. **—*Instructions for Clothing the Dead Who Have Received Their Endowments* (Salt Lake City: Church of Jesus Christ of Latter-day Saints, 1985)**

Bishops and stake presidents are asked to remind those who attend the temple about the importance of dressing appropriately. Brethren and sisters should wear clothing that is appropriate for sacrament meeting when they go to the temple.[6] **—*Bulletin*, Oct./Nov. 1985**

....

In accordance with the decision of the Council of the First Presidency and Quorum of the Twelve, the following policy will now apply in the issuance of a temple recommend to a person married to a spouse who has not been endowed …

A person who is married to an unendowed spouse may receive a recommend when he or she has provided the bishop with written

5. According to the 1998 handbook: "Although the Church does not normally encourage cremation, the body of an endowed member who is being cremated should be dressed in temple clothing if possible" (70).

6. This refers to street clothing worn to the temple. Once inside, people change into white clothing.

consent of the spouse and both the bishop and the stake president are satisfied through appropriate interviews that the responsibilities assumed with the endowment will not impair marital harmony.[7] **—Ezra Taft Benson, Gordon B. Hinckley, and Thomas S. Monson, circular letter, Feb. 12, 1986**

....

The General Authorities are experiencing an increase in the number of requests made by families and couples for them to perform temple marriages.[8] The Brethren are reluctant to decline these requests, but because of their many responsibilities and demands on their time, we have asked them to limit acceptance of such requests to members of their own family and to close personal friends.

In counseling with those planning temple marriages, bishops and stake presidents are requested to encourage families and couples to utilize the temple sealers who have been called to officiate in this sacred ordinance. **—Ezra Taft Benson, Gordon B. Hinckley, and Thomas S. Monson, circular letter, Sept. 20, 1988**

Church members who have been clothed with the garment in the temple have made a covenant to wear it throughout their lives. This has been interpreted to mean that it is worn as underclothing both day and night. This sacred covenant is between the member and the Lord. Members should seek the guidance of the Holy Spirit to answer for themselves any personal questions about the wearing of the garment. Church leaders and others including temple workers should refrain from giving unauthorized instructions and opinions concerning when the garment might be removed. The promise of protection and blessings is conditioned upon worthiness and faithfulness in keeping the covenant.

---

7. Note that the new policy not only allows a woman to receive her endowments without permission from a non-practicing or nonmember husband, but a man is also required to receive permission from a non-practicing or nonmember wife, thus creating gender parity for the first time in this area.

8. While no reason is given for the surge in these requests, it may have corresponded to the increase in the number of general authorities. Beginning in 1984, several new members of the First Quorum of Seventy were called to five-year terms instead of to the usual lifelong service (until retirement at seventy years old). The temporary Seventies were later designated as the Second Quorum of the Seventy. See James B. Allen and Glen M. Leonard, *The Story of the Latter-day Saints,* 2d rev. ed. (Salt Lake City: Deseret Book, 1992), 655.

The fundamental principle ought to be to wear the garment and not to find occasions to remove it. Thus, members should not remove either all or part of the garment to work in the yard or to lounge around the home in swimwear or immodest clothing. Nor should they remove it to participate in recreational activities that can reasonably be done with the garment worn properly beneath regular clothing. When the garment must be removed, such as for swimming, it should be restored as soon as possible.

The principles of modesty and keeping the body appropriately covered are implicit in the covenant and should govern the nature of all clothing worn. Endowed members of the Church wear the garment as a reminder of the sacred covenants they have made with the Lord and also as a protection against temptation and evil. How it is worn is an outward expression of an inward commitment to follow the Savior. Bishops and stake presidents should take the opportunity during interviews to teach the spirit of wearing the garment, giving emphasis to the covenants and the attendant blessings that are related to this sacred privilege. **—Ezra Taft Benson, Gordon B. Hinckley, and Thomas S. Monson, circular letter, Oct. 10, 1988**

To accommodate the rapid worldwide expansion of work for the dead, it has been decided to simplify further the clearance of proposed temple ordinances for the deceased.

In considering ordinances for the deceased, we need not attempt to determine individual worthiness, whether an ordinance will be accepted, or the probable feelings of other deceased individuals affected by the proposed ordinance. In order to be binding in eternity, any ordinance in behalf of the dead must be accepted by the individuals involved, merited by individual worthiness, and sealed by the Holy Spirit of Promise. These determinations must, of necessity, be made beyond the veil.

Accordingly it has been determined that:

- A deceased couple who lived together as man and wife may be sealed even though there may be no documentary evidence of marriage.
- A deceased child is usually sealed to his or her natural parents. However, where there is justification a child may also be sealed to other parents, such as adoptive parents, stepparents, foster parents, or grandparents.

• A deceased woman sealed in life to one husband may also be sealed to another man with whom she lived as a wife.

• Temple ordinances for individuals without a conclusive death date may be performed after ten years from the time of disappearance in all cases of those missing in action, lost at sea, legally dead, or where death is apparent but no body is recovered. **—Ezra Taft Benson, Gordon B. Hinckley, and Thomas S. Monson, circular letter, Dec. 8, 1988**

....

A recommend is required for admission to a temple. The three types of recommends to enter a temple are—

1. *Temple Recommend* for those previously endowed and those being endowed, authorizing them to participate in all temple ordinances.

2. *Recommend for Living Ordinances* for those being endowed, those being sealed to a spouse, and those being married in the temple for time only. This recommend can be used only with a current, valid Temple recommend.

3. *Limited-Use Recommend* for unendowed members to (a) be baptized and confirmed for the dead, (b) be sealed to their parents, and (c) observe sealings of their living brothers and sisters to their parents. …

A member who is eight or older must have a valid recommend to enter a temple. Children under eight who are to be sealed to parents do not need recommends.

A valid recommend admits a member to all temples. …

A bishop may issue only a Limited-Use Recommend to anyone who has been a member of the Church for less than one full year. Only the First Presidency may authorize exceptions. A bishop may issue a Limited-Use Recommend to worthy new members over twelve years of age to perform proxy baptisms and confirmations. …

A worthy person married to an unendowed spouse, member or nonmember, may receive a recommend when (1) the bishop receives the written consent of the spouse and (2) the bishop and stake president are satisfied that the responsibility assumed with the endowment will not impair marital harmony.

A spouse's letter of consent is not required for a man or woman who is divorced or legally separated. If the spouse (1) has been absent because of desertion for at least one year and reconciliation appears unlikely or (2) has been absent for at least five years, a letter is not necessary.

Young single adults receiving recommends must be both worthy and sufficiently mature to understand and keep the sacred covenants made in the temple. Generally, unmarried members do not receive recommends until they are called as missionaries or until they become established in their vocations or professions and need to be strengthened further in righteous living.

Married members may be recommended for sealing to their parents only after receiving their own endowments …

Bishops are to judge the need and qualification of members who have mental handicaps to receive temple ordinances. Bishops may seek the assistance of professional advisers in judging mental capacity. Persons with mental handicaps who are eight or older who, despite their handicap, are sufficiently accountable to be baptized must be baptized before being sealed to parents. Those who do not have this mental capacity do not need to be baptized before being sealed. Bishops should refer questionable cases to the office of the First Presidency.[9] …

Members with physical handicaps who have sufficient mental capacity may receive their own endowments. They also may do temple work for the dead if they can care for themselves without help or are accompanied by relatives or friends who can provide the help needed.

Blind members should have members of the same sex accompany and assist them. Guide dogs are not permitted in temples. …

Members who are divorced, legally separated, or whose marriages have been annulled and who have not committed serious transgressions may qualify for recommends if found to be worthy in regular worthiness interviews. …

Church members who have been clothed with the garment in the temple have made a covenant to wear it according to the instructions given in the endowment. This sacred covenant is between the member and the Lord. Members should be guided by the Holy Spirit to answer for themselves personal questions about wearing the garment. The promise of protection and blessings is conditioned upon worthiness and faithfulness in keeping the covenant.[10]

---

9. Note that proxy ordinances for the mentally handicapped are no longer performed.

10. The 1998 handbook changed the wording to read: "The garment provides a constant reminder of the covenants made in a temple. When properly worn, it provides protection against temptation and evil. Wearing the garment is also an

Endowed members should wear the garment as underclothing both day and night. They should not alter garments from the authorized design. When two-piece garments are used, members should always wear both pieces. For those who are bedfast or who have severe physical handicaps, necessary adjustments can be made, bearing in mind the covenant between the member and the Lord.

Members should keep their garments clean and repaired. …

Only the First Presidency can change the status of a temple sealing. …

A couple married outside the temple may be sealed after one full year from the time of the civil marriage. The one-year waiting period does not apply, however, in the following cases:

1. The temple in which the couple is married is in a country that requires a civil marriage and does not recognize a marriage in the temple.

2. The couple lives in a country where there is no temple and the laws of the country do not recognize a marriage performed outside the country.

3. An unchaperoned couple's travel to a temple will require one or more overnight stops.

In these exceptional cases, couples should receive their endowments and be sealed as soon as possible after their civil marriage.

Worthy members who have been married in a civil ceremony and who have been members of the Church for at least one year may receive their own endowments and participate in all other temple ordinances except their marriage sealing within the year following civil marriage. …

A worthy couple who could not be married in the temple because one or both had not been a member of the Church for one year may be endowed and sealed any time after both have been members for at least one year. ...

A worthy couple married civilly or in the temple for time only while awaiting cancellation of the wife's previous sealing may be sealed any time after they receive a letter from the President of the Church notifying them that the former sealing has been canceled. They must present the letter at the temple in which they will be sealed. ...

---

outward expression of an inward commitment to follow the Savior" (69). The benefit was explicitly stated to be spiritual rather than physical protection, in other words.

A member sealed to a spouse may marry after the spouse's death or following a divorce. A worthy man in these circumstances may have his current wife sealed to him if she is not already sealed to a former husband.

A woman who has been sealed to a former husband and then divorced must receive a cancellation of sealing before she can be sealed to a new husband in her lifetime.

All divorce proceedings must be final before a divorced member can remarry. …

If a man or woman who has been sealed to a spouse commits adultery, he or she cannot be sealed to the partner in the adultery unless authorized by the First Presidency. …

A living woman not already sealed may be sealed to a deceased former husband, even if they were divorced. However, she must have the signed consent of her present husband (if any) and of the surviving widow (if any) of the deceased man to whom she is to be sealed. She must present the signed statements at the temple at the time of the sealing, where they will be retained.

A deceased woman sealed in life to one husband may also be sealed to another man with whom she lived as a wife. In order to be binding in eternity, any ordinance in behalf of the dead must be accepted by the individuals involved, merited by individual worthiness and sealed by the Holy Spirit of Promise. …

If a woman wants her sealing canceled, her local Church leader should obtain the form Application for Cancellation of Temple Sealing from the office of the First Presidency. Instructions on how to proceed are on the form.

Sealings of male members do not require cancellation.

The excommunication of either the husband or the wife suspends but does not cancel their sealing. …

Unendowed members who are married or are twenty-one or older may not attend sealings or be sealed to parents.

Children born after their mother has been sealed to a husband in the temple are born in the covenant of that sealing. If a woman who has been sealed to a former husband remarries, her children of the latter marriage are born in the covenant of the first marriage.

A child must be sealed to two parents, a husband and wife, and not to one parent only. …

The excommunication of either or both covenant parents or the cancellation of their sealing does not affect the sealed status of children previously born in the covenant or sealed to parents. …

A living member who was excommunicated or whose name was removed from the records of the Church after being endowed is not endowed again. Such a person becomes a member of the Church again by baptism and confirmation. Then, after approval by the First Presidency, the priesthood and temple blessings are restored by assignment of the First Presidency. …

If a person was endowed while living but no valid record of a prior baptism exists, either the testimony of witnesses must be obtained … or a baptism and confirmation must be performed. After the baptism, the bishop notifies the First Presidency of the circumstances and of the dates of all prior priesthood and temple ordinances the person has received. The First Presidency then can ratify (1) these ordinances, (2) the ordinance work that the person has performed by proxy in the temple, and (3) in the case of brethren, the priesthood ordinances in which the person has officiated. …

This instruction does not apply to persons who have been excommunicated. …

If a person was thought to have been baptized while living but is now deceased and the baptism cannot be verified after diligent search, even though it was relied upon to perform the person's endowment, a proxy baptism and confirmation must then be performed. **—*General Handbook of Instructions* (Salt Lake City: Church of Jesus Christ of Latter-day Saints, 1989), 6-1 to 6-7**

The Church continues its growth and expands into ever-increasing numbers of countries across the world, each with its own language and culture. There is pressing need for less complex temple procedures and reduced personnel requirements. Accordingly, we have prayerfully determined that it is no longer necessary to permanently record the names of proxies, witnesses, or officiators for any temple ordinances for the deceased.

Present temple operating policies will be used to assure that appropriate proxies, witnesses, and officiators are used. The names of individuals participating in vicarious ordinances may be preserved in personal and family records. The permanent temple record will consist of the names of individuals for whom the work has been done with the temple and dates it was performed, with the temple recorder's certificate that the work was done properly.

The implementation of this decision will substantially reduce the complexity of temple operation and simplify record storage. However, temples will no longer be able to provide stakes and wards with patron attendance information. **—Ezra Taft Benson, Gordon B. Hinckley, and Thomas S. Monson, circular letter, Sept. 20, 1989**

....

The sacredness of the garment should be uppermost in the mind of the wearer. The wearer should avoid exposing the garment to the view of those who do not understand its significance. When conditions make this unavoidable, it may be best to lay the garment aside reverently, and put it on again when conditions permit. ***—Instructions for Priesthood Leaders on Military Relations*** **(Salt Lake City: Church of Jesus Christ of Latter-day Saints, 1990), 3**

In harmony with the Temple Department and with approval of the First Presidency, a concept has been developed which is described as "Temple Excursion Ordinance Workers." Under this concept, individuals who are approved will be called as ordinance workers to function as such only when their stake or ward is participating in the temple as an excursion group or when the temple ordinance worker participates as an individual in a temple session. This concept will permit leaders such as bishops and members of stake presidencies to be called to function as ordinance workers.

To call such ordinance workers, the appropriate Confidential Report on Proposed Temple Ordinance Workers ... will be filled out by the bishop and confirmed by the stake president, to be presented to the temple president. When the candidate meets the requirements of the approved policy, the temple president is authorized to extend the call and use the individual for ordinance work in the temple, respecting the fact that the individual will only function as a temple ordinance worker when in the temple according to his or her own schedule.

Experience from other temple districts indicates that most stakes recommend between 80 and 200 men and women to serve as temple ordinance workers to fulfill the ever-increasing need for qualified ordinance workers. This concept does not replace the need to call regular temple ordinance workers. **—F. Burton Howard,[11] F. Enzio Busche,[12] and W. Eugene Hansen[13] to Stake Presidents of the Northeast Area in the Washington DC Temple District, May 9, 1990**

Temple recommend holders sometimes have a difficult time attending the temple because they cannot afford to rent temple clothing.

When a bishop feels that a member requires assistance for renting temple clothing, he may confidentially provide that assistance from fast offering funds. **—Ezra Taft Benson, Gordon B. Hinckley, and Thomas S. Monson, circular letter, June 6, 1990**

....

Members being married in a temple should not ask all of their wedding guests to dress in white. Only those members who enter the sealing room directly from the Celestial Room must wear white clothing. Members who come to a wedding directly from an endowment session may wear their ordinance clothing. ...

A couple may not be married for time only in the temple unless the woman is already sealed to a previous husband. ...

To clarify the meaning of the temple recommend interview reference to a divorce cleared by appropriate priesthood authorities, replace questions 11 and 12 in the interview with the following question:

Question 11. Have you ever been divorced or are you now separated from your spouse under order of a civil court? If yes,

a. Are you current in your support payments and other financial obligations for family members, as specified by court order or in other written binding commitments?

b. Were there any circumstances of transgression in connection with your divorce or separation that have not been previously resolved with your bishop? ...

When a limited-used recommend is issued solely for baptisms and confirmations for the dead, only the bishop or counselor should interview the member, not a member of the stake presidency.

---

11. Fred Burton Howard (1933-) was a member of the First Quorum of Seventy from 1978 to 2005.

12. Frederick Enzio Busche (1930-) was a member of the First Quorum of Seventy from 1977 to 2000.

13. W. Eugene Hansen (1928-) was called to the First Quorum of Seventy in 1989 and served in the presidency of the Seventy from 1993 to 1998.

When a bishop or counselor issues a limited-use recommend to a young member of college age who may attend more than one temple, temple workers can validate the recommend and the young person can retain it. All other limited-used recommends are to be retained at the temple until they expire.

If a bishop or counselor issues a limited-used recommend to a person who intends to retain it until it expires, the bishop or counselor should either cut away or cross out the additional lines on the recommend so other names cannot be added.[14] …

As has always been the policy, only members who have valid recommends and have received their own endowments may attend the marriage sealing of a couple in the temple. **—*Supplement to the 1989 General Handbook of Instructions,* 1991, pp. 8-9.**

....

The endowment of "power from on high" in modern temples has four main aspects. First is the preparatory ordinance, a ceremonial washing and anointing, after which the temple patron dons the sacred clothing of the temple.

Second is a course of instruction by lectures and representations. These include a recital of the most prominent events of the Creation, a figurative depiction of the advent of Adam and Eve and of every man and every woman, the entry of Adam and Eve into the Garden of Eden, the consequent expulsion from the garden, their condition in the world, and their receiving of the plan of salvation leading to the return to the presence of God … The endowment instructions utilize every human faculty so that the meaning of the gospel may be clarified through art, drama, and symbols. All participants wear white temple robes symbolizing purity and the equality of all persons before God the Father and his Son Jesus Christ. …

Third is making covenants. The temple endowment is seen as the unfolding or culmination of the covenants made at baptism. …

Fourth is a sense of divine presence. … Temple ordinances are seen as a means for receiving inspiration and instruction through the Holy Spirit, and for preparing to return to the presence of God. **—Alma P. Burton, "Endowment," *Encyclopedia of Mormonism,* ed. Daniel H. Ludlow (New York: Macmillam Publishing Company, 1992), 2:455**

---

14. See also Ezra Taft Benson, Gordon B. Hinckley, and Thomas S. Monson, circular letter, Apr. 5, 1990.

The white undergarment worn by those members who have received the ordinance of the temple endowment is a ceremonial one. All adults who enter the temple are required to wear it. In LDS temples, men and women who receive priesthood ordinances wear this undergarment and other priestly robes. The garment is worn at all times, but the robes are worn only in the temple. Having made covenants of righteousness, the members wear the garment under their regular clothing for the rest of their lives, day and night, partially to remind them of the sacred covenants they have made with God.

The white garment symbolizes purity and helps assure modesty, respect for the attributes of God, and, to the degree it is honored, a token of what Paul regarded as taking upon one the whole armor of God (Eph. 6:13; cf. D&C 27:15). It is an outward expression of an inward covenant, and symbolizes Christlike attributes in one's mission in life. Garments bear several simple marks of orientation toward the gospel principles of obedience, truth, life, and discipleship in Christ. **—Evelyn T. Marshall, "Garments,"** ***Encyclopedia of Mormonism,*** **2:534**

The sealing together of husband, wife, and children in eternal family units is the culminating ordinance of the priesthood, to which all others are preparatory. It must be performed by one holding the sealing power and today in an LDS temple dedicated to God. ...

To receive temple sealing ordinances, Church members must receive a temple recommend from a proper Church authority attesting that they are living prescribed Church standards. They then visit a temple and receive initiatory ordinances and the blessing referred to as the temple endowment. This entails the receipt of instruction and being put under covenant to obey eternal laws set forth by God, which, as observed, will ensure a superior standard of morality, marriage, and family life. The sealing ordinances can then be administered, the full benefit of which can be secured only by continued obedience to the divine laws set forth in the gospel of Jesus Christ.

A sealing ceremony is an inspiring and solemn ordinance performed in specially designated and dedicated rooms of a temple. The couple to be married or the family to be sealed kneel at an altar. The officiator is one who has received the sealing power under the highest priesthood authority in the Church ... **—Paul V. Hyer, "Temple Sealings,"** ***Encyclopedia of Mormonism,*** **3:1289**

Washings and anointings are preparatory or initiatory ordinances in the temple. They signify the cleansing and sanctifying power of Jesus Christ applied to the attributes of the person and to the hallowing of all life ... Women are set apart to administer the ordinances to women, and men are set apart to administer the ordinances to men. ... A commemorative garment is given with these ordinances and is worn thereafter by the participant ...

Participants in white temple clothing assemble in ordinance rooms to receive [the endowment's] instruction and participate in the unfolding drama of the Plan of Salvation. They are taught of premortal life; the spiritual and temporal creation; the advent of Adam and Eve, and their transgression and expulsion into the harsh contrasts of the mortal probation; the laws and ordinances required for reconciliation through the atonement of Christ; and a return to the presence of God. The endowment is a series of symbols of these vast spiritual realities, to be received only by the committed and spiritual-minded ...

During the endowment, solemn covenants are made pertaining to truthfulness, purity, righteous service, and devotion. ...

This order of instruction and covenant making culminates in the celestial room, which represents the highest degree of heaven, a return to the presence of God, a place of exquisite beauty and serenity, where one may feel and meditate "in the beauty of holiness" (Ps. 29:2). ...

Marriage and sealing covenants are performed in temple sealing rooms convenient to the celestial room. Officiators and close family and friends often attend the couple. Kneeling opposite each other at the altar, the bride and groom are placed under mutual covenants to each other, and are married through the sealing power of Jesus Christ; their children will thus be born in the covenant, and the family kingdom will become a nucleus of heaven. If the couple has been previously married under secular authority and now has children, the husband and wife are sealed in the temple under the new and everlasting covenant and their children are then brought to the altar and are sealed to them. All subsequent children born to this family are born in the covenant. **—Allen Claire Rozsa, "Temple Ordinances,"** ***Encyclopedia of Mormonism,*** **4:1444–45**

Temple recommends are given to members of the church who have completed the preliminary steps of faith, repentance, baptism, and confirmation. Adult males must also have been ordained to the Melchizedek Priesthood. Temple recommends are usually issued by a bishop and countersigned by a member of the stake presidency in interviews conducted in private. ... [The bishop] seeks to discern personal worthiness and standards of Christlike living and counsels appropriately with those whose lives are in need of any change or repentance. ... Worthiness requirements include being honest, keeping the commandments, such as chastity—sexual continence before marriage and fidelity within marriage—obeying the laws of tithing and the Word of Wisdom, fulfilling family responsibilities and avoiding affiliation with dissident groups. **—Robert A. Tucker, "Temple Recommend," *Encyclopedia of Mormonism,* 4:1446**

Some brides have brought inappropriate wedding dresses to the temple for the marriage ceremony. Brides and their parents or guardians should understand the requirements clearly before they make or purchase the wedding dress. They should also be aware that lovely and tasteful wedding dresses are available at the temple for use during the endowment and marriage ceremonies.

All dresses worn in the temple should be white, have long sleeves, be modest in design and fabric, and be free of elaborate ornamentation. Sheer fabric should be lined. Woman's pants are not permitted in the temple. The dress should not have a train unless it is removable so that it will not be encumbering during the temple ceremonies, though it could be worn for photographs following the marriage or at a later reception. **—*Bulletin,* 1992-1, p. 2**

Some items of temple clothing that may be of value to Church members with special physical needs are now available through the garment distribution centers by special order. A garment designed like a hospital gown is available for those who are confined to rest homes or who may be otherwise bedridden for an extended period of time.

Also available is a special, shorter temple robe that some members with wheelchairs may find more convenient. **—*Bulletin,* 1992-2, p. 3**

The First Presidency and the Quorum of the Twelve have approved the following change in policy for Limited-Use Recommends:

1. A group recommend issued to a ward youth group to do baptisms and confirmations for the dead may be used for only one temple visit.

2. If parents take older children to the temple to perform baptisms for the dead, the patrons will keep recommends issued, whether to one youth or more than one in the same family, and will present them whenever they come to a temple. The present expiration policy for these recommends remains unchanged.

3. Unchanged is the present policy that allows college-age youth and members over twenty-one to keep limited-use recommends that were issued to them individually. **—Ezra Taft Benson, Gordon B. Hinckley, and Thomas S. Monson, circular letter, Nov. 19, 1992**

....

Individual Church members are not authorized to mark commercially produced underclothing for their own use.

Beehive Clothing is authorized, upon request, to sew marks in the commercially produced underclothing which meets the Church standards of style, design, and modesty for members with special needs.[15] **—Gordon B. Hinckley and Thomas S. Monson, circular letter, May 28, 1993**

....

Effective immediately a man who has been previously sealed and later divorced, who desires to be married and sealed in the temple, must first obtain a clearance from the First Presidency.

It is intended that this requirement will help to reemphasize the significance and sacredness of the temple marriage covenants. **—Ezra Taft Benson, Gordon B. Hinckley, and Thomas S. Monson, circular letter, Feb. 3, 1994**

When valid legal regulations or officials in authority prevent an endowed member from wearing the garment, this does not affect that member's religious status, provided his or her worthiness to wear the garment remains unchanged.

When endowed members are compelled to discontinue wearing the temple garment for a time, we encourage them to keep themselves worthy and to pray for protection and blessings so that they may be

15. See also *Guide to Garment Fabrics* (Salt Lake City: Church of Jesus Christ of Latter-day Saints, 2002): "The temple garments distributed by Distribution Services are produced by Beehive Manufacturing using the approved pattern and designs. Fabric and trim are carefully selected, evaluated, and wear-tested to ensure high standards of quality and wearability. New fabric developments are researched and every effort is made to provide a selection of fabrics for comfort in differing climates."

able to resume the appropriate wearing of the garment as soon as possible. **—Ezra Taft Benson, Gordon B. Hinckley, and Thomas S. Monson, circular letter, May 24, 1994**

Please remind your stake presidents, who should in turn train their bishops, that for temple recommend interviews, they should use the questions as indicated in RECOMMEND INSTRUCTIONS, APRIL 1993 (Form 32605). Specifically, please remind them of the following:

1. Do not ask delicate questions regarding what happens in the bedroom.

2. If a member does not attend auxiliary functions, he/she should not be restricted in receiving a temple recommend.

3. Quotas are never, ever given by a stake president, a bishop, or a priesthood quorum leader regarding temple attendance. **—North America Northwest Area Presidency, Memorandum to All Regional Representatives in the North America Northwest Area, May 25, 1994**

We desire that more members of the Church do whatever is necessary to receive or renew their temple covenants and blessings.

Many of our adult brethren and sisters have not yet been endowed. Still others have been endowed but have not returned to the House of the Lord for many years. Some of our otherwise active members are lax in their attendance at the temple.

The restored gospel focuses on the ordinances of the Holy Temple as an essential step toward eternal life. As more members of the Church attend the temple, they and their families will enjoy needed blessings.

We request that stake and mission presidents, bishops, and branch presidents urge all adult members to qualify for a temple recommend even if no temple is immediately available to them. **—Howard W. Hunter, Gordon B. Hinckley, and Thomas S. Monson, circular letter, Aug. 25, 1994**[16]

Temples are sacred for the closest communion between the Lord and those receiving the highest and most sacred ordinances of the holy priesthood. It is in the temple that things of the earth are joined with the things of heaven. **—Howard W. Hunter, "The Great Symbol of Our Membership," *Ensign,* Oct. 1994, p. 2**

---

16. See also "First Presidency Emphasizes Temple Worthiness," *Ensign,* Nov. 1994, p. 109.

....

In a symbolic way, the teachings and rituals of the temple take us on an upward journey toward eternal life, ending with a symbolic entrance into the presence of God. The characters depicted, the physical setting, the clothing worn, the signs given, and all the events covered in the temple are symbolic. When they are understood, they will help each person recognize truth and grow spiritually.

Some of the symbols are straightforward, and the meaning is readily apparent. ...

The temple clothing is also symbolic. When we enter the temple, we change from street clothes into white temple clothing. ... [M]embers who receive temple ordinances and make covenants with God wear special garments (underclothing) throughout the rest of their lives. These garments are symbolic. **—*Endowed from on High: Temple Preparation Seminar, Teacher's Manual* (Salt Lake City: Church of Jesus Christ of Latter-day Saints, 1995), 23**

The endowment is another ordinance performed in our temples. It consists of two parts: first, a series of instructions, and second, promises or covenants that the person receiving the endowment makes—promises to live righteously and comply with the requirements of the gospel of Jesus Christ. The endowment is an ordinance for the great blessing of the Saints—both living and dead. Thus it is also an ordinance performed by the living in behalf of deceased individuals; it is performed for those for whom baptismal work has already been performed. **—Howard W. Hunter, "A Temple-Motivated People," *Ensign*, Feb. 1995, p. 2**

....

If a temple is located within the mission boundaries, you may give permission for specific missionaries to leave their assigned proselyting area to go to the temple on preparation day. If the temple is within the same metropolitan area but outside mission boundaries, you must obtain authorization from the Area Presidency for missionaries to go to the temple. Your permission is required for each instance when missionaries go to the temple.

Missionaries must live close enough to the temple that they can leave for the temple in the morning and return to their proselyting area in time to begin their evening proselyting. Overnight temple excursions are not authorized. The excursion must be safe and inexpensive.

If the temple is closed on the normal preparation day, you may occasionally authorize missionaries to take their preparation day on a different day in order to go to the temple.

The opportunity to go to the temple should be granted equally to all missionaries who qualify within these guidelines and should not be used as an incentive or reward. **—*Mission President's Handbook* (Salt Lake City: Church of Jesus Christ of Latter-day Saints, 1996), 48**

....

Church officers are responsible to see that no unworthy person enters the house of the Lord.[17] …

The bishop, or his counselors as authorized by him, interviews and issues temple recommends to worthy ward members. The bishop personally interviews members who (1) are preparing to receive their own endowment, (2) are planning to be married in a temple, and (3) have not lived in the ward continuously for at least one year. Only in the most urgent cases when he is absent may he authorize one of his counselors to issue recommends in these circumstances.[18]

Following the interview by a member of the bishopric, a member of the stake presidency interviews the person and signs the recommend if the person is worthy. The stake president personally interviews members who are receiving their own endowment and members who are planning to be married in a temple. …

A waiting period of at least one full year after baptism and confirmation is required before a worthy adult may be endowed. Only the First Presidency may authorize exceptions. During a person's first year of membership, the bishopric may issue a limited-use recommend for baptisms and confirmations for the dead according to the guidelines …

Most single members will be interviewed for a recommend for their own endowment when they are called as missionaries or when they are to be married in a temple.[19] Worthy single members who have

17. The 2006 handbook added: "Temple recommend interviews must be private. They should not be rushed. Interviewers should not add any requirements to those that are outlined in the temple recommend book" (76).

18. The 2006 handbook added: "Before a recommend is issued in any of these three circumstances, the bishop should carefully review the person's membership record to verify that it does not include a comment about a sealing or ordinance restriction or unresolved Church discipline" (76).

19. See also Gordon B. Hinckley, Thomas S. Monson, and James E. Faust, circular letter, Nov. 12, 2002: "Single members in their late teens or early twenties

not received their endowment in connection with a mission or marriage may become eligible for a recommend interview when the bishop and the stake president determine that they are sufficiently mature to understand and keep the sacred covenants made in a temple. Such eligibility should be determined individually for each person rather than using routine criteria such as reaching a certain age or leaving home for college or employment. …

Bishops should not issue temple recommends to young, unendowed prospective missionaries until they have received a mission call from the President of the Church. …

Endowment. Members who have physical disabilities may receive their own endowment.

Melchizedek Priesthood holders and sisters who have mental disabilities may receive their own endowment if the bishop determines that they have sufficient mental capacity to understand it and to make and keep the associated covenants.[20] If the member lives with his or her parents, the bishop counsels with them.

Sealing to Parents. Persons with mental disabilities who are eight or older and are sufficiently accountable must be baptized before being sealed to their parents. Those who are not accountable do not need to be baptized before being sealed. Bishops refer questions about specific cases to the stake president, who may refer the questions to the First Presidency.

Members older than 21 who do not have sufficient mental capacity to understand the endowment may be sealed to parents without being endowed. …

If a member has been divorced or legally separated or has had a marriage annulled, the bishop and stake president carefully interview him or her in the first subsequent temple recommend interview. They also review events that led to the breakdown of the marriage. If the member has not committed serious transgression, a temple recommend may be issued according to the usual procedure.

---

who have not received a mission call or who are not engaged to be married in the temple should not be recommended to the temple for their own endowment. They can, however, receive a Limited-Use Recommend to perform baptisms for the dead. The desire to witness temple marriages of siblings or friends is not sufficient reason for a young adult to be endowed."

20. The 2006 handbook added: "The bishop should seek the direction of the Spirit in making this determination" (77).

Members Who Have Been Readmitted by Baptism after Excommunication or Name Removal

Members Who Were Not Previously Endowed. After baptism, these members may be issued limited-use recommends to do baptisms and confirmations for the dead ... There is no waiting period. Brethren must be ordained to the priesthood before they may be issued limited-use recommends.

These members may not be issued recommends to receive their own endowment until one full year after their baptism.

Members Who Were Previously Endowed. These members may not be issued recommends, including limited-use recommends, until their temple blessings are restored through the ordinance of restoration of blessings ...

A member who has committed a serious transgression may not receive a temple recommend until he or she has repented. The waiting period between the transgression and the issuing of a recommend is left to the bishop's discretion. It should be sufficient to determine that the person has genuinely repented. ...

A member who has undergone an elective transsexual operation may not receive a temple recommend.[21] ...

Bishops and their counselors must take exceptional care when issuing recommends to members whose parents or other close relatives belong to or sympathize with apostate groups. Such members must demonstrate clearly that they repudiate these apostate religious teachings before they may be issued a recommend. ...

Garments and Temple Clothing for Members Who Have Disabilities

For members who are bedfast or who have severe physical disabilities, necessary adjustments may be made in wearing the garment. If recommended by a member's bishop, a garment designed like a hospital gown is available by special order for those who are bedfast.

Shorter temple robes are available to meet the needs of members who are in wheelchairs. ...

Where possible, endowed members should be buried in temple clothing when they die. Where cultural traditions or burial practices make this inappropriate or difficult, the clothing may be folded and placed next to the body in the casket.

21. A later passage states that a "transsexual operation ... may be cause for formal Church discipline," although without telling what the variables might be.

Only members who have been endowed may be buried in temple clothing. An endowed person who stopped wearing the garment before his or her death may be buried in temple clothing if the family so requests. An endowed person who has committed suicide may be buried in temple clothing. However, persons whose blessings have not been restored after excommunication or name removal may not be buried in temple clothing.

Temple clothing that is used for burial need not be new, but it should be clean. The member's own temple clothing may be used.

Bishops and Relief Society presidents should know what temple clothing is available for burial and how to dress a deceased member in temple clothing.

A member who is to be buried in temple clothing may be dressed by an endowed family member of the same gender. If a family member is not available, the bishop assigns an endowed man to dress a deceased man. The bishop asks the Relief Society president to assign an endowed woman to dress a deceased woman. …

In some areas only a licensed funeral director or an employee of the director is allowed to handle a deceased body. In these cases, an endowed family member of an endowed person who is assigned by the bishop or Relief Society president should ensure that the clothing has been properly placed on the body. …

A man and a woman must each be endowed before they may be married and sealed in a temple. They must each have a valid Recommend for Living Ordinances and a valid temple recommend. …

Couples may be married in a temple "for time only" if all of the following requirements are met:

1. The woman is already sealed to a previous husband who is deceased or from whom she is divorced.
2. Temples marriages are legal marriages in the country where the temple is located.
3. Both the man and the woman are endowed, have current temple recommends, and have a marriage license that is valid where the temple is located.

Bishops encourage such worthy couples to marry in a temple. In some circumstances, these couples may later be sealed in a temple[22] …

22. See also Gordon B. Hinckley, Thomas S. Monson, and James E. Faust, circular latter, Nov. 12, 2003: "A couple who were married in a temple for time

A living woman may be sealed to only one husband. If she is sealed to a husband and later divorced, she must receive a cancellation of that sealing from the First Presidency before she may be sealed to another man in her lifetime …

A deceased woman may be sealed to all men to whom she was legally married during her life. However, if she was sealed to a husband during her life, all her husbands must be deceased before she can be sealed to a husband to whom she was not sealed during life. …

If a husband and wife have been sealed and the wife dies, the man may have another woman sealed to him if she is not already sealed.

If a husband and wife have been sealed and later divorced, the man must receive a sealing clearance from the First Presidency before another woman may be sealed to him … *A sealing clearance is necessary even if the previous sealing has been canceled.*

Deceased Men

A deceased man may have sealed to him all women to whom he was legally married during his life if they are deceased or if they are living and not sealed to another man. …

When a woman has been sealed and divorced, she may apply for a cancellation of the previous sealing. The bishop and stake president submit an Application to the First Presidency form to seek this cancellation.

When a man has been divorced from a woman who was sealed to him and is worthy and prepared to have another woman sealed to him, he may apply for a sealing clearance. The bishop and stake president submit an Application to the Fist Presidency form to seek this clearance. …

If a person who has been sealed to a spouse commits adultery, he or she may not be sealed to the partner in the adultery unless:

---

only may later be sealed if the woman receives a cancellation of her previous sealing from the First Presidency. The letter from the First Presidency notifying the woman of the cancellation must be presented at the temple in which she will be sealed. We trust local priesthood leaders will be sensitive to the tender feelings of all couples desiring to be married for time only in a temple." The 2006 handbook amended: "Marriage in a temple for time only may be performed only when all of the following requirements are met: 1. The man and the woman are each already sealed to a spouse who is deceased. 2. Neither the man nor the woman has been involved in any divorce while a member of the Church. 3. Both the man and the woman have current temple recommends and have been issued a Recommend for Living Ordinances. 4. Temple marriages are legal marriages in the country where the temple is located and the couple has a valid marriage license" (82-83).

1. The President of the Church authorizes the sealing as part of his action on an application for cancellation of sealing or sealing clearance, or

2. The restriction against such a sealing is thereafter lifted by the President of the Church. A couple who desire the lifting of the restriction so they can be sealed may seek an interview with their bishop and stake president. If these leaders feel to recommend removal of the restriction, they may write separate or joint letters to the First Presidency, summarizing their recommendations and commenting on the applicants' temple worthiness and the stability of their marriage for at least five years. The couple should also write a letter of request to the First Presidency. The stake president should submit all of these letters to the First Presidency. …

… Generally, members may perform temple ordinances for deceased persons one year or more after the date of death without regard to the person's worthiness or cause of death. …

The one-year waiting period for temple ordinances does not apply to worthy members who were prevented from going to a temple in life for reasons beyond their control. …

If a worthy member dies within the year after being baptized, temple ordinances may be completed when one year has passed since the baptism.

If a worthy member dies within one year of a civil marriage, the sealing of the couple may be performed when one year has passed since the marriage. …

Temple ordinances are not performed for stillborn children, but no loss of eternal blessings or family unity is implied. …

No baptism or endowment is performed for a child who died before age eight. Only sealings to parents are performed for such children. If the child was sealed to parents while he or she was living, or if the child was born in the covenant, no vicarious ordinances are performed. …

Temple ordinances for deceased persons who had mental disabilities are performed the same as for other deceased persons. …

In all other cases of missing persons, temple ordinances may not be performed until 110 years have passed from the time of the person's birth. …

Unless they were excommunicated or had their names removed

from Church membership records at the time of death, persons who have taken their own lives may have temple ordinances performed for them one year or more after the date of death. …

First Presidency approval is required to perform temple ordinances for deceased persons who, at the time of their death, were excommunicated or had their names removed from Church membership records. …

Endowed persons who were excommunicated (or who had their names removed from Church membership records) and were later readmitted by baptism can receive their temple blessings only through the ordinance of restoration of blessings. Such persons are not endowed again, since these blessings are restored through the ordinance….

First Presidency approval is required to perform this ordinance for the dead. … **—*Church Handbook of Instructions: Book 1* (Salt Lake City: Church of Jesus Christ of Latter-day Saints, 1998), 66-76**

In temples, worthy Church members receive ordinances that are essential for exaltation. Each ordinance includes covenants and promised blessings. In this way members receive important knowledge and "things which have been kept hid from before the foundation of the world" (D&C 124:41).

Temples are places of safety and refuge from the world. They are sources of strength for righteous living. They strengthen families as members learn sacred truths and serve those who have died without receiving the ordinances of the gospel. …

The washing and anointing are the first part of the endowment. They are also called initiatory ordinances. They are administered to each person privately. They promise blessings in the present and the future (see D&C 124:39).

The endowment ordinance explains the purpose of life, the mission and Atonement of Jesus Christ, and Heavenly Father's plan for the exaltation of His children. Through this ordinance, Church members enter into covenants of sacrifice, consecration, and fidelity. They also receive a gift of power from God (see D&C 38:32, 38; 95:8; 105:12, 18, 33, 109:13, 22). …

The ordinances of baptism, confirmation, Melchizedek Priesthood ordination (for men), and the temple endowment and sealing are required for exaltation for all accountable persons. Many people have died without receiving these ordinances. As part of His plan of salvation, Heavenly Father has prepared a way for the dead to hear the gospel and receive these ordinances. People who died without a knowledge of the gospel, but who would have received it, are promised they will be heirs to the celestial kingdom (see D&C 137:7–10). ...

The people in the spirit world may exercise faith in Jesus Christ and accept the gospel message, but because they do not have physical bodies, the gospel ordinances must be performed vicariously for them on earth. Church members have a responsibility to provide these ordinances for their own ancestral families. This work is performed in temples. Ordinances that have been performed for the dead are effective when the deceased persons choose to accept them and become qualified to receive them (see D&C 138:19, 32–34). **—*Church Handbook of Instructions: Book 2, Temple and Family History Work* (Salt Lake City: Church of Jesus Christ of Latter-day Saints, 1998), 261**

We encourage all endowed members to have their own temple clothing and to use it when performing temple ordinances. Those who do not have their own temple clothing can obtain what is needed through Church distribution outlets. ...

Great blessings come to those who regularly attend the temple.[23] The preparation and care of one's own temple clothing will enhance the feeling of reverence and gratitude for this sacred work.[24] **—Gordon B. Hinckley, Thomas S. Monson, and James E. Faust, circular letter, Oct. 6, 1998**

....

Interview Questions for Recommends to Enter a Temple, Spring 2000

1. Do you have faith in and a testimony of God the Eternal Father, His Son Jesus Christ, and the Holy Ghost?

---

23. In a circular letter of Mar. 11, 2003, the First Presidency (Gordon B. Hinckley, Thomas S. Monson, and James E. Faust) called for "the youth of the Church" and others to "consider ways in which more frequent daytime temple attendance could occur."

24. There was nevertheless increasing concern about people wearing white "non-ceremonial" clothing (white blouses and skirts or white shirts and slacks) outside the temple. "Inasmuch as there is significant symbolism attached to changing from everyday street clothing to white clothing," it was thought that the white articles of clothing should not be worn outside the temple (Ronald A. Rasband, Executive Director of the Temple Department, to temple presidents, Nov. 7, 2004).

2. Do you have a testimony of the Atonement of Christ and of His role as Savior and Redeemer?

3. Do you have a testimony of the restoration of the gospel in these the latter days?

4. Do you sustain the President of the Church of Jesus Christ of Latter-day Saints as the Prophet, Seer, and Revelator and as the only person on the earth who possesses and is authorized to exercise all priesthood keys? Do you sustain members of the First Presidency and the Quorum of the Twelve as prophets, seers, and revelators? Do you sustain the other General Authorities and local authorities of the Church?

5. Do you live the law of chastity?

6. Is there anything in your conduct relating to members of your family that is not in harmony with the teachings of the Church?

7. Do you support, affiliate with, or agree with any group or individual whose teachings or practices are contrary to or oppose those accepted by the Church of Jesus Christ of Latter-day Saints?

8. Do you strive to keep the covenants you have made, to attend your sacrament and other meetings, and to keep your life in harmony with the laws and commandments of the gospel?

9. Are you honest in your dealings with your fellowmen?

10. Are you a full-tithe payer?

11. Do you keep the Word of Wisdom?

12. Do you have financial or other obligations to a former spouse or children? If yes, are you current in meeting those obligations?

13. If you have previously received your temple endowment: Do you keep the covenants that you made in the temple? Do you wear the garment both night and day as instructed in the endowment and in accordance with the covenant you made in the temple?

14. Have there been any sins or misdeeds in your life that should have been resolved with priesthood authorities but have not been?

15. Do you consider yourself worthy to enter the Lord's house and participate in temple ordinances? **—"Temples: Worthiness to Enter,"** ***Fair Wiki*** **(Foundation for Apologetic Information and Research, a group dedicated to defending LDS teachings online), at http://en.fairmormon.org**

INDEX

About the Editor

Devery S. Anderson is co-editor of *Joseph Smith's Quorum of the Anointed, 1842-1845* and *The Nauvoo Endowment Companies, 1845-1846*, which together won the Mormon History Association's 2006 Best Documentary Book Award. The current volume continues the same theme. Anderson recently completed a book about the murder of African American teenager Emmett Till in Mississippi in 1955 and has now begun a biography of LDS Apostle Willard Richards. He has published in *Dialogue: A Journal of Mormon Thought* (Best Article Award, Dialogue Foundation, 1999), the *Journal of Mormon History*, *Southern Quarterly*, and elsewhere.